The Ethics of War and Peace

D0078030

'A *tour de force*, which engages in a fascinating discussion of the complex moral and ethical dilemmas associated with just war theory. Especially noteworthy is the discussion of the morality of terrorism, particularly in view of the killing of Osama bin Laden. The book succeeds brilliantly in setting out the major issues involved in the contemporary debates about just war theory and in revising the orthodox school as represented by Michael Walzer.'

Robert Weiner, *University of Massachusetts, Boston, USA*

'This is a thorough introduction to contemporary philosophical debates relating to the ethics of war and peace that should appeal to philosophy students and may be adopted by courses in that field. It is well written and argued in a good philosophical style.'

Alex Bellamy, *The University of Queensland, Australia*

When is it right to go to war? When is a war illegal? What are the rules of engagement? What should happen when a war is over? How should we view terrorism?

The Ethics of War and Peace is a fresh and contemporary introduction to one of the oldest but still most relevant ethical debates. It introduces students to contemporary just war theory in a stimulating and engaging way, perfect for those approaching the topic for the first time.

Helen Frowe explains the core issues in just war theory, and chapter by chapter examines the recent and ongoing philosophical debates on:

* theories of self-defence and national defence
* *jus ad bellum*, *jus in bello* and *jus post bellum*
* the moral status of combatants
* the principle of non-combatant immunity
* the nature of terrorism and the moral status of terrorists.

Each chapter concludes with a useful summary, discussion questions and suggestions for further reading to aid student learning and revision. *The Ethics of War and Peace* is the ideal textbook for students studying philosophy, politics and international relations.

Helen Frowe is a lecturer in Philosophy at the University of Kent, UK, and was previously a lecturer and Leverhulme Early Career Fellow in Philosophy at the University of Sheffield, UK.

The Ethics of War and Peace

An introduction

Helen Frowe

Routledge
Taylor & Francis Group

LONDON AND NEW YORK

This edition published 2011
by Routledge
2 Park Square, Milton Park, Abingdon, Oxon OX14 4RN

Simultaneously published in the USA and Canada
by Routledge
711 Third Avenue, New York, NY 10017

Routledge is an imprint of the Taylor & Francis Group, an informa
business

British Library Cataloguing in Publication Data
A catalogue record for this book is available from the British
Library

Library of Congress Cataloging in Publication Data
Frowe, Helen.
The ethics of war and peace : an introduction / by Helen Frowe.
p. cm.
Includes bibliographical references and index.
1. War—Moral and ethical aspects. 2. Just war doctrine. 3. Military ethics. I. Title.
U22.F76 2011
172'.42—dc22
2011002340

ISBN: 978-0-415-49239-3 (hbk)
ISBN: 978-0-415-49240-9 (pbk)
ISBN: 978-0-203-80816-0 (ebk)

Typeset in Garamond and Gill Sans
by Prepress Projects Ltd, Perth, UK

Printed and bound in Great Britain by
TJ International Ltd, Padstow, Cornwall

For my dad, Ian

Contents

Acknowledgements

Many people have given me help and advice on this book. I am very grateful to Andréas Lind for comments on Chapters 3, 4 and 5, as well as helpful conversations about the book as a whole. I would also like to thank Jimmy Lenman and Stephen Chappell for comments on Chapter 4, David McNaughton for comments on Chapters 5 and 6, Jeff McMahan and Saba Bazargan for comments on Chapter 2 and Lionel McPherson for comments on Chapter 8. I also owe thanks to three anonymous referees who gave me very useful comments on the whole manuscript, to Tony Bruce at Routledge for first proposing the book, to Adam Johnson at Routledge for help along the way, and to Rob Vinten for doing the index at unreasonably short notice. Thanks also to Seth Lazar for organising various events at the Oxford Institute for Ethics, Law and Armed Conflict that gave me ideas and inspiration, and for many thought-provoking conversations about war and self-defence. I am also very grateful to the Leverhulme Trust for funding received during the writing of the book.

Introduction

Few activities raise as many moral questions as the activity of war. War is, by its very nature, an exercise in destroying lives and property, usually on a very great scale. Those people who engage in warfare transgress some of our most fundamental moral convictions about the wrongness of taking life and inflicting harm. And, yet, those who perpetrate these transgressions – the soldiers and their political leaders – are often praised as heroes. Children aspire to be soldiers. Parades are held for those returning from conflicts. We honour those who die in combat, and decorate those who show particular courage or skill on the battlefield. Why do we regard killing in war as not only morally permissible, but also morally *admirable*? How can we explain these apparent exceptions to our usual prohibitions on the inflicting of harm?

Just war theorists have, over the centuries, produced a vast literature that tries to answer these questions, amongst others. The primary task of just war theory is to determine and explain the *rules of war*, with respect to both the initial resort to war and the way in which a war is fought. On some issues, a considerable degree of consensus has been reached. Most writers, for example, accept that there is a morally significant distinction between those who fight – combatants – and those who do not. But in many other respects, there is profound disagreement about when war is justified, and how wars should be fought.

Unsurprisingly, the current political climate has led to a surge of interest in these most ancient of questions amongst philosophers, legal scholars, political scientists and ordinary citizens. The emergence of terrorism as a central issue on the international stage, combined with the recent and controversial wars in Iraq and Afghanistan and the growing awareness of humanitarian crises in developing countries, has triggered in many people deep reflection upon fundamental questions about justice, rights and the causes for which people may kill and be killed. Debates that many of us living in Western democracies thought to be long settled have re-emerged as genuinely divisive issues with significant practical implications. Are there circumstances in which governments are allowed to torture their political opponents? Is indefinite detention without trial acceptable, provided that the detainees are (suspected) terrorists? Countries that have led the way in establishing the ideal of universal human rights are now accused of violating these rights both at home and abroad. Faced as we are with this changing character of warfare, in which the role of sub-state groups begins to rival that of states themselves, just war theorists have approached anew many of the traditionally dominant views of both just war theory and international law.

The aim of this book is primarily to inform readers about contemporary debates in just war theory, and to encourage them to reflect on their own views and develop their own position on the ethics of war. I should emphasise at the outset some important features regarding the scope of this book. First, this is a book written by a philosopher, and it is intended to serve as an introduction to the philosophical issues that arise in war. This focus on the work of philosophers is not a denial of the relevance or importance of work in other disciplines. War raises interesting questions in many subject areas, such as political science, international relations and psychology, to name but a few. My aim is not to introduce the reader to how war has been approached in these myriad disciplines, a task that would be beyond me and, I suspect, anyway rather ill-advised. But I do hope that the book will be of interest to those who approach war from a non-philosophical background, and who want an introduction to the philosophical questions that war raises.

Like many philosophers, I often use fictional examples to illustrate ideas pertaining to war. This might strike some readers as odd – surely, we might think, history is full of real-life examples that could better serve this purpose. But using fictional examples helps us to identify principles that can be obscured by the complexities of historical cases. For example, many people already have firm views about the political morality of the United States. Using a historical example that concerns the actions of the United States might thus throw up more problems than it solves if we are tempted to evaluate those actions on the basis of what we already know or believe about a particular case. When we're trying to identify general rules or principles, we want to abstract from features that might exert an illicit influence on our judgements. Fictional cases help us to do this.

Second, the book's focus is upon the moral, and not the legal, dimension of war. These two aspects of war often converge, and I sometimes take the law as a starting point for outlining certain aspects of just war theory. And, since the book is intended to inform the reader about war, I sometimes offer fairly detailed summaries of the current state of the laws of armed conflict. But, in general, reference to the 'rules of war' should be understood as referring to the moral rules of war as they are studied by just war theorists, and not to the legal rules of war as codified in international law.

Third, my aim is to give the reader a sense of what philosophers working in this field are currently arguing about. With this in mind, the book concentrates almost exclusively on recent work – much of it published within the last ten years or so – and does not offer a historical survey of the origins or development of just war theory up to the present day. Such a survey is, however, an invaluable part of a comprehensive understanding of just war theory, and I would recommend that anyone interested in this topic read at least one of the many books that take this perspective. Paul Christopher's *The Ethics of War and Peace* gives a good overview of the historical development of just war theory, covering key thinkers such as Augustine, Vitoria and Grotius.[1] The other piece of essential reading for anyone interested in the ethics of war is Michael Walzer's *Just and Unjust War*, the most influential piece of work in just war theory in the last fifty years.[2] Walzer's book has come to represent what is now called the 'orthodox' view of just war theory, and is the inspiration (and the target) for much of the subsequent literature in the field. Whilst we will consider several aspects of Walzer's view here, it really is worth reading the original text, not least for the wealth of useful historical examples that Walzer includes.

The purpose of this book, then, is not to replace or rival such texts, but to offer an accessible, critical introduction to what is happening *now* in just war theory, which has become one of the most important, and exciting, areas of philosophical research. So whilst I do set some theories or ideas aside, this is not because they are not worth discussing. Constraints of space mean that I focus on the topics currently generating the most interest amongst philosophers working in this field. Inevitably, some people will disagree with my choice of topics. But I hope that those I have included will serve to give some indication of the breadth and depth of contemporary just war theory.

Fourth, I should stress that my intention is emphatically not to persuade the reader of any particular view. When teaching a course, I find it off-putting if an introductory text leaves its readers with the impression that there is a right or favoured view in a given debate, or that the views the author rejects are generally agreed to be false. There are few views in philosophy so utterly implausible that no sensible person could hold them: this is what makes philosophy the richest, most interesting, of subjects. So, whilst I offer criticisms of the various positions under discussion, I do not mean to imply that these objections are fatal and that the positions in question can be safely ignored. With this in mind, I largely refrain from drawing overall conclusions about the comparative merits of the views on offer. My job is to explain these views: it is for the reader to decide which is the most attractive or promising, and how they might go about defending it.

However, I do assume without argument (along with most just war theorists) that some form of moral realism is true – that is, that there are moral facts, and that moral claims are capable of being true or false. Given this, I sometimes talk about 'what morality requires' in a way that will raise the philosophical hackles of those who deny realism, or who object to the way in which I have helped myself to the realist perspective. I even, on occasion, make assumptions about how most people would react to a particular moral problem. Although common in the recent just war literature, this way of doing philosophy is far from universal and by no means uncontroversial. But where I make these assumptions, they are explicit, and the conclusions that I draw from them are thus explicitly hypothetical – if the reader agrees with me about how we ought to proceed in a given case, they may also agree with the inferences that I draw from it. I would, however, urge readers to disagree with me as often as possible, and I hope that making use of this methodology, far from stunting debate, will help generate discussion about the problems at hand.

Finally, it is worth pointing out that there are scholarly approaches to war that do not fall into the realm of just war theory. Alex Bellamy suggests that the wider 'just war tradition' is made up of legal, moral and political perspectives on war, and that the narrower 'just war theory' properly refers to work undertaken from the moral perspective.[3] I am rather sceptical about how Bellamy draws these distinctions, but he is certainly correct in that the just war theorists' way of studying war is not the only way of studying war. It is, however, the approach upon which we will focus. And, as I mentioned above, our interest will be not in identifying the evolution of various features of just war theory, but in looking at how these features are treated by those currently working in this field.

There are also moral approaches to war that fall outside the scope of just war theory. Just war theorists, as I understand the label, think that it is at least theoretically possible that war can be just, and that it is at least theoretically possible that there are moral rules that apply to the fighting of war. But there are some people who deny either one or both of these claims. Strict pacifists think that force is never justified as a means to achieving any goal, no matter how desirable. I thus take pacifism to be a rejection of just war theory, rather than a position within just war theory, since pacifists deny that there can be times when war is even theoretically justified. On this view, the just war theorists' enterprise of establishing the rules of war fails from the outset. There are persuasive and important arguments in favour of pacifism, but I do not address these here.

At the other end of the spectrum, *realism* offers an alternative to just war theory. Realists come in various guises, but are united by their common rejection of the idea that war is an activity governed by moral rules. Since the idea of having moral rules for war strikes many people, even those sympathetic to just war theory, as peculiar, we will spend some time looking at the realist position in Chapter 5. But I do not offer here a defence of the just war theory project *per se*. Rather, we will proceed on the basis of the two assumptions mentioned above: that war is, at least theoretically, sometimes justified, and that the fighting of war is governed by rules that we should seek to understand.

Chapter outlines

It is often by thinking about the rules that govern the use of force between individuals – the rules of self-defence – that contemporary just war theorists approach the use of force between states. Exactly how much we can learn about war from looking at the defensive rights of individuals is the subject of a great deal of debate. But the morality of self-defence has been sufficiently influential in just war theory to warrant some examination here. In Chapter 1, then, we will look at some of the most influential accounts of self-defence. We will pay particular attention to the aspects of individual defence that are most obviously relevant to war, namely the requirements of necessity and proportionality, the doctrine of double effect (DDE) and the duty of other-defence.

In Chapter 2, we will look in more detail at how people have understood the relationship between war and self-defence. We will outline Walzer's claim that it is only by employing the *domestic analogy* – a comparison of states and civil society – that we can understand the idea of international aggression. We will then address the individualist claim that this is no mere analogy; rather, war is an extension of 'ordinary life', and is governed by the same moral rules. We will examine the debate between individualist and collectivist approaches to war, looking at recent work by Jeff McMahan, Christopher Kutz, David Rodin and Henry Shue. The aim of this chapter is not to pronounce on the best way to understand the ethics of war, but rather to make the reader aware of the ongoing debate regarding these more abstract issues. In the subsequent chapters, I largely set these issues aside, and focus on debates about specific areas of just war theory.

Just war theorists divide war into three stages: *jus ad bellum*, *jus in bello* and *jus post bellum*. *Jus ad bellum* translates as 'justice before the war'. It is the rules (or, as I will sometimes refer to them, the *conditions*) of *jus ad bellum* that determine whether or not one has a just cause for war. *Jus in bello* translates as 'justice during the war'. The *in bello* rules govern the methods of warfare, and are sometimes referred to as the rules of engagement. These rules dictate the sorts of weapons one may use, the sorts of targets one may strike, the amount of force that one may use, and so on.

Jus post bellum translates as 'justice after the war'. This third stage of war is probably the most under-developed in just war theory, although it is beginning to attract more scholarly attention with the proliferation of war crimes tribunals, and the ongoing Western presence in Iraq and Afghanistan. The scope of *jus post bellum* is much broader than the other stages of war. It covers, amongst other things, the ethics of occupation, war crimes tribunals, reparations, punishment and reconciliation. Given this broad scope, *jus post bellum* is less well understood as a set of rules or conditions. Some of the relevant issues are susceptible to rules, for instance the imposing of war reparations or the procedures for war crimes trials. But others, such as how we ought to facilitate reconciliation between previously warring groups, are less obviously so, and require a different sort of approach.

In Chapter 3, then, we will look at the rules of *jus ad bellum*. The chapter begins by outlining the seven formal *ad bellum* conditions on which just war theorists largely agree: that a war must have a just cause, be proportionate, have a reasonable chance of success, be waged by a legitimate authority, be waged for the right intention, be a last resort, and be publicly declared. Many just war theorists think that a war is just if, and only if, it meets all these conditions. I describe these as the *formal* conditions of *jus ad bellum* because whilst we might agree in principle that, for example, war must be a proportionate response to aggression, there is little substantive agreement about what *counts* as a proportionate response. The lack of consensus regarding the substantive content of these conditions will become apparent as the book progresses. However, two conditions in particular have occupied the attention of some of the most influential contemporary just war theorists, namely just cause and proportionality. In the second part of this chapter, we will look in detail at the some of the arguments concerning these two *ad bellum* conditions.

Chapter 4 continues our study of *jus ad bellum* by examining wars with controversial causes. The Bush administration threw open the debate about the difference between preventive war and pre-emptive war with the 2002 *National Security Strategy* (NSS), in which they declared their commitment to seeking out, and averting, 'emerging threats'.[4] To most people, this sounded like a commitment to impermissible prevention rather than permissible pre-emption. We will look at whether the NSS can find support in just war theory. This chapter also looks at the idea of punishment as a just cause for war, and the permissibility of wars of humanitarian intervention.

In Chapter 5, we will examine the relationship between *jus ad bellum* and *jus in bello*. Traditionally, just war theorists have deemed these two stages of war morally independent of one another, such that it is possible for combatants to fight a war justly even if their side lacks a just cause. The primary explanation of this independence is that it would be unfair to hold combatants responsible for fighting in an unjust war. It is their leaders, and not they, who are responsible for ensuring that the conditions of *jus ad bellum* are met. Combatants need concern themselves only with fighting justly: with obeying the rules of *jus in bello*. This chapter outlines the various rules governing *jus in bello*, such as those pertaining to the protection of non-combatants and the treatment of prisoners of war.

Chapter 6 tackles one of the most important debates in contemporary just war theory: the moral status of combatants. We begin this chapter by looking at Jeff McMahan's influential critique of the idea that the rules of *jus in bello* can be satisfied independently of the rules of *jus ad bellum*. One of the most significant implications of rejecting this independence is that it undermines the idea that combatants do not act wrongly simply in virtue of fighting for an unjust cause. We will examine at McMahan's arguments for why combatants act wrongly if they fight in unjust wars, such that these 'unjust combatants' are not the moral equals of the 'just combatants' whom they kill. We will then consider how McMahan's critics have tried to defend the moral equality of combatants in the face of these arguments.

In Chapter 7, we will address in detail the principle of non-combatant immunity (PNI), a fundamental tenet of just war theory. The idea that non-combatants are morally immune from attack underpins many of the *jus in bello* rules. But, as we will explore in this chapter, this does not mean that non-combatants cannot be permissibly killed. The DDE has been widely used to justify the collateral harming of non-combatants in war. But several writers argue that the distinction between intending harm and merely fore-seeing that harm will result from one's action is insufficient to explain the permissibility of collateral killings. We will look at suggested revisions of the DDE, and also at suggested alternatives.

In the second part of the chapter, we will look at some problems with justifying the PNI itself. It is far from obvious which morally significant feature explains the different treatment of combatants and non-combatants. The historical assumption that non-combatants do not threaten is plausible only under a very narrow understanding of what it is to pose a threat. We will explore various attempts to sustain the PNI, along with some alternative accounts of the moral status of non-combatants.

Chapter 8 addresses one of the now-central debates in just war theory, namely the nature and morality of terrorism. As mentioned above, terrorism seems to be an increasingly prominent part of warfare. A charge frequently levelled at just war theory is that its failure to properly accommodate ter-rorism shows it to be outdated and irrelevant to contemporary warfare. Certainly, just war theory primarily evolved in the context of inter-state relations, and the phenomenon of terrorism presents new challenges to what are often very old ideas. In this chapter, we will look at how contemporary philosophers have tried to analyse both the concept and the morality of ter-rorism within the context of just war theory, using the notions of legitimate authority and non-combatant immunity to capture the sense that terrorism is impermissible in a way that ordinary warfare is not. However, we will also look at how philosophers such as Lionel McPherson have argued that just war theory itself needs revision in light of the challenges presented by terrorism.

Chapter 9 continues our investigation of terrorism, looking at the dif-ficulties surrounding the legal classification of terrorism. On the one hand, terrorists clearly seem to be combatants (at least, they do not seem like *non-*combatants). But on the other hand, allowing that sub-state groups, acting independently of any government, can count as combatants comes very close to granting that such groups can be engaged in genuine warfare. The ramifi-cations of counting terrorists as ordinary combatants, and the implausibility of counting them as non-combatants, have led to their acquiring the peculiar label of *illegitimate combatants*. In this chapter, we will critically examine the suggestion that terrorists are not entitled to protection under the Geneva Convention even though they are engaged in genuine warfare.

This chapter also addresses the high-profile debate regarding the use of torture as a military tactic. This debate usually takes place within the con-text of a 'ticking time bomb' scenario, where only if we torture a terrorist to extract information can we save thousands of people from their terrorist attack. We will look at utilitarian arguments both for and against the use of torture, and at the suggestion that torture can be justified as a legitimate form of self-defence.

The final chapter looks at some of the key issues in *jus post bellum*. Bellamy divides accounts of the ethics of ending war into minimalist and maximalist accounts. Minimalists seek only to restrict the excesses of victors; maximalists seek to impose obligations upon victors to ensure that defeated states are left able to function. We will consider, in particular, the idea that victors have obligations of reconstruction towards defeated countries. In the second part of the chapter, we will explore some of the moral questions that pertain to war crimes. We will outline the superior orders defence of war crimes, which has afforded combatants general protection from prosecution for wrongs they commit under orders. We will also look at the idea of granting amnesties for war crimes in the name of furthering reconciliation in the aftermath of conflict.

Notes

1. P. Christopher, *The Ethics of War and Peace: An Introduction to Legal and Moral Issues*, Englewood Cliffs, NJ: Prentice Hall, 2004, 3rd edn.
2. M. Walzer, *Just and Unjust Wars*, New York: Basic Books, 1977.
3. A. Bellamy, *Just Wars: From Cicero to Iraq*, Malden, MA: Polity Press, 2006, p. 8.
4. *The National Security Strategy of the United States*, 2002, available at http://georgewbush-whitehouse.archives.gov/nsc/nss/2002/nss.pdf, (accessed 15 December 2010).

1 Self-defence

Many just war theorists have sought to explain the permissibility of killing in war by pointing out that there are other exceptions to the general prohibition on taking life. Most notable amongst these is the exception that permits the killing of an attacker in self-defence or in defence of other people. When our lives are threatened, most of us think that it is permissible to try to defend ourselves even if we can do so only by inflicting very great or even lethal harm upon our attacker. We also think that someone who defends us against such an attack, even if they kill our attacker, is pretty heroic. So, if a case can be made that killing in war is a form of defensive killing, we may have the beginnings of an explanation of why killing in war is permissible.

The idea of war as self-defence has had a profound influence upon just war thought across the centuries. But the relationship between war and self-defence is less than straightforward, not least because there is no general consensus amongst either philosophers or legal theorists about when or why self-defence is permissible. Nor is there consensus about how strongly we should interpret the relationship between war and self-defence. However, since many just war theorists grant the existence of at least some relationship between war and self-defence, it will be worth our while to look at some of the main tenets of influential accounts of permissible self-defence. Several of the concepts that we use in just war theory, such as the requirements of necessity and proportionality, certainly seem to have their roots in thoughts about self-defence, even if they are to be understood differently when they are used in the context of war. Once we have familiarised ourselves with some important aspects of self-defence, we can look in more detail at the relationship between war and self-defence.

Proportionality and necessity

Some people believe that it is never morally permissible to use force against another person. This position is usually described as *pacifism*. A committed pacifist will think that even when one's own life is threatened by a murderous attacker, morality does not permit one to use force to prevent that attack. Nor can one use force to defend other people's lives. Most people are not pacifists. Most people think that, under certain circumstances, it can be permissible for one to use force, including lethal force, against another person.

The sorts of circumstance that people making this claim usually have in mind are those in which the force will save either one's own life, or someone else's life. But the permission of self-defence is not unlimited. For example, most people think it permissible to use force only when doing so is *necessary*. And, most people think that there are limits to when I can use even necessary force to save my own life. I probably shouldn't kill you and eat you even if doing so is necessary to ward off the starvation that will otherwise kill me. The purpose of philosophical accounts of self-defence, then, is to explain when, and why, using defensive force is permissible.

Proportionality

That defensive force must be *proportionate* is a standard requirement upon permissible defence. As we will see, judging proportionality in the context of war has proved both complex and controversial. For our purposes here, however, we can stick to a fairly basic account of proportionality. Roughly, the proportionality condition stipulates that the harm I inflict upon my attacker must not significantly outweigh the harm that they threaten to inflict upon me. Whilst I can permissibly break their leg to stop them from breaking my leg, I cannot break their leg to stop them from pinching me.

How can we tell if a defensive harm is proportionate to a threatened harm? When the two harms are equal, this seems easy enough. If I kill you to stop you from killing me, the threatened harm that I avert (death) is the same as the defensive harm that I inflict (death). Killing you thus seems proportionate. But most people think that it is not only when I face a lethal threat that I may lethally defend myself. I may also lethally defend myself against non-lethal harms such as rape, torture, paralysis or kidnap.

There seem to be two possible explanations of how such defensive killings could meet the proportionality requirement. The first is to suggest that whilst these harms of rape, torture and so on are not the same as death, they are nonetheless of the same *magnitude*. We might argue that being raped or tortured is as bad as being killed, and thus these harms are in fact equal to death. This would explain why I can kill a person who will otherwise rape or torture me without falling foul of the proportionality condition.

But even if we can make this case for rape or torture, it seems somewhat less plausible with respect to paralysis or kidnap. Being paralysed is certainly a very serious harm. But it does not seem as bad being killed, at least when the paralysis is only partial. Similarly, kidnapping does not in itself seem to be a harm comparable to death. It may be terrifying, and a gross invasion of one's liberty, but in the absence of *additional* harms, such as torture or rape, being kidnapped does not seem to be a harm of the same magnitude as being killed. Of course, we could simply deny that it is proportionate to use lethal force to prevent these non-lethal harms. But if we think that people are allowed to lethally defend themselves against at least some lesser harms, we will need to adopt an alternative account of proportionality that does not insist that the level of defensive force be no greater than the threatened harm.

An alternative strategy, then, is to argue for a threshold approach to proportionality. This approach does not require that one be threatened with a harm *equal* to death before lethal defence is proportionate, but only that one be faced with a *sufficiently serious* harm. Since rape, torture, paralysis and kidnap are all very serious harms, perhaps this is enough to make it permissible to lethally defend oneself against them. On this understanding of proportionality, we have a sort of ranking of harms, whereby one can inflict a defensive harm that is greater than the threatened harm, but still *comparable* to the threatened harm. This would explain why I can break an attacker's leg not only if he will otherwise break my leg, but also if he will otherwise break my arm or my ankle. A broken leg seems undeniably worse than a broken ankle, but the two harms are nonetheless comparable, such that breaking the assailant's leg to protect my ankle does not seem disproportionate.

Necessity

The *necessity* condition is also a standard requirement of permissible defence. This condition forbids using more force than one has to in the course of defending oneself. If I can prevent you from killing me either by stamping on your foot or by shooting you in the chest, morality requires that I choose the least harmful means and stamp on your foot. Note, however, that shooting you in the chest would not be *disproportionate*, since you do pose a lethal threat to me. Also note that the mere fact that a harm is necessary cannot make it proportionate. Even if breaking your leg is the *only* way in which I can stop you from pinching me, it is impermissible to break your leg. In such a case, I must submit to the infliction of the minor harm rather than inflict a serious harm in self-defence.

Some people describe the necessity condition as a requirement of 'last resort'. One should use force only if one has no other option. Several accounts of self-defence thus endorse the idea that a person must try to retreat from their attacker rather than use force. If I can flee without exposing myself to any great risk, I ought to do so. A notable exception to this, however, might be the issue of retreating within one's own property. Some legal systems do not require that a person leave their home rather than confront an attacker *even if they can safely do so*. This reflects many people's intuitions that it would be permissible to stay and forcefully defend oneself against an attacker in one's own home, although people differ on how much force one could use rather than flee. If, in order to stay, one will have to use lethal force against an attacker, we might think that morality requires one to flee if it is safe to do so.

People also disagree about the permissibility of using significant force to avert an intrusion into one's home if the intrusion is not accompanied by a threat of physical harm. The case of Tony Martin – the British man who shot two would-be burglars, killing one and wounding the other – sparked an enormous debate over the defensive rights of homeowners. Part of the controversy comes from whether it can ever be proportionate to inflict serious physical harm to protect against some non-physical harm such as theft. Some people think that whilst I am permitted to inflict minor harm – to punch you or shove you – to stop you from stealing my purse, I cannot stab you to stop you from stealing it, no matter how much money is in it. Property alone is not usually thought to be of sufficient importance to make serious harm a proportionate means of protection. But we might think that our homes are more than mere property: that they are 'our part of the world', in which we have the right to feel safe. On this view, invading our homes threatens more than just our property rights. This might explain some people's intuition that it is permissible to inflict serious harm or lethal harm in order to stay in our homes, even if we could safely retreat from them.

Of course, that force is necessary and proportionate is only part of what makes the use of force an act of permissible defence. As I suggested above, killing and eating a person to ward off starvation could be described as a necessary and proportionate force if it is the only way in which I can save my life. However, it hardly seems like permissible self-defence. So, what we must investigate now are the *other* conditions that must be met if defence is to be permissible.

The culpability account

Imagine the following scenario:[1]

> *Truck:*
> You are standing in a meadow, innocently minding your own business. Villain, who hates you, is driving towards you in a truck, intent upon running you down. There is nowhere to run. Luckily, you have your anti-tank gun with you. You can blow up the truck, killing Villain, to save your own life.

Most people think it permissible for you to blow up the truck even though doing so will kill Villain. And an intuitive explanation of this permissibility is that Villain is, after all, a *villain*. He is maliciously trying to kill you, an innocent person. On the culpability account of self-defence, it is Villain's malicious intention that makes it permissible to kill him (along with the necessity and proportionality of doing so). Some people interpret this as the claim that Villain *deserves* to be killed, such that killing him in self-defence does not wrong him, or as the claim that Villain's culpability means that he forfeits any right he has that you not kill him.

The culpability account can also explain an important feature of self-defence, namely our intuition that should you try to defend yourself against Villain, Villain cannot then invoke a right of self-defence against *you*. Even though you will now threaten each other, the culpability account will hold that, since you are innocent, you are not a legitimate target of force.

The culpability account is certainly appealing. But it has limitations. For example, consider the following case:[2]

Elevator:
You are in an elevator with Stranger, who is a schizophrenic. Stranger suddenly, and faultlessly, goes into an extremely violent schizophrenic episode and attacks you. You can stop Stranger from throttling you to death only by killing him.

Again, most people think that you are permitted to defend yourself in a case like *Elevator*. But we cannot explain this permissibility on a culpability account of self-defence. Stranger is not culpable for the attack on you: we can suppose that this is the first time Stranger has had a schizophrenic episode, and that he has no reason to think that he might pose this sort of danger to others. Because of his lack of control (or *agency*) over the threat he poses, Stranger is what is usually described in the literature as an *innocent* or *non-responsible* threat.

Some accounts of self-defence bite the bullet in cases like *Elevator* and insist that you are not permitted to kill Stranger in self-defence. But the culpability account also rules out using self-defence in a case like *Vehicle*:[3]

Vehicle:
Driver is a very conscientious car-owner, who keeps his car well maintained and who drives very carefully. One day, however, a freak event causes the brakes to fail in Driver's car. Driver loses control of the car and careers towards you as you walk past. He will hit and kill you unless you use your anti-tank gun to blow up both the car and Driver.

Even people who think that you are not permitted to kill a wholly non-responsible attacker like Stranger tend to think that you may defend yourself against Driver. Driver bears at least *some* responsibility for the threat that he poses to you. But Driver isn't a culpable attacker – he isn't maliciously trying to kill you. Indeed, unlike Stranger, Driver isn't *trying* to kill you at all. A culpability account will thus have to prohibit your killing Driver in self-defence.

If we think that these limitations on the scope of a right to self-defence are plausible, we might support the culpability account. But if we think that an account of self-defence ought to be able to permit killing people like Stranger and Driver, we will have to look elsewhere for an explanation of when and why self-defence is permissible.

The rights-based account

Rights-based accounts of self-defence begin by assuming that people have a right not to be killed. So, if it is permissible to kill a person, we must explain what happens to their right not to be killed, such that killing them does not violate that right. These accounts seek to explain the permissibility of killing a person in self-defence by describing the conditions under which a person can be said to have lost their right not to be killed.

One of the most influential rights-based accounts of self-defence comes from Judith Jarvis Thomson. Thomson argues that the right not to be killed is a *claim right*. Claim rights confer upon other people both a duty of non-interference and a duty of assistance. A duty is a morally binding obligation to behave in a particular way. If you are under a duty of non-interference with respect to a person's right, you must refrain from interfering with that right. If you are under a duty of assistance with respect to a person's right, you must (help to) ensure that the right is fulfilled.

For example, children have a claim right to an education. This claim is held against their parents (amongst other people). This means that parents have a duty to (a) *refrain from preventing* their children from going to school and (b) *actively ensure* that their children go to school. The right not be killed is a claim right that is held against people in general. It requires both that other people refrain from killing me and that other people help me defend myself if I am unjustly attacked. We will return to this idea of defending others – other-defence, as it is usually called – in more detail below.

Thomson's explanation of how a person loses their right not to be killed turns upon her understanding of what it is to fail in the duty not to kill someone. Thomson explains the permissibility of your using force in *Truck* in the following way. In *Truck*, Villain has no right to kill you. He therefore has a duty *not* to kill you. He will fail in this duty, and violate your right not to be killed, if he does in fact kill you. Because Villain is on course to violate your right not to be killed, he lacks the right that you not kill him. So, if you kill Villain, you do not violate his right not to be killed, because he no longer *has* such a right. This explains why it is permissible for you to kill Villain.

Thomson's view accommodates our intuition that Villain may not fight back against you as you try to defend yourself. On Thomson's view, one can lethally defend oneself against a person *only* if that person will otherwise violate one's right not to be killed (or violate some other sufficiently important right). Since Villain has lost his right not to be killed, you will not violate Villain's right by killing him. Thus, Villain cannot lay claim to a right to defend himself against you.

Thomson's account also generates the result that it is permissible to kill Stranger in *Elevator*. We might think that, given Stranger's lack of control, it sounds implausible to say that he violates your right by killing you. But on Thomson's account of rights, provided that we agree that Stranger has no *right* to kill you, which seems plausible, it *is* possible to say that Stranger will violate your right if he does kill you. Once we say that Stranger lacks a right to kill you, we are committed, she claims, to saying that Stranger has a duty not to kill you. Stranger fails in this duty just in case he does in fact kill you. And for Thomson, to fail in a duty that one owes to a person *just is* to violate their right. On her account, then, one can fail in a duty (and thus violate a right) without being morally responsible for that fact. Thomson's view of self-defence thus denies the need for culpability or even moral responsibility on the part of the person posing the threat. What is crucial for permissible defence is that the person whom you will kill in self-defence will otherwise violate your rights.

It is this criterion of permissible defence that limits the scope of the right of defence on Thomson's account. Consider the following case:[4]

Hungry:
Villain has locked you in his dungeon. You are slowly starving to death. One day, Villain lowers a plump baby into the dungeon, along with a knife and fork. You can prevent your death from starvation only by killing and eating the baby. If you do not eat the baby, Villain will remove it, and it will survive.

It seems to me a good test of any account of permissible defence that it prohibit killing the baby in *Hungry*. Thomson's account passes this test. Even though killing the baby is necessary to save your life, and the harm to the baby is proportionate to the harm that faces you, the baby is not on course to violate your rights. You have a right not to be killed that Villain is violating by starving you to death in his dungeon. But the baby is not violating that right, and thus you may not use force against the baby to avert harm to yourself.

Many people have objected to Thomson's claim that it is possible for a person to violate your right not to be killed even if they are not morally responsible for killing you. Consider the following case:[5]

Ray Gun:
Falling Person has been blown by the wind down a well, at the bottom of which you are trapped. Falling Person will crush you to death unless you vaporise her with your ray gun. If you do not vaporise her, your body will cushion Falling Person's landing, saving her life.

Falling Person is not even acting as she threatens you. Unlike Stranger, there is no sense at all in which we might say that Falling Person is *trying* to kill you. But it still sounds implausible to say that she has a *right* to kill you. Given this, Thomson's account holds that Falling Person has a duty not to kill you. Just like Villain, she will therefore violate your right not to be killed if she kills you. Falling Person therefore lacks a right not to be killed. You are permitted to lethally vaporise Falling Person on precisely the same grounds as you are premitted to kill Villain and Stranger.

However, if we are cautious of the idea that a schizophrenic can violate a person's rights, we are likely to be downright sceptical of the idea that a person who is helplessly falling can violate a person's rights. Michael Otsuka argues that even if we agree with Thomson that Falling Person will kill you, we cannot think that she violates your rights in doing so:

Surely one would not be tempted to make the same claim about a stone that falls on you after being lifted into the air by a tornado. Could things really be any different if it is an unconscious human being that falls on you after being lifted into the air by a tornado? I do not see how the rights-violating power of such a human object could be any greater than the rights-violating power of a chunk of granite. But talk of rights violations has, I think, gone too far if it is based on a theory that implies that a falling stone can violate a human right.

(M. Otsuka, 'Killing the Innocent in Self-Defense', *Philosophy and Public Affairs* 23, No. 1, 1994, 74–94, p. 80)

Falling Person is what is often called an *agency-lacking* threat. She endangers your life, but she has no control over this fact. Her movements do not proceed from her moral agency in the way that we would normally require if we were to describe her as *acting* rather than simply moving. It is this lack of agency that has led several commentators to compare agency-lacking threats to inanimate objects or animals.[6] We can agree that falling stones and charging tigers kill people. But do we want to be committed to the idea that stones and tigers *violate rights*? Otsuka argues that such a view is simply implausible, and that we should therefore reject both the permissibility of killing Falling Person and Thomson's account of self-defence.

Otsuka certainly seems to be right that falling stones and charging tigers cannot violate human rights. But many people nonetheless share Thomson's intuition that one may defend oneself against both a violent schizophrenic and an innocent falling person. It seems extremely morally demanding to require that you simply allow yourself to be killed in *Elevator* and *Ray Gun*. Certainly, the law would not require you to refrain from using self-defence in such cases. After all, you are innocent too. Can we defend Thomson against Otsuka's criticism?

Here's a passage from David Rodin, in which Rodin elaborates on precisely what he thinks has gone wrong in Thomson's argument to produce the conclusion that a stone rolling down a hill can violate human rights. Rodin suggests that Thomson is mistaken to infer that simply because something has no right *to* fall on you, it has a duty *not* to fall on you:

The reason why the stone on the hill has no right to fall on you is that it is just not the kind of entity that could be the subject of rights and duties. From the fact that the stone fails to possess a right to fall in this sense, it obviously cannot be inferred that it has a duty not to fall. The correct conclusion is that the stone has neither a right to fall on you nor a duty to abstain from falling, because it is not a moral subject at all. But precisely the same is true of the falling fat man. He is a moral subject, but *qua* falling object he is just like the stone, neither the subject of a liberty to fall on you, nor of a duty not to fall. The falling is not something he does so his falling cannot be in violation of any duties he owes you. Hence, in crushing you he violates none of your rights.

(D. Rodin, *War and Self-Defense*, New York: Oxford University Press, 2002, p. 86)

I think that most of us would agree with Rodin that the stone cannot be the subject of rights and duties. But if the reason for this is that the stone is not a moral subject *at all*, this argument fails to show that Falling Person cannot be the subject of rights and duties. After all, if she were really *just like* the falling stone, it would obviously be true that one is permitted to vaporise her, since vaporising stones is morally unproblematic.

If Rodin wants to resist this implication of his analogy, he must hold that Falling Person is enough of a moral subject to have a right not to be killed. But the portrayal of Falling Person as a sort of quasi-moral subject, with a right not to be killed but no duty not to kill others, might strike us as rather *ad hoc*. Perhaps Thomson's critics cannot have it both ways. If Falling Person is not the sort of thing that can have duties, perhaps she is not the sort of thing that can have a right not to be killed. If so, you will not violate her right if you kill her. If, however, Falling Person *can* have a right not to be killed, there seems to be at least some reason to think that she can have duties as well. But if we grant this, it seems possible that Thomson's argument succeeds, if it is true that Falling Person has no right to kill you to begin with.

Say that we interpret Thomson's argument as applying only to those things that are moral subjects in general, which seems like quite a plausible restriction of her view. In this interpretation, her argument seems to escape the perils of falling stones and charging tigers. She can avoid the peculiar conclusion that stones have a duty not to fall on people, because stones are not moral agents in general. And Rodin and Otsuka cannot really deny that Falling Person is a moral agent in general if they want to hold onto the claim that Falling Person, unlike the stone, can have rights. In this version of her argument, Thomson's account seems to withstand Rodin's and Otsuka's objection.

There might be other reasons, however, to be cautious of Thomson's account of self-defence. For example, even if her account of rights can overcome the sort of objection that Otsuka and Rodin pose, we might wonder whether she is right about what it takes to fail in a duty to someone, and thereby violate their right. Is it enough that Falling Person will kill you to make it the case that she has failed in a duty she owes you? Or must she *intentionally* kill you (or at least kill you through her reckless behaviour) if we are to say that she has failed in this duty?

On the one hand, we usually think that to say that someone *ought* to do something entails that they are *able* to do it (summarised in the philosophical slogan of 'ought implies can'). How can it be true, then, that Falling Person has a duty to refrain from killing Victim if she is not able to so refrain? But, on the other hand, it seems perfectly possible to say that, for example, a person forgot to do something that she ought to have done, like keep a promise. Forgetting, by its very nature, does not proceed from a person's agency (this is why it sounds odd to remonstrate with a person that she *shouldn't* have forgotten). But we don't usually think that simply because a person forgot to keep their promise, they had no duty to keep their promise. Rather, we think that they failed in a duty even though, in one sense, we realise that they could not help doing so. I am not sure which side of the fence we should fall down on here, but it is worth bearing in mind that there may be these more general issues surrounding Thomson's conception of rights, even if her account of self-defence can overcome the specific objection posed by Otsuka and Rodin.

We also noted earlier that Thomson can explain why Villain in *Truck* cannot employ counter-defence against you, because on her account Villain lacks the right not to be killed. But since Thomson's account of permissible defence does not distinguish between culpable attackers and innocent attackers, she cannot allow Falling Person to fight back either. Even though Falling Person is morally innocent, Thomson's account will not allow her to defend herself against you. This implication of Thomson's view might push our intuitions too far if we feel that Falling Person's innocence ought to make at least *some* difference to her moral status. Even if we think that you can defend yourself against Falling Person, we might think that her innocence at least grants Falling Person the right to fight back. But it isn't clear how we can allow for such a permission if we endorse Thomson's account.

The responsibility account

An alternative to both the culpability account and Thomson's rights-based account is the responsibility account of self-defence. The most influential contemporary proponent of this account is Jeff McMahan. McMahan understands permissible defence as foremost a matter of *justice*. An account of self-defence should tell us who, as a matter of justice, ought to bear a harm, given that someone has to bear it. For example, consider *Truck* again, where Villain is intent on running you down. In this case, either you must kill Villain or Villain will kill you. The question, then, is how this harm – death – ought to be distributed between you and Villain. It seems obvious to most of us that it is only fair that Villain be the one to bear the harm. He is, after all, culpably attacking you. McMahan agrees, arguing that justice requires that Villain bear the harm, and thus you may kill him rather than bear the harm yourself.

However, on McMahan's view, it is not, strictly speaking, Villain's *culpability* for the threat that makes it fair that he bear the harm. Rather, what matters is Villain's *moral responsibility* for the threat. Of course, Villain is *also* culpable for the threat. But whilst culpability entails moral responsibility, the reverse is not true. Recall the *Vehicle* case, in which Driver helplessly loses control of his car. Even though Driver is not culpable for posing a threat, McMahan argues that he is *morally responsible* for doing so.[7] Driver chose, voluntarily, to engage in driving, knowing that driving poses a small but genuine risk of serious harm to others. McMahan argues that Driver's moral responsibility for the fact that someone must now bear a harm makes it permissible for you to ensure that Driver suffers the harm rather than you.

McMahan summarises this claim by saying that Driver is *liable to defensive killing*. To say that a person is liable to defensive killing is to say that killing them does not wrong them and does not violate their rights. A person who is liable to be killed has no justified complaint against being killed. McMahan thinks that one can become liable to defensive killing only if one is *morally responsible for an unjust threat*. An unjust threat is a threat of harm that will wrong the person upon whom it is inflicted: it is a threat of harm directed at a person who is not liable to that harm. So, Driver poses an unjust threat to you in *Vehicle* because you are not unjustly threatening anyone, and are thus not liable to be killed. If he kills you, Driver will inflict an unjust harm upon you. And, because he is morally responsible for posing this unjust threat, he will *wrong* you in killing you. It is thus Driver's moral responsibility for an unjust threat that grounds your permission to kill Driver in self-defence.

However, notice that this account will not generate a permission of self-defence in cases like *Elevator* or *Ray Gun*. It is true that you are not liable to be killed in either of these cases. Stranger and Falling Person thus pose unjust threats to you. But neither Stranger nor Falling Person is *morally responsible* for the unjust threat that they pose, and therefore they are not liable to be killed by you in self-defence. On McMahan's view, neither Stranger nor Falling Person will wrong you if they kill you. But you will wrong *them* if you kill them, because they are not liable to be killed. Hence the defensive threat that you pose will be unjust, and you will be morally responsible for inflicting it because your defence will be deliberate. So whilst the responsibility account is more permissive than the culpability account, it is more restrictive than Thomson's rights-based account.

The doctrine of double effect

The final account of self-defence that we will consider is based upon the doctrine of double effect (DDE). The DDE is not exclusively an account of permissible self-defence: double-effect reasoning is used extensively in moral theory, including in just war theory. The DDE finds its roots in Catholic theology, and is an attempt to reconcile the Catholic ideal of 'doing no harm' with our intuition that inflicting defensive harm is sometimes permissible. Of course, one need not hold with Catholicism to think the DDE plausible: secular writers have made frequent use of double-effect reasoning to explain why it can sometimes be permissible to cause harm.

The DDE rests upon an alleged distinction between what I *intend* to cause by my actions (or what I intend to allow through my inaction) and what I merely *foresee* I will cause by my actions (or what I foresee I will allow through my inaction). There are, undeniably, some cases in which it seems plausible to distinguish between effects I intend and effects I merely foresee. For example, the more electricity I use, the larger the electricity bill I run up. But it would be odd to insist that I turned on the light *with the intention* of running up a large electricity bill. Rather, I intend to improve the lighting in the room, and merely foresee that I will receive a larger bill as a result. Here, the lighting of the room and the increasing of my bill seem to be separable effects of the action of switching on the light, such that I can properly be said to intend one but not the other. Proponents of the DDE often emphasise this separateness by pointing out that in the lucky event that I receive a small electricity bill, I will not be disappointed or feel that I have been unsuccessful in achieving some goal of mine. The DDE can explain this, because on this view I had no intention of running up a large bill, and thus my failure to do so is not a frustration of my intentions.

Of course, the DDE does not hold only that we can conceptually distinguish the effects that I intend from the effects that I foresee. It also holds that there is a morally significant difference between these two effects. The DDE claims that whilst it is always impermissible to intend harm, it is nonetheless sometimes permissible to cause harm as a foreseen *side-effect* of an action if doing so is necessary to achieve some proportionate good. The double-effect explanation of self-defence, then, insists that it would be wrong to *intend* harm to one's attacker. However, causing harm to the attacker can nonetheless be permissible provided that it is merely a foreseen side-effect of pursuing the good end of saving one's life. In other words, the permissibility of self-defence lies in the fact that the defender does not aim at doing harm, but aims only at the morally permissible end of saving their life.

Double-effect reasoning has been similarly employed to argue for the permissibility of other sorts of killing, such as euthanasia. According to the DDE, it would be morally impermissible for a physician to intend to kill their patient by giving them a lethal dose of some drug. But it is permissible to intend to relieve the patient's suffering by giving them a lethal dose of the drug, even if the physician foresees that the patient will be killed as a side-effect.

Unsurprisingly, this divorcing of intended consequences from foreseen consequences has attracted a great deal of criticism. In some cases, the two effects of an action – the good end and the harmful side-effect – seem too closely entwined for one to plausibly claim that one intended to produce only the good effect. Consider the *Ray Gun* case again. The 'closeness' objection insists that it is wholly implausible that you might vaporise Falling Person, but intend only to save your life, and not to kill her. Sustaining the intended/foreseen distinction is particularly difficult in such cases because the harm is what *achieves* the good. That Falling Person is vaporised is *what makes it the case* that your life is saved. There are not two things here: the saving of your life and the vaporising of Falling Person. Rather, your being saved consists in her being vaporised, and to vaporise her is to kill her. It is quite a stretch of our ordinary language to describe the killing of Falling Person as a side-effect of an action that saves your life.

It can also be difficult, particularly in cases of self-defence, to meet the DDE's requirement that the harm not be intended as a means. Imagine that the only way that I can stop you from attacking me is to cause you so much pain that you have no choice but to desist. When I stab you in the leg, causing you pain seems to be clearly instrumental in saving my life. It is not a mere side-effect of stabbing you: it is *the reason why* I stab you, because your being in pain is the means to my escaping. Stabbing you seems clearly permissible even though I intend to cause you pain. But the DDE holds that harm is permissible only if it is unintended: the harm must not be a means of achieving the end.

So, there are what look like instances of permissible defence that the DDE cannot allow. And there are what look like instances of impermissible defence that the DDE seems to permit. Consider the following case:[8]

> *Bomb:*
> A runaway trolley is heading towards you as you lie trapped on the trolley tracks. You will be killed unless you throw a grenade at the trolley and destroy it. However, the blast from the grenade will also kill an innocent person who is lying unconscious by the side of the tracks.

Now, most accounts of self-defence hold that it is impermissible for you to throw the bomb if doing so will kill the innocent person. But the innocent person's death would not be intended. It would be merely a foreseen side-effect of saving your life. How can proponents of the DDE prohibit killing this innocent person?

They might do so by arguing that this killing fails the proportionality requirement. How so? Well, the death of one innocent person certainly seems *comparable* to the death of another innocent person, so they could not do so on the threshold interpretation of proportionality that I suggested earlier. But they might opt instead for the simple outweighing model of proportionality, and insist that one may inflict harm only if the good achieved is *in excess* of the harm caused. Since in *Bomb* the harm inflicted would be equal to the harm avoided, the killing would be prohibited by this understanding of proportionality. This strategy would prohibit killing innocently threatening people, such as Falling Person. But we might think this a reasonable stance: perhaps such killings *are* impermissible.

Of course, if proponents of the DDE adopt this strategy, they will have to endorse the idea that the life of an innocent person is worth more than the life of a culpable person. Only in this way could the DDE permit the killing of a culpable attacker to save one's own life. But, again, we might think that this is correct. Perhaps harming a culpable person is not as morally bad as harming an innocent person because harm to the culpable person counts for less.

However, this explanation of the impermissibility of throwing the grenade in *Bomb* might still be problematic, because it is now unclear whether the DDE can permit you to kill a culpable attacker to prevent a lesser harm than

death. Recall my suggestion above that lethal force seems like a proportionate response to a threat of paralysis or kidnapping. If it is indeed permissible
to kill a culpable attacker to prevent such harms, the doctrine of double effect
must hold, in effect, that these harms are not just equal to, but *worse than*,
the death of a culpable person. We now seem to be attributing *significantly*
less weight to the culpable person's life on this account. Furthermore, most
people think that I may kill more than one culpable attacker to prevent them
from inflicting serious harm upon me. But, if this is true, this means that the
life of a culpable person must be worth very little indeed, if I may kill numerous would-be kidnappers rather than let myself be kidnapped.

Mark Timmons suggests that, at root, the DDE does nothing more than
offer alternative, but equally true, descriptions of the same action. The permissibility of the action then depends on which description one chooses to
endorse, as in the euthanasia case described above:

> So describing the action of the physician in one way yields the verdict
> that her action is an intentional killing, but when the action is described
> in another way, the [DDE] yields the verdict that her action is not an
> intentional killing. This means that the verdict we get using the [DDE]
> depends on how we describe the physician's action. Clearly something
> is wrong here. Either the physician's action is morally wrong or it is not
> morally wrong. It is nonsense to say that her action is wrong if described
> one way but not wrong if described another way, where both descrip-
> tions apply truly to her action.
>
> (M. Timmons, *Moral Theory: An Introduction*, Lanham, MD:
> Rowman and Littlefield, 2002, p. 91)

Timmons' complaint is echoed by many writers. What ought to concern
us is whether an action that will inflict a certain harm is morally permissible.
But the DDE seems to tell us that whether or not an action is permissible
depends upon how we *describe* the action. On some descriptions, the action
will be permissible. But on other, no less accurate, descriptions the action
will be wrong.

There lurks behind this complaint a deeper suspicion that although the
DDE might be used to justify a given action, it does not really explain *why*
the action is permissible. Rather, it simply offers support for our prior
convictions about an action's permissibility. When the end and the 'side-
effect' are closely entwined, we can adopt the description that best suits our
purposes. If we think killing in self-defence permissible, we can adopt the
description that pronounces the harm an unintended side-effect. If we think
it impermissible, we can insist that the harm is intended. The DDE offers us
no independent argument for preferring one description over the other – for
judging whether something really is a side effect or an end – but it is *this* that
would tell us whether or not killing in self-defence is morally permissible.
More generally, we might feel that the DDE cannot do justice to the idea that
harm caused in self-defence is morally permissible even when it is intended.

The DDE fails to capture the sense that I am *allowed* to kill a person who will otherwise kill me, and that I need not try to justify or excuse my killing by invoking some different goal or re-description of my action that the DDE will deem permissible.

As we can see, attempts to use double-effect reasoning to explain self-defence are beset with problems. However, in other areas of moral theory, the DDE is perhaps more persuasive. Certainly, it seems sometimes to make a moral difference whether I intend to cause something, or merely foresee that I will cause it. The famous trolley problem,[9] for example, is often explained by invoking the DDE:

Trolley:
A runaway trolley is heading towards five people who cannot get out of the way before it hits them. The trolley will kill them if it hits them. You are standing next to a switch that you can use to divert the trolley down a side track. However, the trolley will then kill a single individual who is stuck on the side track.

Most people think that you may divert the trolley. An obvious explanation of the permissibility of doing so is the difference in the numbers involved. Five people will die if you do nothing, but only one person will die if you divert the trolley. But if it is numbers that do the work, we commit ourselves to all sorts of unwelcome conclusions.

For example, consider *Transplant*:[10]

Transplant:
The trolley has hit the five people, and they are all badly injured. In order to survive, each person needs a different organ transplant. Luckily, the one on the side track is unharmed. You, the surgeon, can cut up the one and distribute his organs amongst the five, saving their lives. The one will, of course, die.

In this case, very few people think that you may save the five people at the cost of the one's life. But if what made diverting the trolley permissible was the difference in numbers, there should be no difference between the two cases. This tells us that it is not the numbers doing the moral work in the original *Trolley* case. What might be doing the moral work, however, is the DDE. In *Trolley*, you do not intend to kill the one. You would, after all, divert the trolley even in his absence. And, as Philippa Foot says, should the one miraculously survive being hit by the trolley, you would not pick up a spare bit of track and proceed to beat him to death with it.[11] Killing the one is not part of your aims: all that you aim at is the (permissible) end of saving the five.

It is hard to make this story stick in *Transplant*, though. Here, your plan to save the five depends upon the presence of the one. Without him, there is no rescue plan. And so you cannot very well claim to have merely foreseen his death, since killing him is part of the plan. Of course, we might argue that you don't *intend* to kill him. All you intend to do is remove his organs. You merely foresee, with an appropriate sense of regret, that he will die if you do this. But now we run into the closeness objection again. The closer the end to the alleged side-effect, the harder it becomes both to separate those effects, and to plausibly postulate some morally significant difference between that which is intended and that which is merely foreseen. Removing the one's organs *constitutes* killing him, and thus it's hard to see how the intended/foreseen distinction can have any purchase in this case.

So, what one intends seems relevant when dealing with some moral problems, but not others. With respect to just war theory, the DDE is primarily used to justify the collateral killing of non-combatants. Whilst non-combatants are not usually regarded as legitimate targets in war, just war theorists have often argued that killing non-combatants as a foreseen side-effect of attacking a military target can be morally permissible. We will consider this application of the DDE in Chapter 7.

Other-defence

An important aspect of any theory of self-defence is what it tells us about the permissibility of *other-defence*. Other-defence occurs when a third party comes to the aid of a person who is under attack. We usually think that if a person is unjustly attacked, it is morally permissible for others to come to their rescue. We might even think that rendering such assistance is, at least *prima facie*, morally *required*. We generally condemn those who stand by and do nothing when a person is under attack, which suggests that we conceive of other-defence as a duty rather than a mere permission. Indeed, the early Christian just war theorist St. Ambrose believed that defensive force could be permissibly employed *only* in defence of other people's lives, and that such force could be 'actually demanded on moral grounds'.[12]

Given this, our account of other-defence has the potential to play an important role not only in individual defence, but in the context of war. There are two readily apparent ways in which other-defence is relevant to war. One is in terms of combatants who are engaged in a defensive war against aggression. The combatants might well be understood to be defending themselves. But they are also defending the other citizens of their nation. For writers like Ambrose, this is crucial to the permissibility of the war. It also has significant implications for things such as proportionality in war. If the threat that I am averting is a threat to many lives, the amount of force that I may employ in averting that threat will be correspondingly greater.

The second obvious role that other-defence can play in the ethics of war is in explaining the permissibility of humanitarian wars of intervention. There is a growing consensus amongst just war theorists, and people in general, that it is not only when a nation wages a defensive war that its use of military force is permissible. We also think it can be permissible for a nation to use its armed forces to defend citizens in another country, against either external or internal threats. If the permissibility of such wars is explained by the fact that they are instances of other-defence, we can perhaps explain, for example, the condemnation that followed the failure of countries like the USA to intervene in Rwanda in 1994. Since other-defence is often conceived of as a duty, we have good grounds for thinking that wars of intervention are not only morally permissible, but morally required.

Consider the following case:

> *Rescue:*
> Villain is chasing Damsel because he hates her and he wants to kill her. Poor Damsel has no means of defence. Luckily, Knight comes riding past. Knight can easily kill Villain and save Damsel's life.

I expect that nearly all of us will think that Knight is morally permitted to save Damsel by killing Villain. And many of us might think that not only is Knight permitted to do this, but he is an under *obligation* to do this. He would act wrongly if he simply kept riding, and ignored Damsel's plight when he could so easily rescue her.

The obligatory nature of other-defence is often explained by the idea that Damsel has a right not to be killed. As I described above, people usually understand the right not to be killed as a claim right that confers duties of non-interference and of assistance on other people. Damsel is permitted to defend herself against Villain because, in trying to kill Damsel, Villain fails in the duty of non-interference that he owes her. Doing so violates Damsel's right. And if Knight fails to assist Damsel, he fails in the duty of assistance that he owes her, and also violates her rights.

But what should we say about *Retreat*?:

> *Retreat:*
> Villain is chasing Damsel, because he hates her and he wants to kill her. Poor Damsel has no means of defence. Knight comes riding past. Knight knows Villain, and knows what a skilled swordsman Villain is. Knight knows that his chances of defeating Villain without suffering serious injury to himself are very slim. Knight can safely retreat without attracting Villain's attention.

Is Knight required to try to save Damsel even at serious risk to himself? Most people think that he is not so required. This suggests that even if other-defence is a duty, rather than a mere permission, it is a *defeasible* duty. Our duty to assist is not so stringent as to require us to bear a significant risk of serious harm to help others (although it might require that we bear some risks of harm).

We might invoke the idea of an agent-relative reason to explain why this is the case. An agent-relative reason is a reason that has genuine weight for the agent, but that does not have weight for others. For example, imagine that a man can either save his wife from drowning or save a stranger from drowning. The fact that one of the drowning people is his wife gives the man a very good reason to save her instead of the other person – we might even think that it gives him a morally conclusive reason. But he could hardly expect this same fact – that she is *his* wife – to give the coastguard a good reason to save her rather than the other drowning person. From the coast-guard's perspective, this agent-relative reason is no reason at all.

Similarly, we might think that when it comes to a choice between saving his own life and saving Damsel's life, Knight has good reason to choose to save his own life. His agent-relative reason to prefer his own survival justi-fies his decision to fail to intervene on Damsel's behalf. The reason is not so strong that it could justify his deciding to let Damsel be killed rather than suffer some minor harm in rescuing her. But, at some point, the risk to Knight will be sufficiently great that he may permissibly refuse to intervene rather than take that risk. He would still be *permitted* to intervene, of course. But such intervention would be an act of supererogation, not of obligation.

We can also think of cases in which a third party might not have even a *permission* of other-defence, let alone a duty. Recall the *Ray Gun* example, in which you are about to be crushed to death by Falling Person. In the discus-sion of Thomson's view, I drew attention to the fact that Thomson denies that Falling Person may defend herself against you. Falling Person lacks a right not to be killed that could ground her right to self-defence. And on the very same grounds, Thomson *affirms* a permission for third parties to kill Falling Person on your behalf. Since you, unlike Falling Person, are about to suffer a violation of your right not to be killed, a third party may intervene to prevent this violation.[13]

Whether or not we think this is correct will probably depend on whether we agree with Thomson about the impermissibility of Falling Person's defending herself against you. If we share Thomson's view that Falling Person is not permitted to use counter-defence against you, we might be amenable to the idea that third parties are permitted to kill Falling Person on your behalf. But if we are hesitant about this first claim, I suspect we will be similarly hesitant about what third parties may do to Falling Person. We might think that part of what explains your permission to kill Falling Person is the existence of an agent-relative reason to prefer your own survival, just as we might think that Knight is allowed to prefer his survival to Damsel's. But since this is an agent-relative reason, it can have no weight for a third party. If this is right, then third parties lack sufficient reason to choose your life over that of another, equally innocent, person. But, again, this seems to undermine Thomson's view that it is rights-violation that does all the work in self-defence.

Chapter summary

Most people think it permissible to use defensive force against an attacker, provided that the force is necessary and proportionate. But these two restrictions on the use of force are only part of the story. Rival accounts of self-defence aim to give us a more complete understanding of self-defence. Culpability accounts invoke the fault of an attacker to explain why defensive force is permissible. Rights-based accounts rely on showing that an attacker has lost the right not to be killed. Responsibility-based accounts like McMahan's focus upon liability to defensive killing, where this is acquired through moral responsibility for an unjust threat. And accounts based upon the doctrine of double effect argue that defensive force is permissible if, and only if, the defender merely foresees the harm that she causes. As we have seen, these different accounts generate different scopes of permissible defence.

While self-defence is usually conceived of as a right or permission, other-defence is usually thought to be a duty. If I can easily rescue someone from unjust harm, I have a duty to do so. But this duty is not absolute. I do not have to expose myself to a significant risk of serious harm in order to save someone else from an even greater harm. And there may be cases in which a person is permitted to defend themselves, but in which a third party is not permitted to assist them. Thus, whilst the duty of other-defence is seemingly grounded in the assisted person's own right to self-defence, it does not follow that I may do in other-defence *whatever* they may do in self-defence.

Questions for discussion

1 Is it permissible to kill Stranger in *Elevator*? Why?
2 Which account of self-defence strikes you as the most plausible?
3 Do you agree that other-defence is a duty, or is coming to the aid of others always supererogatory?
4 How plausible is the doctrine of double effect?
5 Is it permissible to throw the grenade in *Bomb*? Why?

Notes

1. Based on Judith Jarvis Thomson's case in 'Self-Defense', *Philosophy and Public Affairs* 20, No. 4, 1991, 283–310, p. 283.
2. Based on George Fletcher's case in 'Proportionality and the Psychotic Aggressor', *Israel Law Review* 8, 1973, 367–390, p. 371.
3. Based on Jeff McMahan's case in 'The Basis of Moral Liability to Defensive Killing', *Philosophical Issues* 15, Normativity, 2005, 386–405, p. 393.
4. Based on Thomson's case in 'Self-Defense', p. 291.
5. Based on Robert Nozick's case in *Anarchy, State and Utopia*, Malden, MA: Basic Books, 1974, p. 34.
6. See M. Otsuka, 'Killing the Innocent in Self-Defense', *Philosophy and Public Affairs* 23, No. 1, 1994, 74–94; J. McMahan, *The Ethics of Killing: Problems at the Margins of Life*, New York: Oxford University Press, 2002,

p. 409; and D. Rodin, *War and Self-Defense*, New York: Oxford University Press, 2002, pp. 81–83.

7. McMahan, 'The Basis of Moral Liability to Defensive Killing', p. 394.
8. Otsuka, 'Killing the Innocent in Self-Defence', p. 85.
9. P. Foot, 'The Problem of Abortion and the Doctrine of Double Effect', *Oxford Review* 5, 1967, 5–15.
10. J. J. Thomson, 'Self-Defense and Rights', in W. Parent (ed.), *Rights, Restitution and Risk*, Cambridge, MA: Harvard University Press, 1986, p. 34.
11. Foot, 'Abortion and Double Effect', p. 9.
12. L. J. Swift, 'St. Ambrose on Violence and War', *Transactions and Proceedings of the American Philological Association* 101, 1970, 533–543, p. 535.
13. Thomson, 'Self-Defense', p. 308.

Suggested reading

Judith Thomson, 'Self-Defense', *Philosophy and Public Affairs* 20, No. 4, 1991, 283–310.
One of the classic papers in the self-defence literature, this paper defends a rights-based account of self-defence that permits the killing of innocent threats.

Michael Otsuka, 'Killing the Innocent in Self-Defence', *Philosophy and Public Affairs* 23, No. 1, 1994, 74–79.
This paper offers the most influential critique of Thomson's account, arguing against a permission to kill innocent threats.

Noam Zohar, 'Innocence and Complex Threats: Upholding the War Ethic and the Condemnation of Terrorism', *Ethics* 114, 2004, 734–751.
This paper looks specifically at the implications of Thomson's account of self-defence for the ethics of war.

Jeff McMahan, 'The Basis of Moral Liability to Defensive Killing', *Philosophical Issues* 15, Normativity, 2005, 386–405.
This paper outlines McMahan's criticisms of several accounts of self-defence, and develops his own responsibility-based account. Given the importance of McMahan's work in just war theory, it's a good idea to read this article.

2 War and self-defence

Having considered some of the most prominent theories of self-defence, we can turn now to the relationship between self-defence and war. As I have already indicated, the nature and extent of this relationship is a source of considerable disagreement. On the one hand, *collectivists* argue that war is to be understood as a relationship not between persons, but between collectives. We must thus treat the actions of combatants as undertaken on behalf of the collective, which means that we cannot judge these actions by the standards we apply to individuals. On the other hand, *individualists* argue that the rules governing killing in war can be reduced to the rules governing defensive killing between individuals. Killing does not take on a different moral character simply because it is practised on a large scale or has political ends.

The debate about which perspective we should adopt when judging war has emerged as an important theme of contemporary just war theory. Whilst the majority of this book focuses on particular issues within war, it is worth taking some time to consider some of the arguments at this more abstract level.

STATES AND CITIZENS

The domestic analogy

When one state wrongfully attacks another, we call this *aggression*. Michael Walzer argues that in order to understand aggression between states, we must look to civil society:

> Every reference to aggression as the international equivalent of armed robbery or murder, and every comparison of home and country or of personal liberty and political independence, relies upon what is called the *domestic analogy*. Our primary perceptions and judgements of aggression are the products of analogical reasoning. When the analogy is made explicit, as it often is among the lawyers, the world of states takes on the shape of political society the character of which is entirely accessible through such notions and crime and punishment, self-defense, law enforcement, and so on.
>
> (M. Walzer, *Just and Unjust Wars*, New York: Basic Books, 1977, p. 58)

Walzer argues that it is only because we recognise assaults on our person and property that we can recognise international aggression, which is the international equivalent of these assaults. But on Walzer's view, thinking about civil society not only helps us identify acts of aggression between states, but also explains why states may forcefully rebut aggression: why states have the right to use defensive force.

Walzer argues that the primary good defended in war is not human life or property, but rather the 'common life' that citizens develop.[1] This common life is a *way* of living, shaped by the citizens' own interests and preferences, that might involve having a particular political system, practising a certain religion or adhering to certain values. In waging a defensive war, states protect the rights of their citizens not only to live, but to live in a manner of their choosing. Indeed, it is often only indirectly that the lives of the citizens come under attack. Much of the violence of war is conditional violence. It is only if the victims of aggression resist that they find their lives (as opposed to their way of living) at risk.

In order that a state may protect and facilitate the common life, it must have *sovereignty*. Sovereignty can be summarised as the rights of political and territorial integrity. These rights require that outsiders not try to forcefully interfere with the workings of a state's political system, or occupy or control its land. These rights belong to states, says Walzer, 'but they derive ultimately from the rights of individuals, and from them they take their force'.[2] On this view, the defensive rights of states are simply the defensive rights of citizens in 'their collective form'.[3]

How do citizens transfer their defensive rights to the state, such that the state may permissibly wage war in their name? Walzer argues for a roughly contractualist answer to this question, whereby citizens consent to their state's acting on their behalf. But it is a 'special sort' of consent that is given – tacit rather than explicit, and demonstrated not by avowals but by participation.[4] It is by a process of 'association and mutuality' – by *living* in the state and forming a common life within it – that citizens agree to their state's forceful protection of them.[5] In the event that a state does not protect the common life, or if there is no common life to protect, Walzer suggests that the state in question lacks the right to wage defensive wars.

I expect that most people will agree that the right of a state to use defensive force must be in some way rooted in the rights of its people. What is usually disputed is whether a state's defensive rights are not only *grounded in* the rights of its citizens, but also *determined by* those rights. Even if states have defensive rights only because their citizens have certain rights, it does not follow that the content of states' rights must be identical to the content of individuals' rights.

The collectivist account

Walzer suggests that once we move beyond establishing that a state is justified in declaring war, and focus on the actual fighting of war, we move beyond

what individual rights can tell us about the ethics of war. The domestic analogy 'is of little help here. War as an activity (the conduct rather than the
initiation of the fighting) has no equivalent in a settled civil society.'[6]

The idea that the conduct of war *has no domestic equivalent* is extremely
influential amongst just war theorists. Many people think that the rules of
war are *sui generis*: there is nothing else like war, and the rules governing it
are thus unique. War must therefore be judged on its own terms, and these
judgements must pay attention to the sort of thing that war is. War as we
know it involves deliberately killing and maiming people, activities that are
generally morally impermissible in ordinary life. How could an enterprise so
very alien to ordinary life be judged from within civil society, by the rules
of ordinary life? Walzer argues that in trying to apply the rules of ordinary
life to war, all that the individualist achieves is a description of what morality
would require in war, 'if war were a peacetime activity'.[7] Since war is, by definition, *not* a peacetime activity, the individualist project is largely confused
or misplaced.

Walzer claims that, 'war itself isn't a relation between persons but between
political entities and their human instruments.'[8] This claim summarises the
collectivist position: that there is something more to war than groups of
people engaged in fighting. Imagine the following case:

> *Hooligans:*
> A group of football fans encounter some members of a rival club whilst
> on a night out. The fans attack and kill several members of the rival club.

The football fans are clearly engaged in wrongful killing – murder – and each
should be held to account for their role in the attack. But, according to the
collectivist, things are very different in the following scenario:

> *Combatants:*
> Nation A wages an unjust war of aggression against Nation B. The com-
> batants of Nation A attack and kill a great many combatants who are
> trying to defend Nation B.

On the collectivist view, war is not like a brawl between the fans of rival
football teams. War is essentially *political*, and we must reflect this dimension
of war in our judgements of it. When combatants fight for their country,
they fight not as individuals but as representatives of their state. This makes
a great deal of difference to how we ought to morally evaluate their actions.
We cannot, therefore, determine what combatants can do in war solely by
looking at what individuals may do in self-defence.

Noam Zohar, for example, argues that '[t]rying to make sense of warfare
as though it were an aggregate of individual confrontations can only produce moral vertigo.'[9] Zohar argues that self-defence requires some kind of
guilt or fault on the part of the aggressor. But in combatants – even those on
the unjust side – this guilt is lacking. A combatant who obeys his country's

orders to fight, perhaps believing that his war is just, is not, Zohar claims, culpable in the way that we require for defensive killing. And often, combatants are not even *aggressors* in any obvious sense. Zohar argues that the range of legitimate wartime targets includes many people – army drivers, chefs and so on – who could not plausibly be described as threats in ordinary life.[10] If we judge war by the rules governing defence between individuals, we will have to deem killing combatants impermissible even if they are fighting an aggressive war. The only way in which we can permit killing these combatants is to allow that during war people can be killed because they are part of a guilty collective, even if they are morally innocent as individuals.

However, Zohar does not want to claim that *all* members of the enemy nation can be viewed as part of the guilty collective, and can thus be permissibly killed. Rather, he restricts his claims to combatants by arguing that only they can be said to truly represent the collective in their actions. Zohar argues for a dual perspective in war, one that reflects both the individual and collective aspects of citizens:

> War is perceived and described properly only when we see it as being waged between nations rather than simply between two hosts of individual soldiers . . . It is the soldiers, rather than the civilians, who are subsumed under the collective identity. Civilians too are members of the nation, but their identity as individuals is paramount, whereas those who wear the national uniform are rightly identified as embodying the nation's agency.
>
> (N. Zohar, 'Innocence and Complex Threats: Upholding the
> War Ethic and the Condemnation of Terrorism', *Ethics* 114, 2004,
> 734–751, p. 739)

We can attack combatants even if they are innocent because they mark themselves out as acting on behalf of the collective. And, since they act on behalf of the collective, and not as individuals, we need a different set of rules to understand and judge their actions. This means that something that would be morally prohibited between individuals might be morally permissible between agents of a collective.

Christopher Kutz invokes Jean Jacques Rousseau's idea of the political will to help defend the collectivist account. Rousseau's *Social Contract* develops an account of people within states as multifaceted beings who are at once citizens who govern and individuals who are governed.[11] That citizens can be self-legislating is, according to Rousseau, a prerequisite of their being a sovereign body with political authority and freedom. Crucially, our actions as a collective cannot be reduced to the actions of individuals, because sovereignty is about the relationship *between* individuals: it is necessarily group-based. Kutz argues that since war is a relationship between these sovereign collectives, which cannot be reduced to their individual members, we have to judge war as a collective activity. And:

[w]hen individuals' wills are linked together in politics, this affects the normative valence of what they do individually as part of that politics, even to the point of rendering impunible what would otherwise be criminal.

(C. Kutz, 'The Difference Uniforms Make: Collective Violence in Criminal Law and War', *Philosophy and Public Affairs* 33, No. 2, 2005, 148–180, p. 157)

Kutz thus describes combatants as having, 'an essentially *political* permission to do violence' that stems from their role in the collective.[12]

But *how* does the fact that a course of action is undertaken collectively change its moral character? What's so special about group action that the usual moral rules do not apply? Jeff McMahan argues that the collectivist view, 'presupposes a form of moral alchemy' by which people can, by agreeing amongst themselves to pursue a given goal in an organised fashion, licence themselves to do what would otherwise be impermissible.[13] And this kind of self-legislation hardly seems plausible. If it is wrong for me to steal, and it is wrong for each of my friends to steal, it cannot become permissible for us to steal provided that we all do it together. We cannot, in virtue of our joint plan to steal, make stealing permissible.

Of course, the collectivist account is intended to apply only to *political* action. Perhaps my light-fingered friends and I cannot be self-legislating because we are not engaged in a political project: we are not, as Kutz puts it, trying to form a state or similar institution.[14] But, again, it's hard to see exactly what it is about political goals that enables them to render permissible that which would otherwise be wrong:

Goals that are paradigmatically political may also be paradigmatically evil – for example, the goal of eliminating a people in order to create an ethnically 'pure' society. It is morally impossible that the collective pursuit of such goals could be self-justifying [. . .] What matters is not whether a goal is *political* but whether it is *just* – for example, whether it involves the prevention or correction of a wrong.

(J. McMahan, 'Collectivist Defences of the Moral Equality of Combatants', *Journal of Military Ethics* 6, No. 1, 2007, 50–59, p. 53)

Generally speaking, the fact that a large number of us are systematically trying to bring about some end doesn't make our actions morally permissible if the end is itself unjust. And that the unjust end is political doesn't seem to alter this. As McMahan points out, political ends can be wrong just as easily as any other sort of end – that I steal from an immigrant family in order to make a political statement, rather than to feed my drug habit, doesn't make the theft any more morally respectable. Rousseau may well be right that being self-legislating is part of political freedom and authority. But the fact that something is a necessary condition of our being free doesn't explain why we get to do things to people *outside* of our political collective, who necessarily lie outside the scope of our political authority. Our authority over ourselves cannot grant us authority over others.

So, whether we endorse the collectivist project seems to depend on whether we think that by trying to establish or defend a state, or similar political institution, groups acquire rights of self-determination that are so important that they override normal moral constraints. Even if the group's end is unjust, perhaps the right of self-determination can allow the group to authorise its members to pursue that end. If we think that group action of this sort ought to be (or can only be) judged by different rules to those that pertain to individuals, this supports the collectivist view. If, on the other hand, we think that group action does not take on a distinctive moral character in this way, we seem to be inclined towards the individualist approach to war.

The individualist account

Individualists hold that individual rights not only form the moral basis of states' rights, but also shape the content of those rights. What a state may do to protect itself is just an extension of what individuals can do to protect themselves. Whilst Walzer's domestic analogy is *mere* analogy, intended to explain the crime of aggression by comparing it to crimes of domestic life, the individualist takes war to be a continuation of domestic life.

The individualist account draws support from the way that just war theorists use terms like 'proportionate force' and 'last resort' to describe the constraints on killing in war. These ideas, or at least their labels, are taken directly from the constraints governing self-defence. Individualists deny that killings carried out by political groups acquire a privileged moral status simply *because* they are perpetrated by those groups (or rather, by individuals acting on behalf of those groups). What may be done in the name of a group is nothing more or less than may be done in the name of the individuals who compose that group. So, when we think about what a nation may do to defend itself during war, we must try to establish what it would be permissible for an individual to do in self-defence in comparable circumstances.

Of course, the obvious rejoinder here is that there are no circumstances in ordinary life that are similar to war. How can we tell what a country can do to prevent, say, the annexing of part of its land by thinking about what a person might do in self-defence? It is not as if persons can be annexed or invaded. Comparisons with individuals might thus seem unhelpful or unilluminating. But the individualist claim is not that situations in war are identical to situations in which one might use self-defence, but that they are, at root, subject to the same moral principles. And it often doesn't take a great deal of imagination to envisage domestic situations that can illuminate the ethics of war.

Think of a farmer who finds squatters trying to forcibly remove his tenants from their homes on his land. The would-be settlers have already shot one of the tenants, and are threatening the others with lethal force. If the farmer can defend his tenants' lives and homes only by force, is he permitted to do so? Note that in stipulating that this is the only way in which he can protect his tenants, I rule out the possibility of calling the police to remove the squatters (perhaps the farm is in a very remote area). This stipulation reinforces the similarity with war, in which there are no police who will come to right the wrongs. But, if you prefer, think about what the police might do to defend the tenants and the land. Could they forcibly remove the squatters in the famer's defence? Could they use lethal force to protect his tenants? What if the squatters are yet to actually shoot anyone, but make clear that their intention is to occupy the land and enslave the tenants? Could the police use lethal force to prevent the squatters from inflicting these sorts of harms?

These are not intended as rhetorical questions. The answers might be far from obvious. We might think that we must fill in more details before we can pass judgement on what the police, or the farmer, may do in defence of the land and its occupants. We might think that if the tenants are able to flee, then they ought to do so, and the farmer should accept the loss of his land. What the individualist will urge is not that lethal force must be permissible if it is aimed at defending the land, because nations can use force to defend land in war. Rather, they will urge that the same moral considerations that matter in this situation are also what matter at the national level. Thus, what we judge permissible in the domestic case will be similarly permissible in the comparable wartime case. If it is permissible for me to shoot you if that is the only way that I can avoid being enslaved by you, it will be permissible for a group of citizens to use lethal force to prevent an invading nation from enslaving them. If it is wrong for you to kill me in order to steal my land, it is wrong for members of an invading army to kill native citizens in order to steal their land.

What the individualist denies, then, is that once we reach a certain scale of violence, or once we are dealing with violence with political ends, the rules of the game change such that what would be impermissible between individuals becomes permissible between members of the collectives. As McMahan puts it, when it comes to the morality of defensive killing, the conditions of war 'change nothing at all; they simply make it more difficult to ascertain relevant facts.'[15]

Rodin's critique of individualism

One way in which just war theorists have tried to undermine individualism is by pointing to apparent differences between what an individual may do in self-defence and what states (or their representatives) may do in national defence. David Rodin identifies several such differences. For example, Rodin argues that the range of permissible lethal activities in war extends, 'well beyond what could be justified in terms of the personal right of self-defense alone.'[16] Combatants often attack unarmed members of the enemy army, such as chefs or truck drivers, as well as combatants who are sleeping or in retreat.

They also use pre-emptive force, laying traps and mines to avert future threats posed by enemy combatants. Such tactics are, says Rodin, 'clearly no part of self-defense'.[17] If we think that these tactics are permissible in war, but agree with Rodin that they cannot be grounded in self-defence, it looks as if individualism must be false.

Rodin also tries to undermine individualism by highlighting the requirement of retreat that applies to self-defence. As we discussed in Chapter 1, the necessity condition of self-defence means that people should usually try to flee an attacker rather than use defensive force. If we understand the rules of war as entirely determined by the rules of self-defence, Rodin argues, it follows that states that can avert war by appeasing aggression ought to do so.[18] But orthodox just war theory endorses almost the opposite view, with a presumption in favour of *confronting* aggression in the name of deterrence. Rodin suggests that this lack of fit between self-defence and the rules of war shows that 'national-defense cannot be reduced to the defensive rights of individuals'.[19]

Scope and necessity

How persuasive is Rodin's critique of individualism? Let's begin with the claim that the rules of war are more permissive in scope than the rules of self-defence. Rodin argues that self-defence does not include, for example, a right to employ pre-emptive force against a prospective attacker.[20] Individuals may defend themselves only against *imminent* threats. But the rules of war permit combatants to lay traps to kill people who will threaten in the future, and to kill people who have threatened in the past but who are now running away! Surely this shows that killing in war is not constrained by the rules of self-defence?

Rodin's observations point us towards the complex nature of the threat that is posed by a nation, and its army, during wartime. The aggression of a state is not composed of a single threat, posed by a single attacker. It is a complex array of threats posed by thousands of combatants engaged in hundreds of separate offensives. Taken together, these offensives constitute the threat that the defending nation is trying to rebut. Any attempt to understand defensive killing in war by thinking about self-defence must therefore take into account the scale and complexity of the threat involved in war. This will require us to think carefully about exactly how the necessity condition of defence applies in the context of a multifaceted threat of this kind. But, contrary to what Rodin says, it isn't clear that these differences in scale prove that the rules of self-defence and the rules of war are different in type.

Rodin concedes that if one could know that defence is necessary before a harm becomes imminent, pre-emptive force would be permissible between individuals. What he denies is that one *can* know that defence is necessary before the harm is imminent. But consider the following case:[21]

Hostage:
A hostage knows that their captor plans to kill them at the end of the week. At the beginning of the week, an opportunity arises for the hostage to kill their captor.

It seems to me that the hostage may kill their captor now, even though the captor does not imminently threaten their life. Sometimes, one can know with reasonable certainty that force is necessary even before a threat is imminent. Killing the captor seems to be a clear instance of permissible self-defence.

Of course, such cases are unusual in self-defence. Since pre-emptive action is rarely necessary, it is rarely permissible. It is perhaps this that makes it seem as if self-defence does not include a right to use pre-emptive force. But pre-emptive action often *is* necessary during war. War *just is* a state in which one's enemy declares their intention to attack, repeatedly, until a ceasefire is agreed. Given this, combatants can assume that a unit currently in retreat will threaten in the future. As McMahan argues, in war, 'there are no police to capture and restrain a retreating army, and retreats in war are presumptively strategic unless accompanied by a declaration of surrender.'[22]

This alleged difference between self-defence and war, then, shows only that, as a contingent matter, pre-emptive force is unlikely to be necessary on an individual level. It does not show that self-defence excludes a right to use pre-emptive force and that the individualist account is thus incorrect. (We might even argue about whether the use of force in these cases really is pre-emptive, since in both the *Hostage* case and in the wartime case an attack is already under way, even if lethal harm is not yet imminent. But whether or not we call it pre-emption is unimportant for defending the individualist project. All that matters is whether what combatants may do in war can be mirrored in individual defence. If the use of force is permissible in a case like *Hostage*, the kind of military tactics that Rodin describes can be plausibly understood as an extension of self-defence in the way that the individualist requires.)

This more careful analysis of these kinds of tactics partly undermines Rodin's critique of individualism. But it doesn't explain why the range of legitimate targets seems so much broader in war than in self-defence, something mentioned in the discussion of collectivism above. This objection concerns a central aspect of just war theory – the distinction between combatants and non-combatants – to which we return in Chapter 7.

Retreat and appeasement

How might an individualist deal with the fact that the rules of self-defence are widely agreed to include a requirement of retreat, whereas the rules of war are widely thought to favour fighting aggression? One possible reply is to argue that the orthodox presumption of confronting aggression is mistaken.

As we will see in Chapter 4, some writers have urged that we ought to be less permissive when it comes to deeming wars just. Sometimes it is better to acquiesce to aggression than fight it.

However, we need not take this view in order to defend individualism. Rodin's objection is that if the requirement of retreat applies in war, states will have to appease aggression 'if it were possible to avoid bloodshed in this way'.[23] But it's not obvious that the state equivalent of retreat is appeasement. The natural meaning of 'retreat' on an individual level is that of simply running away from one's attacker. If a woman can either kill her would-be rapist or flee to safety, most accounts of permissible defence hold that she ought to flee to safety. But, clearly, states threatened with invasion or other aggression cannot run away. If this is what retreat means, it is not possible for states to retreat.

Nevertheless, we might think that appeasement is the next best thing to retreat. If so, and if the individualist view is correct, perhaps states ought to appease rather than fight. But it does not follow from the fact that one ought to retreat if doing so will avoid bloodshed that one ought to appease if doing so will avoid bloodshed. If a woman threatened with rape cannot flee her attacker, she might nonetheless have a choice between trying to kill her attacker and submitting to the rape. Submitting to the rape – appeasement – will avoid bloodshed. But most accounts of self-defence do not demand that she appease the rapist in this way. Rather, they permit her to try to kill the rapist even if she could have avoided bloodshed by appeasing him.

The difference between retreat and appeasement is that the requirement to retreat is operative only when one can *safely* retreat. I should flee my attacker only if I can do so without exposing myself to a harm comparable to that with which I am threatened. In the event that fleeing will be dangerous – say it requires me to jump from a great height – there is no obligation to retreat rather than try to kill my attacker. Rodin's mistake, I think, is to assume that because appeasement between states would avoid bloodshed (and perhaps avoid any physical harm to citizens) it will therefore avoid harm altogether. This implies that appeasement is akin to safely retreating. But this assumption is false. The meaning of appeasement is that one absorbs a lesser harm in order to avoid a greater harm. This is a very different idea to retreat, which is required only if it will mean that one can avoid the occurrence of any serious harm *at all*. And whilst a state might avoid bloodshed it if appeases an aggressor, it is unlikely to avoid serious harm if it does so.

Imagine that the Spanish government demand that the French relinquish power over Provence, a demand backed by the threat of war. France can avoid a bloody conflict by giving Provence to the Spanish. But can France really be said to *avoid harm* by appeasing Spain in this way? On the contrary – she will forfeit a substantial part of her territory, with all the financial and political burdens that this entails. Appeasement in this case will avoid bloodshed, but it will hardly avoid serious harm. And because appeasement is required only when the lesser harm is not in itself serious, France is not obliged to appease in this case. It will almost never be the case that appeasement of aggression between states avoids serious harm, once we recognise that serious harm is not limited to loss of life or limb. And as long as the harm that could be absorbed in appeasement is *sufficiently* serious, appeasement is not required between either states or individuals.

THE LAWS OF WAR

Morality and law

So, Rodin's critique seems unsuccessful as a rebuttal of the individualist account. But there are further, more fundamental, objections to the individualist project. Henry Shue has argued that the individualist account cannot provide a basis for the laws of war (set down in the Geneva Conventions and formally known as the Laws of Armed Conflict).[24] For example, the current laws of armed conflict hold that combatants do not act illegally simply by fighting in a war, even if they fight on the unjust side. Thus, 'unjust combatants' have the same legal status as 'just combatants'. A corollary of this view is that unjust combatants do nothing illegal if they kill just combatants (assuming that the just combatants have not surrendered or are not prisoners of war).

However, we could not possibly support this position if the laws of armed conflict were based upon the morality of self-defence. In self-defence, there exists a clear moral inequality between an unjust attacker and their victim. Attackers do wrong in attacking their victim in the first place, and they certainly do wrong if they kill them. Victims, in contrast, do not act wrongly if they kill their attacker in order to save their own lives. The individualist account thus yields the result that unjust combatants are not the moral equals of just combatants, because unjust combatants act wrongly by fighting.[25] If we based the laws of armed conflict upon the individualist account, this would make it illegal to fight on the unjust side of a war. All unjust combatants would be in breach of this law and liable to criminal prosecution.

The practical implications of such a law are enormous. Consider the familiar phenomenon of 'victor's justice'. It is bad enough that those involved in unjust aggression sometimes win their wars. But it would be even worse if they could then prosecute the defeated just combatants as criminals under international law. Such trials would compound the injustice that these combatants, and their country, have already suffered. Implementing the individualist account of war could increase the likelihood of such injustices by creating legal scope for such prosecutions. Basing the laws of war upon the individualist account would also be problematic even when victory is claimed by the just side. After the Second World War, there were millions of surviving combatants who had fought against the Allies on (let us assume) the unjust side of the war. What would have been the cost of prosecuting these combatants, both in terms of paying for the trials and in terms of undermining the recovery of the world's economy? Having all that was left of a generation of young men behind bars would have delayed economic growth in Germany for years. And whilst it hardly seems fair to make the states that were the victims of aggression pay for trials, Germany and her allies were already crippled by war reparations. Adding to their debts would have placed their fragile economies under even further strain.

More generally, many people think that it is morally wrong to blame or prosecute combatants for fighting in their country's war. Many combatants are young, uneducated men who are ordered to fight by their leaders, and face being ostracised and punished if they refuse. As McMahan himself points out, these people are already wronged by being ordered to fight an unjust war. How could it be fair to punish them for fighting as well?[26]

In light of these sorts of concerns, McMahan argues that we should not base the laws of war on the moral rules of war. Sometimes, the laws we should adopt do not directly correspond to morality. For example, even if we think that morality requires that a person not cheat on their spouse, it does not follow that we think the law ought to criminalise adultery. The effects of such a law – the invasion of people's privacy, for example – would make it undesirable even if it accurately reflected the morality of adultery. Similarly, McMahan thinks that morality requires combatants to behave in particular ways, such as not fighting in unjust wars. But he does not think that we should therefore criminalise fighting in unjust wars, because of the sorts of difficulties just described. Rather, we must have a 'two-tier' approach to war, distinguishing between the morality of war and the laws of war.

The deep morality of war

The central claim of McMahan's account is that it matters a great deal for the purposes of morality whether or not one's war is just. Those fighting for just causes can permissibly do things that those fighting for unjust causes cannot. The problem with *legislating* on the basis of this claim is that since most people believe that *their* side is the just side, whatever is deemed lawful for the just combatants will also be adopted by the unjust combatants.

For example, according to McMahan, the distinction between those who are morally liable to be killed in war and those who are not does not correspond to the distinction between combatants and non-combatants. This is unsurprising when we recall McMahan's account of self-defence, upon which a person can be liable to defensive killing if killing them will help avert an unjust threat for which they are morally responsible. Non-combatants often contribute to the threats that their countries pose in war. Thus, on McMahan's view, it is theoretically possible for non-combatants to render themselves liable to defensive killing under certain circumstances. Although McMahan takes steps to try to limit non-combatant liability (as we will discuss in Chapter 7), his individualist account cannot offer a moral basis for a universal principle of non-combatant immunity, upon which non-combatants are never legitimate targets. Rather, it supports the claim that just combatants may sometimes permissibly attack non-combatants. But since combatants on *both* sides of a war will believe that *they* are the just combatants, changing the law to reflect this claim would lead to attacks on non-combatants on both sides. This is clearly the worst possible outcome. Changing the law would not ensure that only individuals who are liable to be killed are attacked, but rather would increase the number of attacks on people who are *not* so liable.

So, McMahan does not advocate changing the laws of armed conflict so that they are in line with what he thinks are the moral rules of war as revealed by the individualist account. Rather, he suggests that we have reasons – moral reasons – for keeping many of the laws of war the same, even though they do not reflect what he calls the 'deep morality' of war.[27] The deep morality of war is that some non-combatants may be liable to defensive killing (although such cases will in practice be rare). But the *laws* of war should hold that non-combatants are never legitimate targets. In other words, McMahan advocates a kind of 'levelling down' of the laws of war. Even though just combatants are morally permitted to do certain things, we must legally restrict their actions in order to reduce unjust harm overall. Given that both sides will view themselves as the just side, 'the laws of war must at present be neutral between just and unjust combatants'.[28]

McMahan supports his suggestion by drawing an analogy with the law on rape. Suppose we agree that what rapists deserve, morally, is the death penalty. But if we imposed the death penalty upon rapists, we would eliminate a major incentive that rapists have not to rape *and murder* their victims, since the penalty for rape and murder would be no more severe than the penalty for rape alone. Since 'morality itself requires that the formulation of the law take account of the likely consequences of its promulgation and attempted enforcement',[29] the law should not impose the death penalty for rape, even if rapists deserve to die. By the same token, we might agree that, morally speaking, non-combatants contributing to an unjust war are liable to attack. But we should still have a law that prohibits attacking them, because morality requires that we minimise the likelihood of *innocent* non-combatants being attacked.

McMahan claims that the crucial difference between morality and the law is that the law is devised by humans. The law has a *purpose* in a way that morality does not. It can thus be altered and shaped to meet human ends, because it is humans who determine what the law is, and what it is meant to do. Morality, on the other hand, simply 'is what it is'.[30] We cannot alter morality because it does not suit our purposes. It exists independently of our ends or preferences. If we think that the law should aim to reduce overall unjust harm, we can shape the laws in the way that we think most likely to further that end, perhaps by having laws that protect all non-combatants from attack. But we cannot thereby override or cancel out the fact that, as a matter of basic morality, some non-combatants are liable to attack, just as some rapists might deserve to die.

The morally best laws of war

McMahan's defence of the individualist project seems *prima facie* plausible. We are all familiar with the idea that the law and morality sometimes diverge, and that what morality permits can conflict with what the law prohibits (and vice versa). Perhaps we can thus make sense of the idea that the laws of war must be informed by different considerations from those at work in the ethics of self-defence.

However, as McMahan himself acknowledges, the sorts of considerations that speak in favour of imposing particular laws are *themselves* moral reasons. We should not impose the death penalty on rapists because this endangers the lives of other rape victims. But then, as Shue argues:

> this is not actually an example of the 'divergence between law and moral-ity'. It is a divergence between the best law, moral considerations (like the assumed difference in moral seriousness between death and rape) taken into account, and what morality might otherwise have required if one were not designing a system of general law . . . The law, then, is not diverging from 'morality' in some overall sense. It is diverging from what desert specifically is assumed to require, but the departure from the moral judgement about desert is for the sake of implementing another moral judgement, namely, that one ought not to provoke murders while trying to deter rapes. 'Morality' is on both sides, or rather, at least one moral consideration is on each side.
>
> (H. Shue, 'Do We Need a "Morality of War"?', in D. Rodin and H. Shue (eds), *Just and Unjust Warriors*, Oxford: Oxford University Press, 2008, pp. 92–93)

Shue is surely right that what McMahan presents as the conflict between law and morality is simply a conflict between competing moral demands: desert on the one hand and saving lives on the other. If, on balance, we deem that the moral requirement to save lives outweighs the moral requirement to give rapists what they deserve, then we do not reject morality in favour of law, but rather pronounce on what morality requires *all things considered*.

The law that gives murderers harsher punishments than rapists is an example of what Shue describes as the *morally best laws*. With respect to war, the morally best laws are those that take into account 'all the moral consid-erations that the conduct of a war could take into account'.[31] Shue maintains that what just war theorists should strive to determine are the morally best laws for war. When we establish what these laws are and enact them, we elim-inate the tension that McMahan identifies between the laws of war and the morality of war. The laws of war will not diverge from morality, but rather will *correspond* to what morality requires, all things considered.

For example, consider the principle of non-combatant immunity, which McMahan's account of liability undermines. McMahan argues that because changing the law that prohibits attacks on non-combatants would result in an overall increase in unjust harm, we ought not to change the law. But the claim that we should not increase unjust harm is a *moral* claim. And the judgement that it is better overall that the law prohibit attacking non-combatants is a *moral* judgement. If this judgement is correct, the law protecting all non-combatants from intentional attack is the morally best law. *This* law does not conflict with morality. It *reflects* morality, once all the morally relevant facts are taken into account.

Conflicting obligations

Shue also draws attention to a further difficulty with the sort of two-tier approach to war that McMahan defends. Shue argues that this approach gives rise to perpetual conflict between morality and law in a way that makes it very hard for us to offer guidance to combatants in war. Which of these two 'levels' of war takes precedence when a combatant is trying to decide what they ought to do?

Imagine the following case:

> *Weapon:*
> A group of non-combatant scientists are on the verge of developing a weapon that will give their country a decisive advantage in their unjust war. A just combatant fighting against this unjust war realises that if he kills the scientists, he will significantly increase the chances of defeating the unjust war.

McMahan's moral rules of war will tell the just combatant that the scientists are liable to be killed. They may even tell the combatant that he is *required* to kill them to help his country win their just war. But the laws of war will tell the combatant that, as non-combatants, the scientists are not legitimate targets. He is thus prohibited from intentionally attacking them. What ought he to do? McMahan argues that in a case like *Weapon*, morality triumphs over the law. The combatant ought to kill the scientists, and then defend his actions by appeal to the 'higher form of justification' that morality provides.[32] Offering this justification shows that the combatant still has respect for the law – he is not trying to deny that he acted illegally. He is simply claiming that moral obligations can sometimes require breaking the law.

What about a different case, where the law is more permissive than morality?

> *Attack:*
> A unit of unjust combatants happen upon a unit of just combatants guarding a bridge crucial to the transporting of supplies to the unjust side. The unjust combatants are well concealed, and can easily kill all the just combatants, gaining control of the bridge.

McMahan tells us that under the moral rules of war, unjust combatants are prohibited from killing just combatants. And, he argues that when morality prohibits what the law permits, 'one ought to obey the prohibition'.[33] McMahan suggests that this kind of case does not represent a serious form of conflict. It is obvious that one ought to obey the more restrictive source of authority, which will in this case be the moral rules.

But as Shue points out, and is made apparent by the case above, this seems like a mistake on McMahan's part. This kind of conflict, and McMahan's proposed resolution, will have far-reaching effects on what combatants do in war, because it is precisely this kind of conflict that arises *every time* an unjust combatant is ordered to kill a just combatant. If, faced with such conflicts, unjust combatants must follow the moral prohibition instead of the law, McMahan's view requires perpetual and pervasive disobedience from unjust combatants. This seems to be an example of what Shue has in mind when he says that the individualist account will *prohibit* war rather than govern it.[34] Unjust combatants who try to apply the moral rules of ordinary life to war will simply be unable to fight.

Well, we might say, what's wrong with that? Isn't it *good* that unjust wars don't get fought? Shue agrees that, in an ideal world, it would be good if unjust wars were not fought. The problem is that once the war is being fought, things are already less than ideal. The laws of armed conflict are intended to tell combatants what they are allowed to do *given that they are fighting*. Shue alleges that the only guidance McMahan's approach can offer is an iteration of the claim that if the war is unjust, then they ought *not* to be fighting it. It gives them no guidance whatsoever about how to behave in war once they have already decided to fight. As long as the combatant believes that their war is just, they will not be guided by rules telling unjust combatants what to do.

As Shue argues, recognising the *possibility* that one's war might be unjust could be useful in terms of provoking regular reflection on one's general beliefs about the war. But:

> [W]hat it will not do is lead one to act as if [those beliefs] are mistaken, while one still believes them. What one would not decide is not to attack anyone on the other side, even though one had decided that one ought to participate in the fighting.
>
> (Shue, 'Do We Need a "Morality of War"?', p. 108)

Shue concludes that McMahan's suggested resolution of conflicts between law and morality is 'next to useless as an action-guiding principle for the conduct of war.'[35]

In Shue's view, the rules we have in ordinary life do not apply in war because they are just not compatible with the sort of thing that war is. Using these rules to judge war would not make war a rule-governed activity that more fairly distributed harms. It would simply make war impermissible. Combatants cannot discriminate on the basis of morality liability, which will likely be indiscernible on the battlefield. Rather, they must discriminate on the basis of more readily apparent facts, such as the wearing of uniforms, the possession of weapons, and so on. But Shue is not suggesting that we reject individualism in favour of a collectivist account of liability:

> [T]he mistake that I believe that McMahan is making is not that he has formulated the wrong criteria of moral liability for the circumstances. The mistake is to assume that decisions within war can be based on any criterion of moral liability whatsoever. The mistake is to attempt to operate with a criterion of moral liability at all; the mistake is not to have one set of moral criteria rather than another.
>
> (H. Shue, 'Laws of War', in S. Besson and J. Tasioulas (eds), *The Philosophy of International Law*, New York: Oxford University Press, 2010, p. 519)

Shue's claim, then, is not that the more readily apparent facts, such as the wearing of a uniform, can be taken as evidence of moral liability (recall Zohar's suggestion that we can view combatants in uniform as part of a guilty collective). It is that if we want combatants to constrain their killing and maiming, we must do so on the basis of facts that they can determine. And, sadly, these facts will not correspond to moral facts about whether a person bears moral responsibility for the war. It is thus a tragic, but inescapable, feature of war that the innocent are killed along with the guilty. But constraining the killing in this way is better than failing to constrain it at all. Allowing combatants to discriminate on the basis of non-moral facts might simply be the best that we can do within the realms of what it is *possible* for us to do.

Regulating wrongdoing

Part of the alleged difficulty of applying the rules of ordinary life to the rules of war is that those things that are prohibited by law in ordinary life – rape, theft, armed robbery and so on – are wrong in all, or very nearly all, circumstances. War, in contrast, is *not* always wrong: one is sometimes morally permitted, or even morally required, to go to war. A just war is a war that one *ought* to fight. And so, we might think, one cannot ban war as one can and should ban rape.

This argument warrants closer examination. After all, whilst war is not always wrong, *unjust* war is always wrong. This is why unjust war is illegal. But, says Shue, what we must deal with is the reality that some people will think that their unjust war is just, and will act accordingly. Our primary concern, then, is one of trying to minimise the damage that these people do.

Since people are going to fight unjust wars, believing that they are just, the law should allow them to kill combatants on the condition that they don't kill non-combatants.

Could we, then, run a similar argument about other crimes, such as rape? After all, whilst having sex is not always wrong, *rape* is always wrong. This is why rape is illegal. Nonetheless, we might say, what we must deal with is the reality that some people will think that their act of rape is an act of consensual sex (perhaps they believe that having sex with a person who is unconscious through intoxication isn't rape), and will act accordingly. Our primary concern, then, should be trying to minimise the damage that these people do. Since some people are going to commit rape, believing that theirs is an act of consensual sex, we should allow them to engage in this act provided that, say, they use protection. For example, we might have a law that unmarried couples may engage in consensual sex only if it is protected sex. Our rapist, thinking that his is an act of consensual sex between unmarried people, dutifully uses a condom. He thus ensures that he won't, in addition to inflicting the harm of rape upon his victim, inflict the further harms of sexually transmitted diseases and unwanted pregnancy.

The structure of this case is pretty similar to the structure of Shue's argument: given that people are going to engage in this wrongful act, we must focus our efforts on minimising the harm they cause, even if the best way to do this is to grant that they may legally cause some harms, but not others. To some people, this seems obviously correct. *Of course* we should urge rapists to use condoms. But to others, there is something very worrying about the idea that we might confer the title of a 'morally best law' upon a law that allows people to perpetrate rape provided that they use a condom. This worry is only exacerbated if we commit ourselves to the claim that those who follow the morally best laws do not act wrongly.

This is not to deny that there are reasons in favour of such a law. After all, as things currently stand in the absence of such a law, there are an equal number of rapes, but they are often unprotected rapes. The absence of this law thus results in more unjust harm overall. Nonetheless, we might well think that there are some things that the law should simply refuse to sanction, even if making them legal on occasion would reduce their harmful effects overall. And if rape is one of those things, then killing and maiming innocent people look like good candidates too. Shue emphasises that the laws of war do not say 'kill combatants', but rather say 'kill only combatants' or 'do not kill non-combatants'.[36] We might think that it is therefore too strong to say that these laws *sanction* the killing of combatants. But there remains the fact that unjust combatants are deemed not to act illegally if they kill innocent just combatants. These killings are not criminal, even if they are not lauded. If we object to the idea that we should simply accept certain wrongdoing, such as rapes and unjust wars, as inevitable and legislate accordingly, we might object to Shue's claim that the primary function of the laws of war is the reduction of harm.

Chapter summary

The debate between collectivists and individualists is ongoing, and raises fundamental questions about how we view the relationship between citizens and their state, and how we understand the relationship between morality and law. International law is currently more reflective of the collectivist stance, but there are, I think, genuine difficulties in providing a principled explanation of how collective action attains the special moral status that the collectivist view requires. Nor is the individualist account without its problems, especially when it comes to devising policies that can guide combatants who want to know how they ought to fight. We cannot hope to resolve these tensions here, but the reader should be aware of these more abstract debates about the project of just war theory as we proceed with our analysis of more specific issues.

Questions for discussion

1 How might the our characterisation of other collectives, such as corporations, inform our understanding of the collectivist approach to war? Can the 'actions' of corporations be sensibly attributed to their individual members?
2 How plausible is it to compare war to the defence of land and property in ordinary life? What role does the 'common life' play in justifying war?
3 Can McMahan's account of war offer guidance to combatants?
4 Can we make sense of the 'deep morality' of war that is not reflected in the laws of armed conflict?

Notes

1. M. Walzer, *Just and Unjust Wars*, New York: Basic Books, 1977, p. 54.
2. Walzer, *Just and Unjust Wars*, p. 53.
3. Walzer, *Just and Unjust Wars*, p. 54.
4. Walzer, *Just and Unjust Wars*, p. 54.
5. Walzer, *Just and Unjust Wars*, p. 54.
6. Walzer, *Just and Unjust Wars*, p. 127.
7. M. Walzer, 'Response to McMahan's paper', *Philosophia* 34, 2006, 43–45, p. 43.
8. Walzer, *Just and Unjust Wars*, p. 36.
9. N. Zohar, 'Collective War and Individualist Ethics: Against the Conscription of "Self-Defense"', *Political Theory* 21, No. 4, 1993, 606–622, p. 615.
10. N. Zohar, 'Innocence and Complex Threats: Upholding the War Ethic and the Condemnation of Terrorism', *Ethics* 114, 2004, 734–751, p. 742.
11. J.-J. Rousseau, *The Social Contract*, trans. C. Betts, Oxford: Oxford University Press, reissued 2008.

12. C. Kutz, 'The Difference Uniforms Make: Collective Violence in Criminal Law and War', *Philosophy and Public Affairs* 33, No. 2, 2005, 148–180, p. 173.
13. J. McMahan, 'Collectivist Defenses of the Moral Equality of Combatants', *Journal of Military Ethics* 6, No. 1, 2007, 50–59, p. 53.
14. Kutz, 'The Difference Uniforms Make: Collective Violence in Criminal Law and War', p. 156.
15. J. McMahan, 'Killing in War: Reply to Walzer', *Philosophia* 34, 2006, 47–51, p. 47.
16. D. Rodin, *War and Self-Defense*, New York: Oxford University Press, 2002, p. 128.
17. Rodin, *War and Self-Defense*, p. 128.
18. Rodin, *War and Self-Defense*, p. 128.
19. Rodin, *War and Self-Defense*, p. 128.
20. Rodin, *War and Self-Defense*, p. 128.
21. P. Robinson, *Criminal Law Defenses* 2, St. Paul: West Group Publisher, 1984, p. 78. See also J. McMahan, 'War as Self-Defense', *Ethics and International Affairs* 18, No. 1, 2004, 75–80, for a discussion of a similar case.
22. McMahan, 'War as Self-Defense', p. 76.
23. Rodin, *War and Self-Defense*, p. 128.
24. H. Shue, 'Do We Need a "Morality of War"?', in D. Rodin and H. Shue (eds) *Just and Unjust Warriors*, Oxford: Oxford University Press, 2008, pp. 87–111.
25. J. McMahan, 'On the Moral Equality of Combatants', *Journal of Political Philosophy* 14, No. 4, 2006, pp. 377–393.
26. J. McMahan, 'The Morality of War and the Law of War', in D. Rodin and H. Shue (eds), *Just and Unjust Warriors*, Oxford: Oxford University Press, 2008, p. 29.
27. J. McMahan, 'The Ethics of Killing in War', *Ethics* 114, 2004, 693–733, p. 730.
28. McMahan, 'The Morality of War and the Law of War', p. 28.
29. McMahan, 'The Morality of War and the Law of War', p. 34.
30. McMahan, 'The Morality of War and the Law of War', p. 35.
31. Shue, 'Do We Need a 'Morality of War'?', p. 96.
32. McMahan, 'The Morality of War and the Law of War', p. 39.
33. McMahan, 'The Morality of War and the Law of War', p. 37.
34. Shue, 'Do We Need a 'Morality of War'?', p. 96.
35. Shue, 'Do We Need a 'Morality of War'?', p. 108.
36. Shue, 'Laws of War', p. 516.

Suggested reading

Christopher Kutz, 'The Difference Uniforms Make: Collective Violence in Criminal Law and War', *Philosophy and Public Affairs* 33, No. 2, 2005, 148–180.
Kutz defends the collectivist account of war.

Jeff McMahan, 'Laws of War', in S. Besson and J. Tasioulas, (eds), *The Philosophy of International Law*, Oxford: Oxford University Press, 2010.
This is McMahan's most recent publication to date on the laws of war.

David Rodin, *War and Self-Defense*, New York: Oxford University Press, 2002.
Especially Chapters 5, 6 and 7, in which Rodin argues that the defensive rights of nations cannot be reduced to the defensive rights of individuals.

3 The conditions of *jus ad bellum*

Jus ad bellum is about whether or not one has a just cause for going to war: whether the war as an enterprise is morally permissible. The first part of this chapter will introduce the seven formal *jus ad bellum* conditions that are the generally accepted requirements for a just war, and will outline some of the substantive disagreements concerning them. The second part of the chapter will consider in more detail the ways in which contemporary just war theorists have conceived of the substantive content of two of the most controversial *jus ad bellum* conditions, just cause and proportionality.

JUS AD BELLUM

The rules of *jus ad bellum*

The *ad bellum* rules of war emerged from the writings of various ancient and medieval thinkers as they sought to understand the morality (and legality) of war. Over the centuries, a general consensus has been reached about the formal conditions that make up *jus ad bellum*, although there is a great deal of debate about how each condition ought to be interpreted: about what I will call the *substantive content* of each condition. There are seven conditions that are widely agreed to make up the requirements of *jus ad bellum*:

1. just cause;
2. proportionality;
3. a reasonable chance of success;
4. legitimate authority;
5. right intention;
6. last resort;
7. public declaration of war.

When all of these conditions are met, we can say that a state has an *overall just case* for war: that the war as an enterprise is just. Then, and only then, is it morally permissible for the state to declare war. We will consider each of the *ad bellum* conditions in turn.

Just cause

It might seem odd to talk of a just cause for war as one of the conditions of *jus ad bellum*, rather than the result of meeting those conditions. In ordinary language, we often describe a state as having a just cause for war when it satisfies all the *jus ad bellum* conditions, taking 'just cause' to be an all-things-considered judgement about the morality of a war. But it is important to distinguish between a just cause, understood as the sort of wrong appropriate to form the basis of a case for war, and the justness of the *overall case* for war, where this takes into account all of the *jus ad bellum* conditions.

Properly understood, the rules of *jus ad bellum* allow that one can have a just cause for war, and yet lack an overall just case for war. For example, a state might be in violation of some international agreement, where this violation is the sort of thing that could warrant military intervention. But if diplomatic efforts might have a good chance of resolving the situation without the need for military force, war would not be a last resort. War would thus be impermissible, even though there is a just cause. Just cause should thus be understood as the foundation of a case for war – the trigger that begins the debate about whether war could be morally permissible.

Early just war theorists like Augustine identify peace as crucial for 'advancement towards human purity and a closer relationship with God'.[1] Augustine argued that only when a society is stable – free from outside interference – can there be the organised Christianity that enables individuals to seek the all-important 'divine redemption.'[2] Whilst the motivation from organised religion is lacking in more recent accounts of just cause, Augustine's general claim that wars must be fought for the purposes of justice (and not self-interest) persists, and influences several of the *ad bellum* conditions.

A just cause for war is usually defined as a military act that violates (or threatens to violate) a state's sovereignty. A military act need not involve violence against people, but could include, for example, the illegal occupation of land. 'Sovereignty' refers to the political and territorial integrity of a state. For a state to have sovereignty is for it to have authority over its political system and its borders. Hence, the paradigmatic just war is a war of self-defence that aims to repel violations of sovereignty. Violations of sovereignty are usually termed *aggression*. Invading another country or assassinating its head of state are examples of aggression.

Most people think that wars of other-defence or collective self-defence are also just. States are permitted to go to the aid of another state that is trying to repel aggression. Collective self-defence usually refers to states that have signed mutual defence treaties, where these treaties deem an attack on one signatory an attack on all. Both forms of defence are legally protected by Article 51 of the UN Charter, which states that nothing in that Charter, 'shall impair the inherent right of individual or collective self-defence if an armed attack occurs against a Member of the United Nations (UN), until the Security Council has taken measures necessary to maintain international peace and security.'[3]

We distinguish between territorial integrity and political integrity because whilst an invasion or occupation is often backed by political ambition, such ambition is not a necessary feature of aggression. For example, a foreign power may seek to obtain a valuable natural resource by invading another country's territory, but have no designs on the governance of that country. However, the invasion still counts an act of aggression that can be permissibly resisted on grounds of self-defence because the foreign power threatens the country's sovereignty by threatening its rights over its land.

It is natural to think that what we defend in war are our lives and our land, and that our right to defend these goods stems from our individual rights to defend ourselves and our property. But as Michael Walzer has argued, war threatens more than these physical goods. Walzer argues that political and territorial integrity matter because they are prerequisites of what he calls 'the common life'.[4] As we saw in Chapter 2, Walzer envisages a social contract between citizens and states that confers upon states the right to use forceful means to protect the citizens again invasion:

> The protection extends not only to the lives and liberties of the individuals but also to their shared life and liberty, the independent community they have made, for which individuals are sometimes sacrificed. The moral standing of any particular state depends upon the reality of the common life it protects and the extent to which the sacrifices required by that protection are willingly accepted and thought worthwhile. If no common life exists, or if the state doesn't defend the common life that does exist, its own defense may have no moral justification.
>
> (M. Walzer, *Just and Unjust Wars*, New York: Basic Books, 1977, p. 54)

It is not, then, the ownership of the land *per se* that gives people the right to defend themselves against invasion. Rather, owning the land gives people a space in which they can develop a way of life and in which they can be self-determining to a lesser or greater extent. It is this that sovereignty protects, and it is this that provides states with a just cause for war.

The other primary just cause for war is the prevention of humanitarian abuses in another country. Humanitarian wars are often thought to come under the remit of permissible other-defence. We will consider the nature and justness of wars of humanitarian intervention in Chapter 4. The same chapter will also consider the legitimacy of punitive wars: wars waged in response to a suffered wrong even in the absence of an imminent or ongoing attack. Revenge was often cited as a just cause for war by early just war theorists. If such wars are permissible, however, they move us beyond the scope of what can be justified by a right of defence.

An example of a just cause for war on the basis of the violation of political integrity is the assassination of Archduke Ferdinand in 1914. Ferdinand, heir to the Austro-Hungarian empire, was shot by Serbians seeking independence from the Austro-Hungarian regime. Whilst the gunmen were not acting under authority from Serbia's leaders, Serbia's failure to investigate the killing was seen as a form of complicity with the attack. Since the assassination was a serious attack on the Austro-Hungarian political system, it violated Austro-Hungary's political integrity in a way that made it a candidate just cause for war (although this is not to say that there was an overall just case for the ensuing First World War). Other paradigm just causes for war include the occupation or annexing of land, the invasion of territory and physical attack. The 9/11 attacks on the World Trade Center in New York in 2001 were the right sort of event to form the basis of a case for war (although a war against whom is not entirely clear), as were the German invasion of Poland in 1939 and the Iraqi invasion of Kuwait in 1990.

Paradigmatic *unjust* causes include the expansion of one's territory, the pursuit of natural resources, the imposition of religious change, the effecting of regime change and displays of military prowess. Many people cite these last two causes as the motivating force behind American involvement in Vietnam, where fear of communism encouraged the USA to fight a long and costly war trying to prevent the installation of a communist government in South Vietnam. The USA also wanted to recover its reputation as a force to be reckoned with after recent military embarrassments such as the failed Bay of Pigs invasion in 1961. Vietnam is generally regarded as a clearly unjust war.

A state can be said to have a just cause for war either if it is about to suffer an appropriate wrong or if the appropriate wrong has already occurred. We can illustrate this first sort of cause by thinking about the analogy with self-defence. An individual may use force against an imminent threat – that is, a threat that is anticipated but yet to occur. She need not wait until her attacker lands the first blow before she defends herself, provided she can be reasonably certain that the attack is about to take place. And, once the attack is in progress, she may continue to try to forcefully prevent the infliction of future blows. Likewise, a state may use force to avert imminent harm. It may also use force to prevent future attacks after the initial wrong. We can think of this as the state equivalent of an ongoing attack.

The question of what counts as an imminent harm has become increasingly pressing as the technology of warfare has advanced. On an individual level, it is usually quite obvious if one is about to be attacked. If one is being chased by a man waving a gun and shouting threats, we can agree that the threat of harm is immediate, or 'clear and present'. But the development of long-range weaponry and the capacity to move large numbers of troops at short notice makes it hard to judge whether a state poses a threat. There might be few external or incontrovertible signs that one's enemy is planning for war. When one can attack another country from the air within a matter of minutes, or fire a missile from one's own territory, one need not give any clear indication of plotting aggression at all. This means that a state might have only inconclusive evidence that an attack on its soil is imminent, making it very difficult to establish whether a war would be a legitimate act of pre-emptive defence. We will consider pre-emptive wars in detail in Chapter 4.

Proportionality

In order for a war to be just, it must be a proportionate response to the suffered wrong. As we discussed in Chapter 1, it is not permissible to kill a person even if this is the only way in which you can prevent them from stealing your wallet, because your right to your wallet does not warrant protection by lethal force. Similar considerations apply to the waging of war. The good that you are protecting must be worth the harm that you are inflicting. How are we to go about deciding whether war is a proportionate response to a received or anticipated injury?

Well, we might begin by trying to gauge how bad things will be if the aggressor succeeds in their goal, be it to take control of a particular piece of land, to destabilise a region or to topple a government. What sort of harm will this inflict upon the people of the victim state? Once (or if) we establish an answer to this question, we must try to predict the harms that will be inflicted if we try to avert the attack. How much damage will we cause to enemy civilians if we try to defend ourselves? How many of our soldiers will be killed or injured? What will be the economic cost of fighting the war? And, perhaps hardest of all, we must then judge whether the harms we will inflict by fighting are outweighed by the goods that fighting will protect.

Clearly, this process of judging a war's proportionality is no easy task. There are two main reasons why this is the case. First, there are significant epistemic problems in trying to calculate whether a war would be proportionate. We simply cannot know, or perhaps even reliably predict, the damage that will be caused in the course of a war, or the damage that might result if aggression is not resisted. We can only make a best guess at what the likely civilian casualties will be, or how much property will be damaged, or how many of our soldiers will die. Once begun, wars can rapidly escalate, and even an educated guess at the resulting losses might be wildly off-target.

Consider the war in Vietnam in 1965. Setting aside the question of whether the Americans had a just cause against which they could weigh the harms of war, the Vietnam War is a classic case in which the losses that the Americans anticipated at the outset of the war were greatly exceeded by the actual number of deaths, both of Vietnamese civilians and of their own troops. The Americans misjudged, at great cost, the level of resistance that they would encounter. But their estimated losses at the start of the war may nonetheless have been plausible given the evidence available. Even the most well-founded predictions of the losses of war might be mistaken. It is because of this that the *ad bellum* requirement is to be understood not as a one-off assessment, but as an ongoing evaluation of the war's justness. Things change in war; it might well become apparent that a war that appeared proportionate at its outset is no longer so, and is thus no longer just.

As well as the epistemic uncertainty surrounding losses in war, we also face the more abstract problem of how to go about identifying and weighing the goods and harms that are to be balanced in this sort of calculation. When an individual uses self-defence, it is usually pretty obvious what the relevant goods and harm are. For example, in a standard case of defence against a lethal threat, the relevant good is the victim's life, and the relevant harm is the damage that her defence will cause (to her attacker and perhaps to any bystanders). It seems quite straightforward to weigh this good against this harm, since we are comparing different physical harms. But judging proportionality in *jus ad bellum* can require us to compare harms of radically different sorts, as David Rodin explains:

> The difficulty of applying the test of proportionality in the *jus ad bellum* is this: if the balance we are required to make is between the harms inflicted in the course of war (measured in terms of number of dead, destruction to property) and the protection of a state's rights of sovereignty, then it seems very difficult to know how to go about making this comparison. For, phrased in these terms, the task seems to require the comparison of incommensurables.
>
> (D. Rodin, *War and Self-Defense*, New York: Oxford University Press, 2002, p. 115)

Rather than compare harms within a single category, the proportionality requirement in war requires us to compare harms *across* categories in a way that it is hard to mimic on the individual level. We have to try to judge the value of certain moral goods, like the right to self-determination, in a way that allows comparison with the methods of warfare. But how do we determine how many deaths control over one's border is worth? How much property can one damage in order to maintain political independence? These are very hard questions. Indeed, Rodin argues that they are *so* hard to answer that international law has simply side-stepped them, preferring 'to simply assume that war is always a proportionate response to unlawful use of force which threatens the sovereignty of the victim state.'[5] In other words, because it is so difficult to make these judgements, it has become common practice to grant territorial and political control such great weight that it is *always* deemed proportionate to wage war to defend it. We can thus avoid the need to make proportionality calculations at all, because we stipulate that any cost is worth paying to retain our sovereignty.

Whilst this might be common legal practice, it is philosophically unsatisfying. We will therefore return to the issue of proportionality and relevant goods in more detail in the second part of this chapter. For now, though, it might be helpful to push our analogy with self-defence a little further. After all, not *all* cases of self-defence involve a threat to a person's life. Imagine that I can stop you from stealing my wallet only by breaking your leg with my baseball bat. Is this permissible? In this scenario, the required force seems disproportionate, and thus defending my wallet seems impermissible. But what if, in order to steal my wallet, you have broken into my house? You don't cause me any more *physical* harm by breaking into my house to steal my wallet than you do by stealing my wallet on the street. But now it seems like it might well be proportionate to break your leg, because now I seem to be defending more than just a wallet. As Thomas Hurka argues:

> [F]orcible entry into a person's home invades space that should be personal; this is why its victims feel violated. While the parallel with rape must not be exaggerated, it seems that just as in that case the violation of intimate space increases the seriousness of the crime and the amount of force permitted to prevent it, so invasion of one's home justifies more defensive force than other crimes against property.
>
> (T. Hurka, 'Proportionality in the Morality of War', *Philosophy and Public Affairs* 33, No. 1, 2005, 34–66, pp. 55–56)

Many people, and most legal systems, hold that we may use significant force to prevent forcible entry into our own space or territory. Whilst we might not be able to precisely judge what counts as proportionate force in these cases, we do nonetheless seem able to weigh the good of what is, essentially, a form of sovereignty over one's territory against physical harm. Comparisons across categories of goods and harms thus seem to be possible in at least some cases.

However, Hurka argues that whilst these judgements can be made (and be made meaningfully, such that we do not *always* grant defence of sovereignty the status of a proportionate just cause), the diversity of the values in play means that we must rely on 'direct intuition'.[6] Such intuition might give us clear answers at either end of a proportionality spectrum (condoning waging a brief war to prevent an overwhelming invasion of sovereignty at one end, and prohibiting waging a long and bloody war to prevent a minor infraction of sovereignty at the other). But it will not provide definitive answers in those cases that cover the middle ground.

A reasonable chance of success

The requirement that one wage war only if one has a reasonable chance of success prohibits the fighting of a war 'against all odds', even if one is resisting unjust aggression. If a state is invaded with an overwhelming level of force that it cannot possibly hope to match, it must surrender rather than fight. This condition does not stipulate that one can wage only those wars that one is certain to win, or is even likely to win. But it does require at least a reasonable prospect of success.

Why would we want to include such a condition in our requirements for a just war? There doesn't seem to be any similar requirement in self-defence.[7] If an innocent person is attacked by a culpable aggressor, she may arguably use force against her attacker even if she knows that her struggle will be fruitless.

But this feature of self-defence is in itself somewhat peculiar, because it isn't clear how it fits with the necessity condition of defensive force. Can I believe it *necessary* to, say, scratch my attacker's face even if I know that this will not cause him to desist from his attack? In one sense, we can view such force as permissible because we tend to think that the conditions of necessity and proportionality together sanction the use of *up to* a certain amount of force. If an attacker is going to kill me, I am permitted to inflict up to and including lethal harm upon him. Thus, it looks as though scratching the attacker's face, a much lesser harm than killing him, must fall within the scope of necessary force. But in another sense, the necessity condition can be understood as saying that I may use force sufficient to avert the attack. If I know that the harm I am going to inflict – scratching his face – will not be sufficient, how can I nonetheless be justified in inflicting it?

If we think that I am so justified, perhaps this is because we think that the scratching counts as a *punitive* harm, rather than a defensive harm. I am allowed to scratch my attacker not on grounds of self-defence, but rather on the grounds that he deserves to be punished, and scratching him is one (albeit rather mild) way of doing this. However, we don't usually allow individuals to dish out punishment to those who deserve it; only the state can determine and administer appropriate punishment for this sort of wrong. Moreover, most people agree that punishment must be *intentional*. One cannot, for example, inflict punishment by accident, even if one accidentally inflicts a harm that is deserved. Given this, scratching the attacker can be punitive only if the victim of the attack regards it as punitive. But it seems quite plausible that the victim of the attack would regard the scratching not as punitive or vengeful, but rather as a form of defence.

Perhaps, then, the harm is not punitive, but rather a special part of the right of self-defence that allows us to inflict *symbolic* harm on an attacker. Permitting the infliction of such harm could be one way of demonstrating the value that we place upon the right threatened by an unjust attack. But if the right of defence permits the infliction of symbolic harm, why can't a state mount a similarly symbolic war even when it lacks any reasonable prospect of military success? If individuals have such a right, there seems a *prima facie* case for thinking that states have it too. Furthermore, requiring a reasonable chance of success seems to unfairly disadvantage less well-off states that have only limited means of defence, and cannot hope to defeat a wealthy country with a highly trained and well-equipped army. The constraint seemingly requires that these states always surrender to aggression (although we might point to the Vietnam War as showing that even technologically primitive armies can defeat a superior power at times).

I suspect that the primary rationale behind this *jus ad bellum* requirement is that when the leaders of a state decide to fight a war, they do not generally do the fighting themselves. Rather, they send their military to do it. And we might think that whilst it is permissible to order one's troops to fight wars that they have a realistic chance of winning, it is not permissible to send them to be slaughtered. Leaders may not sacrifice the lives of others for hopeless causes. It is quite possible that many, if not all, of one's soldiers will survive an aggressive invasion if the invasion is not resisted. Perhaps it cannot be just to declare war when this will add needlessly, and fruitlessly, to the death toll.

What if the army *volunteer* to fight to defend their homeland? Is it still impermissible to mount a defensive war? Well, we should remember that war risks not only soldiers' lives, but also the lives of civilians. The fact that the soldiers have agreed to fight a war does not mean that the civilians have consented to be put at risk in this way.[8] Of course, the civilians of the victim state may support the war. But war inflicts civilian casualties on *both* sides. It is not clear that we can justify causing the deaths of civilians on the aggressor's side by waging a defensive war if there is only a very remote chance that the war will succeed. When the chances of achieving the good end are slight, it is hard to see how it can be permissible to inflict serious harm as a side-effect of pursuing that end. It might seem rather hard justice to require restraint out of concern for the citizens of the invading state. But the welfare of those citizens is one of the things that the requirement of proportionality demands we consider before undertaking any war, even a war to resist unjust aggression.

However, there have been cases of private (i.e. non-state) resistance undertaken against all the odds that seem not only morally permissible, but morally admirable. For example, the Warsaw Ghetto Uprising of 1943 is often cited as a heroic example of defiance against the tyranny of the Nazis. Those who tried to defend Warsaw against Nazi attempts to send the Jews to concentration camps knew that they were heavily out-numbered and vastly out-gunned. And yet, they decided to resist. Such resistance hardly seems morally objectionable, even in the absence of a reasonable prospect of success. Again, the symbolic value of the uprising seems to make it permissible and even desirable.

But there are three crucial features that distinguish the Warsaw Uprising from a typical war of national defence. The first is that the resistance fighters *chose* to fight; they were not ordered to do so. The second is that, in all likelihood, those resisting were going to die anyway. As I suggested above, this may not be true in all cases of aggression. The third is that there were so few civilians left in the area that the chances of the resistance fighters killing civilians were minimal, especially given their scant weaponry. And, again, any Jewish civilians faced death in the camps even if they survived the uprising.

If these features were shared by a case of a state facing invasion, we might think that it would in fact be permissible to fight a defensive war even if one lacked a reasonable prospect of success. Perhaps states are not required to submit to the prospect of a malevolent invasion if both their troops and their citizens support a war of resistance, even if it is a war that they have virtually no chance of winning. But there would be strict limitations on the sort of collateral damage that could be permissibly inflicted in the course of such a war. Choosing to risk one's own life does generally not entitle one to risk the lives of others.

Legitimate authority

The rules of *jus ad bellum* specify that a war can be just only if it is fought by an appropriate body, or *legitimate authority*. This usually means that a war can be just only if it is sanctioned by the head of the warring state, such as the president, prime minister, or monarch, or by the elected representative body such as Congress or Parliament. A legitimate authority is the person or group who has the authority to speak for the state and who represents the state on the international stage. Since war is usually understood as a relation between states, only those who speak on behalf of states are deemed competent to declare war.[9]

How one becomes a legitimate authority in this sense is the source of a great deal of debate in political philosophy. As we have seen, some just war theorists favour some form of social contract account, whereby citizens authorise a person or group to represent them. The nature of this authorisation varies between states. It might take the form of a democratic election, or stem from the kind of participation in the state that we discussed in Chapter 2, where this participation counts as a kind of tacit endorsement of the state, even if the citizens do not explicitly consent to the state's authority.

Of course, the requirement of legitimate authority is not only a constraint on whether a war is *just*. It is, for many, a constraint on whether a use of force counts as a war *at all*. The fact that, for example, the Second World War was unjust on the German side did not undermine Hitler's status as a legitimate authority – as the appropriate person to declare war on Germany's behalf. Hitler's war, though unjust, was still a war. But the idea that only a head of state, or some other suitable representative, can declare war has been the subject of a great deal of attention in recent years. As the military focus of the West has shifted away from states and towards terrorists groups like Al-Qaeda, wars seem to be increasingly fought against non-state actors. The very notion of a 'war on terror' implies that it is possible to be at war not only with other states, but also with non-state organisations. If this is indeed possible, we must re-assess the traditional definition and role of a legitimate authority. We will return to this idea in Chapter 9.

Of course, terrorism is not the only example of military force being used by non-state actors. The possibility of civil war suggests that it is at least conceptually coherent to describe non-state actors as engaging in genuine warfare. But even though those engaged in civil war might not represent the state, they are usually representatives of some identifiable group, often an ethnic or religious group. For example, the Sri Lankan government fought a lengthy civil war with the Liberation Tigers of Tamil Eelam, or Tamil Tigers. Whilst the Tamil Tigers did not represent a state, they could plausibly claim (at least at the outset of the war) to represent the Tamil people. They were also striving to obtain a state for the Tamil people. Indeed, many civil wars are motivated by the desire of some group to achieve the status of an independent state. It is perhaps this that encourages us to distinguish between a civil war and, say, a turf war between rival gangs. Whilst those leading one side of a civil war may not be state actors proper, they usually seek to *become* state actors, and regard themselves as genuine representatives of a people. Many civil wars erupt precisely because part or parts of the population feel that the current government does not represent them, and they thus dispute the government's status as a legitimate authority with the power to speak on their behalf.

Right intention

The condition of right intention is closely connected to the idea of just cause. Augustine held that state-sanctioned killing can be permissible only when it is aimed at preventing or correcting an injustice, and that a state may use its combatants only for just ends.[10] Brian Orend suggests that the condition is aimed at ruling out duplicity: that '[h]aving the right reason for launching war is not enough: the actual motivation behind the resort to war must also be morally appropriate.'[11]

For example, if it had been true that Saddam Hussein had weapons of mass destruction, his possession of which violated international agreements, Great Britain and the USA may well have had a just cause for the 2003 war in Iraq. But if the real reason that they invaded had been not to locate these weapons, but rather to topple the Ba'ath regime and help secure Western access to oil, the war itself would have been unjust. The *ad bellum* condition of right intention specifies that one cannot use a just cause as an excuse to wage a war that is not really being fought in response to the received or anticipated wrong, but rather for some other purpose such as regime change or economic advantage.

However, we should distinguish between fighting a war for the *wrong* reasons and fighting a war for *several* reasons. Wars often have multiple aims, and this does not in itself render them unjust. Tony Blair made much of relieving the suffering of the Afghan people when he made his case for the war in Afghanistan in 2001. He also pointed out that the war could help stop the flow of heroin from Afghanistan to the streets of Britain. That a war might bring such benefits certainly seems to be a point in its favour. But Blair did not present these benefits as providing the basis of a case for war. They were, rather, the icing on the cake, with Afghanistan's harbouring of the terrorists behind 9/11 providing the just cause.

The difficulty of establishing the intention behind a war can make it difficult to know how much weight we ought to place upon this particular *ad bellum* condition (and, Orend suggests, explains why it is not included in international law[12]). For a start, it is not clear how we could know the true intentions of a leader who declares war (although observation of the strategy employed during the war might reveal much about their genuine motivations).

More generally, we might wonder why intention really matters. If the appropriate sort of wrong has occurred – such as the 9/11 terrorist attacks – and this *would* justify war, does it matter if the war is ultimately fought for other reasons? Consider the following case:

> *Lucky:*
> Murderer is about to shoot poor Victim, who is innocent and defenceless. Unbeknown to Murderer, Enemy is lurking outside and sees Murderer about to kill Victim. Enemy doesn't care about Victim, but he does hate Murderer, and is overjoyed at this chance to kill Murderer whilst having a legal defence.

What are we to say about Enemy's actions? Does he act rightly? Does he do the right thing for the wrong reason? Is what he does morally permissible (even if it speaks badly of his character)? The difficulty of making these judgements comes from the fact that Murderer is liable to be killed in virtue of the unjust threat that he poses to Victim. As we saw in our discussion of other-defence in Chapter 1, we might think that because of this threat, Enemy has a moral obligation to kill Murderer to save Victim's life. But does this obligation mean that Enemy acts permissibly if he performs the same action – killing Murderer – but for a different reason, such as hatred or personal satisfaction? On the one hand, we might think that Enemy does act permissibly, because, after all, he ought to save Victim. And Murderer hardly seems to have grounds for complaint if Enemy kills him – he is, after all, about to unjustly kill Victim. On the other hand, it sounds odd to say that someone who killed a person out of hatred did the morally right thing, or a morally praiseworthy thing. It still seems to matter that Enemy kills Murderer not for the reasons that make Murderer liable to be killed, but for *other* reasons that do not themselves justify killing Murderer.

The requirement of right intention in war raises similar questions. To use our language from self-defence, the Afghan government seemed to have rendered itself liable to attack by harbouring terrorists. We might think that the leaders of the Taliban regime hardly had grounds for complaint if they were, in fact, attacked not because they harboured terrorists, but because they perpetrated widespread humanitarian abuses and encouraged the exporting of hard drugs. But, as mentioned above, part of why intention matters in war is that war involves states sending other people – combatants – to fight for them. So whilst a war fought for the wrong reasons might not wrong the Taliban – they could not complain about the infringing of their sovereignty – it could still wrong the combatants who are being asked to fight against the Taliban. If we think states owe it to their armed forces to use them only for just causes, this helps explain the importance of fighting wars for the right intention.

Last resort

The requirement of last resort plays a role similar to the requirement of necessity in self-defence. It stipulates that a war can be just only when all other means of averting a threat or seeking redress have been exhausted. These alternative measures include diplomatic pressure and negotiation, economic sanctions, trade bans and the issuing of UN Security Council resolutions to warn states of the perils of their behaviour. Often, the attempt to avoid using military force will involve a combination of these tactics. Of course, it can be argued that war is never the last resort, since one can always try more diplomacy or more sanctions. But most writers understand the condition of last resort as requiring only that all these measures have been tried, not that they be tried endlessly. And, as Paul Christopher reminds us, 'the "last resort" condition is meant to restrain nations that are considering initiating hostilities – it is not relevant to nations that have already been attacked!'[13] If one is the subject of an invasion, one need not try to repel the attack by first opening talks and then applying trade sanctions. The condition of last resort applies only to the *starting* of a war. It is supposed to prevent wars taking place unnecessarily, and thus does not apply if the war is already under way.

This helps to explain why states often respond to humanitarian crises abroad by using economic sanctions to try to pressure foreign governments into action. Since a country that declares a war of humanitarian intervention in some sense *initiates* the conflict, it must first take all reasonable measures to avoid doing so. However, many people oppose the use of economic sanctions on the grounds that they only worsen the situation for those in need. Even targeted sanctions, carefully designed to limit the impact on the general population, can have a widespread effect on the wellbeing of citizens, whilst having minimal effect on those perpetrating abuses. If those committing or allowing abuses are those in charge of a state, overseeing the flow of food and other supplies, it is extremely difficult for outsiders to control how these resources are distributed.

Of course, as we discussed in Chapter 2, it is sometimes possible for a state to avoid war by appeasing an aggressor's demands. It might be that what we face is the possibility of a 'bloodless invasion', where our citizens' lives are at risk only if we resist an invasion. But few people think that a state is required to appease aggression. Of course, the presumption that war can be justified even if one faces a bloodless invasion will be subject to the requirement of proportionality, as we will discuss in more detail below. Some people dispute the idea that it is always proportionate to wage war to defend one's sovereignty, and might thus endorse the idea that, sometimes, one ought simply to hand over the land rather than wage war in the name of sovereignty. But generally speaking, the lack of a requirement to appease is explained both by the wider danger of appearing militarily weak and by the idea that what is at risk when our sovereignty is threatened is more than just individual lives and pieces of land. Even a bloodless invasion can threaten the common life that Walzer describes.

Public declaration of war

The final condition of *jus ad bellum* is that, once all the other conditions have been satisfied, the war be publicly declared. The Hague Convention of 1907 requires that war 'must not commence without previous or explicit warning, in the form either of a declaration of war, giving reasons, or of an ultimatum with conditional declaration of war.'[14] Requiring that a war be made public is important in several respects. It allows the people of a state to debate the war, lending credence to the status of the war as representative of a state rather than of an individual or group of individuals. It also makes it possible for the target of the war to try to seek a last-minute peaceful solution to avoid war. In doing so, the public declaration helps to satisfy the condition that war is a last resort. And, if a peaceful solution is not forthcoming, the declaration enables the evacuation of civilians from cities and other likely targets. The public declaration also makes clear that the laws of war now apply to relations between the two states.

JUST CAUSE AND PROPORTIONALITY

Violations of sovereignty

There is no clear consensus on the relationship between the justness of one's cause and the proportionality of waging war to further that cause. On some views, *any* action that violates or threatens to violate a state's sovereignty counts as a just cause for war. However, most theorists do not accept the position that war is always a justified response to aggression. Jeff McMahan gives the following example in which it seems clearly disproportionate to wage war even though one's sovereignty has been violated:[15]

> *Land:*
> State A owns a piece of uninhabited land at the edge of its territory of approximately one acre in size. State A uses the land as a rubbish dump. The citizens of State B, A's neighbour, regard the land as a sacred holy site. One day, a group of soldiers cross the border from State B and try to annexe the land.

This example raises two questions: (a) does State A have a just cause for war and (b) would war be a proportionate response to State B's actions?

On the one hand, we might argue that the fact that State B is now occupying A's land is the appropriate type of wrong to form the basis for a case for war. It is an act that violates State A's territorial rights, and thus State A does have a just cause for war. But what do we then say about question (b)? Well, we might take the view that the justness of a cause is wholly independent of the proportionality of war. Given this, we could claim that even though State A does have a just cause for war, a war would fail the proportionality condition. The harm that war would cause cannot be justified on the basis of reclaiming a seemingly worthless bit of land. Thus, State A lacks an overall just case for war.

Alternatively, we might follow Michael Walzer in arguing that aggression always justifies a military response, because any aggressive act threatens the rights of citizens. It forces citizens to choose between ceding their rights to the aggressor and risking their lives in war:

> [E]very violation of the territorial integrity or political sovereignty of an independent state is called aggression . . . This refusal of differentiation makes it difficult to mark off the relative seriousness of aggressive acts – to distinguish, for example, the seizure of a piece of land or the imposition of a satellite regime from conquest itself, the destruction of a state's independence . . . But there is a reason for the refusal. All aggressive acts have one thing in common: they justify forceful resistance, and force cannot be used between nations, as it often can between persons, without putting life itself at risk . . . Aggression is a singular and undifferentiated crime because, in all its forms, it challenges rights that are worth dying for.
>
> (Walzer, *Just and Unjust Wars*, pp. 52–53)

Walzer thinks that any illegal encroachment onto another's land violates rights of 'enormous importance', namely the rights of territorial and political integrity.[16] Even if this violation is manifested in a relatively minor encroachment, it nonetheless constitutes a serious offence that warrants a military response. As he points out, the aggressor forces the citizens to choose between their rights and their lives, since it is the nature of military engagement that only by endangering their lives can the citizens protect their rights. If we think that it is always wrong to force such a choice upon others, we might think that the victims of aggression are always allowed to choose to risk their lives rather than surrender their rights to the aggressor.

However, McMahan and Larry May have both disputed Walzer's claim that any violation of sovereignty warrants a military response. They deny that State A in *Land* has a just cause for war, because war is not a proportionate response to the annexing of a worthless piece of land. On this view, the notion of a just cause has proportionality built into it, such that something can qualify as a just cause only if it is both an appropriate *type* of wrong and a *sufficiently serious* wrong. McMahan argues that the mere infraction of one's sovereignty is not enough to give one a just cause for war. Rather, he argues that since war unavoidably involves the serious harms of killing and maiming, only those causes that warrant killing and maiming in response count as just causes. This view is echoed by May:

> Just causes for war are not merely violations of territorial integrity, but only ones that involve threats to the lives, or human rights, of the members of a state. Just causes for war are not merely violations of a

state's sovereignty by another state, unless the state whose sovereignty is violated is protecting the human rights of its members, or where its collapse jeopardises human rights in some significant way. Just causes for war thus involve only certain wrongs committed by the state that is to be attacked, namely wrongs that threaten the lives or human rights of a sufficiently large number of people to offset the threat to lives and human rights that is involved in the waging of the war in question.

> (L. May, 'The Principle of Just Cause', in L. May (ed.), *War: Essays in Political Philosophy*, New York: Cambridge University Press, 2008, p. 57)

Because it is the nature of war to inflict great and widespread harm, such methods can be proportionate only if they are aimed at averting or correcting some other comparable wrong, which May identifies as the violating or jeopardising of the lives or human rights of a significant number of people. And the right that citizens have over territorial control is not enough on its own to provide a just cause for war. It would provide a just cause for war only if the annexing threatened sufficiently important human rights – if, for example, the land was inhabited and the aggression was aimed at forcefully eradicating or undermining the inhabitants' way of life.

However, to claim that these violations would cross the threshold of a just cause for war is not to say that war is *necessarily* a proportionate response to such violations. McMahan argues that whilst *only* these serious violations can be just causes, it does not follow that they will *always* be so. On McMahan's view, proportionality has only a limited role in the notion of just cause: it tells us whether something has passed the threshold for *consideration* as a just cause, but whether war is proportionate is a separate question. Beyond establishing this threshold, 'considerations of scale are irrelevant to just cause.'[17]

To clarify this view, consider the following case:

> *Grenade:*
> Victim is attacked by Murderer, who has a gun and is about to shoot Victim. Victim can defend himself only by throwing a grenade at Murderer. However, the blast from the grenade will kill Family, who are enjoying a picnic nearby.

Certainly, Murderer's attack on Victim is of the right type and magnitude to warrant a lethal response: killing him would be proportionate to the threat he poses. Murderer has, by virtue of his attack on Victim, rendered himself liable to be killed by Victim. We can, on McMahan's view, say that Victim has a just cause for killing Murderer. But would throwing the grenade be a proportionate response? Well, no, because, unfortunately, throwing the grenade will also kill Family. Wiping out not only Murderer, but Family as well, would be disproportionate. As a result, Victim has a just cause for using defensive force, but lacks an overall just case for such force.

With this is mind, consider *Strategy*:

Strategy:
State X is the victim of a violation of its sovereignty by State Y that causes serious violations of State X's citizens' human rights. However, the only weapon that State X possesses is an atomic bomb. If they drop the bomb on State Y, they will wipe out nearly a fifth of State Y's population.

Again, the wrong that State X suffers is a wrong of the appropriate type and magnitude to warrant a military response. But if the only military force available to them is an atomic bomb, war might nonetheless be disproportionate. As May puts it, 'even when the cause appears to be just, there are severe restrictions on what a state can do to another state.'[18]

Liability and proportionality

We have considered whether a just cause for war must be not only a certain *type* of wrong, but also a wrong of a certain *magnitude*. What I want to consider now is whether, if one has a just cause of the appropriate type and magnitude, one may then include subsidiary aims of a war when one considers whether that war is proportionate. For example, let's assume that the aggression of State Y in *Strategy* did not by itself warrant State X's use of an atomic bomb. But what if dropping the bomb would achieve other legitimate goals as well, such as stopping State Y from perpetrating widespread humanitarian abuses in its own country? Could this further goal help to make dropping the bomb proportionate?

Shortly before the war to reclaim the Falkland Islands from Argentina, Margaret Thatcher declared that 'Wherever naked aggression occurs it must be overcome. The cost now, however high, must be set against the cost we would one day have to pay if this principle went by default.'[19] Thatcher's claim that no violation of Britain's sovereignty could be ignored, lest it give rise to future, further violations, might be thought to explain Walzer's view that war is *always* a proportionate response to such violations. Even if war does not seem a proportionate response to a particular wrong, the future effects of not defending one's sovereignty can make war a proportionate response. One must consider not only the harm of losing rights over a particular piece of land, but also the harm of appearing weak and unwilling to commit troops to war. Every act of aggression threatens not only the rights that would be violated by that very act, in this case the rights over the Falklands, but also the rights that are imperilled by the general undermining of sovereignty.

Is it true that part of what could make war with Argentina proportionate, and therefore just, was the deterrent effect that war would have with respect to other would-be aggressors? McMahan and Hurka give different answers to this question. (McMahan has subsequently changed his mind about the nature of proportionality. However, it will nonetheless be instructive to examine how his earlier view differs from Hurka's.[20])

Hurka suggests that how we answer this question depends on how we understand liability to defensive harm. Hurka distinguishes between *global liability* and *specific liability*. Global liability theorists hold that once a state commits a wrong sufficiently serious to warrant a military response, it can be permissible to include in the proportionality calculation not only the correction of that specific wrong, but also associated benefits of waging war. Specific liability theorists, in contrast, maintain that there is a robust connection between the wrong that renders a person or group liable to attack in the first place and the aims that can be permissibly included in the *ad bellum* proportionality calculation.

For example, whilst it is not permissible to wage a war solely in order to disarm another country, a global liability theorist will allow that disarmament is a relevant good once the country has rendered itself liable to attack by committing some sufficient wrong. So, they will permit the inclusion of disarmament in the proportionality calculation about whether there is an overall just case for war. With respect to the Falklands, Hurka suggests that 'deterrence may have done more to make the war proportionate than its initial just cause did.'[21] This implies that Hurka thinks that the repossession of the Falklands was an independently just cause for war – a cause sufficiently serious to warrant military force. It also shows that Hurka endorses a global view of liability, upon which one can invoke something that is not a just cause in its own right – deterrence – in order to make a war proportionate.

If one recalls McMahan's view of self-defence, it will be no surprise that he favours the specific liability account. On this view, a state renders itself liable to attack if it is morally responsible for a wrong that is sufficiently serious to warrant its prevention or correction by the means of killing and maiming. But the liability extends only to harms aimed at redressing or preventing *that wrong*. It does not issue carte blanche for the victim of aggression to inflict harm for other purposes: 'the just causes for war are limited to *the prevention or correction of wrongs that are serious enough to make the perpetrators liable to be killed or maimed.*'[22]

McMahan argues, contra Hurka, that if some potential benefit of a war does not in itself warrant the status of just cause, it cannot be included in the calculations to determine whether the war is proportionate.

> It may seem that the expectation of alleviating religious oppression could contribute to the justification for war by weighing against the bad effects in the proportionality calculation, at least if those warred against were responsible for the oppression. But this seems to imply that the pursuit of an end that is insufficient to justify killing and maiming – namely, alleviating religious oppression – can contribute to the justification for an activity – war – that necessarily involves killing and maiming. And that makes no sense. It seems, therefore, that the only ends that can

weigh against the bad effects of war in the proportionality calculation are those specified by the just causes or causes for war.

(J. McMahan, 'Just Cause for War', *Ethics and International Affairs* 19, No. 3, 2005, 1–21, p. 19)

On this view, even though stopping the flow of drugs from Afghanistan to Britain would be an undeniable benefit of a war in Afghanistan, this benefit cannot be added to the good ends that must be balanced against the harmful effects of war. Since stopping the drugs trade would not independently render the Afghan government liable to killing and maiming, it cannot render it so liable by being attached to another cause for war. A cause that does not warrant killing and maiming cannot lend support to an activity that necessarily involves killing and maiming.

Does this mean that Thatcher was wrong to invoke deterrence as a partial justification for the case for war in the Falklands? For those who advocate a specific account of liability, this depends on whether the Argentinians had rendered themselves specifically liable to harm aimed at deterring aggression. If it were true that by capturing the Falklands, the Argentinians had encouraged others to engage in aggression, the Argentinians' moral responsibility for encouraging this aggression would make them legitimate targets of harms aimed at discouraging it. Such harm would be part of what the Argentinians were specifically liable to. But one could not, for example, wage a particularly harsh war against the Argentinians in order to deter others even if the Argentinians' actions had not encouraged others to aggress. Imagine that, for example, Iran had *already* been threatening aggression against Britain prior to the Argentinian occupation of the Falklands. McMahan argues that one cannot factor in the value of deterring Iran when considering the proportionality of going to war with Argentina if the Argentinians lack responsibility for the fact that the Iranians pose a threat.

But Hurka disputes whether this specific liability view fits with our intuitions about the permissibility of, say, punishing an individual in order to deter others from committing a crime. Hurka argues that, 'while deterrence cannot by itself justify punishment, once someone has acted criminally the fact that imprisoning him will deter others is on most views a legitimate and vital goal of punishment . . . if punishing the perpetrators of these acts somewhat more harshly will improve deterrence further, is doing so not permissible?'[23]

Again, one's response to this will likely depend on whether one takes a view of liability that holds people globally liable once they commit a wrong, or only specifically liable for that wrong. If, on the one hand, we think that it is permissible to use a criminal in this way, making him suffer more in order to reduce crime generally, this implies a global view of liability. The criminal leaves himself open not only to redress for his specific wrong, but also to harms directed at achieving other goods. If, on the other hand, we think it impermissible to inflict more suffering than the wrong itself warrants, this implies that McMahan is correct that liability extends only to harm proportionate to the wrong itself.

Chapter summary

In this chapter, we have outlined the seven traditional conditions of *jus ad bellum*: that one have a just cause, that the war be a proportionate response to that cause, that it have a reasonable chance of success, that it be fought by a legitimate authority, that it be fought with the right intention, that it be a last resort and that it be publicly declared. As we have seen, there is considerable disagreement about how these conditions are to be interpreted. In the second part of the chapter, we looked in detail at how some just war theorists have argued for more restrictive accounts of just cause, whereby acts of aggression must threaten important rights if they are to warrant a military response. We also looked at McMahan and Hurka's competing accounts of proportionality in *jus ad bellum*. Whilst Hurka argues for a form of global liability that allows the inclusion of subsidiary aims in the proportionality calculation, McMahan argues that only wrongs that are themselves serious enough to warrant killing and maiming may contribute to whether a war is *ad bellum* proportionate.

Questions for discussion

1 Does it matter if a war is fought for the 'right intention'?
2 Do you think it permissible for a state to order its soldiers to fight a war that they have little hope of winning?
3 Michael Walzer argues that a state is always justified in resisting aggression, no matter what its form. Do you agree?
4 Does the notion of a just cause have a requirement of proportionality 'built in'? What sort of causes do you think meet this requirement?
5 Should we include the subsidiary aims of a war in our calculation to determine whether a war is proportionate?

Notes

1. A. Bellamy, *Just Wars: From Cicero to Iraq*, Cambridge: Polity Press, 2006, p. 27.
2. Bellamy, *Just Wars: From Cicero to Iraq*, p. 27.
3. Charter of the United Nations, 26 June 1945, Article 51, available at http://www.un.org/en/documents/charter/index.shtml (accessed 14 May 2011).
4. M. Walzer, *Just and Unjust Wars*, New York: Basic Books, 1977, p. 54.
5. D. Rodin, *War and Self-Defense*, New York: Oxford University Press, 2002, p. 115.

6. T. Hurka, 'Proportionality in the Morality of War', *Philosophy and Public Affairs* 33, No. 1, 2005, 34–66, p. 57.
7. See S. Uniacke, 'Self-Defence, Necessary Force and a Reasonable Prospect of Success' (unpublished manuscript, on file with the author) for an excellent discussion of this idea.
8. J. McMahan, *Killing in War*, New York: Oxford University Press, 2009, p. 57.
9. See, however, J. T. Johnson, *Just War Tradition and the Restraint of War*, Princeton, NJ: Princeton University Press, 1981, pp. 150–171, for a useful discussion of the controversy over the notion of legitimate authority in the Middle Ages. Of particular interest at this time is the right of the Church to declare war in order to 'preserve the faith'. Whilst some writers (e.g. Gratian of Bologna) grant the Pope the right to declare war, this view is rejected by later writers such as Thomas Hobbes and Hugo Grotius, both of whom endorse the sovereign-based model of legitimate authority found in current international law.
10. Bellamy, *Just Wars: From Cicero to Iraq*, p. 28.
11. B. Orend, 'War', in E. N. Zalta (ed.), *Stanford Encyclopedia of Philosophy*, Fall 2008 edn, available at http://plato.stanford.edu/archives/fall2008/entries/war/ (accessed 13 December 2010).
12. Orend, 'War'.
13. P. Christopher, *The Ethics of War and Peace: An Introduction to Legal and Moral Issues*, Englewood Cliffs, NJ: Prentice Hall, 1998, 3rd edn, 2004, p. 88.
14. Hague Convention (III) relative to the Opening of Hostilities, The Hague, 18 October 1907, Article 1, available at http://www.icrc.org/ihl.nsf/FULL/190?OpenDocument (accessed 6 January 2010).
15. J. McMahan, 'Just Cause for War', *Ethics and International Affairs* 19, No. 3, 2005, 1–21, p. 4.
16. Walzer, *Just and Unjust Wars*, p. 53.
17. McMahan, 'Just Cause for War', p. 11.
18. L. May, 'The Principle of Just Cause', in L. May (ed.), *War: Essays in Political Philosophy*, New York: Cambridge University Press, 2008, p. 61.
19. M. Thatcher, Speech to the House of Commons, 14 April 1982, transcript available at http://www.margaretthatcher.org/document/104918 (accessed 6 January 2010).
20. See McMahan, *Killing in War*, p. 26, and the related note 23, where McMahan retracts the view that I discuss here.
21. T. Hurka, 'Liability and Just Cause', *Ethics and International Affairs* 21, No. 2, 2007, 199–218, p. 202.
22. McMahan, 'Just Cause for War', p. 11.
23. Hurka, 'Liability and Just Cause', pp. 204–205.

Suggested reading

Thomas Hurka, 'Proportionality in the Morality of War', *Philosophy and Public Affairs*, 33, No. 1, 2005, pp. 34–66.
This paper outlines Hurka's account of how we should understand the role of proportionality in *jus ad bellum*.

Jeff McMahan, 'Just Cause for War', *Ethics and International Affairs*, 19, No. 3, 2005, pp. 1–21.
This paper outlines McMahan's influential account of the causes that can (and cannot) make war proportionate.

Thomas Hurka, 'Liability and Just Cause', *Ethics and International Affairs*, 21, No. 2, 2007, pp. 199–218.
This paper responds to the above paper by McMahan.

4 Just wars?

The previous chapter outlined the rules of *jus ad bellum* – the conditions that a war must meet if it is to be considered just. As we saw, the paradigm example of a just war is a war of self-defence against either an ongoing or an imminent attack. In the first part of this chapter we will focus upon the permissibility of pre-emptive war. In particular, we will examine what makes a war pre-emptive rather than preventive. This distinction is both legally and morally significant. Most contemporary just war theorists deem pre-emptive war permissible and preventive war impermissible, a distinction reflected in international law. In the second part of this chapter we will consider the ethics of punitive war. Early just war theorists generally thought that punitive wars could be morally permissible. But contemporary writers typically argue that punishment alone cannot justify war. We will look in particular at how the requirement to discriminate between combatants and non-combatants has been thought to render punitive war impermissible. In the third part of the chapter we will consider the permissibility of wars of humanitarian intervention. Despite their moral appeal, such wars are legally precarious because of their apparent tension with a state's right to control its borders. We will consider arguments for the permissibility of intervention based upon the view that sovereignty is a conditional good and that intervention is a legally protected form of other-defence.

PRE-EMPTION AND PREVENTION

Definitions

International law defines aggression as an act that either violates or threatens to violate sovereignty. So, states can claim to be responding to aggression even if they are responding to the *imminent threat* of an attack, and not to an actual attack. Wars waged in response to imminent threats are called *pre-emptive* wars.

Pre-emptive wars are usually contrasted with preventive wars. People disagree about how we should define 'preventive' in this context. For example, Lawrence Freedman suggests two ways in which a war can count as preventive. On Freedman's first account, preventive war 'exploits existing strategic advantages by depriving another state of the capability to pose a threat'.[1] This suggests that prevention aims at removing the capacity to pose a threat in the future, that is, at *stopping the creation* of a threat. So, for example, we might fight a war to prevent our neighbour from building a nuclear weapons factory in order to prevent them from threatening us in a few years' time. This understanding of preventive war is pretty uncontroversial.

However, Freedman also says that 'prevention provides a means of confronting factors that are likely to contribute to the development of a threat before it has had the chance to become imminent.'[2] Later, he describes prevention as intended 'to deal with a problem before it becomes a crisis'.[3] These descriptions imply a second way in which a war can be preventive: if it aims to *halt the further development of an existing threat* before harm becomes imminent.

On the first understanding, the aims of prevention are different in *kind* to the aims of pre-emption. Preventive war aims at eliminating the capacity to threaten, in the absence of any actual threat, whereas pre-emptive war aims at averting a specific threat of an imminent harm. On the second understanding, however, the difference between prevention and pre-emption is described as one of *degree*. Whether a war is preventive or pre-emptive will depend on how well developed a threat is when the war is waged. Halting a threat in the early stages of development will be preventive war; halting a threat in the final stages of development will be pre-emptive war.

Of course, for this second understanding of prevention to be of any use, we have to be able to judge when a threatened harm becomes imminent, such that a war waged to prevent the harm counts as pre-emptive rather than preventive. Whilst the concept of imminence does not lend itself to precise definition – there will inevitably be grey areas about whether something counts as imminent or not – people have suggested general standards by which imminence can be judged. The most commonly invoked standard is that stipulated by Daniel Webster, US Secretary of State at the time of the *Caroline* incident. In 1841, British forces attacked the crew and passengers of the *Caroline*, which was being used by Canadians rebelling against British rule in Canada. The British argued that by attacking and destroying the ship, they were acting in pre-emptive self-defence. Webster argued that a right of pre-emptive defence applies only in cases where the need is 'instant, overwhelming, leaving no choice of means, and no moment for deliberation.'[4] Webster denied that the attack on the *Caroline* met these conditions, and thus denied that the attack could be construed as legitimate defence. As we will see below, however, people have objected both to Webster's understanding of imminence and to the idea that imminence is morally relevant to permissible defence.

Most just war theorists hold that, under certain circumstances, pre-emptive war is permissible, since it counts as a form of defence. Preventive war, in contrast, is usually thought to be impermissible. But preventive war has not always been so out of favour. Consider the following extract from Francis Bacon's *Of Empire*, written in 1607, in which Bacon argues that the role of the sovereign is to 'keep due sentinel, that none of their neighbors do ever grow so (by increase of territory, by embracing of trade, by approaches, or the like), as they become more able to annoy them, than they were'.[5] The idea that an increase in a neighbour's strength or prosperity can be a just cause for war is representative of the historical view that war ought to be used as a way of maintaining the status quo between states. In the past, preventive war was deemed just if it was intended to prevent shifts in power that might threaten the position of currently dominant states.

I expect that these days most of us are likely to be sceptical of the idea that one might permissibly wage war in order to maintain an existing balance of power: to stop countries that we currently exceed in wealth or influence from challenging our position. It would clearly be unjust to, for example, respond to the rapid economic growth of India and China by staging or threatening a military invasion to curtail their development. The *capacity* of one's enemy to wage war does not translate into an *intention* to do so. We cannot make an assumption of belligerence the default response to what may or may not be belligerent activities. To do so, and to wage war on the basis of this assumption, seems manifestly unjust. As Walzer argues, in such a case 'hostility is prospective and imaginary, and it will always be a charge against us that we have made war upon soldiers who were themselves engaged in entirely legitimate (non-threatening) activities.'[6]

Rethinking pre-emption

The 2003 invasion of Iraq has thrown open the debate about the legitimacy of preventive war. Although the Bush administration was careful to phrase its intentions in the language of pre-emption, rather than prevention, the US security strategy at that time had more than echoes of preventive war. The 2002 *National Security Strategy of the United States* (NSS) acknowledged that the USA's policy diverged from common usage of 'pre-emptive', but insisted that the new sort of threat posed by terrorism necessitated a revision of what counts as pre-emptive war.

> [A]s a matter of common sense and self-defense, America will act against such emerging threats before they are fully formed. We cannot defend America and our friends by hoping for the best. So we must be prepared to defeat our enemies' plans, using the best intelligence and proceeding with deliberation. History will judge harshly those who saw this coming danger but failed to act. In the new world we have entered, the only path to peace and security is the path of action [. . .] Legal scholars and international jurists often conditioned the legitimacy of pre-emption on the existence of an imminent threat – most often a visible mobilization of armies, navies, and air forces preparing to attack. We must adapt the

concept of imminent threat to the capabilities and objectives of today's adversaries.

[*The National Security Strategy of the United States*, 2002, pp. 4–19, available at http://georgewbush-whitehouse.archives.gov/nsc/ nss/2002/ (accessed 15 December 2010)]

This statement represents a really quite radical departure from contemporary understandings of pre-emptive war. It suggests that since we often cannot show that terroristic harm is imminent, we must change what counts as imminent. We should look to the *capabilities and objectives* of a group as the determining factors in whether or not that group can be said to pose an imminent threat. The claim is that force used against a group with harmful capacities and objectives is not preventive, but rather pre-emptive, and is thus permissible. But even if the label has changed, the primary focus of the NSS is nonetheless on factors that usually serve as the rationale for preventive war. The emphasis is not on what a state or group is doing, but on what it *could* do or would *like* to do.

The mere capacity to threaten clearly seems insufficient to constitute a just cause for war on grounds of pre-emption. But does the combination of capacity and intention suffice? There seem to be two ways in which one might go about defending the position adopted by the Bush administration. The first is to argue that capacity and objective can constitute a threat of imminent harm, even in the absence of more traditional signs of belligerence such as the mobilising of troops. The second is to deny that imminence is a condition of permissible defence.

The first strategy is implied by the section of the NSS quoted above. However, it strikes me as unattractive. It seems false that because one is willing and able to φ, one's φ-ing is imminent. I may have booked and paid for a trip to India that I am very willing to take, but if the trip is not due to commence for another twelve months, it can hardly be said that my going to India is imminent. Similarly, a group may well have the objective of threatening harm, and may well be able to threaten harm. But it just does not follow from these facts alone that the harm is imminent. If pre-emptive wars tackle only imminent threats, wars aimed at those who have merely the capacity and objective of attacking us will not count as pre-emptive.

The role of imminence

The second strategy looks more promising. Perhaps, contrary to popular opinion, pre-emptive force does not require that harm be imminent. Perhaps all that pre-emption requires is that the threat of harm be real, where 'real' means that the threat is sufficiently well developed that one can be confident that it will *become* imminent. Indeed, other parts of the NSS suggest this interpretation of pre-emption, suggesting that the USA will use, 'anticipatory action . . . even if uncertainty remains as to the time and place of the enemy's attack.'[7] If one is uncertain about the time at which an attack will take place, one can hardly claim that one knows harm to be imminent. But if one denies that pre-emption requires that harm be imminent, provided that the threat is real, this uncertainty will not matter.

Is this account of pre-emption plausible? Imminence is often presented as an independent condition of permissible defence at both the individual level and the state level. Recall Webster's claim that only when the need for force is 'instant, overwhelming' can we be said to face an imminent harm that we may pre-emptively avert. This account of legitimate pre-emption hardly seems to fit with the idea that one might claim to be using pre-emptive force even if one does not know when an attack is set to take place. But the rationale behind Webster's insistence that pre-emption is justified only when the need for force is urgent is that only under such circumstances can defence be truly *necessary*. Until one reaches the point at which harm seems inevitable unless action is taken to avert it, one cannot be sure that one needs to use force.

Once we recognise this, however, we can see that the imminence condition is not really an independent condition of permissible defence at all. Rather, it is merely an indicator for whether or not the necessity condition of permissible defence has been satisfied. As David Rodin suggests, the imminence condition 'is simply the application of the necessity requirement subject to epistemic limitations. The point is that we cannot know with the required degree of certainty that a defensive act is necessary until the infliction of harm is imminent.'[8] Imminence matters simply because the fact that a harm is imminent increases the probability that force will be necessary to avert it. When a danger is 'clear and present', one can more reliably predict the need for force.

If what really matters for the permissibility of defensive force is the necessity of using force, ought we to insist that harm be imminent before we grant that defence might be permissible? This depends on whether we agree with Rodin that we cannot know with the requisite certainty that defence is necessary until a harm is imminent. If Rodin is right, then we can satisfy the necessity condition only when harm is imminent. The position of the NSS will thus be untenable, since it will permit the use of force in cases where we cannot be sure that force is required.

I suspect, however, that Rodin is wrong. Consider the following case:

> *Isolation:*
> Murderer, as usual, wants to kill Victim. He has chased Victim into the desert, where Victim is hiding in an abandoned, but well-fortified, building. There are no means of communication with the outside world. Murderer is waiting outside, shouting to Victim that he doesn't plan on going anywhere. Victim knows that it will take Murderer several days to penetrate the building's defences, but that once he does, Victim's chances of a clear shot at him will be much smaller.

Is Victim permitted to shoot Murderer now, days before Murderer will be able to kill Victim? I think he is. I don't think many people would require that Victim wait until Murderer breaks into the building if doing so will significantly lessen Victim's chances of successfully defending himself. Even though the threatened harm is not imminent, the threat itself is very real, having reached the stage at which Victim can be confident that, if unimpeded, Murderer will kill him in the future. And, given the circumstances, I think that Victim *can* be sufficiently certain that killing Murderer is necessary to save his own life. But Victim is not trying to prevent the creation of a threat, or halt a threat in the early stages of development. His actions are not preventive. Rather, in killing Murderer, he defuses an *existing* threat before it can eventuate in harm. Thus, the harm that he inflicts seems to fall under the scope of pre-emption.

If this is correct, it looks like force used against a current threat can count as permissible pre-emption even in the absence of imminent harm. Of course, things are very much simpler in a case like *Isolation* than they are on the state level. But *Isolation* shows that there is no essential connection between the temporal imminence of a harm and the permissibility of using defensive force. If a scenario relevantly similar to *Isolation* took place at the level of states, it seems that using force against a real, but non-imminent, threat could count as permissible pre-emptive force. What we must investigate now, then, is what counts as a 'real' threat for the purposes of pre-emptive war.

Pre-emption and just cause

We ought to notice, first, an ambiguity in the term 'threat'. A threat can be a physical danger or it can be a verbal warning (or a combination of the two). In 2005, Iranian President Mahmoud Ahmedinejad was widely reported to have declared Iran's desire to 'wipe Israel off the map'. Let us assume, for the sake of argument, that Ahmedinejad did in fact express such a wish. Such a declaration could indeed be described as threatening. But is it the right sort of threat for the purposes of justifying pre-emptive war? No. Such posturing is the state equivalent of provocation between individuals. And whilst being provoked into violence can mitigate fault on an individual level, it cannot excuse waging war on the state level. Given the power they wield, we require our leaders to exercise much more restraint than can perhaps be expected of the average citizen. As Michael Walzer says, '[i]nsults are not occasions for war, any more than they are (these days) occasions for duels.'[9] Verbal threats, unless backed by evidence of a physical threat, cannot warrant a physical response.

Walzer suggests three conditions that a group or state must fulfil if they are to count as posing a sufficiently developed threat, such that force used against them would be classed as pre-emptive rather than preventive. The first is that the group or state must display a *manifest intent to injure*. The second is that they must have undertaken a degree of *active preparation* 'that makes intent a positive danger'.[10] The third is that the situation must be such that not fighting will significantly *increase the risk to oneself*.[11] Recall the stipulation in *Isolation* that by waiting until Murderer penetrates the building, Victim will significantly lessen his chances of successful defence. Walzer's conditions of pre-emption include such a stipulation. If a state could adequately defend itself at a later time, it ought not to strike pre-emptively. But if waiting will significantly reduce its capacity to mount an effective response, pre-emption can be permissible.

Walzer suggests that his conditions identify a middle ground between the overly permissive nature of preventive war and the overly demanding urgency required by Webster:

> Instead of . . . rapacity and ambition, current and particular signs are required; instead of an 'augmentation of power,' actual preparation for war, instead of the refusal of future securities, the intensification of present dangers. Preventive war looks to the past and future, Webster's reflex action to the immediate moment, while the idea of being under a threat focuses on what we had best call simply *the present*. I cannot specify a time span; it is a span within which one can still makes choices, and within which it is possible to feel straitened.
>
> (M. Walzer, *Just and Unjust Wars*, New York: Basic Books, 1977, p. 81)

The most opaque of Walzer's criteria is perhaps the requirement that there be a degree of active preparation. Judging preparation for war can be usefully compared to the area of criminal law that deals with attempted crimes. Merely purchasing a weapon is not sufficient to render one guilty of attempted murder. But at some point between purchasing a hammer and hitting someone over the head with it, one crosses the line from lawful activity to criminal attempt. Where we draw this line poses, in some respects, the same question as where we draw the line of a sufficiently developed threat that can trigger a case for war. And, indeed, it is likely to be not so much a clear line as an attempt to delineate a general area within which a plausible case can be made that preparation is under way. To decide what this area covers, we must consider both *how much* preparation a state must undertake before it crosses the threshold that Walzer identifies and what *sort* of activity counts as preparation.

George Fletcher and Jens Ohlin suggest that the requisite degree of preparation should be that which provides evidence (in the form of publicly observable facts) that convinces the world that force is necessary:

> When the facts are laid bare – when the threatened attack is manifested in troop movements, missile deployments, and the like – the world will know which side to support in the struggle. Outside powers are

permitted only to support the defender against aggression, and therefore there must be some public test of aggression. When there is persistent disagreement about the evidence, as there was in the case of Iraq, the invading powers might believe their action is justified, but a large number of states, particularly those who identify with the victim state, will treat the invaders as aggressors and criminals.

(G. Fletcher and J. Ohlin, *Defending Humanity: When Force is Justified and Why*, New York: Oxford University Press, 2008, p. 169)

Fletcher and Ohlin identify the evidence presented by the USA during the Cuban missile crisis as a textbook example of how to demonstrate active preparation of a serious military threat. The USA showed photographs that proved that the Cubans had acquired long-range missiles from the Soviet Union that would enable them to launch a nuclear attack on US soil. Fletcher and Ohlin claim that, in the context of US–Cuban relations at the time, these photos were sufficient to convince the world that the Cubans meant business. Less impressive, they suggest, was Colin Powell's evidence of the threat posed by Saddam Hussein prior to the 2003 invasion of Iraq: 'Powell projected a photograph of a trailer and said, essentially, "This is where Saddam is manufacturing chemical weapons." '[12] The ongoing debate as to the legality of the second Iraq war supports Fletcher and Ohlin's view that the amount of demonstrable illegal activity on the part of the Iraqis was insufficient to warrant the use of force.

However, it is not the amount, but the *nature*, of preparation to which the Bush administration draws attention in its NSS. The NSS argues that the sort of preparation that writers like Walzer and Fletcher and Ohlin have in mind – the visible manoeuvring of troops and so on – does not always apply to modern-day warfare.

Rogue states and terrorists do not seek to attack us using conventional means. They know such attacks would fail. Instead, they rely on acts of terror and, potentially, the use of weapons of mass destruction – weapons that can be easily concealed, delivered covertly, and used without warning.

(*The National Security Strategy of the United States*, p. 15)

It certainly seems possible that a state could, for example, launch a long-range missile into the territory of another state without showing many outward signs of planning aggression. In addition, most states have standing armies that negate the need to actively recruit in readiness for war, and also have reserves of weapons that can be accessed without drawing attention. One could, conceivably, quietly prepare for an offensive on foreign soil.

But we should remember that a state that is poised to launch an attack needs to prepare not only its offensive, but also its defences. It is often planning for the *aftermath* of an attack, rather than the attack itself, that indicates belligerence. And whilst a non-state group that lacks a territory to defend may be able to bypass these parts of war, states must take steps to protect their borders and citizens – steps that it will usually be hard for observers to miss. Unlike terrorists, states cannot hide from reprisals, but must instead ready themselves for a military response. It would be a very reckless state that launched an attack, however covertly prepared, but that did not take measures to protect itself from retaliation. Moving troops to the borders, stockpiling food and medical supplies (which will often be imported), moving civilians out of the cities into rural areas and recalling one's diplomatic ambassadors all signify that war is on the cards. Given this, it is hard to see how one could be sufficiently sure that a state posed a threat in the absence of any significant amount of defensive preparation. Even very secretive states, such as North Korea, would find it hard to batten down the hatches in this way without detection. The US position, then, is perhaps less than convincing when applied to states.

What about terrorist groups? These groups have no borders to guard, nor civilians to protect. They are unlikely to manifest the signs of preparation described above. But it is not clear where or how one would strike at a terrorist group even in retaliation for an *actual* attack, unless it is a group that is clearly supported by a particular government. Striking in *anticipation* of a non-specific attack thus seems very difficult to justify. The signs that an attack is planned are likely to be less than conclusive if one cannot show details of a particular, imminent threat. It is therefore difficult to see how force against such a group to prevent the infliction of a non-imminent harm could meet the necessity condition.

PUNITIVE WARS

Punishment as just cause

We have so far examined the permissibility of waging war at various stages before an attack, and to deflect an ongoing attack. But what about waging war *after* an attack as an act of punishment? Can punitive wars ever be just? Justifications of punishment typically focus on two aims: retribution and deterrence. Retribution is backwards-looking, seeking to restore the balance of justice by making a wrongdoer pay for their crimes. Deterrence is forward-looking, aiming at discouraging both the wrongdoer and others from committing crimes in the future. Punitive wars are best understood as having both retributive and deterrent aims. They are primarily intended to make an aggressor pay for some past injury, and return the victim of aggression to their former status, both by retrieving stolen goods and by reasserting the state's authority. But punitive wars can also have forward-looking aims, and be intended to reduce the likelihood of future aggression by deterring both the target state and other states from waging aggressive wars.

Early just war theorists typically accepted that revenge or punishment could be a just cause for war. In order to reconcile the intentional killing of war with Christian doctrine, St Augustine argued that wars were justified *only* when they were undertaken to punish aggression, because aggression is a sin.[13] Stopping one's enemies from sinning is an act of beneficence. Even those not trying to reconcile war with Christianity cited punishment as a just cause for war. Cicero, writing in the first century BC, claims that 'only a war waged for revenge or defence can actually be just'.[14] This inclusion of revenge as a just cause for war can perhaps be attributed to the value placed upon honour at the time Cicero was writing. As mentioned above, to challenge a man's honour was historically regarded as cause for a duel. Similarly, to challenge or subvert the honour of a state by inflicting some injury was regarded as a cause for war. Even if an aggressor had desisted, and force was no longer necessary to ward off an attack, force could nonetheless be justified as a necessary means of reasserting the dignity and standing of the victim state.

These days, not many theorists think that war can be legitimately employed as a solely punitive or vengeful measure. Of course, there can be punitive *aspects* of a just war. For example, the disarming of Germany after the First World War was not only a practical measure intended to prevent Germany from waging war again, but also a punitive measure taken in recognition of Germany's wrongdoing (the accompanying shame played no small part in engendering support for the Nazis in later years). The assigning of 'war guilt' and the imposition of reparations were also ways of punishing German aggression. But punishment is no longer generally recognised as an independently just cause for war, even if punitive aims may be pursued as part of a just war.

There are two main reasons why punishment is not thought to be a just cause for war. The first is that we usually allow only those in an appropriate position of authority to inflict punishment. Even if a person is rightly convicted of a crime, and deserves to be punished, we do not let just anyone inflict punishment. We do not even let the victim of the crime inflict punishment. Rather, we allow only the state, through its representatives, to decide upon and impose punishment. But, the argument goes, since there is no appropriate authority that can adjudicate between states as a state can between its citizens, there can be no justified punishment of one state by another. (Those accused of war crimes and tried by the International Criminal Court sometimes refuse to recognise the authority of the court on similar grounds.) This is not to deny that a state might *deserve* to be punished. But in the absence of a person or body who may rightfully decide upon and impose punishment, it is impermissible for even warranted punishment to be administered. Individuals, and individual states, do not have the right to mete out punishment.

We might object that there *is* an appropriate body that can adjudicate between states. The UN contains representatives from nearly every country in the world, and is generally thought to have the authority to issue resolutions condemning the actions of particular states, or to impose sanctions to coerce states to behave in certain ways. All the member states consent, at least in theory, to be subject to the UN's decisions on such matters. But despite its inclusiveness, the UN is not a democratic or impartial body. As Rodin explains, the structure and hierarchy of the UN make it unsuitable as a judge and jury capable of dishing out punishment:

> The five permanent members of the Security Council each have a veto right on decisions pertaining to the use of force and they therefore possess the power to exempt themselves and their clients from legal sanctions. The permanent members routinely utilize their power to shape UN decisions so as to accord with their own national interest. Because of this the United Nations is not a truly impartial authority and it is difficult to view the military expeditions it authorizes as legitimate forms of punishment or law enforcement.
>
> (D. Rodin, *War and Self-Defense*, New York: Oxford University Press, 2002, p. 180)

We usually require impartiality on the part of those who work in the legal system. We condemn as corrupt those who allow their own interests or preferences to shape judicial policy. We would not, for example, think it just to allow a judge to rule on a case in which he had a personal vested interest. But, at the moment, the UN does allow that a state can refuse to authorise uses of force in cases where such force might conflict with its own interests. Of course, this might not be the ostensible reason for the veto. But, as Rodin argues, it would be naive to assume that states are never moved by these sorts of considerations.

However, these features of the UN that make it unsuitable as an adjudicating body are by no means fixed or insurmountable. It is not beyond the realms of possibility that a universal body could be set up that lacked the bias of the UN and that could be fairly employed to settle disputes between states. But even if such a body existed, it would still be unlikely to sanction war as a method of punishment.

The requirement of discrimination

This brings us to our second argument against the permissibility of punitive war. This argument is based upon the principle of discrimination that forms part of the *jus in bello* rules of war. Put simply, the principle of discrimination requires that we punish only the guilty. It is morally impermissible to punish the innocent for the wrongs of others. But the nature of warfare is that innocent people are caught in the crossfire. War inevitably inflicts harm on the guilty and innocent alike, no matter how carefully combatants follow the laws of war.

Of course, this is true of war in general, not only of punitive war. But other wars, such as wars of defence, can justify such collateral damage by the fact that it is inflicted in the course of saving other, innocent lives. The deaths caused by a war of defence are in some sense necessary, in that they are an unavoidable part of defending one's own citizens from attack. But punitive harm lacks this sort of necessity justification. Unlike defence, which involves the *distribution* of harm that someone – either victim or attacker – must bear, punishment involves the *creation* of harm that nobody need bear.

It is thus much harder to justify killing or harming innocent people in pursuit of punitive goals than it is to justify such killings that result from trying to defend one's own people against aggression. Of course, this is not to say that *any* amount of harm that one inflicts on the innocent in the course of defending others can be justified. Such harm is subject to requirements of proportionality and steps must be taken to minimise the harm to innocent people even when one is engaged in a just defensive war. But the good end of defence is able to balance out the harm of collateral damage in a way that the end of punishment seems less able to do. This difference is supported by most people's intuition that it is better that ten guilty people go free than that one innocent person be wrongfully punished. To catch innocent people in the net whilst trying to punish the guilty seems morally worse than letting the guilty escape punishment, even when we feel that punishment is richly deserved. If this intuition is right, we can see why punitive wars are generally thought to be unjust. Punishment that will inflict harm not only upon those who deserve it, but also upon the innocent, cannot be a just cause for war.

HUMANITARIAN INTERVENTION

I mentioned in Chapter 3 that whilst the paradigm just cause for war is self-defence, most people also think it permissible to wage war in defence of others. Usually, such wars take the form of coming to the aid of an ally to help it deflect external aggression. The first Gulf War exemplified this sort of other-defence, with the USA and Britain (amongst others) assisting Kuwait's attempt to repel an Iraqi invasion. Given that Kuwait welcomed this assistance, most people think that this use of force was morally permissible. But is it permissible to enter a state without its leaders' permission in order to defend its citizens against *internal* aggression?

These so-called 'wars of humanitarian intervention' can seem like the most morally admirable sort of war. What could be a more just cause than stopping the widespread, and often horrific, abuse of innocent people at the hands of their fellow citizens? As the media increasingly bring horrors from abroad into our living rooms, the idea of 'the world standing by' as people are maimed and massacred strikes many of us as morally abhorrent. And, yet, wealthy countries like the USA failed to intervene to prevent the genocide in Rwanda (said by President Clinton to be his biggest regret from his time in office). And little has been done to prevent the current humanitarian crisis in Darfur, despite widespread reporting of the ethnic cleansing of black Sudanese by Arab Sudanese, or to curb the ongoing crisis in the Democratic

Republic of the Congo. Why is there a reluctance to wage wars of humanitarian intervention even in the face of overwhelming evidence that atrocities are being committed?

Intervention and sovereignty

Part of the answer to this question is political: state leaders always have an eye on cost and public support. Fletcher and Ohlin argue that

> the U.S. public needs a really good reason to accept their soldiers coming home in body bags. The images of the World Trade Center collapsing on 9/11 provided exactly this kind of reason. Not surprisingly, the image of a starving family, or a burning village in Darfur, does not.
>
> (Fletcher and Ohlin, *Defending Humanity: When Force is Justified and Why*, p. 132)

The American political theorist Samuel P. Huntington put things rather more strongly, claiming that, 'it is morally unjustifiable and politically indefensible that members of the [US] armed forces should be killed to prevent Somalis from killing one another.'[15] Things are perhaps not as straightforward as Huntington and Fletcher and Ohlin suggest. Many Americans protested against the war in Afghanistan, despite 9/11. And many campaign for intervention to relieve humanitarian suffering. But it is certainly true that many people have a sense that provided that other countries are not engaged in aggression, they should be left to sort out their own problems.

Moreover, humanitarian intervention is fraught with legal and political dangers. A moment's reflection on the emphasis that the *jus ad bellum* rules place on defence of sovereignty gives us an indication of the source of these dangers. The rules of war are primarily designed to enable states to retain control of their politics and their land. This control is believed to be so important that defending it is the primary – and some think only – justification for war. If sovereignty is so very important, how can it be permissible to simply disregard a state's sovereignty and send one's troops over their border against their wishes? Many leaders are uneasy with the idea of other states interfering in their internal affairs, and fear that legitimising humanitarian intervention might erode the power of sovereignty, with disastrous consequences of its own.

Kosovo

The tension between sovereignty and humanitarian concern was brought into sharp focus by the North Atlantic Treaty Organization (NATO)'s intervention in Kosovo in 1999. In the later part of the twentieth century, the historically difficult relationship between Kosovo and Serbia became increasingly acrimonious. Kosovars were seeking independence from Serbian rule and, after a period of unsuccessful non-violent resistance, Kosovar guerrillas began attacking Serbian targets on a regular basis. By the end of the nineties, the Serbs and the Kosovars were effectively engaged in civil war. Reports of ethnic cleansing of Kosovars by Serbs began to filter out of Kosovo. The UN issued resolutions condemning the violence on both sides. A temporary peace was reached, but was shattered in January 1999, when Serbia executed a group of alleged Kosovar terrorists. Serbia refused to allow the UN's chief war crimes prosecutor to investigate the killings. Subsequent peace talks failed when Serbian President Slobodan Milosevic refused an agreement that would permit NATO troops to enter Yugoslavia. The second round of talks failed on similar grounds. In the meantime, violence against civilians was widely reported to be escalating as Serbia tried to quash the rebellion. Massive displacement had left thousands homeless and pointed towards a looming humanitarian disaster. NATO began airstrikes against Serbia in March 1999 in an attempt to force Milosevic to sign the peace treaty. Hostilities ceased in June when Serbia withdrew from Kosovo and agreed to the deployment of a NATO peace-keeping force.

NATO constitutes an alliance formed in 1949 between twenty-eight countries from North America and Europe. Its members undertake to defend each other against aggression, holding that an attack against one NATO member will be treated as an attack on all members. But the Treaty explicitly subordinates the power of NATO to that of the United Nations, specifying that the UN retains overall responsibility for international peace-keeping and security. NATO members are bound to act within the confines of what the UN permits. With respect to Kosovo, critics allege that NATO intervention overstepped the boundaries of what the UN had authorised.

Of course, the UN need not authorise self-defence; NATO members can defend themselves and other NATO members against aggression. But Kosovo was not a NATO member, and the UN did not explicitly authorise NATO to intervene in the Kosovars' struggle. The legal debate therefore focused on whether the previous Security Council resolutions condemning Serbia's actions, and the failure of Serbia to comply with the resolutions' demands, could suffice to legitimise NATO intervention in the absence of a further resolution authorising the use of 'all necessary means' – the UN's code for military force.

The member states were divided on this issue (and it is an issue that has reared its head again recently with respect to the 2003 Iraq war). Carl Ceulemans represents the general consensus when he says that from a legal point of view, 'NATO didn't have a leg to stand on.'[16] NATO's use of force went beyond what the UN had authorised. But there is also a general consensus that NATO was *morally* justified in using force because of the developing humanitarian crisis on the ground. Waiting to obtain a further UN Security Council resolution would have allowed the humanitarian situation to worsen (and there was reason to think that Russia and China would anyway have vetoed a resolution permitting the use of force).

Many writers therefore argue that NATO was right to intervene, even if its doing so went outside the law. Certainly, morality sometimes obliges us to break the law, especially if the law is unjust. Women's suffrage and anti-slavery movements often involved breaking the law in the course of trying to change it, and we usually judge these infractions to have been morally right. Perhaps, then, we can defend the NATO intervention in the same way: as illegal, but nonetheless the morally right thing to do.

However, Ceulemans draws our attention to the wider implications of allowing the moral status of a *cause* of war to play a role in determining who is a *legitimate authority* to declare war:

> From a Just War Theory point of view, the opponents argue that it is very dangerous to allow the gravity of the just cause to determine the outcome of the Legitimate Authority analysis. It not only implies the end of Legitimate Authority as an independent principle, it also puts us on a slippery slope heading to the hell of a holy war ... The international security system provided for by the United Nations and international law could be profoundly destabilized if the legal restraints on the use of force are loosened by an appeal to vague and general moral principles. Thus, for some NATO members such as Belgium there was reluctance to treat the Kosovo war as a precedent for other forms of intervention.
> (C. Ceulemans, 'The NATO Intervention in the Kosovo Crisis',
> in B. Coppieters and N. Fotion (eds), *Moral Constraints on War*,
> Lanham, MD: Lexington Books, 2008, p. 213)

As we discussed in Chapter 3, it is not always clear whether or not a person or body qualifies as a legitimate authority. Civil wars and terrorism cast doubt on the traditional model of a sovereign (the head of state) as the only entity capable of declaring war. But this lack of clarity normally comes from an uncertainty about who truly represents an identifiable group, and has the right to speak on its behalf. It does not come from uncertainty about the justice of the *cause* of the war (recall the observation that Hitler was certainly the appropriate person to wage war on Germany's behalf, even though the war he waged was unjust). If we try to condone NATO's actions by declaring it a legitimate authority on the grounds that its cause was morally good, we reduce the condition of legitimate authority to nothing more than the reaffirmation that one has a just cause.

Fletcher and Ohlin similarly question the wisdom of trying to show that whilst NATO's intervention was technically illegal, it was nonetheless morally required. To do so is to 'sacrifice the rhetorical high ground ... one cannot walk into the Security Council conceding that a course of action violates international law and expect to prevail.'[17] Fletcher and Ohlin emphasise the importance of not undermining the rules of war laid out by Article 51,[18] arguing that destabilizing the Charter in this way would be used to the advantage not only of those waging just humanitarian wars, but also of those with aggressive intentions. Once we provide for circumventing Article 51, we leave the door open to those who will take advantage of this precedent for less than moral reasons.

Nevertheless, the fact remains that many people think humanitarian intervention morally desirable. We will thus consider two ways in which people have recently argued in favour of humanitarian intervention. The first is by invoking a notion of conditional sovereignty, whereby a state has a right to control over its borders only if it meets certain humanitarian criteria. This approach goes outside the parameters of the UN Charter and argues for additional circumstances, other than self-defence or collective defence, under which force can be permissible. The second approach tries to subsume humanitarian intervention under Article 51's provision for self-defence, arguing that the international law on genocide gives rise to a right to defence on the part of both state and sub-state groups.

Conditional sovereignty

What is it that makes sovereignty so valuable? Fletcher and Ohlin suggest that one answer to this question has emerged from the recent interest in the idea of universal human rights. This answer holds that sovereignty matters because, and only if, it enables a government to protect its citizens' human rights. The purpose of sovereignty – of political and territorial authority – is to enable one to provide one's citizens with the basic living conditions to which all people are entitled. Since these entitlements (or rights) are of fundamental moral importance, and as sovereignty enables their fulfilment, sovereignty is itself very important.

However, notice that in this explanation of why sovereignty matters, sovereignty is taken to be *instrumentally* valuable, rather than *intrinsically* valuable. For something to have intrinsic value is for it to be valuable in its own right. Happiness seems an obvious example of something that is intrinsically valuable. If I ask you why you play football, you might answer that you play because it makes you happy. It would be odd for me to then to ask the further question of *why* you want to be happy. The pursuit of happiness doesn't require further explanation because happiness is valuable in itself. But in the picture of sovereignty just sketched, sovereignty is not valuable in itself. Rather, it is valuable only because it helps one achieve other valuable things, such as a healthy life or a life free from persecution. Sovereignty's value is conditional upon whether it helps citizens to achieve basic human goods. If sovereignty does not in fact help a state's citizens achieve these goods, then, according to the conditional sovereignty view, it lacks any value and we need not respect it. Under such circumstances, the government of the state in question can be said to have forfeited its authority over its territory.

In the sorts of scenario in which we might consider waging a humanitarian war, the government will either be responsible for widespread human rights abuses or be intentionally failing to prevent them. (If it simply lacks the resources to prevent the abuses, we might think that it is not *intentionally* failing to prevent them. However, if this is the case, it should accept assistance from other states, and issues of contravening sovereignty should not arise. If it refuses such assistance, I think we can say that it counts as intentionally failing to prevent the abuses, since it has a chance to stop them that it intentionally fails to take.) Under such circumstances, its sovereignty over its borders is not doing what it ought to do, namely protect its citizens' human rights. On a conditional understanding of sovereignty, this means that the government's sovereignty is forfeit, and thus other states do not violate that right in sending their troops over the border. Advocates of this view thus deny that humanitarian intervention conflicts with sovereignty. The sorts of states in which intervention is required are states that *lack* sovereignty.

This view raises some difficulties for the conventional understanding of what it is to be a state. The idea of a state is usually thought to be bound up in the idea of sovereignty, such that one cannot be properly described as a state at all if one does not have rights over one's territorial and political integrity. But those who think sovereignty contingent deny this sort of identity relationship. They think it possible for a state to exist but to lack rights of sovereignty. We can interpret this as the claim that one must be a state in order to *qualify* for sovereignty, but sovereignty does not *follow* from statehood. Statehood is only a necessary, and not a sufficient, condition of sovereignty. This additional dimension of governance must come from fulfilling or protecting basic human rights.

Michael J. Smith defends both the conditional view of sovereignty and its implications for the permissibility of humanitarian intervention:

> A genocide is no less 'a common threat to humanity' . . . if it occurs within borders than if it crosses them. The basic principle that should guide international intervention is this: Individual state sovereignty can be overridden whenever the behavior of the state even within its own territory threatens the existence of elementary human rights abroad and whenever the protection of the basic human rights of its citizens can be assured only from the outside. State sovereignty, in short, is a contingent value: its observance depends upon the actions of the state that invokes it. Members of the international community are not obliged to "respect the sovereignty" of a state that egregiously violates human rights.
> (M. J. Smith, 'Humanitarian Intervention: An Overview of the Ethical Issues', *Ethics and International Affairs* 12, No. 1, 1998, 63–79, p. 78)

This view is certainly appealing. It gives governments an incentive to strive to protect their citizens' basic rights, since their own legal rights to their borders may well depend on it. It avoids fetishising sovereignty at the cost of widespread killing, raping and maiming. And it recognises what many of us think to be a sound moral principle: that our moral obligations extend beyond our immediate community to those suffering deprivation and abuse elsewhere. But Fletcher and Ohlin voice concern that, the Universal Declaration of Human Rights notwithstanding, intervention based on these grounds would still not be *legal*, because 'there is nothing in these human rights treaties that implies that states have abrogated their sovereignty if they fail to protect them.'[19] As described above, allowing that a moral argument can supersede Article 51 would set a dangerous precedent of exceptions. If we want to make a case for humanitarian intervention whilst preserving international law on the use of force, Fletcher and Ohlin argue that we cannot rely on moral arguments, but must show legal grounds.

Intervention as other-defence

A natural interpretation of humanitarian intervention is that it is a form of other-defence. In most circumstances in which a person is allowed to defend herself, others may assist her defence. Fletcher and Ohlin use this notion of other-defence to argue for the permissibility of humanitarian intervention, claiming that, 'the world community can come to the aid of any nation who has a legitimate claim to self-defense against armed attack.'[20] The crucial feature of this account of intervention is that it conceives of intervention as a *legal* right arising from Article 51, rather than a primarily moral obligation. Article 51 affirms the 'natural' right that its members have to defend both themselves and each other from armed attack. But if this affirmation can ground humanitarian intervention, why all the fuss about the legality of interventionist wars?

Well, notice that Ohlin and Fletcher talk of the right of *nations* to defend themselves. But Article 51 has historically been implemented on the assumption that it applies to *states*. It does not apply to subgroups within states. Consider the following extract from the International Court of Justice (ICJ) ruling regarding Israel's construction in 2002 of a wall in the West Bank to prevent terrorist attacks from Palestine:

> Article 51 of the Charter . . . recognizes the existence of an inherent right of self-defence in the case of armed attack by one State against another State. However, Israel does not claim that the attacks against it are imputable to a foreign State. The Court also notes that Israel exercises control in the Occupied Palestinian Territory and that, as Israel itself states, the threat which it regards as justifying the construction of the wall originates within, and not outside that territory . . . therefore Israel could not in any event invoke those resolutions in support of its claim to be exercising a right of self-defence. Consequently, the Court concludes that Article 51 of the Charter has no relevance in this case.
>
> [*Legal Consequences of the Construction of a Wall in the Occupied Palestinian Territory (Request for advisory opinion)*, available from the International Court of Justice website (http://www.icj-cij.org/docket/files/131/1677.pdf) (accessed 14 December 2010)]

Article 51 was never intended to deal with internal conflicts, but rather was aimed at international affairs. Israel cannot claim a legal right of self-defence against the terrorist threat from Occupied Palestine because, being under Israeli control, threats from Occupied Palestine are not external threats of the sort that Article 51 is intended to cover. Moreover, since the threats come from terrorists, rather than state actors, the ICJ ruling holds that Israel cannot invoke Article 51 to govern her dealings with these groups.

Ohlin and Fletcher describe this ruling as 'the most extreme example of international law's myopic fixation on states to the exclusion of other entities.'[21] Ohlin and Fletcher seek to undermine this fixation by distinguishing between states and nations. States are political by nature. They are 'geographically defined, constituted by governments (whether legitimate or not) and recognized by the world community as states with legal personality.'[22] States are easy to identify and count. Nations, on the other hand, are rather more vague concepts. Multiple groups with distinct national identities can be subsumed under a single state. The Tamil people are part of the Sri Lankan state. The Basque region is part of the Spanish state. Tibet is ruled by the Chinese. None of these places counts as a state at the moment – they have no official representative on the international stage. But they do seem to be identifiable national groups, with distinctive languages and cultural practices.

Ohlin and Fletcher support the relevance of international law to sub-state groups by pointing out that laws about genocide are framed in terms of 'peoples' rather than states. Genocide is usually understood as an attempt to eradicate a particular ethnic group, and is condemned in the strongest terms as a crime against humanity. And, as Ohlin and Fletcher argue:

> the prohibitions protect nations and national groups – not states. One might infer from these protections that nations have the basic right to exist under international law and that violating this right by killing individuals who belong to a particular ethnic group is the most serious breach of international law possible.
> (Fletcher and Ohlin, *Defending Humanity: When Force is Justified and Why*, p. 138)

If this is correct, then it seems that the right of sub-state groups to defend themselves against aggression has a place in international law. And, if the right of states to use self-defence explains the legality of mutual defence between states, it looks as though the right of sub-state groups to use self-defence can similarly support permission for others to come to their aid.

The basis of Ohlin and Fletcher's account of intervention, then, is that both states and sub-state groups have a right of defence under Article 51. The existence of such a right of sub-state groups is evidenced by the international laws prohibiting genocide. Since a group is clearly permitted to defend itself against genocide, and presumably against other forms of abuse, others may assist this defence as stipulated by the part of Article 51 that permits collective defence.

On this account, the state's forfeiting of sovereignty seems comparable to the way in which states forfeit the right to sovereignty by waging an aggressive war. If an aggressor invades another state, we do not think it impermissible or illegal for the victim state to defend itself by dropping bombs on the aggressor's territory. It would be very odd if we were required to obtain the aggressing state's consent before we bombed their home turf. Similarly, Ohlin and Fletcher argue that 'it would be absurd to require state consent before defense of others is undertaken.'[23] If the state is either perpetrating or failing to prevent humanitarian abuses, asking for permission to cross its borders is like the victim of an attack asking her attacker for permission to shoot him. Since we certainly do not require that individuals obtain such permission, we should not require that states do so.

However, we should recall from our discussion in Chapter 1 that other-defence is often conceived of as an obligation, not as a mere permission. Indeed, the Genocide Convention of 1948 requires that signatories undertake to prevent and to punish genocide. This suggests not only that states are *allowed* to defend sub-state groups, but that they have a *duty* to do so. But few countries regard themselves as legally obliged to prevent genocide, even if they feel the moral pull of the requirement to prevent such harms. Ohlin and Fletcher similarly phrase their argument as a *right* of states to intervene on humanitarian grounds, but they do not argue that states *must* intervene. How can we account for this, if intervention is justified by the considerations of other-defence?

Well, we could argue that positing a duty to always intervene to prevent humanitarian abuses is simply unrealistic, both because of the costs of war and because of the inherent risks. The state of the world is such that it would simply be unfeasible for even wealthy countries to dedicate the vast resources needed for war to each humanitarian cause, which are, sadly, many and varied. This consideration doesn't speak against construing intervention as a duty, but rather invokes something along the lines of 'ought implies can' with respect to the *scope* of the duty. If a person can save only one of two people, she does not fail in her duty to save by rescuing only one. She cannot have a duty to save both if she is not *able* to save both. Similarly, whilst we might have a duty to intervene to prevent humanitarian abuses, it will not follow that we fail in this duty if we do not prevent *all* such abuses.

Alternatively, we might argue against construing humanitarian intervention as a duty at all by invoking the intrinsic risks of war. Unlike acting in other-defence at an individual level, war inevitably involves the loss of life. If individuals are not obliged to risk their lives to save other people's lives, perhaps states are not obliged to send their soldiers to save others people's lives. We might therefore think that wars of intervention are always supererogatory on the part of states that wage them.

Chapter summary

The paradigm just cause for war is defence against aggression. In this chapter, we have looked at other possible just causes: punishment, prevention and humanitarian intervention. We looked at how the requirement of discrimination speaks against allowing the infliction of gratuitous, punitive harms of the sort that would result from a punitive war. We also looked at the distinction between prevention and pre-emption, paying particular attention to the US *National Security Strategy* of 2002. The second part of the chapter explored the idea of humanitarian intervention as a just cause for war, using NATO's intervention in Kosovo as an example of a morally justified intervention that may nonetheless have breached international law. As we have seen, Fletcher and Ohlin argue that international law *does* provide for wars of intervention by stipulating the right of peoples (and not just states) to exist. Fletcher and Ohlin argue that this stipulation gives rise to a legal right for states to come to the defence of those at risk of aggression from within their own state.

Questions for discussion

1 David Rodin suggests that we cannot know that defensive force is necessary unless a harm is imminent. Is he right?
2 Should humanitarian intervention be construed as a right, or as a duty (or neither)?
3 Was NATO right to intervene in Kosovo?
4 Is the distinction between pre-emption and prevention morally significant? Why?

Notes

1. L. Freedman, 'Prevention, Not Pre-emption', *The Washington Quarterly* 26, No. 2, 2003, 105–114, p. 106.
2. Freedman, 'Prevention, Not Pre-emption', p. 106.
3. Freedman, 'Prevention, Not Pre-emption', p. 107.
4. Letter of Secretary of State Daniel Webster to Special Minister Ashburton, dated 24 April 1841. The correspondence between Webster and Ashburton is available at http://avalon.law.yale.edu/19th_century/br-1842d.asp#ashdes1 (accessed 15 December 2010).
5. F. Bacon, *Of Empire*, London: Penguin Books, 2005, pp. 31–32.
6. M. Walzer, *Just and Unjust Wars*, New York: Basic Books, 1977, p. 80.
7. *The National Security Strategy of the United States*, 2002, p. 15, available at http://georgewbush-whitehouse.archives.gov/nsc/nss/2002/ (accessed 15 December 2010).
8. D. Rodin, *War and Self-Defense*, New York: Oxford University Press, 2002, p. 41.

9. Walzer, *Just and Unjust Wars*, p. 81.
10. Walzer, *Just and Unjust Wars*, p. 81.
11. Walzer, *Just and Unjust Wars*, p. 81.
12. G. Fletcher and J. Ohlin, *Defending Humanity: When Force is Justified and Why*, New York: Oxford University Press, 2008, p. 161.
13. Augustine, *City of God*, trans. Henry Bettenson, London: Penguin Books, 1972, Book XIX, Ch. 7.
14. Cicero, *The Republic*, trans. C. W. Keyes, Bury St Edmunds: St Edmundsbury Press, 12th edn, 2000, p. 212.
15. S. P. Huntington, 'New Contingencies, Old Roles', *Joint Forces Quarterly* 2, Autumn 1993, 38–44, p. 42.
16. C. Ceulemans, 'The NATO Intervention in the Kosovo Crisis', in B. Coppieters and N. Fotion (eds), *Moral Constraints on War*, Lanham, MD: Lexington Books, 2008, p. 215.
17. Fletcher and Ohlin, *Defending Humanity: When Force is Justified and Why*, p. 134.
18. Charter of the United Nations, 26 June 1945, Article 51, available at http://www.un.org/en/documents/charter/index.shtml (accessed 20 March 2011).
19. Fletcher and Ohlin, *Defending Humanity: When Force is Justified and Why*, p. 135.
20. Fletcher and Ohlin, *Defending Humanity: When Force is Justified and Why*, p. 146.
21. Fletcher and Ohlin, *Defending Humanity: When Force is Justified and Why*, p. 137.
22. Fletcher and Ohlin, *Defending Humanity: When Force is Justified and Why*, p. 136.
23. Fletcher and Ohlin, *Defending Humanity: When Force is Justified and Why*, p. 151.

Suggested reading

Judith Lichtenberg, 'The Ethics of Retaliation', *Philosophy & Public Policy Quarterly* 21, No. 4, 2001, reprinted in Verna Gehring (ed.), *War After September 11*, Lanham, MD: Rowman and Littlefield, 2002.
Lichtenberg gives an accessible discussion of the idea of war as punishment.

George P. Fletcher and Jens D. Ohlin, *Defending Humanity: When Force in Justified and Why*, New York: Oxford University Press, 2008, especially Chapter 6.
This book has more emphasis on the legal aspect of war than much of literature that I have used, and offers an interesting discussion of various relevant topics. Chapter 6 offers a good discussion of the issue of humanitarian intervention.

Cindy Holder, 'Responding to Humanitarian Crises', in L. May (ed.), *War: Essays in Political Philosophy*, Cambridge: Cambridge University Press, 2008. Holder offers an interesting argument against humanitarian intervention.

Michael J. Smith, 'Humanitarian Intervention: An Overview of the Ethical Issues', *Ethics and International Affairs* 12, No. 1, 1998, 63–79.

Henry Shue and David Rodin (eds), *Preemption*, Oxford: Oxford University Press, 2007.
This anthology contains many excellent recent papers on the ethics of pre-emptive war.

Nicholas J. Wheeler, *Saving Strangers: Humanitarian Intervention in International Society*, New York: Oxford University Press, 2000.
This book offers a good analysis of intervention from the perspective of international relations and political science.

5   The conditions of *jus in bello*

So far, we have considered the circumstances in which a war as an enterprise might be considered just by examining the conditions of *jus ad bellum*. In this chapter, we will look at the *jus in bello* rules that govern the fighting of war. We will begin by looking at the way in which realists have tried to undermine the idea that there are moral rules that govern the fighting of war. We will then consider how just war theorists have traditionally conceived of the relationship between the justness of one's war *overall* and the justness of how the war is fought. In the second part of the chapter, we will look specifically at the rules of *jus in bello* as they pertain to combatants, legitimate targets, legitimate tactics and prisoners of war.

THE IDEA OF *JUS IN BELLO*

Realism

We can understand why we have rules about whether a war is just. The rules of *jus ad bellum* are designed to reduce the number of wars, constrain aggression and so on. But if there is going to be a war, does it make sense to try to enforce rules about how that war ought to be fought? A view that is usually called *realism* appears throughout the centuries of just war thought, neatly summarised by Cicero's phrase *inter arma enim silent leges* ('laws are silent when arms are raised').[1] In short, realists argue that the nature of war defies legal or moral constraint. In the absence of these constraints, state leaders act (or should act) only in the national interest. Beyond doing what is best for their own state, there are no rules about what they can do in war. Brian Orend describes realists as emphasising 'power and security issues, the need for a state to maximize its expected self-interest and, above all, their view of the international arena as a kind of anarchy, in which the will to power enjoys primacy.'[2]

Given this, realism is not so much a view within just war theory, which is concerned with the rules governing war, as an alternative to just war theory, according to which there *are* no rules governing war. Since this is a book on just war theory, we will not spend a great deal of time examining the realist position. But it is worth outlining why people have found such a view appealing.

There are a variety of realist positions on the table, most of which fall into two main camps. The first camp is broadly consequentialist, suggesting that the absence of rules is better for the warring nation. War is a hellish enterprise, and hellish enterprises should be brought to a close as quickly as possible. Having rules for waging war restricts the manoeuvres open to combatants, slowing them down and making war more cumbersome than it need be. Without rules, we could simply wage a brief offensive of massive force, overwhelming the enemy in a short space of time. A war without rules would perhaps be more brutal, but it would be shorter and, in the long run, better. This argument offers pragmatic reasons against trying to regulate war, and suggests that we make a mistake in thinking that war is improved by restrictions on tactics, targets and the like. Orend calls this view prescriptive realism because it advocates warfare fought in the absence of rules.[3]

It is certainly possible that a short, brutal war could have fewer casualties than a drawn-out conflict that lasts several years. But this view seems to overlook the fact that people care a great deal about how combatants behave during war. They blame and condemn those who kill civilians in a way that they do not usually condemn even enemy combatants who stick to killing other combatants. Some communities shun even those people on 'their' side who engaged in torture of the enemy or other war crimes. Part of the motivation behind having rules of war, then, is that the rules themselves make reconciliation much easier. Bringing peace to a region that has seen widespread massacre, genocide, torture or mutilation is much harder than bringing peace to a region where the rules of war have largely been followed. These simmering tensions that persist long after particularly brutal wars sometimes lead to further wars that might have been avoided had the rules of *jus in bello* been followed in the first place. So, it is far from obvious that consequentialist considerations support the abolition of the laws of war. Such a policy might well lead to more wars of increased brutality rather than fewer wars of shorter duration. Of course, since this realist position is broadly consequentialist, it could in fact endorse having rules of war if following such rules would be better than not following them. But the reasons given for these rules would be markedly different from those usually offered by just war theorists. The rules would be purely contingent – they would not reflect moral principles of the sort that just war theorists envisage, but would simply be the best way of satisfying the national interest.

The second realist position is rather more defeatist. Orend calls it descriptive realism.[4] On this view, the problem is not that we *shouldn't* regulate war, but that we *cannot* regulate war. We might pretend to be imposing rules upon combatants, but we are fooling ourselves if we think that those in the field use these rules to inform their deliberations about what to do. The nature of war, and the nature of humanity, make it a futile exercise to try to restrain people's actions in what are the most dire situations that mankind can imagine. David Luban describes Paul Fussell's mockery of those 'armchair moralists' who think that rules can apply to warfare:

Fussell heaps sarcasm on the 'sensitive humanitarian' who 'was not so socially unfortunate as to find himself down there with the ground forces, where he might have had to compromise the purity and clarity of his moral system by the experience of weighing his own life against someone else's'. Marines 'sliding under fire down a shell-pocked ridge slimy with mud and liquid dysentery shit into the maggoty Japanese and USMC corpses at the bottom, vomiting as the maggots burrowed into their own foul clothing' simply cannot take seriously the notion of war as a realm governed by rules and restraints.

(D. Luban, 'War Crimes', in L. May (ed.), *War: Essays in Political Philosophy*, New York: Cambridge University Press, 2008, p.269. Quoted material from P. Fussell, 'Thank God for the Atom Bomb', in *Thank God for the Atom Bomb and Other Essays*, New York: Summit Books, 1988, pp. 34–36)

The horrors of war will undeniably lead combatants to do terrible things for which we do not blame them. But, as Luban argues, it matters a great deal whether we refrain from blaming them because we think that they did nothing wrong or because we think they can be excused for what they did. We might well accept that a combatant is excused because of duress. We might also accept a diminished responsibility defence of their actions. But such defences seek not to show that the agent did nothing wrong, but rather that they were not responsible for what they did. In other words, these considerations do not show the absence of rules in war, but merely show that, at times, combatants may not be able to follow those rules.

Of course, if combatants were *never* able to follow rules, Fussell would have a point. Stipulating rules of war would be a rather futile exercise. But it seems empirically false that combatants can never follow rules in war. Combatants usually hold *themselves* to strict moral codes in a way that seems at odds with Fussell's realist view. This has become especially apparent with the recent rise in terrorism. Professional soldiers who want to distinguish themselves from terrorists often emphasise that they, unlike terrorists, follow the rules of *jus in bello* – that they fight honourably in a way that marks them out from a rampaging militia or terrorist group. The notion of the honourable warrior appears in nearly all cultures, both ancient and contemporary (think of the Stoics or the samurai).

If we argue that during war there can be no rules restraining what people can do, and that therefore combatants are justified in doing even terrible things, we endorse the idea that one is permitted to do 'whatever it takes' to defeat one's enemy. Certainly, there have been times when people have used such arguments. The bombings of Hiroshima and Nagasaki were justified (rightly or not) as the only way in which the Second World War could be brought to a close. But most people restrict these arguments to cases of 'supreme emergency', in which the consequences of not acting are unthinkable – even more terrible than what one proposes to do. We distinguish between war and war crimes precisely because we *don't* think that just anything goes in war, even in the most hostile of circumstances. And combatants themselves endorse these rules, which would be an odd thing for them to do if they felt the rules to be wholly alien to their occupation.

It also seems false to think that all warfare takes place under anything like the conditions that Fussell describes. Modern warfare is often remote, employing unmanned aircraft and long-range weaponry. Most wars are fought by standing armies, whose members are well-equipped and well-trained. The trench warfare that Fussell describes might well have pushed ordinary people, many of them conscripts, to do things that violated the rules of war. But we cannot infer from this that there is no place for rules in war, or that combatants are not willing or able to be guided by these rules. As Michael Green argues, all parties to a conflict have reason to urge restraint:

> Nations will wish to limit war so that the possibility of their nation being totally destroyed is minimized, or at least significantly reduced. Most will wish that enough of their country remain so that their country can be rebuilt and their way of life continued after hostilities. A nation will wish to preserve its cultural, educational, and religious sites, its reproductive capacity (traditionally represented by women and children), and its non-military economic assets. Thus, it will wish to restrict war as far as possible to military and military-related activities, and it will wish actions against these to be circumscribed by rules of appropriate conduct.
>
> (M. J. Green, 'War, Innocence and Theories of Sovereignty',
> *Social Theory and Practice* 18, 1992, 39–62, p. 57)

Since all sides of a conflict will care about protecting their citizens, heritage and infrastructure, it is in the interests of all parties to have rules governing the sorts of damage that can be permissibly inflicted in war.

Those who endorse this 'mutual interest' account of war sometimes talk of the 'just war convention' rather than of just war theory. The use of 'convention' emphasises the idea that the rules of war are merely mutually beneficial agreements rather than the result of fundamental moral principles. The conventionalist view is, essentially, a more moderate form of realism. However, rather than grounding the rules solely in the national interest, the conventionalist view holds that we are *all* better off if we have these rules, since they reduce suffering and better enable reconstruction after the war. We ought therefore to obey them, but we are mistaken if we think them 'true' in any deeper sense.

Most contemporary just war theorists reject both the realist and conventionalist positions. Much of the recent work in just war theory assumes that there is at least some connection between morality and war, and that we can make sense of the idea that there are rules governing war just as there are rules governing morality in ordinary life. Of course, as we saw in Chapter 2, not everyone agrees about whether these are the *same* rules: people like Walzer deny that we can apply the rules of everyday life to the arena of war. But whatever the moral foundations of the *jus in bello* rules, most people agree that there are some things that one cannot do in war and some things that one must do in war, and that these rules are more than useful conventions.

The independence of *jus in bello*

We might think it obvious that a combatant can only fight justly if their war is just. How could they fight justly in the name of an unjust cause? But according to what we will call the orthodox view of just war theory, *jus ad bellum* and *jus in bello* are logically independent of one another. In other words, the overall justness of a war – whether it fulfils the rules of *jus ad bellum* – does not determine whether its combatants fight justly. This orthodox view, which is reflected in current international law, stems primarily from the idea that *jus ad bellum* is a political matter. It is politicians who decide whether or not to fight a war, and it is thus they who are morally and legally responsible for the overall justness of that war. State leaders can be guilty of the crime of aggression if they elect to wage an unjust war. But since combatants have no control over the sort of war that their leaders decide to wage, it would be unfair to label *their* actions criminal (or to label the combatants guilty) on the basis of political considerations about *jus ad bellum*. Combatants have control over military matters, not political decisions.

So, the orthodox view holds that combatants need pay attention only to the rules of *jus in bello* – the rules about how the war is fought. Provided that they obey these rules, combatants can rest assured that their actions are legal, even if their war is unjust. As Michael Walzer argues, fairness to the combatants demands that we do not condemn them for the crimes of their leaders:

> [S]o long as they fight in accordance with the rules, no condemnation is possible. The crucial point is that there are *rules* of war, though there are no rules of robbery (or of rape or murder). The moral equality of the battlefield distinguishes combat from domestic crime. If we are to judge what goes on it the course of a battle, then 'we must treat both combatants', as Henry Sidgwick has written, 'on the assumption that each believes himself in the right'.
>
> (M. Walzer, *Just and Unjust Wars*, New York: Basic Books, 1977, p. 128)

It is perfectly possible, on this view, that a just war be unjustly fought, and that an unjust war be justly fought. The combatants of a state engaged in a just war of defence might use illegal weapons, disregard proportionality or intentionally kill civilians. These combatants could be convicted of war crimes even if their war is just. Conversely, the combatants of a state pursuing an unjust war might follow the *in bello* rules to the letter. These soldiers will not be deemed criminals under international law, even if their political leaders are intent on criminal aggression.

Because of this divorcing of *jus ad bellum* from *jus in bello*, there is a certain peculiarity about the moral and legal status of war. We would think it very odd if someone were to suggest making laws about how one ought to go about committing domestic crimes. Take something like armed robbery. Since the very activity of armed robbery is illegal, we do not to try to legislate how one ought to go about it (perhaps by specifying the sort of weapon that one should use, or identifying particular banks that ought to be targeted). And, yet, this is precisely how international law approaches the issue of war. Whilst acknowledging that unjust wars are illegal, the law nonetheless requires that combatants pursuing such a war obey the *jus in bello* rules. Despite its illegality, unjust war is a law-governed activity.

Of course, as Walzer notes and as we discussed in Chapter 2, nearly all combatants will believe themselves to be fighting a just war, even if they are not. Thus, even if the laws of *jus in bello* were applied only to those fighting a just war, most armed forces would try to adhere to them anyway, since they would perceive the rules as applying to them. But, in addition to the idea that it is unfair to hold combatants responsible for the wars they fight, there are good reasons to explicitly extend the *in bello* rules to combatants engaged in unjust wars.

Consider the alternative. If we deny that combatants fighting an unjust war can fight legally by obeying the *in bello* rules, we brand them criminals from the outset. And this removes a major incentive that the combatants have to care about things like minimising civilian casualties or protecting prisoners of war – things that we have very good reason to want them to do. If a combatant is pretty sure that his state is waging an unjust war, he will know that he is already regarded as a criminal no matter what he does, and will perhaps fail to take steps to minimise the harm he causes. By separating the justness of *how* one fights from the fact *that* one fights, we can give those combatants reason to avoid committing atrocities, which seems pretty desirable for all concerned.

Divorcing *ad bellum* rules from *in bello* rules can also make surrender more likely. If a combatant thinks that he will be arrested for fighting as soon as the war ends, he is unlikely to hasten that outcome by surrendering. Wars might drag on longer than necessary as combatants try to avoid arrest. By making it legal for combatants to fight even unjust wars, we remove this incentive to prolong war. However, despite these advantages of divorcing *jus ad bellum* from *jus in bello*, some contemporary just war theorists have sought to undermine the orthodox view of these two stages of war. Most notable amongst these critics is Jeff McMahan. McMahan denies that combatants can fight justly even if their war is unjust. He also rejects the concomitant claim that combatants who fight on the unjust side of a war are the moral equals of those who fight on the just side. McMahan's critique represents one of the most important shifts in recent just war thought, and we thus return to it in detail in Chapter 6.

THE RULES OF *JUS IN BELLO*

The rules of *jus in bello* can be divided into four categories. The first category specifies the conditions that a person must meet if they are to qualify as a combatant. The second governs the targets that one may legitimately attack in war. The third describes the sorts of tactics one may use, in terms of both the scale of attacks and the sorts of weapons or strategies that can be permissibly employed. The fourth category details the rules that govern the treatment of prisoners of war.

The *jus in bello* rules are legally enshrined by two sets of conventions. The Hague Conventions of 1899 and 1907 detail the 'customs of war', specifying the types of weapons that one may employ in war and laying down certain humanitarian rules of combat. Much of the substance of the Hague Conventions is iterated by the Geneva Convention of 1949 and the subsequent Geneva Protocols of 1977.[5] The Geneva Conventions also lay down rules for the treatment of vulnerable parties in war, namely wounded combatants, prisoners of war and non-combatants.

Qualifying as a combatant

The great moral weight that rests upon the division between combatants and non-combatants means that we want to be pretty clear about who counts as a combatant and who doesn't. This is partly because of the impermissibility of targeting non-combatants, as we will discuss below. But it is also because of the importance of according combatants prisoner of war (POW) status, which grants them protected status under law and confers particular duties upon their captors. Attaining this status gives one certain immunities and privileges that are not extended to non-combatants who engage in hostilities. As we will see in Chapter 9, the increase in inter-state terrorism has raised difficult questions about how we ought to identify combatants. However, the conventional means of identification laid out by the Geneva Convention give us a good place to start.

When it was drafted in 1949, the Convention stipulated that to qualify as a combatant, a person must:

- be part of a hierarchical group, such that there is a recognisable chain of command;
- wear a distinctive emblem that is visible from a distance;
- bear arms openly;
- obey the rules of *jus in bello* as laid out in the Convention.

The first requirement holds that unless there is a clear sense in which a person can be said to be either giving or following orders as part of a larger organisation to which they are accountable, they will not qualify as a combatant. This stipulation that combatants be part of a group with a recognisable structure of authority distinguishes combatants from mobs or other groups that might use force during a conflict, but who lack the organisation and accountability of a legitimate military group. Part of what protects combatants against criminal charges is that when they inflict damage, they are following orders. A member of the US army who took it upon himself to blow up even a military target would be criminally liable for the damage he caused. Damage must be *authorised* if it is to fall within the scope of *jus in bello*. A group without a recognisable hierarchy is rather like a group of combatants who do nothing but inflict damage 'off their own bat'. A chain of command ensures that there is scope for punishment and discipline within a group that enforces obedience to *jus in bello*, and also enables the group to negotiate with other parties in the conflict.

The requirement that combatants wear a distinctive emblem means that combatants must identify themselves *as* combatants. By wearing uniforms, combatants mark themselves out as legitimate targets. In so doing, they protect non-combatants, since their uniforms make it clear who is a legitimate target and who is not. If combatants did not distinguish themselves in this way, the chances of accidentally targeting non-combatants would be greatly increased. However, the Additional Protocols of 1977 slightly revised the conditions about distinguishing oneself as a combatant and bearing arms openly:

> Recognising [. . .] that there are situations in armed conflicts where, owing to the nature of hostilities an armed combatant cannot so distinguish himself, he shall retain his status as a combatant, provided that in such situations, he carries his arms openly: (a) during each military engagement, and (b) during such time as he is visible to the adversary while he is engaged in a military deployment preceding the launching of an attack in which he is to participate.
>
> [Additional Protocol to the Geneva Convention (Protocol 1), Geneva, 1977, Article 44.3]

The exceptions described are most commonly manifested by guerrilla warfare, where combatants routinely blend in amongst the non-combatant population. In recent times, this type of warfare has been most successfully employed by the Vietcong in the Vietnam War (although the notion of guerrilla warfare is far from recent: references to this sort of combat are found as far back as 500 BC in the writings of the Chinese writer Sun Tzu). The Vietcong capitalised on the fact that the Americans couldn't distinguish them from non-combatants. They dressed the same as the local population, lived in the villages and often helped villagers work the land in return for shelter. To the untrained eye, there was little to tell Vietcong members from local peasants – hardly surprising, since most of them *were* local peasants. However, this strategy resulted in high civilian casualties on the Vietnamese side. Since the Americans couldn't distinguish combatants from non-combatants, they often erred on the side of caution (as it were) and killed both.

Despite this danger, the revised Geneva Convention does not deny guerrillas combatant status. This would unfairly disadvantage smaller, less well-equipped forces who cannot win wars by conventional means. Given their (initially) small numbers and lack of weaponry, requiring the Vietcong to wear uniforms would have denied them any chance of success against the military might of the US forces. Provided that they met the third qualifying condition of bearing their arms openly immediately prior to military engagement, and whilst actually engaging the US soldiers, the Vietcong thus retained their status as combatants even without the wearing of any distinctive emblem. The requirement that one bear arms openly is again intended to enable combatants to identify each other to the exclusion of non-combatants. Concealing weapons about one's person deceptively implies that one does not pose a threat and is not engaged in hostilities. Again, if combatants frequently hide their weapons, it is likely that many non-combatants will be targeted by mistake.

The final condition for qualification as a combatant is that one obey the rules of *jus in bello*. However, violation of the rules does not automatically disqualify one from combatant status. As I described above, part of the rationale behind requiring hierarchy in military groups is that it enables combatants who break the rules to be disciplined. If a combatant who breaks the *jus in bello* rules is held to account by their own superiors, they are still deemed a combatant. Such a combatant would, for example, be eligible for POW status in the event of their capture. However, members of a group that persistently fail to punish breaches of *jus in bello* would probably forfeit their combatant status, even if the group has a clear chain of command. As we will discuss in Chapter 9, their persistent and deliberate violating of *jus in bello* is a primary argument against granting terrorists combatant status.

Legitimate targets

The requirement of discrimination

As mentioned above, one of the primary reasons for distinguishing combatants from non-combatants is that only combatants are legitimate targets. The rules of war prohibit aiming force at non-combatants. However, the distinction between legitimate and illegitimate targets does not always map onto the distinction between combatants and non-combatants as neatly as we might like. For example, the category of combatant can include some political leaders. Of course, some state leaders, such as Burma's military rulers, clearly identify themselves as part of the armed forces, and most state leaders have ultimate authority over their armed forces. But even those politicians without military roots or affiliation can be legitimate targets if they are instrumental in the orchestrating of the war. And some members of the military, such as doctors and clergy, are not legitimate targets, and are not counted as combatants for the purposes of *jus in bello*. These people are deemed to perform civilian roles, and are legally protected from attack (although military doctors are allowed to be armed in order to defend themselves). One is permitted to kill 'active' combatants (i.e. those who are not *hors de combat* through surrender, capture or injury) whenever doing so would afford one a military advantage.

In Chapter 7 we will look at objections to the idea that there is a morally significant difference between combatants and non-combatants that explains why it is permissible to target combatants, but not non-combatants. In particular, we will look at how we ought to classify those who are not members of the armed forces, but who work for them (perhaps by making weapons or equipment). For now, however, we will assume that the combatant/non-combatant distinction is sufficiently robust to ground the various parts of *jus in bello* that prohibit the targeting of non-combatants.

The Geneva Convention forbids all intentional violence towards non-combatants, and towards those members of the armed forces who are *hors de combat*. Even though one can capture wounded combatants as prisoners of war, one cannot intentionally inflict further injury upon a combatant once he or she is unable to take part in the battle.

> To this end, the following acts are and shall remain prohibited at any time and in any place whatsoever with respect to the above-mentioned persons: (a) Violence to life and person, in particular murder of all kinds, mutilation, cruel treatment and torture; (b) taking of hostages; (c) outrages upon personal dignity, in particular humiliating and degrading treatment; (d) the passing of sentences and the carrying out of executions without previous judgement pronounced by a regularly constituted court, affording all the judicial guarantees which are recognized as indispensable by civilized peoples.
>
> [Convention (IV) Relative to the Protection of Civilian Persons in Time of War, Geneva, 1949, Article 3, available at http://www.icrc.org/ihl.nsf/FULL/380?OpenDocument (accessed 22 March 2011)]

The intentional killing of non-combatants counts as a war crime. Such a violation of the laws of war is usually punished internally by one's own military organisation, as described above. For example, a combatant accused of deliberately killing civilians would ordinarily face a court martial rather than a criminal trial. However, there have been cases in which combatants have been tried by criminal courts for violations of *jus in bello*, such as the trial of Trooper Kevin Williams for the murder of an Iraqi civilian in 2003. In addition, large-scale violations of *jus in bello* might fall under the jurisdiction of the International Criminal Court rather than any individual military organisation.

Non-personal targets

The basic rule of thumb regarding legitimate non-personal targets (i.e. buildings and so on) is that one can strike targets that have a military function, the destruction of which will afford one a military advantage. The obvious examples are military headquarters or bases, factories providing weapons, ammunition or equipment to the military, and military vehicles. But one can also strike at those things that play a more general role in enabling the military to function. For example, armed forces sometimes rely on communications networks such as telephone exchanges. These networks count as legitimate targets. Television and radio stations can also be legitimate targets, as can transport networks, such as roads, railways and tunnels, and power plants (although one cannot target nuclear or hydroelectric plants). It is also permissible to target research centres that are being used to develop military technology. For example, in the First World War, the Kaiser Wilhelm Institute of Physical Chemistry and Electrochemistry was used by the Germans to develop chemical weapons. This military function of an otherwise civilian building renders it a legitimate target.

Illegitimate targets are basically non-military buildings, for example hospitals, places of worship, schools, and 'cultural' buildings such as libraries or museums. Anything with a civil, rather than a military, function is an illegitimate target. (But, again, these sorts of buildings can *become* legitimate targets if, as often happens, the military take them over during the war, for example as research units, military headquarters or army barracks.)

Bombing a purely or largely residential area is impermissible. One of the criticisms of the Allied forces in the Second World War stemmed from their use of firebombing against German cities such as Dresden. As we will discuss below, the indiscriminate nature of firebombing – that it spreads uncontrollably from military to non-military targets – makes it hard to argue that one could use it in a targeted way as required by the *in bello* rules. And, even though Dresden contained some military facilities, it was widely reported that combatants were under no instructions to aim at these facilities rather than residential areas. The Dresden offensive thus violates the *jus in bello* rules (and firebombing was banned as a method of warfare after the Second World War). The Geneva Convention also prohibits intentionally destroying medical equipment or vehicles.

Remember that we're talking here about legitimate and illegitimate *targets*. One cannot *aim* at a school or hospital during wartime. But one can permissibly destroy such buildings in the course of targeting something else, such as a power plant or military base. Whether this 'collateral damage' is permissible depends on whether the attack meets certain conditions, for example proportionality and necessity. It is to these further conditions of a legitimate attack that we now turn.

Legitimate tactics

Military necessity

All legitimate attacks in war must meet the conditions of military necessity and proportionality. Military necessity requires that an offensive be intended to confer some sort of military advantage. The instantiation of this requirement in law draws heavily on the formulation of Francis Lieber, a law professor and veteran of Waterloo, and author of the *Lieber Code*. The US government adopted the *Lieber Code* in its Instructions for the Government of Armies of the United States in the Field in 1863:

> Military necessity, as understood by modern civilized nations, consists in the necessity of those measures which are indispensable for securing the ends of war, and which are lawful according to the modern law and usages of war. Military necessity admits of all direct destruction of life or limb of armed enemies, and of other persons whose destruction is incidentally unavoidable in the armed contests of the war; it allows the capturing of every armed enemy . . . it allows of all destruction of property, and obstruction of the ways and channels of traffic, travel or communication, and of all withholding of sustenance or means of life from the enemy . . . Military necessity does not admit of cruelty – that is, the infliction of suffering for the sake of suffering or for revenge, nor of any maiming or wounding except in fight, nor of torture to extort confessions.
>
> [Instructions for the Government of Armies of the United States in the Field (*Lieber Code*), 24 April 1863, available at http://www.icrc.org/ihl.nsf/FULL/110?OpenDocument) (accessed 22 March 2011)]

The requirement of military advantage explains why only those things with military connections are legitimate targets. Blowing up a school or a church will not help one secure a military advantage, but blowing up an airbase or a munitions factory might. The damage that one intends must be instrumental in winning the war.

Note, however, that military necessity requires commanders to think about what will improve their chances of a *military* defeat of the opposition. They should think about how the offensive will enable them to fight more effectively, reduce the number of enemy combatants or force the enemy to retreat. In other words, military commanders must be firmly focused upon the opposing military force. They cannot consider what are sometimes called 'political' ends, such as whether a particular attack will scare their opponents' political leaders into surrender. Bombing a school could have a political advantage, in that the government might be so horrified by what the enemy is prepared to do that it surrenders immediately. But this would not count as part of a legitimate military campaign.

Recall the discussion of NATO intervention in Kosovo in the previous chapter. Although NATO justified its use of force on primarily humanitarian grounds, there was also a political motive of coercing Serbia into signing a peace treaty. According to the rules of *jus in bello*, whilst it was fine for NATO's political leaders to be concerned with this goal, it should not have influenced commanders on the ground. This might seem a rather odd requirement. As Burrus Carnahan argues;

> Any major military operation will emanate from both military and political motivations . . . if the legality of an attack turns on the motivation or predominant purpose of the highest governmental authority approving it, it will be impossible for an objective observer to determine whether the attack was justified by military necessity.
> (B. Carnahan, 'Lincoln, Lieber and the Laws of War: The Origins and Limits of the Principle of Military Necessity', *American Journal of International Law* 92, No. 2, 1998, 213–231, p. 222)

In other words, much as with the *jus ad bellum* requirement of right intention, there are parts of the requirement of military necessity that are hard to establish. It might well be the case that sometimes a military commander cannot help but have an eye on the political game. But the inclusion of a requirement that emphasises *military* necessity (and not just necessity) helps iterate the division between *jus ad bellum* and *jus in bello*, reminding combatants that though the war as a whole is a political project, their role in it must be restricted to military concerns. Walzer argues that, '[g]enerals may well straddle the line, but that only suggests that we know pretty well where it should be drawn.'[6] Once combatants begin to concern themselves with the wider politics of war, it becomes harder to sustain the idea that they lack responsibility for *ad bellum* considerations about the justness of the war as a whole. And, as described above, undermining the *ad bellum/in bello* divide has significant implications for the moral status of combatants.

Proportionality

Military attacks are constrained not only by the sorts of ends that commanders may have in mind, but also by considerations of proportionality. Much as in self-defence, the harm that one inflicts must be proportionate to the good that is protected, and must be the least harmful means available of achieving the good. A pressing question, then, is what counts as a relevant good or harm during war. In the discussion of *ad bellum* proportionality in Chapter 3, we saw the different ways in which people conceive of relevant goods with respect to whether a war has a just cause. For example, even if deterrence would be a benefit of waging war, it may not follow that it is a relevant good in terms of whether war would be proportionate. Similarly, we must identify the sorts of goods and harms that matter to the *in bello* proportionality considerations. Thomas Hurka suggests that the relevant *in bello* goods are defined by the *ad bellum* just cause for war.[7] What can weigh against causing harm during war must be the furtherance of the good aims that justified resort to war in the first place. So, helping to secure or defend sovereignty, or helping to eradicate humanitarian abuse, would be a relevant good that could be balanced against relevant harms.

The primary relevant harm in war is going to be the taking of life. Whilst damage to infrastructure is important, its significance usually derives from the impact on the death toll. Damage to sewage or water works, for example, can often indirectly kill people. But the proportionality calculation in war is not as straightforward as weighing lives saved against deaths caused. Not all lives count equally under the rules of *jus in bello*, as is made apparent by the prohibition on targeting non-combatants.

We can distinguish between four 'types' of lives that are at risk during war. There are the lives of enemy combatants, the lives of enemy non-combatants, the lives of our combatants and the lives of our non-combatants. Just war theorists disagree about how these categories compare to each other when it comes to judging proportionality. For a start, most accounts of proportionality in war do not count the deaths of enemy combatants as a harm to be weighed against the pursuit of some good. All enemy combatant deaths are thus 'free'. Provided that killing them achieves a military advantage (the deaths must be necessary in this sense), one can kill any number of enemy combatants.

This permissive view is usually explained by the claim that combatants have signed up to fight: they have volunteered to put themselves at risk. By enlisting, they waive their right not to be killed in battle by the other side. They are therefore not wronged by being killed, and thus their deaths don't weigh as harms against the good being pursued. This idea is sometimes compared to the principle that one may kill any number of lethal attackers (or, at least, of culpable attackers) in self-defence. When a person chooses to try to kill you, they waive their right not to be harmed in self-defence. Killing two, three or even ten culpable attackers is not deemed disproportionate by most accounts of self-defence, because none of the attackers is wronged by being killed. Similarly, if killing a great number of enemy combatants is necessary to achieve some military advantage, one can discount the harm to those combatants. Even a great number of enemy combatant deaths will not make an offensive disproportionate.

What about the harm to enemy *non*-combatants? Nearly all just war theorists think that one must include the lives of these non-combatants in one's proportionality calculations. In most offensives, the loss of civilian life will be the main factor in determining whether a course of action is proportionate. The Geneva Convention prohibits killing or harming non-combatants at a level 'which would be excessive in relation to the concrete and direct military advantage anticipated.'[8] We might think, however, that this seems rather at odds with the part of the Convention quoted earlier forbidding violence against non-combatants. How can it be permissible to cause even proportionate harm to non-combatants if the Geneva Convention forbids violence towards non-combatants?

Most answers to this question will invoke something along the lines of the doctrine of double effect. What the Convention prohibits is the *targeting* of non-combatants – the use of the word 'violence' is meant to capture this intentional aspect of harm. But the Convention does not prohibit killing non-combatants as a foreseen side-effect of an offensive aimed at gaining some military advantage. Despite the misgivings that many people have about the DDE's philosophical viability, double-effect reasoning has an established place in the ethics of war. Hurka, for example, argues that, 'the targeted/ collateral distinction is central to just war theory . . . In fact the distinction is implicit in the very idea of *in bello* proportionality.'[9] Hurka argues that the only way to allow for the accidental or incidental killing of non-combatants – which is an inevitable part of war – is to draw a distinction between those killings that one intends as a means to achieving a military end and those killings that one foresees or predicts but that are not themselves conducive to the military end. The very existence of the *in bello* proportionality condition assumes that there are some non-combatant killings that are permissible. We avoid sanctioning the more general killing of non-combatants by restricting permissible killing to that which is both unintended and proportionate to the military good.

Do the lives of enemy non-combatants count as much as the lives of 'our' non-combatants? When we put the question like this, I expect that most people will think that they do. It is hard to believe that, say, the life of a German child in the Second World War was any less valuable or worthy of protection than the life of a British child. But is the life of a German child as worthy of protection *by the British* as the life of a British child? Our answer to *this* question might be rather different.

Hurka argues that states can have an obligation to prefer the interests of their own citizens to those of other citizens, much as parents can have obligations to give their own children's interests more weight than the interests of other children.[10] Hurka supports his argument with the following case:

> Help:
> Daughter is attacked by Murderer. Father can save Daughter only by throwing a grenade at Murderer. However, the blast from the grenade will not only kill Murderer, but will also kill Bystander, who cannot get out of the way in time.

Hurka argues that whilst a stranger would not be permitted to throw the grenade, it is permissible for Father to do so. Part of why Father can do this is that Daughter is *his* daughter, and he is allowed to choose her life over that of Bystander. But the permissibility is also explained by the fact that Father does not intend the harm to Bystander, but merely foresees it. Bystander's death is 'collateral damage'.

Compare *Help* with *Shield*:

> *Shield:*
> Murderer throws a spear at Daughter. Father can save Daughter only by grabbing Bystander and using her as a human shield, making sure that the spear impales her rather than Daughter.

Few people think that Father is permitted to do *this* to save Daughter, even if he may sometimes choose Daughter's life over the life of a stranger. And the DDE explains why this is. In *Shield*, the harm to Bystander is not a side-effect of saving Daughter's life. It is part of the plan to save Daughter's life. The role that the DDE attributes to intention enables it to explain why killing Bystander in *Help* is permissible, but killing Bystander in *Shield* is not.

Hurka claims that the DDE also explains why a government can be permitted to kill some foreign citizens in order to save its own citizens' lives, provided that the deaths of foreign citizens are merely foreseen and not intended:

> The situation of a nation weighing its own against enemy civilians' lives is analogous [to *Help*]. The nation is, say, attacking a government that has sponsored terrorist attacks against its citizens and finds that, while directing force only at that government's agents, it will unavoidably kill some enemy civilians. I think that in this case the nation's government is permitted to give somewhat greater weight to its own civilians' lives, and the case for partiality here may even be stronger than in that of individual defense.
>
> (T. Hurka, 'Proportionality in the Morality of War', *Philosophy and Public Affairs* 33, No. 1, 2005, 34–66, p. 62)

I don't know how many of us will share Hurka's intuition about the permissibility of Father's throwing the grenade in *Help*. It certainly seems true that if both Daughter and Bystander were being attacked by Murderer, and Father could save only Daughter *or* Bystander, he would be permitted to save Daughter. Similarly, in the context of war, it seems permissible (or even required) for the British army to rescue British non-combatants rather than foreign non-combatants if both are under attack.

However, does this permission of partiality extend to the *killing* of foreign non-combatants as part of a bid to save British lives? If Hurka is right that Father may kill Bystander as a side-effect of saving Daughter, he may well be right that governments may exhibit similar preferences. But if we do not share Hurka's intuition at the individual level, we might be reluctant to endorse it at the state level. Perhaps Father is just excused for acting as he does: he acts wrongly, but we don't blame him for doing so. If we take this view, we seem to favour the position that non-combatant lives on all sides of a conflict are to be weighed equally in proportionality calculations.

What about the final category: the lives of our combatants? How do these compare with the other types of life that we have considered? The fact that it is permissible to intentionally kill combatants certainly suggests that their lives are to count for less than the lives of non-combatants. Certainly, many governments will seek to minimise non-combatant losses over combatant losses. We might explain this by reference to the earlier observation that combatants have signed up to fight. In doing so, they agree that their lives may be sacrificed in order to save others. But they perhaps intend only that their lives may be sacrificed to save the lives of their fellow citizens. Even if we think it preferable that one of our combatants is killed rather than one of our non-combatants, do we think the same is true when the choice is that between our combatant and an enemy non-combatant?

Imagine that a military commander has the following dilemma:

> *Offensive:*
> Commander can use any of three strategies to achieve a significant military advantage. Strategy A will involve minimal risk to his combatants, but will probably kill ten enemy non-combatants as a side-effect. Strategy B will involve a higher risk to the combatants – three will probably be killed – but anticipated non-combatant losses will be much lower – about three people will be killed. Strategy C will incur much greater losses on the part of the combatants – about six will be killed, but the risk to non-combatants will be negligible.

Which strategy should Commander adopt? Strategy A will result in a higher total loss of life, but will avoid casualties amongst Commander's own troops. If we weigh the lives involved equally, A seems to be prohibited because it is not the least harmful means of achieving the goal, and proportionality requires that one do no more harm than is necessary. If the deaths of combatants and enemy non-combatants count for the same, it cannot be permissible to kill ten people if one can achieve the same goal by killing six.

Strategy B shares the deaths equally among the combatants and non-combatants. If we weigh their lives equally, B seems to distribute the risk fairly between the two groups. Strategy C imposes the greatest risk on the combatants in order to protect the non-combatants, but does not increase the overall loss of life compared with B. If the lives are weighed equally, B and C are equally harmful, and thus the proportionality constraint will allow either.

But *ought* we to weigh the lives equally? Is there anything to choose between B and C, given that six people will be killed either way? Paul Christopher and Michael Walzer both argue that in cases like *Offensive*, the onus is on the combatants to shoulder the risks, not only to save their non-combatants, but to save enemy non-combatants as well. Christopher argues that 'risking one's life is part of what it means to be a soldier. Taking the position that minimizing the risk to soldiers is the basis for choosing among alternatives undermines the very notion of distinguishing between combatants and non-combatants.'[11] Walzer argues that it is not enough that combatants do not intend to kill non-combatants. What is required from them is a 'positive commitment to save civilian lives':

> Not merely to apply the proportionality rule and kill no more civilians than is militarily necessary – that rule applies to soldiers as well; no one can be killed for trivial purposes. Civilians have a right to something more. And if saving civilian lives means risking soldiers' lives, the risk must be accepted.
>
> (Walzer, *Just and Unjust Wars*, p. 156)

Walzer and Christopher thus reject the idea that we might weigh the lives of the combatants and non-combatants equally in *Offensive*, and opt for Strategy B. Non-combatants are entitled not merely to equal consideration, but to *greater* consideration. Commander must employ Strategy C. Hurka, on the other hand, argues that the two considerations in play – national partiality towards one's own citizens, including combatants, on the one hand, and the voluntary nature of soldiering, on the other – balance each other out. Commander must allow the lives of the combatants and non-combatants equal weight. On Hurka's account, Commander ought to employ Strategy B.

Weapons and tactics

As well as the general conditions of military necessity and proportionality, the rules of war stipulate the sorts of weapons and techniques that one can permissibly employ in warfare. As with much of law, these stipulations are primarily negative. In other words, they outline what one must not do, with an assumption that what is not prohibited is permitted by default.

There are two guiding principles behind the laws of weaponry. The first is, again, the principle of discrimination between combatants and non-combatants. The Geneva Convention requires that combatants 'shall direct their operations only against military objectives.'[12] This effectively prohibits the use of weapons that cannot be directed against only military objectives, either because they are 'blunt instruments' or because they cannot be sufficiently well controlled. The V-2 rockets used in the Second World War fall into the class of blunt instrument, because they can only be used against entire cities. Firebombing is prohibited because the spread of the fires cannot be restricted to military targets. Part of the campaign against landmines cites their indiscriminate nature, but as yet there is no consensus about the impermissibility of land mines (rather, countries such as the USA have tried to make landmines safer, for example by developing mines with batteries that expire after a certain length of time, with the aim of reducing civilian casualties).

The second guiding principle with respect to weaponry is the demand that parties to a conflict not employ 'weapons, projectiles and material and methods of warfare of a nature to cause superfluous injury or unnecessary suffering.'[13] This part of the Geneva Convention has been used in particular to outlaw certain types of bullet, such as those that explode on impact and disperse inside the combatant's body. Since standard bullets are sufficient to render a combatant *hors de combat*, the additional damage done to a combatant by an exploding bullet is deemed unnecessary and impermissible.

We are all by now painfully familiar with the phrase 'weapons of mass destruction' (WMDs). Iraq's alleged possession of such weapons was the primary cause of the 2003 invasion of Iraq. Weapons of mass destruction is the name given to the group of weapons that includes chemical, biological and nuclear weapons. The Geneva Protocol of 1925 banned the use of 'asphyxiating, poisonous or other gases [and] analogous liquids, materials or devices in war'.[14] Biological weapons, for example anthrax, originate from living organisms such as bacteria. Perhaps surprisingly, these weapons can be the most destructive of WMDs, and are particularly harmful to non-combatants. Paul Christopher suggests that this indiscriminate aspect of biological weapons has led to a general consensus regarding their impermissibility: 'The reason that these weapons have been considered inappropriate has nothing to do with their effect on soldiers – that is, they do not cause "unnecessary suffering" – but because of their potential effects on innocent and friendly non-combatants.'[15] Historically, there has been less agreement about the impermissibility of using chemical weapons, which can be more accurately targeted at combatants and don't seem significantly more harmful than conventional weaponry. Many countries thus agreed not to use chemical weapons first in a conflict, but did not rule out that they might be used in response to a chemical attack by one's enemy. Chemical weapons were used extensively in the First World War. However, in 1997, the Convention on Chemical Weapons came into force. The Convention currently has 184 signatory states. This Convention prohibits the development and stockpiling of chemical weapons, and requires that all signatory states destroy their existing reserves of such weapons.

Much of the current debate about WMDs is about whether nuclear weapons are different in kind from chemical weapons, or merely different in degree. If they are merely different in degree, their use would seem to fall under the rules governing chemical weapons. However, if they are different in kind, the use of nuclear weapons might fall into a gap in the law, with their use not covered by the rules about chemical warfare. Christopher argues, however, that there is good reason to think that nuclear weapons should be outlawed because they fall foul of the principle of discrimination:

> There is certainly at least one aspect of nuclear weapons that offers strong evidence for considering them *different in kind* from conventional weapons, namely the long-term effects of radiation and nuclear fallout. No other weapons system has such far-reaching and long-lasting destructive

capability. This seems to make their use in war at least questionable, because by their very nature they tend to be indiscriminate in whom they harm *in the long term*.

(P. Christopher, *The Ethics of War and Peace: An Introduction to Legal and Moral Issues*, Englewood Cliffs, NJ: Prentice Hall, 1998, 3rd edn, 2004, p. 210)

Unlike, say, nerve gas, radiation hangs around. The effects of the nuclear bombs used in Hiroshima and Nagasaki at the end of the Second World War are still keenly felt in Japan. Subsequent generations have been scarred by birth defects, illness and environmental devastation. And, yet, there is no ban on the use of nuclear weapons, although recent years have seen some states resolve to reduce their nuclear arsenal. The Comprehensive Test Ban Treaty,[16] which prohibits experimental nuclear explosions, has not been signed by India, Pakistan or North Korea. It has been signed but not ratified by the USA, China, Egypt, Indonesia, Iran and Israel. The overwhelming destructive power of these weapons makes their use unlikely – not least because of the improbability that their use would be proportionate – but it is this power that makes states reluctant to be without their nuclear weapons while other states retain nuclear capacity.

So, this gives us an idea of the sorts of thing that one is *not* permitted to do in war. Counted amongst the *legitimate* tactics, then, are some sorts of bombing, the use of some missiles, the sinking of ships, the intentional shooting of combatants, the capturing of combatants, sabotage, espionage, ambush and blockades. Blockades take place on water – usually coastal waters – and are designed to stop the importing and exporting of goods. The most recent example of such a tactic is Israel's blockading of Lebanon in 2006. The land equivalent of a blockade is a siege. Whilst sieges were historically common, the changes in international law have made lawful sieges virtually impossible. The law allows one to restrict the access of supplies to the military in order to force surrender. But the Geneva Convention prohibits the starving of non-combatants. Since, these days, any area worth besieging is likely to have a sizeable non-combatant population, the besieging force would have to allow aid to get through the barriers. Once inside, it would be practically impossible to prevent the supplies from reaching the military, undermining the purpose of the siege.

Prisoners of war

There are strict and detailed rules laid out in the Third Geneva Convention regarding the treatment of prisoners of war. All captured combatants should be treated as prisoners of war, which means treating them humanely at all times. This precludes the infliction of any injury, the use of torture, and the use of prisoners for medical or scientific experimentation. The Convention also prohibits the degrading treatments of prisoners, and their use as 'objects of curiosity'. What this means is that a prisoner of war ought not to be paraded as a symbol of victory or success. This rule was recently broken when Saddam Hussein's medical examination, carried out whilst he was in US custody, was filmed and shown around the world. Even though parading Hussein probably helped decrease morale amongst those fighting against US troops in Iraq, the Geneva Convention forbids this sort of exhibiting of prisoners of war.

When a combatant is captured, his own force should be informed as soon as possible, and he should be safely evacuated from the combat zone. He should be able to write to his family at the earliest opportunity. Combatants are obliged to inform their captor of their name, rank, affiliation and date of birth, but they are not obliged to give up any further information. They can be questioned, but should not be threatened, insulted or coerced into giving up information. All combatants must be issued with an identity card that they should keep in their possession at all times.

There are also clear rules about the sorts of conditions in which prisoners of war can be kept. By imprisoning enemy combatants, the capturing force – or Detaining Power – takes on responsibility for their welfare. They are charged with the protection of their prisoners, in terms of both shielding them from the dangers of the war and providing food, shelter and medical care. Prisoners should be kept with their comrades, be allowed to keep their personal possessions and be allowed to practise their religion. Prisoners may be put to work, but they must be paid for this work, and cannot be forced to do work of a dangerous or unhealthy nature or asked to contribute to the Detaining Power's own military effort.

In keeping with the division between *jus ad bellum* and *jus in bello*, prisoners of war are not to be judged as criminals even if their war is unjust. Thus, they cannot be punished simply for fighting. However, they can be punished for offences committed whilst under the authority of the Detaining Power. International law distinguishes between disciplinary punishments and judicial punishments. Disciplinary punishments are a sort of internal sanction, akin to those issued by one's own superiors for mild offences. One might forfeit pay, incur additional labour duties, and so on. Judicial punishments are reserved for serious offences of the sort that would usually be the subject of a court martial. The Convention requires that prisoners of war be treated no more harshly than members of the Detaining Power's own troops, and that defendants have a right to a fair trial with adequate means of defence. Finally, once the war is over, all prisoners of war must be repatriated as soon as possible.

Again, it is clearly in the interests of all parties to a conflict that their prisoners be treated in accordance with these rules. And ensuring the humane treatment of prisoners of war can help bring reconciliation once the war ends. The reports of the mistreatment of prisoners of war in Japanese prison camps generated significant animosity towards the Japanese that persisted long after the end of the war, and perhaps played no small part in explaining the general lack of condemnation immediately after the dropping of the nuclear bombs on Hiroshima and Nagasaki. As we will see in Chapter 9, the privileged moral status of combatants explains why it matters so much whether we class terrorists as combatants.

Chapter summary

We began by briefly outlining two forms of realism. The first holds that we should not try to restrain war by imposing rules. The second holds that we cannot restrain war by imposing rules. Just war theorists reject realism. Whilst there is often disagreement about what the rules of war are, it is the essence of just war theory that there are such rules. And most just war theorists think that these rules apply to the fighting of even an unjust war. This division between *jus ad bellum* and *jus in bello* is largely premised on the idea that we ought not to condemn combatants from the outset if their country happens to be waging an unjust war. We then looked in detail at the rules of war. These rules cover the conditions for qualifying as a combatant, the restrictions on targets, the restrictions on tactics and the treatment of prisoners of war. We will return to the restrictions on targets in Chapter 7 when we address the issue of non-combatant immunity.

Questions for discussion

1   Would it be better if we did away with the laws of war?
2   Should guerrilla fighters who hide amongst non-combatants qualify as combatants?
3   Is it permissible for Father in *Help* to throw the grenade to save Daughter even though doing so will kill Bystander? If so, does this means that states may kill foreign non-combatants to save the lives of their own non-combatants?
4   Should Commander in *Offensive* employ Strategy A, Strategy B or Strategy C?

Notes

1. Cicero, *Pro Milone*, Bristol: Bristol Classic Press, 1991.
2. B. Orend, 'War', in E. N. Zalta (ed.), *Stanford Encyclopedia of Philosophy*, Fall 2008 edn, available at http://plato.stanford.edu/archives/fall2008/entries/war/ (accessed 13 December 2010).
3. Orend, 'War'.
4. Orend, 'War'.
5. See http://www.icrc.org/ihl.nsf/INTRO?OpenView (accessed 22 March 2011).
6. M. Walzer, *Just and Unjust Wars*, New York: Basic Books, 1977, p. 39.

7. T. Hurka, 'Proportionality in the Morality of War', *Philosophy and Public Affairs* 33, No. 1, 2005, 34–66, p. 44.
8. Protocol Additional to the Geneva Conventions of 12 August 1949, and relating to the Protection of Victims of International Armed Conflicts (Protocol 1), 8 June 1977, Article 51 (5b), available at http://www.icrc. org/ihl.nsf/FULL/470?OpenDocument (accessed 22 March 2011).
9. Hurka, 'Proportionality in the Morality of War', p. 62.
10. Hurka, 'Proportionality in the Morality of War', p. 61.
11. P. Christopher, *The Ethics of War and Peace: An Introduction to Legal and Moral Issues*, Englewood Cliffs, NJ: Prentice Hall, 1998, 3rd edn, 2004, p. 155.
12. Protocol Additional to the Geneva Conventions of 12 August 1949, and relating to the Protection of Victims of International Armed Conflicts (Protocol 1), 8 June 1977, Article 48, available at http://www.icrc.org/ihl. nsf/FULL/470?OpenDocument (accessed 22 March 2011).
13. Protocol Additional to the Geneva Conventions of 12 August 1949, and relating to the Protection of Victims of International Armed Conflicts (Protocol 1), 8 June 1977, Article 35, available at http://www.icrc.org/ihl. nsf/FULL/470?OpenDocument (accessed 22 March 2011).
14. Protocol for the Prohibition of the Use of Asphyxiating, Poisonous or Other Gases, and of Bacteriological Methods of Warfare, Geneva, 17 June 1925, available at http://www.icrc.org/ihl.nsf/FULL/280?OpenDocument (accessed 22 March 2011).
15. Christopher, *The Ethics of War and Peace: An Introduction to Legal and Moral Issues*, p. 204.
16. See   http://www.ctbto.org/fileadmin/content/treaty/treaty_text.pdf (accessed 22 March 2011).

Suggested reading

Thomas Hurka, 'Proportionality in the Morality of War', *Philosophy and Public Affairs* 33, No. 1, 2005, 34–66.
This influential paper outlines and defends Hurka's views on distributing risk between combatants and non-combatants.

Jeff McMahan, 'The Just Distribution of Harm Between Combatants and Noncombatants', *Philosophy and Public Affairs* 38, No. 4, 2010, 342–379. McMahan pays particular attention to the fair distribution of risk in cases of humanitarian intervention.

Thomas Nagel, 'War and Massacre', *Philosophy and Public Affairs* 1, No. 2, 1972, 123–144.
Nagel's paper is a classic of the just war literature, exploring the moral basis of the rules of war.

6   The moral status of combatants

In Chapter 5, I outlined the view that the rules of *jus in bello* are logically independent of the rules of *jus ad bellum*. This view, which I called the orthodox view of just war theory, has been the dominant view of how we should understand the relationship between *jus ad bellum* and *jus in bello* since Hugo Grotius's work in the early seventeenth century. As we saw, one of the central motivations for divorcing these two stages of war is the belief that it would be unfair to hold that combatants act wrongly simply in virtue of their leaders' wrongful decision to wage an unjust war.

Because of this alleged unfairness, most just war theorists have defended the *principle of the moral equality of combatants*. Endorsed by international law, this principle holds that combatants do no wrong in fighting wars even if they fight on the unjust side. Combatants on the unjust side of a war (unjust combatants) are thus the moral and legal equals of combatants on the just side (just combatants). In this chapter, we will look at how this view has been defended and how more recent just war theorists have sought to undermine it. In particular, we will look at Jeff Mahan's arguments for a radical shift in how we understand both the morality of killing in war and the moral status of the combatants who carry out those killings. McMahan argues against the divorcing of *jus in bello* from *jus ad bellum*, claiming that a combatant cannot fight justly if his war lacks a just cause to begin with. If McMahan is right, it seems that combatants whose wars are *ad bellum* unjust cannot be the moral equals of combatants whose wars are *ad bellum* just.

THE ORTHODOX VIEW

The moral innocence of combatants

The orthodox view of just war theory is that combatants need concern themselves only with how they fight, and not with why they fight. Combatants should follow the orders of their superiors and, provided that they do not breach the rules of *jus in bello*, they do nothing wrong even if their war is unjust. As Samuel Huntington puts it, the goal of a combatant 'is to be an instrument of obedience; the uses to which that instrument is put are beyond his responsibility.'[1] The wider political goals of the war are not the combatants' concern.

Michael Walzer similarly argues that combatants on both sides of a conflict are merely 'pawns in a game' played by their political leaders.

> [T]he enemy soldier, though his war may well be criminal, is nevertheless as blameless as oneself. Armed, he is an enemy; but he isn't *my* enemy in any specific sense; the war itself isn't a relation between persons but between political entities and their human instruments. These human instruments . . . are 'poor sods, just like me', trapped in a war they didn't make. I find in them my moral equals.
>
> (M. Walzer, *Just and Unjust Wars*, New York: Basic Books, 1977, p. 36)

In Chapter 5, I outlined some pragmatic reasons for granting unjust combatants legal immunity for their actions, such as hastening surrender and discouraging war crimes. But the orthodox view makes a much stronger claim about the status of unjust combatants. This claim is that combatants *do nothing to lose their moral innocence* merely by fighting in war, even if they fight on the unjust side. So, not only do we have prudential reasons to *treat* unjust combatants *as if* they are equal to just combatants; according to orthodox view, unjust combatants *really are* the moral equals of their just counterparts.

This view is representative of both the law and many people's intuitions. That war is a political struggle between states, not between individual combatants, is a historically pervasive view. Even when combatants are engaged in a war that is widely thought to be unjust, it is rare for condemnation to be aimed at the combatants themselves. For example, Cheyney Ryan draws attention to the intriguing phenomenon of those who explicitly criticise the wars in Iraq and Afghanistan, labelling George Bush and Tony Blair murderers and war criminals, whilst displaying bumper stickers demanding that people 'Support Our Troops'.[2] This putative distinction between combatants and the wars they fight seems firmly embedded in our attitudes towards war. But it is, after all, the combatants who perpetrate the harms of war. They are the ones who do the killing and the maiming that make war, especially unjust war, so morally objectionable. Why is it, then, that we focus our moral criticism almost exclusively on those calling the shots rather than on those firing them?

Walzer's models of combat

Walzer suggests that we can explain this attribution of responsibility in war by thinking about the reasons why combatants fight wars. Walzer describes these reasons as fitting two models of combatant: the *gladiatorial model* and the *boxing model*.

On the gladiatorial model of combat, combatants are forced to fight by their states. In this case, combatants are like Roman gladiators, each of whom must fight if they are to survive. Given that it is in everyone's best interests to fight (since otherwise they will all suffer their states' wrath), the combatants do no wrong by fighting.

On the boxing model of combat, combatants are akin to boxers who have all consented to get into the ring and fight. Just as boxers agree to punch and be punched, combatants agree to kill and be killed. Walzer describes his view thus:

> [T]he moral reality of war can be summed up in this way: when soldiers fight freely, choosing one another as enemies and designing their own battles, their war is not a crime; when they fight without freedom, their war is not their crime.
>
> (Walzer, *Just and Unjust Wars*, p. 37)

If either or both of these models can be plausibly applied to combatants in war, this would seem to explain the widespread belief that combatants are morally equivalent. Either the combatants have no choice but to fight, in which case they are all morally innocent, or they mutually consent to fight, thereby absolving each other of wrongdoing and, again, making them all morally innocent.

The gladiatorial model, whilst perhaps plausible at some points in history and with respect to some armies, doesn't seem to present an accurate description of most modern-day combatants. Setting aside the separate issue of shooting combatants who desert in the midst of battle, there are not many states which execute combatants for refusing to fight in a war, even if they might impose other sanctions. If the other sanctions are non-lethal, the claim that it is rational for combatants to agree to kill and be killed in war seems unfounded. It could of course be rational to fight under *some* circumstances. Perhaps if there were a very small chance of being killed in war, and the alternative was life imprisonment, it might be rational to fight. But since the chances of being killed in war are often high, and the sanctions often comparatively mild, this reasoning could hardly apply to most or even many combatants.

The gladiatorial model might therefore be a suitable for understanding the position of a small percentage of combatants, such as those from particularly oppressive regimes, or child soldiers who have been forced to fight by brutal militia groups. But the moral equality of combatants is supposed to be a *universal* principle.[3] We thus need an explanation that can account for the moral innocence of all combatants, not just a small percentage of them. The gladiatorial model thus has few contemporary proponents as an explanation of the moral equality of combatants.

More popular are variations of the boxing model of combat. On this model, combatants are understood as voluntarily participating in the war. By enlisting in the armed forces, each combatant waives his right not to be killed by the enemy. This means that no combatant is wronged by being killed, just as no boxer is wronged by being punched. If unjust combatants don't wrong just combatants by killing them, the unjust combatants do nothing to detract from their own moral innocence by killing just combatants. Thus, unjust combatants and just combatants are morally equal.

Many people think that this is an accurate description of how our modern-day armed forces operate. Even if they do not explicitly invoke Walzer's analogy with boxers, most people will think it morally relevant that combatants consent to go to war. A country's standing army is made up of people who have *signed up* to fight, in full knowledge of the risks that this involves. As I described in the previous chapter, this consent is meant to explain why combatant deaths are 'free' in the *in bello* proportionality calculation.

Combatants' reasons for signing up are likely to be many and varied: financial gain, a desire for travel or adventure, a desire to learn a trade, a lack of alternative employment opportunities or a sense of patriotic duty. But, irrespective of why they join, they are all willing participants in the dangerous activity that is war. We often hear it said of combatants who have been killed in war that they 'knew the risks involved' or that they 'died doing what they loved'. And we have plenty of anecdotal evidence that combatants themselves do not think that they are wronged by enemy combatants who try to kill them (think of the popular stories of Allied forces playing football with German soldiers on Christmas day – hardly the behaviour of people who think the other side a bunch of murderers). These facts seem to support the idea that combatants accept the risks posed to them by combatants on the other side, and that this explains why combatants on both sides are moral equals.

Thomas Hurka endorses this position, arguing that those who voluntarily enlist in the armed forces freely waive their right not to be killed. This absolves enemy combatants who kill them of any wrongdoing. Of course, combatants do not agree to be killed under *any* circumstances. They should not be killed if they have surrendered to the enemy, for example. But they do agree that, unless they are *hors de combat*, the enemy can try to kill them. And, Hurka says, this includes agreeing that even enemy soldiers who are pursuing an unjust war may try to kill them.

Hurka suggests that we can see this by noticing that voluntary enlistment constitutes a general waiving of one's rights. Combatants agree not only to be killed by particular enemy soldiers in a particular war, but to be killed by *all* enemy soldiers in *all* future wars.[4] This global surrendering of their rights results from the nature of the military institutions that the combatants join. These institutions do not want combatants who consent selectively, agreeing to fight only in particular wars. They want combatants who agree to fight in any war in which they are told to fight. These are the terms of the contract between the military and individual combatants. Since the combatants agree to these terms, they agree to the possibility that they will end up fighting on the unjust side of a war.

However, Hurka argues, combatants would presumably not agree to this possibility unless they believed that they would be permitted to use force whilst fighting such a war. It would suicidal to agree to fight in unjust wars unless one believed that one would be permitted to defend oneself. But defending oneself in these cases is going to mean killing *just* enemy combatants. If combatants agree that they will fight such wars, then they must do so believing that killing just combatants is permissible. So Hurka's claim is that by signing up to join the military, combatants themselves endorse the idea that it is morally permissible to kill just combatants. Their enlisting constitutes an affirmation of the moral equality of combatants. Hurka's account is thus a refined version of Walzer's boxing model. It is their consenting to fight that makes combatants moral equals.

Undermining the orthodox account

An obvious problem with applying Walzer's analysis of the moral status of combatants is that he seems to assume that in any given war, combatants on both sides will be fighting for the same reasons. Either the fighting will be of gladiatorial style on both sides – with both sets of combatants forced to participate – or it will fit the boxing model on both sides – with both sets of combatants freely consenting. But this assumption could easily be false. Combatants on one side of a war might readily consent to fight, and thus represent the boxing model of combat. But those on the other side might fight only reluctantly as a result of coercion by their oppressive state, thereby representing the gladiatorial model.

Since these reluctant combatants do not really seem to *agree* to being killed by the consenting combatants on the other side – they are rather forced into it under terrible duress – it does not look as if the consenting combatants are absolved of wrongdoing if they kill the reluctant combatants. The appropriate comparison here would be that between a slave forced into gladiator battles by his owners and a professional gladiator who voluntarily fights slaves in order to make money. That the professional gladiator consents to fight does not make it permissible for him to kill slaves who do not so consent. And thus, even if we grant that it is permissible for consenting combatants to fight other consenting combatants, it doesn't follow that they may fight combatants who have not so consented.

However, as I mentioned above, most contemporary defences of the moral equality of combatants ignore the gladiatorial model and try to argue that all combatants fall under the consent model. We can call these accounts *consent-based accounts*. McMahan offers three main arguments against these accounts.[5] The first questions the soundness of the claim that all combatants can be plausibly understood as consenting to be killed. The second tackles the validity of consent-based accounts, suggesting that it does not follow from the fact that a person consents to being killed that it is permissible to kill her. The third addresses the scope of consent-based accounts, reminding us that it is not only combatants who are killed in war.

McMahan's first argument invokes the moral status of combatants who enlist to fight in a single conflict to show that consent-based accounts cannot support the supposed universality of the moral equality principle. Whilst we might agree that combatants in a standing army issue a global waiver of their rights of the sort that Hurka describes, it is hard to see how this argument could explain the position of someone who enlists to fight only in one particular war. Individuals who enlisted in the Allied forces in the Second World War were not agreeing to fight in any war to which their political leaders saw fit to commit them. They were agreeing to fight in one specific conflict and, moreover, a conflict that seemed to be obviously just.

Combatants like this seem to be a counter-example to Hurka's claim that combatants issue a general waiver of their right not to be killed when they join the military. Since these combatants do not agree to fight in war generally, but only in particular wars, we cannot say that they have agreed to fight in an unjust war in the future. Therefore, there are some combatants who have *not* affirmed the idea that they would be permitted to kill even just combatants in future conflicts. A person might enlist to fight what they think is a just war whilst still thinking that killing just combatants morally impermissible. If the principle of moral equality relies upon combatants affirming it, as Hurka suggests, and if there are cases in which combatants do not affirm it, we cannot claim that the moral equality principle applies universally as the orthodox view requires.

In addition, McMahan argues that accepting a risk of being killed is not the same as consenting to be killed. Consider a person who crosses the street despite knowing that there is a risk they will be hit by a drunk driver. We can say that they accept the risk of being hit, where this means that they voluntarily cross the road whilst knowing about the risk. But it would be strange to say that they consent to being hit by a drunk driver and, furthermore, that the drunk driver therefore does nothing wrong if he hits them. Accepting risks of harm does not generally amount to consenting to *being* harmed. Thus, showing that a combatant accepts the risk of being killed by the enemy does not show that they consent to being killed by the enemy.

McMahan's attack on the validity of the consent-based account focuses on the assumption that the mere fact that a person consents to being killed makes it permissible to kill her. This assumption perhaps gains credence from claims about the moral permissibility of euthanasia. Many of us think that a person who faces a life of severe pain and suffering can consent to be killed, and that killing a person under these circumstances would be morally permissible. But many of us also think that killing them would be impermissible if they refused their consent. This implies that it is consent that makes the difference between permissible and impermissible killing. But McMahan argues that this is a mistake. It is not consent *alone* that makes it permissible to carry out euthanasia. It is consent combined with the fact that the person is facing a life of pain and suffering. The permissibility of euthanasia relies upon both consent *and* a lesser-evil justification about the harm that the person will otherwise suffer. McMahan argues that in the absence of that further justification, killing a person who has consented is morally impermissible.

If McMahan is right, it is only unjust combatants who can be permissibly killed in war. Even if combatants on both sides consent to be killed, the further lesser-evil justification will apply only to the killing of unjust combatants. Their deaths are a lesser evil than the success of their unjust war. But the killings of just combatants are not a lesser evil, since killing them frustrates their just war. Killing unjust combatants is thus morally permissible, but killing just combatants is not. If so, those who kill just combatants cannot claim to be the moral equals of those who kill unjust combatants.

McMahan's third argument draws attention to the fact that defenders of the consent-based account need to explain more than the permissibility of unjust combatants killing just combatants. They also need to explain the permissibility of unjust combatants inflicting collateral harms on non-combatants. Any consent that the combatants issue cannot extend to cover non-combatants too. The consent-based account thus lacks the resources to explain the permissibility of these incidental killings (unless it stipulates that non-combatants *also* consent to be killed in war; but not only is this stipulation false, it undermines the prohibition on targeting non-combatants, which a defender of the orthodox view will certainly want to retain). Since war inevitably involves combatants killing non-combatants, it seems that the consent-based account must say not that *both* sides fight permissibly, but rather that *neither* side fights permissibly. And such a position can hardly support the orthodox view that combatants do no wrong in fighting.

THE MORAL INEQUALITY OF COMBATANTS

McMahan's account

Until recently, the principle of the moral equality of combatants was generally accepted by both just war scholars and international law. But over the past decade, McMahan has mounted a sustained and, in philosophical circles at least, increasingly influential assault on the idea that the rules of *jus in bello* can be followed independently of considerations of *jus ad bellum*. McMahan argues that combatants cannot fight justly if their war is *ad bellum* unjust: if they lack a just cause. On McMahan's account of war, a combatant who fights in, say, an aggressive invasion is morally doomed from the outset. They *cannot* fight justly, no matter how hard they try, because they lack a just cause for fighting in the first place. We saw in Chapter 5 that the rules of war are meant to restrict attacks to legitimate targets. McMahan's central claim is that unjust combatants have no legitimate targets. Any harm that unjust combatants cause is morally impermissible.

As we saw in Chapter 2, McMahan endorses an individualist account of war. He thinks that the rules of killing in war are to be understood by thinking about the rules governing defensive killing between individuals. One of

McMahan's most powerful arguments for why the orthodox view of combatants is wrong draws upon an analogy with self-defence. If a person tries to defend themselves against an unjust attack, we do not think that they and the attacker are on a moral par because each is now using force against the other. Rather, we think that the attacker acts wrongly, forfeits their right not to be harmed and so on. In McMahan's terminology, attackers render themselves *liable to be killed*, such that killing them will no longer wrong them as it usually would. Victims, in contrast, remain morally innocent as long as their defence is necessary and proportionate. If this asymmetry is correct as 'a matter of basic morality', as McMahan claims, why would we think it any less accurate a description of the relationship between just and unjust combatants?[6] An unjust war is simply an unjust attack on a large scale. If victims of aggression are not the moral equals of their attackers, just combatants are not the moral equals of unjust combatants. Unjust combatants are liable to be killed; just combatants are wronged by being killed.

McMahan's view draws support from certain features of what we might call 'commonsense morality'. As we saw, Walzer himself notes the peculiarity of having laws for unjust (and thus illegal) wars. McMahan's view emphasises that this is not merely a legal oddity, but a *moral* oddity. It seems plain to most of us that if a certain end is unjust – say, robbing a pensioner of their savings – then there cannot be just means by which one can permissibly bring about that end. We don't think that deceiving the pensioner into giving us their bank details is just, whereas rifling through their belongings to find those details is unjust. If what one is trying to achieve is morally wrong, *any* methods that one employs to try to achieve it are similarly wrong. But the orthodox view of war commits us to precisely the opposite claim. It holds that even if combatants have unjust, immoral ends, they are nonetheless *morally permitted* to try to bring those ends about provided that they employ certain tactics. Understandably, McMahan finds this position rather puzzling. And the implications of this puzzle are far-reaching within just war theory.

In particular, McMahan argues that once we pay proper attention to the fact that unjust combatants have unjust ends, we can see that it is almost impossible for them to meet the proportionality requirement of *jus in bello*.[7] (Hurka also makes this objection to the orthodox view.[8]) The proportionality requirement demands that one weigh the harm that one will cause against the good end that one will achieve. So, it might seem proportionate to blow up a munitions factory even though one will kill three non-combatants as a side-effect if one will make significant progress towards one's military goals by eliminating the factory. But this assumes that one's military goals are *good* goals: goals that can counteract the harm of killing three non-combatants. This is why, on McMahan's view, just combatants may permissibly inflict incidental harm on non-combatants. Just combatants can invoke the importance of achieving their goals as justification for these harms.

However, such justification is generally unavailable to the unjust combatants. The doctrine of double effect was never intended to justify incidental harm caused in the pursuit of an end that *is itself harmful*. If a combatant's goals are not good, but are rather part of an unjust war, they cannot counterbalance the harm of killing the non-combatants. In other words, if unjust combatants have no good outcomes that they can balance against collateral damage, *any* collateral damage they cause is disproportionate and therefore impermissible.[9]

Even more puzzling, perhaps, is that not only does the orthodox view permit people to try to bring about deeply immoral ends, but it requires that these people be viewed as morally equivalent to those who are trying to *prevent* those unjust ends. But showing that just and unjust combatants mutually threaten each other it is not enough, says McMahan, to show them to be morally equal. That an attacker and his victim threaten each other does not make them morally equal:

> People don't lose moral rights by justifiably defending themselves or other innocent people against unjust attack; therefore, unless they lose rights for some reason other than acquiring combatant status, just combatants are innocent in the relevant [moral] sense. So, even when unjust combatants confine their attacks to military targets, they kill innocent people. Most of us believe that it's normally wrong to kill innocent people even as a means of achieving a goal that's *just*. How, then, could it be permissible to kill innocent people as a means of achieving goals that are *unjust*?
>
> (J. McMahan, 'On the Moral Equality of Combatants', *Journal of Political Philosophy* 14, No. 4, 2006, 377–393, p. 379)

That just combatants are material threats to the unjust combatants – that they are engaged in causing harm – does not show that they have lost their right not to be killed. They must do something else to bring this about. As we have seen, McMahan rejects the most popular candidate for this something else, namely that combatants consent to be killed. And if nothing *else* explains why the just combatants have lost their rights, we must assume that they have *not* lost them – that they retain their rights not to be killed even though they participate in the war. Since the unjust combatants have no objective justification for killing the just combatants, they act wrongly if they kill them.

In effect, McMahan's view holds that unjust combatants murder just combatants if they kill them. They unjustly kill innocent people who have a right not to be killed. And in defending themselves against these murderous attacks, just combatants do nothing wrong, and do not cease to be morally innocent. Just and unjust combatants are therefore far from morally equivalent.

Institutional stability

Samuel Huntington argues that,

> [L]oyalty and obedience are the highest military virtues . . . When a military man receives an order from an authorized superior, he does not argue, he does not hesitate, he does not substitute his own views; he obeys instantly. He is judged not by the policies he implements, but rather by the promptness and efficiency with which he carries them out.
> (S. P. Huntington, *The Soldier and the State: The Theory and Politics of Civil–Military Relations*, Cambridge, MA: Harvard University Press, 1957, p. 73)

Huntington argues that beyond their legal duty, combatants also have a *moral* duty to follow orders. This moral duty arises from their obligation to their institution: they have committed themselves to fight for the military, and morality requires them to fulfil this commitment. A combatant's moral duty is fully discharged provided that they follow orders. There is no further duty on their part to ensure that the orders are legal or moral. As we will discuss in Chapter 10, recent changes in international law cast doubt on as strong a position as Huntington's. Combatants are required to disobey orders that are manifestly unlawful, such as an order to shoot an obviously unarmed civilian. But the law still allows Huntington's basic intuition – that combatants may follow orders without worrying about the content of those orders – plenty of weight. And many people do think that it is beyond the remit of combatants to ponder the justness of their orders.

One of the implications of McMahan's view is that this traditional picture of what morality requires of a 'military man' is profoundly misguided. McMahan's account holds that combatants have moral responsibilities that extend far beyond those attributed to them by the orthodox view. They should not blindly follow orders, viewing themselves as mere instruments in the hands of their leaders. Rather, they should question their superiors' claims about the justness of their cause. They should investigate the case for war for themselves. If they conclude that the war they are being ordered to fight is unjust, they must refuse to fight it.

Many people have therefore objected to McMahan's account on the grounds that it would produce widespread instability in military institutions. The armed forces rely, inherently, on the ability to command their troops and receive unquestioning obedience from them. Once we start telling combatants that they ought not to simply obey their superiors, but must first stop and think about the justness of what their superiors are telling them to do, we threaten to unravel the military's ability to fight wars at all. Undermining the chain of command is fundamentally at odds with the nature of the military.

Of course, it might be no bad thing if a military is unable to fight an unjust war. If *this* is the result of McMahan's urging of reflection on the part of combatants, we might think that it serves only to bolster McMahan's view. But what if telling combatants to question their orders also frustrates the military's ability to fight *just* wars? Imagine a combatant who serves as part of a military institution that is overall just – that is, an institution that normally pursues only good ends. Is it a good idea to urge this combatant to question their orders, even at the risk of undermining this overall just institution?

McMahan suggests that someone might support this objection to his view by drawing an analogy with the criminal justice system.[10] Imagine the following case:

> *Conscience:*
> A convict has undergone a fair trial, and has been found guilty of a crime by a jury of his peers. He has been sentenced to life imprisonment. Despite the fact that the justice system is overall just, the prison guard becomes convinced of the convict's innocence. He has an opportunity to free the convict early into his sentence.

We might think that even if the guard is correct that the convicted man is innocent, he should not release him from prison. The justice system simply couldn't function if prison guards took it upon themselves to free people they believed to be innocent. Even if the guard correctly believes that imprisoning the convict is unjust, he ought to adhere to his orders, since the wider stability of the justice system depends on it.

So, this looks like a pretty good argument against McMahan. Even if unjust combatants think that they are occasionally ordered to fight an unjust war, this does not show that they ought to refuse to fight those wars. The obligation to uphold the institution can require a person to defer to that institution, even if he has doubts about the justice of a particular order.

But of course, this argument works only if we assume that the institution in question is overall just. If, in contrast, *most* of the inmates at the prison have been wrongly convicted, our intuitions about the guard's obligations might be rather different. His deference to the system is warranted only if he has good reason to think the system worth preserving, which will require that the system gets convictions right most of the time. Similarly, a combatant can invoke an obligation to preserve his military only if that military is overall just. If it is not – if the military often fights unjust wars – then he cannot cite the importance of its preservation as justification for following a particular unjust order to fight. And this matters a great deal for the moral equality of combatants. For, as we have seen, this principle is meant to be universal. And, thus, if we were to use this argument to support equal treatment of all combatants we would have to show that *all* combatants fight for institutions that are overall just. But it is clearly false that all combatants serve such an institution, or that they could even believe that they serve such an institution. And so this argument cannot support the orthodox principle of universal moral equality.

McMahan is also sceptical that even an overall just military institution can demand the unfailing obedience of its troops in the pursuit of unjust wars. There are limits to what the obligation to uphold an institution can require. Imagine a variation of *Conscience* in which the convict has been sentenced to death, and his executioner similarly comes to believe that he is innocent. Ought the executioner, like the guard, defer to the system and kill the man anyway? McMahan suggests that he should not. And war is a lot more like this case than it is the original *Conscience* case, since war involves killing and maiming as one seeks to uphold one's institution. Even if protecting just institutions can generate some obligations, it cannot, says McMahan, generate an obligation (and hence a right) to kill innocent people. And, thus, even those who are confident in their military's overall justness cannot invoke this as a justification for partaking in a particular war that happens to be unjust.

Finally, McMahan offers a third argument against the idea that preserving a just military could morally oblige combatants to fight in unjust wars. Consider the following case:[11]

> *Oops:*
> Nation A launches one of its long-range missiles towards Nation B, where it will unjustly kill hundreds of Nation B's children. Just after launching the missile, Nation A realises that its war is unjust, and tries to detonate the missile mid-air. But it is too late. The only way in which Nation A can prevent this disaster is to divert the missile back to its own territory. However, the missile will then kill hundreds of Nation A's children.

McMahan argues that:

> when an institution malfunctions in a harmful way, those who designed, direct, participate in and benefit from the institution are liable to pay the costs . . . It would be unjust if they were to impose the costs of its malfunctioning on others.
>
> (McMahan, 'On the Moral Equality of Combatants', p. 387)

On his account, it looks as if Nation A ought, as a matter of justice, to divert the missile back to its own territory. It is A's political system that has malfunctioned, and A's citizens must bear the cost of that malfunction.

Analogously, if our overall just government malfunctions, and tries to wage an unjust war, we cannot justify participating in this war by citing the cost to us, and our country, if our just institution is undermined. That it will be bad for *us* if our military no longer functions effectively, perhaps leaving us more vulnerable to aggression, cannot justify our fighting in an unjust war because this would illegitimately shift the costs of our malfunction onto another state.

The argument from ignorance

We might agree that if combatants know that they are fighting an unjust war, then they ought not to fight it. And if they fight it anyway, we might agree that they act wrongly, and cannot claim to be the moral equals of any just combatants whom they kill. But what we might dispute is the claim that combatants *can* know, or can be expected to know, whether their war is just or unjust. After all, there is often significant disagreement about the justness of a war. Almost thirty years on, even supposed experts contest the justness of the Falklands War. If people who are well-versed in the laws of war cannot agree on whether a particular war had a just cause, it hardly seems fair to demand that combatants – many of whom are young and relatively uneducated – establish the justness of their war before agreeing to fight it.[12] There could be all kinds of obstacles to their doing this, such as the difficulty of acquiring relevant or reliable information about a war, or of finding the time to assess this material. Even if they did find reliable information, and they did take the time to reflect upon it, they still might not be able to tell whether the war was really just or unjust.

Given these difficulties, we might think that combatants can legitimately defer to their leaders on the assumption that these people are better informed about the facts of the war, and are in a better position to determine its justness. The argument from ignorance thus supports the moral equality principle by claiming that combatants on both sides of a war are justified in deferring to their leaders about which wars to fight, and thus are justified in fighting if they are ordered to do so. If combatants on both sides are justified in fighting, the argument goes, this supports the principle of combatant equality.

McMahan rejects the argument from ignorance on two main grounds. The first is that it employs a notion of justification that suggests that a mistaken belief can make it *permissible* for a person to bring about harm. Such a view implies that a teenage boy who, after years of indoctrination, believes it right to carry out terrorist attacks would be justified in perpetrating those attacks.[13] McMahan argues that at best such ignorance could generate an *excuse* for the attacks. It could not generate a justification for them.

Second, McMahan argues that even if ignorance could generate justifications, only *reasonable* ignorance about the unjustness of one's war could create a justification for fighting. And, he argues, not even the majority of combatants can lay claim to such reasonable ignorance, let alone all of them.

McMahan identifies certain features as clear (if only *prima facie*) indicators regarding the justness of one's war.[14] For example, combatants who are told that their war is a defensive war should consider whether they're being ordered to fight on their own territory, or whether they will be sent abroad to fight. If, on the one hand, they are being ordered to fight on home turf, this lends credence to their leaders' claim that the war is defensive and just. If, on the other hand, they are told that the war involves fighting abroad, on someone else's territory, it is much harder to credit the claim that this is nonetheless a just war of defence.

However, it's not impossible that this could be the case – it might be a war of other-defence, such as the first Gulf War in Kuwait. But in Kuwait, US and British troops fought alongside Kuwaiti troops. If combatants are ordered to go abroad to fight *against* a native army, however, the idea that this is some sort of defensive war becomes less plausible. Again, it's not impossible that it could be a just war. It could be a war of intervention that aims to defeat the army of an unjust regime. But here, too, combatants can consider whether local people or human rights groups have appealed for intervention. If not, there are grounds for scepticism about the justness of the war.

McMahan also points out that if we grant that no war can be just on both sides, this means that at least half the wars that have ever been fought were unjust. This gives combatants only a fifty–fifty chance of being on the just side of a war, which should at least give them pause for thought. And when we note that wars can be *unjust* on both sides (for example, when two colonial powers fight for control over a neutral piece of land), the statistics tell us that a combatant's war is actually far more likely to be unjust than just. Combatants should also realise that many people who fight in unjust wars believe that they are fighting in just wars. Unless the combatants grant themselves some sort of privileged status, they should be open to the possibility that are similarly mistaken in their belief that their war is just, especially in light of the unfavourable odds just described. Finally, McMahan argues that it is well-known that governments sometimes lie about the reasons behind a war. Combatants thus know that they have grounds for scepticism about what their leaders tell them.

What's important about McMahan's observations is that arriving at these conclusions requires no particular analytical skill, nor any great knowledge of just war theory or of the military intelligence behind a particular war. It requires only a rudimentary amount of reflection on the nature of war in general. Any combatant with the mental capacity to serve in the armed forces should be able to recognise these facts about war. Given this, the majority of combatants are not in the position of needing to defer their judgement about the justness of a war to their leaders. They already have important information about the nature of war. And this means that we should not so readily assent to the idea that combatants can reasonably believe that their war is just even if it is unjust.

McMahan also argues that the standard for what counts as a *reasonable* belief varies, depending on what the belief is about and what turns on it. I might reasonably believe that my neighbour is out because her car is not in her driveway. On the basis of this belief, I might play my music loudly, or carry out some un-neighbourly DIY. When nothing much turns on whether or not she is out, I don't need to gather much evidence in order to claim a reasonable belief that she is out. But if my neighbour's house catches fire, the fact that her car is not in her driveway doesn't seem to be sufficient grounds for telling the fire-fighters that she is out and that they needn't bother looking for her. What is a reasonable belief for the purposes of playing loud music is not a reasonable belief for matters of life and death.

Similarly, McMahan claims that given the very high stakes of war, a combatant cannot claim a reasonable belief that their war is just unless they have undertaken a serious investigation of the evidence.[15] Often this investigation will not yield the result that the war is just, and it then becomes morally incumbent upon combatants to refuse to fight:

> This means that we must stop reassuring soldiers that they act permissibly when they fight in an unjust war, provided that they conduct themselves honorably on the battlefield by fighting in accordance with the rules of engagement. We must cease to regard them as mere instruments or automata and recognize that they are morally autonomous and therefore morally responsible agents. And we must insist that they too recognize their own moral autonomy and abandon the comforting fiction that all responsibility for acts they do in obedience to commands lies with those who command them, so that it is only when they disobey, or when they breach the norms governing their professional action as warriors, that they become responsible for wrongdoing.
>
> (J. McMahan, *Killing in War*, New York: Oxford University Press, 2009, p. 95)

McMahan's view is certainly demanding: it speaks against how we have treated our armed forces for centuries. And it does so not only by pointing to the moral shortcomings of combatants who fail to adequately reflect on their wars, but also by identifying the comprehensive failure of societies to provide combatants with the training and resources that they need to carry out their moral obligations. In McMahan's view, we have consistently and gravely wronged combatants by telling them that the orthodox view is true, and that they are morally innocent pawns in someone else's game. Correcting this injustice will require serious investment in the education of our armed forces.

Just and 'justified' combatants

Uwe Steinhoff argues that McMahan is mistaken to think that unjust combatants always act wrongly in killing just combatants.[16] Steinhoff argues that it can be permissible for unjust combatants to kill just combatants in order to protect the non-combatants on the unjust side. As McMahan acknowledges, combatants on the just side of a war often kill innocent non-combatants as a side-effect of their military offensives. Now recall from Chapter 1 that McMahan's account of self-defence holds that a person is liable to defensive harm only if they are morally responsible for an unjust threat, or if they have consented to be harmed. When a person is liable to defensive harm, this means that harming them doesn't *wrong* them – they have no right not to be harmed in this way.

If the non-combatants whom just combatants kill as a side-effect are morally innocent, and do not consent to being killed, McMahan's own account holds that the non-combatants are not liable to be killed. Since the just combatants seem to be morally responsible for these collateral killings – they act deliberately, foresee that the deaths will occur and so on – it would appear that the just combatants wrong the non-combatants when they kill them. Given this, McMahan's view seems to suggest that the just combatants must be liable to defensive killing. Steinhoff argues that if this is the case, McMahan is wrong to say that unjust combatants do not have any legitimate targets in war, and that they always act wrongly when they kill just combatants. The unjust combatants can permissibly kill the just combatants to prevent them from posing these unjust threats to the non-combatants on the unjust side.

Of course, as we have seen, McMahan thinks that just combatants can invoke the importance of winning their just war as a justification for killing non-combatants. It is this good end that they weigh in their proportionality calculations. McMahan argues that this end also prevents the just combatants from becoming liable to defensive killing. McMahan famously claims that *justification defeats liability*. This means that if a person has *objective moral justification* for posing an unjust threat, they do not become liable to be killed by posing it. Rather, they retain their usual rights against attack. And, sometimes, one can permissibly harm even an innocent, non-liable person if one has a sufficiently weighty moral justification.

McMahan illustrates this principle using the following case:[17]

> *Pilots:*
> A group of pilots, whose country is fighting a just war of defence, need to blow up a factory. To do so, they will need to drop multiple bombs that will also incidentally kill several innocent civilians who live across the border in a neutral country. These deaths are proportionate to the good that destroying the factory will produce, and the pilots are thus objectively justified in dropping the bomb. The civilians have an anti-aircraft gun that they can use to shoot the pilots in self-defence.

On McMahan's view, the pilots escape liability to defensive harm because they have objective justification for dropping the bombs. Therefore, even though the pilots are inflicting unjust harms on the civilians, they would still be wronged if the civilians killed them in self-defence.

However, McMahan does not argue that it would therefore be impermissible for the civilians to use self-defence. Rather, he argues that there are mutual permissions of defence between the pilots and the civilians. The civilians may try to kill the pilots, because otherwise the pilots will wrong them. But since harm aimed at the pilots will wrong the pilots, the pilots are permitted to fight back against the civilians. McMahan thinks that it would be impermissible, however, for a third party to intervene on behalf of either the pilots or the civilians. He therefore denies that the unjust combatants are allowed to come to the aid of the civilians and kill the just combatants in defence of the civilians' lives. Unjust combatants still have no legitimate targets in war.

Is McMahan right that the civilians may try to defend themselves? Compare this case with *Train*:

> *Train:*
> A runaway train is hurtling towards a hundred people, who are stuck on the track and cannot get out of the way. They will all be killed if the train hits them. Controller can flip a switch that will divert the trolley down a side-track. But the train will then kill Pedestrian, who cannot get out of the way. Pedestrian has a grenade that he can throw at the switch, which will destroy the switch and make it impossible to divert the train towards him. (Controller will be unhurt.)

Assume that saving a hundred lives gives Controller objective justification for diverting the train, even though the train will then kill Pedestrian. Is Pedestrian permitted to throw the grenade to stop Controller from doing this? It is not obvious to me that he *is* so permitted. Pedestrian doesn't seem to be liable to be killed: he is not morally responsible for an unjust threat. And, he would be acting in self-defence – destroying the switch is the only way to save his life. But all the same, I am not sure that he is permitted to throw the grenade.

The case is difficult because whilst Pedestrian could not throw the grenade if the grenade would also *kill* 100 people, since this would be to cause disproportionate harm, it's less clear whether the fact that 100 people will *not be saved* if he throws it makes throwing it disproportionate. Proportionality is usually about the harm that one will cause compared with the harm that one will avert, and it is debatable whether Pedestrian *causes* harm to the 100 people if he destroys the switch. He certainly ensures that harm will befall them (but notice that had Controller not been present, harm would have befallen them in this case too). If we think that Pedestrian is not permitted to throw the grenade to prevent Controller from diverting the trolley, we might also have doubts about whether the civilians in *Pilots* are permitted to try to stop the pilots from dropping their bombs. Morality might require them to suffer the harm rather than prevent the pilots achieving their objectively justified goal.

If so, McMahan will be wrong to say that the civilians are allowed to try to kill the pilots, and *this* will explain why the pilots are allowed to shoot back at the civilians. In terms of sustaining the inequality of combatants, this conclusion is not detrimental to McMahan's overall position, since if the civilians may not defend themselves, others may not defend them either. This means that, contrary to Steinhoff's claims, the unjust combatants still have no legitimate targets. But since McMahan and Steinhoff agree that the civilians may defend themselves, we should look at why Steinhoff thinks this undermines McMahan's claim about the moral status of combatants.

Steinhoff rejects McMahan's claim that the pilots and the civilians are on some sort of moral par, with neither party being liable to attack. It matters, Steinhoff argues, that the pilots *initiate* a non-defensive threat of harm to the civilians, whereas the civilians threaten only defensively, reacting to the threat that the pilots pose. That the pilots' threat to the civilians is non-defensive makes them liable to be killed, in Steinhoff's view. He supports this view by considering how we would treat compensation claims from relatives of civilians killed by the pilots. Steinhoff suggests that it would be perfectly reasonable for these relatives to seek compensation from the pilots' government.

> Suppose, however, that the nation or the pilots responsible for the attacks reply: 'Well, and you have to compensate us for the pilots you shot down!' That seems to be simply outrageous. Obviously, the adequate rejoinder to that counter-claim would be: but *you* attacked *us*, you *initiated* the unjust attack. *We* simply *defended* ourselves against your attack.
>
> (U. Steinhoff, 'Debate: Jeff McMahan on the Moral Inequality of Combatants', *Journal of Political Philosophy* 16, No. 2, 2008, 220–226, p. 224)

That the pilots, but not the civilians, were liable to be killed would explain this difference in compensation rights. The civilians are due compensation because, since they were not liable to be killed, the pilots wronged them by killing them. But the civilians do not owe the pilots compensation because the pilots *were* liable to be killed. Killing the pilots in self-defence did not wrong them.

Steinhoff also rejects McMahan's claim that third parties cannot permissibly intervene to protect the civilians.

> Suppose the innocent civilians are children. Would not their parents be permitted to intervene on their behalf? It seems obvious that they would. And why should third parties not be allowed to intervene in such a situation on behalf of their spouses, lovers, friends and, most importantly in this context, compatriots?
>
> (Steinhoff, 'Debate: Jeff McMahan on the Moral Inequality of Combatants', p. 223)

If Steinhoff is right, it seems that McMahan is mistaken that third parties cannot permissibly intervene on behalf of those about to be wronged. And this implies that unjust combatants who kill just combatants in defence of non-combatants act permissibly, thereby undermining McMahan's view that unjust combatants have no legitimate targets. Steinhoff suggests a relabelling of just combatants as 'justified combatants' to reflect the fact that even if their war is overall just, they still inflict harms that wrong people.

We might partly respond to Steinhoff's critique by suggesting that even if we agree that third parties may defend the civilians, it seems no less plausible that the pilots' comrades may come to *their* aid. Should the pilots come under attack from the civilians, it seems rather implausible to think that other members of the unit may not, for example, give them information about the location of the anti-aircraft gun. The pilots are, after all, in danger only as a result of following a legitimate, justified order. But if third parties may intervene on both sides, we do not have an asymmetry that shows that the pilots are liable to harm whereas the civilians are not.

However, perhaps we should not be so quick to grant the claim that third parties may come to the aid of the civilians. Having us imagine that the civilians are children is bound to trigger the response that Steinhoff wants: that their parents may surely rush to their aid. But there are lots of cases in which it is intuitively attractive that a parent may defend their child in which it is nonetheless implausible to think the target of defence *liable to be killed*.

Imagine that a young child picks up a gun, thinking it a toy, aims it at you and goes to pull the trigger. Knowing as you do that the gun is both real and loaded, I think you may permissibly defend yourself against the child. But Steinhoff's plea that surely the child's mother could shoot you to stop you from killing her child is no less intuitive here, even though you are clearly not liable to be killed by the mother – you have done nothing to forfeit your right against attack. The argument becomes only less compelling, I think, as we move from parents to friends to compatriots. Whatever moral weight these relationships have, they cannot confer liability to defensive killing on those who act with objective justification.

What about the argument concerning compensation? Steinhoff seems to be right that only the civilians are entitled to claim compensation for losses that they suffer. But can this difference be explained only by a difference in liability? Steinhoff's argument makes two claims. The first is that the pilots' government owes the civilians compensation, and this shows that that the civilians were not liable to be killed. The second is that the civilians don't owe the pilots' government compensation, and this shows that the pilots are liable to be killed.

However, the second of these claims seems false. Consider *Storm*:

Storm:
A group of pilots on the just side of the war blow up an isolated factory with no civilian casualties. As they are flying home, an unforeseen violent storm blows the pilots uncontrollably off course. Their planes hurtle towards a group of civilians, who will be killed unless they blow up the planes with their anti-aircraft gun.

I think that the civilians are permitted to blow up the planes, and I do not think that they would owe the pilots' government compensation if they did so. But I do not think that the reason for this is that the pilots were liable to be killed. The pilots were not morally responsible for unjustly threatening the civilians, even if we agree that they did unjustly threaten them. If I am right, this suggests that the absence of an obligation to pay compensation for killing a person does not show that the person was liable to be killed. And so Steinhoff's observation that the civilians in *Pilots* do not owe compensation for killing the pilots does not show that the pilots were liable to be killed.

What else could explain the asymmetry in compensation rights, other than a difference in liability to defensive harm? Well, we should remember that the pilots' government had decided to sacrifice the civilians in order to secure a greater benefit for themselves. It seems plausible that the civilians would have been owed compensation even if they had had no means of defence, and thus the pilots had not intentionally tried to kill them in self-defence, but rather had only killed them incidentally whilst bombing the factory. That they owed the civilians compensation from the outset could explain why they still owe them compensation after intentionally killing them to prevent them from shooting the planes down. On this account, the asymmetry in compensation rights does not come from the fact that the pilots initiated the threat and that the civilians merely reacted defensively to it. It comes from the fact that the pilots' government owed the civilians compensation for deciding that their lives were to be sacrificed for the greater good.

Chapter summary

This chapter investigated what has become a contentious issue amongst just war theorists: the principle of the morality equality of combatants. We outlined Walzer's two models of combat, upon which combatants either fight freely and consent to be killed or fight through coercion and are permitted to try to kill each other. We looked at McMahan's critique of this picture and at his claim that we cannot divorce the morality of fighting a war from the morality of the war itself. We considered two arguments that McMahan offers as a rebuttal of the claim that combatants are not morally responsible for unjust wars: the argument from institutional stability and the argument from ignorance. We also explored Steinhoff's critique of McMahan's claim that unjust combatants have no legitimate targets.

Questions for discussion

1 In *Oops*, what should Nation A do?
2 Is McMahan right that the executioner should not kill the convicted man if he correctly believes that he is innocent?
3 Is Pedestrian in *Train* allowed to throw the grenade? What are the implications of your answer for the permissibility of the civilians' trying to defend themselves in *Pilots*?
4 Can a combatant reasonably, but mistakenly, believe that his war is just? If so, does this show that even unjust combatants are justified in fighting?

Notes

1. S. P. Huntington, *The Soldier and the State: The Theory and Politics of Civil–Military Relations*, Cambridge, MA: Harvard University Press, 1957, p. 73.
2. C. Ryan, 'Popular Sovereignty and Military Service: Democratic Duty and the Unjust Soldier', unpublished manuscript, on file with the author. Ryan discusses this idea in a later version of this paper, 'Democratic Duty and the Moral Dilemmas of Soldiers', *Ethics* (forthcoming).
3. J. McMahan, *Killing in War*, New York: Oxford University Press, 2009, p. 64.
4. T. Hurka, 'Liability and Just Cause', *Ethics and International Affairs* 21, No. 2, 2007, 199–218, p. 210.
5. McMahan, *Killing in War*, pp. 51–57.
6. J. McMahan, 'On the Moral Equality of Combatants', *Journal of Political Philosophy* 14, No. 4, 2006, 377–393, p. 379.
7. J. McMahan, 'The Ethics of Killing in War', *Philosophia* 34, No. 1, 693–733; J. McMahan, 'Just Cause for War' *Ethics and International Affairs* 19, No. 3, 2005, 1–21.
8. T. Hurka, 'Proportionality in the Morality of War', *Philosophy and Public Affairs* 33, No. 1, 2005, 34–66, p. 45.
9. McMahan does suggest that under certain circumstances unjust combatants might be permitted to cause collateral harm. For example, if combatants on the just side of the war are carrying out war crimes to further their just cause, the unjust combatants may permissibly defend people against such attacks. However, such justifications will be rare (see *Killing in War*, p. 24).
10. McMahan, 'On the Moral Equality of Combatants', p. 384.
11. The case I have used here is adapted from F. M. Kamm's example in 'Failures of Just War Theory: Terror, Harm and Justice', *Ethics* 114, No. 4, 2004, 650–692, p. 682.

12. S. Lazar, 'The Responsibility Dilemma for *Killing in War*: A Review Essay', *Philosophy and Public Affairs* 38, No. 2, 2010, 180–213, p. 194.
13. McMahan, 'On the Moral Equality of Combatants', p. 389.
14. McMahan, On the Moral Equality of Combatants', p. 391.
15. McMahan, On the Moral Equality of Combatants', p. 390.
16. U. Steinhoff, 'Debate: Jeff McMahan on the Moral Inequality of Combatants', *Journal of Political Philosophy* 16, No. 2, 2008, 220–226.
17. McMahan, 'The Basis of Moral Liability to Defensive Killing', *Philosophical Issues* 15, Normativity, 2005, 386–405, p. 388.

Suggested reading:

Michael Walzer, 'The Rules of War', in *Just and Unjust Wars*, New York, Basic Books: 1977.
Walzer articulates and defends the orthodox view of the moral status of combatants.

Jeff McMahan, 'On the Moral Equality of Combatants', *Journal of Political Philosophy*, 14, No. 2, 2006, 377–393.
McMahan sets out and defends the main arguments for his view in this article. For a more detailed discussion, in which he responds to some of his critics, see Jeff McMahan, *Killing in War*, Oxford: Oxford University Press, 2009.

Thomas Hurka, 'Liability and Just Cause', *Ethics and International Affairs*, 21, No. 2, 2007, 199–218.
Hurka offers a critique of McMahan's view, defending the idea that consent can ground the moral equality of combatants.

Uwe Steinhoff, 'Debate: Jeff McMahan on the Moral Inequality of Combatants', *Journal of Political Philosophy* 16, No. 2, 2008, 220–226.
Steinhoff defends the orthodox view of combatants against McMahan, arguing that the need to defend non-combatants against unjust harm can make it permissible for unjust combatants to fight.

7 Non-combatants in war

In this chapter, we will look in more detail at some of the philosophical issues surrounding the idea of non-combatant immunity in war. In particular, we will look at why the principle of non-combatant immunity permits the collateral killing of non-combatants, but prohibits the intentional killing of non-combatants. Usually, this position is explained by invoking the doctrine of double effect (DDE). Since the collateral harms are merely foreseen, rather than intended, this is thought to affect their permissibility. We will look at criticisms of the DDE and consider how just war theorists have sought to revise this doctrine to make it more plausible. We will also consider some suggested alternatives to the DDE. In the second part of the chapter, we will look at the difficulty of explaining or justifying the principle of non-combatant immunity itself. We will focus on attempts to distinguish combatants from non-combatants, and will consider whether there is a plausible criterion that explains why combatants may be attacked, but non-combatants may not.

COLLATERAL DAMAGE

The doctrine of double effect

In Chapter 1, we looked at how the doctrine of double effect is used to explain the permissibility of inflicting certain harms. The DDE holds that there is a morally significant difference between harm that I *intend* to cause and harm that I merely *foresee* I will cause. Of course, this difference alone cannot suffice to make inflicting harm permissible, as illustrated by cases such as *Meeting*:

> Meeting:
> I am driving to an important meeting. You are crossing the road in front of me. I foresee that I will hit you and harm you if I keep driving. But I do not intend to harm you; all that I *intend* is to get to my important meeting on time. I would carry on driving whether you were crossing the road or not.

If all that matters for permissibility is that I do not intend harm, even if I foresee it, our account of permissibility will be rather implausible. It will deem it permissible for me to run you over provided all that I intend is that I make my meeting. In order to avoid sanctioning cases like *Meeting*, the DDE is usually thought to include a proportionality requirement. The foreseen harm must be outweighed by the good that I intend to achieve. Even if my meeting is important, it is very unlikely to be *so* important that the good of attending it outweighs the harm of running you over. The inclusion of the proportionality requirement thus makes the DDE more restrictive.

One of the moral difficulties of war is that it is practically impossible to fight a war without killing at least some non-combatants. But non-combatants are supposed to be immune from harm in war. If we are to fight wars, we need to explain how killing these supposedly immune people can be morally permissible. Many just war theorists have used the DDE to provide such an explanation, arguing for a morally significant distinction between the collateral harming of non-combatants and the intentional harming of non-combatants.

The following two cases are often invoked to illustrate this difference.

Tactical Bomber:
A bomber drops a bomb on a munitions factory in order to secure his side a significant military advantage. The bomber knows that fifty non-combatants in a nearby children's hospital will be killed as a side-effect of the blast.

Terror Bomber:
A bomber drops a bomb on a children's hospital in order to kill fifty non-combatants. This will terrorise the local munitions workers into quitting their jobs, thus securing his side a significant military advantage.

The tactical bomber and the terror bomber cause the same amount of harm in order to achieve the same end. But the laws of war, and the orthodox rules of *jus in bello*, hold that the tactical bomber acts permissibly, whereas the terror bomber acts impermissibly. The tactical bomber foresees that he will kill fifty non-combatants, but, it is said, he does not intend their deaths. The terror bomber, in contrast, intends to kill the non-combatants. Their deaths are part of his plan for securing the advantage for his side.

Cases like this are thought not only to illustrate the DDE, but also to show that it must be *true*. Many people firmly believe that the tactical bomber acts permissibly and that the terror bomber acts impermissibly. The DDE gives us a way to explain this difference by pointing to the different intentions of the two bombers.

But can the fact that the tactical bomber merely foresees the harm, whereas the terror bomber intends it, really make a difference to the permissibility of their actions? Judith Jarvis Thomson argues that even when we include a proportionality requirement, the DDE cannot show that there is a morally significant difference between the two bombings. Thomson imagines a pilot asking his superior officers whether or not he may carry out a mission that will involve dropping a bomb where it will kill some non-combatants. And she imagines his superiors giving the following reply:

> 'Well, it all depends on what your intentions would be in dropping the bombs. If you would be intending to destroy the munitions factory and thereby win the war, merely foreseeing, though not intending, the deaths of the children, then yes, you may drop the bombs. On the other hand, if you would be intending to destroy the children and thereby terrorize the [enemy] and thereby win the war, merely foreseeing, though not intending, the destruction of the munitions factory, then no, you may not drop the bombs.' What a queer performance this would be! Can anyone really think that the pilot should decide whether he may drop the bombs by looking inward for the intention with which he would be dropping them if he dropped them?
>
> (J. J. Thomson, 'Self-Defense', *Philosophy and Public Affairs* 20, No. 4, 1991, 283–310, p. 293)

Thomson rejects the idea that the difference between intending an outcome and merely foreseeing that it will occur can make the difference between permissibility and impermissibility. The permissibility of my action cannot rest on the mental state that I happen to be in at the time of performing the action. That I don't intend to kill you by dropping the bomb cannot settle the question of whether or not I may drop the bomb, if I know that dropping the bomb *will* kill you. Thomson thus denies that we can account for collateral killing in war by invoking a difference in intention of the sort stipulated by the DDE. She suggests that, in principle, it may be the case that the terror bomber's action is not morally different to the tactical bomber's action.[1]

Thomson's objection reflects a fairly general concern that its heavy reliance on intention renders the DDE too flimsy, in the sorts of ways that we described in Chapter 1. Even those who do not entirely reject the relevance of intention to permissibility might think that more work needs to be done to show that the DDE is a plausible account of permissible killing in war. If we want to sustain the moral distinction between collateral damage and intended damage, then, we might try to revise the DDE so that it can do better in the face of objections such as Thomson's. Or we might replace the DDE with some other principle of permissible killing that avoids these objections altogether.

Double effect and double intent

Michael Walzer argues that we can profitably revise the DDE by including a requirement of what he calls *double intention*.[2] The standard DDE requires that the agent have an intention of achieving the good effect (e.g. halting weapons production). Double intention requires that the agent also have a further intention of reducing the foreseeable bad side-effects as far as possible. The agent must try to minimise the harm to non-combatants, 'accepting costs to himself' in the process.[3] This addition is supposed to make the DDE more demanding. A combatant cannot render the infliction of harm permissible simply by lacking an intention to harm. He must also have the intention of *avoiding* harm to non-combatants as far as possible. This intention must be sufficiently sincere that the combatant is willing to incur additional risks to his own safety in order to protect non-combatants from harm.

Walzer's claim, then, is that by combining the DDE with a 'positive commitment' to saving non-combatant lives, we can show that the tactical bomber's actions are morally different to those of the terror bomber.[4] The terror bomber can hardly claim to be trying to minimise non-combatant losses if he deliberately targets non-combatants. This does not display a positive commitment to saving non-combatants' lives. The tactical bomber, in contrast, could display such a commitment. If, for example, he bombs the factory at night because the nearby hospital has fewer patients at night, he demonstrates an active commitment to reducing non-combatant harm. This is especially true if attacking at night is more dangerous – the combatant is then demonstrating his commitment to protecting non-combatants by shouldering additional risks to that end.

Several writers have echoed Walzer's suggestion. Tony Coady talks of a 'pre-condition' for the DDE that requires combatants to use the least harmful means available to them.[5] Coady argues that this means that collateral damage is permissible only when it is the *only* way in which a proportionate good can be achieved. So, whilst he thinks that Walzer's inclusion of double intent is along the right lines, Coady emphasises that minimising harm can mean seeking alternative methods of achieving the good end that inflict no collateral damage *at all*.

However, others have argued that Walzer's attempt to rescue the DDE fails. Noam Zohar argues that if this additional criterion is to improve upon the DDE, seeking to minimise harm must amount to more than simply lacking an intention to harm (since the DDE already specifies that the agent must not intend his harmful effects). And, indeed, a requirement that combatants seek to minimise harm does sound more demanding than not intending harm: it 'implies an active effort, in addition to motivation.'[6] As described above, this effort would be demonstrated by, for example, opting for a less harmful course of action over a more harmful course of action, especially if the less harmful course of action increases risks to the combatants.

But, Zohar says, what if there *is* no alternative that involves less harm to civilians? In such a case, how would seeking to minimise harm manifest itself? It seems that sometimes, 'the "seeking" boils down to the counterfactual assertion, "If there were another option, he would have taken it." '[7] In such a case, we judge the permissibility of the combatant's action by the presence of a disposition to act in a certain way. And this is, in effect, to attribute the permissibility of the combatant's action to his mental state in just the way that Thomson rejects. Walzer's revision thus offers 'scant comfort' to those troubled by Thomson's original complaint.[8]

But Zohar is perhaps too hasty here. After all, to seek does not mean to find. How could a combatant know that there is no alternative course of action available to him unless he had bothered to look for one? And this will involve not just a counterfactual assertion – a claim to a certain disposition – but actually investigating alternatives, be they attacking on a different day or at a different time of day, or using a different type of weapon, or trying to evacuate or warn the non-combatants. One must not only have a counterfactual disposition to act differently: one must *actually* make sure that one cannot act differently. And making sure that this is the case will not simply be a matter of having a certain mental state. If so, Walzer's revision seems to withstand Zohar's objection.

A more worrying problem, it seems to me, is that the terror bomber might also be able to undertake the kind of 'minimising' activities that Walzer has in mind. Imagine that the terror bomber accurately predicts that he needs to kill thirty people if his attack is going to effectively generate fear amongst the munitions workers. He knows that the hospital has an average population of 100 non-combatants during the day and of fifty non-combatants during the night. He chooses to attack at night in order to avoid killing any more people than necessary to achieve his goal of terrorising the munitions works. Couldn't this meet the requirement of seeking to minimise harm? Perhaps attacking at night is even more dangerous for him and so, in choosing this alternative, he accepts greater costs to himself in order to minimise non-combatant deaths. If the terror bomber has no other way to stop production at the factory (perhaps the factory is underground and cannot be directly attacked), he is choosing the least harmful means available to him. Of course, we can still point to the difference in intention – the terror bomber still intends to kill non-combatants. Their deaths are part of his plan. But the requirement of minimising harm was introduced precisely because the difference between intending and foreseeing harm doesn't seem able to support the difference in permissibility on its own.

Alternatives to double effect

Foreseeable harm

What about simply giving up on the DDE, and trying to give some other account of collateral damage? Colm McKeogh, for example, rejects the DDE, arguing that while damage to civilian property can be outweighed by the achievement of a greater good, harm to civilians themselves cannot be so outweighed.

It is unjust to trade in human life, to balance and trade off innocent human lives against any good. It is wrong to kill an innocent person so that another innocent life may be saved. It is wrong to kill an innocent person even so that an entire nation may be saved.

(C. McKeogh, *Innocent Civilians: The Morality of Killing in War*, New York: Palgrave Macmillan, 2002, p. 166)

In place of the DDE, McKeogh defends what Stephen Nathanson calls the *foreseeable harm principle*.[9] According to this principle, only the genuinely accidental killing of non-combatants can be excused. And a killing is genuinely accidental only if it is both 'unforeseen and reasonably unforeseeable'.[10] According to this principle, both the tactical bomber and the terror bomber act impermissibly because both foresee the harm they will cause to non-combatants. If an agent knows that an action of theirs will cause a certain harm, and they perform the action anyway, they cannot plausibly claim that the harm was an accident.

Clearly, a view like this has significant implications for just war theory. The majority of non-combatant deaths in war are foreseeable and, indeed, foreseen. This is true with respect to the killing of specific non-combatants in specific offensives, such as in our tactical bomber case. And it is also true more generally, when we take a broader view of the war as an enterprise. Even before a war begins, we know that some non-combatants will be killed, even if we do not yet know which ones. The foreseeable harm principle suggests that, since we can confidently predict that these deaths will occur, we act wrongly if we nonetheless act in a way that brings them about. In other words, permitting only accidental harm to non-combatants seems to effectively prohibit the fighting of war altogether. Some pacifists use this line of reasoning to argue that war is never justified.

McKeogh, however, suggests that we would be permitted to fight wars were we able to restrict the foreseeable harm done in war to only civilian property, rather than civilians themselves. Whilst such attacks are currently illegal, and would still be a compromise of the principle of non-combatant immunity, they would, he says, 'be welcome if they were accompanied by a genuine immunity for civilian life in war.'[11]

However, it's not clear what sorts of target McKeogh thinks it appropriate to attack under this kind of strategy. He cites, rather approvingly, 'the sort of victory of which a senior US Air Force commander dreams':

Just think if after the first day, the Serbian people had awakened and their refrigerators weren't running, there was no water in their kitchens or bathrooms, no lights, no transportation system to get to work ... they would have asked: 'All this after the first night? What is the rest of this [war] going to be like?'

> (Quoted by T. Barela in 'To Win a War', *Airman* 43, No. 9, 1999, 2–3, and cited in McKeogh, *Innocent Civilians: The Morality of Killing in War*, p. 171)

This particular dream seems to involve cutting off water and electricity to the civilian population – hardly compatible with McKeogh's emphasis on respect for civilian life. McKeogh then quotes another senior member of the US Air Force who suggests targeting '*anything* not absolutely indispensable' for human survival.[12] But at least some of those things on the list of suggested targets (which includes factories, plants, shops and banks) do seem rather indispensable for human survival, at least for those living in towns and cities.

For example, it's hard to see what sort of plants would be worth attacking other than those providing power or clean water. To be an effective military strategy, the attacks would have to be aimed at facilities offering more than mere recreation or convenience. But once we start to destroy important infrastructure, it seems inevitable that access to basic goods will be affected. Simply cutting off or even restricting something like fuel supplies to a town could foreseeably result in civilian deaths by impeding the work of the emergency services. Cutting off the electricity supply to residential areas endangers the life of anyone who relies on home medical equipment (a ventilator, for example). If so, and if causing foreseeable harm makes an action impermissible, I'm not sure that McKeogh's suggestion manages to avoid the pacifist conclusion that the foreseeable harm principle implies. By the lights of McKeogh's theory, if we can foresee that just one civilian death will result from such a strategy, the strategy is impermissible.

Nathanson ultimately rejects the foreseeable harm principle as too restrictive. But he does offer an alternative suggestion for why this principle need not lead directly to pacifism. We can resist this conclusion by restricting our application of the principle to specific offensives within war, rather than to the war as a whole. After all, there are plenty of activities that inevitably and predictably result in death, but that are nonetheless permissible.[13] We know, for example, that a certain percentage of minor operations will result in death, but we do not think that the inevitability of these deaths makes the practice of performing minor operations wrong. We also know that a certain number of people will be killed on roads each year, but we don't refuse to build roads as a result. Rather than prohibit these practices, we insist that precautions be taken to limit the number of deaths that arise from them. We impose high standards of hygiene and training upon those carrying out each specific operation. We improve road-building techniques to try to make each specific instance of road-building safer.

> With those cases in mind, it is possible to claim that it is not arbitrary to restrict the foreseeable harm principle to evaluating tactics and actions

within wars and not to apply it to war itself. Accepting this restriction does not deprive the foreseeable harm principle of critical force. It can be used to show that types of weapons or tactics that especially endanger civilians are immoral.

(S. Nathanson, *Terrorism and the Ethics of War*, New York: Cambridge University Press, 2010, p. 260)

So, Nathanson suggests that the foreseeable harm principle need not prohibit war altogether, because we can plausibly restrict its application to specific offensives in war. Is he right? I am not sure that he is. In the sorts of cases that Nathanson cites, like road-building, we can explain the permissibility of the enterprise as a whole by noticing that the group of people at risk of bearing the costs are the same as those who will enjoy the predicted benefits. The drivers who will be killed on the road are part of the group who will benefit from the road. The people who will die in surgery are part of the group who will benefit from successful surgery. These people also consent to the risks when they participate in the risky activity.

Of course, it's not always clear how we define the relevant group in such cases, and there are usually some counter-examples. A pedestrian who has never driven a car might be hit by a driver. But even she might indirectly benefit from the road, even if she does not use it herself. Perhaps it makes it easier for the fire brigade to reach her house in an emergency, or for her relatives to visit or for her town to develop economically. The important point is that, by and large, the people who are at risk of being harmed by the enterprise are also the people who will benefit from that enterprise.

But this is not likely to be the case in war. Combatants are usually inflicting collateral damage on non-combatants on the *other side*. When we think about whether we should wage war, we are partly wondering whether the benefits that will accrue to us outweigh the costs that our combatants and the enemy non-combatants will bear. We can justify the costs to our combatants by the fact that they are part of the group that will benefit if we win the war. They are on our side. But we cannot justify the costs to the enemy non-combatants in this way. *They* will not share in our benefits if we win the war. So the fact that looks likely to justify risky practices such as building roads and carrying out operations – that those at risk of being harmed are also those who stand to gain – does not obtain in war. Given this, it's not clear that we can assume that the overall practice of war is justified, and thus plausibly restrict the foreseeable harm principle to specific offensives in war in the way that Nathanson suggests. The pacifist conclusion thus seems hard to escape.

Even if Nathanson is right, however, that the foreseeable harm principle does not essentially entail pacifism, it might still require pacifism in practice. The principle would severely restrict the fighting of war by permitting offensives only if collateral damage is not foreseen or reasonably foreseeable. If we know that a particular attack or weapon is likely to cause harm to non-combatants, the principle will prohibit their use. This approach might still rule out wars in practice, at least at the moment, because too many specific offensives will involve foreseeable harm. Until we develop equipment or strategies that make harm to non-combatants very unlikely, our chances of meeting this interpretation of non-combatant immunity will make war a practical impossibility.

The precautionary principle

Nathanson argues that we ought to reject the foreseeable harm principle in favour of what he calls the *precautionary principle*. Whilst the foreseeable harm principle prohibits the inflicting of either foreseen or *reasonably foreseeable* harms, the precautionary principle demands that combatants do *everything that they can* to predict collateral damage. Nathanson argues that the standard of investigation required by the precautionary principle thus exceeds that of the foreseeable harm principle. And he argues that it is this higher standard that is required by the Geneva Convention, which demands that combatants take 'constant care' to try to protect non-combatants against collateral damage.[14] They must do 'everything feasible' to confirm that their targets are military targets, and take 'all feasible precautions' with respect to weapons and tactics to avoid or minimise harm to non-combatants.[15] If we use this feasibility standard to judge whether combatants have taken adequate precautions, we can see that 'the precautionary principle imposes demands on fighting that neither the double effect principle nor the foreseeable harm principle imposes'.[16]

However, in other respects, the precautionary principle is more permissive than the foreseeable harm principle. If combatants have taken the extensive measures required of them to guard against collateral damage, and yet cannot avoid causing some harm to non-combatants, inflicting this harm can be permissible even if it is foreseen.[17] Thus, the precautionary principle will not restrict permissible offensives to the same extent as the foreseeable harm principle. Combatants may cause non-accidental harm provided that they have done their utmost to minimise that harm.

Nathanson acknowledges that someone might object to the precautionary principle on the grounds that it permits reckless harm. The legal understanding of reckless behaviour, as expressed by the American Model Penal Code, includes behaviour that 'consciously disregards a substantial and unjustifiable risk'.[18] Since the precautionary principle allows combatants to act knowing that there is a substantial risk that they will cause harm to non-combatants, it looks as though it sanctions the reckless harming of non-combatants. But, argues Nathanson, this objection fails in two ways. First, he suggests that those who undertake the measures required by the precautionary principle cannot be sensibly described as consciously disregarding a risk. On the contrary, they have actively tried to *lessen* that risk. That after these protective measures have been exhausted some risk remains is not enough to describe the combatants as acting recklessly.

Second, for behaviour to count as reckless, the risk in question must be not only substantial, but *unjustifiable*. Nathanson suggests that it is here that proportionality plays a role. Whether or not a risk is justifiable will depend upon whether the expected benefits sufficiently outweigh the expected collateral damage. And '[i]f constant care is taken to protect civilians and foreseeable harms are proportionate, then the attacks can be morally justified.'[19] If so, combatants adhering to the precautionary principle cannot be described as reckless.

Of course, by including this role for proportionality in the precautionary principle, it isn't clear that Nathanson will be able to permit unjust combatants to cause collateral damage. As we have already discussed in Chapter 6, writers such as Thomas Hurka and Jeff McMahan argue that unjust combatants lack good ends that can weigh against bad side-effects in a proportionality calculation. Whilst the foreseeable harm principle applies equally to just and unjust combatants, simply disallowing the infliction of any foreseen harm, the precautionary principle seems applicable only to just combatants. Only they will be able to *justifiably* impose risks, because only their offensives have the potential to produce benefits.

Nathanson tries to resist this outcome partly by invoking the sort of 'damage limitation' approach to the rules of war that is favoured by Henry Shue, and that we explored in Chapter 2. Nathanson claims that Hurka and McMahan fail 'to take seriously the effects of rules of war'; it is better for everyone if we do not have different rules for just and unjust combatants.[20] We will not revisit this argument here. Rather, I want to consider the other part of Nathanson's reply to Hurka, which holds that Hurka 'overstates the extent to which the overall value of an endeavor completely determines the morality of individual acts performed as part of that endeavor.'[21]

> Consider again the highway designer. Suppose that she is working on a road that has little to no value. It is a 'road to nowhere,' promoted by corrupt politicians and highway companies. Hurka's view suggests that we should evaluate all the actions done in creating the highway as wrong. Yet surely we should distinguish the actions of a conscientious highway designer who strives to make this useless road as safe as possible from the actions of a designer who takes no such steps.
>
> (Nathanson, *Terrorism and the Ethics of War*, p. 274)

By the same token, Nathanson thinks that we can morally distinguish between the actions of unjust combatants who try to carry out proportionate attacks and unjust combatants who make no such efforts. The precautionary principle can therefore be usefully employed by unjust combatants, because it is better that their unjust attacks are proportionate than that they are disproportionate.

However, the comparison of an unjust war with a road that has 'little to no value' is hardly sound. Unjust wars are not of little value, or even of neutral value. They are of enormous *dis*value. They are not just unhelpful or useless;

they are very bad indeed. Nathanson might be right that when an enterprise is of little or no value, it can nonetheless be undertaken in morally better or worse ways. Consider John Rawls' famous grass-counter, who dedicates her life to counting blades of grass.[22] Assume (although this is by no means agreed upon) that the activity of endlessly counting blades of grass is morally neutral. There is nothing good about it, but there is nothing wrong with it either. All the same, we might think better of the grass-counter who uses environmentally friendly fertilisers to grow her grass than we do of the grass-counter who uses polluting chemicals to that same end. There can be morally better or worse ways of going about activities that are themselves morally neutral.

However, I am not sure that the same is true of activities that have such huge disvalue as the fighting of an unjust war. A more apt analogy for unjust war is not the conscientious designer of a useless road, but the conscientious rapist who wears a condom so as to avoid transmitting diseases to his victim. Rape, like unjust war, is an enterprise with significant disvalue. By Nathanson's lights, though, it sounds as if we must 'surely' draw important moral distinctions between the rapist who tries to avoid inflicting additional harms on his victim by using a condom and the rapist who is indifferent about inflicting such harms and does not use a condom. I suspect, however, that some of us might be rather reluctant to draw such distinctions.

Of course, we can agree that the victim might prefer that the rapist use a condom. It does make the rape less harmful. But this doesn't commit us to judging the conscientious rape to be somehow morally better than the indifferent rape. Sometimes, the overall value of an endeavour *does* completely determine the morality of individual acts performed as part of that endeavour. And it seems likely that the sort of endeavours of which this is true are those which have very great disvalue, which must include unjust wars.

We might level a similar objection at the other part of Nathanson's claim that if combatants do all they can to minimise risks of harm, they cannot be said to disregard those risks. Whether or not this is plausible also depends, I think, on the overall value of the endeavour. Imagine a joyrider who, whilst determined to reach top speeds on a motorway, is also anxious to avoid killing anyone in the process. So, he picks Sunday night (a quiet time on the roads) as the best time for his adventure, avoids alcohol all day, steals a car with a good safety record, and checks the brakes carefully as he sets off. Is the joyrider reckless? Is he consciously disregarding the risks that he imposes on others? Well, according to Nathanson's view, it looks as if he does not. On the contrary, the joyrider has given considerable thought to minimising the risks to others. Of course, Nathanson might reply that the joyrider counts as reckless because he has not done *all that he can* to minimise these risks, because he could simply forgo the joyride. Indeed, this is clearly what he ought to do. But the same is true of unjust combatants. Just combatants need to cause collateral damage to achieve their morally good end. We might say that they lack morally viable alternatives (after all, that their war is just means that it is a last resort). But unjust combatants do have a morally viable (indeed, perhaps a morally required) alterative. They should simply forgo fighting altogether. And thus unjust combatants who choose to fight never do all that they can to minimise risks to non-combatants. They can thus never meet the terms of the precautionary principle. Given this, it doesn't look as though Nathanson's precautionary principle can be universally employed in the way he assumes it can.

These are some of the difficulties surrounding the application of the principle of non-combatant immunity. Exactly how we interpret this principle – as prohibiting intended harm, as an absolute ban on all predictable harm, as requiring strict attempts to minimise harm – will greatly influence our account of the *jus in bello* rules. But we should not take the principle itself for granted. The discussion above proceeded on the assumptions that we can distinguish combatants from non-combatants, and that there is something wrong with killing non-combatants that does not extend to the killing of combatants. In the rest of the chapter, we will examine these assumptions.

COMBATANTS AND NON-COMBATANTS: DRAWING THE LINE

Both orthodox just war theory and the laws of armed conflict deem non-combatants immune from intentional attack. The typical explanation of this immunity is that non-combatants have done nothing to lose their usual rights against such attacks. All people have, as a default position, a right not to be killed. If non-combatants do nothing to forfeit that right, killing them will violate that right. Thus, even though some non-combatants will inevitably be incidentally killed in the war, as we have discussed above, they are not to be intentionally killed. The principle of non-combatant immunity is thought to be universal: it holds for all non-combatants in all conflicts.

The difficulty with sustaining this principle comes from identifying what it is that combatants do that means that they, and only they, have forfeited their right not to be killed. As Larry May emphasises, the distinction between combatants and non-combatants is supposed to explain the principle of non-combatant immunity, identifying what it is about combatants that renders their rights against attack forfeit. But the principle of non-combatant immunity is a *moral* principle. It makes claims about how morality requires that we treat people. We therefore need to identify something that not only factually distinguishes combatants from non-combatants, but does so on the basis of a morally relevant feature. As May points out, 'we can form groups by stipulation in an infinite number of ways, but this will not tell us who should be morally distinguished from whom.'[23] We could argue that, for example, the difference between combatants and non-combatants is that combatants sleep on bases or in camps. But even if this were true of all and only combatants, it is not *this* that results in the loss of their right not to be killed. A purely non-moral difference between combatants and non-combatants cannot ground a moral principle like the principle of non-combatant immunity.

But, as we will see, most of the moral features that look like good candidates for this role either cast their nets too wide, including all combatants but also some non-combatants, or cast it too short, excluding all non-combatants but also some combatants. Given the difficulties with showing that there is a clear line between combatants and non-combatants, several writers have argued that we should abandon the view that there is some deep moral principle that forbids attacking non-combatants.

Guilt and non-combatant immunity

The notion of non-combatant immunity in war, although central to contemporary just war theory, is notably absent in the writing of St Augustine, one of the earliest and most influential just war theorists. As we saw in Chapter 4, Augustine argued that war could be justified as an act of punishment.[24] But we noted that it is hard to justify using war as a form of punishment because war inflicts harms upon the guilty and innocent alike. Augustine tried to overcome this problem by arguing that *all* members of aggressing states are guilty. Part of Augustine's account, then, is that we can properly view the members of a state as one body, sharing in each other's wrongdoing. If the French army invades Spain, all French citizens are guilty, and all may be punished. Thus, Augustine's account of the just war does not recognise any moral distinction between combatants and non-combatants.

McKeogh suggests that this view of guilt as attaching to each and every member of an aggressing state was essential for showing that the Christian ideal of treating people as individuals – with each getting what he or she deserved – was compatible with causing non-combatant deaths in war.[25] Wartime tactics at Augustine's time often included, for example, sieges of towns or cities, which would predictably result in the deaths of non-combatants along with combatants. Causing these deaths seems *prima facie* incompatible with Christian teachings on not killing the innocent. By deeming each citizen individually guilty, and thus liable to punishment, Augustine could explain why causing these deaths was morally justified.

However, given that, until fairly recently, states were usually ruled by unelected monarchs who were wholly unaccountable to their subjects, it is hard to credit Augustine's attribution of national guilt for military aggression. In these authoritarian regimes, political power was either inherited or obtained by force. The idea that ordinary citizens (or, more accurately, ordinary subjects) might widely participate in government, and wield political power, would have been an alien concept to most early just war theorists.

Indeed, this kind of political climate probably explains the emergence of the view that responsibility for war lies solely with a state's political leaders. Ordinary citizens were often uneducated, poor and physically isolated, living in rural communities with minimal links to the rest of the country. McKeogh argues that as armies became increasingly composed of these ordinary people, it became harder to deem even the combatants fighting for the unjust side morally guilty. Knights who were politically aligned with their monarch might plausibly have been said to share in the monarch's aggressive aims, and thus share in their guilt. But as armies expanded to include more ordinary people with no particular political affiliation or influence, 'the grounds for the ascription of guilt to soldiers on the side without a just cause grew even weaker.'[26]

The decisive shift from Augustine's 'collective guilt' view to the endorsing of non-combatant immunity (and the moral equality of combatants) came with Hugo Grotius's writings on international law. Grotius rejected Augustine's claim that collective guilt justifies killing in war, devising secular laws of war that permitted the killing of combatants, 'because of the customary acceptance in the Western world that members of the armed forces may in war be treated as instruments, both by their own commanders and by their enemy's.'[27] It is here that the distinction between those who are threatening – who are the lethal instruments of the state – and those who are not begins to emerge as the foundation of non-combatant immunity.

Posing a threat

That combatants threaten probably strikes many people as the most obvious difference between combatants and non-combatants. Combatants are out fighting the battles that make up the war. They are the ones doing the killing and the maiming. Non-combatants do not do these things. And so, we might think, what makes it the case that combatants forfeit their rights against attack is that they are attacking other people. And, equally, what makes it the case that non-combatants do not forfeit their rights is that they are not attacking other people.

We have already looked at one argument for why this view fails. If McMahan is right that merely posing a threat is not enough to forfeit one's right not to be killed, then the mere fact that combatants threaten will not show that they have forfeited their rights. But not everyone accepts that the rules of killing in war can be reduced to the rules of self-defence in the way that McMahan supposes. If war is not based upon the rules of individual defence, those combatants who pose even just defensive threats might forfeit their rights against intentional attack. So, let's set McMahan's view aside for now, and consider the merits of this argument on its own terms. Can the criterion of posing a threat provide a plausible basis for the principle of non-combatant immunity?

To do so, the notion of posing a threat will have to enable us to distinguish between combatants and non-combatants. At the very least, it will have to show that only combatants pose threats. And, ideally, it will also show that *all* combatants pose threats, if we are to allow that all combatants are legitimate targets. Whether it can do this will depend on how narrowly we understand the idea of posing a threat. If we employ a very restricted account of 'threatening', whereby we count only those actually killing combatants on the other side as posing a threat, we can certainly rule that only combatants threaten. Non-combatants do not kill enemy combatants.

However, whilst this restricted account will generate the result that *only* combatants threaten, it will not generate the result that *all* combatants threaten. After all, only a fraction of an armed forces' members actually fight on the frontline. Many are employed in gathering intelligence, training, providing tactical information, transporting supplies and the like. All these activities contribute to the threats posed by the military: the people performing them seem like instruments of the state of the sort that Grotius describes. But none of them involve actually killing people. If we restrict our account of what it is to pose a threat to only those people actually firing guns or dropping bombs – to those doing the killing – the majority of combatants will not count as posing a threat. So, this narrow account of posing a threat seems unpromising if we want to defend anything like the orthodox view that all combatants are legitimate targets. It casts the net of legitimate targets too short.

If we want to include all combatants as legitimate wartime targets, then we must broaden our account of what counts as posing a threat. One way to do this is to hold that making a material contribution to a threat counts as posing a threat (even if one doesn't directly inflict harm oneself). So, those who provide technical support for offensives will count as posing a threat, as will those training other soldiers and transporting guns. This approach will enable us to count all the behind-the-lines military personnel as threats, since they all play a role in bringing about the harms that the frontline soldiers inflict. We can therefore class all combatants as legitimate targets.

The difficulty is that this broader account of posing a threat cannot exclude non-combatants. After all, if we include as threats those driving guns to the front line, what principled reason could we offer for excluding those making the guns? Both groups make clear causal contributions to the threats posed by those on the frontline. Both contributions are essential to the harms being inflicted on enemy combatants. But the munitions factories are manned not by combatants, but by ordinary people. Thus, this account of what it is to pose a threat seems to cast its net too wide, catching plenty of non-combatants along with the combatants.

Guns and food

In light of this difficulty, some writers have bitten the bullet (as it were) and argued that munitions workers count as posing a threat, and can be permissibly attacked. But they nonetheless try to sustain the idea of non-combatant immunity by arguing that these workers count as combatants. Thus, deeming them threats does not undermine the idea that only combatants threaten during war – that only combatants are the 'instruments' that Grotius describes.

This position is often supported by alleging a morally relevant distinction between the *sorts* of contributions made by non-combatants (we can call this the *functionalist* view of non-combatant immunity). Grotius, for example, suggests a distinction between the things that a state needs specifically to wage war, for example weapons, and things that it needs in peacetime, such as food. The weapons are part of the wartime threat, but the food is not. Hence, people supplying the weapons are posing threats and count as combatants, but those supplying the food do not. Grotius' view is echoed in Michael Walzer's assertion that there is a difference between the things that soldiers need *qua* soldier, and the things they need *qua* human beings:

> An army, to be sure, has an enormous belly, and it must be fed if it is to fight. But it is not its belly but its arms that make it an army. Those men and women who supply its belly are doing nothing peculiarly warlike. Hence their immunity from attack: they are assimilated to the rest of the civilian population.
>
> (M. Walzer, *Just and Unjust Wars*, New York: Basic Books, 1977, p. 146)

Walzer's distinction is often invoked to explain why we cannot kill, for example, farmers who are supplying an army with food, or companies that supply medical equipment. Food is not really part of the war effort (or so the story goes), because the members of the army would have to eat whether or not they were at war. So, the farmer isn't doing anything other than that which he would do during peacetime, and thus we cannot fairly construe his actions as threatening. The same goes for medical supplies: people get injured and sick whether or not there is a war on, and so workers providing these kinds of goods are not doing anything peculiarly warlike, to borrow Walzer's phrase. Munitions workers, on the other hand, are making weapons precisely *because* there is a war on. Their efforts are 'directed towards' helping combatants inflict harm, and it is this that makes them legitimate targets.

Even if the functionalist view is correct, we should notice that it will nonetheless broaden the range of legitimate targets quite considerably. Weapons are not the only peculiarly warlike things that non-combatants supply to the armed forces. They supply a whole range of things that the combatants need *qua* combatants, such as parachutes, sophisticated reconnaissance equipment, armoured vehicles and so on. Parachutes and armoured vehicles are not things that ordinary people use in ordinary life. The scientists who developed nerve gas during the First World War were not supplying things that combatants 'need to live, like all the rest of us', as Walzer puts it.[28] If we include as a threat anyone making a peculiarly warlike contribution, the scope of legitimate wartime targets is going to trample all over the distinction between combatants and non-combatants.

Cécile Fabre, however, argues that we should be sceptical of the functionalist distinction between types of causal contributions. Fabre argues that it isn't clear that there is a morally significant difference between making peculiarly warlike contributions and making other sorts of contributions, if both are necessary for posing a threat:

> For although it is true that, strictly speaking, it is the guns as used by combatants which kill, not their specialized rations or wound dressing, it is equally true that combatants are not able to kill if hunger or untreated wounds make it impossible for them to lift their arms and train those guns on the enemy. Generally, meeting combatants' material need for food, shelter, appropriate clothing, and medical care goes a long way toward enabling them to kill in war, even if the resources in question do not in themselves constitute a threat.
>
> (C. Fabre, 'Guns, Food, and Liability to Attack in War', *Ethics* 120, No.1, 2009, 36–63, pp. 43–44)

Fabre also denies that we can so easily divide up the sorts of contributions that people make into 'warlike' and 'non-warlike'. Combatants do not just need food – they need specially designed rations that provide them with the appropriate calories and nutrition to keep them fit in physically demanding conditions. They don't just need clothing – they need clothing that protects them in conditions of extreme heat, humidity or cold, and that enables them to camouflage themselves against their environment.[29] It is misleading to present the provision of these specialist goods as non-warlike contributions. Applying the functionalist distinction between guns and food, then, doesn't seem like a very promising basis for the principle of non-combatant immunity.

Proximate threats

Some people have instead tried to sustain the principle of non-combatant immunity by distinguishing not the *types* of causal contribution that people make to a war, but rather the *directness* with which those contributions are made. The idea is that even though non-combatants might well contribute to their country's war effort, they do not pose *direct* threats to the combatants on the other side. And, according to this account of liability to defensive harm, only those posing direct threats forfeit their rights against intentional attack. Such a view is endorsed by *The Manual of the Law of Armed Conflict*:

> Only combatants are permitted to take a direct part in hostilities. It follows that they may be attacked. Civilians may not take a direct part in hostilities and, for so long as they refrain from doing so, are protected from attack. Taking a direct part in hostilities is more narrowly construed than simply making a contribution to the war effort. Thus working in a munitions factory or otherwise supplying or supporting the

war effort does not justify the targeting of civilians so doing. However, munitions factories are legitimate military targets and civilians working there, though not themselves legitimate targets, are at risk if those targets are attacked. Such incidental damage is controlled by the principle of proportionality.

(UK Ministry of Defence, *The Manual of the Law of Armed Conflict*, Oxford: Oxford University Press, 2005, 2.6.3)

We might be sceptical of the idea that one can make a 'contribution to the war effort' without taking a 'direct part in the hostilities'. Such a distinction seems artificial. But David Rodin has offered a philosophical account of why the directness of a threat might be relevant to liability to intentional attack.

Rodin argues that it is a necessary condition of liability to defensive force that one be currently engaged in an unjust attack.[30] Of course, it isn't readily apparent how we should determine whether or not someone counts as currently engaged in an attack. Imagine the following case:

Trap:
Son is impatient to get his hands on his inheritance. He sets a trap on the family estate, hoping to kill Father. A week later, Father is walking in the woods and stumbles over the tripwire. The wire triggers the release of a spear that heads straight for him.

Son certainly seems to be engaged in an unjust attack when he sets up the trap. But once he has set the trap, he need carry out no *further* actions in order to see his cunning plan come to fruition. Is he still engaged in an unjust attack when, a week later, the spear flies towards Father?

Rodin argues that he is, and that this shows that we should not understand being currently engaged in an attack as a temporal condition. It doesn't matter, for the purposes of liability, that Son set the trap a week ago. He is still engaged in an attack when Father trips the wire because he is what Rodin calls the *proximate cause* of the threat to Father's life. Being the proximate cause of a threat doesn't require that one's action fall within any particular timeframe. Rather, it requires that one's action be the last morally responsible action in the causal chain that produces the threat (we can exclude Father's accidental tripping of the wire from the category of proximate cause, since his ignorance precludes his being morally responsible for tripping the wire).

Rather than adopting a temporal measure of what it is to be currently engaged in an unjust attack, then, Rodin argues for a *principle of intervening agency* that will identify the proximate cause of a threat. The principle holds that if two or more agents create an unjust threat between them, and both meet a threshold of minimal moral responsibility, the agent whose action came last in the causal chain is the proximate cause of the threat. Rodin further argues that only this agent – the proximate cause – is a permissible target of defence.[31] Rodin offers the following example to illustrate this claim:[32]

Provocation:
Villain culpably provokes Attacker into attacking Victim. Victim can save his life either by killing Attacker or by lethally trampling over Villain as he makes his escape.

Rodin argues that it would be impermissible for Victim to save himself by killing Villain. Rodin grants that Villain bears perhaps greater moral responsibility for the unjust threat to Victim's life than Attacker does. But Villain is not currently engaged in an unjust attack because his engagement has been superseded by Attacker's intervention. This intervention transfers liability to defensive force from Villain to Attacker.

Similarly, non-combatants might bear greater moral responsibility for a war than, say, an unwilling conscript on the front line. But non-combatants are causally remote threats, whereas combatants are causally proximate threats. Since combatants are morally responsible intervening agents, only they are liable to defensive killing. It follows that that non-combatants are not liable to attack in war. Intervening agency thus gives us a principled way of sustaining non-combatant immunity in war, even if we grant the role of non-combatants in contributing to wartime threats.

Rodin's account probably coheres quite well with many people's intuitions about the relationship between citizens and their military. We employ the military to fight for us, to take risks for us and, we might say, to be targeted instead of us. That is their job: they accept that they are legitimate targets, and they accept this in order that non-combatants might avoid being targeted. But despite its appeal, I don't think this account can give us a plausible picture of liability to defensive killing. Whilst it might show us that only combatants can be legitimate targets, because only they are proximate threats, it's not clear how it can show that *all* combatants are legitimate targets.

For example, the officer who orders his troops to fire is part of the causal chain that leads to the posing of a threat, but he isn't a proximate agent of that threat. Rodin acknowledges this, but suggests that, 'those persons who play a defined role within the command structure of an organization engaged in the infliction of harm are deemed to participate in equal measure in the proximate agency of delivering unjust harm.'[33] So, the officer can be treated as a proximate threat because he is part of the command structure of the threatening organisation.

But, of course, it isn't only those giving the orders in the military who are not proximate threats. As we saw above, plenty of people in the armed forces – often its lowest ranking members – will be involved in activities such as transporting weapons. They might also feed bullets into a gun that is then fired by someone else. To capture these members of the armed forces as legitimate targets, Rodin will have to widen his suggestion to include not only those who are part of the command structure of the organisation engaged in the inflicting of harm, but anyone who is part of the threatening organisation. And whilst Rodin obviously has the military in mind when he talks of an organisation engaged in the infliction of harm, I'm not sure that we can grant this assumption.

After all, in most countries, the military is under the command of the government. But if the government is the relevant organisation, Rodin's account cannot obviously exclude other government workers, such as people employed at government-owned factories making goods used in the war effort. These people also seem to be part of an organisation involved in the inflicting of harm. Without an argument for restricting the notion of proximate cause to only the armed forces, Rodin's account doesn't seem able to support the principle of non-combatant immunity. And as we have seen, restricting causation to only the armed forces is far from easy to justify.

BEYOND THE PRINCIPLE OF NON-COMBATANT IMMUNITY

A useful convention

George Mavrodes argues that attempts to sustain the principle of non-combatant immunity fail because their authors are confused about the sort of thing that this principle is. As we have seen, most attempts to defend the principle proceed by trying to identify something about non-combatants that makes killing them wrong (or something about combatants that makes killing them permissible). The prohibition on killing non-combatants is thought to result from this rather elusive feature. As Mavrodes puts it, the authors, 'have construed the immunity of non-combatants as though it were a moral fact which was independent of any actual or envisaged convention or practice.'[34] And this, according to Mavrodes, is why their attempts fail.

Mavrodes asks us to consider a political leader who is contemplating waging a war. The war has a just cause, but the costs of fighting the war are very high indeed; so high, in fact, that the ends could not justify the means. In the terminology we used in Chapter 3, the politician has a just cause for war, but he concludes that he lacks an overall just case for war, because the war will be disproportionate.

Then, the politician has an idea. Wouldn't it be useful if the dispute giving rise to the just cause could be settled by some other means – means that would not incur such enormous costs as waging all-out war? What if, for example, both countries agreed to send forth a single champion to fight in mortal combat, on the understanding that the victor's country would be deemed to have won the dispute, and the losing country would acquiesce to their demands just as if they had lost a war? Such a convention would drastically reduce the cost of settling disputes. It is, Mavrodes says, a very attractive prospect.

However, it is also, Mavrodes says, perhaps too utopian 'to be given serious thought'.[35] In practice, losing countries would probably refuse to abide by the outcome, and would fight the war anyway. But somewhere between hellish unrestrained warfare and idealised single combat, there might be a feasible middle way. This middle way might make it possible to fight wars whose costs are not so high as to always outweigh the benefits of winning, even if it cannot reduce those costs to the extent envisaged in our single combat example. Mavrodes suggests that the persistent battle to limit military operations to counter-forces strategies, and to avoid killing non-combatants, is an attempt to find this middle way.[36] The principle of non-combatant immunity is the result of these efforts. As such, however, the principle does not reflect any deep truth about the moral status of non-combatants that philosophers can uncover. Rather, the principle of non-combatant immunity has emerged as a useful convention for limiting the damage of war: a convention that countries broadly agree on, and that can be relatively easily employed by making combatants wear uniforms.

Mavrodes is not arguing that we have no moral reason not to kill non-combatants in war. What he denies is the general assumption that these reasons give rise to the convention that forbids the killing of non-combatants. Rather, the relationship works the other way – it is the convention that gives rise to the reasons. Far from being a moral fact independent of our practices, the principle of non-combatant immunity is a, 'convention-dependent obligation'.[37]

By way of example, Mavrodes describes the convention of driving on a particular side of the road. In Britain, I have moral reasons to drive on the left, because doing so reduces the risk that I will kill people. But it does so only because, in Britain, there is a convention of driving on the left. It is only by making reference to the established practice of driving on the left that we can explain my moral obligation to do so. Once such a convention exists, we have an obligation to adhere to it.

Of course, this means that the existence of the convention is itself explained by moral reasons. Fewer lives are lost if we all drive on the same side of the road, and saving lives is a moral consideration. Mavrodes is not arguing, then, that the convention of protecting non-combatants lacks moral grounding – it is grounded in a general moral concern to limit the harms of war. His claim is that the existence of this *particular* convention is not explained by some special moral fact about non-combatants (any more than driving on the left is explained by some special moral fact about the left-hand side of the road). It may simply be the case that the best way to limit deaths in war is to divide a population into 'targets' and 'non-targets', and make the targets wear uniforms so as to avoid confusion between the two.

One objection to the convention-based approach to non-combatant immunity is that allows for the possibility that the prohibition on targeting non-combatants could simply break down over time. Those who try to ground non-combatant immunity in some independent moral fact about non-combatants can explain why, even if one's opponent is attacking non-combatants, one ought to refrain from doing so oneself. The obligation not to attack non-combatants is independent of whether or not people actually do attack them. But, as Mavrodes acknowledges, conventions are, by their nature, about what everyone else is doing.[38] If the combatants in other armed forces begin to systematically attack non-combatants, it seems that there is no longer any convention to speak of. And if the convention no longer exists, it cannot give rise to any obligations.

Mavrodes' response to this objection is to emphasise the importance of trying to establish the convention afresh. Wartime conventions are fragile, relying as they do upon conformity. But, Mavrodes suggests, this

> [A]lso bears on the way in which they may be adopted. One such way, perhaps a rather important way, is for one party to the hostilities to signal his willingness to abide by such a convention by undertaking some unilateral restraint on his own part.'
>
> (G. Mavrodes, 'Conventions and the Morality of War',
> *Philosophy and Public Affairs* 4, No. 2, 1975, p. 130)

The long-term benefits of establishing a convention could warrant forgoing the short-term benefits of attacking non-combatants.

However, this is a time-limited offer. If the other party fails to reciprocate, there will come a point at which the costs of adhering to non-combatant immunity in the absence of a general adherence will become too great. In these circumstances, Mavrodes says that one must 're-evaluate' one's approach.[39] And it's hard to see what this re-evaluation could mean, other than that one also abandons the convention and engages in unrestrained warfare. The convention-dependent approach to non-combatant immunity is, at root, a contingent approach. In so far as adhering to the convention reduces the harms of war, we have reason to adhere to it. But since the convention is justified in purely functional terms, it cannot give us reason to uphold non-combatant immunity should it become apparent that it no longer fulfils its function.

Moral responsibility

Perhaps it is time to take a closer look at a claim that we considered earlier. McKeogh suggests that as the armed forces began to be increasingly composed of ordinary citizens, the case for attributing guilt to the members of the armed forces correspondingly weakened. The idea that ordinary citizens – combatants or otherwise – might be morally responsible for their country's aggression was roundly rejected by Grotius, and by subsequent international law. But we might make use of McMahan's recent work and argue that this historical stance is a mistake. After all, whilst McMahan does not generally talk of guilt, he does insist that combatants are morally responsible for the wars that they fight. He urges combatants to engage in moral reflection, and to refuse to fight in unjust wars. Combatants who fight in unjust wars are, generally, morally responsible for posing unjust threats.

McMahan's account might thus give us the resources for explaining one side of the principle of non-combatant immunity. It tells us that unjust combatants are legitimate targets because they are morally responsible for unjust threats (although it won't, of course, tell us that just combatants are legitimate targets). But McMahan's responsibility-based account doesn't look as though it can give us the resources for the sustaining other side of the principle. It is not only combatants who can be morally responsible for unjust threats. Non-combatants can support the war just as much as, or even more than, combatants. They can vote for it, fundraise for it and make other material contributions of the sorts that we have already considered.

Non-combatants might also play important political roles in bringing the war about. McMahan cites the role of the United Fruit Company (UFC) in the Guatemalan conflict of the 1950s as an example of this. The UFC lobbied the US government to overthrow the Guatemalan government after the Guatemalan president nationalised some of the UFC's land. This seems to be a clear (albeit rare) example of non-combatants who bear considerable moral and causal responsibility for the threats posed by their country in war.[40] McMahan also suggests that Israelis who settle land in the West Bank are 'not just conscious and willing participants but enthusiastic and indeed fanatical instigators and perpetrators' of a plan to wrongfully dispossess Palestinians of their land.[41]

It looks as if, on McMahan's view, non-combatants who are responsible for unjust threats in war are legitimate targets. And McMahan does conclude that the principle of non-combatant immunity 'is false as a moral doctrine'.[42] Invoking the kind of distinction we explored in Chapter 2, McMahan argues that even though we should maintain the illegality of attacking non-combatants, it can in principle be morally permissible to attack them. Non-combatants on the unjust side of the war can be morally responsible for unjust threats, and if attacking them will avert these threats, they can, in principle, be liable to attack.

However, McMahan suggests that even if non-combatants responsibly threaten in war, there are still several reasons why attacking them could be generally morally impermissible. Some of these problems are largely practical. For example, even if we know that, for example, over half a country's non-combatant population voted for the war, it could still be impossible to identify how any particular non-combatant voted. Thus, even if we know that some non-combatants are morally responsible for unjust threats, we cannot know whether *this particular* non-combatant is so responsible. In the absence of that knowledge, it would be impermissible to attack particular non-combatants.

McMahan also uses the idea of proportionality to try to sustain widespread non-combatant immunity, even if he cannot support an absolute prohibition on attacking non-combatants. In his recent work, McMahan develops a more nuanced account of proportionality that distinguishes between two proportionality requirements: *narrow proportionality* and *wide proportionality*. Which particular proportionality requirement is relevant to a particular use of force depends on whether the target of force is *potentially liable* to harm. A person is potentially liable to harm if, for example, they are engaged in an unjust attack. A harm is narrowly disproportionate if it exceeds the amount of harm to which the target is potentially liable. A harm is widely disproportionate if it exceeds the amount of harm that can be inflicted on a person who is not potentially liable to any harm at all.

So, imagine that you are culpably trying to break my arm. I can stop you, but only by (a) breaking your leg, whilst (b) painfully grabbing hold of a nearby stranger in order to balance myself. Since you are culpably trying to break my arm, you are potentially liable to some level of defensive harm. It seems likely that a broken leg falls within the threshold of what you are liable to. Since breaking your leg will avert your attack – the defensive force will be effective – McMahan holds that you are liable to a broken leg. Inflicting this harm on you is narrowly proportionate. If, however, I were to shoot you in the chest and kill you, this would be narrowly disproportionate. Killing you exceeds the defensive force to which you are liable.

What about my painful grabbing of the nearby stranger? Being wholly innocent, she is not potentially liable to any harm at all. McMahan argues that harms to people like this are governed by wide proportionality. I can inflict some mild, temporary pain upon the stranger, given that doing so is necessary for averting a pretty serious harm to myself. Grabbing her to balance myself is widely proportionate. But I could not, for example, break her arm to stop you from breaking my arm. That would be widely disproportionate – it exceeds the harm that can be permissibly inflicted upon her, given that she is not liable to bear any harm at all.

McMahan argues that attacks on non-combatants usually violate both of these proportionality requirements. He suggests that non-combatants rarely bear what he calls 'a significant degree of responsibility' for their country's unjust war:

> Most civilians have, on their own, no capacity at all to affect the action of their government. They may pay their taxes, vote or even campaign for particular political candidates [. . .], participate in the culture from which the country's political leaders have emerged, fail to protest their country's unjust war, perhaps because they correctly believe that to do so would be ineffective, or perhaps because they approve of the war, and so on; but none of these things, nor even all of them together, is ordinarily sufficient for the forfeiture of a person's right not to be attacked and killed. Military attack exceeds what a person may ordinarily be liable to on the basis of these comparatively trivial sources of responsibility.
>
> (J. McMahan, *Killing in War*, New York: Oxford University Press, 2009, p. 225)

So, even if non-combatants are potentially liable to *some* harm on McMahan's account, he thinks that intentionally killing them exceeds the scope of that liability. Intentionally killing non-combatants is thus narrowly disproportionate, and therefore impermissible. And attacking non-combatants who are not potentially liable to any harm almost always violates wide proportionality as well.

Thus, McMahan's view, with its emphasis on individual moral responsibility, cannot support any intrinsic difference between combatants and non-combatants that supports a universal principle of non-combatant immunity. But it does have some resources that can limit the impact of undermining this principle, offering non-combatants a more contingent form of protection against intentional attack.

Chapter summary

The permissibility of inflicting collateral damage upon non-combatants is a persistent theme in just war theory, as is the impermissibility of intentionally harming non-combatants. Many just war theorists have invoked the doctrine of double effect to explain this apparent inconsistency, arguing that there is a morally significant difference between harms that I intend to cause and harms that I merely foresee that I will cause. As we have seen, however, the various problems with the DDE have led some writers to try to revise or replace this explanation of the permissibility of collateral damage. Walzer argues that we must include a requirement of double intention alongside the requirement of double effect. McKeogh argues for a prohibition on all non-accidental harms. Nathanson argues for a precautionary approach that seeks to minimise harms as far as possible without prohibiting foreseeable harms altogether.

A more fundamental problem for the principle of non-combatant immunity is the difficulty of explaining why non-combatants are immune from intentional attack in the first place. We considered various criteria that might distinguish combatants from non-combatants, but none seems to result in the sharp line that is assumed by much of just war theory and international law. With this is mind, we considered George Mavrodes' claim that the notion of non-combatant immunity is a mere convention that arises out of attempts to limit the harms of war. We also looked at the implications of Jeff McMahan's responsibility-based account of war for non-combatant immunity.

Questions for discussion

1 What is the most plausible account of the permissibility of collateral damage?
2 Would a 'war on property' of the sort that McKeogh describes be morally desirable?
3 Is there a plausible way to distinguish combatants from non-combatants?
4 Is there a morally significant difference between those who provide combatants with medical aid and supplies and those who supply them with weapons?
5 Can it ever be permissible to intentionally kill non-combatants?

Notes

1. J. J. Thomson, 'Self-Defense', *Philosophy and Public Affairs* 20, No. 4, 1991, 283–310, p. 297.
2. M. Walzer, *Just and Unjust Wars*, New York: Basic Books, 1977, p. 155.
3. Walzer, *Just and Unjust Wars*, p. 155.
4. Walzer, *Just and Unjust Wars*, p. 156.
5. C. A. J. Coady, 'Collateral Immunity in War and Terrorism', in I. Primoratz (ed.), *Civilian Immunity in War*, New York: Oxford University Press, 2007, p. 152.
6. N. Zohar, 'Double Effect and Double Intention: A Collectivist Perspective', *Israel Law Review* 40, No. 3, 2007, 730–742, p. 734.
7. Zohar, 'Double Effect and Double Intention: A Collectivist Perspective', p. 734.
8. Zohar, 'Double Effect and Double Intention: A Collectivist Perspective', p. 734.
9. S. Nathanson, *Terrorism and the Ethics of War*, New York: Cambridge University Press, 2010, p. 255.
10. C. McKeogh, *Innocent Civilians: The Morality of Killing in War*, New York: Palgrave Macmillan, 2002, p. 170.
11. McKeogh, *Innocent Civilians: The Morality of Killing in War*, p. 172.
12. McKeogh, *Innocent Civilians: The Morality of Killing in War*, p.171. Quoted material from Charles J. Dunlap Jnr, 'The End of Innocence: Rethinking Noncombatancy in the Post-Kosovo Era', *Strategic Review*, Summer 2000, 9–17, p. 12.
13. Nathanson, *Terrorism and the Ethics of War*, pp. 259–260.
14. Protocol Additional to the Geneva Conventions of 12 August 1949, and relating to the Protection of Victims of International Armed Conflicts (Protocol 1), 8 June 1977, Article 57, available at http://www.icrc.org/ihl.nsf/FULL/470?OpenDocument (accessed 29 March 2011).

15. Protocol Additional to the Geneva Conventions of 12 August 1949, and relating to the Protection of Victims of International Armed Conflicts (Protocol 1), 8 June 1977, Article 57, available at http://www.icrc.org/ihl.nsf/FULL/470?OpenDocument (accessed 29 March 2011).
16. Nathanson, *Terrorism and the Ethics of War*, p. 263.
17. Nathanson, *Terrorism and the Ethics of War*, p. 263.
18. *Model Penal Code*, Section 2. 2, Philadelphia: American Law Institute, 1980, available at http://www1.law.umkc.edu/suni/CrimLaw/MPC_Provisions/model_penal_code_default_rules.htm (accessed 17 December 2010).
19. Nathanson, *Terrorism and the Ethics of War*, p. 273.
20. Nathanson, *Terrorism and the Ethics of War*, p. 273.
21. Nathanson, *Terrorism and the Ethics of War*, p. 274.
22. J. Rawls, *A Theory of Justice*, Cambridge, MA: Harvard University Press, 1971, pp. 432– 433.
23. L. May, 'Killing Naked Soldiers: Distinguishing between Combatants and Non-Combatants', *Ethics and International Affairs* 19, 2005, No. 3, 39–53, p. 41.
24. Augustine, *City of God*, trans. H. Bettenson, London: Penguin Books, 1972, Book XIX, Ch. 7.
25. C. McKeogh, 'Civilian Immunity: Augustine to Vattel', in I. Primoratz, (ed.), *Civilian Immunity in War*, New York: Oxford University Press, 2007, p. 65.
26. McKeogh, 'Civilian Immunity: Augustine to Vattel', p. 70.
27. McKeogh, 'Civilian Immunity: Augustine to Vattel', p. 75.
28. Walzer, *Just and Unjust Wars*, p. 146.
29. C. Fabre, 'Guns, Food, and Liability to Attack in War', *Ethics* 120, No. 1, 2009, 36–63, p. 44.
30. D. Rodin, 'The Moral Inequality of Soldiers: Why Jus in Bello Asymmetry is Half Right', in D. Rodin and H. Shue (eds), *Just and Unjust Warriors*, New York: Oxford University Press, 2008, p. 49.
31. Rodin, 'The Moral Inequality of Soldiers', p. 52.
32. Rodin, 'The Moral Inequality of Soldiers', p. 48.
33. Rodin, 'The Moral Inequality of Soldiers', p. 50, n. 14.
34. G. Mavrodes, 'Conventions and the Morality of War', *Philosophy and Public Affairs* 4, No. 2, 1975, 117–131, p. 126.
35. Mavrodes, 'Conventions and the Morality of War', p. 125.
36. Mavrodes, 'Conventions and the Morality of War', p. 125.
37. Mavrodes, 'Conventions and the Morality of War', p. 127.
38. Mavrodes, 'Conventions and the Morality of War', p. 128.
39. Mavrodes, 'Conventions and the Morality of War', p. 130.
40. McMahan, *Killing in War*, p. 224.
41. McMahan, *Killing in War*, p. 223.
42. McMahan, *Killing in War*, p. 235.

Suggested reading

Seth Lazar, 'The Responsibility Dilemma for Killing in War: A Review Essay', *Philosophy and Public Affairs* 38, No. 2, 2010, 180–213.
Lazar's article offers an excellent critique of McMahan's position on both combatants and non-combatants.

George Mavrodes, 'Conventions and the Morality of War', *Philosophy and Public Affairs* 4, No. 2, 1975, 117–131.
Mavrodes gives an influential account of non-combatant immunity as a useful convention rather than as a reflection of the moral status of non-combatants.

Larry May, 'Killing Naked Soldiers: Distinguishing between Combatants and Non-Combatants', *Ethics and International Affairs* 19, No. 3, 39–53.
May emphasises the need for a moral distinction between combatants and non-combatants, and argues that current approaches to this distinction are too rough-grained.

Cécile Fabre, 'Guns, Food and Liability to Attack in War', *Ethics* 120, No. 1, 2009, 36–63.
Fabre undermines many of the arguments that try to distinguish the types of contributions that non-combatants make in war.

8   The moral status of terrorism

The recent surge of interest in just war theory is attributable in no small part to the significant and prolific rise in terrorist activity over the past decade. Of course, terrorism is not a new phenomenon. The term 'terrorism' was first coined during the French Revolution in the eighteenth century, and terroristic activities go back as far as Ancient Rome. The IRA (Irish Republican Army) employed a sustained campaign of terrorism against the British in the 1970s, and ETA (Euskadi Ta Askatasuna) have been blowing things up in Spain for the past forty years. What has lately changed is the amount of *inter-state* terrorism. In the past, terrorism was a largely domestic problem, with small groups using violence against their own governments or occupying forces in a bid to change domestic policies. Now, terrorism has an undeniably international dimension, crossing borders in a way that seems to take it beyond the realm of 'ordinary' criminal violence and into the realm of warfare. These international terrorists primarily seek to change not the domestic policies of their own countries, but the foreign policies of the countries they target. In this chapter, we will look at whether there is anything conceptually distinctive about terrorism, and whether there is anything morally distinctive about terrorism. We will also consider whether terrorism can ever be morally justified.

WHAT IS TERRORISM?

It is unlikely that there is any single feature (or group of features) that is found in all and only terrorist acts. For example, some people characterise terrorism as violence perpetrated by non-state actors – that is, by people who do not represent the state. But we can think of countless acts of violence perpetrated by non-state actors that are clearly not terrorism. A pub brawl is violence perpetrated by non-state actors, but it is not terrorism. Moreover, some writers argue that there are actions that are terroristic but not violent, such as failed terrorist attacks and terrorist threats.

So, rather than try to identify a single defining feature of terrorism, we will look at a group of features that are commonly thought to be relevant to assessing whether an action counts as terrorism:

1. It is politically motivated.
2. It is aimed at non-combatants.

3. It is perpetrated by non-state actors.
4. It is violent.
5. It is intended to generate fear.

Some instances of terrorism will display all of these features, but others may display only some. We will consider each feature in turn.

Political motivation

That terrorism is politically motivated is perhaps the least contested aspect of terrorism. It is this feature that is usually thought to distinguish terrorists from a common or garden mass murderer or serial killer. Jack the Ripper may have killed innocent people and spread terror amongst the population of London, but not many people think that the Ripper was a terrorist. The most obvious difference between the Ripper and, say, Al-Qaeda, is that the Ripper's killings were not politically motivated. Unlike ordinary murderers, terrorists have a *political agenda* that their attacks are intended to further.

This agenda might be to induce a state to cease the occupation or invasion of another state, to ban animal experimentation, to halt the development of nuclear weapons or to reduce environmental damage. Whatever its content, the agenda matters because it is this that gives terrorist attacks their instrumental (or, as it is sometimes called, their *symbolic*) nature. Terrorist attacks are not ends in themselves; they are part of a broader plan. For example, animal rights terrorists do not try to stop animal experimentation by systematically killing all scientists involved in such experiments. Rather, they kill a few scientists in order to scare *other* scientists into halting their experiments, and to induce citizens in general to pressurise their government into banning animal experimentation. The effectiveness of the initial killings in achieving the terrorists' goal comes not from preventing the targeted scientists from carrying out experiments, but from the wider political effects of the killings. Ultimately, terrorist attacks are not about killing people, but about getting people to behave in ways that further the terrorists' goals.

It is, in part, this instrumentality of terrorism that distinguishes it from other forms of political violence. Take the Rwandan genocide in 1994, in which hundreds of thousands of Tutsis were slaughtered by Hutus seeking to ethnically cleanse Rwanda. Such slaughter is obviously political violence in the extreme. But the aim of the killings was not to spread fear amongst, or manipulate, the Tutsi population. Rather, the aim was to achieve the goal of 'ethnic purity' by systematically eradicating Tutsis. There was nothing symbolic about these killings – they were ends in themselves. This explains why we do not typically describe such killings as terrorism, even though they are clear examples of politically motivated violence.

So, that an action furthers a political agenda is not sufficient to make it an act of terrorism. But is a political agenda nonetheless a *necessary* condition of terrorism? Well, whilst an agenda of some sort seems necessary to capture the instrumental nature of terrorist attacks, we might question whether it needs to be a *political* agenda. Imagine that Jack the Ripper had the agenda of deterring prostitution in London. He might have hoped that by killing some prostitutes, he could induce others to change their behaviour. If so, he certainly seems to have an agenda. Does this mean that we ought to classify him as a terrorist?

One argument against doing so is that there is a difference between trying to exert illicit influence upon a political system and trying to influence the non-political behaviour of a small group of individuals. To reiterate an earlier point, many people take sovereignty – including political integrity – to be of immense importance. Whilst what the Ripper did was very bad indeed, he did not try to manipulate the political integrity of a state for his own ends. His actions, even if successful, would have had much more limited ramifications than those of someone with a specifically political agenda. Of course, it doesn't follow from this that his actions were morally any better or worse than those of a politically motivated terrorist. But they might nonetheless be different in *kind* to the actions of the politically motivated terrorist, because the Ripper's actions do not undermine, or threaten to undermine, the sovereignty of the state in which he operates.

Of course, that we *can* draw this distinction between political and personal agendas does not entail that we *ought* to draw it. Whether we ought to draw it will depend on how broad an account of terrorism we want to endorse. An advantage of a broad account will be that it is more likely to capture all of the actions that strike us as terrorism. But a disadvantage of such an account is that it will not capture only those things that strike us as terrorism. Counting as terrorism any violent action that furthers any agenda will lessen the moral force that attaches to the label 'terrorism'.

Compare our use of the concept 'torture'. If we define torture as simply 'the intentional infliction of pain', we are committed to a very broad account of torture that will probably include all those actions that strike us as torturous. The abuse of detainees in Abu Ghraib will count as torture on this account. But this account will also include actions that don't strike us as torturous, such as a mother smacking her child or a person's inflicting defensive harm. Even if we think that smacking children is wrong, we probably don't think that it is an act of torture. And, since these intentional inflictions of pain are much less obviously wrong than the abuse of prisoners in Abu Ghraib, counting them as torture dilutes the moral connotations of the term itself. Saying that an action is torture will no longer tell us much about its moral content.

By opting for a narrower account of torture, we need not deny that non-torturous inflictions of pain can be wrong. Perhaps smacking one's child *is* wrong. But the narrower account better captures the idea that torture is a distinctive *sort* of infliction of pain. Similarly, by opting for a narrower account of terrorism, which holds that only politically motivated actions count as terrorism, we can preserve terrorism's alleged distinctiveness.

Of course, not all politically motivated groups are terrorist. Indeed, we might think that not all politically motivated *violent* groups are terrorist. Armies are politically motivated violent groups. It is precisely the desire to demarcate terrorism within the broader field of political violence that gives rise to attempts to identify something distinctive about the sort of political violence that terrorists perpetrate. With this in mind, let's examine the other features listed above.

Attacking non-combatants

When we hear about terrorist attacks in the news, what is typically emphasised is that these were attacks that killed (or were intended to kill) 'innocent people'. In the context of war, the term 'innocent person' is often taken to be synonymous with 'non-combatant'. It is the fact that terrorists *intentionally* kill non-combatants that is generally thought to mark terrorist killings out from the collateral killings perpetrated by combatants in war.

As we saw in the previous chapter, it is not obvious that non-combatants can lay claim to innocence when their countries are engaged in fighting a war. Nor is it obvious that the intending/foreseeing distinction makes a difference to an action's permissibility. These debates might influence our moral assessment of terrorist attacks. But that terrorists usually aim at civilian targets, rather than military targets, might still be a distinctive conceptual feature of terrorism. It seems to distinguish terrorism from combatant killings and from guerrilla warfare. But it does so by seemingly conceding an important claim to terrorists, namely that they are engaged in genuine warfare. 'Non-combatant' is a military term (as is 'civilian'), and makes sense only when contrasted with combatants (who are, by implication, legitimate targets).[1]

If we want to deny, as many people do, that terrorists are engaged in warfare, it doesn't make much sense to offer an account of terrorism that relies upon these military distinctions. But if we remove these military terms from our analysis, we seem to be left with the claim that what is distinctive about terrorism is that it involves intentionally killing people. And this raises similar concerns to those noted above with respect to the broadness of our account. After all, ordinary murderers intentionally kill people all the time, as do state executioners and people engaged in self-defence. We do not want our account of terrorism to label all such killings terroristic.

Focusing exclusively on the *targets* of terrorist killings to identify terrorism's distinctiveness thus seems to undermine the idea that there is something conceptually distinctive about terrorism, since the killing of innocent people is a feature of more than just terrorism. But if we combine the targeting of non-combatants with the criterion of political motivation, we might be better able to capture what is distinctive about terrorism. Just as euthanasia is distinguished from other kinds of intentional killing because of the agent's benevolent motivation, perhaps terrorism is distinct from other kinds of killing (and other kinds of other violence) because of both its distinctively political basis *and* its targeting of non-combatants.

However, it is worth noticing that there have been attacks upon combatants that some people think qualify as terrorist attacks. For example, the group behind a planned attack on an Australian army base in 2009 were described as terrorists, even though it seemed clear that their plan involved killing only combatants. President Bill Clinton described the attack on the US Navy ship *USS Cole* in 2000 as an act of terrorism. Why would we call these attacks on obviously military targets acts of terrorism? The most obvious answer is that the attacks were sponsored and organised by terrorist groups – that is, groups that are responsible for other politically motivated attacks on non-military targets. Al-Qaeda claimed responsibility for the *Cole* attack, and the planned attack on the Australian base is alleged to have been backed the Somali group al-Shabaah, who also have links to Al-Qaeda. Describing these attacks as terrorist implies that any attack carried out by a terrorist group – whether aimed at non-combatants or not – is itself terrorist. It also reflects the assumption that terrorism is about what we might call the *pedigree* of the perpetrators. The attack on the *Cole* was an act of terrorism not because of the nature of the target, but because of the nature of the attackers. It is to the idea of terrorism as non-state violence that we now turn.

Non-state violence

As we saw in Chapter 3, one of the *ad bellum* requirements of a just war is that the war be fought by a legitimate authority. We also noted that, for many people, this is a condition not only of a war's being a just war, but of its being a war at all. Only legitimate authorities – usually understood as heads of state – have the capacity to declare war. If terrorists are not legitimate authorities, this might give us a way to clearly distinguish the killings carried out by terrorists from the killings carried out by regular combatants in war. Unlike regular combatants, who are employed by their state to carry out military operations, terrorists act independently: they are non-state actors. Perhaps terrorism can thus be characterised as unauthorised political violence.

The importance of legitimate authority stems from the idea that the state should have a monopoly on political violence. On entering society, citizens give up what Thomas Hobbes calls their 'natural right' to use violence, transferring this right to the state in return for the state's provision of security and order.[2] Thus, whilst states (and their representative agents) can legitimately use force, private individuals cannot. Of course, a private individual can use self-defence if necessary. But the explanation of the permissibility of self-defence is that, in a situation where my life is threatened and defence is necessary, the state has failed in its part of our bargain. It has not provided me with security, and thus I re-acquire my natural right to use force. With the exception of these cases, however, it is only the state that has a right to use force.

There is an obvious worry with defining terrorism as political violence carried out by non-state actors. As Robert E. Goodin puts it, such a definition 'conceptually immunizes' agents of the state against allegations of terrorism, making the idea that state actors might engage in terrorism conceptually incoherent.[3] Goodin points out that, for example, the definition of terrorism endorsed by the US government in the *United States Code* stipulates that ' "terrorism" means premeditated, politically motivated violence perpetrated against noncombatant targets by *subnational groups or clandestine agents*' (emphasis added).[4] This account of terrorism precludes, in principle, that a person acting on behalf a national body – the state – might be guilty of terrorism:

> The *US Code*'s definition of 'terrorism' would have us think [that] states and their official agents can commit many wrongs strictly analogous to those committed by terrorists, perhaps; but they cannot commit the particular wrong peculiar to 'terrorism', which is (as with 'piracy') doing those things 'privately' rather than on the authority of some state.
> (R. E. Goodin, *What's Wrong with Terrorism?*, Cambridge: Polity Press, 2006, p. 55)

Goodin's interpretation of the Americans' stance does seem to fit well with their frequent focus on the illegitimacy of terrorist actions (that terrorists are 'unlawful combatants'), which implies that the pedigree of terrorists is central to the concept of terrorism. Terrorists, unlike states, lack the proper authority to engage in political violence.

We can of course see why it would be advantageous for a state to endorse definitions of crimes that have built into them the notion that they are things that other people do. But using such a definition of terrorism is implausible for a number of reasons. For a start, it seems to involve mistaken assumptions about the scope of state authority. Notice that the *US Code*'s definition of terrorism talks about violence *aimed at non-combatant targets* (a stipulation which is, incidentally, hard to reconcile with Clinton's assertion that the attack on the *USS Cole* was an act of terrorism). But violence aimed at non-combatants is prohibited by international law. If international law 'trumps' domestic law, it is hard to see how a state could be properly said to *authorise* such violence. States do not have the authority to override the laws of armed conflict. So, even if a state actor is ordered to carry out such an attack by their superiors, this order cannot grant them the authority to carry it out, any more than you or I could grant them that authority.

We might also object that it is simply false that states cannot engage in terrorism. Indeed, we might think that the vast majority of terrorism is perpetrated by states. States can engage in terrorism by sponsoring terrorist groups: by giving them financial support, trading arms with them, providing them with a safe haven for evading capture and allowing the terrorists to set up training camps within their territory. Several countries, including the

USA, have refused to recognise a distinction between terrorists and those who 'harbour' them in this way. If supporting a terrorist group is enough to make one a terrorist, it seems that plenty of states engage in terrorism.

State-sponsored terrorism can also involve much more direct interaction with terrorists. Many people thought that the Libyan government orchestrated the 1998 Lockerbie bombing – the Libyan government itself eventually acknowledged responsibility and paid compensation to the victims' relatives. But the involvement of the Libyan government – of the state actors – doesn't seem to make the Lockerbie bombing any less an act of terrorism. Indeed, the USA has a 'terrorism exception' in its Foreign Sovereign Immunities Act (FSIA). The FSIA emerged out of trade disputes between US companies and overseas contractors. Under customary law, states were immune from prosecution in foreign courts. But as states became increasingly involved in international trade, their assumed independence was seen as giving states an unfair advantage in trade disputes. Companies could be held to legal account should they breach an agreement, but states could not. The USA, along with the UK, began to revise the law on prosecuting states, rejecting absolute immunity in favour of a more limited immunity.[5] And in 1996, Congress passed legislation permitting people to bring lawsuits in the USA against states that were responsible for terrorist acts involving US citizens even if those attacks had occurred abroad. The very existence of this exception suggests that the USA is not consistently committed to the idea that only actions perpetrated by subnational or clandestine agents can count as terrorism.

The second way in which a state might engage in terrorism is by employing so-called *state terror*. Many states use violent secret police forces to routinely imprison, torture and kill their own citizens. These tactics are intended to spread fear amongst the population, and are usually politically motivated. Such tactics seem clearly terroristic in nature. However, as Samuel Scheffler points out, despite these similarities, state terror is different in character to 'ordinary' terrorism.[6] Ordinary terrorism aims at destabilising a regime in order to effect change. State terror is almost always about bolstering control in order to maintain the status quo. Of course, preserving an existing regime is a manifestly political agenda, and presumably state terror has the same effect as ordinary terrorism, namely of getting people to behave in ways that further the authors' ends. But it isn't clear whether state terror undermines sovereignty as other forms of terrorism do. On the face of it, maintaining control seems like a way of preserving sovereignty, since sovereignty is all about power over one's territory and political system.

However, perhaps state terror undermines sovereignty in a different way. Recall the idea of conditional sovereignty from our discussion of humanitarian intervention in Chapter 4. This was the view that states can jeopardise their claim to sovereignty by systemically violating or failing to protect their citizens' human rights. This erosion of sovereignty paves the way for wars of intervention. States that engage in state terror might undermine their sovereignty in *this* way – not by causing internal instability, but by lessening the strength of their claim that other states not interfere in their affairs. If so, state terror can also threaten a state's sovereignty, albeit in a way unintended by the authors of the terror.

Thinking about state-sponsored terrorism and state terror makes it seem rather implausible that only those actions that are perpetrated by non-state actors can count as terrorism. Whilst it may be true of many instances of terrorism that they are so perpetrated, it seems unlikely that this is what *makes* them terrorist. To borrow from Goodin, there is good reason to think that states can be terrorists, too.

More violence

It might seem obvious that terrorism must be violent. This doesn't mean that it must involve violence against people. But if we include blowing up buildings, vehicles and the like as violent acts, this will probably cover most instances of terrorism that spring to mind. We might also count certain attempts at violence as terroristic too. Richard Reid's attempt to blow up a plane using explosives hidden in his shoes seems like terrorism, even though it was not, in the end, violent. This suggests that terrorism is a more 'holistic' concept than, say, murder. If a person tries and fails to commit murder, we say that they are guilty of attempted murder. But Reid is universally described not as an attempted terrorist, but as a terrorist. When we identify something as terrorism, then, we seem to place a significant amount of weight on actions leading up to the final attack, classifying these preceding actions as terrorism in and of themselves. Because of this, however, it looks as if an action does not have to be violent in order to count as terrorism. Actions leading up to a terrorist attack – buying explosives, boarding a plane and so on – are not themselves violent, but most people nevertheless count them as terrorism.

Goodin agrees that not all terrorist actions must be violent. For example, warnings of terrorism can count as terrorism. Imagine that someone makes a phone call to a shopping centre, warning of a bomb that is about to go off. If the caller is a police officer intending to get the building evacuated in order to save lives, this hardly seems like an act of terrorism. But if the caller is issuing a bomb threat in order to cause fear and panic, this *does* seem like an act of terrorism, even though phone calls are not themselves violent. And, making the phone call still seems like terrorism even in the event that the call is a hoax.

Goodin argues that this is because it is the agent's aims that distinguish acts of terrorism – that '[w]hat makes those warnings wrongful acts of terrorism is precisely the intention lying behind the acts, the intention to instil fear for political advantage.'[7] His claim that making threatening phone calls about bombs in order to induce fear and panic counts as terrorism seems plausible (even in the absence of actual bombs). But Goodin argues that the range of non-violent acts of terrorism goes far beyond these sorts of cases.

He suggests that a significant amount of mainstream political rhetoric and argument counts as terrorism. There is a difference between *warnings about terrorism*, such as the call from the police officer just described, and *terroristic warnings*. Warnings about terrorism are intended to inform people of a threat in order to avert harm. Such warnings might generate fear, but that is not the intention behind their issuance. Terroristic warnings, in contrast, aim at creating fear by reference to impending violence. And Goodin argues that some politicians issue warnings that aim to do just this.

This is not a new idea. Politicians are often accused by their opponents of 'peddling the politics of fear' – of trying to manipulate citizens into voting or behaving in particular ways by appealing to their anxieties. For example, the British government has been accused of playing on people's fear of terrorism in order get Parliament to pass legislation undermining civil liberties, presenting this legislation as 'counter-terrorism'. The government is not violent in its methods of manipulation, but Goodin thinks that such manipulation is nonetheless terrorism.

Goodin supports his claim by pointing out that whilst political leaders often insist that only violent attempts at political manipulation count as terrorism, other, more neutral, accounts do not endorse this view. For example, Goodin cites the *Oxford English Dictionary*'s definition of a terrorist:

> 'One who entertains, professes or tries to awaken or spread a feeling of terror or alarm; an alarmist, a scaremonger'. So insofar as politicians' warnings count as 'alarmist', they would indeed meet the dictionary's definition of 'terrorist' . . . The point is just this: people who do nothing more than issue warnings with the intention of instilling fear are in those other connections [e.g. the shopping centre case] deemed 'terrorists', provided they issue those warnings purely or predominantly for political purposes. Why not say the same of the public officials who do just the same?
>
> (Goodin, *What's Wrong with Terrorism?*, pp. 99–100)

Goodin is not denying that violence is part of terrorism. What he is denying is that all acts of terrorism must *themselves* be violent. There are terrorist actions that are not themselves violent, but rather 'piggyback' on the violent actions of others.

So, the hoax caller who issues the fake bomb threat at the shopping centre is engaged in terrorism, even though the phone call is non-violent, because the fear that the caller intends to create invokes or relies upon violence, albeit the violence of others. It is because terrorist groups have, in the past, planted bombs in shopping centres that bomb threats are effective tools of manipulation even when they are hoaxes. And, according to Goodin, politicians similarly rely upon the violence of others in creating fear that they can use for their own ends. It is because people are scared of attacks by Al-Qaeda that they accept the erosion of certain civil liberties by their government.

Of course, this need not commit us to the claim that there are no moral differences between politicians who deliberately engender and manipulate fear and terrorists who go around blowing up buildings. We can distinguish, morally, between different *sorts* of terrorism. Terrorism that involves killing people is worse than terrorism that does not. But if what is crucial to terrorism is the use of fear as a political weapon, and if acts of terrorism need not be violent, there seems to be at least a *prima facie* case for thinking that Goodin is right that politicians often employ terroristic tactics to achieve their goals.

This broad claim about what counts as terrorism might raise concerns similar to those I noted earlier about diluting the content of terrorism. But, unlike the killings of Jack the Ripper, the kinds of action that Goodin has in mind do seem to commit the particular wrong of undermining a state's political integrity. We might thus think that whilst the difference between paradigmatic terrorists and the Ripper is a difference in kind, the difference between paradigmatic terrorists and terrorising politicians is one of degree.

Fear

Scheffler suggests that 'if we define [terrorism] in a way that effaces or even breaks the connection between terrorism and terror . . . then we are liable to miss some of the moral saliences toward which the word "terrorism" gestures'.[8] Surprisingly, it is the 'terror' part of terrorism that is often neglected in accounts of terrorism, which tend to focus more on the targets and political objectives of terrorists. But, as we have seen in Goodin's analysis, the intentional creation of fear as a weapon does seem to make terrorism conceptually distinctive. Other crimes may cause fear, but they usually do so incidentally – as a side-effect of pursuing some other goal. For terrorists, the fear is crucial to their wider plans. The point of terrorism is to make people feel unsafe – to make them feel as if their government cannot protect them. This, in turn, can cause them to distrust their government and put pressure on them to bow to the terrorists' demands, or even seek to replace the government altogether.

Thinking about the sorts of targets that terrorists choose to attack, such as aeroplanes or high-profile political gatherings, can highlight the way in which terrorists deliberately cultivate fear. We all know that, for example, airport security is now incredibly rigorous. Every passenger is searched, scanned and questioned about their luggage. There are surveillance cameras, sniffer dogs and specialist police officers. Getting a bomb or other dangerous device onboard a plane is really quite difficult. And yet, even now, terrorists persist in their attempts to blow up planes. Why? Why target a plane, with all the inevitable obstacles, instead of a hospital or a cinema, which will have virtually no security and will be a comparatively easy target?

Disruption is one answer. Grounding planes causes massive inconvenience and costs governments and businesses money. But another answer, I suspect, is that hospitals and cinemas are *too* easy. It doesn't take a great deal of skill, resources or knowledge to plant a bomb in a hospital. Getting a bomb onto a plane, in contrast, requires resources, expertise, contacts and training. By blowing up planes, terrorists let us know that *even the very best* security that our government can provide cannot stop them. No matter how sophisticated or stringent the security measures, terrorists can and do overcome them. And that is pretty frightening in its own right. It tells us that the terrorists are well-organised, clever and well-connected: that they are part of larger organisations that train and fund them. They can blend in, undetected by the very people who are supposed to be watching for them, and who are specially trained to identify them. This assertion of the terrorists' power is as much a part of generating fear as the bombings themselves, and it is rendered all the more apparent if someone manages to get a bomb onto a plane than if they attack an unprotected hospital.

Of course, the seemingly most obvious way in which terrorists create fear is by randomly killing innocent people. The sense of vulnerability created by random attacks is powerful indeed. But, in fact, terrorist killings are not often entirely random. In terms of the *group* that is targeted, terrorists are usually very specific. They have to be, if they want to further a specific political agenda. They will target the British, the Israelis, people working for particular companies or in particular industries, and so on, picking the group best placed to bring political pressure to bear in a way that will further the group's ends. Where the process becomes random is with respect to the individuals *within* that group who are killed. By randomly killing within particular groups, terrorists make everyone who is a part of the group feel threatened, maximising the number of people who identify with the victims.[9]

This technique is especially effective at creating fear when the targeted group is one that cannot be easily exited, or cannot be exited at all, such as a national or ethnic group. Since the British cannot help but be British, terrorist attacks that kill randomly within this group create a feeling of helplessness and persistent vulnerability amongst its members. It is these sorts of attacks that best fit Michael Walzer's description of terrorism as attacks aimed at people not because of what they are doing, but because of who they are.[10]

For example, attacks that target military bases or politicians do not tend to spread fear amongst the general population. They might give rise to a sense of indignation or anger. But most people do not feel as if they themselves are in danger, since they do not identify with the group perceived to be at risk. In contrast, when terrorists kill randomly within a group that cuts across social boundaries, perhaps by blowing up a train on the London Underground, they are able to cause significant unrest amongst the society at large. As Scheffler says, '[f]iguratively and often literally, terrorism offers the biggest bang for one's buck'.[11] Hitting a target that resonates across a significant cross-section of society enables one to maximise the impact of a single attack.

Is the intention to create fear a necessary condition of something's counting as terrorism? I think Scheffler is probably right that accounts that overlook this feature are in some way bereft. The fear-based element is intrinsic to the *workings* of terrorism. Terrorists don't achieve political goals by killing off anyone and everyone who stands in the way of those goals (as in the case of the Rwandan genocide). The killings are not *eliminative* in this way. Rather, terrorists kill some people in order to influence others, and this influence comes about primarily because people are afraid of what else the terrorists will do.

Imagine that an animal rights group kill a couple of politicians who were planning to vote against a ban on animal experimentation. The killings are intended to scare other politicians into voting in favour of the ban. This seems like terrorism: the killings are politically motivated, and are intended to create fear as a means of manipulating behaviour. If, in contrast, the group simply murdered every member of Parliament who had planned to vote against the ban, this would be a very different method of achieving their goals. These people would be violent political activists. But I do not think they would be terrorists, because causing terror is not part of their plan. Such an approach would have more in common with the eliminative technique of genocide than the instrumental technique of terrorism.

WHAT'S WRONG WITH TERRORISM?

In the above discussion, we examined various features of terrorist actions without taking a stance on the overall moral character of terrorism. Analysing the morality of terrorism is by no means an easy task. There are two main issues that such analyses usually seek to address. The first is whether terrorism is morally *distinctive*. To say that something is morally distinctive is not to say that it is worse than other actions, or to say that it is always wrong. Euthanasia is a morally distinctive form of killing – it is not like abortion, and it is not like self-defence – but acknowledging this fact does not entail any claim about whether euthanasia is right or wrong, or whether it is better or worse than other forms of killing.

Of course, most of us probably think that terrorism is at least presumptively wrong. Terrorism often involves killing or maiming people who have not consented to be killed or maimed. Actions that cause these sorts of harm require strong moral justification. So, the second issue that moral analyses of terrorism address is whether such justification is possible.

The notion of justified terrorism is, on some views, an oxymoron, akin to justified murder. Since murder *just means* 'wrongful killing', it makes no sense to wonder if murder might sometimes be right, because this amounts to asking whether something that is wrong might be right. Similarly, some people defend a view of terrorism in which it is just part of the meaning of the word 'terrorism' that it is unjustified. We will not explore these arguments here, but rather will rather keep an open mind about whether terrorism could, under certain circumstances, be justified.

Killing non-combatants

That terrorists intentionally kill non-combatants strikes most people as not only conceptually distinctive, but also morally distinctive. But, as mentioned above, it is the *intentional* aspect of the killings, rather than the killings themselves, that is the focus of most people's condemnation of terrorism. Terrorist killings are not like combatant killings, we think, because terrorists aim at non-combatants.

However, we have already seen that some people reject the moral significance of the distinction between intended harm and merely foreseen harm. Combatants *know* that they are going to kill non-combatants. This is why collateral killings are described as *incidental*, rather than accidental. Of course, they do not intend the killings, and intentions often play a role in our moral judgements of actions. But, as Lionel McPherson argues, it is not obvious that intentions are *so* important that they can sustain the alleged moral distinction between terrorism and collateral damage:

> Acts of conventional war [. . .] are not as susceptible to evaluation through this feature of commonsense morality. The harm done to non-combatants through many of these acts is likely, foreseeable, avoidable, and extensive – which would appear to largely overshadow the relevance of the combatant's intentions to permissibility. Commonsense morality recognizes that agents might not be morally culpable when, despite what they reasonably could expect, they do unwarranted harm. But when the unwarranted harm can reasonably be expected, commonsense morality is not committed to recognizing that the agents' intentions make a moral difference. . .
>
> (L. K. McPherson, 'Is Terrorism Distinctively Wrong?', *Ethics* 117, No. 3, 2007, 524–546, p. 537)

McPherson suggests that even if we allow that intention is sometimes morally relevant, it does not follow that it always makes the difference between permissibility and impermissibility.

This becomes especially apparent when we think of those who generate unintended harm as a side-effect of pursuing a morally bad or neutral goal. Consider a factory owner who dumps his factory's waste into a local river because this is cheaper than disposing of it safely. His intention is only to save money. He does not intend to pollute the river and cause environmental damage. But few of us would think that this matters very much for our moral judgement of his action. Provided that he knew that the pollution was likely or even possible, we would probably hold him just as responsible for the damage as if he *had* intended it. That polluting the river was a side-effect of his action, rather than his end, does not make polluting the river permissible.

If so, it seems that there are times when intention makes little or no difference to the morality – and permissibility – of an action. As we saw in Chapter 7, some just war theorists argue that causing *any* foreseeable harm to non-combatants is impermissible – that the distinction between intending and foreseeing is simply irrelevant. McPherson's own view is that the difference in intentions simply pales into insignificance alongside the magnitude of the harms being inflicted. If he is right, invoking the difference in intentions between terrorists and combatants is not enough to show that terrorist killings are wrong in a way that collateral killings are not.

Legitimate authority and representative authority

However, McPherson is not claiming that terrorism is therefore permissible, or that all collateral killings are therefore impermissible. McPherson offers another explanation for why terrorism is wrong in a way that the violence of regular combatants is not. We have already encountered the objection that terrorists lack the legitimate authority to employ political violence. But McPherson argues that this objection does not quite hit the nail on the head. There is, he suggests, an important difference between a *legitimate authority* and a *representative authority*.[12] The criteria for legitimate authority make a poor vantage point from which to criticise terrorism because these criteria themselves lack moral credibility. One can, for example, be a legitimate authority by the lights of a Hobbesian social contract theory just in case one provides order and security for one's citizens. But this very minimal condition for legitimate authority confers legitimacy on even the most morally bankrupt of states. A harsh totalitarian regime can offer security for its people and count as a legitimate authority. But can we really judge the rightness or wrongness of terrorism by whether it fits with a notion of legitimacy that confers authority upon those sorts of states? McPherson thinks not. Failing to satisfy the 'morally weak, Hobbesian account of legitimate authority hardly seems a compelling reason for judging that nonstate terrorism is wrong.'[13]

What matters for the legitimacy of political violence is not whether one is a legitimate authority in the Hobbesian sense. Rather, McPherson argues, what matters is whether one can lay claim to representative authority, which results from an appropriate process of consultation with the people that one claims to represent:

> The deeply distinctive problem for nonstate terrorists now emerges. That they lack legitimate authority is only a rough indication of the problem. Political violence by nonstate actors is objectionable when they employ it on their own initiative, so that their political goals, their violent methods, and, ultimately, their claim to rightful use of force do not go through any process of relevant public review and endorsement. Nonstate terrorism's distinctive wrongness does not lie in the terrorism but rather in the resort to political violence without adequate licence from a people on whose behalf the violence is purportedly undertaken.
> (McPherson, 'Is Terrorism Distinctively Wrong?', p. 542)

Representative authority matters, in McPherson's view, because peoples are entitled to self-determination. Even in less than ideal states, there are usually processes of consultation that allow the citizens to influence how their state behaves. Thus, in the case of regular combatants, we can usually assume that they carry out the will of at least a majority of those whom they represent. But terrorist groups who claim to represent a people rarely give the members of that people the opportunity to endorse or reject them. McPherson's argument against terrorism is thus broadly Kantian, stressing that respect for peoples' autonomy requires allowing them to control what is done in their name. Terrorists who employ violence 'on behalf of' a people without properly consulting that people fail to respect its members' autonomous rights.

McPherson is not arguing that terrorist groups can never have representative authority of the sort that he describes. Some terrorists groups, such as the African National Congress (ANC), could lay claim to such authority. But that one is a representative authority is not sufficient to make the use of political violence permissible. No group – state or otherwise – is entitled to use force simply because it represents a people. Most terrorist groups not only lack representative authority, but also lack a just cause. However, like Scheffler, McPherson does not rule out the possibility that a terrorist group might have such a cause, and that, under certain circumstances, their use of terrorism might be permissible.

One difficulty with McPherson's account is that of discerning which groups count as 'peoples' of the sort that can confer authority upon their members to violently pursue their goals. McPherson grants that such peoples can emerge as a result of 'self-ascribed nationality, ethnicity, culture, or religion, or on the basis of being victims of common oppressors'.[14] But if we allow a great many shared features to form the basis of a people, nothing prevents, for example, fundamentalist Islamic militants from claiming this status. After all, they are all fundamentalist Islamic militants – they share this particular cultural or religious feature. It looks as if, by McPherson's lights, such a group can qualify as a people and bestow representative authority upon themselves.

Whilst acknowledging this worry, McPherson suggests that it is not as serious as it first appears.[15] Terrorist groups rarely claim to represent only a small minority, but tend to rather grander assertions about representing, for example, all Muslims or all Palestinians. McPherson argues that this is precisely because such claims give a more plausible impression of 'representative authority that is morally compelling.'[16] If this is the case, it implies that terrorist groups themselves endorse the idea that they must have wider endorsement than merely their own 'parochial source that answers only to the edicts of leaders who lack relevant public approval.'[17]

But it's not clear that this will satisfy those who level this objection. For a start, it seems a merely contingent fact that terrorists often make these claims. Such a fact cannot rebut the theoretical objection that McPherson's account gives us no way in which to restrict what counts as a people. Moreover, there are explanations of terrorist proclamations of representation that do not support McPherson's analysis. It seems possible that, for example, those terrorists who claim to represent all Muslims might really believe that they represent these people, and that their methods are approved by them. But this doesn't meant that they take their actions to be morally permissible *because* of this approval. It seems more likely that they think them permissible because of the 'parochial source' to which McPherson refers. *This* is the source of the morally credible licence. They just happen to (mistakenly) believe that other Muslims endorse this source too. So we cannot be so quick to assume that terrorists accept the need for endorsement by those whom they claim to represent. They might simply assume this endorsement because of prior assumptions that the Qur'an confers legitimacy on their actions, and that all Muslims endorse the Qur'an. For these people, there might not be any relevant public approval that invoking the Qur'an fails to satisfy.

Furthermore, only *some* terrorist groups seek to present themselves as acting on behalf of a wider people. Others, like animal rights activists and environmental terrorists, do not claim to act on behalf of *people* at all. Who ought to be consulted about the decision to use violence to further the cause of animal welfare? Who should have the power to sanction or prohibit violence in the name of this cause? In so far as we can make reasonable judgements about what the animals themselves would prefer, the onus would seem to be on those opposing the activists to show that their actions are not genuinely representative of the animals' preferences.

Still other terrorists do not claim to represent a people because they take their orders directly from some divine being (thinking that they are God's messengers on Earth, for example). If we assume, for the sake of argument, that there is no God, such a group or person cannot commit the wrong of violating God's autonomy by failing to engage him or her in a proper process of consultation. If what is distinctively wrong with terrorism is that terrorists claim to represent a group whilst failing to appropriately consult that group, thereby violating that group's rights of autonomy and self-determination, there will be a significant number of terrorist groups who do nothing distinctively wrong (although, should they lack a just cause, their action will still be wrong in the way that other unjust violence is wrong). Only those who lay claim to wide representation whilst failing to genuinely engage with that group will undermine that group's autonomous rights in the way that McPherson describes.

Using as a mere means

McPherson's rejection of intention as a way of distinguishing between terrorism and collateral damage also warrants closer attention. For example, Scheffler argues that it is not simply that terrorist killings are *intended* that makes them morally different from combatant killings. The distinctive wrong of terrorism is more specific. Terrorists don't just intentionally kill non-combatants – they also *make use* of their victims in a morally distinctive way.

Recall the earlier description of how terrorists typically choose their targets – that they select a specific group, and then randomly kill a subset of that group. Scheffler describes the members of this subset as the terrorists' primary victims. But these victims are not only intentionally killed. They are also *used*: it is their deaths that enable the terrorists to spread fear and instability amongst the remaining members of the target group. Scheffler calls these remaining members of the target group the secondary victims of terrorism, because it is they whom the terrorists intend to terrorise. These secondary victims are also used as mere means in their turn, since it is they who are manipulated into bringing political pressure to bear on their leaders. The secondary victims, just like the primary victims, are crucial tools in achieving the terrorists' goals. Scheffler thus argues that terrorism is morally distinctive not simply because terrorists intend the deaths of their primary victims, but because they use those victims as a *means to a means*, an extreme violation of the Kantian prohibition on using people.

Kant argued that we should always treat people as ends in themselves, respecting them as autonomous individuals with their own projects and goals. If I go on a date with you just to make somebody else jealous, I fail to treat you as an end in this Kantian sense. By regarding you merely as a way of getting what I want, I fail to accord you the proper respect that you deserve as a human being. I don't think about *your* goals or projects, but only about how you can help me further mine. You could rightly complain that in dating you, I was just *using* you. Terrorism, according to Scheffler, abuses people in the extreme of this Kantian sense. All members of the target group are viewed as tools to be manipulated in the pursuit of some goal that they do not share. Such treatment is the epitome of lack of respect for persons:

> Those who engage in this kind of terrorism do not merely display callous indifference to the grief, fear and misery of the secondary victims; instead, they deliberately use violence to cultivate and prey on these reactions. This helps to explain why there is something distinctively repellent about terrorism, both morally and humanely.
> (S. Scheffler, 'Is Terrorism Morally Distinctive?', *Journal of Political Philosophy* 14, No. 1, 2006, 1–17, p. 10)

By deliberately engendering 'fear and misery', terrorists do something not only morally *distinctive*, but, in Scheffler's eyes, morally abhorrent. When terrorists mount a sustained campaign of attacks, they create an environment where people live in perpetual fear, unable to carry out their normal lives. Scheffler echoes Hobbes' claim that, '[c]ontinual fear – not momentary anxiety but the grinding, unrelenting fear of imminent violent death – is unspeakably awful . . . A life of continual fear is scarcely a life at all.'[18] Scheffler does not, however, argue that terrorism is always wrong, even though he does think it a *prima facie* evil.[19] He leaves it open whether there could be circumstances that are themselves so awful that the use of terrorism is justified as a way of overcoming those circumstances.

Goodin's account of the moral distinctiveness of terrorism is also broadly Kantian, and reflects his claim that the conceptual distinctiveness of terrorism comes from the use of fear to achieve political goals. Goodin argues that fear-mongering in this way subverts citizens' capacity to reason clearly, causing them to vote or lobby reactively, rather than rationally. In other words, terrorists erode what Kant identifies as most valuable about people, namely their 'capacity for autonomous self-government, both individually and collectively.'[20]

Goodin describes this as a primarily political wrong, rather than a moral wrong, although of course the two are not mutually exclusive. Terrorism is morally distinctive, and morally bad, because it threatens our ability to rationally participate in the state, thereby threatening our ability to shape our own lives. Of course, neither Scheffler nor Goodin denies that much of the moral *gravity* of terrorism comes from the fact that terrorists intentionally kill people. It is the killing that makes terrorism morally serious. But Kantian analyses can show us why terrorism also seems morally different.

Permissible terrorism?

Tony Coady argues that terrorism is clearly wrong. But, he says, it may be that terrorism is like lying – usually wrong, but sometimes justified: 'The really interesting moral issue is thus not whether terrorism is generally wrong, but whether it is nonetheless sometimes morally permissible.'[21] As we have seen, several contemporary just war theorists are at least open to the idea that terrorism could, under certain circumstances, be justified. Most people do, after all, accept that it can be permissible to incidentally kill some non-combatants in a just war. If non-combatant lives can be weighed against just ends, it seems possible that they can be so weighed not only by states, but also by terrorists. And even if we think that intentional killing requires much *more* justification than incidental killing, this is compatible with thinking such justification possible. The threshold, though high, might yet be attainable. So what sort of causes might be so morally important as to warrant intentional killing of the sort that terrorists employ?

Saul Smilansky argues that, in the absence of gratuitous poverty or severe oppression, merely being under foreign rule cannot justify terrorism. Smilansky's view echoes the ideas put forth in Chapter 3 regarding proportionality and just cause. Recall May's and McMahan's claims that even if a nation suffers the appropriate sort of wrong to have a just cause for war, such as the illegal annexing of its land, war can nonetheless be disproportionate and therefore unjust. Similarly, even if the group whom the terrorists represent (and might *genuinely* represent in the way that McPherson requires) have suffered an appropriate wrong, it does not follow that terrorism is a proportionate response.

Smilansky argues that to have a chance of being justified, terrorism must be employed for a proportionate just cause, and be a last resort after all other means have been exhausted. As an indication of the sort of historical causes which might have met these conditions, Smilansky lists the 'almost genocidal' situations of Biafra, Cambodia, Rwanda, Sudan and East Timor.[22] These are cases in which the cause is clearly proportionate, since 'there is clear danger to a group's very existence or [of] the mass extermination of noncombatants.'[23]

He also suggests that terrorism might be warranted as a means of drawing the world's attention to poverty in the Developing World, where the catastrophic effects of famine and deprivation have been allowed to rage largely unchecked.[24] If a state inflicted this amount of suffering upon another state in an act of aggression, this would be a proportionate cause for war. And since the suffering is so *very* great, it could plausibly serve as a proportionate cause for terrorism as well.

Finally, Smilansky suggests that terrorism could be a permissible means to toppling tyrannical regimes. Where a regime is undemocratic and severely oppressive, it is often only by forcefully ousting its leaders that change can be brought about. In such cases, Smilansky suggests that 'limited and narrowly focused terrorism' could be justified (assuming that such force had a good chance of being effective).[25]

However, Smilansky concludes that what is interesting about terrorism is that it is widely employed in cases where it is obviously unjustified, and only rarely employed in cases where it would be justified. People have used terrorism extensively in the name of religious extremism, but not, for example, to try to galvanise the West into combating poverty in the Developing World:

> Our result implies that the world is curiously disjointed. Perhaps there are situations where terrorism has been contemplated but not pursued as a result of good moral reasoning. Still, in a striking way the role of adequate moral reflection is shown in its emptiness – both when the efforts at justification ought to yield negative results and when they ought perhaps to yield positive ones. Within the societies and cultures that have generated terrorism, or support it, moral deliberation has failed to be effective. The thought that terrorism can be adequately guided by processes of justification is an illusion . . . Our conclusion, in brief, is that the connection between justification and actualization is severed: under such conditions, engaging with the issues in the hope of 'fine tuning' the permission of terrorist activity is far too risky. We should err on the side of not allowing terrorism.
>
> (S. Smilansky, 'Terrorism, Justification and Illusion', *Ethics* 114, 2004, 790–805, pp. 799–800)

Smilansky's claim is that we do grave harm, and no good, by entertaining the possibility that terrorism can be justified. By failing to unequivocally condemn terrorism, we give succour to those who 'justify' their causes by some parody of moral deliberation. Smilansky suggests that the sort of people who resort to terrorism are, by and large, the sort of people who bypass moral reasoning altogether, being motivated instead by religious fanaticism and ancient feuds. He argues that we are obliged, given the apparent irrelevance of justification in cases of actual terrorism, to denounce terrorism across the board, lest those with malevolent causes make use of our arguments for their own ends. He cites Bernard Williams's observation that engaging in moral philosophy is itself morally perilous, since 'we may run the risk of misleading people on important matters.'[26]

Whilst it might be true as a matter of empirical fact that terrorists abuse the notion of justification for their own ends, Smilansky's thoughts on how we should respond to this abuse are both surprising and, I think, unattractive. Of course, we can be mindful of the practical implications of advancing particular views. But there are a great many arguments in moral philosophy that are open to abuse. Offering justifications for euthanasia runs the risk that one's arguments will be gleefully adopted by some grasping relative keen to bump off granny before her time. But even if this might be a good argument for making euthanasia illegal, it is not a good argument for prohibiting moral discussion of euthanasia.

Moreover, if we're talking about practical implications, Smilansky's own view is that the sort of people who engage in terrorism don't really care about moral justification, being motivated instead by religious fanaticism and ancient feuds. But such people are then unlikely to be any more swayed by an unequivocal condemning of terrorism than they are by the revelation that their cause in fact fails the justification test.

The sort of people who might care about justification, however, are the sort of people whom Smilansky identifies as *having* a just cause, such as those facing genocide or horrific oppression. Such people are not motivated by religious fundamentalism, or by nationalistic hatred, but rather by a desperate need to defend their own lives. A case that is notable by its absence in Smilansky's discussion is that of the ANC, whose use of terrorism in a bid to overthrow the South African government and end apartheid seems to exactly fit Smilansky's description of limited and narrowly focused terrorism aimed at abolishing tyranny. And the ANC began as non-violent group, becoming increasingly militant only after peaceful means failed to produce results.

Given the terrible conditions imposed upon black South Africans during apartheid, and given that terrorism did seem to be a last resort in this case, many people think that it is precisely cases like this that make it worth discussing whether terrorism can be justified. And given Smilansky's own acknowledgement that terrorism is sometimes justified, and his claim that unjustified terrorists don't care about morality anyway, it seems that, by his lights, we can only make things *worse* by universally condemning terrorism. Doing so will not discourage those who lack just causes, but it may discourage those whose cause *is* just.

Chapter summary

In this chapter, we have examined both the nature and the morality of terrorism. We explored the features most commonly supposed to make terrorism distinctive, such as the use of force against non-combatants, and by non-state actors in pursuit of political ends. I suggested that different instances of terrorism might exhibit some or all of these features, and that there is unlikely to be one single characteristic that enables us to define what it is for something to be an act of terrorism. In the second part of the chapter, we moved from considering the conceptual nature of terrorism to examining the moral nature of terrorism. We looked at how just war theorists have tried to capture our sense that terrorists commit a peculiar wrong that makes terrorism unlike other forms of political violence. But I suggested that we should remain open to the idea that terrorism can, sometimes, be justified. In the final part of the chapter, we looked at the sorts of causes that might warrant terrorism, and considered Smilansky's suggestion that the risks of trying to justify terrorism are so great that we ought to simply prohibit it absolutely.

Questions for discussion

1 Do you think that there is any single feature of terrorism that makes it conceptually distinctive?
2 Is the fact that terrorists (often) kill people the most morally important feature of terrorism?
3 Should the state have a monopoly on political violence?
4 Do you think that terrorism might sometimes be justified? Under what conditions?
5 Could terrorism ever be preferable to open warfare (if, for example, it would lead to fewer non-combatant casualties)?

Notes

1. R. E. Goodin, *What's Wrong with Terrorism?*, Cambridge: Polity Press, 2006, p. 14.
2. T. Hobbes, *Leviathan*, New York: Oxford University Press, 1996, p. 86.
3. Goodin, *What's Wrong with Terrorism?*, p. 50.
4. *United States Code*, available at https://www.cia.gov/news-information/cia-the-war-on-terrorism/terrorism-faqs.html.
5. See M. B. Feldman, 'The United States Foreign Sovereign Immunities Act of 1976 in Perspective: A Founder's View', *International and Comparative Law Quarterly* 35, No. 2, 1986, 302–319, for an interesting discussion of the development of the FSIA.
6. S. Scheffler, 'Is Terrorism Morally Distinctive?', *Journal of Political Philosophy* 14, No.1, 2006, 1–17, p. 11.

7. Goodin, *What's Wrong with Terrorism?*, p. 102.
8. Scheffler, 'Is Terrorism Morally Distinctive?', p. 17.
9. Scheffler, 'Is Terrorism Morally Distinctive?', p. 7.
10. M. Walzer, *Just and Unjust Wars*, New York: Basic Books, 1977, p. 200.
11. Scheffler, 'Is Terrorism Morally Distinctive?', p. 9.
12. L. K. McPherson, 'Is Terrorism Distinctively Wrong?', *Ethics* 117, No. 3, 2007, 524–546, p. 539.
13. McPherson, 'Is Terrorism Distinctively Wrong?', p. 540.
14. McPherson, 'Is Terrorism Distinctively Wrong?', p. 543.
15. McPherson, 'Is Terrorism Distinctively Wrong?', p. 543.
16. McPherson, 'Is Terrorism Distinctively Wrong?', p. 543.
17. McPherson, 'Is Terrorism Distinctively Wrong?', p. 544.
18. Scheffler, 'Is Terrorism Morally Distinctive?', p. 4.
19. Scheffler, 'Is Terrorism Morally Distinctive?', p. 1.
20. Goodin, *What's Wrong with Terrorism?*, p. 158.
21. C. A. J. Coady, 'Terrorism and Innocence', *Journal of Ethics* 8, 2004, 37–58, p. 58.
22. S. Smilansky, 'Terrorism, Justification, and Illusion', *Ethics* 114, 2004, 790–805, p. 797.
23. Smilansky, 'Terrorism, Justification, and Illusion', p. 797.
24. Smilansky, 'Terrorism, Justification, and Illusion', p. 798.
25. Smilansky, 'Terrorism, Justification, and Illusion', p. 798.
26. Smilansky, 'Terrorism, Justification, and Illusion', p. 790.

Suggested reading

Samuel Scheffler, 'Is Terrorism Morally Distinctive?', *Journal of Political Philosophy*, 14, No. 1, 2006, 1–17.
Scheffler outlines a Kantian analysis of the moral nature of terrorism.

Lionel K. McPherson, 'Is Terrorism Distinctively Wrong?', *Ethics*, 117, No. 3, 2007), 524–546.
McPherson gives an interesting account of the wrongness of terrorism based on the idea of representative authority.

Robert E. Goodin, *What's Wrong with Terrorism?* Cambridge: Polity Press, 2006.
Goodin explores various conceptual aspects of terrorism and defends a broad account of what counts as terrorism.

Strictly speaking, this isn't further reading, but the Philosophy Talk Show (www.philosophytalk.org) has an interesting discussion with Alan Dershowitz on terrorism, posted on 6 January 2004.

9   Terrorists, torture and just war theory

The changing character of modern warfare has thrown up questions about some of our most fundamental assumptions about war, particularly the idea that only states can engage in warfare. It has also sparked a surprising and, for many, unwelcome debate about the permissibility of using torture as a means of combating political violence. In this chapter, we will consider the nature of conflicts between states and non-state groups. We will examine the suggestion that although terrorists are engaged in armed conflict of the sort governed by international law, they are not to entitled protection under the Geneva Convention. The second part of the chapter will investigate an issue that has been explored primarily in the context of counter-terrorism and the 'war on terror', namely the use of interrogational torture in 'ticking time bomb cases'.

THE LEGAL STATUS OF TERRORISTS

Combatants or criminals?

As noted in the previous chapter, terrorism is not a new phenomenon. What is new is its importance on the international stage. Many states have experienced domestic terrorist attacks, and have dealt with these attacks under domestic criminal law. If Spanish terrorists bomb a train in Madrid, this hardly seems a matter for international law. And even if the terrorists are not Spanish, but carry out attacks on Spanish soil, their prosecution still seems to fall within the remit of the Spanish government. We would not take seriously the terrorists' claims that they are combatants and should be treated as prisoners of war.

Things are more difficult, however, when the attacks are orchestrated from abroad by non-state actors, and are not isolated incidents but rather part of a prolonged campaign of violence. Prior to the attacks on the World Trade Center in 2001, Al-Qaeda was responsible for a series of attacks against American targets, such as the attack on the *USS Cole* in 2000, the bombing of the US embassies in Kenya and Tanzania in 1998 and the first attack on the World Trade Center in 1993. In a co-authored article, John C. Yoo and James C. Ho argue that the organised nature of Al-Qaeda's campaign, combined with the scale of the attacks and the fact that they were organised by a foreign group, qualify the 2001 World Trade Center attacks as an act of war (or, as it called in law, 'international armed conflict').[1]

Traditionally, of course, war has been conceived of as something that happens between states. But in the current political climate, the importance of the debate over legitimate authority has become ever more apparent. As I have described, there are those who take the *ad bellum* condition of legitimate authority to be a restriction not only on whether something is a *just* war, but on whether it is a war at all. But there is no longer a consensus on this point. Until recently, such debates would have been purely academic, because only states would have had the military capacity to launch attacks on a scale that could serve as a cause for war. When only states have the *capacity* to wage war, the question of whether non-state groups *could* wage war was practically redundant. This is no longer the case. Terrorists have shown that they have the capacity to cause massive devastation both at home and abroad. The question of legitimate authority amongst non-state groups is no longer academic, but politically pressing.

Yoo and Ho reject the assumption that only states can engage in war. The Geneva Convention clearly allows for the possibility of wars involving non-state groups when it refers to 'armed conflict not of an international character'.[2] This reference was intended to include civil wars under the terms of the Convention, but there is no reason why it shouldn't also apply to other forms of conflict waged by non-state groups. Yoo and Ho therefore maintain that international law clearly allows that non-state actors can engage in armed conflict, claiming that

> [I]t has long been recognized that formal concepts of 'war' do not constrain application of the laws of armed conflict and that non-state actors are properly bound by certain minimum standards of international law when they engage in armed hostilities.
> [J. C. Yoo and J. C. Ho, 'The Status of Terrorists', UC Berkeley: Boalt Hall, 2003, p. 7, available at http://www.escholarship.org/uc/item/7kt6n5zf (accessed 17 December 2010)]

In other words, Yoo and Ho reject the idea that our academic debates about the concept of war determine the scope of the international laws governing armed conflict. The two can come apart – even if terrorists are not engaged in war by the abstract standards of just war theory, they are engaged in armed conflict for the purposes of international law.

Classing terrorism as armed conflict implies that terrorists are combatants. This in turn implies that they ought to be entitled to protected status under the Geneva Convention. But Yoo and Ho deny that this follows. Yoo and Ho argue that terrorists cannot be protected by a treaty between *states*, since they are not represented at the state level. This is one reason why terrorists are not to be treated like armed forces who act on behalf of states that have signed the Convention. But, argue Yoo and Ho, even if terrorists *were* state actors, and could in principle be entitled to protection under the Convention, they would still be ruled out in practice from enjoying that protection. Whilst the international laws of armed conflict apply to all armed conflicts, the protections of the Geneva Convention apply only to *legitimate* combatants, that is, those who meet the qualifying conditions for combatants laid out in the Convention itself. Because terrorists fail to meet these conditions, they are *illegitimate* combatants. As such, they are not entitled to protection under the Geneva Convention.

Terrorists as illegitimate combatants

Let's remind ourselves of the conditions for qualifying as a combatant as laid out in the Geneva Convention. These conditions require that combatants:

- be part of a hierarchical group, such that there is a recognisable chain of command;
- wear a distinctive emblem that is visible from a distance;
- bear arms openly;
- obey the rules of *jus in bello* as laid out in the Convention.

Can terrorists meet these conditions? They could certainly meet the first. Terrorist groups are often well-organised, with a clear chain of command in which some members of the groups are subordinate to, and take orders from, others. The second and third conditions are more problematic. Terrorists notoriously try to blend in amongst the non-combatant population, eschewing uniforms and other signs that they are engaged in hostilities. They also tend to conceal their weapons (for example by wearing suicide belts or by carrying bombs in rucksacks).

However, as we discussed in Chapter 5, an Additional Protocol to the Geneva Convention allows that someone can fail the condition of wearing a distinctive uniform or emblem, and yet be granted combatant status. This Protocol also allows that combatants need not always bear arms openly. Provided that they bear arms openly whilst engaging the enemy or deployed on a mission, they do not forfeit their combatant status. Many guerrilla fighters meet only this weaker version of the condition. But perhaps terrorists cannot do even this. Even if a terrorist bears arms openly whilst engaged in an attack, he does not usually do so whilst 'visible to the adversary while he is engaged in a military deployment preceding the launching of attack', as required by the Convention.[3]

There are some attacks, however, where one is not visible to the enemy before or perhaps even during an attack. Guerrilla fighters often employ ambush techniques where they are hidden from the enemy until the moment of engagement. They also use snipers to kill from concealed vantage points. Indeed, plenty of regular combatants use such tactics. If one need only bear one's arms openly whilst visible to the enemy, and one is *not* visible to the enemy, it seems that concealing one's weapons prior to engagement doesn't always fall foul of the Convention. Of course terrorists are usually visible prior to attacks, and they hide their weapons whilst they are so visible. But if they concealed themselves before launching an attack, terrorists would appear to meet the revised condition of bearing arms openly.

It's hard to believe, however, that those opposed to granting terrorists combatant status would change their minds if only terrorists stuck to ambush-style assaults of the sort employed by guerrillas. This seems a pretty contingent fact upon which to hang the widespread condemnation of terrorism. What appears to most obviously disqualify terrorists from claiming combatant status, then, is their failure to meet the fourth condition. Terrorists do not obey the rules of *jus in bello*, because terrorists attack non-combatants and other civilian targets.

But even this failure does not straightforwardly preclude terrorists' being granted combatant status. Article 44.2 of the Additional Protocols of the Geneva Convention stipulates that while combatants are bound by the laws of war, 'violations of these rules shall not deprive a combatant of his right to be a combatant or, if he falls into the power of an adverse Party, of his right to be a prisoner of war.'[4] So, in fact, regular combatants do not forfeit their status as combatants (or as prisoners of war) even if they break the rules of *jus in bello*, provided that they bear arms in a way that meets the revised condition of the Convention.

The Convention also states that even when a combatant forfeits his right to be a prisoner of war because he has *not* borne his arms openly, 'he shall, nevertheless, be given protections equivalent in all respects to those accorded to prisoners of war by the Third Convention and by this protocol.'[5] This provision implies that, in fact, it is *not* a condition of being a combatant that one obey the rules of *jus in bello*, because it describes *as a combatant* someone who fails to adhere to those rules. And whilst strictly speaking such a person is not a prisoner of war, he is nonetheless to be *treated* as a prisoner of war.

Given this, it's not obvious that we can exclude terrorists from the class of combatant on the grounds that they break the rules of *jus in bello*, or that we can justify their extraordinary treatment on the grounds that they are not genuine prisoners of war. This position is supported by the part of the Convention that stipulates that combatants must be fairly tried before they can be convicted of breaching the *in bello* rules. Since the terms of the Convention prohibit trying prisoners of war for breaches of *jus in bello*, Detaining Powers cannot strip combatants of their legal status.

The ambiguity surrounding the criteria for qualifying as a combatant seems to support the idea that terrorists might qualify for protection under the Geneva Convention even if they breach the rules of *jus in bello*. Of course, they are still not state actors. But as we saw above, Yoo and Ho themselves emphasise a 'provision common to all four Geneva Conventions' that shows that the Convention applies to armed conflicts between non-state groups, because it applies to civil wars.[6] So, contrary to what Yoo and Ho claim, the

Convention does not apply only to state actors, and it is not only state actors who may be granted combatant status.

Terrorists as combatants

So, the case for viewing terrorists as illegitimate combatants seems less than compelling. But many people, especially regular combatants, baulk at the idea of granting terrorists legitimate combatant status. Members of the armed forces do not want to be ranked alongside those systematically breaking the rules that, in their eyes, constitute the moral fabric of war. And they may be right. Perhaps it is a mistake to confer a sort of legitimacy on terrorists by equating them with people who (generally speaking) obey the rules of *jus in bello*.

Those who want to resist the extension of normal combatant status to terrorists might insist that there are both legal and moral differences between members of a group who, as a matter of policy and general practice, adhere to the *in bello* rules and members of a group who, as a matter of policy and general practice, breach the *in bello* rules. When a person is a member of a regular armed force, the presumption should be that they are innocent of war crimes unless proven guilty. They should therefore retain their combatant status until they can be fairly tried. When a person is a member of a terrorist organisation, however, the presumption should be that they *are* engaged in committing war crimes. This is, after all, what terrorists do. They should therefore be denied combatant status.

However, this idea of guilt by association is itself indicative of combatant status. When a person is a member of the regular armed forces, he can be legitimately killed in virtue of that fact. His membership of the group makes him a legitimate target under international law. But non-combatants, even criminals, cannot usually be killed simply for belonging to particular groups. Nor can they be deemed guilty of crimes simply for belonging to a particular group. We cannot convict and punish one Mafia member for the crimes of another. So, if terrorists are criminals, and not combatants, it is hard to justify practices such as killing or imprisoning them on the basis of their group membership. This would make fighting against terrorist groups very difficult.

These difficulties might make us think that, despite our misgivings, it makes sense to treat terrorists as combatants. After all, the sorts of goals that terrorists pursue are akin to those pursued by states in war – territorial control, regime change and so on. Regarding terrorists as combatants would certainly fit with how terrorists view themselves. It might also give us a fairer fight against them. As mentioned above, combatants can be killed *for being combatants*. Classifying terrorists as combatants would eliminate the legal problem of attributing guilt (or liability) by association. Combatants can also be killed on the basis of *future* threats that they may pose. This is why one can kill enemy combatants even if they are in retreat. But one cannot kill non-combatants if they currently pose no threat, even if one believes that they will threaten in the future. Thus, classing terrorists as combatants makes it easier to kill them.

In terms of what some people might call the *dis*advantages of classing terrorists as combatants, we have the sorts of concerns that motivate Yoo and Ho's reluctance to endorse this status. Most significantly, such endorsement will entitle terrorists to prisoner of war status (they will no longer be the 'detainees' that we're so used to hearing about). This will mean, amongst other things, that they cannot be subjected to 'enhanced interrogation' by the Detaining Power. One of the functions of places like Guantánamo Bay is to extract information from suspected terrorists. If terrorists are counted as prisoners of war, the Geneva Convention protects them from attempts to obtain information about future attacks. They can be questioned, but they must not be threatened, insulted or coerced into giving up information. On the one hand, this will strike many people as a good thing. It will result in an unambiguous prohibition on the sort of methods currently employed against the residents of various 'detention centres', such as water-boarding, sleep deprivation, and so on. But on the other hand, it probably decreases the likelihood of obtaining information about future attacks on non-combatants.

In addition, terrorist prisoners of war who are not themselves convicted of attacks against non-combatants will have to be returned to their home countries once the war is over. The Geneva Convention prohibits trying or punishing combatants for fighting, even if their war is unjust. So, people known to be active members of terrorist groups could not be prosecuted unless there was evidence tying them to a specific breach of *jus in bello*.

Of course, the Convention stipulates that prisoners of war are to be returned home *once the war is over*. A further complication with asymmetric warfare is that it is often unclear when a war fought against terrorists *is* over. But this problem might be largely resolved by rejecting the idea that we can group all terroristic warfare as a single target in a 'war on terror'. We could individuate between terrorist campaigns just as we individuate between conventional wars. Sometimes, peace agreements can be reached with terrorist groups just as they are reached between states, such as that achieved with the IRA in Northern Ireland. Such agreements could serve as marking the end of the conflict, and the point at which prisoners should be returned. One could hardly justify, for example, holding onto IRA prisoners in Northern Ireland on the grounds that Al-Qaeda are still active in Pakistan.

Distinguishing between terrorist campaigns, then, could largely eliminate the problem of determining when a war with terrorists is over. Of course, terrorist campaigns often last much longer than conventional wars, and the more pressing concern might not be judging when the war is over, but knowing what to do with captured terrorists in the interim. Prisoners of war in 'normal' wars can usually expect to be released within a number of years at most. Terrorist campaigns can go for decades. Holding onto prisoners of war for this length of time without prosecuting them has its own moral, legal and practical difficulties.

Of course, the biggest theoretical implication of treating terrorists as combatants is that it undermines the idea of war as a conflict between states. In effect, we would be giving non-state groups the power to declare and wage war. Political violence would cease to be the monopoly of the state, and international affairs would no longer be conducted or shaped by heads of state. But, whilst this represents a significant shift in just war theory, it is, as Yoo and Ho suggest, perhaps already the case in practice. Some just war theorists have started to refer to 'asymmetric war' as a way of distinguishing between traditional inter-state war and the sort of war waged by non-state groups. Whether we like it or not, military threats are increasingly posed by irregular forces, be they insurgents, terrorists, guerrillas or freedom fighters. Counter-terrorism has become the primary focus of military strategists, security specialists and governments. It seems undeniable that war is no longer the exclusive domain of states.

TORTURING TERRORISTS

Liz Cheney (Mitt Romney's foreign policy advisor) was recently reported to have claimed that 'terrorists have no rights'.[7] The Keep America Safe organisation (of which Cheney is a leading member) criticises the Obama administration's policy of 'giving foreign terrorists the same rights as American citizens'.[8] And Cheney is certainly not alone in thinking that terrorists can be legitimately subjected to treatment usually shunned by liberal democracies. Thousands of suspected terrorists have been imprisoned without trial by the USA, occupying a legal black hole of the sort that we have just been examining. And nowhere has the debate become more heated than with respect to revelations that the USA, and some of its allies, have employed what strikes most people as torture against suspected terrorists.

What the Bush administration described as 'enhanced interrogation' includes water-boarding (to induce a sense of drowning), sleep deprivation, and forcing prisoners to stand for long periods of time (reportedly up to forty hours at a time), often in so-called stress positions. Of course, the right not to be tortured is generally thought to be a fundamental human right. The UN Torture Convention states that, '[n]o exceptional circumstances whatever, whether a state of war or a threat of war, internal political instability or any other public emergency, may be invoked as a justification of torture.'[9] The Convention gives the following definition of torture:

> Any act by which severe pain or suffering, whether physical or mental, is intentionally inflicted on a person for such purposes as obtaining from information, punishing him, intimidating or coercing him, when such

pain or suffering is inflicted by or at instigation of a public official or
other person acting in an official capacity.

[United Nations Convention Against Torture and Other Cruel,
Inhuman or Degrading Treatment or Punishment, 26 June 1987,
available at http://www2.ohchr.org/english/law/pdf/cat.pdf, Article
1.1 (accessed 22 March 2011)]

The first part of the definition seems plausible enough: torture is the
intentional infliction of severe pain or suffering upon a person as a means
of achieving of certain goals. The reference to persons acting in an official
capacity probably wouldn't strike most of us as part of a definition of torture,
but its inclusion here is indicative of the fact that the UN Convention is an
agreement between states that they will not engage in torture for political
ends. And the Convention is clear: no circumstances, no matter how dire,
justify torture.

So what is it about torture that makes it so abhorrent? David Sussman suggests that the wrongness of torture lies at least partly in the way that torture
subverts autonomy, forcing the subject into 'colluding against himself'.[10]

> Torture does not merely insult or damage its victim's agency, but rather
> turns such agency against itself, forcing the victim to experience herself
> as helpless yet complicit in her own violation. This is not just an assault
> on or violation of the victim's autonomy but also a perversion of it, a kind
> of systematic mockery of the basic relations that an individual bears both
> to others and to herself.
>
> (D. Sussman, 'What's Wrong with Torture?', *Philosophy and
> Public Affairs* 33, No. 1, 2005, 1–33, p. 30)

Sussman likens the wrong of torture to the wrong of rape, where it is
not so much the physical pain that makes the act abhorrent, but rather the
violation of the person and their autonomy. Some writers think that these
features make torture morally worse than killing. Henry Shue, for example,
suggests that we might think that, 'while killing destroys life, it need not
destroy dignity'.[11] But, as we will see, even if we all agree that torture is very
bad indeed, not everyone agrees that it is always wrong.

Ticking time bombs

Imagine that a terrorist has planted a bomb in a crowded shopping centre.
You, the local Chief of Police, capture the terrorist, but they refuse to tell
you where they have hidden the bomb. Only by torturing them can you get
them to reveal the bomb's location. If you do not torture them for the information, the bomb will go off and hundreds, perhaps thousands, of people
will be killed. Should you torture the terrorist?

We can divide the most popular arguments in favour of torturing the terrorist into two main camps. The first camp is utilitarian. These arguments hold that the harm that you will inflict upon the terrorist is outweighed by harm that you will thereby avert. It is the production of the greater good that justifies torturing the terrorist. The second set of arguments are deontological, and invoke the idea that torture can be a form of defence. Just as one may kill an attacker to save either oneself or an innocent third party, so may you torture the terrorist to save the lives of those in the shopping centre.

Utilitarian arguments for torture

The basic utilitarian argument for torturing the terrorist is clear. The amount of harm that you will cause the terrorist is massively outweighed by the saving of hundreds of lives. Even those not normally given to consequentialist leanings will be hard-pushed not to feel the force of this argument. Shoving needles under a person's fingernails is a horrible thing to do, but it is clearly justified by the enormous amount of suffering that it will avert.

One problem with utilitarian arguments of this sort is that they pay no heed to the difference between the guilty and the innocent. In our example, the person to be tortured is a terrorist. But what if, instead of capturing the terrorist, you have in your custody the terrorist's (wholly innocent) wife. By torturing her and broadcasting it over the internet, you will induce the terrorist to contact you with the bomb's location. The amount of pain that you will cause is the same, and the number of lives that you will save is the same. May you torture the terrorist's wife? What about his child? If all that matters is maximising the good, we can offer no reason why these innocent people are not to be tortured if that too will enable us to find the bomb.

Since most people do not think it permissible to torture an innocent person to find the bomb, the utilitarian argument is usually run alongside some other argument about the terrorist's guilt or responsibility. By planting the bomb, the terrorist makes it the case that he has no right not to be tortured if torturing him is necessary to save many lives. We can perhaps justify the inclusion of this condition on utilitarian grounds, citing the disutility of the fear we would produce if we allowed innocent people to be tortured along with the guilty. People's terror that they could be subjected to torture even if they do nothing wrong might change the outcome of the utilitarian analysis. If this argument is successful, it seems that utilitarian reasoning shows that you should torture the terrorist.

However, we cannot be so hasty. As Vittorio Bufacchi and Jean Maria Arrigo argue, a more careful study of the consequences of torturing the terrorist might not generate the result that the torture is permissible. Echoing a widespread complaint, Bufacchi and Arrigo draw our attention to a number of artificial aspects of the ticking time bomb scenario that could never be replicated in real life.[12] If it is these idealised aspects that make the torture permissible in a hypothetical case, torturing in a real-life time bomb case might still be impermissible.

Perhaps the most important artificial aspect of the hypothetical case is the stipulation that the torture will *work*. This assumption entails a number of further assumptions: that you have the right person; that if you torture him, he will talk; that the information he gives up will be reliable; that you will find the bomb in time; and that you will be able to defuse it before it detonates. In an actual case, perhaps only the first of these could be guaranteed. The others will be mere speculation. Information obtained through torture is not always (or even usually) reliable. And, even if you did acquire the bomb's location, you still might not succeed in defusing it in time. The case also stipulates that torturing the terrorist is the *only* possible way of finding the bomb. Again, in an actual case, there might well be other ways in which the bomb could be located. And the number of lives at risk in the hypothetical cases is always very great. Whilst some terrorist attacks do kill large numbers of people, many kill in much smaller numbers. The utilitarian pull on our intuitions might be considerably weaker in such cases.

So, we should be mindful of the fact that even if we think torture justified in our hypothetical case, this might be only because of the artificial stipulations that accompany it. However, it might be argued that the condition that I suggested as the only one likely to be satisfied in real life – that of knowing that you have the right person – is the only one that matters. The others are secondary, because provided we know that the terrorist is responsible for the attack, we are permitted to torture him even if there is only a *chance* that the torture will succeed. And this is not implausible. We can admit that the torture might not work or that the terrorist might give us false information. But surely we are allowed to *try* to stop the bomb, even if we ultimately fail? Why should we allow hundreds of people to die rather than torture the terrorist, simply because of the risk that he might not tell us the truth? The claim that the torture would be permissible if it would work does not entail that it is permissible *only* if it works. (Of course, we might be hard-pushed to justify this on a utilitarian basis. In cases where the chances that the terrorist will talk are small, we cannot straightforwardly trade the harm of torture against the benefit of saving lives.)

For the sake of argument, however, let's say that the chances of getting the terrorist to talk are high, and that the torture is thus expected to produce a net benefit. Even if we recognise that the stipulations of the hypothetical case are unlikely to be replicated in real life, then we could still judge the torture permissible in an actual case where the chances of success are high. But Bufacchi and Arrigo argue that this overlooks the *most* artificial aspect of the ticking time bomb case, namely the illusion that the torture takes place in some kind of social vacuum:

> We believe the ticking-bomb argument ultimately fails as a consequentialist argument because it ignores the intensive preparation and larger social consequence of state-sponsored torture. The validity of any consequentialist argument rests on a costs and benefit analysis. We argue that empirical evidence clearly suggests that institutionalizing torture

interrogation of terrorists has detrimental consequences on civil, military and legal institutions, making the costs higher than the benefits.

(V. Bufacchi and J. M. Arrigo, 'Torture, Terrorism and the State: A Refutation of the Ticking-Bomb Argument', *Journal of Applied Philosophy* 23, No. 3, 2006, 355–373, p. 362)

Allowing government agencies to employ torture as a form of counter-terrorism would require a veritable institution of people working to produce the most effective forms of torture. This institution would incorporate medical personnel, lawyers, scientists and members of the armed forces. Doctors and nurses would be required to, for example, advise on the sort of torture that a suspect could or could not withstand, or that might be more or less effective in a given case. They would have to resuscitate suspects who lost consciousness in order that they might be tortured again. Our societal image of the role of medicine would be radically altered. Doctors would no longer just help people. They would use their skills to facilitate the intentional infliction of pain and suffering. Bufacchi and Arrigo allege that where torture has been practised, the complicity of medical professionals has led to deep divides in the medical community.[13] And doctors who refuse to participate have themselves become targets of torture. These wider consequences of state-backed torture must be included in a utilitarian analysis of its permissibility.

So too must be the effects of torture on those doing the torturing. The torturers – usually members of the armed forces – will have to undergo 'desensitisation' training to enable them to carry out their duties. This training, designed to brutalise and degrade the torturers so that they can in turn stand to brutalise and degrade others, often causes the recruits to 'resort to denial, psychological compartmentalization, alcohol, or drugs'.[14] Bufacchi and Arrigo allege that the stigmatisation of torturers amongst even their own armed forces and communities results in yet more ruined lives, all of which count against a utilitarian justification for torture. And, they suggest, the use of torture would not stop with a few government agencies dealing with counter-terrorism. Other areas of law enforcement would demand similar powers. The harmful effect of torture on those doing the torturing would be multiplied accordingly. Bufacchi and Arrigo conclude that even if a utilitarian analysis of a single ticking time bomb case produces a net benefit, an analysis of the sort of *system* that practises state-sanctioned torture would surely not.

Bufacchi and Arrigo's arguments militate against the idea, advocated by Alan Dershowitz, that states should issue torture warrants that sanction the use of torture in extreme circumstances. Dershowitz argues that, under certain circumstances, government agencies will use torture whether or not doing so is legal.[15] Given that torture is inevitable, it is better that it be done openly, by people who can then be held accountable, than practised in secret and later denied or covered up. Dershowitz's justification is consequentialist – he thinks that the existence of a system of warrants would reduce the amount of torture carried out.

Certainly, there is something appealing in the idea that if a state is going to carry out torture, it should do it openly and accountably rather than behind closed doors. But is Dershowitz right that the best way to reduce the use of torture is by introducing official warrants? Bufacchi and Arrigo suggest that he is not:

> Dershowitz fails to appreciate that the time constraints of the ticking-bomb argument work against the accountability envisioned by legalizing torture interrogation and requiring prior 'torture warrants' from judges. Because destruction is imminent, the captors of the terrorists will not want to lose time obtaining a search warrant [. . .] Since the capture of the ticking-bomb terrorist is entangled with ongoing operations, where lives of agents and future counterterrorist operations are at risk, intelligence officers will not submit evidence of guilt to judges, whom they consider naïve and poor security risks.
>
> (Bufacchi and Arrigo, 'Torture, Terrorism and the State: A Refutation of the Ticking-Bomb Argument', p. 366)

Bufacchi and Arrigo have a point. It is supposed to be the very nature of these cases that time is of the essence. For the torture warrants to be anything more than a formality, the issuing judge would have to take the time to familiarise themselves with the case, assessing the evidence of an imminent threat, the subject's involvement and the likelihood of acquiring relevant information. This is the sort of time that is supposed to be lacking in the ticking time bomb cases.

If torture warrants were to play any role, it seems likely to be one of retrospective endorsement, with officials making the case for torture after the event. But denying warrants retrospectively will hardly stand in the way of torture that has already happened. In any case, torture that failed to yield results would likely be covered up, as it is now. The circumstances in which the warrants would be applied for *prior* to the torture seem likely to be those in which the need is less urgent and more speculative, for example when we believe that a person has valuable information, but we do not know of any particular imminent attack that the information might help avert. But in such cases, the necessity and purpose of the torture that are supposed to serve as its justification are much less apparent. It is precisely the fear that torture will become a common method of interrogation, and not a technique reserved for the direst of emergencies, that makes many people think that the state must enforce a total ban on its use.

Torture as defence

Uwe Steinhoff is also sceptical of the case for torture warrants. But Steinhoff does, however, think that torture can sometimes be permissibly employed. Moreover, he argues that it can be so employed not only in fantastical ticking time bomb cases, where a great many lives are at risk, but also in more mundane cases in which only one person's life might be saved by its use. Steinhoff claims that, '[t]here is no morally relevant difference between self-defensive killing of a culpable aggressor and torturing someone who is culpable of a deadly threat that can be averted only by torturing him.'[16] In Steinhoff's view, torture can be justified as a form of self- or other-defence.

Prima facie, it seems unlikely that we can justify torturing a person by invoking a right of defence. When someone is sufficiently at our mercy that we can torture them, any force used against them hardly seems able to meet the necessity condition of permissible defence. If I am the one torturing you, how I can also be defending myself against you? Shue thus calls torture 'an assault on the defenceless'.[17] Unlike an act of defence, which implies some kind of battle or struggle in which neither party is utterly helpless, torture takes place when the 'victim has exhausted all means of defense and is powerless before the victors'.[18]

However, as Sussman points out, the terrorist in our ticking bomb case is not helpless: he is still threatening even as he sits in police custody. Sussman suggests an analogy:

> *Suffocation:*
> A very obese man is trying to suffocate an innocent person by sitting on him. If the police kill him, or cause him to lose consciousness, they will be unable to shift his dead body and save the innocent man. All the fat man need do to kill his victim is remain where he is.

Sussman argues that the fat man's staying put is comparable to the terrorist's staying silent. Neither needs do anything more in order to kill their victim(s). They must only refuse to do what the police want. In this sense, even though both are powerless with respect to the police – they cannot resist any attempts at force – they are not harmless with respect to their victims.

Another reason why the plea of defencelessness is perhaps unconvincing in a case like the ticking bomb scenario is that the terrorist can avoid being tortured by giving up the bomb's location. Such torture seems to satisfy what Shue calls the *possible compliance constraint*, upon which torture is not an assault upon the defenceless if it is possible for the subject to end the torture by complying with the torturer's demands. But Shue argues that in cases where the subject of torture is committed to their goals, the compliance condition requires a 'betrayal of one's ideals and one's comrades. The possibility of betrayal cannot be counted as an escape.'[19] Shue argues that to avoid the charge of assaulting the defenceless, torturers must offer their subjects an escape that meets a minimum standard of moral acceptability. Requiring that a person betray their deepest commitments does not meet this standard: 'denial of one's self does not count.'[20]

I find it hard to mirror Shue's concern that people not be forced to betray their ideals even when these are ideals are, by Shue's own admission, morally abhorrent, and have endangered the lives of hundreds of people. These seem like precisely the sorts of ideals that people ought to betray. And it is hard to believe that the angst a person feels at selling out their friends and thwarting their own terrorist attack weighs against the possibility of saving hundreds of lives. A mother who tells the police where her dangerously psychotic son is hiding might feel a terrible sense of betrayal, but this doesn't mean that she shouldn't tell them where he is, especially if other people's lives are at risk.

Sussman seems similarly perplexed by Shue's position, although his confusion comes from the belief that terrorists are not entitled to this sort of consideration because of the way that they ignore the laws of war. By refusing to distinguish themselves from non-combatants, Sussman argues that terrorists force regular combatants to make terrible choices that endanger non-combatants, and that tarnish combatants' own integrity.

> Given that the terrorist attacks his enemy's own integrity in this way, it is hard to see how he is entitled to terms of surrender that do not require him to in any way compromise his cause. Plausibly, such terms should be reserved for combatants who accept certain risks (by wearing uniforms, living apart from civilian populations, and so on) and do so in order to allow fighting to proceed without forcing combatants to make such self-disfiguring choices.
>
> (Sussman, 'What's Wrong with Torture?', p. 18)

One of the features of the argument from self-defence, however, is that it does not obviously limit the permissibility of torture to cases involving terrorists. As described above, Steinhoff thinks that torture is no different from other forms of defence, and can be employed against people who would be legitimate targets of defence. Stephen Kershnar similarly argues that torture can be defensive. Kershnar illustrates this claim with the following case:

> *Mafia:*
> A mafia boss orders a hit on a union leader who refuses to pay him protection money. The police find out about the hit and arrest the mafia boss. By issuing various threats (to revoke his probation, and tell his wife about his affairs), they pressure the mafia boss into revealing the time and place of the hit.

Kershnar argues that the pressure that the police apply can be plausibly described as defensive. And:

> [n]othing appears to change in terms of what is done when the police escalate from threats to torture. The notion that the pressure in such scenarios is defensive is appealing because the pressure involves one party intentionally using threats or violence to injure another party and thereby prevent that second party from harming someone else. This

appears to have all the features of paradigmatic self-defense or defense
of others.

(S. Kershnar, 'For Interrogational Torture', *International
Journal of Applied Philosophy* 19, No. 2, 2005, 223–241, p. 228)

Can arguments from self-defence rule out justifying the torture of innocent people? As we saw in Chapter 1, some writers argue that the innocent
are legitimate targets of defensive force. Of course, we might object that
the sort of person whom it would be useful to torture in ticking time bomb
cases is not going to *be* innocent, because they have planted the bomb. But
the example of the terrorist's wife shows that this might not always be true.
Here, torturing the innocent person *is* useful. Could a right of defence permit
torturing the wife?

I think that the best way for defenders of the deontological argument to
avoid this conclusion is by arguing that torturing the wife isn't a form of
defence, because harm can only be properly described as defensive when it is
aimed at someone who will otherwise cause harm. This supports Kershnar's
claim that the torture in *Mafia* is defensive because it is aimed at preventing
the mafia boss from harming someone else. But torturing the terrorist's wife
would be aimed not at preventing *her* from harming someone else, but at
preventing her husband from harming someone else. Torturing her would
therefore not count as an act of defence.

However, even if torture can be properly characterised as defence, it does
not follow that it is *proportionate* defence. I can be properly said to defend
myself against your attempt to steal my wallet if I stab you in the chest, but
such defensive force would be impermissible because it is disproportionate.
So, in order to show that torture is not only defensive, but also *permissible*,
we will have to show that torture is a proportionate means of defence. If we
can show that it is proportionate to torture the mafia boss in order to save a
single life in *Mafia*, we will presumably also show that it is proportionate to
torture the terrorist to save hundreds of lives in the ticking time bomb case.

It is certainly proportionate (and permissible) to *kill* in self-defence a
person who will otherwise kill me. Unless torture is a significantly worse
harm than death, it looks as though torture should also be a proportionate form of defence against a lethal harm. As we saw above, some people
think torture a particularly abhorrent way of treating someone. And we can
certainly imagine forms of severe, prolonged torture that seem to be literally
a fate worse than death. This kind of torture might be a disproportionate
means of defence, at least in cases where only one life is at risk.

However, it's hard to see how this could be true of *all* forms of torture.
To take Dershowitz's suggestion, even if inserting needles under someone's
fingernails is very painful, it's hard to imagine that anyone would rather *die*
than suffer, say, an hour of that sort of pain. People undergo painful operations precisely because suffering some level of pain (especially temporary
pain) is better than dying. Of course, as we discussed above, the wrongness

of torture might not be limited to the physical pain inflicted, but might also include the wrong of violating autonomy. But even if by causing you an hour's worth of pain, I (might) get you to reveal your plans to me and thereby act against your own autonomous preferences, it still seems a stretch to say that what I did was worse than if I had killed you. After all, I may have subdued your will to my ends for an hour, but you still have the rest of your life to go about forming and pursuing autonomous preferences. There would be something odd about a view that urged respect for autonomy, but held temporary violations of autonomy to be worse than its permanent elimination.

Chapter summary

This chapter began by addressing issues surrounding the classification of terrorists. We critically examined Yoo and Ho's claim that whilst Al-Qaeda terrorists are engaged in international armed conflict, they do not count as combatants for the purposes of the Geneva Convention. I suggested that even if terrorists fail to fulfil the rules of *jus in bello*, this does not straightforwardly preclude their being treated as combatants. We outlined some of the objections to treating terrorists as combatants, paying particular attention to the implications of treating terrorists as prisoners of war. In the second part of the chapter, we explored the controversial idea of torturing terrorists. We looked at utilitarian arguments for and against state-sponsored torture. We also examined the idea that torture might be justified as a form of self-defence or other-defence.

Questions for discussion

1 Are terrorists combatants? If so, are they entitled to prisoner of war status?
2 Do you think that the state should issue torture warrants of the sort that Dershowitz suggests?
3 What is the best argument in favour of torturing the terrorist?
4 Could torture be permissible to save one person's life, if the subject of torture were morally responsible for the threat to that person?

Notes

1. J. C. Yoo and J. C. Ho, 'The Status of Terrorists', UC Berkeley: Boalt Hall, 2003, p. 4, available at http://www.escholarship.org/uc/item/7kt6n5zf (accessed 17 December 2010).
2. Geneva Convention Relative to the Protection of Civilian Persons in Time of War, Article 3, 6 U.S.T. at 3518, 1949, cited by Yoo and Ho, 'The Status of Terrorists', p. 7.

3. Protocol Additional to the Geneva Conventions of 12 August 1949, and relating to the Protection of Victims of International Armed Conflicts (Protocol 1), 8 June 1977, Article 44.3 (b), available at http://www.icrc. org/ihl.nsf/FULL/470?OpenDocument (accessed 29 March 2011).

4. Protocol Additional to the Geneva Conventions of 12 August 1949, and relating to the Protection of Victims of International Armed Conflicts (Protocol 1), 8 June 1977, Article 44.2, available at http://www.icrc.org/ ihl.nsf/FULL/470?OpenDocument (accessed 29 March 2011).

5. Protocol Additional to the Geneva Conventions of 12 August 1949, and relating to the Protection of Victims of International Armed Conflicts (Protocol 1), 8 June 1977, Article 44.4, available at http://www.icrc.org/ ihl.nsf/FULL/470?OpenDocument (accessed 29 March 2011).

6. Yoo and Ho, 'The Status of Terrorists', p. 7.

7. See http://www.slate.com/id/2246903/ (accessed 21 May 2010).

8. See http://www.keepamericasafe.com/?page_id=217 (accessed 21 May 2010).

9. United Nations Convention Against Torture and Other Cruel, Inhuman or Degrading Treatment or Punishment, 26 June 1987, available at http:// www2.ohchr.org/english/law/pdf/cat.pdf, Article 2.2 (accessed 29 March 2011).

10. D. Sussman, 'What's Wrong with Torture?', *Philosophy and Public Affairs* 33, No. 1, 2005, 1–33, p. 21.

11. H. Shue, 'Torture', *Philosophy and Public Affairs* 7, No. 2, 1978, 124–143, p. 126, n. 4.

12. V. Bufacchi and J. M. Arrigo, 'Torture, Terrorism and the State: A Refutation of the Ticking-Bomb Argument', *Journal of Applied Philosophy* 23, No. 3, 2006, 355–373, pp. 360–362.

13. Bufacchi and Arrigo, 'Torture, Terrorism and the State: A Refutation of the Ticking-Bomb Argument', p. 363.

14. Bufacchi and Arrigo, 'Torture, Terrorism and the State: A Refutation of the Ticking-Bomb Argument', p. 364.

15. A. Dershowitz, 'Want to Torture? Get a Warrant', *The San Francisco Chronicle*, 22 January 2002.

16. U. Steinhoff, 'Torture – The Case for Dirty Harry and against Alan Dershowitz', *Journal of Applied Philosophy* 23, No. 3, 2006, 337–353, p. 337.

17. Shue, 'Torture – The Case for Dirty Harry and against Alan Dershowitz', p. 140.

18. Shue, 'Torture – The Case for Dirty Harry and against Alan Dershowitz', p. 130.

19. Shue, 'Torture – The Case for Dirty Harry and against Alan Dershowitz', p. 135.

20. Shue, 'Torture – The Case for Dirty Harry and against Alan Dershowitz', p. 136.

Suggested reading

As in Chapter 8, this is not further reading, but the Philosophy Talk Show (www.philosophytalk.org) has a discussion with Nancy Sherman on torture, posted 11 April 2010.

John C. Yoo and James C. Ho, 'The Status of Terrorists', UC Berkeley, Boalt Hall, 2003, available at http://www.escholarship.org/uc/item/7kt6n5zf (accessed 17 December 2010).

David Sussman, 'What's Wrong with Torture?', *Philosophy and Public Affairs* 33, No. 1, 2005, 1–33.
Sussman argues against Henry Shue's critique of torture.

Yuval Ginbar, *Why Not Torture Terrorists?: Moral, Practical and Legal Aspects of the 'Ticking Time Bomb' Justification for Torture*, Oxford: Oxford University Press, 2008.

Vittorio Bufacchi and Jean Maria Arrigo, 'Torture, Terrorism and the State: A Refutation of the Ticking-Bomb Argument', *Journal of Applied Philosophy* 23, No. 3, 2006, 355 – 373.
Bufacchi and Arrigo offer a utilitarian argument against torture.

10 *Jus post bellum*

So far in this book, we have considered the *ad bellum* and *in bello* parts of war. In this chapter, we will look at some of the issues covered by *jus post bellum*: justice after war. The first part of the chapter considers Alex Bellamy's distinction between minimalist and maximalist approaches to *post bellum* obligations. We will also outline Brian Orend's maximalist principles of *jus post bellum*, paying particular attention to the idea of reconstruction as part of a just peace. The second part of the chapter will focus on issues surrounding the prosecution of war crimes. We will consider the superior orders defence of war crimes, the role of duress in excusing war crimes and the principle of command responsibility. We will also look at how non-judicial truth commissions have been used to facilitate reconciliation in the aftermath of conflict.

ENDING WAR

Minimalism and maximalism

The recent conflicts in Iraq and Afghanistan have placed questions about *jus post bellum* to the front and centre of contemporary debates about the ethics of war. Several just war theorists argue that one cannot claim to be waging a just war unless one has a clear 'exit strategy' – a plan for ending the war. As Alex Bellamy describes:

> [a]dvocates of *jus post bellum* insist that if, as Augustine argued, war is only legitimate to the extent that it is fought to preserve a just peace, then it stands to reason that combatants be held to account for the way in which the war is concluded and peace managed.
>
> (A. Bellamy, 'The Responsibilities of Victory: *Jus Post Bellum* and the Just War', *Review of International Studies* 34, 2008, 601–625, pp. 601–602)

Of course, it is usually political leaders (rather than combatants) who determine how a war should be brought to a close. The terms of the peace agreement, and the timetable for withdrawal, are usually matters of policy rather than military strategy. But the general point that (at least sometimes) the justness of a war can be partly judged by the manner in which it is ended seems plausible. Even if a warring state has a just cause and obeys the *in bello* rules, it can undermine its claim to be fighting a just war if, for example, it offers only unfair terms of surrender.

Bellamy distinguishes between *minimalist* and *maximalist* approaches to *jus post bellum*. Minimalism is generally identified with earlier just war scholars such as Hugo Grotius. On the minimalist approach, the *post bellum* rules are designed to rein in the excesses of victorious states. Minimalists thus view the *post bellum* rules as *permissions* – as telling victors what they are allowed to do in victory. Most minimalist accounts of *jus post bellum* limit the rights of victors to actions that 'protect themselves, recover that which was illicitly taken, [and] punish the perpetrators'.[1] In effect, this means that victors may secure the just cause of the war, and deter future aggression by punishing the aggressors.

The idea that the *post bellum* rules aim to restrict what victors may do is probably a reaction to historical instances of victorious nations 'raping and pillaging' their defeated foes (Brian Orend cites the typical Greek and Roman demands that their enemies surrender unconditionally, effectively granting the victors the right to take whatever they liked from the defeated country).[2] On some minimalist accounts, victors may, in addition to securing the just cause, halt serious human rights violations taking place within the defeated country. But whilst a victor may temporarily occupy a defeated country in order to achieve the ends of protection, recovery and punishment, minimal-ists prohibit 'full assumption' of the reins of government.[3] This means that minimalist accounts prohibit, for example, enslaving the inhabitants of the defeated country or attempting to colonise the land.

Maximalism is a more recent development in the *jus post bellum* literature, and is now the dominant view of the role of victors. Maximalists understand the *post bellum* rules as imposing obligations upon the victors rather than granting them permissions. Their concern is not that states will do too much in victory and that these excesses must be curbed. Rather, the worry is that victorious states will do too little, leaving behind them a dysfunctional state that cannot meet its citizens' basic needs. Bellamy suggests that whilst the minimalist rules of *jus post bellum* find their roots in just war theory, invok-ing familiar ideas of just cause and proportionality, the maximalist rules are grounded in more general liberal theory and in international law. These nor-mative sources often require that we not only refrain from inflicting harms, but also assist others in need, and help bring about the conditions under which people can leave minimally decent lives.

Brian Orend suggests a maximalist account of *jus post bellum* based upon the following principles:[4]

1. proportionality and publicity;
2. rights vindication;
3. discrimination;

4. punishment (i);
5. punishment (ii);
6. compensation;
7. rehabilitation.

For Orend, *jus post bellum* is conceptually connected to *jus ad bellum*. It is not possible, in Orend's view, for an aggressor to bring about a just peace. So, his principles are intended to guide the behaviour of a just, victorious state as it devises terms of peace with a defeated aggressor.

The conditions of proportionality and publicity are intended to restrict the severity of the peace terms imposed by the victor. Orend stresses that states must resist the temptation to insist upon harsh terms as a form of revenge, arguing that to 'make a settlement serve as an instrument of revenge is to make a volatile bed one may be forced to sleep in later.'[5]

Nowhere is this more apparent than with the repercussions of the Treaty of Versailles. At the end of the First World War, Germany was forced to accept responsibility for the war (the infamous 'war guilt' clause), and, therefore, to pay crippling reparations to fund the rebuilding of Europe. The resentment created amongst Germans by the terms of the treaty were instrumental in Hitler's rise to power in the 1930s, and in generating support for Hitler's aggression. By imposing requirements of proportionality on peace agreements, then, we might lessen the chances of future aggression. And one way of ensuring proportionality is to make the terms open to public scrutiny, hence Orend's inclusion of a publicity condition.

Orend's second condition – rights vindication – speaks to achieving the just cause of the war. Any peace agreement should secure the rights whose protection warranted the initial resort to war. This principle makes it especially apparent why Orend thinks that a just peace can be achieved only when the victorious side is the just side. If the victors are aggressors, achieving the cause of their war (such as the annexing of land or the theft of natural resources) hardly seems a likely component of a just peace.

The principle of discrimination is rooted in the *in bello* requirement to distinguish between combatants and non-combatants. It requires that the terms of the peace settlement maintain what Orend calls a 'reasonable immunity' of the civilian population.[6] In other words, the financial penalties imposed upon the defeated state should not have too severe an impact on the general population. The rationale for this principle is the (by now familiar) idea that non-combatants lack responsibility for the war, and thus cannot be fairly punished for it. Whilst it would be unrealistic to suppose that the ordinary population will not feel the burden of reparations to some extent, Orend thinks that the principle of discrimination prohibits imposing the kind of crippling reparations that were forced upon Germany after the First World War.

In addition to defeating the unjust aims of the aggressor, Orend argues that a just peace will involve punishing those responsible for the aggression.

Leaders should thus be subjected to fair and public trials for breaching international law. There are three main reasons that warrant pursuing such trials even once the rights threatened by aggression have been secured and any illicit gains made by the aggressor have been undone. The first reason is deterrence: subjecting aggressive leaders to trial and punishment deters both future aggression from the same state and future aggression from other states. The second reason is reform: punishment, Orend says, can 'be an effective spur to atonement, change and rehabilitation on the part of the aggressor.'[7] Third, and, in Orend's view, most importantly, justice requires that we punish those who have inflicted suffering on others. A failure to pursue criminal trials against aggressors 'disrespects the worth, status, and the suffering of the victim.'[8]

Orend's second principle of punishment requires that combatants on both sides who are accused of *in bello* war crimes should be subject to investigation and possibly trial. As we will see in the second part of this chapter, however, prosecutions are usually restricted to high-ranking members of the armed forces and political leaders. Low-ranking combatants who commit war crimes have been largely protected from criminal prosecution by various incarnations of the 'superior orders' defence, which exempts them from responsibility for wrongs committed under the orders of a superior officer.

Orend argues that, in addition to punitive measures, a just peace might include making the aggressor nation pay compensation to the victims of aggression. But, again, he urges that these measures should be fair, and not threaten the aggressor's ability to rebuild after the war or fulfil its citizens' basic human rights. As with the other terms of the peace settlement, frustrating the defeated country's attempts to rebuild can foster dangerous resentment that can lead to further conflicts.

Finally, Orend suggests that political rehabilitation can form part of *jus post bellum*. This rehabilitation is usually directed at preventing future aggression, perhaps by reinstating an usurped government or enforcing some kind of demilitarisation (although harsh demilitarisation is often interpreted as punitive rather than preventive). More controversially, rehabilitation might require the total dismantling and replacing of the existing regime, if that regime is particularly abhorrent or aggressive.

Post-bellum regime change

This sort of extensive regime change can be controversial, not least because regime change is generally regarded as an unjust cause for war. For example, in the first edition of *Just and Unjust Wars*, Michael Walzer argues that the sign of a genuine war of humanitarian intervention is that the intervener is 'in and out', eschewing any kind of state-building.[9] States that linger in other countries whilst attempting political reform leave themselves open to the charge of imperialism. But many just war theorists argue that victors are not only permitted, but required, to leave a defeated state in something better than its pre-war conditions. After all, as Orend points out, to allow it to return it to its pre-war state is to allow it to return to the conditions that led to the war in the first place.[10]

Orend suggests that the goal of political rehabilitation is 'the timely reconstruction of a minimally just political community.'[11] In the event that the aggressor state is 'truly atrocious' or 'still poses a serious and credible threat to international justice and human rights', the victor may remove and replace the regime.[12] A clear example of this sort of rehabilitation is the post-Second World War peace agreement between the Allies and Japan, which gave the Americans the power to completely rewrite the Japanese constitution. The Allies wanted to engender democratic participation in a bid to curb future aggression, and the new constitution thus imported certain liberal principles into Japanese society, such as freedom of religion, freedom of speech, democratic elections and gender equality.

However, as Orend notes, the construction of such a community can be enormously costly. Who ought to bear these costs? Orend argues that rehabilitation of this sort 'would seem to necessitate an additional commitment on the part of [victor] to assist the new regime [in the defeated state] with this enormous task of political restricting . . . until the new regime can "stand on its own"'.[13] He cites the US involvement in post-war Japan as a 'stellar' example of such a commitment.[14] But whilst such commitment may be admirable, it's not clear why Orend conceives of it as morally required – as a commitment 'that must be borne by any [victor] seeking to impose such far-reaching and consequential terms' on a defeated aggressor.[15]

On the one hand, Orend makes the commitment sound optional, in that it falls upon only those who choose (or seek) to attempt a general overhaul of the defeated state. But, on the other hand, if the state in question is either committing ongoing atrocities against its own people, or posing an ongoing threat of the sort that Orend describes, it doesn't look as if dismantling the existing regime is optional at all. It is part of securing the just cause of the war that one neutralise the enemy's aggression. If so, the victor has no choice but to dismantle the existing regime if they are to secure a just peace. If the obligation to rebuild follows from a decision to dismantle, it seems that, on Orend's view, this is not an obligation that victors can avoid.

It may of course be in the victor's *interests* to replace a dismantled regime, and to replace it with a minimally just regime of the sort Orend describes. To leave a country defeated and leaderless might well spark a civil conflict that establishes another aggressive regime. It could also engender hostility towards the victor that later manifests in further conflicts. But prudential interests aside, it isn't clear why a state that successfully wages a defensive war would acquire an *obligation* to replace the aggressive regime and support it until it can stand on its own.[16] Such an obligation could impose significant costs at a time when the victorious state is attempting its own post-war reconstruction.

One possible explanation of such an obligation is that even just, defensive wars inflict harms upon innocent non-combatants in the aggressor nation. These harms can be physical, such as the destruction of life and property. But they can also be more abstract. Causing the collapse of a country's government renders its citizens vulnerable to all kinds of dangers, from a dearth of basic goods to threats of external aggression. Even if the collateral harm done to non-combatants is proportionate to the just cause, it is still harm to people who, as Gary Bass puts it, are not liable to 'the kind of suffering they endured as a consequence of policies adopted in foreign ministries and cabinet meetings.'[17] Since, in the course of defending themselves, the victors have inflicted harms upon innocent people, they may owe it to those people to help rebuild their state as a form of apology or compensation. We can imagine comparable duties arising in individual self-defence. If I trample over you as I flee a murderous attacker, it might be incumbent upon me to later help you up, take you to the hospital, and so on. After all, I have harmed you in the course of protecting myself. Even if harming you is proportionate and permissible, I might still have an obligation to do what I can to make good that harm.

Reconstruction after humanitarian intervention

What if the war in question is not a war of self-defence, but rather a war of humanitarian intervention? Walzer's claim that intervening states should be 'in and out' suggests that states do not have duties of reconstruction after wars of intervention. The rationale behind this claim is that interventions should not be masks for straightforward imperialism. But the lack of an obligation to rebuild in the wake of an intervention might also be explained by thinking about the differences between self-defence and other-defence. Whilst it seems plausible that if I harm you as a side-effect of my self-defence, I should try to assist or compensate you in some way, this is less obviously true if I harm you in the course of rescuing someone else. The duty to compensate seems to fall more naturally to the person being rescued than to the rescuer. After all, they are the beneficiary of the harm that I inflict on you. So, if an intervening state inflicts collateral harms in the course of a humanitarian war, we might think that the burden of making good those harms falls to those who are the beneficiaries of the intervention, and not to the intervening state.

However, Walzer later revises his position on the role of interveners, suggesting that sometimes 'humanitarianism probably requires staying on, in a kind of protectorate role, to keep the peace and ensure the continuing safety of the rescued community.'[18] He also criticises those who, motivated by the mounting costs of war, withdraw too quickly. In Walzer's view, wars of intervention are morally optional, because duties to intervene are imperfect duties that do not attach to any particular state: 'Somebody ought to intervene, but no specific state in the society of states is morally bound to do so.'[19] But, he says, once a state chooses to intervene, it must take on the burdens of reconstruction as part of its having a just overall case for war. A just war requires a plan for peace and, without such a plan, the intervention is unjustified. Bellamy similarly argues that 'states that embark on humanitarian interventions are required to assist the host population in rebuilding their country, though they must not impose their own blueprint for reconstruction on unwilling peoples.'[20]

We should notice an important assumption underlying both Walzer's and Bellamy's claims, namely that the beneficiaries of the rescue will not be able to bear the costs of the reconstruction themselves. This does seem like a plausible difference between individual rescue cases and cases of humanitarian intervention, where persecuted groups are often those with the fewest resources at their disposal. But it seems plausible that if they *could* finance reconstruction themselves, they would be obliged to do so. It would be odd if this duty nonetheless fell to the intervening state. This suggests that the connection between the intervener and reconstruction is more contingent than Walzer and Bellamy allow.

I think, therefore, that we might wonder whether the content of a plan for peace must be as narrowly construed as Walzer and Bellamy claim. Even if it is part of a just war that one have a plan for the war's aftermath, it doesn't follow that that plan must be to shoulder the costs of reconstruction oneself. Indeed, we might think that since the intervening state is bearing the (often substantial) costs of military intervention, it falls to other states to take on the burden of reconstruction. Consider the following example, which I have borrowed from Seth Lazar:[21]

> *Rescue:*
> A child is drowning in a fast-flowing river. The water is sufficiently dangerous that any rescue attempt would be supererogatory. Being a brave soul, you jump in and manage to drag the child to the riverbank. Although still alive, she is in a pretty bad way and needs to get to a hospital. The only way she can get there is if a nearby fisherman drives her in his car.

It seems obvious that even if the fisherman isn't obliged to try to rescue the child from the river, he is obliged to drive her to the hospital. He might even be so obliged if the drive is somewhat risky – perhaps the weather is bad and visibility on the road will be poor – assuming that the child will suffer serious harm if he does not take her. The fact that you have rescued the child from immediate danger does not preclude others from having duties of assistance towards her.

What if you too have a car, and so either you or the fisherman could drive the child to the hospital? Even in this case, it seems that you might fairly insist that the fisherman take her. After all, you have already borne a significant cost to save her, having battled through cold, dangerous water to drag her out of the river. If any further costs of the rescue can be borne by someone else, it seems fair that they are so borne. If this is right, it looks as though third parties can have a duty to assist with the aftermath of a rescue even when they lack an obligation to initiate the rescue.

Walzer's characterisation of humanitarian intervention as a duty that attaches to nobody in particular perhaps lends superficial credence to his claim that only the intervening state has a duty of reconstruction. Both he and Bellamy seem to draw support for their claims from an implicit sense that since the intervening state 'chose to get involved' by waging a war of intervention, they brought the further duty of reconstruction upon themselves. After all, if they hadn't waged an interventionist war, there would be no post-war reconstruction to undertake. It is therefore unfair to expect a third party to take on this duty.

However, cases like *Rescue* show that this kind of 'all or nothing' view isn't plausible, even when the initial rescue is wholly supererogatory. The fact that the child wouldn't need to go to hospital if you hadn't pulled her out of the river doesn't mean that nobody else has a duty to drive her there. So, whilst it might be true that intervening states have a duty of reconstruction if nobody else can bring the reconstruction about, it doesn't look very plausible that they (and only they) have such a duty if the reconstruction could be undertaken by a third party.

We might also object more generally to Walzer's claim that intervention is an imperfect duty. An alternative view is that the duty to intervene attaches to *every* state that can intervene, and that those who fail to intervene (or at least fail to offer to do so) simply fail in this duty. If so, such states *owe* it to the intervening state to take up the slack in the aftermath of the war, having shirked their earlier duty. And even if the intervening state is best placed to organise the reconstruction (perhaps because it has won the trust and support of the local people), this is no bar to having third parties fund the reconstruction, discharging their duty via the intervening state in this way.

Of course, there are interesting questions about what a state ought to do if third parties will not agree to assist in the reconstruction. If they can bear the costs of both the intervention and the reconstruction themselves, they probably ought to do so. But what if they can only bear the costs of the intervention? If a plan for reconstruction really is part of having a just war overall, it looks as though states should not intervene if they cannot rebuild afterwards.

I am not sure whether or not this is true. It would certainly be permissible to rescue the drowning child even if you knew that you couldn't get her to a hospital and that she would almost certainly die anyway once you had pulled her out. But here you risk only your own life, and (as we discussed in Chapter 4) an intervening state risks the lives of its combatants. If there is a significant chance that withdrawing immediately after halting a crisis would only delay (and not prevent) that crisis, it might be hard to justify risking the lives of one's combatants on such a mission. This points us to another aspect of *jus post bellum* that isn't so apparent on Orend's account, namely our obligations to those who have fought on the just side of the war. Securing a just peace doesn't only make amends to innocent people caught in the crossfire and protects threatened rights. It is also one way of ensuring that the sacrifices made by just combatants were not in vain.

WAR CRIMES

Those who break the rules of *jus ad bellum* by waging an unjust war are guilty of the crime of aggression. But those who break the *in bello* rules are also guilty of war crimes. The most serious of these violations – those that form part of a wider policy or plan – are tried by the International Criminal Court (ICC), along with crimes against humanity such as genocide or forced mass deportation. Less systematic violations of the laws of war are prosecuted by national courts. These are usually the courts of the defendant's home country. However, the universal jurisdiction that exists over war crimes means that, strictly speaking, any country can try a person accused of war crimes, even if the crimes were committed on foreign soil against foreign nationals.

However, these criminal trials usually focus on a handful of high-ranking officers and political leaders. In order to bring wrongdoers more generally to account, some countries have set up 'truth commissions' – non-criminal investigations intended to bring a sense of justice to the wider community.

The superior orders defence

In 1968, US soldiers carried out a brutal massacre in the village of My Lai in Vietnam. The members of Charlie Company raped, mutilated and shot several hundred civilians, including women and children. One of the perpetrators, Paul Meadlo, later described his role in the massacre during a television interview with CBS news. But only the unit commander, Lieutenant William Calley, was ever convicted of any crime. The men he commanded, all of whom admitted partaking in the massacre, were either acquitted or not brought to trial at all.

This case illustrates a common assumption that has pervaded both the law and our perception of moral responsibility within the armed forces: when they are following orders issued by a person who is in a position to give them, combatants are not accountable for wrongs that they commit. This placing of responsibility squarely on the shoulders of those who *order* wrongdoing is typically explained by a variety of excusing factors that together form the *superior orders defence*. In its original pre-Nuremberg form, this defence afforded combatants pretty good protection from prosecution for illegal actions. As the legal theorist L. F. L. Oppenheim describes, the law held that, '[i]n case members of forces commit violations ordered by their commanders, the members may not be punished, for the commanders are alone responsible, and the latter may, therefore, be punished as war criminals on their capture by the enemy.'[22]

We can identify three central aspects of the superior orders defence. The first is the *prima facie* legality and moral permissibility of the relationship between a combatant and their commanding officer. The combatant does not act wrongly or illegally in joining the armed forces (assuming that the force question is an overall just force), and their commander does not in general act wrongly or illegally in giving them orders. So, we might argue, the combatant is justified in assuming that the default position of their orders is that they are legal and moral.

A second feature of the superior orders defence is the claim that combatants have a legal obligation to obey their commanding officer. Some people have argued that soldiers also have a *moral* obligation to obey such commands. Recall from Chapter 6 Samuel Huntington's claim that:

> [L]oyalty and obedience are the highest military virtues [. . .] When the military man receives a legal order from an authorized superior, he does not argue, he does not hesitate, he does not substitute his own views; he obeys instantly [. . .] His goal is to perfect an instrument of obedience; the uses to which that instrument is put are beyond his responsibility.
>
> (S. P. Huntington, *The Soldier and the State: The Theory and Politics of Civil–Military Relations*, Cambridge, MA: Harvard University Press, 1957, p. 73)

Whilst acknowledging that a combatant 'cannot deny himself as a moral individual', Huntington argues that even when an order strikes a combatant as immoral, 'rarely will the military man be justified in following the dictates of private conscience against the dual demands of military obedience and state welfare.'[23]

The reasoning behind this view is probably largely pragmatic. As we saw in Chapter 6, one of the most common arguments made against the claim that combatants act wrongly if they participate in an unjust war is that it would undermine the whole institution of the military if combatants began questioning, rather than simply obeying, orders. According to this argument, when combatants enlist, they transfer at least part of their autonomy to the wider organisation. They thereby confer upon their leaders the right to make decisions about what they, as individuals, will do.

Since we have good reason to want to preserve military institutions (at least if they are overall just), and to want those institutions to run efficiently, we have good reason to discourage combatants from asking questions. If this pertains to questions about the justness of the war itself, it also, and perhaps more critically, pertains to questions about the justice of individual actions during the war. The inconvenience of having soldiers question the justness of a war before they embark upon it pales in comparison with the danger of having them routinely question the justness of particular actions within that war. By training and requiring a recruit to always defer to those higher up in the chain of command, we ensure the smooth running of the military that is crucial to its success. And, so, a soldier's obedience to orders is justified by appeal to the necessity of preserving the chain of command.

The third feature of the superior orders defence refers to the pressures of war. Soldiers are in a situation of ongoing mortal peril, in the midst of a bloody conflict with all the pressures and distortion that this brings. We cannot expect combatants in these circumstances to make informed decisions (or so the argument goes), and thus combatants are justified in deferring to the orders of superior officers who are in a better position to judge the legality and morality of orders.

After Nuremberg

During the Nuremberg Trials of 1945, where various members and supporters of the Nazis were prosecuted for war crimes, a new understanding of the superior orders defence emerged. Prior to Nuremberg, a combatant needed to show only that they were following orders to be exempted from wrongdoing. But the Nuremberg defence, as it came to be known, exempted a combatant from responsibility for a crime only if he or she could prove that they committed the crime believing both (a) that the orders were morally and legally permissible and (b) that they had no reasonable alternative course of action that was morally preferable. In the event that a combatant knew that an order was unlawful, they could be prosecuted for following it.

Of course, the difficulty here is that in order to find a combatant guilty of a war crime, the prosecution would have to prove not that the order they followed was in fact unlawful, but rather that the combatant *believed* that it was unlawful. And this could be very difficult to establish. Given this, in 1997 the ICC introduced a further clause requiring combatants to disobey orders that are *manifestly unlawful*. Under this standard, combatants are responsible for the perpetrating of a crime if they *should* have recognised that an order was illegal, even if they did not in fact do so. The ordering of an action that pertains to genocide, for example, constitutes a manifestly unlawful order. A combatant who participates in genocide cannot invoke a defence of superior orders.

I suspect that, these days, a lot of people would agree that soldiers should not blindly follow orders no matter what they are, and that it is not a defence of homicide to insist that somebody else told you to do it, even if that somebody else is usually in a position to give you orders. Part of being a professional soldier, and not a member of a mob or terrorist group, is that one restricts one's activity to lawful orders.

However, even since the ICC introduced the manifest illegality clause, most tribunals have not seen a proliferation in the prosecution of lower-ranking combatants for war crimes. Indeed, in the rare cases where the perpetrators (rather than the organisers) of crimes are prosecuted, some people see this as a failure of justice. During the trial of three Bosnian Serbs accused of rape in 2001, protesters held signs up outside the court reading 'Punishment for the big fish – where are they?'[24] Many people would rather try those who organised (or failed to prevent) atrocities than try those who actually carried them out.

We might think that this is simply a pragmatic preference. Since we cannot prosecute everyone, we should prosecute those who have indirect responsibility for a large number of crimes instead of trying those who are directly responsible for a much smaller number. But it might not be a solely pragmatic consideration. After the Second World War, more than 5,000 Japanese leaders and combatants were convicted of war crimes, including many ordinary, low-ranking combatants. Soon afterwards, a 'parole for war criminals' campaign began, describing these combatants as victims of the war rather than criminals.[25] And this is indeed how many people see ordinary combatants, who are usually young men who have undergone some kind of desensitisation training to numb them to the horrors of war, and who are already breaching the usual moral rules that prohibit killing. They are told that if they don't follow orders, people on their side – both combatants and non-combatants – will die. And they often have only limited information about the circumstances in which they act. What looks to them like an unarmed civilian might be known by those with more information to be a suicide bomber. They are reliant upon a general assumption that others in the chain of command are obeying the rules of war and are not ordering them to break those rules. Many people think that it is wrong to punish these combatants even if they should have known that what they were doing was wrong.

Moral perception

Larry May argues that the ICC is mistaken in its assumption that combatants are always capable of identifying even 'manifestly' unlawful orders. May argues that the current superior orders defence identifies two moral choices that combatants are supposed make. The first is a decision that an order is legal and moral; the second is a decision that there are no morally preferable options available to them. May argues that the defence thus assumes that combatants are capable of making these sorts of decisions – that they can, for example, scrutinise an order and judge whether or not they are allowed to follow it. But May claims that it is often not possible for a combatant to make such choices. In response to people like Michael Walzer, who argue that any normal person would have known that the orders to kill the My Lai villagers were immoral, May argues that we cannot apply the perspective of normal people to the abnormal standards of war.[26]

May suggests three possible perspectives from which we can apply the Nuremberg test of manifest illegality to a case like the My Lai massacre. The first is by asking how a normal person 'unexposed to the vagaries of war' would have reacted to the order to kill the villagers.[27] The second is to ask how a normal person exposed to the same wartime experiences as the combatants at My Lai would have reacted to those orders. The third is how someone just like the combatants at My Lai, having undergone their wartime experiences, would have reacted to those orders.

The third perspective is discounted by May, since 'presumably someone just like the soldier in question *would* react just as the soldier in question *did* react.'[28] And he objects to the first perspective on the grounds that the usual 'jury of peers' standard that we apply to domestic crimes simply doesn't work when the context of the crime is so far outside the experience of the peers. Whilst most people can extrapolate from their own experience to understand the context of a domestic crime, they cannot extrapolate from ordinary life in a way that tells them what is reasonable in war.

This leaves the second perspective – that of a normal person who has undergone the things that combatants undergo in war. How would such a person react to an order to kill the villagers of My Lai? May points out that members of the Vietcong often dressed as members of the local population, blending into villages just like My Lai. The combatants had been told that the village was a Vietcong stronghold and that even children might be carrying weapons. In these circumstances, May argues, it is not obvious that a normal person would have known that their orders to shoot were illegal, because it wasn't obvious that these were non-combatants. What seems manifestly unlawful to normal people in normal circumstances may not be manifestly unlawful to combatants in these circumstances:

> This discussion does not call into question the normal sentiment that innocent life should be preserved. Rather, what is uncertain is the very judgement that a certain adult, or even a child, is to be seen as an innocent person. And yet it is this judgment, really a matter or moral perception, that is crucial to the determination of whether it was indeed an outrage for Lieutenant Calley's unit to kill civilians in the hamlet of My Lai in Vietnam. Normally, things would be clearer. But here we are dealing with several levels of abnormality.
> (L. May, *Crimes against Humanity: A Normative Account*, New York: Cambridge University Press, 2005, p. 190)

May does not argue that Lieutenant Calley should have been acquitted. Rather, he is drawing attention to the difficulty of applying the manifest illegality standard to even those things that appear to be paradigmatic atrocities. Even if, once we add in further details about My Lai, we can conclude that those particular combatants should have known that those particular orders were illegal, May's general point about the difficulty of employing the manifest illegality standard still stands, at least with respect to the killing of non-combatants. (It is, of course, far more difficult to see how mutilations and rapes of the sort that took place at My Lai could seem anything other than manifestly illegal, even under the most abnormal of circumstances.)

Duress

May also argues that, given their belief that their lives were under threat in My Lai, the combatants involved might seek protection under the part of the superior orders defence that excuses combatants who believed themselves to lack morally available alternatives to committing war crimes. May thus suggests that a plea of duress can support the superior orders defence.

The role that duress ought to be allowed to play in excusing combatants who commit war crimes was contested in the ICC. The majority opinion was that duress could mitigate responsibility for killing innocent civilians, but could not constitute a full defence (although it might for less serious crimes). The dissenting view held that duress can be a full defence provided that the duress was *proportionate*. So, a combatant who kills an innocent civilian because they fear for their own life ought to be able to use duress as a full defence.

May argues that the ICC should have adopted the dissenting view that duress is a full defence of homicide. On this view, if a combatant (or anyone else, for that matter) has good reason to think that he faces a significant risk of a serious harm should he fail to comply with an order, then failing to comply with that order is not a moral option that is available to him:

> As the probability increases that one will pay a high price for non-compliance with an order, then non-compliance becomes less and less reasonable, and we are less and less inclined to say that one had a reasonable moral choice not to comply . . . On the assumption that people should only be held responsible for their actions where they have a choice, the assessment of whether an agent is responsible will depend on whether reasonable alternatives are open – that is, whether the agent had alternatives that did not involve a high probability that there would be a high price to pay for choosing that alternative course of action.
>
> (May, *Crimes against Humanity*, p. 193)

So, May offers a particular account of what it is to have a moral alternative, namely an alternative that is (a) morally permissible and (b) does not involve significant costs to the agent.

May draws a comparison with the tort law notion of a 'duty of care' to support his account, defending this comparison (which usually speaks to the accidental infliction of harms) by arguing that what we want to know in war crimes trials is whether the combatants are guilty of 'moral negligence'.[29] Did the combatants in My Lai, for example, have a duty to do more to ascertain whether the villagers were armed, such that their failure to take these additional steps counts as negligence? In tort law, May says, '[t]o ascertain if one had such a duty, one looks, among other things, at what the burden would have been to the agent if the agent had conformed to the duty.'[30] When this burden would have been very great, we do not deem the agent negligent if she does not bear it:

When we speak of whether a person had a moral choice or not, normally we mean whether the alternatives open included ones that were morally permissible. In addition, at least part of the concept of moral choice concerns whether there were alternatives open that could be considered reasonable. In most situations, it is not part of one's moral choices, and hence too much to expect, that one should have done something highly dangerous, or otherwise unreasonable. If the only way we can avoid harming another person is to put our own lives in grave jeopardy, then it is not a moral choice to avoid harming this other person.

(May, *Crimes against Humanity*, p. 193)

May illustrates this idea by hypothesising a case in which three bank robbers recruit a fourth person, Green, to act as their getaway driver. The four clearly conspire with respect to the robbery, and are collectively responsible for it. But May suggests that this responsibility would not necessarily cover *all* the results of the robbery. Imagine that as the four drive off, a pedestrian begins to cross the road, right in the car's path. Green begins to apply the brakes to avoid hitting the pedestrian, but the gang's ringleader, Jones, holds a gun to Green's head and orders her to drive on. May argues that whilst Green clearly had a choice about whether or not to conspire in the robbery, she had 'not much of a choice, if she had a choice at all, about whether to run down the pedestrian.'[31]

In comparable cases in war, where a combatant's own life is threatened should she fail to obey an order, May claims that 'the same conditions should be operative, making us reluctant to say that, in such situations, there is a moral choice available to the soldier.'[32] A combatant might be responsible for getting himself into a combat situation. But this does not make him responsible for the things that he does under proportionate duress.

I am not sure that we can use the tort law notion of a duty of care in the way that May thinks. Negligence usually consists in an omission that leads to the accidental infliction of harm (e.g. a failure to follow safety procedures leads to an explosion at a factory). But this doesn't mean that *all* harms that result from omissions count as negligent harms. Intentionally inflicting harm upon a person seems to me to fall outside the remit of negligence, even if it results from a failure to check that the person really is a threat.

Moreover, even if we did accept that intentionally inflicting harm on someone can count as negligence, May is wrong that the duty of care cannot require me to place my own life in grave danger. If I am having some kind of medical emergency, and can get myself to the hospital only by driving my death-trap of a vintage car, whilst suffering crippling pain and seizures, and unable to find my glasses, the duty of care will not tell me that given the cost to me of not getting to the hospital, I may drive the car. Rather, it will prohibit driving the car, and will do so even though I would not be intending to cause any harm at all. So, even if it were appropriate to employ a tort law standard to the intentional infliction of harm, it doesn't follow that I may cause serious harms to others to avoid similar harms to myself.

May's position also generates rather worrying implications in cases such as *Javelin*:

> *Javelin:*
> A javelin is heading towards you. Only by grabbing hold of a bystander, and using her as a human shield, can you save your own life.

There doesn't seem to be anything in May's account that rules out grabbing the bystander and using her to save oneself. But we do not usually think that the fact that I will be killed unless I kill an innocent bystander means that I have *no real choice* but to kill the bystander. Killing the bystander seems clearly morally impermissible. And I suspect that many of us would be rather sceptical of an appeal to irresistible duress in such a case. The pressures of war are of course different from the pressures of everyday life. But would we accept a plea of duress from a soldier who, say, used a civilian as a human shield? Even with the pressures we can imagine – a hail of bullets, bombs exploding and so on – it seems hard to accept that a soldier had no real alternative – no morally viable option – other than to grab a civilian and use her body to shield himself from the bullets. It seems to me that sometimes sacrificing one's own life just is the only morally available option.

Command responsibility

We might think that it is only when a commanding officer orders his troops to commit a war crime that he can plausibly be held responsible for that crime. But international law does not endorse this view. Rather, the *principle of command responsibility* holds that commanders can be responsible for wrongs that their troops commit even if those wrongs were not the result of orders.

David Luban outlines three ways in which a commanding officer can be found guilty of a crime committed by his troops.[33] The first is to construe a failure to prevent or punish a war crime as being an accessory to the crime on the grounds that it implies some degree of complicity. The second is to construe the failure to punish or prevent a war crime as a crime in itself – as a criminal dereliction of duty. The third is to hold a commander vicariously liable for the crimes committed by those under his command. Luban describes this as the most radical application of the principle, 'because it convicts the commander for the soldier's crimes, as though the soldier were a mere extension of the commander rather than an independent intervening decision maker.'[34]

The most famous conviction on the basis of command responsibility is that of General Yamashita. Yamashita was convicted of war crimes committed by his troops in Singapore and Manila during the Second World War. The case is controversial because Yamashita was not present when the attacks in Manila took place, having been forced to retreat by Allied forces. He did not order the attacks; indeed, the actions of the Allies meant that he was unable to communicate with his troops at all. But the court found that Yamashita was responsible for the crimes on the grounds that he should have trained his troops in such a way that they did not engage in atrocities even when they were outside his direct control. As Luban puts it, 'the wide scope of the atrocities is evidence of a prior command failure, not individual soldiers run amok.'[35]

It is certainly true that the general participation in the slaughter suggests a systemic lack of discipline amongst Yamashita's troops. But holding him responsible for any and all consequences that arise from this lack of discipline is to impose what Luban calls an 'unforgiving' standard upon commanding officers. Can the use of such a standard in the case like Yamashita's be justified? Luban argues that it can, because a commander 'wields an instrument with the power of life and death'.[36] A good way make sure that he wields this instrument carefully is to make him responsible for all that it does.

Walzer, in contrast, argues that whilst we should require commanding officers to take appropriate measures to control their troops, this does not mean that they must do everything that they can to this end. Taken literally, this would leave commanders no time to get on with fighting the war. And, even if they were to do everything possible, this does not guarantee success. All we can ask, says Walzer, 'is serious efforts of specific sorts; we cannot require success, since the conditions of warfare are such that success isn't always possible.'[37] Walzer claims that Yamashita should have been exonerated, and that his trial should have triggered careful reflection about the limits of command responsibility.

Amnesties

The number of war crimes cases tried by criminal tribunals is comparatively small. Places such as the former Yugoslavia and Rwanda saw thousands of breaches of the laws of armed conflict, but only a handful of perpetrators have been prosecuted. There are various reasons for this. Some are financial – it simply isn't viable to prosecute all those suspected of war crimes. But there are other considerations in play as well. Reconciliation has become the focus of much of the reconstruction in places like Rwanda, and also in post-apartheid South Africa. Subjecting all of those accused of war crimes to criminal trials would take decades, keeping the conflict to the front and centre of people's minds and hampering development in other areas. Mexican President Vicente Fox describes this as the danger of governments getting 'worn out and lost in the past'.[38]

Because of concerns like these, some countries have offered amnesties for those who have committed war crimes. These amnesties are sometimes offered as part of a wider truth commission into humanitarian abuses. Truth commissions are official, independent investigations into widespread abuses. They are usually held after specific conflicts, but are sometimes established after a country has undergone an extensive period of political violence. The

Truth and Reconciliation Commission (TRC) in post-apartheid South Africa is generally regarded as a particularly successful example of what truth commissions can achieve. Central to the TRC's powers was the ability to grant amnesties to those who confessed their roles in apartheid, provided that they were able to show that they acted for political (rather than personal) reasons. Though controversial, the system of amnesties enabled the TRC to process a vast number of accusations in a fraction of the time (and for a fraction of the expense) that it would have taken to bring criminal trials against all those accused of atrocities.

The granting of amnesties is controversial because of the kind of concerns that Orend identifies in his account of *jus post bellum*. Many people think that the victims of abuse have a right to see their abusers punished, and that granting self-confessed war criminals amnesty exacerbates the injustice done to those who have suffered persecution. Amnesties allow war criminals to go back to living their ordinary lives, often amongst the victims of their crimes.

But those in favour of amnesties, and truth commissions more generally, argue that there are different sorts of justice, and that criminal trials are often not the best way to foster reconciliation. For example, May argues that post-conflict regions should seek restorative justice rather than retributive justice, since it is restorative justice that 'corresponds to reconciliation, in that restorative justice seeks to remedy the effects of injustice by restoring the society to order.'[39] According to May, victims of abuse may find that they need not only to forgive, but also to temporarily forget, the wrongs that they have suffered. This temporary amnesia can be essential if a country is to reach a point at which it is able to confront the injustices of its past without simply imploding into further violence. Amnesties are one way in which a country can build upon what is often a fragile peace.

But what about the rights of victims in these cases? Do the victims of war crimes have a right that their governments not grant amnesties because they have a right that their abusers be prosecuted? Christopher Wellman argues that there ought to be a presumption against amnesties in the aftermath of conflicts, and thus they should be offered only when doing so is necessary for the achievement of some suitably important good. But he also argues that the *interests* of victims in seeing their abusers prosecuted do not amount to a *right* that they be prosecuted. States, not individuals, have authority over who is to be subjected to criminal trials within their territory:

> And if government officials are well within their rights when they elect not to press charges against a potential defendant (if they decide that it would not be possible to build a sufficiently compelling case against the criminal, for instance), then a state's decision to grant amnesty to a large group of rights-violators (because its legal system could not feasibly manage such a massive load of cases, for example) appears to be just a larger example of what is commonly understood to be squarely within a

state's legitimate sphere of sovereignty over its exercise of the criminal law.

> (C. Wellman, 'Amnesties and International Law', in L. May,
> *War: Essays in Political Philosophy*, New York: Cambridge
> University Press, 2008, p. 254)

Wellman is at pains to emphasise that he is talking about the rights of *legitimate* states to decide against pursuing prosecutions, where a legitimate state is one that protects its people's basic rights. A corrupt state that systematically failed to prosecute wrongdoing would not be safeguarding those rights and would cease to be legitimate. Amnesties from a state like this would lack genuine legal or moral force. And, as mentioned above, Wellman thinks that even legitimate states ought to grant amnesties only when there are very weighty reasons to do so. But when they are granted, they do not violate the rights of victims, since victims do not have a right to prosecution.

Wellman claims that this argument also applies to foreign governments who might try to pressure a country into prosecuting its war criminals. Since war crimes fall under international jurisdiction, it is theoretically possible for any country to prosecute someone accused of such crimes even if they have been granted amnesty by their own state. Amnesties are not legally binding upon other states. But Wellman argues that other states should nonetheless generally respect amnesties, and gives rather short shrift to the notion that there are some crimes that harm humanity at large, and which the international community might thus be entitled to see punished. There is, he says, no persuasive account of (so-called) crimes against humanity that shows that 'an average citizen in Australia, say, is necessarily harmed by even the most horrific crime perpetrated against either a Jew in Germany or a Kurd in Iraq.'[40]

Again, these foreign states and their citizens might have an interest in seeing justice done – accountability for wrongdoing is genuinely important. But this does not amount to their having a *right* that prosecutions take place. When such prosecutions will jeopardise the post-conflict region's chances of recovery, a government can have good reason to grant war crimes amnesties. And, indeed, Wellman argues that it is not only when an amnesty is rational, or in the country's best interests, that the international community ought to respect it. What matters is that the amnesty reflects the will of the people: it is, he says, 'up to a country's own people to make the difficult choices about how to pursue the various (and often mutually exclusive) goals of retributive justice, reconciliation, peace, and stability.'[41]

As an example of why a state might grant an amnesty, Wellman imagines a tyrannical dictator who can be persuaded to leave office only if they are promised amnesty from subsequent prosecution. If this is the best way to prevent more humanitarian abuses, and to allow the country to establish a better regime, the balance of considerations might well tip in favour of offering the dictator an amnesty. The good of achieving justice for the past might be outweighed by the good of preventing future crimes.

Of course, we might think that, once the dictator willingly leaves office, there is no reason why another state should not, all the same, indict them on charges of crimes against humanity. After all, like war crimes, crimes against humanity fall within the jurisdiction of all states. But whilst this might seem appropriate in a specific case, Wellman argues that making such prosecutions the rule would undermine the efficacy of amnesties as a way of ending tyrannical regimes. Amnesties will have value only if they are respected by other states, and the international community should not act in a way that prevents vulnerable states from making use of such a potentially powerful tool.

Chapter summary

The ending of war, and the establishing of a just peace, raises its own set of moral and legal issues. The traditional minimalist approach to a victorious state's obligations has largely given way to maximalist views that impose a fairly demanding set of positive duties upon those who defeat aggression. In particular, many maximalist accounts of *jus post bellum* require the victor to undertake at least some kind of political reconstruction, even in the aftermath of humanitarian intervention. Maximalists also include an obligation to punish both the initial aggression and any subsequent war crimes. However, as we saw in the second part of the chapter, it is unusual for low-ranking combatants to be subjected to criminal trial. Throughout most of history, the superior orders defence has given combatants immunity for wrongs that they commit under orders. Even with the tightening up of this defence in the later part of the twentieth century, most war crimes trials have continued to focus upon high-ranking combatants and political leaders.

Questions for discussion

1 Does a country that successfully defeats aggression incur obligations of reconstruction in the defeated country? If so, why?
2 Who should bear the costs of justified humanitarian interventions?
3 Should General Yamashita have been convicted of the crimes committed by his troops?
4 Do victims of war crimes have a right that the perpetrators be prosecuted? If so, does this right mean that governments may not grant amnesties for such crimes?

Notes

1. A. Bellamy, 'The Responsibilities of Victory: *Jus Post Bellum* and the Just War', *Review of International Studies* 34, 2008, 601–625, p. 605.

2. B. Orend, 'Jus Post Bellum: The Perspective of a Just-War Theorist', *Leiden Journal of International Law* 20, 2007, 571– 591, p. 579.
3. Bellamy, 'The Responsibilities of Victory: *Jus Post Bellum* and the Just War', p. 605.
4. Orend, 'Jus Post Bellum: The Perspective of a Just-War Theorist', pp. 580–581.
5. Orend, 'Jus Post Bellum: The Perspective of a Just-War Theorist', p. 580.
6. Orend, 'Jus Post Bellum: The Perspective of a Just-War Theorist', p. 580.
7. Orend, 'Jus Post Bellum: The Perspective of a Just-War Theorist', p. 580.
8. Orend, 'Jus Post Bellum: The Perspective of a Just-War Theorist', p. 580.
9. M. Walzer, *Just and Unjust Wars*, New York: Basic Books, 1977, p. 105.
10. B. Orend, 'Jus Post Bellum', *Journal of Social Philosophy* 31, No. 1, 2000, 117–137, p. 122.
11. Orend, 'Jus Post Bellum: The Perspective of a Just-War Theorist', p. 581.
12. Orend, 'Jus Post Bellum', p. 126.
13. Orend, 'Jus Post Bellum', p. 126.
14. Orend, 'Jus Post Bellum', p. 126.
15. Orend, 'Jus Post Bellum', p. 126.
16. See Bellamy, 'The Responsibilities of Victory: *Jus Post Bellum* and the Just War', pp. 619–620, for a discussion of this criticism.
17. G. Bass, 'Jus Post Bellum', *Philosophy and Public Affairs* 32, No. 4, 2004, 384–412, p. 407.
18. M. Walzer, Preface to the third edition of *Just and Unjust Wars*, New York: Basic Books, 2000, p. xv.
19. Walzer, Preface to the third edition of *Just and Unjust Wars* , p. xiii.
20. Bellamy, *Just Wars: From Cicero to Iraq*, Cambridge: Polity Press, 2006, p. 214.
21. In discussion at the 12th International Law and Ethics Conference, Belgrade, June 2010.
22. L. F. L. Oppenheim, *International Law: A Treatise, Vol. 2: War and Neutrality*, 2nd edn, London: Longmans, Green and Co., 1912, p. 310.
23. S. P. Huntington, *The Soldier and the State: The Theory and Politics of Civil–Military Relations*, Cambridge, MA: Harvard University Press, 1957, p. 78.
24. 'Serbs Jailed for Using Rape as "Weapon of Terror"', *The Independent*, 23 February 2001.
25. See A. Kentaro, 'The Tokyo Tribunal, War Responsibility and the Japanese People', trans. T. Amos, available at http://www.japanfocus.org/-Awaya-Kentaro/2061 (accessed 10 July 2010).
26. L. May, *Crimes against Humanity: A Normative Account*, New York: Cambridge University Press, 2005, p. 184.
27. May, *Crimes against Humanity: A Normative Account*, p. 186.
28. May, *Crimes against Humanity: A Normative Account*, p. 186.
29. May, *Crimes against Humanity: A Normative Account*, p. 192.
30. May, *Crimes against Humanity: A Normative Account*, p. 192.

31. May, *Crimes against Humanity: A Normative Account*, p. 192.
32. May, *Crimes against Humanity: A Normative Account*, p. 192.
33. D. Luban, 'War Crimes: The Law of Hell', in L. May (ed.), *War: Essays in Political Philosophy*, New York: Cambridge University Press, 2008, p. 282.
34. Luban, 'War Crimes: The Law of Hell', p. 282.
35. Luban, 'War Crimes: The Law of Hell', p. 283.
36. Luban, 'War Crimes: The Law of Hell', p. 284.
37. Walzer, *Just and Unjust Wars*, p. 321.
38. 'Mexico Considers Truth Commission', Human and Constitutional Rights resource page, 2001, available at http://www.hrcr.org/hottopics/mexico.html (accessed 16 July 2010).
39. May, *Crimes against Humanity: A Normative Account*, p. 244.
40. C. H. Wellman, 'Amnesties and International Law', in L. May (ed.), *War: Essays in Political Philosophy*, New York: Cambridge University Press, 2008, p. 258.
41. Wellman, 'Amnesties and International Law', p. 263.

Suggested reading

Alex Bellamy, 'The Responsibilities of Victory: *Jus Post Bellum* and the Just War', *Review of International Studies*, 34, 2008, 601–625.
Bellamy gives an interesting summary of the historical path of *jus post bellum*, and argues against viewing *jus post bellum* as a third component of just war theory.

Brian Orend, '*Jus Post Bellum*: The Perspective of a Just-War Theorist', *Leiden Journal of International Law*, 20, 2007, 571–591.
Orend outlines various issues in *jus post bellum* and defends his own maximalist account.

Larry May, *Crimes against Humanity: A Normative Account*, New York: Cambridge University Press, 2005.
Chapter 10 has a discussion of the superior orders defence, and Chapter 13 deals with amnesties and reconciliation.

Christopher Heath Wellman, 'Amnesties and International Law', in Larry May (ed.), *War: Essays in Political Philosophy*, New York: Cambridge University Press, 2008.
May offers a defence of amnesties on the grounds that victims and other states lack a right that war crimes be prosecuted.

Glossary

Aggression (between states)   an act that violates, or threatens to violate, another state's sovereignty.

Collectivist account of war   the claim that war is to be understood as a conflict between groups.

Combatant   commonly, a member of the armed forces.

Consequentialism   the view that we should morally evaluate actions according to their consequences.

Doctrine of double effect   the claim that it can be permissible to cause harm as a side-effect of pursuing a (proportionate) good.

Domestic analogy   comparison between inter-state relations and relations between people or groups in civil society.

Guerrilla fighter   a combatant outside of a regular armed force, usually employing 'mobile' tactics such as ambushes and raids.

Hors de combat   literally, 'out of the fight'. This term refers to those who are not engaged in fighting, such as captured or injured combatants and non-combatants.

Humanitarian intervention   a war of assistance fought to relieve or prevent widespread suffering or abuse.

Individualist account of war   the claim that war is to be understood as a conflict between (groups of) individuals.

Jus ad bellum   justice prior to war.

Jus in bello   justice during war.

Jus post bellum   justice after war.

Just combatant   a combatant who fights on the just side of a war.

NATO   North Atlantic Treaty Organization.

Non-combatant   a person who is not a member of the armed forces.

Non-state actor   a person who does not act on behalf of a government.

Other-defence   defensive force employed to protect a third party.

Pre-emptive war   a war fought in anticipation of an imminent attack.

Preventive war   a war fought to prevent the creation of a threat.

Prisoner of war   a person captured and imprisoned by the enemy.

Proportionality   roughly, whether the good achieved by an action is sufficient to justify the harms that the action also inflicts.

Sovereignty   rights of political and territorial integrity.

Sovereign   head of state.

Supererogatory   an action that goes beyond what is morally required.

Unjust combatant   a combatant who fights on the unjust side of a war.

Bibliography

Augustine of Hippo, *City of God*, trans. H. Bettenson, London: Penguin Books, 1972.

Bacon, F., *Of Empire*, London: Penguin Books, 2005.

Barela, T., 'To Win a War', *Airman* 43, No. 9, 1999, 2–3.

Bass, G., 'Jus Post Bellum', *Philosophy and Public Affairs* 32, No. 4, 2004, 384–412.

Bellamy, A., *Just Wars: From Cicero to Iraq*, Cambridge: Polity Press, 2006.

——'The Responsibilities of Victory: *Jus Post Bellum* and the Just War', *Review of International Studies* 34, 2008, 601–625.

Bufacchi, V., and Arrigo, J. M., 'Torture, Terrorism and the State: A Refutation of the Ticking-Bomb Argument', *Journal of Applied Philosophy* 23, No. 3, 2006, 355–373.

Carnahan, B., 'Lincoln, Lieber and the Laws of War: The Origins and Limits of the Principle of Military Necessity', *American Journal of International Law* 92, No. 2, 1998, 213–231.

Castle, S., 'Serbs Jailed for Using Rape as 'Weapon of Terror', *The Independent*, 23 February 2001, available at http://www.independent.co.uk/news/world/europe/serbs-jailed-for-using-rape-as-weapon-of-terror-693017.html (accessed 6 January 2001).

Ceulemans, C., 'The NATO Intervention in the Kosovo Crisis', in B. Coppieters and N. Fotion (eds), *Moral Constraints on War*, Lanham, MD: Lexington Books, 2008.

Christopher, P., *The Ethics of War and Peace: An Introduction to Legal and Moral Issues*, Englewood Cliffs, NJ: Prentice Hall, 1998, 3rd edn, 2004.

Cicero, *The Republic*, trans. C. W. Keyes, Bury St. Edmunds: St. Edmundsbury Press, 12th edn, 2000.

Coady, C. A. J., 'Terrorism and Innocence', *Journal of Ethics* 8, 2004, 37–58.

——'Collateral Immunity in War and Terrorism', in I. Primoratz (ed.), *Civilian Immunity in War*, New York: Oxford University Press, 2007.

Dunlap Jnr, C.J., 'The End of Innocence: Rethinking Noncombatancy in the Post-Kosovo Era', *Strategic Review*, Summer 2000, 9–17.

Fabre, C., 'Guns, Food, and Liability to Attack in War', *Ethics* 120, No. 1, 2009, 36–63.

Feldman, M. B., 'The United States Foreign Sovereign Immunities Act of 1976 in Perspective: A Founder's View', *International and Comparative Law Quarterly* 35, No. 2, 1986, 302–319.

Fletcher, G., 'Proportionality and the Psychotic Aggressor', *Israel Law Review* 8, 1973, 367–390.

Fletcher, G. and Ohlin, J., *Defending Humanity: When Force Is Justified and Why*, New York: Oxford University Press, 2008.

Foot, P., 'The Problem of Abortion and the Doctrine of Double Effect', *Oxford Review* 5, 1967, 5–15.

Freedman, L., 'Prevention, Not Pre-emption', *The Washington Quarterly* 26, No. 2, 2003, 105–114.

Fussell, P., 'Thank God for the Atom Bomb', in *Thank God for the Atom Bomb and Other Essays*, New York: Summit Books, 1988.

Ginbar, Y., *Why Not Torture Terrorists?: Moral, Practical and Legal Aspects of the 'Ticking Time Bomb' Justification for Torture*, Oxford: Oxford University Press, 2008.

Green, M. J., 'War, Innocence and Theories of Sovereignty', *Social Theory and Practice* 18, 1992, 39–62.

Goodin, R. E., *What's Wrong with Terrorism?*, Cambridge: Polity Press, 2006.

Hobbes, T., *Leviathan*, New York: Oxford University Press, 1996.

Holder, C., 'Responding to Humanitarian Crises', in L. May (ed.), *War: Essays in Political Philosophy*, Cambridge: Cambridge University Press, 2008.

Huntington, S. P., *The Soldier and the State: The Theory and Politics of Civil–Military Relations*, Cambridge, MA: Harvard University Press, 1957.

——'New Contingencies, Old Roles', *Joint Forces Quarterly* 2, Autumn 1993, 38–44.

Hurka, T., 'Proportionality in the Morality of War', *Philosophy and Public Affairs* 33, No. 1, 2005, 34–66.

——'Liability and Just Cause', *Ethics and International Affairs* 21, No. 2, 2007, 199–218.

Johnson, J. T., *Just War Tradition and the Restraint of War*, Princeton, NJ: Princeton University Press, 1981.

Kamm, F. M., 'Failures of Just War Theory: Terror, Harm and Justice', *Ethics* 114, No. 4, 2004, 650–692.

Keep America Safe, available at http://www.keepamericasafe.com/?page_id=217 (accessed 21 May 2010).

Kentaro, A., 'The Tokyo Tribunal, War Responsibility and the Japanese People', trans. T. Amos, available at http://www.japanfocus.org/-Awaya-Kentaro/2061 (accessed 10 July 2010).

Kershnar, S., 'For Interrogational Torture', *International Journal of Applied Philosophy* 19, No. 2, 2005, 223–241.

Kutz, C., 'The Difference Uniforms Make: Collective Violence in Criminal Law and War', *Philosophy and Public Affairs* 33, No. 2, 2005, 148–180.

Lazar, S., 'The Responsibility Dilemma for Killing in War: A Review Essay', *Philosophy and Public Affairs* 38, No. 2, 2010, 180–213.

Lichtenberg, J., 'The Ethics of Retaliation', *Philosophy & Public Policy Quarterly* 21, No. 4, 2001. Reprinted in V. Gehring (ed.), *War After September 11*, Lanham, MD: Rowman and Littlefield, 2002.

Luban, D., 'War Crimes: The Law of Hell', in L. May (ed.), *War: Essays in Political Philosophy*, New York: Cambridge University Press, 2008.

McKeogh, C., *Innocent Civilians: The Morality of Killing in War*, New York: Palgrave Macmillan, 2002.

——'Civilian Immunity: Augustine to Vattel', in I. Primoratz (ed.), *Civilian Immunity in War*, New York: Oxford University Press, 2007.

McMahan, J., *The Ethics of Killing: Problems at the Margins of Life*, New York: Oxford University Press, 2002.

——'The Ethics of Killing in War', *Ethics* 114, 2004, 693–733.

——'War as Self-Defense', *Ethics and International Affairs* 18, No. 1, 2004, 75–80.
——'The Basis of Moral Liability to Defensive Killing', *Philosophical Issues* 15, Normativity, 2005, 386–405.
——'Just Cause for War', *Ethics and International Affairs* 19, No. 3, 2005, 1–21.
——'Killing in War: Reply to Walzer', *Philosophia* 34, 2006, 47–51.
——'On the Moral Equality of Combatants', *Journal of Political Philosophy*. 14, No. 4, 2006, 377–393.
——'Collectivist Defenses of the Moral Equality of Combatants', *Journal of Military Ethics* 6, No.1, 2007, 50–59.
——'The Morality of War and the Law of War', in D. Rodin and H. Shue (eds), *Just and Unjust Warriors*, Oxford: Oxford University Press, 2008.
——*Killing in War*, New York: Oxford University Press, 2009.
——'The Just Distribution of Harm Between Combatants and Noncombatants', *Philosophy and Public Affairs* 38, No. 4, 2010, 342–379.
——'Laws of War', in S. Besson and J. Tasioulas, (eds), *The Philosophy of International Law*, Oxford: Oxford University Press, 2010.
McPherson, L. K., 'Is Terrorism Distinctively Wrong?', *Ethics* 117, No. 3, 2007, 524–546.
Mavrodes, G., 'Conventions and the Morality of War', *Philosophy and Public Affairs* 4, No. 2, 1975, 117–131.
May, L., *Crimes against Humanity: A Normative Account*, New York: Cambridge University Press, 2005.
——'Killing Naked Soldiers: Distinguishing between Combatants and Non-combatants', *Ethics and International Affairs* 19, No. 3, 2005, 39–53.
——'The Principle of Just Cause', in L. May (ed.), *War: Essays in Political Philosophy*, New York: Cambridge University Press, 2008.
Model Penal Code, Philadelphia: American Law Institute, 1980, Section 2. 2, available at http://www1.law.umkc.edu/suni/CrimLaw/MPC_Provisions/model_penal_code_default_rules.htm (accessed 17 December 2010).
Nagel, T., 'War and Massacre', *Philosophy and Public Affairs* 1, No. 2, 1972, 123–144.
Nathanson, S., *Terrorism and the Ethics of War*, New York: Cambridge University Press, 2010.
The National Security Strategy of the United States, 2002, available at http://georgewbush-whitehouse.archives.gov/nsc/nss/2002/nss.pdf (accessed 15 December 2010).
Nozick, R., *Anarchy, State and Utopia*, Malden, MA: Basic Books, 1974.
Oppenheim, L. F. L., *International Law: A Treatise, Vol. 2: War and Neutrality*, London: Longmans, Green and Co., 2nd edn, 1912.
Orend, B., '*Jus Post Bellum*', *Journal of Social Philosophy* 31, No. 1, 2000, 117–137.
——'*Jus Post Bellum*: The Perspective of a Just-War Theorist', *Leiden Journal of International Law*, 20, 2007, 571–591.
——'War', in E. N. Zalta (ed.) *Stanford Encyclopedia of Philosophy* (Fall 2008 edn.), available at http://plato.stanford.edu/archives/fall2008/entries/war/ (accessed 13 December 2010).
Otsuka, M., 'Killing the Innocent in Self-Defense', *Philosophy and Public Affairs* 23, No. 1, 1994, 74–94.
Rawls, J., *A Theory of Justice*, Cambridge, MA: Harvard University Press, 1971.
Robinson, P., *Criminal Law Defenses* 2, St. Paul, MN: West Group Publisher, 1984.
Rodin, D., *War and Self-Defense*, New York: Oxford University Press, 2002.

——'The Moral Inequality of Soldiers: Why *Jus in Bello* Asymmetry is Half Right', in D. Rodin and H. Shue (eds), *Just and Unjust Warriors*, New York: Oxford University Press, 2008.

Ryan, C., 'Popular Sovereignty and Military Service: Democratic Duty and the Unjust Soldier', unpublished manuscript, on file with the author.

——'Democratic Duty and the Moral Dilemmas of Soldiers', *Ethics* (forthcoming).

Scheffler, S., 'Is Terrorism Morally Distinctive?', *Journal of Political Philosophy* 14, No.1, 2006, 1–17.

Shue, H., 'Torture', *Philosophy and Public Affairs* 7, No. 2, 1978, 124–143.

——'Do We Need a 'Morality of War'?', in D. Rodin and H. Shue (eds), *Just and Unjust Warriors*, Oxford: Oxford University Press, 2008.

——'Laws of War', in S. Besson and J. Tasioulas (eds), *The Philosophy of International Law*, New York: Oxford University Press, 2010, 511–527.

Shue, H. and Rodin, D. (eds), *Preemption*, Oxford: Oxford University Press, 2007.

Slate website, available at http://www.slate.com/id/2246903/ (accessed 21 May 2010).

Smilansky, S., 'Terrorism, Justification, and Illusion', *Ethics* 114, 2004, pp. 790–805.

Smith, M. J., 'Humanitarian Intervention: An Overview of the Ethical Issues', *Ethics and International Affairs* 12, No. 1, 1998, 63–79.

Steinhoff, U., 'Torture – The Case for Dirty Harry and against Alan Dershowitz', *Journal of Applied Philosophy* 23, No. 3, 2006, 337–353.

——'Debate: Jeff McMahan on the Moral Inequality of Combatants', *Journal of Political Philosophy* 16, No. 2, 2008, 220–226.

Sussman, D., 'What's Wrong with Torture?', *Philosophy and Public Affairs* 33, No. 1, 2005, 1–33.

Swift, L. J., 'St. Ambrose on Violence and War', *Transactions and Proceedings of the American Philological Association* 101, 1970, 533–543.

Thatcher, M., Speech to the House of Commons, 14 April 1982, transcript available at http://www.margaretthatcher.org/document/104918 (accessed 6 January 2010).

Thomson, J. J., 'Self-Defense and Rights', in W. Parent (ed.), *Rights, Restitution and Risk*, Cambridge, MA: Harvard University Press, 1986.

——'Self-Defense', *Philosophy and Public Affairs* 20, No. 4, 1991, 283–310.

Timmons, M., *Moral Theory: An Introduction*, Lanham, MD: Rowman and Littlefield, 2002.

Uniacke, S., 'Self-Defence, Necessary Force and a Reasonable Prospect of Success', unpublished manuscript, on file with the author.

United States Code, available at https://www.cia.gov/news-information/cia-the-war-on-terrorism/terrorism-faqs.html (accessed 29 March 2011).

Walzer, M., *Just and Unjust Wars*, New York: Basic Books, 1977.

——'Response to McMahan's paper', *Philosophia* 34, 2006, 43–45.

Webster, D., Letter to Special Minister Ashburton, dated 24 April 1841, available at http://avalon.law.yale.edu/19th_century/br-1842d.asp#ashdes1 (accessed 15 December 2010).

Wellman, C. H., 'Amnesties and International Law', in L. May (ed.), *War: Essays in Political Philosophy*, New York: Cambridge University Press, 2008.

Wheeler, N. J., *Saving Strangers: Humanitarian Intervention in International Society*, New York: Oxford University Press, 2000.

Yoo J. C., and Ho, J. C., 'The Status of Terrorists', UC Berkeley: Boalt Hall, 2003, available at http://www.escholarship.org/uc/item/7kt6n5zf (accessed 17 December 2010).

Zohar, N., 'Collective War and Individualist Ethics: Against the Conscription of "Self-Defense"', *Political Theory* 21, No. 4, 1993, 606–622.
——'Innocence and Complex Threats: Upholding the War Ethic and the Condemnation of Terrorism', *Ethics* 114, 2004, 734–751.

List of cited conventions and other manuscripts

Instructions for the Government of Armies of the United States in the Field (Lieber Code), 24 April 1863, available at http://www.icrc.org/ihl.nsf/FULL/110?OpenDocument (accessed 22 March 2011).

Hague Convention (III) relative to the Opening of Hostilities, The Hague, 18 October 1907, available at http://www.icrc.org/ihl.nsf/FULL/190?OpenDocument (accessed 6 January 2010).

Protocol for the Prohibition of the Use of Asphyxiating, Poisonous or Other Gases, and of Bacteriological Methods of Warfare, Geneva, 17 June 1925, available at http://www.icrc.org/ihl.nsf/FULL/280?OpenDocument (accessed 22 March 2011).

Charter of the United Nations, 26 June 1945, available at http://www.un.org/en/documents/charter/index.shtml (accessed 20 March 2011).

Geneva Convention (IV) Relative to the Protection of Civilian Persons in Time of War, Geneva, 12 August 1949, available at http://www.icrc.org/ihl.nsf/FULL/380?OpenDocument (accessed 22 March 2011).

Protocol Additional to the Geneva Conventions of 12 August 1949, and relating to the Protection of Victims of International Armed Conflicts (Protocol 1), 8 June 1977, available at http://www.icrc.org/ihl.nsf/FULL/470?OpenDocument (accessed 22 March 2011).

United Nations Convention Against Torture and Other Cruel, Inhuman or Degrading Treatment or Punishment, place, 26 June 1987, available at http://www2.ohchr.org/english/law/pdf/cat.pdf (accessed 22 March 2011).

The Manual of the Law of Armed Conflict, UK Ministry of Defence, 2005, available at http://www.mod.uk/NR/rdonlyres/3DBB1299-2722-423F-9D46-3D952C407C7A/0/law_manual_amended_text.pdf (accessed 6 January 2011).

Legal Consequences of the Construction of a Wall in the Occupied Palestinian Territory (Request for advisory opinion), 9 July 2004, available from the International Court of Justice website at http://www.icj-cij.org/docket/files/131/1677.pdf (accessed 14 December 2010).

'Mexico Considers Truth Commission', Human and Constitutional Rights resource page, 2001, available at http://www.hrcr.org/hottopics/mexico.html (accessed 29 March 2011).

Index

From Rhetoric to Reform?

Welfare Policy in American Politics

Anne Marie Cammisa

Understanding Medieval Liturgy

Essays in Interpretation

Edited by

HELEN GITTOS
University of Kent, UK

SARAH HAMILTON
University of Exeter, UK

Routledge
Taylor & Francis Group

LONDON AND NEW YORK

First published 2016 by Ashgate Publishing

2 Park Square, Milton Park, Abingdon, Oxfordshire OX14 4RN
52 Vanderbilt Avenue, New York, NY 10017

Routledge is an imprint of the Taylor & Francis Group, an informa business

First issued in paperback 2018

British Library Cataloguing in Publication Data
A catalogue record for this book is available from the British Library

The Library of Congress has cataloged the printed edition as follows:
Understanding medieval liturgy : essays in interpretation / edited by Helen Gittos and
    Sarah Hamilton.
        pages cm
    Includes bibliographical references and index.
    ISBN 978-1-4094-5150-1 (hardcover)
    1. Liturgics. 2. Church history–Middle Ages, 600–1500.
    I. Gittos, Helen, editor.
    BX1973.U53 2015

    264'.0200902–dc23
    2014043572

ISBN 978-1-4094-5150-1 (hbk)
ISBN 978-0-367-13579-9 (pbk)

Contents

List of Figures and Tables

Figures

Tables

Notes on Contributors

Mette Birkedal Bruun (University of Copenhagen) works on church history and is a specialist on the history of the Cistercians. Her publications include *Parables: Bernard of Clairvaux's Mapping of Spiritual Topography* (Leiden: Brill, 2007) and several articles on monks and ritual. She has also edited the *Cambridge Companion to the Cistercians* (Cambridge: Cambridge University Press, 2012).

Florence Chave-Mahir is an associate researcher with the Centre national de la recherche scientifique (CNRS): Centre Interuniversitaire d'Histoire, Archéologie, Littératures des mondes chrétiens et musulmans médiévaux (CIHAM-UMR 5648-Université Lyon 2). She works on the history of exorcism, is the author of *L'exorcisme des possédés dans l'Eglise d'Occident (Xe–XIVe siècle)* (Turnhout: Brepols, 2011) and is currently working on an edition of a fifteenth-century ritual for exorcisms in collaboration with Julien Véronèse which will be published as *Rituel d'exorcisme ou manuel de magie? Le manuscrit Clm 10085 de la Bayerische Staatsbibliothek de Munich* (Florence: Edizioni del Galluzzo, forthcoming).

William T. Flynn (University of Leeds) lectures in medieval Latin and is a specialist on the interactions among liturgy, music and theology. His publications include *Medieval Music as Medieval Exegesis* (London: Scarecrow Press, 1999) and various publications on liturgical poetry and music produced for women's convents by Hildegard of Bingen and by Peter Abelard.

Helen Gittos (University of Kent) lectures on medieval history and her publications include *Liturgy, Architecture, and Sacred Places in Anglo-Saxon England* (Oxford: Oxford University Press, 2013) and together with M.B. Bedingfield she edited *The Liturgy of the Late Anglo-Saxon Church*, HBS Subsidia Series 5 (London: HBS, 2005). She is currently writing a book about the use of vernacular languages in medieval liturgy.

Louis I. Hamilton (Drew University) is Associate Professor in the Department of Comparative Religion and his research focuses on medieval ritual and liturgical commentaries, especially the central medieval Italian rites for the consecration of churches and the eleventh-century reform. His publications include *A Sacred City: Consecrating Churches and Reforming Society in Eleventh-Century Italy* (Manchester: Manchester University Press, 2010).

Sarah Hamilton (University of Exeter) works on central medieval history, and her research focuses on the early pontificals, especially the rites for penance and excommunication. Her publications include *The Practice of Penance, 900–1050* (Woodbridge: Boydell and Brewer, 2001); *Church and People in the Medieval West 900–1200* (Harlow: Pearson, 2013) as well as several articles.

Carolyn Marino Malone (University of Southern California) works on medieval English and French art and architectural history. Her research focuses on combining archaeological, liturgical and art historical approaches to Romanesque and Gothic architecture. Her publications include *Façade as Spectacle: Ritual and Ideology at Wells Cathedral* (Leiden: Brill, 2004); *Saint-Bénigne et sa rotonde: Archélogie d'une église bourguignonne de l'an mil* (Dijon: Editions universitaires de Dijon, 2008); and *Saint-Bénigne de Dijon en l'an mil, 'totius Galiie basilicis mirabiliorem': interprétation liturgique et théologique*, Disciplina monastica 5 (Turnhout: Brepols, 2009).

Henry Parkes (Yale University) took up a post at the Institute of Sacred Music and Department of Music in 2014 and his publications include *The Making of Liturgy in the Ottonian Church: Books, Music and Ritual in Mainz 950–1050* (Cambridge: Cambridge University Press, 2015).

Frederick S. Paxton (Connecticut College) works on European, deep and big history and his primary research focus has been on death and dying in medieval Europe. His publications include *The Death Ritual at Cluny in the Central Middle Ages*, Disciplina monastica 9 (Turnhout: Brepols, 2013); *Anchoress and Abbess in Ninth-Century Saxony: The Lives of Liutbirg of Wendhausen and Hathumoda of Gandersheim* (Washington, DC: Catholic University of America Press, 2009); and *Christianizing Death: The Creation of a Ritual Process in Early Medieval Europe* (Ithaca, NY: Cornell University, 1990).

Matthew Cheung Salisbury (University of Oxford) lectures in medieval music and his publications include *The Secular Liturgical Office in Late Medieval England* (Turnhout: Brepols, 2015) and *The Use of York: Characteristics of the Medieval Liturgical Office in York* (York: Borthwick Institute, University of York, 2008).

Carol Symes (University of Illinois at Urbana-Champaign) is an historian whose research focuses on the intersection between performance practices and written records. She is also the founding executive editor of *The Medieval Globe*, a new academic journal. Her publications include *A Common Stage: Theater and Public Life in Medieval Arras* (Ithaca, NY: Cornell University Press, 2007); *Cities, Texts, and Social Networks 400–1500: Experiences and Perceptions of*

Medieval Urban Space (Aldershot: Ashgate, 2010), edited with C.J. Goodson and A.E. Lester; 'The Medieval Archive and the History of Theater: Assessing the Written and Unwritten Evidence for Premodern Performance', *Theatre Survey* 52 (2011); and 'A Few Odd Visits: Unusual Settings of the *Visitatio sepulchri*', in *Music and Medieval Manuscripts: Paleography and Performance. Essays in Honour of Andrew Hughes*, ed. J. Haines and R. Rosenfeld (Aldershot: Ashgate, 2004).

Acknowledgements

This collection arises out of discussions with a much larger group of people which were made possible thanks to generous funding from the British Academy and the Arts and Humanities Research Council. These began with a one-day workshop in 2007, funded by the British Academy, on *Recovering Medieval Liturgies: Methodologies for the Study of Liturgical Rites, c. 750–c. 1500*. The conversations we had on that occasion became the foundation for those held under the aegis of the AHRC-funded International Research Network, *Interpreting Medieval Liturgy c. 500–c. 1500 AD: Text and Performance*, which ran from 2009 to 2011. This project brought together researchers working in different disciplines, time periods and intellectual traditions. This book is not intended as a record of the papers delivered to these various meetings, but rather it represents a first attempt to discuss in print some of the problems and questions identified over their course. We would like to thank all those who took part in these meetings: Susan Boynton, Benjamin Brand, Mette Birkedal Bruun, Florence Chave-Mahir, Claire Cross, Jane Flynn, William Flynn, David Ganz, Marie-Pierre Gelin, Louis Hamilton, Sally Harper, Yitzhak Hen, Julian Hendrix, Christopher Hodkinson, Jane Huber, Eddie Jones, Sarah Larratt Keefer, Rob Meens, Eric Palazzo, Henry Parkes, Fred Paxton, Joanne Pierce, Paul Post, Susan Rankin, Matthew Reeve, Tamsin Rowe, Matthew Cheung Salisbury, Carol Symes and Matthew Ward. Paul Barnwell deserves special thanks, not only for taking part, but also for his help in arranging the first meeting. We are especially indebted to John Harper who not only took part in all the meetings, but also organized and directed a re-enactment of a late medieval Sarum rite for the reconciliation of public penitents in a late medieval church: St Teilo's at St Fagan's National History Museum, Cardiff. His effort, energy and expertise helped to make this project work. The contributors to this book have been model collaborators: enthusiastic and forbearing. Alwyn Harrison efficiently compiled the index at short notice. Finally, we would like to thank our partners Stephen Lee and Andy Hudson, united in their preference for football rather than liturgy, for putting up with us.

List of Abbreviations

CCCM	Corpus Christianorum Continuatio Mediaevalis
CCM	*Corpus consuetudinum monasticarum*, ed. Kassius Hallinger et al., vols. 1–9 (Siegburg: Franz Schmitt, 1963–76)
CCSL	Corpus Christianorum Series Latina
CLS	Cistercian Liturgy Series
HBS	Henry Bradshaw Society
Leroquais, *Pontificaux*	V. Leroquais, *Les pontificaux manuscrits des bibliothèques publiques de France*, 4 vols. (Paris, 1937)
MGH	Monumenta Germaniae Historica
MGH SS	Monumenta Germaniae Historica, Scriptores
MGH SS rer ger	Monumenta Germaniae Historica, Scriptores rerum Germanicarum
OR	*Les ordines romani du haut moyen-âge*, ed. Michel Andrieu, 5 vols., Spicilegium sacrum Lovaniense 11, 23, 24, 28, 29 (Louvain: Université Catholique de Louvain, 1931–61)
Palazzo, *History*	Eric Palazzo, *A History of Liturgical Books from the Beginning to the Thirteenth Century*, trans. Madeleine Beaumont (Collegeville, MN: Liturgical Press, 1998); originally published as *Le moyen âge: des origines au XIIIème siècle* (Paris: Beauchesne, 1993)
Pfaff, *Liturgy*	Richard W. Pfaff, *The Liturgy in Medieval England: A History* (Cambridge: Cambridge University Press, 2009)
PL	*Patrologia cursus completus, series latina*, ed. J.-P. Migne (Paris: Garnier, 1844–64)
PRG	*Le pontifical romano-germanique du dixième siècle*, ed. Cyrille Vogel and Reinhard Elze, Studi e Testi 226–7, 269, 3 vols. (Vatican: Biblioteca Apostolica Vaticana, 1963–72)
RED	Rerum Ecclesiasticarum Documenta
SF	Spicilegium Friburgense

Vogel, *Medieval Liturgy*   Cyrille Vogel, *Medieval Liturgy: An Introduction to the Sources*, rev. and trans. William G. Storey and Niels K. Rasmussen (Washington, DC: Pastoral Press, 1986); originally published as *Introduction aux sources de l'histoire du culte chrétien au moyen âge* (Spoleto: Centro italiano di Studi Sull'alto Medioevo, 1966)

Introduction

Helen Gittos and Sarah Hamilton

Most of the contributors to this book would not describe themselves as liturgists. Few have had any training in using liturgical sources or have had their doctoral theses supervised by scholars whose primary interest was in liturgy. But between us, we have spent many decades working with such sources, exploring their potential as evidence for medieval history, and dealing with the problems involved in using them. In recent years there has been a revival of interest in medieval rituals but, despite this flourishing activity, medieval liturgy is rarely taught in universities. This book is a response to these circumstances.

Aims

The main focus of the book is on so-called 'occasional rites' which were actually anything but occasional. This term refers to all those rituals other than the mass and office, such as rites of passage like baptism and burial, the ceremonies associated with major feasts including Candlemas and Palm Sunday, consecration of people and things, for example priests and churches, and legal actions like ordeal and excommunication. However, there is no firm distinction to be made: occasional rites frequently included masses, or took place during a mass or office. Some authors included here primarily work on the mass or office, and many ideas in this book are relevant to all types of medieval Christian ritual. There are several reasons, though, why we have focused on such rites. In part it is because they have received rather less attention than the mass and the office.[1] But it is also because occasional rites are so informative about many different aspects of life in the Middle Ages. And finally there has been much recent work on them that challenges many established ideas, especially about the extent to which rites differed from place

---

[1] For example, the following works focus on the mass and office: Theodor Klauser, *A Short History of the Western Liturgy: An Account and Some Reflections*, 2nd edn. (Oxford: Oxford University Press, 1979; originally published as *Kleine abendländische Liturgiegeschichte*, 5th edn., 1969, trans. by John Halliburton); Pierre-Marie Gy, *La liturgie dans l'histoire* (Paris: Cerf, 1990); John Harper, *The Forms and Orders of Western Liturgy from the Tenth to the Eighteenth Century: A Historical Introduction and Guide for Students and Musicians* (Oxford: Oxford University Press, 1991); Pfaff, *Liturgy*; Matthew Cheung Salisbury, *Hear My Voice, O God: Functional Dimensions of Christian Worship* (Collegeville, MN: Liturgical Press, 2014).

to place and over time, and how the surviving evidence should be interpreted. Modern scholarship has witnessed a shift away from a search for origins in the early Church and a focus on teleological accounts of development, to a renewed emphasis on the diversity of the liturgical record, yet these ideas, and their implications, have not previously been fully articulated in print.

One of the book's primary purposes is to provide guidance to those who are new to the subject, want to know more about it, or wish to conduct research on liturgical topics. These specially commissioned essays offer advice in several different ways. The three contributions to Part I explicitly discuss the practicalities of undertaking research: In Chapter 1 Helen Gittos considers some of the problems and possibilities of working on rites; in Chapter 2 Frederick Paxton illustrates some of these issues by means of an autobiographical case study of his own work on rites for the dying and William Flynn explores current approaches by musicologists in Chapter 3. The two studies in Part II explore the problems caused by uncritical reliance on modern editions of medieval liturgical texts and how to avoid them. Henry Parkes in Chapter 4 examines the presumptions of, and methods used by, Michel Andrieu, Cyrille Vogel and Reinhard Elze to construct their edition of the so-called Romano-German Pontifical, and shows how unrepresentative that edition is of the manuscript record. In Chapter 5 Matthew Cheung Salisbury explains how the debates of nineteenth-century Anglicanism shaped the editions of the late medieval Uses of York and Sarum which are still used today. The three essays in Part III each focus on a different ritual. They provide examples of the range of evidence available for occasional rites, the approaches that can be taken, and the kinds of questions such evidence can help address. Sarah Hamilton explores some of the earliest eleventh-century examples of episcopal excommunication in Chapter 6, and Florence Chave-Mahir sets out the twelfth-century hagiographical as well as liturgical evidence for exorcism in Chapter 7. Mette Birkedal Brunn and Louis Hamilton in Chapter 8 approach the rite for church dedication from the different perspectives of sermons and liturgical rites and show how taking into account a range of sources enriches our understanding of the meaning and experience of this rite. These three case studies also illustrate one of the key themes of all recent work on the field: the extent of diversity one finds in the sources. The two contributions to Part IV are concerned with how the surviving sources relate to the way liturgy was actually practised. In Chapter 9, Carolyn Marino Malone demonstrates the value of reading the liturgical evidence of monastic customaries alongside the surviving architectural record, through case studies of Saint-Bénigne, Dijon and Wells Cathedral, whilst Carol Symes in Chapter 10 addresses problems of interpretation that frequently surface in other chapters as well from the point of view of a specialist in drama.

All the contributions refer to key resources and the aim has been to show the ways in which they may be used, their strengths and weaknesses, rather than to provide a comprehensive bibliography.[2] In order to convey the range of approaches that can be adopted and types of questions asked by people working in different disciplines, we solicited contributions from scholars with various disciplinary backgrounds: history, theology, musicology, architectural history, drama and English literature. One of the themes of this collection is that in this field it is vital to draw on as wide a range of sources as one can, even if reconciling them can be tricky. So, William Flynn emphasizes what is to be gained by cross-disciplinary collaboration, whilst Florence Chave-Mahir, Mette Birkedal Brunn and Louis Hamilton explore such an approach by examining the types of information that can be sought from different sources for the same ritual. These last three authors, alongside Carolyn Marino Malone and Carol Symes, concentrate on sources of evidence that are not often central to liturgical study, including saints' lives, sermons and church architecture. We hope that this mixture of practical guidance, case studies and bibliographical orientation will be both helpful and stimulating.

We also hope that this book will be of value to those who know a great deal about the subject as well as to beginners. In this regard we have three main aims. One is to articulate more clearly than has been done before some of the major recent changes in the ways that liturgical sources are being interpreted. Another is to invigorate the subject by encouraging greater co-operation between traditional scholarly communities. There are enduring divisions between people working on medieval liturgy which are chronological, geographical and disciplinary. We hope to demonstrate the value of greater communication by showing that a number of common concerns cross-over these groupings. The third aim is to address the historiographical legacy that we have inherited. This is a particular focus in Chapter 3 where William Flynn considers the musicological historiography and Chapters 4 and 5 in which Henry Parkes and Matthew Cheung Salisbury draw attention to the problematic nature of some of the editions of texts that have been considered landmarks in medieval liturgical history. In short, we hope this will be a helpful and provocative book.

Having set out what this book aims to be, it is worth explaining what it is not. This is not intended to serve as a replacement for existing accounts of the development of medieval liturgy. Nor is it intended as a critique of all previous

---

2   For bibliographies see Vogel, *Medieval Liturgy*; Richard W. Pfaff, *Medieval Latin Liturgy: A Select Bibliography*, Toronto Medieval Bibliographies 9 (Toronto: University of Toronto Press, 1982); Angelus A. Häussling, Martin Klöckener and Burkhard Neunheuser, 'Der Gottesdienst der Kirche: Texte, Quellen, Studien', *Archiv für Liturgiewissenschaft* 42 (2000): 106–202; 43/44 (2001–02): 97–221; Paul F. Bradshaw, ed., *The New SCM Dictionary of Liturgy and Worship* (London: SCM Press, 2002); F.L. Cross and E.A. Livingstone, eds., *The Oxford Dictionary of the Christian Church* (Oxford: Oxford University Press, 2005).

scholarship: an enormous amount of scholarly effort has been invested in the edition of liturgical texts, and in investigating the relationships between particular manuscripts; work which, whatever the problems identified below and in the chapters in this collection, remains absolutely fundamental to current and future research. Nor has it been our aim to write a detailed account of the development of occasional rites. Instead our hope is that the ideas presented here, by providing various perspectives on these materials, will help stimulate future research. What follows is intended as a brief introduction to some issues that those interested in occasional rites should be aware of.

Being Aware of the Scholastic Inheritance

Modern historians of medieval liturgy are heirs to a considerable historiographical inheritance which continues to shape the field in profound ways. Even the word 'liturgy' itself is an early modern construct. Medieval churchmen never used *liturgia*, and its related adjectives, to describe the prayers and rites which structured both private and communal worship. The word only began to be used in this way in the mid-sixteenth century at a time when there was considerable debate about religious ceremonial.[3] In the Middle Ages, it was more common either to refer to specific types of texts – prayers, chants, *ordines* – or types of books – such as sacramentaries, antiphonaries, pontificals and rituals.[4] When a collective noun was used it tended to be *officia* (offices).[5] The modern use of 'liturgy' to apply to a more or less wide range of medieval ceremonies is therefore

---

[3]   Symes, Chapter 10 below, 239–40; Christopher A. Jones, 'Performing Christianity: Liturgical and Devotional Writing', in *The Cambridge History of Early Medieval English Literature*, ed. Clare A. Lees (Cambridge: Cambridge University Press, 2013), 427–50, at 428. On the relative rarity of the term before the twentieth century see Simon Ditchfield, 'Giving Tridentine Worship Back Its History', in *Continuity and Change in Christian Worship*, ed. R.N. Swanson, Studies in Church History 35 (Woodbridge: Boydell Press, 1999), 199–226, at 203–204. See also the discussion of the significance of Reformation polemic about religious ceremony in Philippe Buc, *The Dangers of Ritual: Between Early Medieval Texts and Social Scientific Theory* (Princeton, NJ: Princeton University Press, 2001), 164–202.

[4]   *Ordo* (plural *ordines*) is generally used to refer to texts with directions for performance of particular religious services; *sacramentary* is a service book containing all the prayers needed to celebrate mass on each day of the year, often together with *ordines* for pastoral rites (such as baptism, penance, funerals), blessings and other texts; *antiphonary* or antiphonal contains a collection of antiphons; *pontifical* contains those rites that could only be celebrated by a bishop (such as confirmation, clerical ordination, church dedication); *ritual* or *rituale* (or *manual*) contains rubrics and texts for celebrating rites performed by a priest. For an introduction to liturgical books see Palazzo, *History*.

[5]   Jones, 'Performing Christianity', 428.

anachronistic. All the contributors to this volume have self-consciously used 'liturgy' in its modern sense. However, it is fair to say that there are disagreements about what should be considered as liturgy and the whole topic of how church rituals were classified in the Middle Ages merits further investigation.[6]

The debates of the sixteenth and seventeenth centuries among and between Roman Catholics and Protestants did not just provide us with a specious vocabulary. They also shaped the study of what we now know as medieval liturgy in terms of modern scholars' chronological and geographical emphases, the questions they ask, and materials they study. These battles were largely fought over the mass and, to a lesser extent, the round of daily prayer known as the office. The Protestants' quest for authenticity led them to become interested in the history of the practices of the early Church before (as they saw it) the liturgy had been corrupted by Rome. And the Catholics sought validity for their ceremonies by trying to demonstrate continuity with apostolic practices and across Christian history.[7] The search for authority has left its mark in present-day scholarship, especially in the English-language history of pastoral rites such as baptism where attention has largely focused on Late Antiquity and the early Middle Ages.[8]

It was, however, late medieval liturgy which shaped the rituals of both sides in the early modern period. In England many of the medieval rites characterized as Sarum were adapted into the Book of Common Prayer (1549).[9] The service books which emerged in the wake of the Council of Trent (1545–63) and which were promoted universally throughout Catholic Europe, also had their origins in the late medieval Church; the Roman Pontifical approved by Pope Clement VIII in 1595 is based, essentially, on the late thirteenth-century compilation

---

[6]   For problems of definition see below, Chapters 1, pp. 30–32; 6, pp. 157–58; and 10, pp. 239–41.

[7]   Interpretations of medieval liturgy are inevitably caught up in wider understanding of Christian history; for an overview see Anthony Grafton, 'Church History in Early Modern Europe: Tradition and Innovation', in *Sacred History: Uses of the Christian Past in the Renaissance World* ed. Katherine Van Liere, Simon Ditchfield and Howard Louthan (Oxford: Oxford University Press, 2012), 1–26; the other contributions to this volume are also relevant. An example of the Reformers' interest in the origins of liturgical uses can be found in q. 5 of Archbishop Thomas Cranmer's questionnaire sent to other bishops in 1547, cited by Gregory Dix, *The Shape of the Liturgy*, 2nd edn. (London: A. and C. Black, 1945), 640–42.

[8]   E.C. Whitaker and Maxwell E. Johnson, *Documents of the Baptismal Liturgy*, 3rd edn., Alcuin Club Collections 79 (London: SPCK, 2003); Bryan D. Spinks, *Early and Medieval Rituals and Theologies of Baptism: From the New Testament to the Council of Trent* (Aldershot: Ashgate, 2006). On early Church liturgy see Paul F. Bradshaw, *Reconstructing Early Christian Worship* (London: SPCK, 2009).

[9]   Salisbury, *Hear My Voice*, 65.

of William Durandus (1293–95).[10] The use made of late medieval liturgy was balanced, though, by a renewed emphasis on the regional: local churches looked to validate their past, be it in Italy through local saints' cults, or in England where there was a special interest in the Anglo-Saxon Church as exemplifying an indigenous form of Christianity untouched by the perceived corruption of the later medieval Church.[11] In the sixteenth-century Reformation, there was, then, keen interest in the Late Antique and early medieval Churches and much use made of later medieval rites but perhaps rather less concern for the liturgy of the period in between; that is, of the central Middle Ages.

These tendencies to focus on the earlier and later periods were exacerbated by developments in the nineteenth century. The Liturgical Movement, which was initially Roman Catholic, sought to counteract the trend towards clerically dominated public rites and bring the laity back into active participation, especially through chanting responses in the mass.[12] They looked back to a time before the divisions of the Reformation, viewing the Middle Ages as a period of great lay piety, manifest in church building, and wanted to revive the chants of the period. At the same time, they, like their Tridentine predecessors, sought authority and authenticity in the study of rites from earlier periods. The focus, perhaps inevitably, was on chants for the mass and office. This emphasis helped reinforce the view that the late medieval Church had excluded the laity from active involvement in the liturgy, and that vernacular languages were not widely used in liturgical contexts.[13] In the Church of England, the proponents of the

---

10   Vogel, *Medieval Liturgy*, 255–56.

11   Ditchfield, 'Giving Tridentine Worship Back its History'; Simon Ditchfield, *Liturgy, Sanctity and History in Tridentine Italy: Pietro Maria Campi and the Preservation of the Particular* (Cambridge: Cambridge University Press, 1995); Vivienne Sanders, 'The Household of Archbishop Parker and the Influencing of Public Opinion', *Journal of Ecclesiastical History* 34, no. 4 (1983): 534–47; Angelika Lutz, 'The Study of the Anglo-Saxon Chronicle in the Seventeenth Century and the Establishment of Old English Studies in the Universities', in *The Recovery of Old English: Anglo-Saxon Studies in the Sixteenth and Seventeenth Centuries*, ed. Timothy Graham (Kalamazoo, MI: Medieval Institute Publications, Western Michigan University, 2000), 1–82, esp. 1–2 and n. 2.

12   'Liturgical Movement', in *Oxford Dictionary of the Christian Church*, ed. Cross and Livingstone, 987–88; Katherine Bergeron, *Decadent Enchantments: The Revival of Gregorian Chant at Solesmes* (Berkeley: University of California Press, 1998).

13   For example, Keith Thomas, *Religion and the Decline of Magic: Studies in Popular Beliefs in Sixteenth- and Seventeenth-Century England* (London: Weidenfeld and Nicolson, 1971). For a corrective to views about the exclusion of the laity see Virginia Reinburg, 'Liturgy and the Laity in Late Medieval and Reformation France', *The Sixteenth Century Journal* 23, no. 3 (1992): 526–47; Eamon Duffy, *The Stripping of the Altars: Traditional Religion in England c. 1400–c. 1580* (New Haven: Yale University Press, 1992), 91–130. On the use of vernacular languages in the English liturgy see Helen Gittos, 'The Use of English in the Liturgy in the Middle Ages: A Case-Study from York' (working title, forthcoming); and Bruce Holsinger, *The Work of God: Liturgical*

emerging High Church movement sought to emphasize their Church's descent from the universal Church, and the continuities between its practices and those of the late medieval period: this led to the interest in the late medieval Uses of Sarum and York traced by Matthew Cheung Salisbury in Chapter 5. It is also manifest in the foundation of the Cambridge Camden Society (which later became the Ecclesiological Society) in 1839 and the Henry Bradshaw Society 'for the editing of rare liturgical texts' in 1890. These nineteenth-century concerns helped shape the development of much scholarly work and the creation of editions upon which, whatever their shortcomings, modern researchers still rely.

The confessionalization of scholarship on medieval liturgy has had other legacies too. Until the mid-twentieth century, research on liturgy was largely the domain of professional religious, belonging to both the Catholic and Protestant traditions. In England, for example, with certain notable exceptions such as the Catholic layman Edmund Bishop, this was the case until well after the Second World War.[14] But it is also worth recognizing the contribution made by art historians who, in England at least, helped in the twentieth century lead the turn away from such confessional approaches, for those interested in manuscript art have long recognized the need to understand the liturgical material. Art historians have, however, largely, but not wholly, focused on the evidence for saints' feasts recorded in calendars and litanies, seeking to attribute manuscripts and to trace relationships between different houses.[15] They have been much less interested in occasional rites.

Culture and Vernacular Writing in Britain, 550–1550 (Chicago: University of Chicago Press, forthcoming).

[14] Many of the most influential works on medieval liturgy in the late nineteenth and twentieth centuries are the work of churchmen, including Adalbert Ebner, *Quellen und Forschungen zur Geschichte und Kunstgeschichte des Missale Romanum im Mittelalter Iter italicum* (Freiburg: Herder, 1896); Josef A. Jungmann, *Missarum sollemnia: eine genetische Erklärung der römischen Messe*, 2 vols., 2nd rev. edn. (Vienna: Herder, 1949), trans. Francis A. Brunner as *The Mass of the Roman Rite: Its Origins and Development*, 2 vols. (New York: Benziger Brothers, 1951–55); Dix, *Shape of the Liturgy*; OR; *Le pontifical romain au moyen âge*, ed. Michel Andrieu, 4 vols., Studi e Testi 86–89 (Vatican City: Biblioteca Apostolica Vaticana, 1938–41); Vogel, *Medieval Liturgy*. For Edmund Bishop see his posthumously published papers, *Liturgica Historica: Papers on the Liturgy and Religious Life of the Western Church* (Oxford: Clarendon Press, 1918).

[15] Key figures in English medieval liturgical manuscript studies include Francis Wormald (see for example his *English Benedictine Kalendars before AD 1100*, HBS 72 (London: HBS, 1934)); Christopher Hohler, for whom there is a partial bibliography in Alan Borg and Andrew Martindale, eds., *The Vanishing Past: Studies of Medieval Art, Liturgy and Metrology Presented to Christopher Hohler* British Archaeological Reports, International Series, 111 (Oxford, 1981), 1–6; Derek Turner, for whom there is a bibliography in Janet Backhouse and Shelley Jones, 'D.H. Turner (1931–1985): A Portrait', *The British Library Journal* 13, no. 2 (1987): 111–17; and Nigel J. Morgan (see for example his *English Monastic Litanies of the Saints after 1100*, 2 vols., HBS 119–20 (London: HBS, 2012–13)). See also Eric Palazzo, 'Art and Liturgy in the Middle

Much of the work in the last fifty years has continued along the chronological lines set down by early modern and nineteenth-century churchmen and this helps to explain the relative neglect of the central Middle Ages, and of occasional rites, in the prevailing narratives of liturgical history. Thus accounts tend to focus on either the earlier or the later Middle Ages, and particularly on the early Church and the Carolingian reforms, or the years after the Fourth Lateran Council.[16]

The essays in this book address this legacy in several ways. First, many are concerned with evidence from the tenth to twelfth centuries; this is, in part, to challenge traditional ideas that the foundations of Christian liturgy were laid in the early Church and flourished in the High Middle Ages. Second, we have included some explicit discussion of historiographical topics, especially in Chapters 2, 3, 4 and 5. Given the extent to which past debates continue to shape modern research it is vital to understand the framework within which current narratives have developed. Third, our focus on occasional rites is also intended to address another example of how early modern concerns have skewed contemporary debate. Occasional offices have always received less attention and one reason for this is that the debates of the sixteenth and seventeenth centuries were focused principally on the mass and the office, as these were seen as the most theologically contentious areas. Fourth, all the chapters address one of the most potent legacies of earlier scholarship. This is a series of teleological narratives about how rites developed during the Middle Ages which traces the origins of later collections back to earlier texts, and gives seminal importance to particular works, such as the 'Romano-German Pontifical', and periods, such as the Carolingian Reformation.[17] The attraction of such stories is that they simplify the complexity of the evidence. But, as the contributions to this volume make clear, they are also deeply problematic because they do not take account of the very diverse nature of the rites themselves. It is therefore vital to reassess the nature and influence of traditional landmarks in liturgical history.

Ages: Survey of Research (1980–2003) and Some Reflections on Method', *Journal of English and Germanic Philology* 105, no. 1 (2006): 170–84.

[16]   For example, Palazzo's *History of Liturgical Books from the Beginning to the Thirteenth Century* focuses mainly on the years pre-1000; John Harper's *Forms and Orders*, whilst it begins in the tenth century, focuses its attention on the later Middle Ages; Richard Pfaff's study, *The Liturgy in Medieval England: A History*, devotes some seventy pages to the Anglo-Saxon period, one hundred pages to the years 1066–1215, and some 350 pages to the years after 1215; Andrew Hughes, *Medieval Manuscripts for Mass and Office: A Guide to their Organization and Terminology* (Toronto: University of Toronto Press, 1982) has a similarly later focus.

[17]   For example, see the efforts to construct a genealogy for the evolution of liturgical traditions in Vogel, *Medieval Liturgy*, 399, 403 (Tables A and E).

Challenges

This brief discussion conveys something of the extent to which modern research into medieval liturgy continues to be shaped by early modern and nineteenth-century preoccupations. How can we break away from them? In these studies, and the discussions that helped shape them, several potentially fruitful approaches have emerged. One is that it is essential to recognize and find ways of working with the diversity of the evidence, be it for individual rites, as with excommunication, exorcism or church dedication, or collections of rites, such as those now known as the Romano-German Pontifical. It is also useful to pay attention to the contexts in which individual rites were recorded. For example, it is instructive to ask: Why was this rite written down?[18] There is much that can be learnt here from the approaches taken by relevant research in musicology and drama.[19] Other ways in which to contextualize rites include trying to answer questions like: How were these texts read? What was the audience for a particular manuscript? Why were some rites viewed as core to most collections, whilst others, such as those for exorcism and excommunication, seem to have been more peripheral?[20] In asking these questions, scholars need to be mindful, as Carol Symes points out in Chapter 10, that medieval manuscripts of liturgical rites were rarely, if ever, intended simply as a prescription for how the service should be conducted, as with some modern service books. By focusing on the local and the particular scholars may identify fresh ways in which to interpret, and understand, medieval rites. One example of this is Sarah Hamilton's comparison of excommunication rites in Chapter 6 which helps explain how and why the collections in which they appear were compiled. It is also helpful to make use of other types of evidence in addition to the rites themselves. Considering other genres and media alongside liturgical texts can be very revealing, as Florence Chave-Mahir, Mette Birkedal Bruun, Louis Hamilton and Carolyn Marino Malone demonstrate in Chapters 7, 8 and 9.

We hope these essays convey something of the excitement of current work in the field, the potential value of the evidence, and some directions for future research. Liturgy should not be a marginal subject, of interest only to those who

---

[18] For an example of this approach, see S. Hamilton, Chapter 6 in this book.

[19] See, for example, Susan Rankin, 'From Memory to Record: Musical Notations in Manuscripts from Exeter', *Anglo-Saxon England* 13 (1984): 97–112; Carol Symes, 'The Appearance of Early Vernacular Plays: Forms, Functions, and the Future of Medieval Theater', *Speculum* 77 (2002): 778–831; eadem, 'The Medieval Archive and the History of Theater: Assessing the Written and Unwritten Evidence for Premodern Performance', *Theatre Survey* 52, no. 1 (2011): 29–58.

[20] Hamilton, Chapter 6 and Chave-Mahir, Chapter 7 below.

study the lives of medieval professional religious.[21] Occasional rites, in particular, were often directed towards, and involved, the laity as well as the clergy. And the liturgy was not nearly as static as often supposed: it was continually adapted to meet new circumstances. Investigating how and why this was offers not only new ways of understanding medieval liturgical evidence, but also of improving our understanding of the Middle Ages.

---

[21]   Unfortunately Arnold Angenendt's pioneering work in this respect is yet to be fully taken up by English-language scholarship: see his *Geschichte der Religiosität im Mittelalter* (Darmstadt: Wissenschaftliche Buchgesellschaft, 1997) and his *Liturgik und Historik. Gab es eine organische Liturgie-Entwicklung?* (Freiburg: Herder, 2001). Other examples of recent books that attempt to integrate liturgy and social history include Eric Palazzo, *Liturgie et société au Moyen Age* (Paris: Aubier, 2000) and Sarah Hamilton, *Church and People in the Medieval West, 900–1200* (Harlow: Pearson, 2013).

PART I
Researching Rites

Chapter 1

Researching the History of Rites

Helen Gittos

Preliminaries

Thousands of medieval manuscripts containing materials for use in so-called 'occasional' rites such as baptism, burial and Palm Sunday survive from Western Europe.[1] Yet their value as historical sources has hardly begun to be realized. There are two main reasons for this. The first is the enduring perception that the medieval liturgy was conservative – traditional, slow to change, and therefore not very useful for historians to study. Here, for example, is the end of an essay by John Blair about baptismal fonts in Anglo-Saxon England:

> Encouraged by the materials that they study, liturgists tend to lay great stress on uniformity. From a liturgist's perspective this paper is rather iconoclastic, proposing as it does a high degree of diversity and informality in English local practice during the ninth to eleventh centuries.[2]

Although some previous generations of liturgists did emphasize uniformity, Blair's statement could not be less true of current work in the field. The diversity in early medieval baptismal rites that he proposes on the basis of the archaeological evidence is precisely what one finds in the liturgical sources. Susan Keefe, in her

---

[1]   For example, more than 450 manuscripts are listed in Thomas Davies Kozachek, 'The Repertory of Chant for Dedicating Churches in the Middle Ages: Music, Liturgy, and Ritual' (unpub. Harvard University DPhil thesis, 1995), 382–91; and Richard Kay, *Pontificalia: A Repertory of Latin Manuscript Pontificals and Benedictionals* (Lawrence, KA: published online by Digital Publishing Services, University of Kansas Libraries, at http://hdl.handle.net/1808/4406, 2007) lists 1249 pontificals and benedictionals. For the term 'occasional rites' see p. 1 above.

I am immensely grateful to everyone who participated in the *Interpreting Medieval Liturgy* network from whom I learnt so much and without whom I could not have written this. I have benefited from comments on a draft of this chapter from Mette Birkedal Bruun, Louis Hamilton, Sarah Hamilton, Andy Hudson, Christopher A. Jones, Carolyn Marino Malone, Henry Parkes, Fred Paxton, Matthew Salisbury, Carol Symes and Ben Whitworth. Yitzhak Hen kindly sent me some of his unpublished articles. Moira and Brian Gittos provided crucial logistical support.

[2]   John Blair, 'The Prehistory of English Fonts', in *Intersections: The Archaeology and History of Christianity in England, 400–1200: Papers in Honour of Martin Biddle and Birthe Kjølbye-Biddle*, ed. Martin Henig and Nigel Ramsay, British Archaeological Reports, British Series 505 (Oxford: Archaeopress, 2010), 149–177, at 177.

work on baptism in the Carolingian Empire repeatedly stresses this: 'one can truly be amazed at the amount of liturgical diversity'; 'diversity … characterized public worship'.[3] It is the degree to which medieval liturgy was diverse, informal, and frequently revised and rewritten that makes it so valuable as historical evidence.

The second reason why liturgical sources are undervalued is that they are perceived as being difficult to use:

> Liturgical history is pure scholarship: painstakingly detailed, extremely technical, highly esoteric … Its practitioners, like the initiates of an ancient mystery cult, pour the fruits of their researches into learned journals with splendidly arcane titles like *Ephemerides Liturgicae* and *Sacris Erudiri*. It is hard for a mere layman to penetrate these mysteries ….[4]

In fact liturgical sources present only the same kinds of problems as other types of medieval texts such as charters, writs or law codes. Just as with other sources, in order to be able to use liturgical manuscripts one needs to familiarize oneself with the conventions of the genre but they are far from being impenetrable and arcane. In this chapter I will discuss the potential of liturgical rites as sources, some practical ways in which one can work with this material, some problems that are likely to be encountered, and some possible directions for future research. My focus is on how one can go about doing such work rather than providing a survey of the historiography.

Potential: What are Rites Evidence For?

Medieval liturgical sources for rites such as Palm Sunday, baptism and penance are of immense value for many reasons. One of these has already been mentioned: these rituals were repeatedly revised and never standardized – it is rare to find

---

3   Susan A. Keefe, *Water and the Word: Baptism and the Education of the Clergy in the Carolingian Empire*, 2 vols. (Notre Dame, IN: University of Notre Dame Press, 2002), 1:137 (this whole volume is relevant but see especially 42, 67, 131–37, 152). For further discussion about liturgical diversity see the papers by Hen, McKitterick and Cubitt in R.N. Swanson, ed., *Unity and Diversity in the Church: Papers Read at the 1994 Summer Meeting and the 1995 Winter Meeting of the Ecclesiastical History Society*, Studies in Church History 32 (Oxford: Blackwell, 1996); and Richard E. Sullivan, 'The Carolingian Age: Reflections on Its Place in the History of the Middle Ages', *Speculum* 64, no. 2 (1989): 267–306, esp. 293–94, 295.

4   Jeffrey Richards, *Consul of God: The Life and Times of Gregory the Great* (London: Routledge & Kegan Paul, 1980), 119. This quotation was drawn to my attention by John F. Romano's *MedievalLiturgy.com* website: http://medievalliturgy.com/introduction_bibliography. html.

any version of a ritual that is identical to any other. One of the recurring features of manuscript-based studies of such rites is that their authors remark on the comparative diversity of whatever ritual they are considering. Susan Keefe's previously cited characterization of baptismal rites in the Carolingian period is particularly emphatic but essentially typical; similar statements have been made about the diversity of Anglo-Saxon rites for blessing holy oils, liturgies for excommunication and the consecration of churches from the central Middle Ages, blessings of pilgrims and crusaders in the twelfth and thirteenth centuries, and rites for public penance in thirteenth- and fourteenth-century France.[5] Contemporaries were aware of this. Walahfrid Strabo, abbot of Reichenau (Germany), writing in c. 840–42 discusses at length the 'great diversity in the liturgy' in his own time and mentions the different versions of the psalms used, and the many variations in baptismal practices. He was tolerant of these differences and, for example, willing to accept the validity of triple or single immersion or effusion.[6] He was aware that much of the liturgical material available in his day had been written only recently and was content that 'new compositions ... are not to be rejected' so long as they were doctrinally orthodox.[7] Later on, in the eleventh century, Lanfranc, archbishop of Canterbury (1070–89), was involved in various disagreements with John, archbishop of Rouen, about vestments. In a surviving letter he draws on his own experience: 'I have often watched various bishops of different provinces dedicating churches, and I have observed most

---

[5]   Christopher A. Jones, 'The Chrism Mass in Later Anglo-Saxon England', in *The Liturgy of the Late Anglo-Saxon Church*, ed. Helen Gittos and M. Bradford Bedingfield, HBS Subsidia 5 (London: HBS, 2005), 105–42, esp. 130; Christopher A. Jones, 'The Origins of the "Sarum" Chrism Mass at Eleventh-Century Christ Church, Canterbury', *Mediaeval Studies* 67 (2005): 219–315, esp. 231–32; Chapters 6 and 8 below; M.C. Gaposchkin, 'Origins and Development of the Pilgrimage and Cross Blessings in the Roman Pontificals of the Twelfth and Thirteenth Centuries', *Mediaeval Studies* 73 (2011): 261–86, esp. 262; Mary C. Mansfield, *The Humiliation of Sinners: Public Penance in Thirteenth-Century France* (Ithaca, NY: Cornell University Press, 1995), esp. 16, 161, 189–90. Paul F. Bradshaw, *The Search for the Origins of Christian Worship: Sources and Methods for the Study of Early Liturgy*, 2nd. edn. (Oxford: Oxford University Press, 2002), esp. 191, emphasizes the diversity of liturgical practice in the early Church up to the fourth century. For the Carolingian period see also F.S. Paxton, *Christianizing Death: The Creation of a Ritual Process in Early Medieval Europe* (Ithaca NY: Cornell University Press, 1990), esp. ch. 5 and 207–9.

[6]   Alice L. Harting-Corrêa, *Walahfrid Strabo's* Libellus de exordiis et incrementis quarundam in observationibus ecclesiasticis rerum: *A Translation and Liturgical Commentary*, Mittellateinische Studien Und Texte 19 (Leiden: E.J. Brill, 1996), 1 (for the date), 162–63 (for the quote 'tanta ... in ipsis diversitas officiis'), 168–81 (psalms and baptism).

[7]   '... noviter componi, quae non sint, ... abicienda', in ibid., 160–61, and see 136–37, 172–73.

scrupulously all that they did. In some respects their practice differed'.[8] In relation to a detail in the rite for ordaining a subdeacon, he talks about the different rubrics found in 'our own books of episcopal *ordines*, of which we have many from different parts of the world'.[9] This letter is fascinating because it provides evidence for an interest in liturgical minutiae, the importance of witnessed precedents ('I was present when St Leo himself, supreme bishop of the Roman see, dedicated the church of Remiremont ...'), and for the academic study of liturgical books.[10] Even in the late Middle Ages, diversity had not disappeared: a late fifteenth-century scribe somewhat exasperatedly introduced the rite for dedicating a church in a manuscript from Besançon by saying: 'Concerning the dedication or consecration of churches there is so much variety among various rites, that not only do they not agree in many things, but they can even contradict one another'.[11] It is not yet clear when liturgies became more stable because less work has been done on the rites of the later Middle Ages than those of earlier periods. However, it has been suggested that this only happened once texts intended to be authoritative and official began to be printed by Pope Pius V in the 1560s.[12]

The extent of diversity is such that where one does, occasionally, find evidence for a group of texts that are substantially similar, this is notable.[13] The

---

[8]　'Diuersos enim diuersarum prouinciarum praesules aecclesias dedicare sepe conspexi, omnibusque quae ab eis acta sunt quantam potui curam adhibui. Qui etsi in nonnullis dissimilia egerunt'; Helen Clover and Margaret Gibson, eds., *The Letters of Lanfranc Archbishop of Canterbury* (Oxford: Oxford University Press, 1979), 84–85.

[9]　'In nostris episcopalis ordinis codicibus, quos ex diuersis regionibus multos habemus'; ibid., 86–87 (translation adapted).

[10]　'Denique sanctus Leo Romanae sedis summus antistes Romericensem me praesente aecclesiam dedicauit'; ibid., 84–85.

[11]　'Circa dedicacionem sive consecracionem ecclesiarum apud varios est varietas tanta, ut non solum in multis non conveniant, sed eciam sibi contradicunt'; Besançon, Bibliothèque Municipale, Mss 115-116-117, fol. 90, transcribed in Leroquais, *Pontificaux*, 1: 77, and translated and discussed in Kozachek, 'Repertory', 1–2, and see also Louis Hamilton, this book, 178–79. Keefe, *Water and the Word*, 1:128, for earlier, ninth-century, evidence that bishops were aware of liturgical diversity.

[12]　John F. Romano, 'Joy in Waiting?: The History of Gaudete Sunday', *Mediaeval Studies* 72 (2010): 75–124, at 107–8; Natalia Nowakowska, 'From Strassburg to Trent: Bishops, Printing and Liturgical Reform in the Fifteenth Century', *Past and Present* 213 (2011): 3–39; Matthew Cheung Salisbury, *The Secular Liturgical Office in Late Medieval England* (Turnhout: Brepols, 2015), introduction.

[13]　Some rites seem to have become 'petrified', apparently through disuse: Mansfield, *Humiliation of Sinners*, 160–61, 245–46. Sometimes when one finds identical *ordines* in several manuscripts it is because the rite is brand new; see for example Helen Gittos, *Liturgy, Architecture, and Sacred Places in Anglo-Saxon England* (Oxford: Oxford University Press, 2013), 113–15 (a ceremony for Candlemas). In some cases rites which have been considered to be 'rather static'

eleventh-century customaries associated with the monastery of Cluny (France) are one example and are discussed in Chapter 9. In this case it appears that their homogeneity reflects the authority that Cluny had. Sometimes Cluniac monks used a written customary as part of the process of reforming another monastery.[14] More often, though, the Cluniac customaries were not used as practical documents to guide daily life but as 'inspirational texts' which 'offered their readers the opportunity to learn about admirable monastic lives'.[15] These customaries sometimes offered models of how to live a good life rather than rules for how to do so. Most of the time, though, medieval rites were 'living' texts that were regularly tinkered with and therefore provide evidence for current ideas and concerns.[16]

The extent of diversity results from many different causes. Sometimes one can uncover the precise historical contexts in which these changes were made. It is clear, for example, that rites were repeatedly revised by liturgists at Canterbury Cathedral throughout the later tenth and eleventh centuries, and enough manuscripts survive that one can see in some detail the successive changes that were made.[17] In some cases these can be associated with particular individuals, such as Archbishop Dunstan's (959–88) interest in the Candlemas ceremony, or the changes to the Palm Sunday service made by Lanfranc (1070–89).[18] In other cases they can be related to particular circumstances, such as the monasticization of the cathedral, or the desire to control the proliferation of newly constructed local churches.[19] Many other examples could be cited. We have, for example,

---

actually were not as S. Hamilton argues in the case of excommunication rites (Chapter 6, this quote on 134).

[14]   Isabelle Cochelin, 'Customaries as Inspirational Sources', in *Consuetudines et regulae: Sources for Monastic Life in the Middle Ages and the Early Modern Period*, ed. Carolyn Marino Malone and Clark Maines, Disciplina monastica 10 (Turnhout: Brepols, 2014), 27–72, at 27–28 and n. 5. I am grateful to Carolyn Marino Malone for this reference.

[15]   Ibid., 32.

[16]   This metaphor has frequently been deployed: see, for example, Keefe, *Water and the Word*, 1:154; Bradshaw, *Origins of Christian Worship*, 5; Jones, 'Chrism Mass', esp. 130–38; Sharon L. McMillan, *Episcopal Ordination and Ecclesial Consensus* (Collegeville, MN: Liturgical Press, 2005), 3; Parkes, this book, 77 below.

[17]   Jones, 'Chrism Mass'; Jones, 'Origins'; Gittos, *Liturgy*, 45–50, 113–21, 124–28, 220–30; Helen Gittos, 'Sources for the Liturgy of Canterbury Cathedral in the Central Middle Ages', in *Medieval Art, Architecture and Archaeology at Canterbury*, ed. Alixe Bovey (Leeds: British Archaeological Association, 2013), 41–58.

[18]   Gittos, *Liturgy*, 113–15; Gittos, 'Sources for the Liturgy of Canterbury Cathedral', 47–48. For another example of a rite written by an identifiable person see Paxton, this book, 47.

[19]   Monasticization: *The Canterbury Benedictional (British Museum, Harl. Ms. 2892)*, ed. R.M. Woolley, HBS 51 (London: HBS, 1917), produced in the second quarter of the eleventh century, is an intriguing manuscript which deserves further study. Its compiler revised several rites to make them accord better with the directions in the *Regularis concordia*. Both complete

evidence for the rite written by Hincmar, archbishop of Rheims (845–82), for the coronation of Charles the Bald as king of Lotharingia in 869.[20] We can read the new liturgies created by Goscelin of Saint-Bertin for the saints of St Augustine's abbey, Canterbury in preparation for their move into the rebuilt church at the end of the eleventh century.[21] One can trace the creation of new rites for consecrating cemeteries in the tenth century as bishops tried to control popular enthusiasm, or for blessing crusaders in the twelfth century, or the revival of interest in celebrating Gaudete Sunday as part of an attempt by Pope Innocent II (1130–43) to establish himself in Rome.[22] When it is possible to identify the circumstances in which particular rites were created their value as evidence increases substantially.

This is especially true when texts and the manuscripts in which they are found can be associated with particular people. Although liturgical books were usually compiled anonymously, they were often personal books, commissioned by particular individuals for their own use, even if these persons are not named. Amongst the best sources for occasional rites are pontificals and manuals, books containing rites to be conducted by bishops and priests respectively. There is evidence that these were often treated as personal books and sometimes subsequently preserved as memorials of the people for whom they were made. We seem to have the pontificals made for Dunstan and Anselm, archbishops of Canterbury (959–88 and 1093–1109), Hugues de Salins, archbishop of Besançon (1031–66), Gundekar, bishop of Eichstätt (1057–75), David de Bernham, bishop of St Andrews (1240–53), and the benedictional (a book containing episcopal blessings for use in the mass) of Æthelwold, bishop of Winchester (963–84) amongst many others.[23] Sometimes there may be good

---

surviving copies of the *Regularis concordia* were made in Canterbury in the mid-eleventh century so it seems likely that the interest in the text at that time was associated with a reform of the community to make it a totally Benedictine house. On the difficulty of telling precisely when this happened see Nicholas Brooks, *The Early History of the Church of Canterbury: Christ Church from 597 to 1066* (London: Leicester University Press, 1984), 255–60. This is a topic I hope to examine in more detail in future. Control of local churches: Jones, 'Chrism Mass', esp. 130–38; Helen Gittos, 'Introduction', in *Liturgy of the Late Anglo-Saxon Church*, ed. Gittos and Bedingfield (London: 2005), 1–11, at 9–10.

[20] Jinty Nelson, 'Coronation Rituals and Related Materials', in *Understanding Medieval Primary Sources: Using Historical Sources to Discover Medieval Europe*, ed. Joel T. Rosenthal (London: Routledge, 2012), 114–30, at 117–21.

[21] Richard Sharpe, 'Goscelin's St Augustine and St Mildreth: Hagiography and Liturgy in Context', *Journal of Theological Studies* n.s. 41, no. 2 (1990): 502–16.

[22] Gittos, *Liturgy*, 39–54; Gaposchkin, 'Pilgrimage and Cross Blessings'; Romano, 'Gaudete Sunday', 90–102, 120–21.

[23] Gittos, 'Sources for the Liturgy of Canterbury Cathedral'; Sarah Hamilton, 'The Early Pontificals: The Anglo-Saxon Evidence Reconsidered from a Continental Perspective', in *England*

reason to think the commissioners of these books were the deans and precentors who were really in charge of the liturgy, rather than often-absent figureheads, but even so they remain useful evidence for the state of the liturgy in those cathedrals at that time, perhaps for the process of negotiation undertaken with an incoming incumbent: a book may have been produced by a cathedral to try to persuade a new bishop that these were the local customs he should follow.[24] Although we rarely know the names of the priests for whom manuals were written, the surviving manuscripts, which tend to be small, workaday books, are precious evidence for the decisions of their owners, and historians are increasingly paying attention to them. We have, for example, the liturgical manuscripts of a priest ministering in south-eastern Gaul probably in the late seventh century, another belonging to someone working near Liège, Belgium c. 800, and a third from a priest associated with Sherborne Cathedral, Dorset c. 1060; there are many more that deserve study.[25] Even when they are anonymous, it is possible to recover a great deal of information about the authors and compilers of specific liturgies and particular manuscripts.

---

and the Continent in the Tenth Century: Studies in Honour of Wilhelm Levison (1876–1947), ed. David Rollason, Conrad Leyser and Hannah Williams, Studies in the Early Middle Ages 37 (Turnhout: Brepols, 2010), 411–28; *Pontificale ecclesiæ S. Andreæ: The Pontifical Offices Used by David de Bernham, Bishop of S. Andrews*, ed. C. Wordsworth (Edinburgh: Pitsligo Press, 1885).

[24] For the last point see Hamilton, 'Early Pontificals', 427–28.

[25] Yitzhak Hen and Rob Meens, eds., *The Bobbio Missal: Liturgy and Religious Culture in Merovingian Gaul*, Cambridge Studies in Palaeography and Codicology 11 (Cambridge: Cambridge University Press, 2004), esp. editors' conclusion 219–22; Yitzhak Hen, 'A Liturgical Handbook for the Use of a Rural Priest (Brussels, Br 10127–10144)', in *Organising the Written Word: Scripts, Manuscripts, and Texts*, ed. Marco Mostert (Turnhout: Brepols, forthcoming); Yitzhak Hen, 'Knowledge of Canon Law among Rural Priests: The Evidence of Two Carolingian Manuscripts from around 800', *Journal of Theological Studies* n.s. 50, no. 1 (1999): 117–34; Christopher Hohler, 'The Red Book of Darley', in *Nordiskt Kollokvium II: I Latinsk Liturgiforskning 12–13 Maj 1972, Hässelby Slott* (Stockholm: Institutionen för Klassiska Språk vid Stockholms Universitet [1972]): 39–47; Helen Gittos, 'Is There Any Evidence for the Liturgy of Parish Churches in Late Anglo-Saxon England? The Red Book of Darley and the Status of Old English', in *Pastoral Care in Late Anglo-Saxon England*, ed. Francesca Tinti, Anglo-Saxon Studies 6 (Woodbridge: Boydell Press, 2005), 63–83. See also Frederick S. Paxton, '*Bonus Liber*: A Late Carolingian Clerical Manual from Lorsch (Bibliotheca Vaticana Ms Pal. lat. 485)', in *The Two Laws: Studies in Medieval Legal History Dedicated to Stephan Kuttner*, ed. Laurent Mayali and Stephanie A. J. Tibbetts, Studies in Medieval and Early Modern Canon Law 1 (Washington, DC: Catholic University of America Press, 1990), 1–30; Carine van Rhijn, 'The Local Church, Priests' Handbooks and Pastoral Care in the Carolingian Period', in *Chiese locali e chiese regionali nell'alto medioevo*, Settimane di studio del Centro italiano di studi sull'alto medioevo 61, 2 vols. (Spoleto: Fondazione Centro Italiano di Studi Sull'alto Medioevo, 2014), 2: 689–710; Yitzhak Hen, 'Priests and Books in the Merovingian Period', in *Early Medieval Priests*, ed. Yitzhak Hen and Rob Meens (Hilversum: Verloren, forthcoming).

Sometimes one can use rites to make inferences about the decisions taken by individuals but more often they enable one to examine changes in political, theological or social ideas. This is partly because rites tended to be created and altered by making use of material that already existed:

> One of the advantages for the historian in studying any ritual is the potential it can offer for observing processes within a defined matrix, rather than simply apprehending a single event or series of events caught in a particular moment ... ritual provides a structural framework in which ... relationships ... can be understood over a long period.[26]

The existence of diversity within common forms means such sources are ideal for making comparisons between periods and regions. They offer 'spyholes through which we could look to pinpoint elements of a social reality' of the kind advocated by Chris Wickham for the purposes of writing comparative history.[27] Because liturgy was so diverse, because people did have considerable freedom in how it was celebrated, because there was so little aspiration to uniformity, the surviving written sources are richly informative. As Susan Keefe says – and the other chapters in this book repeatedly emphasize – such texts 'tell of resistance and cooperation, borrowing and independence, conformity and non-conformity, local sensitivities, preferences, needs'.[28]

Historians cannot, however, assume that these differences had much, if anything, to do with how the liturgy was practised.[29] It is clear that liturgical manuscripts were created for many more reasons than was appreciated by earlier generations of scholars.[30] Given the oral nature of the transmission of liturgy in the Middle Ages it is even more important than ever to ask: Why were texts written down?[31] Sometimes it was for a practical purpose: in order to manage long and complex services, for use when out in the field, to note

---

[26]   Andrew Jotischky, 'Holy Fire and Holy Sepulchre: Ritual and Space in Jerusalem from the Ninth to the Fourteenth Centuries', in *Ritual and Space in the Middle Ages: Proceedings of the 2009 Harlaxton Symposium*, ed. Frances Andrews, Harlaxton Medieval Studies 21 (Donington: Shaun Tyas, 2011), 44–60, at 45.

[27]   Chris Wickham, 'Problems in Doing Comparative History', in *Challenging the Boundaries of Medieval History: The Legacy of Timothy Reuter*, ed. Patricia Skinner, Studies in the Early Middle Ages 22 (Turnhout: Brepols, 2009), 5–28, at 12.

[28]   Keefe, *Water and the Word*, 1:154.

[29]   On the last point see below Chapter 8, esp. 183 and Chapter 10.

[30]   For the 'variety of intellectual contexts in which a single text could potentially reside' see Parkes, this book, 92.

[31]   Thanks to Sarah Hamilton for repeatedly demonstrating to me how useful it is to ask this question; for further discussion of this issue see her chapter in this book, esp. 128. On oral transmission see Symes, this book, 247–49; Cochelin, 'Customaries', 27–28 and n. 5; Steven

down recently encountered texts and chant, to try to ensure revisions were carried out as anticipated, to mitigate the problems caused by a rapid turnover of people, to establish definitive texts.[32] But there were other reasons too. It has been argued that liturgies could be written down in order to control, suppress, limit or fossilize particular practices.[33] In particular, written rituals may have been intended to try to curtail improvisation. This was certainly something that worried Walahfrid Strabo in the ninth century who made a clear distinction between what was written and what was improvised: 'and we see that even today readings and collects and different kinds of praises are being added to an almost superabundance of things ... But we must consider, as blessed Augustine says, "that we should sing what is written but what is not written we should not sing".[34] Another reason for writing liturgies down was to deliberately obscure regional differences in order to emphasize unity. The *Regularis concordia*, a Benedictine customary promulgated at Winchester c. 966, is an example of a text that was probably intended to do several of these things: to suppress some contemporary liturgical practices (in which attempt it was unsuccessful), and to make a statement about unity in the context of the newly created kingdom of the English.[35] This makes it an extremely valuable source – but as evidence for the ideals of King Edgar and Bishop Æthelwold and only at best indirectly for the state of the liturgy in Anglo-Saxon England at the time. Whilst in the past it has been assumed that customaries such as this were compiled as guides to the rules by which a community should live, it is becoming increasingly clear that it is not safe to assume this. One example of this has already been cited: the evidence that many early medieval customaries,

---

Vanderputten, ed., *Understanding Monastic Practices of Oral Communication (Western Europe, Tenth–Thirteenth Centuries)*, Utrecht Studies in Medieval Literacy 21 (Turnhout: Brepols, 2011).

[32]   I have borrowed the last phrase from Carol Symes, 'The Medieval Archive and the History of Theatre: Assessing the Written and Unwritten Evidence for Premodern Performance', *Theatre Survey* 52, no. 1 (2011): 29–58, at 50. For a rite written down in detail because of its novelty, see Romano, 'Gaudete Sunday', 96; for attempts to control doctrine see Bradshaw, *Origins of Christian Worship*, 225. For an example of a reason why a text was written down see Paxton, this book, 52.

[33]   See this book, Chapters 8 and 10.

[34]   '... cum videamus usque hodie et lectiones et collectas et diversas laudum species iam paene abundantibus omnibus superaddi ... Sed videndum est, sicut beatus Augustinus ait, "ut ea cantentur, quae ita scripta sunt, quae autem non ita scripta sunt, non cantentur."' Harting-Corrêa, *Walahfrid Strabo's* Libellus de exordiis, 136–37. On improvisation see Chave-Mahir, this book, 173–74; Symes, this book, 249–50; and for a late Anglo-Saxon reference to improvisation in private prayer see Christopher A. Jones, 'Performing Christianity: Liturgical and Devotional Writing', in *The Cambridge History of Early Medieval English Literature*, ed. Clare A. Lees (Cambridge: Cambridge University Press, 2013), 427–50, at 441.

[35]   Symes, 'Medieval Archive', 30.

including those of Cluny, were created as inspirational rather than normative documents.[36] These are some examples of the reasons why texts were written down other than simply being for practical use in a particular ceremony.

More evidence of the multifarious motivations for the creation of written liturgies comes from research into pontificals. The creation of this new type of liturgical book seems to have been part of a strategy to emphasize the power of bishops in the later ninth and early tenth centuries.[37] In some cases pontificals were associated with attempts by archiepiscopal sees to assert control over bishops within their provinces.[38] It has been suggested that the inclusion of didactic texts in them indicates that they were intended as texts from which to teach priests rather than for use in services.[39] Some functioned, even if they were not originally intended, as repositories of local information.[40] One example is the early tenth-century pontifical of Sens which contains an unusual and detailed rite for crowning a queen. This new rite appears to have been drawn up by Archbishop Walter of Sens c. 888–922 in order to demonstrate the rightful rule of successive West Frankish rulers whom he crowned. It was legitimized by being placed next to an older coronation rite for a king. In the tenth and eleventh centuries, oaths of fidelity of suffragan bishops were entered into this book in several places, including in the margins of the queen's coronation rite, which seems therefore to have been read as testimony of the authority of the archbishops of Sens.[41] Some manuscripts were intended both to memorialize the pontificates of individual bishops and serve as institutional histories. The Litlyngton Missal, a large-scale, deluxe mass book which includes some *ordines*, was produced for Westminster Abbey

---

[36] Cochelin, 'Customaries', esp. 32–41 where it is also argued that this changed from the twelfth century onwards, especially in the context of the rise of monastic orders in which different houses were tied together by institutions which could be regulatory, such as general chapters and visitations.

[37] Eric Palazzo, 'La liturgie de l'occident médiéval autour de l'an mil: Etat de la question', *Cahiers de civilisation médiévale* 43 (2000): 371–94, at 377–83; Palazzo, *History*, 199; Niels Krogh Rasmussen, with Marcel Haverals, *Les pontificaux du haut moyen âge: Genèse du livre de l'évêque*, Spicilegium Sacrum Lovaniense: Etudes et Documents 49 (Leuven, 1998); S. Hamilton, Chapter 6 in this book for discussion about why early pontificals were created and pp. 126–27 for their use as statements of episcopal authority.

[38] Hamilton, 'Early Pontificals', 415–16.

[39] Ibid., 420–21; S. Hamilton, this book, 127.

[40] Hamilton, 'Early Pontificals', 421–28. For an example, see Yitzhak Hen, ed., *The Sacramentary of Echternach (Paris, Bibliothèque Nationale, Ms. lat. 9433)*, HBS 110 (London: HBS, 1997), 39–40.

[41] Shane Bobrycki, 'The Royal Consecration *Ordines* of the Pontifical of Sens from a New Perspective', *Bulletin du centre d'études médiévales d'Auxerre* 13 (2009): 131–42, at 4–6 and 8n29 in the online edition; Hamilton, 'Early Pontificals', 422.

in 1383/84, and was commissioned to enshrine Abbot Nicholas Litlyngton into the history of the institution.[42] This book was so huge it would have been extremely unwieldy to use. It would be foolish to study the rites in such a book as if they were created primarily as texts from which to perform the liturgy.[43] As these examples demonstrate, rites *may* provide clues about how liturgy was performed but they can only be used as such with a great deal of care. Far from limiting their historical value, that makes them valuable for understanding the initiatives of particular individuals, for regional traditions, for institutional history, for ideas and ideals and – sometimes – for practice.

Process: How can Rites be Read?

In order to make sense of any one version of a ritual it needs to be placed within its widest possible context, especially:

- in relation to other versions of the same rite
- in relation to other rituals to which it is related
- within its manuscript context
- within the historical contexts of the place and time when it was written and read.

How can one achieve this? The last two points will be familiar to anyone working with manuscript sources. As far as possible it is desirable to try to answer questions such as: Where and when was the manuscript written? Who was it written and/or commissioned by and for? What else is in the manuscript? For what purposes was it created? Was it used and, if so, is there evidence for how? What else can be discovered about the manuscript's later history?

In terms of the text of a particular rite, in order to be able to interpret it one needs to know what in it is common and what is unusual, what is old and what may be new.[44] It is only possible to do this by adopting a comparative approach and by seeking out comparative material – from earlier and later periods, different regions, sometimes even from different religions depending on the questions one is addressing: 'the comparative perspective heightens the contrasts and makes ... some of the different developments ... easier to see,

---

[42] Jayne Wackett, 'The Litlyngton Missal: Its Patron, Iconography and Messages' (unpub. PhD thesis, University of Kent, 2015). For a definition of the word '*ordo*' see 4n4 above.

[43] Pfaff, *Liturgy*, 228. See also Parkes, this book, 98–99.

[44] Susan Rankin, *The Music of the Medieval Liturgical Drama in France and England*, 2 vols. (New York: Garland, 1989), 1:3, 7, 73.

perhaps even to explain'.[45] It can be helpful to cast the net widely to begin with before narrowing down the group of materials that are particularly useful, rather like an archaeologist undertaking surveys and opening up trial trenches to get a sense of the terrain and work out where activity should best be focused. You may be lucky to find that someone else has already done the spade-work and written a history of the ritual in question.[46] However, even so, one must be cautious about trusting secondary sources of this kind. There are several reasons for this. Few studies have been founded on extensive manuscript-based research; many more rely on edited canonical texts. This is problematic because of the misleading nature of such editions, which is discussed in Chapters 4 and 5. Also, the pervasiveness of misplaced ideas about the influence of the liturgies of major centres such as Rome and Salisbury has tended to skew interpretation.[47] The labelling of liturgies as 'Gallican', 'Roman' or 'of Sarum Use' in the Middle Ages often seems to have been intended as a mark of orthodoxy, a stamp of approval, rather than a statement that this was how things were done in Gaul or Rome or Salisbury.[48] In the Carolingian period, it appears that any baptismal rite could be called 'Roman' if it included the scrutinies, the preparatory meetings that took place in the week beforehand: '"The Roman ordo of baptism" meant a type of rite, of which there could be numerous legitimate variations'.[49] Additionally, the tendency to elide difference by writing about *ordines* as if they were literary texts (for example, the First and Second English Coronation *ordines*) and regional differences as though there were national rites ('Gallican'/ 'Mozarabic'/ 'Irish') means that the surviving evidence is often misrepresented.[50] In other words, one is likely to find that the manuscript evidence is much more diverse and complex

[45]　Wickham, 'Problems in Doing Comparative History', 27, talking about a different example of comparative history.

[46]　For useful bibliographic sources see the references cited in the Introduction, 3n2 above. The introductions to two editions are bibliographic mines, though they lack subject indices: *The Leofric Missal*, ed. Nicholas Orchard, 2 vols., HBS 113–14 (London: HBS, 2002); *The Sacramentary of Ratoldus (Paris, Bibliothèque nationale de France, lat. 12052)*, ed. Nicholas Orchard, HBS 116 (London: HBS, 2005).

[47]　See this book, Chapter 2, 48, and Chapters 4 and 5; Hen, 'Liturgical Handbook'; Keefe, *Water and the Word*, 1, esp. 98–115, 131–37; Mansfield, *Humiliation of Sinners*, 13.

[48]　I am grateful to Matthew Salisbury for articulating this point so clearly to me. See this book, Chapter 2, 48, and Chapter 5. Paxton, *'Bonus Liber'*, 16 and n.69; Keefe, *Water and the Word*, 1:42, 67–68, 150–53; Matthew Cheung Salisbury, *The Use of York: Characteristics of the Medieval Liturgical Office in York*, Borthwick Paper 113 (York: Borthwick Institute, University of York, 2008), esp. 40.

[49]　Keefe, *Water and the Word*, 1:67–69, 150–53 (quote on 150).

[50]　For example: 'the native Gallican rite', Gerald Ellard, *Ordination Anointings in the Western Church before 1000 AD* (Cambridge, MA: Medieval Academy of America, 1933), 18; 'the various "national" usages', Cornelius Bouman, *Sacring and Crowning: The Development of the Latin Ritual for the Anointing of Kings and the Coronation of an Emperor before the Eleventh Century*

than one would expect from the way it has been presented in the historiography. Finally, it is often the case that current ideas about the dates and places of origins of key manuscripts have changed considerably since older studies were written and this can have a considerable impact on the conclusions reached. So, while it is always worth seeking out earlier studies of a particular ritual, not least because they are likely to guide you to a core repertory of prayers and a range of sources, their conclusions must be handled cautiously.

It is therefore important to look at as many manuscript witnesses as possible. Printed editions are a quick way of doing this but one needs to be careful when using synthetic editions based on several manuscripts which claim to reconstruct a text that cannot be shown ever to have existed, like the Romano-German Pontifical: this issue is discussed in Chapters 4 and 5.[51] *Ordines* tend to be found in pontificals, manuals and sacramentaries, so these are sensible places to look. Edmond Martène's early eighteenth-century collection of editions of *ordines* remains useful as do the descriptive catalogues produced by Victor Leroquais.[52] Other especially valuable resources are the handlist of pontificals compiled by Richard Kay and the editions produced by the Henry Bradshaw Society.[53] As more manuscripts are digitized it is becoming increasingly easy to look them up directly rather than having to work initially via intermediaries. This is likely to have a radical effect on the whole discipline.[54]

At an early stage it is helpful to identify the core material of a ritual: prayers, chant and readings that were often compiled early in the history of a rite and are commonly found.[55] This is where synthetic editions of texts can be useful. Consulting editions of the early medieval Supplemented Hadrianum, *Ordines Romani*, *PRG*, and later medieval 'Sarum' rite can be a fast way of identifying

---

(Groningen: J.B. Wolters, 1957), xiii. Bradshaw, *Origins of Christian Worship*, 145, discusses the tendency to emphasize similarities rather than differences, and see Parkes, this volume, 79–80.

51   *PRG*.

52   Edmund Martène, *De antiquis ecclesiæ ritibus*, 2nd edn., 4 vols. (Antwerp: Joannis Baptistae de la Bry, 1736–38). It needs to be used in conjunction with Aimé-Georges Martimort, *La documentation liturgique de Dom Edmond Martène: Etude codicologique*, Studi e Testi 279 (Vatican City: Biblioteca Apostolica Vaticana, 1978) which identifies the modern shelfmarks of many of the manuscripts; Leroquais, *Pontificaux*; V. Leroquais, *Les sacramentaires et les missels manuscrits des bibliothèques publiques de France*, 4 vols. (Paris: n.p., 1924).

53   Kay, *Pontificalia*.

54   There is currently an online catalogue of Digitized Medieval Manuscripts at http://digitizedmedievalmanuscripts.org/ and the Digital Image Archive of Medieval Music is also useful: http://www.diamm.ac.uk/. There are substantial collections of microfilms of medieval manuscripts at the Hill Museum and Manuscript Library, St John's University, US, and the Institut de recherche et d'histoire des textes, Centre National de la Recherche Scientifique, France. For examples of digitized texts see the ones discussed in Chapter 6.

55   Rankin, *Music of the Medieval Liturgical Drama*, 1:12–15.

common texts. Such work can be supplemented by the collation tables found at the back of some editions.[56] The identification of a common core of materials is helpful because it makes it easier to spot things that appear to be distinctive to the manuscript(s) in question.

The distinctive material – of whatever kind, whether prayers, rubrics, or ritual actions – can help to identify the 'family' of texts to which the ritual belongs. Occasionally one will find a copy of a text that exists in other manuscripts. More often it will share affinities, more or less closely, with other rites. The word 'family' has been used in several recent studies and is a useful analogy for describing rites that are more or less textually related to one another. People talk about identifying 'tell-tale signs', 'markers', 'signature features', 'symptoms', 'traits' or 'text elements' of one type of rite or another.[57] An example is the 'breviculum' type of rite for blessing holy oils, so-called because of its 'unusual provision that each ampoule shall bear a *breviculum* ("label" or "tag") identifying the oil that it contains'.[58] Often the simplest way of identifying such families is by distilling the rites in question down to their principal constituent parts: the sequence of ritual actions. This usually reveals major differences between families.[59] But other features may help to do so, such as the titles they are given or the musical notation included in them.[60] I have repeatedly found in my own research that patterns are much easier to spot the more evidence one has. If you only look at a few sources it is hard to see what features are worth attending to, so it is important to examine material written over a long time span and from a wide geographical area.

Having cast the net widely, one can then return to the particular text or texts in question with a better sense of their chronological and geographical affinities. Often one will be interested in interrogating them further to ask

---

[56]   Some key texts are cited in Chapters 2–5.

[57]   Mansfield, *Humiliation of Sinners*, 193–96; Jones, 'Chrism Mass', esp. 114–15; Christopher A. Jones, 'Wulfstan's Liturgical Interests', in *Wulfstan, Archbishop of York: The Proceedings of the Second Alcuin Conference*, ed. Matthew Townend, Studies in the Early Middle Ages 10 (Turnhout: Brepols, 2004), 325–52, at 344–45; Rankin, *Music of the Medieval Liturgical Drama*, 1:60.

[58]   Jones, 'Chrism Mass', 114.

[59]   Robert Taft, 'The Structural Analysis of Liturgical Units: An Essay in Methodology', *Worship* 52 (1978): 314–29 for an example in this volume see L. Hamilton, 180–81.

[60]   'Ordines tend to reveal something of their pedigree in their very titles ... titles in particular may tell us something about the principal exemplar a scribe had before him': Kozachek, 'Repertory', 33. On the value of music in this context see Rankin, *Music of the Medieval Liturgical Drama*, 1:13; Kozachek, 'Repertory', esp. 83–84, 319–21 (where he argues that the notation of only a few antiphons in a particular rite suggests this was because the antiphons – and their music – were new), 323–26 (for the suggestion that the sporadic provision of notation in a ritual was for its use on 'a specific occasion'); Chapter 3, 66–67 below.

questions like: How did this rite change over time? Where and when did it originate? Where and when was it revised? This usually involves trying to work out the relationships between texts within a group and attempting to place them in a chronological sequence. This is difficult to do; it is particularly hard to establish hypotheses capable of verification or falsification. This is because only a small proportion of the evidence survives, one is dealing with a textual tradition in which scribes were not aiming to reproduce literary texts faithfully, and there was a great deal of cross-fertilization between families of texts.[61] One also has to remember that the dates when particular rites were compiled may be different from the dates of the manuscripts in which they are found. The appearance of old rites in later books may not necessarily be due to slavish copying: for example it has been suggested that an ancient *ordo* for the blessing of the oils may have been 'rediscovered and proudly adopted in the course of the tenth-century revival' in England.[62] Nonetheless research has to focus on the surviving evidence. People tend to proceed by drawing up tables which summarize the structure and content of each rite as accurately as possible.[63] This allows one to see which rites share most material with one another. Often you can identify prayers or ritual actions added into an earlier rite which subsequently became part of the standard repertory.[64] At times one can glimpse this process in action where, for example, a scribe has several exempla open on the desk and s/he is selecting between them.[65] Sometimes

---

[61] Rankin, *Music of the Medieval Liturgical Drama*, 1:146; Bradshaw, *Origins of Christian Worship*, 5; Jones, 'Chrism Mass', esp. 128; Mansfield, *Humiliation of Sinners*, 193–94; Pfaff, *Liturgy*, 156, 'the comparative-textual method is irreplaceable but limited, in both scope and accuracy. We cannot operate without it, but it is unlikely ever to reveal a whole story'.

[62] Jones, 'Chrism Mass', 112.

[63] Examples: Sarah Hamilton, 'Rites for Public Penance in Late Anglo-Saxon England', in *Liturgy of the Late Anglo-Saxon Church*, ed. Gittos and Bedingfield, 93–103; Jones, 'Chrism Mass', 139–40; Jones, 'Origins', 288–315; Helen Gittos, 'Hallowing the Rood: Consecrating Crosses in Late Anglo-Saxon England', in *Cross and Culture in Anglo-Saxon England: Studies in Honor of George Hardin Brown*, ed. Karen Louise Jolly, Catherine E. Karkov and Sarah Larratt Keefer (Morgantown: West Virginia University Press, 2008), 242–75, at 269–73, 275; Gittos, *Liturgy*, Tables 1–4, pp. 46–47, 116–18, 125–27, 246–55.

[64] S. Hamilton, this book, 155 for an example.

[65] For example, in the church dedication ceremony in the later tenth-century Egbert Pontifical (Paris, Bibliothèque Nationale de France, Ms. latin 10575) the scribe appears to have had several rites in front of him and on one occasion copied out a rubric commonly found in tenth-century Frankish pontificals and then, noticing that this conflicted with contemporary Anglo-Saxon practice, struck it out, and copied out a rubric found in several other Anglo-Saxon manuscripts: *Two Anglo-Saxon Pontificals (the Egbert and Sidney Sussex Pontificals)*, ed. H.M.J. Banting, HBS 104 (London: HBS, 1989), 42–43; Kozachek, 'Repertory', 303n16, 305–6, 313n30; Gittos, *Liturgy*, 223, fig. 79. For other examples see Jones, 'Chrism Mass', 128–30, and S. Hamilton, 142–43 below.

one can see that a medieval liturgist has chosen features characteristic of one type of rite and inserted them into another. In early versions these can appear as marginal additions, which then get incorporated into later copies.[66] One recurring characteristic of the history of rites is that to begin with only the key texts required by the celebrant and skeletal rubrics are recorded. In later versions, the service gets more complex, and more detail is written down. This tendency may then be checked as it becomes desirable to slim down *ordines* in part to make them more usable. It does not follow that the simplest rites are the earliest, but it is often the case.[67] It is also common to find new material placed at the end of a rite; only in later versions does it get moved into its proper, intended location, displacing earlier texts.[68] Using all this information it should be possible to work out the simplest explanation for how the various rites within a family are related to one another – and to those in other families.[69] All the time one needs to keep an eye on the manuscript contexts of the texts in question. It may be possible to test one's resulting hypothesis by collating the texts of prayers to see whether variants follow the predicted pattern.[70]

It is worth saying here that whilst there has been an understandable backlash against the desire to seek the origins of rites, it is not a completely futile enterprise. The reason for the negativity is that in the past liturgical scholarship was dominated by a search for origins and an erroneous belief that there was once a single early text which could be reconstructed. This meant that the surviving manuscripts were not considered as valuable evidence in their own right and attempts were made to reconstruct ancient texts that never existed and establish evolutionary models that were false.[71] However, new rites *were* created – sometimes surprisingly late – and the process can sometimes be recovered and be of considerable historical interest.[72]

---

[66] Jones, 'Chrism Mass', 128.

[67] J. Brückmann, 'The Ordines of the Third Recension of the Medieval English Coronation Order', in *Essays in Medieval History Presented to Bertie Wilkinson*, ed. T.A. Sandquist and M.R. Powicke (Toronto: University of Toronto Press, 1969), 99–115, at 110; Rankin, *Music of the Medieval Liturgical Drama*, 1:12; Bradshaw, *Origins of Christian Worship*, 9; Symes, this book, 251–52; for an example of a streamlined rite see S. Hamilton, this book, 143–53.

[68] For an example see Jones, 'Origins', 280n169; Kozachek, 'Repertory', 254.

[69] Examples of diagrammatic representations of such hypotheses: Mansfield, *Humiliation of Sinners*, 194–95; Gittos, *Liturgy*, figs. 10, 35, 84. For the difficulties in doing such research see Parkes, 79–80 below.

[70] For an example along these lines, see Jones, 'Origins', 280.

[71] Bradshaw, *Origins of Christian Worship*, 1–13; Parkes, this book, Chapter 4; Salisbury, this book, Chapter 5, esp. 104; Flynn, this book, 58.

[72] Gittos, *Liturgy*, 39–54 (for the consecration of cemeteries), 235–36 (for relaying pavements moved from elsewhere).

When all this is done it is possible to read the rites much more attentively and to suggest where, when and by whom a version of a rite was created and for what reasons.

Problems

Having suggested a way of proceeding, it is worth considering some of the problems that are likely to be encountered. These liturgical sources pose challenges owing to the very diversity that makes them so interesting. Such a small proportion of the evidence survives that major changes can be obscured from view. The vast majority of evidence is unpublished, sometimes either uncatalogued or poorly catalogued, and is likely to remain so.[73] This is why the digitization of manuscripts will have a particularly significant impact on this field. The degree of difference encountered can be hard to manage, especially for complex rites such as the dedication of churches or royal coronations. For this reason studies tend to aim broadly but end up tackling only aspects of a rite, or material from a limited chronological or geographical area.[74] Because of the need to deal with very large numbers of manuscripts it can be hard to keep a firm grip on the evidence for the dates and places of origins of those that one is not working on directly. One often finds that histories of rites are marred by errors of this kind, which can seriously undermine the conclusions drawn. It is worth spending time on this; *Scriptorium Online* is a useful bibliographic resource for published work on medieval manuscripts.[75]

Another type of problem is encountered with those rituals that have a rather unusual textual history, of which two examples are discussed in Chapters 6 and 7. The excommunication rites considered by Sarah Hamilton only began to be written down some time after they were first used and continued to be viewed as being 'peripheral to the content of pontificals'.[76] They were initially recorded in legal manuscripts alongside canon law and later on tended to be added into liturgical manuscripts, often in an ad hoc manner. As Florence Chave-Mahir reveals, exorcisms are even more elusive – they were rarely written down at all

---

[73]   The situation today is little different from the one depicted just after the war: 'Every study in this field ... is bound, despite extensive consultation of manuscripts, to be incomplete and provisional ... and the student will notice that many roads are as yet unpaved and that even the highways are not always reliable'; Ernst H. Kantorowicz, *Laudes regiae: A Study in Liturgical Acclamations and Mediaeval Ruler Worship*, University of California Publications in History 33 (Berkeley: University of California Press, 1946), ix.

[74]   For example, McMillan, *Episcopal Ordination*, 2, and Paxton, this book, 41–42.

[75]   www.scriptorium.be last accessed 23 April 2015.

[76]   See 140 below.

until the very end of the Middle Ages.[77] Why this was remains to be discovered: perhaps both were considered too potent and dangerous to be routinely written out as *ordines* in pontificals. Certainly these examples demonstrate that one needs to be alert to the possibility that evidence may lurk in unlikely places.[78] This is also a useful reminder of the extent to which only a limited amount of what was performed ever got written down.

Even when one does have an *ordo*, it is highly unlikely to be in any sense complete.[79] A fundamental aspect of liturgical books is that they were usually designed to be used by a particular person and to contain only those parts of the service required by that individual.[80] So, for Palm Sunday, one may find additional material in a processional (a book containing chant for use in processions) that is not included in an *ordo*. It is also common to find only the *incipits* of chant rather than full texts, and this can alter the apparent rhythm of a rite considerably. In a re-enactment of a late medieval rite for reconciling penitents on Maundy Thursday, those participants used to reading liturgical texts were a little taken aback by how long it took to sing the seven penitential psalms – a rubric of only a few words actually took almost twenty minutes to complete.[81] This point is made forcibly in Fred Paxton's attempt to create a full text of all the elements in the death ritual from a late eleventh-century customary from Cluny: the result is many times longer than the original *ordo*.[82] One aspect of learning to read rites is knowing where else to look to find texts that are not given in full.

Another problem is knowing how to recognize rites in the first place. In the nineteenth and early twentieth centuries, editors tended to make judgements about the genre to which texts belonged, many of which now look inappropriate. Eager to seek the origins of European drama, vernacular texts displaying what were perceived to be dramatic characteristics were identified and printed in such a manner that they were completely detached from their manuscript contexts. The text known as 'Sponsus', for example, a 'liturgical play' in Latin and Occitan

---

[77]   Chapter 7.

[78]   For baptismal *ordines* in manuscripts intended for educational purposes or as exempla, see Keefe, *Water and the Word*, 1:21–30.

[79]   S. Hamilton, this volume, 153–58 for an example.

[80]   John Harper, *The Forms and Orders of Western Liturgy from the Tenth to the Eighteenth Century: A Historical Introduction and Guide for Students and Musicians* (Oxford: Clarendon Press, 1991), 59, ch. 4.

[81]   This was organized by John Harper and took place at St Teilo's church, St Fagans National History Museum, Cardiff, in June 2010. A film of it can be seen at the AHRC Interpreting Medieval Liturgy Network website (http://projects.exeter.ac.uk/mlnetwork/workshop3.php) and on YouTube (http://www.youtube.com/user/MedievalLiturgy). See also p. 70.

[82]   Frederick S. Paxton, *The Death Ritual at Cluny in the Central Middle Ages / Le rituel de la mort à Cluny au moyen âge central*, Disciplina monastica 9, fontes 2 (Turnhout: Brepols, 2013); and see below 50–56.

for the Easter Vigil, was printed in a facsimile as if it were a discrete item in the manuscript, starting on its own line. In fact, it follows on directly from the preceding liturgy. It is found in a late eleventh-century proser-troper (which contains sung embellishments for use in the mass and office) from the abbey of Saint-Martial, Limoges: there is no reason to think that contemporaries would have seen this as anything other than liturgy. As Carol Symes says, 'Plays independent from liturgical context are what scholars have wanted to see, and they will occasionally go to great lengths in order to ensure that this is all there is to be seen.'[83] Parallels can be made with a group of Latin and Old English texts known as the 'Cattle Theft Charms' for use when a horse or cow was stolen. These 'charms' tend to be found in legal manuscripts. Once interpreted as pagan survivals, they are now being considered as examples 'of episcopal performative power in a realm that falls somewhere between our modern labels of liturgy and law'.[84] I suspect even this may be unnecessarily tentative and they are best considered simply as liturgical texts. Anglo-Saxon medical remedies and other kinds of charms have also suffered from having been gathered up and mislabelled. It is only in very recent times that scholars are finally willing to see that some, if not all, of these are best understood as prayers, blessings and liturgical rites. This is despite the number of clues available: they sometimes contain liturgical Latin, are found in liturgical books, and refer to their being carried out by priests in churches.[85] These are examples of how the assignment of texts to particular

---

[83] Carol Symes, 'The Appearance of Early Vernacular Plays: Forms, Functions, and the Future of Medieval Theatre', *Speculum* 77, no. 3 (2002): 778–831, at 795; Carol Symes, 'A Few Odd Visits: Unusual Settings of the *Visitatio sepulchri*', in *Music and Medieval Manuscripts: Paleography and Performance: Essays Dedicated to Andrew Hughes*, ed. John Haines and Randall Rosenfeld (Aldershot: Ashgate, 2004), 300–22, at 301–12.

[84] Tracey-Anne Cooper, 'Episcopal Power and Performance: The Fugitive-Thief Rite in Textus Roffensis (Also Known as the Cattle-Theft Charm)', in *Textus Roffensis: Law, Language and Libraries in Early Medieval England*, ed. Bruce O'Brien and Barbara Bombi (Turnhout: Brepols, forthcoming). Thanks to the author for sending me a copy of this prior to publication. Geoffrey Koziol, 'The Early History of Rites of Supplication', in *Suppliques et requêtes: le gouvernement par la Grâce en Occident, XIIe–XVe siècle*, ed. Hélène Millet (Rome: Ecole française de Rome, 2003), 21–36, at 29 argues that early medieval petitions 'were essentially prayers'.

[85] For relevant discussion see John D. Niles, 'The Æcerbot Ritual in Context', in *Old English Literature in Context: Ten Essays*, ed. John D. Niles (Cambridge: D.S. Brewer, 1980), 44–56, 163–64; Karen Louise Jolly, *Popular Religion in Late Saxon England: Elf Charms in Context* (Chapel Hill: University of North Carolina Press, 1996), 113–23, 132–68; Stephanie Hollis, 'Scientific and Medical Writings', in *A Companion to Anglo-Saxon Literature*, ed. Phillip Pulsiano and Elaine Treharne (Oxford: Blackwell, 2001), 188–208, esp. 203; John Blair, *The Church in Anglo-Saxon Society* (Oxford: Oxford University Press, 2005), 484–85; R.M. Liuzza, 'Prayers and/ or Charms to the Cross', in *Cross and Culture in Anglo-Saxon England: Studies in Honor of George Hardin Brown*, ed. Karen Louise Jolly, Catherine E. Karkov and Sarah Larratt Keefer (Morgantown: West Virginia University Press, 2007), 279–323; Rebecca M.C. Fisher, 'The Anglo-Saxon Charms:

genres in modern times continues to influence the way material is classified and interpreted.

My final example of a problem is also partly a solution. In this chapter I have focused on *ordines* because they are of fundamental importance. However, there are likely to be a very large number of other types of sources for the history of any given rite including sermons, saints' lives, expositions of the liturgy, artistic depictions, architectural settings, other narrative sources, even account books listing payments for materials and work in preparation for a particular service. Ideally one would take all of this material into account.[86] However, this is often impractical, and instead scholars tend to focus on particular types of sources. This is not ideal because different genres of source tend to provide insights which may be complementary but can be apparently contradictory. Chapter 8 explores this by comparing the types of information about rites for dedicating churches that can be gained from liturgical books and sermons. By looking across a range of sources we may understand more about how rituals were experienced and considered. Attention to other sources is crucial when few *ordines* survive and in Chapter 7 Florence Chave-Mahir explores the use of hagiography as a source for liturgical practice. As we learn to ask better questions, there are likely to be many more inferences that can be made about liturgical practices from church buildings themselves and in Chapter 9 Carolyn Marino Malone gives some examples of what can be learnt by combining texts and buildings.[87] Wherever

---

Texts in Context', in *Approaching Methodology*, ed. Frog and Pauliina Latvala, with Helen F. Leslie (Helsinki: Finnish Academy of Science and Letters, 2012), 221–47; Jones, 'Performing Christianity', 441–43; Rebecca M.C. Fisher, 'Genre, Prayers and the Anglo-Saxon Charms' in *Genre, Text, Interpretation: Multidisciplinary Perspectives on Folklore and Beyond*, ed. Kaarina Koski (University of Helsinki, forthcoming); and now particularly Ciaran Arthur, 'The Liturgy of Charms in Anglo-Saxon England' (working title for unpub. PhD thesis, University of Kent, in progress). I am grateful to Ciaran Arthur and also former students on my special subject *Ritual, Ceremony and Magic in the Early Middle Ages* and on the University of Kent's MA in Medieval and Early Modern Studies for helping me explore this material, especially Ruth Stone, and to Rebecca Fisher for sending me an advance copy of her forthcoming article.

[86]   Examples of studies of individual rites that draw on several genres of evidence include Robert Bartlett, *Trial by Fire and Water: The Medieval Judicial Ordeal* (Oxford: Clarendon Press, 1986); Mansfield, *Humiliation of Sinners*, with comments on sources at 14–16; Joseph H. Lynch, *Christianizing Kinship: Ritual Sponsorship in Anglo-Saxon England* (Ithaca, NY: Cornell University Press, 1998); Sarah Hamilton, *The Practice of Penance, 900–1050* (Woodbridge: Boydell Press, 2001); Florence Chave-Mahir, *L'exorcisme des possédés dans l'Eglise d'Occident (Xe–XIVe siècle)*, Bibliothèque d'histoire culturelle du moyen âge 10 (Turnhout: Brepols, 2011).

[87]   These are useful bibliographies: Sible de Blaauw, 'Architecture and Liturgy in Late Antiquity and the Middle Ages: Traditions and Trends in Modern Scholarship', *Archiv für Liturgiewissenschaft* 33 (1991): 1–34; Eric Palazzo, 'Art and Liturgy in the Middle Ages: Survey of Research (1980–2003) and Some Reflections on Method', *Journal of English and Germanic Philology* 105, no. 1 (2006): 170–84. Examples of other recent studies which adopt a variety

possible, triangulation with other types of sources can greatly help interpretation of the *ordines*.

Possibilities

In order to understand better how liturgical rites were created, revised and used in the Middle Ages, research needs to proceed in several directions:

> A fast rule in the study of liturgical manuscripts generally, and of pontificals especially, is that relations between books as wholes cannot be argued merely on the evidence of this or that single component. And yet the working out of such larger relationships has few options but to proceed ritual by ritual.[88]

In other words, there needs to be more investigation of the history of individual rites, the relationships between individual manuscripts, as well as between families of manuscripts. One question is: Was diversity more acceptable in some rituals – and books of rituals – than others? It is widely accepted that 'as one moved outward from the canon first to the rest of the liturgy of the mass, then to the daily office, and finally to occasional rites like penance, one finds at each step more tolerance for alteration.'[89] It has also been said that pontificals 'tend to be much less conservative than sacramentaries [mass books]'.[90] Are these impressions correct and, if so, what do they suggest about how different types of rituals were classified, and do these observations remain valid throughout the Middle Ages?[91] Another major question is: At what stage do we begin to see a great deal of homogeneity in rites? Is this true for the late Middle Ages? Are

---

of approaches include: P.S. Barnwell, 'The Laity, the Clergy and the Divine Presence: The Use of Space in Smaller Churches of the Eleventh and Twelfth Centuries', *Journal of the British Archaeological Association* 157 (2004): 41–60; Richard Gem, 'How Much Can Anglo-Saxon Buildings Tell Us about Liturgy?', in *Liturgy of the Late Anglo-Saxon Church*, ed. Gittos and Bedingfield, 271–89; Paul Everson and David Stocker, 'The Common Steeple? Church, Liturgy, and Settlement in Early Medieval Lincolnshire', in *Anglo-Norman Studies 27: Proceedings of the Battle Conference 2005*, ed. C.P. Lewis (Woodbridge: Boydell Press, 2006), 103–23; Paul Crossley, '*Ductus* and *Memoria*: Chartres Cathedral and the Workings of Rhetoric', in *Rhetoric Beyond Words: Delight and Persuasion in the Arts of the Middle Ages*, ed. Mary Carruthers (Cambridge: Cambridge University Press, 2010), 214–49; Tomás Ó Carragáin, 'Archaeology of Early Medieval Baptism at St Mullin's, Co Carlow', *Peritia: Journal of the Medieval Academy of Ireland* 21 (2010): 285–302; Gittos, *Liturgy*. See also the references in Paxton, this book, 54n64.

[88]   Jones, 'Chrism Mass', 128.
[89]   Mansfield, *Humiliation of Sinners*, 160.
[90]   Jones, 'Chrism Mass', 111.
[91]   See also S. Hamilton, this volume, 158.

there particular regions in which this happened? Did the availability of printed texts curtail improvisation?[92]

Greater attention to evidence for moments of decision making in the process of putting together a text would be instructive. Occasionally one can see that a scribe had one or more manuscripts open in front of him/her, and was selecting bits from each rite, as is the case with a church dedication rite in the late tenth-century Egbert Pontifical.[93] Such instances give some insight into the process by which rites were revised and the options available at a particular place. More attention to the working documents of liturgists would be useful too. Some of the materials in the commonplace books of Wulfstan, archbishop of York (1002–23) look as if they were gathered up by a man with a keen interest in liturgy.[94] It seems likely that more evidence of this kind will have survived, particularly given the materials for the composition of sermons that are being recovered.[95] Another approach would be to make careful comparisons between manuscripts which are similar: examples I am familiar with are the Dunstan and Anderson pontificals, and two mid-eleventh-century pontificals associated with Leofric, bishop of Exeter (1046–72).[96] Each pair of manuscripts is substantially, though not entirely, alike: working out the ways in which they differ and the inferences that can be made from those differences could be instructive. More work on larger groups of closely related manuscripts also would be helpful. There are some places from which many manuscripts survive, and this allows one to trace change over time in some detail. Fred Paxton and Eric Palazzo have demonstrated how productive such analysis can be in their work on the ninth-century sacramentaries from St Amand and Fulda.[97] Canterbury Cathedral in

---

92   I am grateful to Matthew Salisbury for this suggestion. Analogously, it has been argued that printed texts served to delineate genres of plays: Symes, 'Appearance of Early Vernacular Plays', 828–29. See also p. 16 and n. 12 above.

93   See above, n. 65.

94   Jones, 'Wulfstan's Liturgical Interests'.

95   For example, Ursula Lenker, 'The Rites and Ministries of the Canons: Liturgical Rubrics to Vernacular Gospels and Their Functions in a European Context', in *Liturgy of the Late Anglo-Saxon Church*, ed. Gittos and Bedingfield, 185–212.

96   Paris, Bibliothèque Nationale de France, Ms. latin 943; London, British Library, Additional Ms. 57337; London, British Library, Additional Ms. 28188, an edition of which is being prepared by Christopher A. Jones for publication by the HBS; London, British Library, Ms. Cotton Vitellius A. vii. For discussion and references see Gittos, *Liturgy*, 279–80, 283, 285–86. This is something I hope to pursue.

97   Paxton, *Christianizing Death*, 169–85, and this book Chapter 2; Eric Palazzo, *Les sacramentaires de Fulda: Etude sur l'iconographie et la liturgie à l'époque ottonienne*, Liturgiewissenschaftliche Quellen und Forschungen 77 (Münster: Aschendorff, 1994). Carolyn Malone makes use of the three surviving customaries from Saint-Bénigne, Dijon, in Chapter 9 of this book, pp. 208–25.

the central Middle Ages is one place where it is possible to do this for rites, and some research has demonstrated the potential of the material, but more could be done.[98] Another candidate would be the cathedral of Sens, France, from where many manuscripts survive.[99] These are examples of the kinds of research that would help reveal more about the processes involved in the creation and revision of rites.

Such research feeds into debate about the circumstances in which rites were created and revised. Did this tend to happen in preparation for a particular occasion? Or when a new manuscript was commissioned? Were there moments when a desire for reform led to thorough revision? To what extent were written rites intended to control behaviour, close down options and curtail improvisation?[100] Such questions are bound up with the issue of who was responsible for revising rites: cantors? precentors? librarians? abbots? bishops? deans?[101] Were new rites disseminated from particular centres, such as the cathedrals of Canterbury, Salisbury, York and Rome, or the monastery at Cluny? And in what circumstances were the manuscripts themselves produced? It has been suggested that in late Anglo-Saxon England, 'a new pontifical was created for each archbishop as he took up office'.[102] Mary Mansfield has argued that northern French pontificals from c. 1150 to 1350 'had an average life span of fifty years or so' and from the fourteenth century pontificals 'were increasingly luxury items produced to celebrate the election of a particular bishop rather than to serve the diocese during several episcopates'.[103] Is this true? If so, who was responsible for shaping the contents of these books?[104] Was this used as an opportunity for liturgical revision or were these compilations of rites that had been revised since the last pontifical was made? How influential were pontificals? Were they vehicles for authorizing new ideas or hardly used books largely for display?[105] What purpose did explicatory and theological rubrics serve? One oddity that remains to be explained is that although pontificals contained rites

---

[98] Jones, 'Origins'; Gittos, *Liturgy*, 42–54, 113–21, 124–29, 220–30; Gittos, 'Sources for the Liturgy of Canterbury Cathedral'.

[99] Mansfield, *Humiliation of Sinners*, 162n6, 231–34.

[100] Symes, Chapter 10 below with references to her previous work.

[101] Margot E. Fassler, 'The Office of the Cantor in Early Western Monastic Rules and Customaries: A Preliminary Investigation', *Early Music History* 5 (1985): 29–51; Mansfield, *Humiliation of Sinners*, 163.

[102] David N. Dumville, *Liturgy and the Ecclesiastical History of Late Anglo-Saxon England: Four Studies* (Woodbridge: Boydell, 1992), 93; Gittos, 'Sources for the Liturgy of Canterbury Cathedral', 41–44.

[103] Mansfield, *Humiliation of Sinners*, 162, 230.

[104] Ibid., 163–64.

[105] 'At times, in fact, the liturgical books actually anticipated theological changes'; Mansfield, *Humiliation of Sinners*, 164.

that were designed to be used by bishops they appear to have been owned by a wider range of people and institutions, especially monasteries and nunneries. This seems to have been the case right through the Middle Ages. So far, some possible explanations have been suggested but no sustained research has been done. Such books may have been used as academic resources, especially for the theology of the liturgy, or available for use by visiting bishops, or by abbots when they participated in grand episcopal ceremonies, or they may have been part of the accoutrements of a mitred abbot.[106] Nicholas Litlyngton, the abbot of Westminster whose missal we have previously encountered, seems to have been very keen in that book to demonstrate that he could perform liturgical ceremonies usually restricted to a bishop.[107] The range of possible reasons why places other than cathedrals had copies of pontificals shows how useful it would be to understand the problem better.

And what about manuals, book for priests: how were they put together? Recent research has begun to undermine the negative stereotypes of priests as poorly educated, lazy incompetents. Examples of priestly books and book collections have been studied, though so far only on a small scale.[108] One late eighth- or early ninth-century Carolingian example was written by at least three scribes simultaneously, which led Yitzhak Hen to wonder whether there was 'mass production of similar codices for the use of priests and itinerant missionaries throughout the Carolingian empire'.[109] Were there times when priests compiled their own manuscripts, gathering materials they anticipated would be useful, copying out texts encountered during their training?[110] The fundamental nature of some of these questions illustrates how much remains to be understood.

Conclusion: Performance

In this chapter I have not focused on what rites may reveal about how they were performed because this topic is explored by Carol Symes in Chapter 10. However, in conclusion it is worth making two points about this here. The

---

[106] For further discussion see Henry Parkes, *The Making of Liturgy in the Ottonian Church: Books, Music and Ritual in Mainz 950–1050* (Cambridge: Cambridge University Press, 2015) and this book, Parkes, 98–99. For an eleventh-century example see the discussion of Cambridge, Corpus Christi College, Ms. 44 in Gittos, *Liturgy*, 282, and the references cited there.

[107] See above, 22–23.

[108] See above, n. 25 and Matthew Wranovix, 'Ulrich Pfeffel's Library: Parish Priests, Preachers, and Books in the Fifteenth Century', *Speculum* 87, no. 4 (2012): 1125–55.

[109] Hen, 'Liturgical Handbook'.

[110] This would make sense of the contents of the 'Red Book of Darley': Gittos, 'Is There Any Evidence?', 69.

first is that recent work on medieval and early modern drama is highly relevant to students of medieval liturgy. Current work on performance practices, and the relationship between written texts and actual performances, provides very close parallels with the problems faced by liturgical historians. It is instructive, for example, to think about the different ways in which 'complex performance pieces' were recorded for those who were already familiar with them, or for those who had not encountered them before.[111] Variety in what was written down, and how it was presented, may be explained by differences in the intended audiences as well as changing ideas about what ought to be recorded. A second, related, point worth emphasizing is that liturgical rites are extremely valuable historical sources even if they were never performed, or in very different ways from what was written, or with participants who did not understand them.[112] That is because even in such circumstances, liturgical manuscripts are evidence for decisions made by their compilers and copyists. Because medieval liturgy was neither conservative nor uniform it is extremely revealing – so long as we can learn to read its rites right.

---

[111] Symes, 'Appearance of Early Vernacular Plays', 800–802 (p. 792 for the quote); S. Hamilton, this volume, 153–58.

[112] Bobrycki, 'Royal Consecration *Ordines*', 2; Gittos, *Liturgy*, 8–11.

Chapter 2

Researching Rites for the Dying and the Dead

Frederick S. Paxton

Rites for the dying and the dead have been on my research agenda for thirty-five years. An account of how Benedictine monks responded to a brother's death triggered my first foray into the critical study of medieval texts: a translation and commentary on the care of the dying and the dead in the late eleventh-century monastic customaries of Bernard and Ulrich of Cluny.[1] That project set me wondering how the highly complex rituals in the customaries – the 'customs' of a particular house or order which describe aspects of monastic life not covered in the Benedictine Rule – had evolved. What did they owe to Christian antiquity versus medieval Christianity, for example? Pursuing such questions led to a dissertation and book on the origins and early growth of death rituals in Latin Christianity.[2] Investigations instigated by that research revealed the limits of a strictly liturgical approach to the history of death and dying while also suggesting new ways of presenting liturgical sources for study and reflection. So I went back to the death ritual at Cluny. Monastic customaries did not include the texts of the prayers and chants of liturgical rites, citing them simply by their first few words (or *incipits*). Consequently, my earlier work revealed the overall structure of the death ritual at Cluny but ignored much of its content. It was as if I had used the stage directions and song titles for an opera or musical but not the spoken lines or lyrics. So I set out to reconstruct everything Cluniac monks said or sang in response to death, hunting down the missing texts of the prayers, psalms and chants in other liturgical sources. This study discusses the major tools and methods I used in moving from the Cluniac death ritual to the origins of Latin Christian death

---

[1]   Frederick S. Paxton, 'A Medieval Latin Death Ritual: The Monastic Customaries of Bernard and Ulrich of Cluny', MA thesis, University of Washington, 1980; published under the same title as no. 1 in the series Studies in Music-Thanatology (Missoula, MT: St. Dunstan's Press, 1993).

[2]   Frederick S. Paxton, *Christianizing Death: The Creation of a Ritual Process in Early Medieval Europe* (Ithaca, NY: Cornell University Press, 1990).

rituals and back again.[3] It is a case study of how a generation of developments in liturgical and monastic studies, and in the history of death, dying and the dead, guided, shaped and supported my scholarly research and writing.

The Cluniac Death Ritual in the Customaries of Ulrich and Bernard

My introduction to monastic customaries began with a reading of the Constitutions of Lanfranc, archbishop of Canterbury (1070–89), created for the cathedral chapter of monks over whom he also presided as abbot, as edited and translated by Dom David Knowles (1896–1974).[4] Knowles's work remains, in a revised edition by Christopher N.L. Brooke, one of only two complete modern English translations of medieval customaries for particular abbeys.[5] The extraordinary level of care taken by the monks of Canterbury to attend to the spiritual needs of the dying and the dead made a deep impression on me. Coming at the end of Lanfranc's text, they seemed to mark not just the culmination of the customary but also the place where the monastic liturgy, the 'work of God' (*opus dei*), was most dramatically focused on the needs of a particular individual. That encounter spurred an interest in monastic customaries as sources of medieval ritual life and, in particular, of rites for the dying and the dead. Since Lanfranc's directions for the death ritual at Canterbury clearly derived from the customs of Cluny (in Burgundy, France) and since Cluny's customs were not available in English, I decided to translate the two roughly contemporary versions of the Cluniac customaries and see what they said about death, dying and the dead at Cluny at the height of its influence in the late eleventh century.

It would have been nice to have modern critical editions of the customaries to work with, but while they were major desiderata of the *Corpus consuetudinum monasticarum* (the corpus of monastic customaries), which had produced, under the direction of Dom Kassius Hallinger, seven volumes

---

[3] For a more personal perspective on the same material, see Frederick S. Paxton, 'Listening to the Monks of Cluny', in *Why the Middle Ages Matter: Medieval Light on Modern Injustice*, ed. Celia Chazelle, Simon Doubleday, Felice Lifshitz and Amy G. Remensnyder (London: Routledge, 2012), 41–53.

[4] Lanfranc, *The Monastic Constitutions of Lanfranc*, ed. and trans. Dom David Knowles (London: Thomas Nelson and Sons, 1951); reprinted with minor corrections and a slightly revised introduction as *Decreta Lanfranci monachis Cantuariensibus transmissa*, CCM 3 (Siegburg: Franz Schmitt, 1967); Dom (from Latin *Dominus*) is an honorific for Benedictine monks.

[5] Brooke's revised edition was published in Oxford by the Clarendon Press in 2002. See also *The Customary of the Benedictine Abbey of Eynsham in Oxfordshire*, ed. Antonia Gransden, CCM 2 (Siegburg: Franz Schmitt, 1963); and Christopher A. Jones, *Ælfric's Letter to the Monks of Eynsham* (Cambridge: Cambridge University Press, 1998).

by the late 1970s, they had not yet appeared.[6] In fact, they still have not.[7] As I learned quite quickly, the relationship between the two Cluniac customaries is so fraught with questions about who wrote first, Bernard or Ulrich, and the degree to which the extant editions were contaminated by material from one or the other of the two authors, that no one has been able to sort it out. I thus decided to translate both accounts, comment on their common features and assess the degree to which their differences supported or undermined Dom Hallinger's argument that Bernard's text was written before Ulrich's.[8]

The text of Ulrich's customary was readily available in the *Patrologia Latina*, the massive nineteenth-century collection of works by Christian authors from the second to the thirteenth centuries published by Jacques-Paul Migne.[9] Migne had reprinted an edition of Ulrich's customary done by Jean Luc d'Achery (1609–85), a French Benedictine of the abbey of Saint-Germain-des-Prés in Paris, the head of the so-called Congregation of Saint-Maur, a group of abbeys with a decidedly scholarly bent who looked to medieval Cluny as a model for reforming monastic practice in their own time.[10] Bernard's customary was more difficult to access, for Migne, the publishing impresario behind the *Patrologia* series, did not choose to reprint it.[11] The only available edition was by another monk of Saint-Maur, the German Benedictine Marquard Herrgott (1694–

---

[6]   CCM. I was able to use Giles Constable's edition of the Statutes of Abbot Peter the Venerable (1122–56) in *Consuetudines Benedictinae variae (Saec. XI–Saec. XIV)*, CCM 6 (Siegburg: Franz Schmitt, 1975) for insights into minor but significant changes to the death ritual in the first half of the twelfth century.

[7]   But see note 55 below.

[8]   The major discussions of the issues at that time were by H.R. Philippeau, 'Pour l'histoire de la coutume de Cluny', *Revue Mabillon* 44 (1954): 141–51 (an important study that is often overlooked); and Kassius Hallinger, 'Klunys Bräuche zur Zeit Hugos der Grossen (1049–1109) Prolegomena zur Neuherausgabe des Bernhard und Udalrich von Kluny', *Zeitschrift der Savigny-Stiftung für Rechtsgeschichte: kanonistische Abteilung* 45 (1959): 99–140. For more recent work, see below note 56.

[9]   *Antiquiores consuetudines cluniacensi monasterii*, PL 149: 643–778.

[10]   Luc d'Achery, *Spicilegium sive Collectio veterum aliquot scriptorum qui in Galliae bibliothecis maxime Benedictinorum delituerant*, 3 vols. (Paris: Montalant, 1723, a slightly revised edition of the original, published 1655–77), 1:641–703. On the Maurists and Cluny, see Marc Saurette, 'Excavating and Renovating Ancient Texts: Seventeenth- and Eighteenth-Century Editions of Bernard of Cluny's *Consuetudines* and Early Modern Monastic Scholarship', in *From Dead of Night to End of Day: The Medieval Customs of Cluny*, ed. Susan Boynton and Isabelle Cochelin, Disciplina monastica 3 (Turnhout: Brepols, 2005), 85–107.

[11]   For the story behind the *Patrologia*, see R. Howard Bloch, *God's Plagiarist: Being an Account of the Fabulous Industry and Irregular Commerce of the Abbé Migne* (Chicago: University of Chicago Press, 1994).

1762), who had included it in a collection of customaries published in 1726.[12] Herrgott's book was so rare, however, that I was only able to get photocopies of the most relevant pages. As a result, I limited my research to the chapters in Ulrich's customary that corresponded to what I had available from Bernard's. That was probably a good thing, because had I had the whole text, I might never have had the courage to write on just one small section of it, however important and interesting.

One other helpful publication by a monk of Saint-Maur was available: four volumes of ritual texts drawn from a wide array of medieval manuscripts and organized according to the sacraments by Edmond Martène (1654–1739).[13] Parts of the Cluniac death ritual according to both Ulrich and Bernard, and from other sources based on their customaries, appeared among Martène's sections on rites for the sick, the penitent and the dying. A final source, an edition of a High Medieval missal from Westminster Abbey, published in 1891 by the Henry Bradshaw Society as the first volume of a still ongoing venture to edit and publish important liturgical manuscripts, also had enough affinities with the Cluniac material to aid in understanding them.[14]

As for interpretive frameworks, two works published in 1930 seemed to form a baseline for understanding the Cluniac death ritual as a particularly revealing artefact of medieval monasticism and the Latin liturgy. The first was an essay on the death of a monk by Dom Louis Gougaud that situated the Cluniac death rituals squarely within the context of Benedictine spirituality.[15] The other was a book by a German scholar on how remembering the dead at Cluny connected the monastic community to the world outside its walls.[16] By the time I started working on the subject, the latter approach had gained real traction in

[12]   *Vetus disciplina monastica*, ed. Marquard Herrgott (Paris: Osmont, 1726); see also Saurette, 'Excavating and Renovating Ancient Texts', 105–7.

[13]   Edmond Martène, *De antiquis ecclesiae ritibus*, 2nd edn., 4 vols. (Antwerp: Joannis Baptistae de la Bry, 1736–38; repr. Hildesheim: Georg Olms, 1969). Though I did not know of it at the time, Aimé-Georges Martimort's *La documentation liturgique de Dom Edmond Martène: étude codicologique*, Studi e Testi 279 (Vatican City: Biblioteca Apostolica Vaticana, 1978), which identifies Martène's vague references to his manuscript sources wherever possible, had already made his collection much more valuable to liturgical scholars, who could now in most cases accurately identify the date and provenance of the ritual materials that he had collected all over Europe.

[14]   *Missale ad usum ecclesie Westmonasteriensis*, ed. John Wickham Legg, 3 vols., HBS 1, 5, 12 (London: HBS, 1891, 1893, 1897).

[15]   'The Death of a Monk', in Louis Gougaud, *Anciennes coutumes claustrales* (Ligugé: Abbaye Saint-Martin, 1930).

[16]   Willibald Jorden, *Das cluniazensische Totengedächtniswesen vornehmlich unter den drei ersten Äbten Berno, Odo und Aymard (910–954), Zugleich ein Beitrag zu den cluniazensischen Traditionsurkunden*, Münsterische Beiträge zur Theologie 15 (Münster: Aschendorff, 1930).

German scholarship thanks to the work of Karl Schmid and Joachim Wollasch on liturgical commemoration of the dead.[17] There was something else in the air, though, for the French scholar Philippe Ariès had just laid the foundations for the history of death as a field of historical investigation with the publication of a series of lectures given in 1973 and a monograph that appeared in 1977.[18] Ariès associated each major period of European history, from the early Middle Ages to the present, with a distinct 'attitude toward death'. He called the attitude that prevailed before the twelfth century 'tamed death' (*la mort apprivoisée*). In accordance with this attitude, people accepted death as a natural part of life, anticipating and facing it with calm acceptance. Dying persons directed the ritual action that accompanied their own deaths by drawing on a common stock of gestures and utterances visible in literary texts such as the epic *Song of Roland* and the romance of *Tristan and Iseult*.[19]

Such secondary sources allowed me to situate the response to death and dying at Cluny within both the immediate context of medieval Benedictine monasticism and the more general context of European cultural history. Cluniac spirituality was expressed almost entirely through the liturgy: the monks of Cluny were not scholars or contemplatives; they devoted most of each day to communal prayer and chant, their whole lives long. When a death occurred in the community, they drew on every tool in their arsenal of prayer and gesture, sacrament and song, to ensure the safe and successful passage of a brother's soul from this life to the next. When a monk was dying, the whole community was meant to gather in the chapter house for a mutual confession and absolution, to erase any spiritual or psychological impediments to a successful passing. They were to come together again in the infirmary for a final anointing (not yet defined as the sacrament of extreme unction) and then again to attend their brother's death, even if it meant gathering in the infirmary multiple times when his death seemed imminent. After spending the night in constant vigil over his corpse, they held a funeral mass, procession and burial service. They prayed and chanted before, during and after his death, while preparing the corpse for burial, when moving it into the church and then towards the grave, and daily thereafter for a month, constantly petitioning the heavenly court to receive their dead

---

[17] Two of the foundational studies appeared in the first issue of a new journal that would become the flagship for scholarship on this subject: Karl Schmid and Joachim Wollasch, 'Die Gemeinschaft der Lebenden und Verstorbenen in Zeugnissen des Mittelalters', *Frühmittelalterliche Studien* 1 (1967): 365–405; and Joachim Wollasch, 'Ein cluniacensisches Totenbuch aus der Zeit Abt Hugos von Cluny', *Frühmittelalterliche Studien* 1 (1967): 406–43.

[18] Philippe Ariès, *Western Attitudes towards Death*, trans. Patricia M. Ranum (Baltimore: Johns Hopkins University Press, 1974). I did not learn about his book, *L'homme devant le mort* (Paris: Editions de Seuil, 1977), until the publication of an English translation by Helen Weaver, as *The Hour of Our Death* (New York: Knopf, 1981).

[19] Ariès, *Western Attitudes*, 1–25, and *The Hour of Our Death*, 5–28.

brother into the community of saints. Fearing to presume on God's judgement, they inscribed their brother's name in their necrology, to be recalled each year on the anniversary of his death, so he would not be forgotten, whatever his place in the afterlife.

As much as the death ritual at Cluny reflected Benedictine monastic spirituality, it also fitted Ariès' model of a 'tamed death'. A dying monk himself set the ritual process in motion when he sensed the approach of death and much of what followed resonated with the representations of dying in medieval literature discussed by Ariès. It made sense that secular and sacred texts would concur if 'tamed death' was truly a cultural constant in medieval Europe.

The Medieval Latin Death Ritual from Its Origins to the Tenth Century

When it came time to choose a topic for a dissertation, I first imagined a study of rituals and discourses around death and dying from the ninth to the twelfth centuries, with special attention to canon law. A year's work on Gratian's *Decretum*, the mid-twelfth-century schoolbook also known as the *Concordia discordantium canonum* (The Harmony of Discordant Canons), ended, however, in frustration.[20] There was interesting material there, drawn from councils and other ecclesiastical sources dating back to Christian antiquity, but it did not suggest a narrative or analytical approach other than the reception and use of the past by High Medieval lawyers.[21] Fortunately, Professor Gerard Caspary directed my attention to liturgical sources and anthropological understandings of ritual.[22] I could not have been given better advice. As I had learned, the scientific study of the Christian liturgy was a very old field, having emerged in the course of the debates between Protestants and Catholics in the sixteenth century. Since then, Christian scholars had collected and catalogued ancient and medieval manuscripts, edited the most important of them, and written extensively on

---

[20]   The most accessible edition of Gratian's text is *Decretum magistri Gratiani*, ed. Emil Friedberg, Corpus iuris canonici 1 (Leipzig, 1879), an online version of which is available through the Bavarian State Library at http://geschichte.digitale-sammlungen.de/decretum-gratiani/online/angebot, accessed 7 June 2013.

[21]   The work on the section of the *Decretum* concerned with death did eventually become the basis of the essay 'Gratian's Thirteenth Case and the Composition of the *Decretum*', which appeared in the *Proceedings of the Eleventh International Congress of Medieval Canon Law*, ed. Manlio Bellomo and Orazio Condorelli, Monumenta Iuris Canonici Series C: Subsidia 12 (Vatican City: Biblioteca Apostolica Vaticana, 2006), 119–29.

[22]   For a sense of Professor Caspary as scholar and teacher see his *Politics and Exegesis: Origen and the Two Swords* (Berkeley: University of California Press, 1979) and the memorial minute presented to the University of California, Berkeley, faculty senate, available at http://www.universityofcalifornia.edu/senate/inmemoriam/gerardernestcaspary.html, accessed 7 June 2013.

the history of the mass and the major sacraments. What they had not done, though, was to look at that history dispassionately, outside of theology and arguments over the correctness of one or another form of ritual behaviour. That is where anthropology came in. Editions of liturgical texts would tell me what Christians thought should be done around deathbeds, at funerals and tombs; anthropological theory promised to make sense of it as human behaviour.

Following Professor Caspary's advice, I began looking for the origins of rites for the dying and the dead in Latin Christianity. The best sources were the so-called sacramentaries – mass books, essentially, with prayers for different Sundays and feasts – which came over time to include material on occasional rites as well, such as deathbed penance, anointing and funerals. The Bobbio Missal is a complex manuscript written or compiled in the Rhône Valley, possibly at Vienne c. 700, and marked by just about every early medieval liturgical tradition – Gallican (that is, French), Roman, North Italian, Visigothic and Irish. It was available in an early twentieth-century edition by the great American palaeographer Elias A. Lowe, published by the Henry Bradshaw Society.[23] Another eighth-century text, the Irish Stowe Missal, had appeared in the same series in 1915.[24] Access to the early Spanish (Visigothic) liturgy was possible thanks to the early twentieth-century editorial labours of Dom Marius Férotin and a just-published edition of a Spanish priest's manual.[25] In 1956, a team of Benedictines led by Leo Cunibert Mohlberg had published an edition of the oldest so-called Roman sacramentary, the *Sacramentarium Veronense* or 'Leonine Sacramentary', a private collection of masses traditionally ascribed to Pope Leo I, as the first in an important series of early liturgical sources sponsored by the Vatican.[26] The team followed up over the next five years with editions of the so-called Gelasian Sacramentary, another ostensibly Roman book, and three Gallican missals, all of which contained, in

---

[23] *The Bobbio Missal: A Gallican Mass-Book*, ed. E.A. Lowe and J. Wickham Legg, HBS 53 (London: HBS, 1917), facsimile; 58 (1920) text; and 61 (1924) notes and studies, with A. Wilmart and H.A. Wilson. See also Yitzhak Hen and Rob Meens, eds., *The Bobbio Missal: Liturgy and Religious Culture in Merovingian Gaul*, Cambridge Studies in Palaeography and Codicology 11 (Cambridge: Cambridge University Press, 2004); and my review of that volume in the *Journal of English and Germanic Philology* 105 (2006): 345–47.

[24] *The Stowe Missal*, ed. George F. Warner, HBS 32 (London: HBS, 1915); and see now Sven Meeder, 'The Early Irish Stowe Missal's Destination and Function', *Early Medieval Europe* 13 (2005): 179–94, which argues that it was written for an itinerant priest. (I thank Sarah Hamilton for this citation.)

[25] *Le liber ordinum en usage dans l'église wisigothique et mozarabe d'Espagne du cinquième au onzième siècle*, ed. Marius Férotin, Monumenta Ecclesiae Liturgica 5 (Paris: Firmin-Didot, 1904; repr. with bibliographical supplement on the Spanish liturgy, Rome: Edizioni Liturgiche, 1996); *Liber ordinum sacerdotal*, ed. José Janini, Studia Silensia (Silos: Abadia de Silos, 1981).

[26] *Sacramentarium Veronense*, ed. Leo Cunibert Mohlberg, Leo Eizenhöfer and Petrus Siffren, RED series maior, fontes 1 (Rome: Herder, 1956); 2nd edn. 1966, 3rd edn. 1978.

fact, a mix of Roman and Gallican materials, which made them more complex, but also more interesting.[27] During the same years, one member, Petrus Siffrin, produced concordances to the material in those editions, which greatly facilitated their comparative study.[28] The year of 1961 also saw the completion of Michel Andrieu's multi-volume edition of what he considered to be the surviving *ordines* used in the city of Rome in the early Middle Ages, texts containing the rubrics for the Roman mass, baptism, ordination and other rites, including one for funerals that began at the deathbed (*Ordo* 49).[29] I also made liberal use of Father Damien Sicard's 1978 study of the Latin liturgy of death and dying up to the ninth century.[30] With these sources and tools, I was able to trace what was Roman and what was Gallican in the liturgical books in circulation in eighth-century Francia and compare it to Irish and Visigothic materials.

The most recent work, however, was on the sacramentaries associated with the liturgical reforms of the Carolingian court around Charlemagne. They fell into two groups: a group of manuscripts known to modern historians as the eighth-century Gelasians and another comprising copies of a massbook sent to Charlemagne by Pope Hadrian I (known as the Gregorian Sacramentary or Hadrianum). Together, they spawned a large body of books over the course of the ninth century known as 'mixed Gregorians'. The eighth-century Gelasians may or may not have been a response to the inadequacy of the Hadrianum, which was too closely tied to the papal custom of performing mass at different churches in Rome over the course of the liturgical year to be of general use in Carolingian Francia, but they clearly shared a tendency to collect prayers and rites missing from the book sent by the pope. Recent editions of important examples of the genre, the sacramentaries of Rheinau, Gellone and Autun, supplied evidence of some key ritual innovations around the deathbed in the years just before and after 800.[31]

---

[27]   *Missale Francorum*, RED series maior, fontes 2 (Rome: Herder, 1957); *Missale Gallicanum vetus*, RED series maior, fontes 3 (Rome: Herder, 1958); *Liber sacramentorum Romanae aeclesiae ordinis anni circuli*, RED series maior, fontes 4 (Rome: Herder, 1960), 2nd edn. 1968, 3rd edn. 1981; *Missale Gothicum*, RED series maior, fontes 5 (Rome: Herder, 1961).

[28]   Petrus Siffrin, *Konkordanztabellen zu den römischen lateinischen Sakramentarien*, 3 vols., RED series minor 4–6 (Rome: Herder, 1958–61).

[29]   *OR*. For *Ordo* 49 see *OR* 4:523–30. On Andrieu's endeavours see also the discussion by Henry Parkes in Chapter 4 above.

[30]   Damien Sicard, *La liturgie de la mort dans l'église latine des origines à la réforme carolingienne*, Liturgiewissenschaftliche Quellen und Forschungen 63 (Münster: Aschendorff, 1978).

[31]   *Sacramentarium Rhenaugiense*, ed. Anton Hänggi and Alfons Schönherr, SF 15 (Freiburg, Switzerland: Universitätsverlag, 1970); *Liber sacramentorum Gellonensis*, ed. Antoine Dumas, CCSL 159A (Turnhout: Brepols, 1981), originally from Northern France; and *Liber sacramentorum Augustudonensis*, ed. Odilo Heiming, CCSL 159B (Turnhout: Brepols, 1984).

Tracing developments over the course of the ninth century in even greater detail was made possible thanks to another extraordinary project. This was an edition by the French Benedictine Jean Deshusses of the Hadrianum and its famous Supplement, the first attempt to improve the usefulness of the papal book itself by adding prayers and ritual materials from other liturgical traditions.[32] Long thought to have been the work of Charlemagne's liturgical advisor, Alcuin of York, instead the Supplement was, according to Deshusses, the creation of Benedict of Aniane, who served in that capacity for Charlemagne's son, Louis the Pious.[33] Deshusses added to his edition of the Hadrianum+Supplement two volumes of material that eventually accreted to the main text in the mixed Gregorian sacramentaries of the later ninth century.[34] The third volume was particularly important for me because the mixed Gregorians regularly included full ritual orders for deathbed penance, visiting and anointing the sick and dying, and funerals. Along with editions of the prayers and *ordines*, Deshusses also included detailed descriptions of some fifty liturgical manuscripts, creating a research tool with the features of both a manuscript catalogue and a source of manuscript content.[35] Some of the findings that he published separately were also of particular value to my project. His identification of Benedict of Aniane as the author of the Supplement to the Hadrianum, for example, made sense of the Visigothic elements in some of its prayers for death and burial because Benedict was himself a Goth.[36] It also suggested Benedict was the author of a rite for anointing the sick which was designed to direct anointing away from the dying, in line with certain tendencies of Carolingian liturgical reform.[37]

See also Bernard Moreton, *The Eighth-Century Gelasian Sacramentary: A Study in Tradition* (Oxford: Oxford University Press, 1975).

[32] *Le sacramentaire grégorien: Ses principales formes d'après les plus anciens manuscrits*, ed. Jean Deshusses, 1: *Le sacramentaire, le supplément d'Aniane*, SF 16 (Fribourg: Editions Universitaire, 1971; 3rd revised and corrected edn. 1992).

[33] Jean Deshusses, 'Le "Supplément" au sacramentaire grégorien: Alcuin ou Benoît de Aniane?' *Archiv für Liturgiewissenschaft* 9 (1965): 48–71.

[34] *Le sacramentaire grégorien: Ses principales formes d'après les plus anciens manuscrits*, ed. Jean Deshusses, 2: *Textes complémentaires pour la messe*, SF 24 (1979; 2nd edn. 1988); and 3: *Textes complémentaires divers*, SF 28 (1982; 2nd edn. 1992).

[35] As a consequence, Deshusses's volumes provided more authoritative information on the manuscripts he utilized than the most important catalogue of early liturgical manuscripts to date, Klaus Gamber's *Codices liturgici latini antiquiores*, SF subsidia 1, 2nd edn. (Freiburg, Switzerland: Universitätsverlag, 1968).

[36] The 'Spanish symptoms' in the Supplement had first been noted by Edmund Bishop, *Liturgica Historica: Papers on the Liturgy and Religious Life of the Western Church* (Oxford: Clarendon Press, 1918), 168.

[37] Paxton, *Christianizing Death*, 138–54.

Deshusses's work made it possible to trace ritual developments concerning death and dying in the ninth century in ways that would have been nearly impossible otherwise. I now had a series of texts on the same subject matter spanning some four hundred years. Most importantly, Deshusses's identification of seven key mixed Gregorian manuscripts as the work of the scriptorium of the abbey of Saint-Amand offered a series of similar texts created in one place over twenty-five years (between 851 and 877).[38] Close analysis of their presentation of the rites for the dying and the dead revealed a clear pattern of experimentation as the liturgists of Saint-Amand adapted Benedict of Aniane's anointing ritual for use with the dying and produced a synthesis that marked the third quarter of the ninth century as the point in time when the medieval Latin death ritual coalesced into its more or less final form.[39]

In general, the secondary literature on these subjects was, not surprisingly, organized in relation to the different sacraments involved. Liturgical scholars, almost exclusively monks and priests, wrote on the history of deathbed baptism, penance or communion, extreme unction, and funeral masses and ceremonies but did not consider them as constituent pieces of a larger ritual process. Study of the sacraments had been given a great impetus by the liturgical reforms associated with the Second Vatican Council (1962–65). The council's reform agenda, however, revived the liturgiological debate between Catholics and Protestants over the scriptural or Roman bases of particular ritual acts. Thus scholarship on early medieval rites tended to focus on Roman sources over Insular, Spanish, North Italian or Gallican ones and to assume that the central traditions were always Roman.[40] This tendency was particularly notable in Damien Sicard's study, which may reflect his role as a counsellor on liturgical reform at Vatican II, which he had attended as a young priest with his diocesan superior, the bishop of Montpellier.[41] The Roman *ordo* for the dying and the dead was the standard against which all others were measured.

Seeking an approach outside of this ecclesiastical tradition from which to get a different purchase on the subject led me to the anthropological notion of rites of passage first articulated by Arnold van Gennep in the early twentieth century and revived in the 1960s and 1970s by cultural anthropologists like Victor Turner.[42] While I made some use of van Gennep's and Turner's analyses

---

[38] Jean Deshusses, 'Chronologie des grands sacramentaires de Saint-Amand', *Revue bénédictine* 87 (1977): 230–37; and 'Encore des sacramentaires de Saint-Amand', *Revue bénédictine* 89 (1979): 310–12.

[39] Paxton, *Christianizing Death*, 169–85.

[40] See Helen Gittos's chapter in this volume.

[41] See the author biography on the website of the publisher Les Editions du Cerf (Paris), http://www.editionsducerf.fr/html/fiche/ficheauteur.asp?n_aut=4247, accessed 7 June 2013.

[42] Arnold van Gennep, *Rites of Passage*, trans. Monika B. Vizedom and Gabrielle L. Caffee (Chicago: University of Chicago Press, 1960); Victor Turner, 'Betwixt and Between: The Liminal

of the particular character of the pre-liminal, liminal and post-liminal phases of rites of passage, the real key for me was the structure itself. On the one hand, it suggested that the Latin liturgical traditions of the early Middle Ages were local products of a universal human tendency to organize rites of passage in particular ways. On the other, it suggested a framework for tracking change over time in the body of similar sources at my disposal.[43] I could follow the separate histories of rites in preparation for death (anointing the sick and dying, deathbed penance and communion), for the transition from this life to the next (commendation of the soul at death, funeral and burial), and for the incorporation of the soul into the other world (liturgical commemoration of the dead), with an eye to when and how they coalesced into a single ritual process.

This led to two surprising findings. The first was how long it took Latin Christianity to fully ritualize death as a rite of passage. In spite of the fact that the religion was rooted in the death and resurrection of Christ (or perhaps because of it), little attention was paid to ritual care of the dying or the dead before the fourth and fifth centuries. Baptized Christians in good standing with the church were assured salvation. They neither needed nor demanded ritual care before or after death. The multiple 'Christianities' of the early Middle Ages, however, spawned a diverse set of responses to death, dying and the dead, which were not synthesized into a common ritual structure until the later ninth century.[44] The second surprise was that it was actually the failed Carolingian drive to 'Romanize' the liturgy in the Frankish Empire that created the conditions for that synthesis. Copies of the 'Gregorian' sacramentary of Pope Hadrian became the carrier first for the non-Roman Frankish and Visigothic prayers and rites in the Supplement and then, in the mixed Gregorians, for even more wide-ranging materials, which gained acceptance and influence precisely because they appeared in books purported to be papal and Roman.[45] It was just such *ordines* that the liturgists of Saint-Amand used to come up with a ritual process that had real staying power because it both

---

Period in Rites de Passage', in Turner, *The Forest of Symbols* (Ithaca, NY: Cornell University Press, 1967); Turner, *Dramas, Fields, and Metaphors: Symbolic Action in Human Society* (Ithaca, NY: Cornell University Press, 1974); and, Turner with Edith Turner, *Image and Pilgrimage in Christian Culture: Anthropological Perspectives* (New York: Columbia University Press, 1978).

[43]   See also pp. 24–25.

[44]   See, in general, Thomas F.X. Noble and Julia M.H. Smith, ed., *The Cambridge History of Christianity, vol. 3: Early Medieval Christianities, c. 600–c. 1100* (Cambridge: Cambridge University Press, 2008), and, in particular, my essay on 'Birth and Death' at 383–98.

[45]   Such *ordines* could also circulate independently; see, for example, Frederick S. Paxton, 'Bonus liber': A Late Carolingian Clerical Manual from Lorsch (Bibliotheca Vaticana Ms Pal. lat. 485)', in *The Two Laws: Studies in Medieval Legal History Dedicated to Stephan Kuttner*, ed. Laurent Mayali and Stephanie A.J. Tibbetts, Studies in Medieval and Early Modern Canon Law 1 (Washington, DC: Catholic University of America Press, 1990), 1–30. See also p. 24 in this book.

expressed every nuance of Christian hope and anxiety in the face of death and took the form of a fully realized rite of passage. Thus, thanks to the work of generations of codicologists, palaeographers, editors and anthropologists, I was able to piece together a history of the medieval Latin death ritual that culminated in the decades just preceding the foundation of Cluny in the year 910. I also learned that Philippe Ariès had been wrong. Christians did not die the way they did in medieval literary texts because they were in touch with some primordial European attitude towards death, but because they had been taught to do so by the liturgists of the Christian church.

Reconstructing the Cluniac Death Ritual on the Basis of Bernard's Customary

Not long afterwards I got my own comeuppance: an encounter with a different type of primary source, the *Life* (or *Vita*) of Hathumoda, abbess of a house of canonesses at Gandersheim (Germany). Shortly after Hathumoda's death in 875, a monk from a nearby Benedictine monastery, Agius of Corvey, who was her confessor and confidante, wrote a spiritual biography and poem of consolation for her surviving sisters.[46] I wondered whether or not Hathumoda's *Vita* featured the Latin Christian death ritual in the form that I had asserted was just then taking shape in the Carolingian realms. It did, as it turned out, just as I had hoped, but as a relatively minor part of a larger story about fear of death and nearly inconsolable grief. In Agius's telling, ritual action was less important than the psychological and spiritual struggles of people trying to come to terms with death in a newly Christianized culture. The death ritual may have found its more or less final form, it seems, but it did not put an end to the need for consolation in the face of death.

At the same time, as it happened, I was teaching the history of death to students preparing to comfort the dying with music in the medieval ecclesiastical modes (as opposed to modern key signatures) played on gothic harps.[47] The students were interested in the Cluniac death ritual as a historical precedent for their work, but found it hard to assess it in the form in which I had originally presented it. They related more to the story of Hathumoda's passing because it focused so clearly on care of the dying and consoling the survivors. They were not satisfied with knowing only what Cluniac monks

---

[46]   See Frederick S. Paxton, *Anchoress and Abbess in Ninth-Century Saxony: The Lives of Liutbirga of Wendhausen and Hathumoda of Gandersheim* (Washington, DC: Catholic University of America Press, 2009); and Julia M.H. Smith, 'The Problem of Female Sanctity in Carolingian Europe, c. 780–920', *Past and Present* 146 (February 1995): 3–37.

[47]   Paxton, 'Listening to the Monks of Cluny', gives a short history of the new profession – music-thanatology – which the students were pursuing.

were supposed to do; they wanted to know what they actually said and sang, what it sounded like, if at all possible, and how it facilitated a 'blessed death'.[48] Their questions provided the impetus to return to the Cluniac death ritual with the aim of reconstructing it, translating the results into English, and reporting the new insights that emerged – a project that is now complete.[49]

Much had changed in the two decades since I had first worked on death and dying at Cluny. While there were still no modern editions of Bernard's or Ulrich's customaries, Herrgott's early modern edition of Bernard had become available in an affordable reprint from the publisher of the *Corpus consuetudinum monasticarum*.[50] More importantly, the CCM had produced critical editions of the earliest records of the customs of Cluny, from around the year 1000, and the so-called *Liber tramitis*, created for the Italian monastery of Farfa in the second quarter of the eleventh century.[51] With their help, I was able to uncover some of the ritual developments that had occurred between Cluny's founding in the early tenth century and the end of the eleventh, when Ulrich and Bernard wrote.[52]

As for the death ritual itself, I began with Ulrich's account, which was simpler and more straightforward than Bernard's, posting a draft reconstruction and translation online in 2002.[53] Susan Boynton and Isabelle Cochelin, who were at the time orchestrating a revival of scholarly interest in the Cluniac customaries, convinced me, however, of the value of Bernard's text as the basis for the reconstruction.[54] There were three reasons. First, like all his predecessors, Ulrich did not write his customary for Cluny itself, but for Abbot William of Hirsau, who wanted to reform the German monasteries under his

---

[48] See Therese Schroeder Sheker (the founder of music-thanatology), *Transitus: A Blessed Death in the Modern World* (Missoula, MT: St. Dunstan's Press, 2001).

[49] Frederick S. Paxton, *The Death Ritual at Cluny in the Central Middle Ages/Le rituel de la mort à Cluny au moyen âge central*, Disciplina monastica 9, fontes 2 (Turnhout: Brepols, 2013.)

[50] Edited by the German Benedictine Pius Engelbert (Siegburg: Franz Schmitt, 1999); for the earlier edition, see above note 12.

[51] *Consuetudines Cluniacensium antiquiores cum redactionibus derivatis*, ed. Kassius Hallinger, CCM 7.2 (Siegburg: Franz Schmitt, 1983); *Liber tramitis aevi Odilonis abbatis*, ed. Peter Dinter, CCM 10 (Siegburg: Franz Schmitt, 1980).

[52] Frederick S. Paxton, 'Death by Customary at Eleventh-Century Cluny', in *From Dead of Night to End of Day*, ed. Boynton and Cochelin, 297–318.

[53] The internet version of the reconstruction and translation according to Ulrich's customary is available through the website of the Institut für Frühmittelalterforschung at the Universität Münster: http://www.uni-muenster.de/Fruehmittelalter/Projekte/Cluny/BiblClun/index.html, accessed 7 June 2013.

[54] I do not know if they were responding directly to Joachim Wollasch's call for scholars to work on the liturgy of Cluny in 'Zur Erforschung Clunys', *Frühmittelalterliche Studien* 31 (1997): 32–45, but they were certainly in agreement with him about the importance and timeliness of the task.

influence along Cluniac lines. Bernard was the first Cluniac to write at and for Cluny itself, and the best manuscript of his customary (Paris, Bibliothèque Nationale de France, Ms. latin 13875), while not an autograph, dates to the late eleventh century and contains evidence of regular use at Cluny during the early years of the twelfth century.[55] Second, while questions of priority remain unsolved, an in-depth analysis of the pre-mortem stage of the death ritual in the *Liber tramitis*, Ulrich and Bernard, suggested that Bernard took up his pen at least partially to correct Ulrich.[56] Finally, although Bernard's style is less direct than Ulrich's, his customary is much longer and reflects the care he took to get every detail right, so that there would be no arguments among the community over the customs of the house. This is particularly evident in his account of the death ritual, where he treats every possible response to a death interrupting the daily liturgical obligations of the community. While the prayers, chants, gestures and movements of the Cluniac death ritual are nearly identical in the two accounts, Bernard's has the greater claim on the attention of scholars who want to understand Cluny from the inside out, which was my ultimate goal.

Searching for the full texts of the prayers of the Cluniac death ritual was made easier by the work done in the previous stage of my research, since, as it turned out, the Cluniacs drew all but one of the prayers they used from the liturgical stock inherited from the mixed Gregorian sacramentaries of the ninth century. Three other massive publishing projects also played significant

---

[55]   Isabelle Cochelin, 'Evolution des coutumiers monastiques dessinée à partir de l'étude de Bernard', in *From Dead of Night to End of Day*, ed. Boynton and Cochelin, 50–52. Boynton and Cochelin are preparing a semi-diplomatic edition of the Paris manuscript for the series Disciplina monastica. See *From Dead of Night to End of Day*, 7–9.

[56]   Paxton, 'Death by Customary', 304–8. Cf. Joachim Wollasch, 'Zur Verschriftlichung der klösterlichen Lebensgewohnheiten unter Abt Hugo von Cluny', *Frühmittelalterliche Studien* 27 (1993): 317–49, who posited a common source behind both customaries, a position taken up by his student Burkhardt Tutsch, in 'Die Consuetudines Bernhards und Ulrichs von Cluny im Spiegel ihrer handschriftlichen Überlieferung', *Frühmittelalterliche Studien* 30 (1996): 248–93; and Tutsch, *Studien zur Rezeptionsgeschichte der Consuetudines Ulrichs von Cluny*, Vita Regularis 6 (Münster: LIT, 1998), 41–42. Isabelle Cochelin has rejected that notion and argued cogently for the priority of Ulrich in 'Peut-on parler de noviciat à Cluny pour les Xe–XIe siècles?' *Revue Mabillon*, n.s. 9, no. 70 (1998): 17–52; 'Le pour qui et le pourquoi (des manuscrits) des coutumiers clunisiens', in *Ad libros! Mélanges d'études médiévales offerts à Denise Angers et Claude Poulin*, eds. J.-F. Cottier, Martin Gravel and Sébastien Rossignol (Montreal: Presses de l'Université de Montréal, 2010), 121–38; and 'Appendix: The Relation between the Last Cluniac Customaries, *Udal* and *Bern*', in *Consuetudines et Regulae: Sources for Monastic Life in the Middle Ages and the Early Modern Period*, eds., Carolyn Marino Malone and Clark Maines Disciplina monastica 10 (Turnhout: Brepols, 2014).

roles in this stage of my research: a concordance to the prayers in Deshusses's three volumes of material in the ninth-century Gregorian sacramentaries,[57] the *Corpus orationem*, which contains editions and source information on many of the prayers contained in medieval ritual books,[58] and the *Corpus antiphonalium officii*, which identifies antiphons and related chant pieces in manuscript sources from throughout the Middle Ages.[59] An edition of a ritual book clearly derived from Ulrich's customary provided contemporary wording for many of the prayers.[60] When it came to the psalms, however, and occasional scriptural passages embedded in the spoken or sung material, I turned to the Latin Vulgate text in use at Cluny, as elsewhere in medieval Europe.[61]

In accordance with the editorial principles of the series in which the reconstruction was to appear, the Latin text of the death ritual had to be accompanied by a French as well as an English translation. After transcribing Bernard's description from the manuscript, and expanding its many abbreviations (in effect creating a semi-diplomatic edition of it), I used the sources cited above to fill out the text of the prayers and chants. Except for scriptural passages, Isabelle Cochelin and I independently translated the results into French and English and then reviewed everything in all three languages, trying to get them to reflect each other as closely as possible. For scripture I used an updated version of the only English translation from the Vulgate, the seventeenth-century Douay-

---

[57] Jean Deshusses and Benoît Darragon, *Concordances et tableaux pour l'étude des grands sacramentaires*, SF subsidia 9–14, 6 vols. (Fribourg: Editions Universitaires, 1982–83).

[58] *Corpus orationum*, eds. Eugene Moeller and Jean-Marie Clément, completed by Bertrand Coppieters 't Wallant, 13 vols., CCSL160 (Turnhout: Brepols, 1993–2003).

[59] *Corpus antiphonalium officii*, ed. René-Jean Hesbert, 6 vols., RED series maior, fontes 7–12 (Rome: Herder, 1963–79). The material is now also available online through *Cantus: A Database for Latin Ecclesiastical Chant*, http://publish.uwo.ca/~cantus/, accessed 7 June 2013. I had been ignorant of this essential resource the first time around, relying instead on Carolus (Karl) Marbach, *Carmina scripturarum, scilicet Antiphonas et Responsoria ex sacra scripturae fonte in libros liturgicos* (Strasbourg: F.-X. Le Roux, 1907; repr. Hildesheim: Georg Olms, 1963).

[60] *Das Rheinauer Rituale (Zürich Rh 114, Anfang 12. Jh.)*, ed. Gebhard Hürlimann, SF 5 (Freiburg, Switzerland: Universitätsverlag, 1959), another important source I had previously missed.

[61] *Biblia sacra iuxta vulgatam versionem*, ed. B. Fischer et al., Stuttgart: Deutsche Bibelgesellschaft, 1994; see also now *The Vulgate Bible*, Dumbarton Oaks Medieval Library (Cambridge, MA: Harvard University Press, 2010–, six vols. to date). For a fully searchable open source online edition, see *Biblia sacra juxta vulgatam clementinam*, editio electronica, Michael Tweedale (London: http://vulsearch.sourceforge.net/html/index.html, 2005), accessed 7 June 2013.

Rheims Bible.[62] The French was provided by Louis-Claude Fillion's nineteenth-century translation.[63]

While I still see the value of understanding the Cluniac death ritual as a rite of passage – a subset of common human patterns of behaviour and belief – the new material supported a much thicker description of the ritual process, with less attention to the significance of its overall structure and more to the Christian and Benedictine spiritualities at its heart – and the precise details of its intended performance. Thanks to recent work by archaeologists and architectural historians, it was possible to follow the death ritual step by step through the sacred space of the monastic complex at Cluny, imagining it as a performance in real time.[64] The death ritual was a multi-media event of highly choreographed movements, sounds and smells performed by men who dedicated their whole lives to the liturgy. The prayers and chants, which are always thematically related and often play out as little liturgical dramas, expressed the core beliefs of Christianity as practised by Benedictine monks, balancing fear of God's judgement with faith in His salvation in the face of death. Reconstructing the words of the chants and prayers that Bernard thought the monks should sing and speak showed exactly how they had honed their liturgical tools for the all-important service of intercession at the heavenly court, an activity they pursued for each other, above all, but also for their patrons and benefactors and for all the faithful departed, on a daily basis. The reconstruction also revealed the place of death, dying and the dead in the hierarchy of the sacred at Cluny. For the

---

[62]   *Holy Bible*, Catholic Public Domain Version, Based on the Douay-Rheims version, ed. and trans. Ronald L. Conte, Jr., at http://www.sacredbible.org/index.htm, accessed 7 June 2013. The original version is available as *Holy Bible*, Douay-Rheims version (Baltimore: John Murphy Company, 1899), and online at http://www.biblegateway.com/, accessed 17 June 2013, and in *The Vulgate Bible*, Dumbarton Oaks Medieval Library, which provides the English of Douay-Rheims as a facing-page translation of the Vulgate text.

[63]   *La sainte Bible*, trans. Louis-Claude Fillion (Paris: Librairie Letouzey et Ané, 1889), editio electronica, Editions Magnificat, http://www.magnificat.ca/textes/, accessed 7 June 2013.

[64]   See Carolyn Marino Malone's study in this volume and Neil Stratford, 'Les bâtiments de l'abbaye de Cluny à l'époque médiévale: Etat des questions', *Bulletin monumental* 150 (1992): 383–411; and, in particular Anne Baud, 'La place des morts dans l'abbaye de cluny, état de la question', *Archéologie mediévale* 29 (2000): 99–114; and Baud, *Cluny, un grand chantier médiéval au cœur de l'Europe* (Paris: Picard, 2003); also Anne Baud and Gilles Rollier, 'Liturgie et espace monastique à Cluny à la lecture du *Liber tramitis*, 'descriptione monasterii' et données archéologiques', in *Espace ecclesial et liturgie au moyen âge*, ed. Anne Baud (Lyon: Maison de l'Orient et de la Méditerranée, 2010), 27–42; Kristina Krüger, 'Architecture and Liturgical Practice: The Cluniac *galilaea*', in *The White Mantle of Churches: Architecture, Liturgy, and Art around the Millennium* ed. Nigel Hiscock, International Medieval Research 10; Art History Subseries 2 (Turnhout: Brepols, 2003), 138–59, and Krüger, 'Monastic Customs and Liturgy in the Light of the Architectural Evidence: A Case Study on Processions (Eleventh–Twelfth Centuries)', in *From Dead of Night to End of Day*, ed. Boynton and Cochelin, 191–220.

Cluniacs to adapt their tightly regulated schedule so that as many of them as possible could personally participate, before, during and after a death, indicates how important the death ritual was to the community as a whole. The many specifics provided by Bernard show that only the monks' obligations to the high altar – daily mass and the regular hours – ranked above the death ritual in importance. Finally, the reconstructed ritual provided new insights into the hierarchical structure of the monastic community, of seniors over juniors, oblates over converts, and perfected 'mouth men', whose control of their voices may have signalled an enhanced masculinity vis-à-vis the 'body men' whose lack of control placed them lower in the monastic gender hierarchy, toward the status of boys and women.[65]

Looking at the Cluniac death ritual as a whole, what seems most interesting now is its connection to a larger cultural phenomenon, the 'economy of salvation', in which wealth was exchanged for prayers and other forms of intercession for the dead, which involved almost everyone in medieval society.[66] Before the twelfth century, monks were almost the exclusive brokers of the economy of salvation, and the monks of Cluny were second to none. They had the greatest reputation for comforting souls in the afterlife, even snatching them from the very jaws of hell. Because of this, they received the most gifts of any contemporary monastic community, enough to build the largest and most beautiful church in western Christendom, from which prayers for the salvation of the dead, honed in the ritual response to death itself, rose heavenwards, almost without pause, throughout the medieval centuries.[67]

The story of my journey from a monastic text and the ritual it preserved to their deep history and back again is admittedly idiosyncratic, but I hope of some value to scholars working or thinking about working with medieval liturgical

---

[65]   Lynda L. Coon, *Dark Ages Bodies: Gender and Monastic Practice in the Early Medieval West* (Philadelphia: University of Pennsylvania Press, 2010).

[66]   Paxton, 'Birth and Death'(above, n.44); *The Death Ritual at Cluny in the Central Middle Ages*, 15–52; and Paxton, 'The Early Growth of the Medieval Economy of Salvation in Latin Christianity', in *Death in Jewish Life: Burial and Mourning Customs among the Jews of Europe and nearby Communities*, eds. Stefan Reif, Andreas Lenhardt and Avriel Bar-Levav, Studia Judaica 78 (Berlin: de Gruyter, 2014), 17–41.

[67]   Dominique Iogna-Prat took up this theme in the 1990s in such works as 'Les morts dans la comptabilité céleste des Clunisiens de l'an mil', in *Religion et culture autour de l'an mil: royaume capétien et Lotharingie. Actes du colloque international 'Hugues Capet 987–1987. La France de l'an mil'. Auxerre, 26–27 juin, Metz, 11–12 septembre 1987*, ed. Dominique Iogna-Prat and Jean-Charles Picard (Paris: Picard, 1990), 55–69; English translation: 'The Dead in the Celestial Bookkeeping of the Cluniac Monks Around the Year 1000', in *Debating the Middle Ages*, ed. Lester K. Little and Barbara H. Rosenwein (Malden, MA: Blackwell, 1998), 340–62; and Iogna-Prat, 'Des morts très spéciaux aux morts ordinaires: le pastorale funéraire clunisienne (XIe–XIIe siècles)', *Médiévales* 31 (1996): 79–91.

sources. It shows the effects on fields traditionally dominated by professional religious of bringing monastic and liturgical studies into dialogue with cultural history and social anthropology. It also highlights the debt that anyone who wants to engage in such dialogue owes to those monastic and priestly scholars whose codicological and editorial efforts over four centuries have made much of the vast manuscript sources for the medieval liturgy available for scholarly use. Finally, it illustrates the particular value of moving back and forth between ritual studies, which can anchor specific liturgical remains in the wider context of human behaviour, and liturgy, which reveals the expressions of religious belief that shape rituals at specific times and places.

Chapter 3
Approaches to Early Medieval Music and Rites

William T. Flynn

Mind the Gap: Bridging Disciplinary Differences

The publication, twenty years ago, of David Hiley's *Western Plainchant: A Handbook* is a good starting-point for assessing the work being done by musicologists and its relationship to other work on ecclesiastical ceremonies and rites.[1] Intended to be introductory, it nevertheless contains a large bibliography (sixty-four pages) and text of nearly seven hundred pages, and, some two decades later, it is still the essential synthesis of twentieth-century scholarship on Western chant. The coverage of the book suggests that earlier musicologists tended to defer to liturgical scholars and theologians for basic historical understanding of medieval rites. The book's summary of the work of liturgical scholars takes up only the first forty-six pages, and the rites (baptism, confirmation, ordination, coronation, marriage, burial, and dedication) are given a mere three pages without further bibliographic references, presumably for the reason that 'not all of these services require the performance of music as an essential element'.[2] Much more attention is given to two areas: musicologists first focus on the fundamental work of identifying, inventorying and editing the sources. This has to be accomplished at a level of detail necessary to enable careful analysis of individual genres of chant (such as Introit, Offertory, Communion and each item of the mass proper, as well as the Responsories, and antiphons of the office). Studies of individual genres (defined by a formal analysis of their linguistic and musical structures) then become the focus, since each has a complex history of its own, and the several families of early chant have differing forms within the same portions of the mass and office. The book's historical discussion concentrates on debates about the early history of the music up to the first fully notated – though not pitch-secure – sources and then, in a section that anticipates the direction the field would turn in subsequent years, it summarizes scholarship on chant as it was practised and revised at specific institutions.

---

[1]   David Hiley, *Western Plainchant: A Handbook* (Oxford: Clarendon Press, 1993).
[2]   Hiley, *Western Plainchant*, 42.

Based on Hiley's summary, which I believe is reasonably comprehensive and fair, the contribution of musicology seems to have been curiously inattentive to the historical study of the rites in which music appeared. Questions of how chant functioned within particular rites seem to have been subordinated to others that could be answered by attending to the music alone, often without consideration of the music's connections to the services and wider religious contexts that gave rise to it. Chant was thus treated somewhat reductively as part of a history of musical style that had a tendency to be co-opted into progressive evolutionary narratives which gave the impression of far greater ritual and musical uniformity than was the case. Musicologists, if they were to follow Willi Apel's famous and highly influential proposal to 'reconstruct a picture of the formative processes which led to the final stage of Gregorian chant, as it appears in the earliest manuscripts', had to accept the supposition that the surviving manuscripts represented some kind of relatively closed and very consistent and uniform canon, and the pinnacle of a musical development.[3] Hiley's own remarks throughout his *Western Plainchant* display a thorough awareness of this wider problem, but the rigorous focus on music as the object of study creates very little space in a large book for consideration of the context for which the music was destined by its creators.[4]

Not long after Hiley's book was published, Barbara Haggh-Huglo noted a similar disconnection between the study of church music and church history, from the perspective of someone interested in medieval polyphony.[5] The principal argument of her article is that musicologists have been extraordinarily selective in the kinds of historical sources that they pay attention to, favouring, in addition to the musical sources themselves, those that record the administrative transactions of institutions (such as account books) that yield information about musicians, but neglecting others such as cartularies, obits, wills, foundation charters and narratives. As Haggh-Huglo points out, the value of these sources has often been demonstrated by art historians, who have found in them information on the patronage of books, artworks and architecture. By paying little attention to such evidence, musicologists are in danger of distorting the history of music, because they may miss many references to the music itself (whether still extant or lost), its principal patrons, its religious purposes, and the shifting attitudes towards its

---

3   Willi Apel's chapter title is particularly revealing: 'Conclusion: Prolegomena to a History of Gregorian Style', in his *Gregorian Chant* (Bloomington: Indiana University Press, 1958), 507–15.

4   Typical of his balanced and cautious approach is Hiley's remark that 'a medieval source records only what was understood to be "right" at a particular place and time' (*Western Plainchant*, 400).

5   Barbara Haggh, 'Foundations or Institutions? On Bringing the Middle Ages into the History of Medieval Music', *Acta Musicologica* 68 (1996): 87–128.

use in rites. All of these sources may help one consider in what circumstances and why rites were continually altered. For Haggh-Huglo a more broadly conceived form of archival research is needed to give direction to historical musicology. As she suggests, this would help musicologists make connections with medievalists in allied fields.

Hiley's caveats about musical and ritual diversity and Haggh-Huglo's admonition concerning the need to use a wider variety of documentary sources demonstrate that musicologists themselves were already raising questions two decades ago about how their discipline might come into better dialogue with other medievalists. Haggh-Huglo's article defines the gap in understanding between musicologists and ecclesiastical historians as a kind of blindness to the study of religious history in general. All of the neglected sources she mentions are related to the mechanics of instituting, maintaining and performing ecclesiastical rituals, and so ought to be of key interest to historians of the liturgy. The music that medieval benefactors endowed gave these rituals varying degrees of solemnity and fullness that affected both their form and their content. The music within such bespoke rites was often passed down, but it was also continually adapted and sometimes extensively renewed. Therefore, unless the music is firmly situated within wider spheres of inquiry into the adaptation of rites, little progress can be made in understanding how benefactors, church leaders and musicians all provoked and reacted to ritual change.

However, this gap in understanding flows in both directions: the close connection in the West between music and rite should make it equally difficult for other medievalists to ignore the work of musicologists – even those who have paid closer attention to the musical objects that they uncover than to that music's ritual context. Aside from the basic historical data that can be uncovered by paying attention to musical palaeography and the transmission and distribution of repertories, paying specific attention to the musical content of a rite in performance (to the extent that it is possible to recreate or imagine) provides an alternative reading of texts for that rite that must be considered essential to its understanding. By taking the music of a rite into account one begins to consider questions concerning its effect on a rite's performance and delivery, and therefore on its rhetoric and its diverse audiences.[6]

This gap between ecclesiastical historians and musicologists has since been addressed in many productive ways, but the results are still often couched in intimidating layers of technical language and specialized analysis of both music and medieval ritual that sometimes hide the fact that the common ground shared by all medievalists covers a much greater area than their disciplinary allotments.

---

[6]   These are research questions that have dominated my own work; see William T. Flynn, *Medieval Music as Medieval Exegesis* (Lanham, MD and London: Scarecrow Press, 1999).

We are all working with material sources, especially manuscripts, that give us our sole access to the Middle Ages. The remainder of this chapter therefore focuses on introducing a personal, but hopefully representative, selection of musicological studies and resources, both completed and emerging, that seem to me to bridge – or show greatest potential for bridging – the gap; all of them are the fruits of the last twenty years of internal criticism amongst musicologists concerned about the directions taken by their own discipline.

Recent Approaches to Sources

It is unlikely that musicologists will ever give up the search for the origin of Gregorian chant, but this search is no longer dominated, as it was during the nineteenth and early twentieth centuries, by the need to establish one authentic earliest version of Gregorian chant as it was transmitted from Rome to the Carolingians. Even if one accepts the theory that there was a period of Frankish development and a re-transmission back to Rome, the gradual accumulation of evidence has proved that no single version of chant exists in the written record that represents an original authoritative tradition. The transmission of the chants that eventually formed a corpus of fairly stable texts and melodies and that is now called 'Gregorian' was a mixed literate and oral phenomenon in which a variety of notations conveyed differing amounts of musical information. The least musical information is conveyed by references to partial text (*incipits* or even references that merely list the subject matter to be used). The most information is conveyed by fully written-out texts with at least one kind of music notation (some of which convey information primarily about musical gesture and delivery, and others of which convey information primarily about pitch). The early text-only transmissions differ substantively from each other though the critical editions obscure this.[7] Later notated transmissions show at most a correspondence of about 80–90 per cent of melodic content, unless one makes assumptions that dissimilar notational signs have exactly the same melodic meaning when occurring in similar musical contexts.[8] Although the consensus that a core repertory of Roman-Frankish chant was transmitted with some stability has not broken down, there is at present little agreement on the direction(s) of the transmission and its chronology: what exists are late

---

[7] See remarks on Hesbert's editions below, 61–62.

[8] This is the assumption guiding much of Eugène Cardine's *Gregorian Semiology*, trans. Robert M. Fowels (Sablé-sur-Sarthe: Solesmes, 1982). Although *Gregorian Semiology* has nearly reached classic status, Óscar Octavio Mascareñas Garza demonstrates the assumptions behind the approach and its tendency towards uniformity instead of 'différence' in 'Exposing the *Play* in Gregorian Chant: The Manuscript as an *Opening* of *Re-Presentation*' (unpub. PhD thesis, University of Limerick, 2010).

ninth- and tenth-century fully notated manuscripts that encode similar musical gestures in differing though arguably related semiotic systems that scholars have assumed to record similar melodies.[9] Moreover, this limited consensus has been built without agreement on some fundamental questions that are logically prior: for example, there is currently no agreement about 'What constitutes a significant musical variant?' without which one cannot really state whether one melody is essentially the same or essentially different.[10]

Recently, musicologists' ideas of what might constitute the transmission of a Roman rite in the early Middle Ages have changed dramatically. They are no longer thinking solely that the rites were transmitted as a fundamentally distinct set of texts and melodies, but rather as checklists and guides for selecting good texts for specific feasts, and that the sending of teachers who could give instruction in a regional musical style was crucial.[11] For example, Susan Rankin's recent work on the liturgical florilegium in Alcuin's *De laude Dei* has demonstrated the eclectic mixture of office chants that may have been interpreted as 'Roman' (or at least Romanizing) before the Carolingian reforms. Her work on Carolingian sources themselves demonstrates that a long series of redactions, which probably involved multiple centres, produced the relative stability of the later ninth-century Gregorian repertory.[12] An important consequence of

---

9   The sixty years of scholarship that have led to a current agreement-to-disagree can best be traced in two volumes of reprinted essays collected by Thomas Forrest Kelly, ed., *Oral and Written Transmission in Chant* and *Chant and its Origins* (Farnham: Ashgate, 2009).

10   David G. Hughes has provided work towards a typology of variants; see especially 'The Implications of Variants for Chant Transmission', in *De musica et cantu: Helmut Hucke zum 60. Geburtstag*, ed. Peter Cahn and Ann-Katrin Heimer (Hildesheim: Olms, 1993), 65–73. Recent work by Emma Hornby and Rebecca Maloy uses a statistical method combined with text-music analysis to give greater probability to their readings of pitch-insecure sources in *Music and Meaning in Old Hispanic Lenten Chants: Psalmi, Threni and Easter Vigil Canticles* (Woodbridge: Boydell and Brewer, 2013). Craig Wright (discussing the intellectual context of the notation of Notre Dame polyphony) suggests that in his own scholarly past fundamental questions that 'we failed to ask – nor were encouraged to ask' might be reduced to the 'most basic question: What *is* this document that we see on the page?'; see his 'Quantification in Medieval Paris and How it Changed Western Music', in *City, Chant, and the Topography of Early Music in Honour of Thomas Forrest Kelly*, ed. Michael Scott Cuthbert, Sean Gallagher and Christoph Wolff (Cambridge, MA: Harvard University Press, 2013), 3–26 at 7.

11   For one of the rare examples of such a teacher see Bede's, *Ecclesiastical History of the English People*, ed. and trans. Bertram Colgrave and R.A.B. Mynors (Oxford: Clarendon Press, 1969), 4.18 (pp. 388–91) on John the arch-chanter; for brief but illuminating remarks on him, see Christopher Page, *The Christian West and Its Singers: The First Thousand Years* (New Haven: Yale University Press, 2010), 269–74.

12   Susan Rankin, 'Beyond the Boundaries of Roman-Frankish Chant: Alcuin's *De laude Dei* and Other Early Medieval Sources of Office Chants', in *City, Chant, and the Topography*

such work is that a largely tacit consensus about uniformity of early text-only transmissions of the Roman rite, established by René Hesbert's 1935 edition of the eighth- and ninth-century text-only transmissions of mass repertory, has now broken down.[13] This is for two main reasons, both exemplified by the recent work of Daniel DiCenso: first, by taking into account fragments unknown to (or neglected by) Hesbert, DiCenso proposes to bring together all of the earliest sources of Gregorian chant afresh.[14] Second, ideas about how to edit texts have changed. Editors are now likely to think that the editing of texts designed to convey music should have a different set of conventions from those designed for editing other types of texts.[15] DiCenso's proposed edition of early Gregorian chant sources promises to provide a music-critical analysis in which variants that might be considered insignificant in establishing a text's meaning (for example, transposition of phrases, omission or addition of adverbs or conjunctions) will be carefully examined for the melodic variants that they imply as mnemonic notations of music.

It would not be too strong to say that musicologists dealing with notated sources also accepted the bias of liturgical historians for sources that represented a complete repertory of Gregorian chant, and there has been a healthy turn towards abbreviated and fragmentary sources that give more variegated, although incomplete, pictures of the whole repertory. These neglected sources may helpfully be compared to the fuller and better-known sources to facilitate a thoroughgoing revision (and hopefully clarification) of the history of Carolingian (and later) transmissions of chant. While musicologists will

of Early Music, 229–62. See also Jesse Billet, 'The Liturgy of the "Roman" Office in England from the Conversion to the Conquest', in *Rome Across Time and Space: Cultural Transmission and the Exchange of Ideas, c. 500–1400*, ed. Claudia Bolgia, Rosamond McKitterick and John Osborne (Cambridge: Cambridge University Press, 2011), 84–110; and Susan Rankin, 'The Making of Carolingian Mass Chant Books', in *Quomodo cantabimus canticum: Studies in Honor of Edward H. Roesner*, ed. Rena Mueller and John Nadas, American Institute of Musicology Miscellanea 7 (Middleton, WI: A-R Editions, 2008), 37–63.

[13]   *Antiphonale missarum sextuplex*, edited by René-Jean Hesbert (Brussels: Vromant, 1935; repr. Rome: Herder, 1967).

[14]   DiCenso, 'Sacramentary-Antiphoners as Sources of Gregorian Chant in the Eighth and Ninth Centuries' (unpub. PhD thesis, University of Cambridge, 2012). For the proposed new edition, see Daniel DiCenso's webpage: http://www.danieljdicenso.com where links to very brief project descriptions may be found.

[15]   The University of Stockholm project *Ars Edendi* (project director: Gunilla Iversen) focuses on recent developments in the editing of particular categories of medieval Latin texts, including liturgical texts: http://www.arsedendi.org (accessed 2 July 2014). Even liturgical rubrication can provide guides to interpretation that alter the readings of traditional text editors; see William T. Flynn, 'Reading Hildegard of Bingen's Antiphons for the 11,000 Virgin-Martyrs of Cologne: Rhetorical *Ductus* and Liturgical Rubrics', *Nottingham Medieval Studies* 56 (2012): 171–89.

continue to discuss the earliest sources, the result of recent research suggests that they will not find any single, decisive moment of transmission of what later became known as the Roman rite, and that the continuing diversity within the families of rites that claim Roman origin will be considered more fully than it was in earlier scholarship.

When one comes to the later sources containing musical notations, it is fair to say that two areas of concern have dominated: first discovering and cataloguing the sources; and then producing editions suitable for the purpose of reading and analysing the sound of the music and/or for performing it. Since musicologists can only begin studying the music itself when they have decoded the manuscript witness (that is, when they have reconstructed from it the object of their study), it is not surprising that they have in general been slower to undertake detailed study of the manuscripts for the information these might yield about their production and use. Even though some textual scholars and historians have been engaged in such research, they have seldom treated manuscripts that contain mostly notated music. Recent editions, however, suggest that this tendency is changing. For example, Susan Rankin's commentary to her facsimile edition of the Winchester Troper (Cambridge, Corpus Christi College, Ms. 473) carefully indexes both text and music scribes, and in describing the notation reveals a great range of pitch-clarifying strategies, uncovered through painstaking palaeographical analysis.[16] Not only does this manuscript contain chants that were partially dually notated (where letter names of pitches provide some information), it also contains many pitch-clarifying neumes. Its carefully notated polyphonic lines interact with the chant lines in ways that can be interpreted with the help of music treatises. The edition provides essential material that expands and revises earlier scholarship, especially on the sound of the music and its historical context.

There is still extensive work to be done in all of the areas that have interested earlier musicologists – even basic indexed descriptions of many sources are still lacking. This is partly due to the tendency of palaeographers to mention merely that a source contains music notation (or even ignore it altogether in manuscripts dominated by text only). K.D. Hartzell's *Catalogue of Manuscripts Written or Owned in England up to 1200 containing Music* attempts to rectify these omissions for early medieval English manuscripts.[17] It will prove valuable, though it should not be used without reference to the review by Michael Gullick and Susan Rankin which supplies corrections, supplemental

---

[16] *The Winchester Troper*, ed. Susan Rankin, Early English Church Music 50 (London: Published for the British Academy by Stainer and Bell, 2007).

[17] K.D. Hartzell, *Catalogue of Manuscripts Written or Owned in England up to 1200 containing Music* (Woodbridge: Boydell Press in association with the Plainsong and Medieval Music Society, 2006).

listings of manuscripts, and a critical evaluation of the information given on music palaeography.[18]

Chant scholars are now paying considerable attention to fragmentary sources, not only of texts that were intended to be performed musically, but also of music manuscripts themselves. One of the reasons that musicologists once found it convenient to think of Gregorian chant as a relatively stable and relatively uniform corpus is that they gave priority to comprehensive manuscripts that attempt to record the repertory for the whole of, or large portions of, a rite. Eduardo Henrik Aubert's thesis on Aquitanian fragments before 1100 and his forthcoming catalogue of chant fragments (from four departmental archives in Burgundy – Côte d' Or, Nièvre, Saône-et-Loire and Yonne) provide important resources and perhaps pave the way for larger research projects to address the need for incorporating such sources into music histories.[19]

There is still much work to be undertaken on music treatises. Until recently the priority was to make their texts available in modern editions, but little systematic work has been undertaken on their manuscript transmission. There is a parallel between the study of these texts and those for other educational purposes, but it is not overstating the case to say that historians of grammar and rhetoric have at present taken the lead. Music treatises pose a particular problem in that they seem to have been classified by medieval librarians simply as part of the quadrivium, yet many of them display practical concerns with teaching the music as practiced in institutional liturgies. For example, in a recent study, T.J.H. McCarthy identified an interesting corpus of twenty music-theoretical compilations in manuscripts associated principally with monasteries in Salian Germany, yet it is not clear whether these manuscripts form a coherent corpus, since some contain full texts while others contain excerpts; some are encyclopaedic and comprehensive while others seem much more practical.[20] It is fair to say that we need a better understanding of such miscellanies both in terms of their production, and the purposes that underlie them, and in terms of their use in teaching. A recent chapter by Michel Huglo and Barbara Haggh-Huglo (with Leofranc Holford-Strevens) has begun to address some of these issues, plotting the institutional provenance of all known surviving Parisian music treatises from 900 to 1450. The results of

---

[18]   Michael Gullick and Susan Rankin, 'Review of K.D. Hartzell, *Catalogue*', *Early Music History* 28 (2009): 262–85.

[19]   Eduardo Henrik Aubert, 'Ecrire, chanter, agir: Les graduels et missels notés en notation aquitaine avant 1100' (unpub. PhD thesis, l'Ecole des Hautes Etudes en Sciences Sociales: Paris, 2011). For the catalogue, see Aubert's webpage at http://buscatextual.cnpq.br/buscatextual/visualizacv.do?id=K4231522Y6.

[20]   T.J.H. McCarthy, *Music, Scholasticism and Reform: Salian Germany, 1024–1125* (Manchester: Manchester University Press, 2009). See also my review of this work in *German History* 28 (2010): 572–73.

the survey have pointed out remaining 'gaping lacunae' and provided a list of possible gains to be made from further work: (1) A thorough palaeographic and codicological assessment of music theory codices (many of whose contents are already indexed) needs to be undertaken. At present even the country of origin is imprecise for some. (2) A taxonomy of music theory manuscripts needs to be constructed so that like can be compared with like. (3) Attempts might be made to identify the hands of musicians using localizable and datable music theory manuscripts.[21]

To sum up, there is a notable convergence between the ways historians and musicologists are approaching and reassessing manuscript sources. Musicologists, in abandoning a simple narrative about the origins of chant, have turned their attention more fully to the centres of production and transmission of the manuscripts. The opportunities for interdisciplinary and co-operative projects should be noted. For early medievalists, it is important to recognize that words alone are a powerful form of musical notation, and perhaps the most common form, even after more specialized notations were invented and transmitted by cantors and clerics.[22] All early medievalists looking at liturgical texts should become aware that in doing so they are also probably looking at a kind of musical notation, even if that notation is simply the words of the rite itself.

Recent Approaches to (Genre) Analysis

The analysis of repertories of individual chant genres (Introit, Responsory, etc.) remains an important focus for musicologists, who have recently pushed beyond earlier boundaries that constrained the field because of two factors. First, it is now much easier for scholars to create, use and share digital data and to manipulate large data sets that previously would have required specialist computing assistance. Second, new attention is being paid to the ways in which the grammatical and rhetorical structures of the texts interact with their musical structures.

The use of large data sets underpins Katherine Helsen's thesis on the great-responsory repertory of the early twelfth-century antiphoner, Paris, Bibliothèque Nationale, Ms. latin 12044. Greatly expanding upon and ultimately revising the

---

[21]   Michel Huglo, Barbara Haggh and Leofranc Holford-Strevens, 'The Topography of Music Theory in Paris, 900–1450', in *City, Chant, and the Topography of Early Music*, 275–334, at 314–15.

[22]   See Anna Maria Busse Berger, *Medieval Music and the Art of Memory* (Berkeley: University of California Press, 2005), esp. 1–120, for a consideration of the many possible ways the *artes memorativae* influenced the creators of early medieval music. This should be read together with the review by William Flynn and Jane Flynn in *Early Music History* 28 (2009): 249–62.

conclusions of the seminal work on responsories of Walter Frere, she compares this manuscript with eight other repertories, and points a way forward for such studies.[23] Her meticulous collection of data allows her to catalogue both textual and musical detail and to analyse how melodic material is reused both within and between repertories. Moreover, she is able to demonstrate the existence of a number of house-styles and to demonstrate their characteristic melodic choices. The great value in this approach is that variants that might seem insignificant when casually encountered are shown to create significant and discernable differences in style, even if a singer then and now would not dispute that it is the 'same' piece being sung. Helsen demonstrates one application of this data, using it to localize fragmentary sources (even to identify some very partial fragments). While the thesis itself displays little concern with the structure of the texts, since Helsen's focus is on the musical structures, the careful organization of her database makes further exploration of both the text and music of the repertory practical for any interested scholar.[24]

The new analytical attention given to the dual structures of a text's grammar and its musical setting has been particularly valuable when comparing different liturgical families. Since the families of Old Roman and Gregorian chant share texts, and have related yet very different melodic content, text-analysis has been integral to discerning the differences between the two musical styles in the important studies by Emma Hornby and Rebecca Maloy.[25] Hornby's work has been particularly attentive to the potential mnemonic functions of the structure of liturgical texts. She has demonstrated how the highly formulaic melodic style of Old Roman tracts (psalm texts that are sung between the readings of Lenten masses) work in concert with the texts' grammar to create memorable structures that may not have needed any musical notation beyond

---

[23]   Katherine Eve Helsen, 'The Great Responsories of the Divine Office: Aspects of Structure and Transmission' (unpub. PhD thesis, University of Regensberg, 2008), available online and downloadable at http://epub.uni-regensburg.de/10769/. For Walter Frere's analytical work on the great responsories see his introduction to *Antiphonale Sarisburiense: A Reproduction in Facsimile of a Manuscript of the Thirteenth Century* (London, 1901–24).

[24]   Technological gains are also evident in older databases such as *Cantus* (now at the University of Waterloo: http://cantus.uwaterloo.caa) which still claims to be largely an *incipit* database of the musical items of the Divine Office. Its scope has become considerably broader. *Cantus* now links not only to full texts from René-Jean Hesbert's *Corpus antiphonalium officii*, 6 vols., RED series maior, fontes 7–12 (Rome: Herder, 1963–79), but even supplies full, newly transcribed texts for items not found in Hesbert, as well as links to the manuscript images themselves, where available.

[25]   Emma Hornby, *Gregorian and Old Roman Eighth Mode Tracts: A Case Study in the Transmission of Western Chant* (Aldershot: Ashgate, 2002); Rebecca Maloy, *Inside the Offertory: Aspects of Chronology and Transmission* (New York: Oxford University Press, 2010).

the words themselves for their accurate oral transmission. Furthermore, the interaction between text and music and its potential for emphasizing particular verbal meanings has become a focus of Hornby's analysis and the focal point of Hornby and Maloy's joint project on Old Hispanic Lenten Chant.[26] These works demonstrate the significant amount of musical information that can be obtained from adiastemmatic neumes; that is, neumes that do not represent pitch graphically (for example, on a staff) but instead serve as a mnemonic for a known melody. Even though the pitch content cannot be recovered, significant melodic gestures and cadential structures can be compared with textual structures. When the musical reading goes against the grain of the texts' grammar, points of particular rhetorical emphasis are generated, and these can be examined first within the texts' fuller liturgical context (informed by the emphases and progression of the whole rite) and, second, compared with interpretations (in liturgical commentary, *ordines* and rules) contemporary with the formation and use of the repertory. The engagement with the musical content thus adds to, and sometimes alters, readings available from attending to the texts alone and opens up a whole field in which dialogue between musicologists and historians will prove particularly productive. Hornby and Maloy have already demonstrated that there was a complex relationship between the two major manuscript (and liturgical) traditions that preserve Old Hispanic chant, and it is clear that genre studies are only just reaching their potential for challenging and revising theories of liturgical transmission that have been dominated in the past by textual scholars.

Musical Sources Interpreted in Institutional, Pedagogical, and Ritual Contexts

Musicological work that concentrates on rituals as manifested in specific manuscripts made within particular institutional and pedagogical circumstances is perhaps the most immediately useful for historians interested in liturgy. Although this is also the kind of work that is most fraught with technical difficulty and fragmentary source material, musicologists have been mining the most promising aggregations of source material, which are mostly from the end of the early Middle Ages. Notable examples of such work are James Grier's studies of Adémar de Chabannes (996–1034), and Margot Fassler's two monographs: the first on the sequences associated with the Augustinian canons of St Victor (Paris), and the second on the fabric

---

[26]   Emma Hornby, *Medieval Liturgical Chant and Patristic Exegesis: Words and Music in the Second-Mode Tracts* (Woodbridge: Boydell and Brewer, 2009); Hornby and Maloy, *Music and Meaning*.

and liturgy of Chartres. Grier's extensive manuscript work has demonstrated that Adémar was composer, text- and music-scribe for a large corpus of work (and text- and/or music-scribe for an even larger corpus).[27] Having identified this evidence of liturgical and textual production by a known and important churchman, Grier has been able to investigate Adémar's contributions to the enhancement and promotion of Saint Martial's cult as apostle. Fassler's earlier study of the sequences of the Parisian Victorines shows how this mass genre (important because it precedes the Gospel reading and can directly affect its interpretation) changed in both content and function, in part due to the educational reforms of the early Augustinians.[28] Fassler's more recent study argues that the process of making history in the early medieval West was intimately tied to the liturgy. She makes the basic, but important, point that cantors were especially active in history writing both in cathedral and monastic institutions. Her study therefore examines the role of cantors and the officials of the cathedral (and town) of Chartres in their production of a sacred history in which the liturgy is employed as the primary means of creating a communal memory that promotes the cathedral's famous relic of the Virgin Mary and her cult.[29] Fassler's implicit claim is that a modern critical reading of medieval historical sources is not achievable if their connections to the liturgy go unrecognized by modern historians. In an important article, she argues that the liturgy provided a 'fundamental default mode for the representation of the past in the Latin Middle Ages (especially up to the twelfth century)', exercising an influence that is 'both more beautiful and more terrible than has been imagined'.[30] Such aggregations of liturgical and historical material as survive from Chartres can be found, as Fassler points out, because cantors were not only musically and liturgically educated, but were also often authors

---

[27]   See especially his article 'The Musical Autographs of Adémar de Chabannes (989–1034)', *Early Music History* 24 (2005): 125–68; his monograph, *The Musical World of a Medieval Monk: Adémar de Chabannes in Eleventh-Century Aquitaine* (Cambridge: Cambridge University Press, 2006); his edition of Adémar de Chabannes, *Opera liturgica et poetica: Musica cum textibus*, ed. James Grier, Ademari Cabannensis Opera Omnia Pars 2, CCCM (Turnhout: Brepols, 2012), vols. 245 and 245A; and most recently his article, 'Adémar de Chabannes (989–1034) and Musical Literacy', *Journal of the American Musicological Society* 66 (2013): 605–38.

[28]   Margot E. Fassler, *Gothic Song: Victorine Sequences and Augustinian Reform in Twelfth-Century Paris* (Cambridge: Cambridge University Press, 1993; 2nd rev. edn. Notre Dame, IN: Notre Dame Press, 2011).

[29]   Margot E. Fassler, The *Virgin of Chartres: Making History through Liturgy and the Arts* (New Haven: Yale University Press, 2010).

[30]   Margot Fassler, 'The Liturgical Framework of Time and the Representation of History', in *Representing History 900–1300: Art, Music, History*, ed. Robert A. Maxwell (University Park, PA: Pennsylvania State University Press, 2010), 149–71, at 157.

of institutional and (in Adémar's case universal) chronicles and were in charge of the production of necrologies and cartularies; insofar as history was made, it was made by cantors.[31]

Such innovative work, offering readings of medieval liturgies informed by extensive study of the liturgical manuscripts, relies on evidence that is necessarily partial and often necessarily speculative. Liturgical manuscripts are inherently prescriptive, offering rules and repertories for enacting a rite; they never provide evidence that it was in fact enacted in the way the cantor-scribes intended. Yet, nevertheless, they are the best and fullest witnesses to what might have happened and are certain witnesses to what their creators wanted to happen. For another example of work that situates liturgical innovation within specific institutions, I refer to my own study of liturgies intended for Heloise's abbey of the Paraclete (near Troyes) in the 1130s that were shaped profoundly by the contributions of Peter Abelard.[32] In the 1980s, Chrysogonus Waddell did the essential spadework for the Paraclete liturgy in a lengthy series of publications that provided editions of key sources as well as detailed commentary.[33] The most important sources he edited were a reasonably full late thirteenth-century Old French translation of a somewhat earlier Latin Ordinary giving detailed, though not comprehensive, information about the order of the services in summary form, and a late fifteenth-century Breviary containing principally the offices of Vespers and Lauds (although some other repertory is occasionally included). These two

---

[31] Fassler, 'Liturgical Framework', 168; and Margot E. Fassler, 'The Office of the Cantor in Early Western Monastic Rules and Customaries', *Early Music History* 5 (1985): 29–52.

[32] William T. Flynn, 'Letters, Liturgy, and Identity: The Use of *Epithalamica* at the Paraclete', in *Sapientia et Eloquentia: Meaning and Function in Liturgical Poetry, Music, Drama, and Biblical Commentary in the Middle Ages*, ed. Gunilla Iversen and Nicolas Bell (Turnhout: Brepols, 2009), 301–48; '*Ductus figuratis et subtilis*: Rhetorical Interventions for Women in Two Twelfth-Century Liturgies', in *Rhetoric Beyond Words: Delight and Persuasion in the Arts of the Middle Ages*, ed. Mary Carruthers (Cambridge: Cambridge University Press, 2010), 250–80; and 'Abelard and Rhetoric: Widows and Virgins at the Paraclete', in *Rethinking Abelard: A Collection of Critical Essays*, ed. Babette S. Heelemans (Leiden: Brill, 2014), 155–86.

[33] *The Old French Paraclete Ordinary: Paris Bibliothèque Nationale Ms français 14410 and the Paraclete Breviary: Chaumont, Bibliothèque Municipale Ms 31: Introduction and Commentary*, CLS 3 (Trappist, KY: Gethsemani Abbey, 1985); *The Old French Paraclete Ordinary: Edition*, CLS 4 (Trappist, KY: Gethsemani Abbey, 1983); *The Paraclete Breviary: Edition*, 3 vols., CLS 5–7 (1983); *Hymn Collections from the Paraclete*, 2 vols., CLS 8–9; and *The Paraclete Statutes, Institutiones Nostrae: Introduction, Edition and Commentary*, CLS 20 (Trappist, KY: Gethsemani Abbey, 1987). All of these editions were edited by Chrysogonus Waddell, appeared as photocopies of typescripts in the Cistercian Liturgy Series and were distributed by Cistercian Publications, Kalamazoo, and are now available online from Western Michigan University: http://digitalcollections-wmich.cdmhost.com/cdm/landingpage/collection/p15032coll5 (accessed 4 July 2014).

sources can be compared with a number of twelfth-century texts: Abelard and Heloise's letters including Abelard's Rule for the Paraclete; Abelard's hymns and sermons, and the anonymous *Institutiones nostrae* of the Paraclete whose text is thought to date from Heloise's abbacy. All of these texts have late transmission histories and no manuscript dates from a period earlier than the ordinary, but these sources often legislate for, or provide repertory for, a form of the liturgy that is earlier. Even if this earlier liturgy was instituted fully, it was no longer completely in use by the time the ordinary was copied. But by examining the proposed liturgy as something that was at least intended to be enacted, one gains an insight into Abelard's intent and purpose for the Paraclete and an appreciation for the rhetorical skill with which he created a novel monastic identity for the Paraclete nuns. When there are sources available, as illuminating as those for the Paraclete, it is possible to detect the ways the liturgy was altered intentionally by individuals and evaluate their work.

By way of a conclusion, it should be emphasized that musicologists rightly bring their own experience of reading and performing music to their examination of liturgical sources. Western music notations grew out of liturgical sources after all, and the combination of graphic representation of the music and sufficient verbal directions that one can find in modern scores suggests a form of reading that acknowledges these origins. In the performance of liturgies, structures of time and space can be experienced (rather than simply imagined). For example, a source may give a single rubric stating that a sequence 'Epithalamica' should precede the reading of a Gospel 'Maria Magdalene', but a performance of the ritual involves the singing of this nine-minute dramatic poem, sections of which may be assigned to a variety of singers, solo and choral, during which a candle-lit procession and censing of the Gospel takes place. Interpreting such a rubric is not only a complex matter of tracking down additional sources that might give some insight into the ritual, but is also a matter of going beyond the sources, extrapolating from them to reproduce a ritual. It is arguable that such reconstruction allows for a fuller 'reading' of the liturgical sources and exposes more of the rubricator's tacit and memorized knowledge. Musicologists have recently been emphasizing a need for practice-based research that allows a fuller investigation of the sense of space and time that rubrics and notated music attempt to encode. Perhaps the boldest experiment along these lines to date is John and Sally Harper's AHRC/ESRC-funded project 'The Experience of Worship in Late-Medieval Cathedral and Parish Church'.[34] Even with the luxury of a cathedral (Salisbury) with standing fabric from a time at which one of the versions of its customary was composed, the project discovered innumerable lacunae in the sources through such a practice-based approach. One of the most

---

[34]   The 'Experience of Worship in Late-Medieval Cathedral and Parish Church' website is http://www.experienceofworship.org.uk (accessed 2 July 2014).

important of the lacunae was the huge gap in understanding how the cathedral rite was transferred into parish settings.[35] By making the attempt to transfer it to a completely different space from that for which it was conceived, the project took part in a process that no doubt took place throughout the Middle Ages in churches that wished to be allied with Salisbury (Sarum) Use. The process also exposed both pedagogical and sociological distance between modern and medieval participants. The differences in musical training are perhaps easier to fill in with future research that aims for a practical recreation of performance techniques well documented in the sources, using performance strategies that are recoverable through further research. The even greater differences in sociological expectations regarding class, gender, and belief systems are also somewhat amenable to further research and at the very least need to be accorded critical and methodological weight by liturgical historians. In recognizing the tacit knowledge needed to perform the liturgy, liturgical historians can become attuned to the clues medieval sources occasionally yield when medieval conventions are violated and provoke commentary. While the 'Experience of Worship' project has considerably broader aims than historical investigation, it demonstrates both the value and the limits of a full imaginative reconstruction of an enacted ritual for historical research.[36] All real or imagined reconstructions highlight an irreducible element of invention in historical inquiry. However, if one demurs at investigating the sources in this way, perhaps on the grounds that it is too experimental, or somehow ahistorical, one arguably ends up with an equally invented historicized reading that ignores many features of the sources, the most important of which are the abundant rubrics and music notation. Such features suggest that great care was taken by medieval scribes to aid liturgical celebration and that today a fundamental form of reading these texts must take into account their sound, pacing, and the use of space that they encode and describe. By recognizing these features of our sources, and by using the better analytical tools available, and by incorporating the fuller picture of the sources that is currently emerging, scholars from all disciplines may yet realize their enormous potential for further insight into the history of medieval liturgies.

---

[35]   See also Matthew Cheung Salisbury's discussion of this issue in Chapter 5 below.

[36]   Early medieval institutions that might benefit from such an approach include Winchester in the mid-eleventh century, and any of the many monasteries and several cathedrals that produced tropes and sequences. Gunilla Iversen's monograph, *Laus Angelica: Poetry in the Medieval Mass*, trans. W. Flynn, ed. J. Flynn (Turnhout: Brepols, 2010) gives a rich selection of these rewarding texts and points to the need for further study of the liturgies of the institutions where they were produced.

PART II
Questioning Authority and Tradition

Chapter 4

Questioning the Authority of Vogel and Elze's *Pontifical romano-germanique*[1]

Henry Parkes

> The most important liturgical book of the tenth century, the Romano-German Pontifical, was compiled at the monastery of St Alban in Mainz in 950–963 ... and influenced all of the West.[2]

When medieval historians seek to engage with medieval liturgy, nothing is more useful than a one-sentence summary. None has enjoyed more success, arguably, than that which distils the *Pontifical romano-germanique* (*PRG*), one of the most complicated and mysterious of medieval textual traditions, into an easily digestible sound bite. The quotation at the head of this chapter is not

---

[1]   I am grateful to Mme Daphné Defosset, of the Bibliothèque des Facultés de Théologie, Université de Strasbourg, for her efforts in trying to track down the papers of Michel Andrieu, which subsequently formed the basis of *Le pontifical romano-germanique du dixième siècle*, ed. Cyrille Vogel and Reinhard Elze, Studi e Testi, 226–27, 269, 3 vols. (Vatican: Biblioteca Apostolica Vaticana, 1963–72), the edition which concerns me here. Unfortunately, these could not be located. For evidence of the deposit see *PRG*, 1:vii. Subsequent references to the edited texts within this publication are indicated by '*PRG*' plus a chapter number and, where necessary, a paragraph number. Texts published in the volumes of *Les ordines romani du haut moyen âge*, ed. Michel Andrieu, Spicilegium Sacrum Lovaniense, 11, 23–24, 28–29, 5 vols. (Leuven: Université Catholique de Louvain, 1931–61) are indicated by '*OR*' plus the number of the relevant *Ordo Romanus*. Manuscripts are referred to by the following sigla: *Primary sources:* A = Rome, Biblioteca Universitaria Alessandrina, Cod. 173; B = Bamberg, Staatsbibliothek, Ms. Lit. 53; C = Montecassino, Archivio della Badia, Ms. 451; D = Rome, Biblioteca Vallicelliana, Cod. D. 5; G = Eichstätt, Diözesanarchiv, Cod. B. 4; K = Pistoia, Archivio Capitolare, C. 141; L = Lucca, Biblioteca Capitolare Feliniana, Cod. 607; T = Vienna, Österreichische Nationalbibliothek, Ms. 701; V = Vendôme, Bibliothèque Municipale, Ms. 14; *Supplementary sources:* P = Paris, Bibliothèque Nationale de France, Ms. latin 820; R = Wolfenbüttel, Herzog August Bibliothek, Cod. Guelf. 555 Helmst. (cat. no. 603); J = London, British Library, Additional Ms. 17004.

[2]   'Le livre liturgique le plus important du 10e siècle, le pontifical romano-germanique, a été compilé au monastère Saint-Alban de Mayence en 950–963 ... et à influencé tout l'Occident.' Pierre-Marie Gy, in Pierre Grelot et al., 'Liturgie et vie spirituelle', *Dictionnaire de spiritualité ascétique et mystique, doctrine et histoire*, ed. Marcel Viller et al., 17 vols. (Paris: Beauchesne, 1932–95), 9: cols. 873–939, at col. 905; the article was reprinted as *Liturgie et vie spirituelle* (Paris: Beauchesne, 1977).

unique, but one example among the hundreds (if not thousands) of scholarly books, articles and dictionary entries, all written in the last half-century, whose authors have gravitated towards this touchstone of tenth-century certainty. The reason is quite simple. Within the confusing proliferation of early medieval liturgical books – with their often awkward shapes, ambivalent testimonies and frustrating propensity to resist systematic analysis – the *PRG* has long stood as an irresistible exception: a clearly delineated, named tradition of manuscripts, anchored to a specific locality and a narrow timeframe, and attached to a wealth of historical context. Medieval liturgy might be a difficult subject, one could say, but at least we have the *PRG*.

For this we have to thank Cyrille Vogel and Reinhard Elze, the devoted scholars whose 'definitive' three-volume edition of the *PRG* manuscript tradition, entitled *Le pontifical romano-germanique du dixième siècle*, was published between 1963 and 1972.[3] This monument of liturgical philology opened up a new vista of scholarly opportunity, and its publication was complemented by a series of explanatory articles by Cyrille Vogel, joined in 1963 by the lucid primer for which he is probably best remembered: the *Introduction aux sources de l'histoire du culte chrétien au moyen âge*.[4] With a readily available text and handy commentary, Vogel and Elze thus equipped their readers to learn about the *PRG* as the pre-eminent tenth-century pontifical (that is, a bishop's liturgical book) which combined Frankish ritual texts, Carolingian liturgical exposition and commentary, and sources of Roman authority known as *Ordines Romani*.[5] One could find out about the *PRG* as a watershed moment in the evolution of pontificals. And readers could discover how monks from a German cathedral city had managed to assemble this compendium, which, following a stellar rise in popularity across eleventh- and twelfth-century Europe, as well as its successful implantation in Rome,

---

[3]   The adjective is courtesy of Eric Palazzo, *Le moyen âge: des origines au XIIIème siècle* (Paris: Beauchesne, 1993), 210. For details of the edition see note 1.

[4]   Cyrille Vogel, 'Le pontifical romano-germanique du Xe siècle: éléments constitutifs avec indication des sections imprimées', *Revue des sciences religieuses* 32 (1958): 113–67; Vogel, 'Précisions sur la date et l'ordonnance primitive du Pontifical romano-germanique', *Ephemerides liturgicae* 74 (1960): 145–62; Vogel, 'Le pontifical romano-germanique du Xe siècle: nature, date et importance du document', *Cahiers de civilisation médiévale* 6 (1963): 27–48; Vogel, 'Contenu et ordonnance du pontifical romano-germanique', in *Atti del VI Congresso Internazionale di Archeologia Cristiana, Ravenna 23–30 Settembre 1962* (Vatican City: Pontifico Istituto di Archeologia Cristiana, 1965), 243–65; Vogel, *Introduction aux sources de l'histoire du culte chrétien au moyen âge* (Spoleto: Centro italiano di studi sull'alto medioeva, 1966).

[5]   The adjective *romano-germanique*, first coined in Michel Andrieu, *Immixtio et consecratio: la consécration par contact dans les documents liturgiques du moyen âge* (Paris: Picard, 1924), 63n5, was explicitly designed to account for these different flavours.

set a standard for episcopal books in the Christian West that is said to persist even to this day.[6]

These narratives are by no means watertight, for reasons which I shall explore during the course of this chapter. But the greater problem here is not factual. It is the historiographical allure of a liturgical tradition so neatly packaged. In an ideal world, every medieval liturgical text would be accompanied by a printed edition and a ready explanation. Ritual practices would be considerably easier to grasp, historians could cite with confidence, and liturgists would be liberated from many of the tiresome, expensive, and often fruitless labours of manuscript study. As the present volume is at pains to point out, however, this is an entirely unrealistic hope. Living ritual traditions cannot simply be apportioned into discrete categories, nor can they readily be squeezed together and represented by a single printed text. This is no truer than when dealing with the products of the free-spirited, individualistic century before Gregorian Reform, when innovation seems to have been rife; and it applies no less strongly to the scores of eleventh- and twelfth-century manuscripts identified as '*PRG*' sources, whose mutual differences are actually as marked as their similarities.[7] So we are left in an interesting quandary. What price an accessible medieval liturgical text? And what scholarly premium have we been paying for the particular edition of the *Pontifical romano-germanique* – or, as some know it, the *Romano-German Pontifical* (*RGP*) – whose outward stability and utility, coupled with its now-canonical status, belies what is still one of the least well understood corners of medieval liturgical history?

The Book that (Almost) Never Was

The story of the *PRG* might have turned out very differently had the great liturgical scholar Michel Andrieu not passed away, wholly unexpectedly, in October 1956. When he had retired that summer as Dean of Faculty and Professor of Liturgy at the University of Strasbourg, apparently in good health, Andrieu had anticipated devoting his new freedom to a number of unfinished projects. According to his *Festschrift* of the same year, which was hastily turned into a memorial when news of his death emerged, he had in the pipeline a sixth instalment of his series on *Ordines Romani*, an edition of a thirteenth-century Missal of the Roman Curia, and the eagerly anticipated edition of the

---

[6]   The original author of this last claim was, as with many of these ideas, Michel Andrieu, in *OR*, 1:494–95 and 548.

[7]   For a list of sources by origin see Vogel, 'Le PRG: nature, date et importance', 29–30; and for a more updated version of the same see Sarah Hamilton, *The Practice of Penance, 900–1050* (Woodbridge: Boydell Press, 2001), 220–23.

Pontifical romano-germanique du dixième siècle.[8] 'With him,' wrote his friend and Strasbourg successor Cyrille Vogel, 'disappeared one of the great liturgical historians of our age.'[9] With him, we might add, disappeared the secrets of the *PRG*.

Andrieu had been working on this textual tradition for much of his life, during which time his bold hypotheses had become well known: that, although no original source appeared to have survived, the divergent families of surviving *PRG* manuscripts (comprising some forty sources) could be taken to show that a single text had probably originated at the monastery of St Alban's, Mainz (Germany) shortly after 950; that this text was likely to have been assembled and propagated with the backing of Archbishop William of Mainz (954–68); and that, following a period of intense copying and dissemination, it was brought over the Alps by Otto I (936–73) and subsequently adopted by the papacy.[10] During his career, Andrieu managed to edit a number of the tradition's constituent texts, of which the largest and most famous, *Ordo Romanus* 50 (his title), was sent to the publishers not long before his death and appeared posthumously a few years later.[11] He also categorized the most important manuscripts into four groups, arranged in order of fidelity to a hypothetical original, and here described as Groups I, II, III and IV.[12] Tantalisingly, however, he left no clue as to the intended shape of his *PRG* edition. How had he planned to distil these four manuscript families and some forty divergent manuscript witnesses, each of at least a hundred pages, into a single edited text? How would he define and order the different liturgical components of the compilation, given that every source presents them in a different light? And, most intriguingly of all, after three decades of work and still no edition, did he really believe that this project could feasibly be brought to completion?

After his death, no one was really in a position to know, least of all his colleagues Cyrille Vogel and Reinhard Elze, to whom the project was suddenly entrusted in the autumn of 1956.[13] In the circumstances, theirs was a Herculean

---

8   *Mélanges en l'honneur de Mgr Andrieu*, Revue des Sciences Religieuses, Volume Hors Série (Strasbourg, 1956), 6. For a sense of anticipation (and disappointment) see Cornelius Bouman, *Sacring and Crowning* (Groningen: J.B. Wolters, 1957), 28 n 1.

9   Cyrille Vogel, 'Mgr Michel Andrieu (1886–1956)', *Ephemerides liturgicae* 71 (1957): 34–6, at 34: 'Avec lui disparaît un des plus grands historiens de la liturgie de notre époque'.

10   See, chiefly, *OR*, 1:511–14.

11   *OR*, vol. 5.

12   For the disposition of these groups see *OR*, 1:526–45. Note that different categorizations have been applied over time: in 'Le PRG: éléments constitutifs', Vogel arranged the manuscripts into Groups A to D; in 'Le PRG: nature, date et importance', he regrouped them by geographical origin.

13   The editors tell the story of their involvement in the introduction to *PRG*, 1:vii–x.

effort. By 1963 a complete text had been published, and an introduction and indexes followed a few years later.[14] But the editors were quick to emphasize the modest state of their work. This edition was not the lost masterpiece of Andrieu, they stressed, nor was it fully theirs. In difficult and constrained circumstances, they had produced something from Andrieu's papers which might be worthy of his memory. They had not attempted what they perceived as the 'hazardous' reconstruction of Andrieu's hypothetical Mainz original, and yet nor had they made any concerted attempt to reconsider or overturn his ideas in the light of their own work.[15] Avowedly and openly, this edition was a compromise.

Crucial as it is for our understanding of the PRG edition, this state of compromise has never fully been recognized. Vogel and Elze tended to defer to Andrieu's wisdom on most matters of interpretation, giving an outward impression of absolute consensus when inwardly they may have felt unqualified to disagree. And as Andrieu's remarkable hypotheses have been replicated reverently from article to article, and have assumed concrete form through the publication of successive editions, theory has coalesced slowly into fact. In this last respect much of the blame must lie with Vogel, whose speculative conclusions reached an international audience in his otherwise well-respected and indispensable *Introduction aux sources*, later translated into English as *Medieval Liturgy: An Introduction to the Sources*.[16] In the absence of any concerted interrogation of the *PRG* concept over the last century, therefore, and with the benefit of a growing canon of past discourse which has taken these ideas for granted, this twentieth-century creation continues to flourish unchallenged in the literature. For this reason above all, an exposé of the original 1963 edition – the underlying philological premises, the editorial policies, and the particular exigencies which led to its current state of compromise – is now long overdue.

The Nature of the *PRG* Edition

An Edition without a Primary Source

In many respects, it was much to their credit that Vogel and Elze decided against trying to recover Andrieu's putative Mainz archetype. Liturgy, they rightly pointed out, cannot be treated like classical literature.[17] That is to say, ritual traditions vary by their very nature, and former stages of transmission

---

[14]   *PRG*, vols. 1 and 2 (1963); vol. 3 (1972).
[15]   Ibid., 1:xi.
[16]   Vogel, *Introduction aux sources*; Vogel, *Medieval Liturgy*.
[17]   *PRG*, 1:xi.

cannot be imputed by logic alone. They opted instead for a synthetic edition which combined texts from nine complete manuscripts, hand-picked from the forty or so which Andrieu had identified as '*PRG*'.[18] Eschewing the traditional process of divination, by which the philologist freely postulates the shape of an earlier textual layer, the editors spoke of their overriding desire to 'keep to the manuscript tradition which has actually been preserved'.[19] This strategy had a number of benefits. Chiefly, it avoided having to adjudicate on the competing claims of the two main manuscript families, Group I and Group II, to the contested status of 'original', and it shifted onto the reader the onus of sifting through these various surviving texts.[20] In fact, as the editors argued, there was probably no one 'original' source to be found anyway. If the scriptorium at St Alban's, Mainz had had the means to produce one influential liturgical volume around 950, they intuited, it had probably produced many. In that case, there was no reason to choose between the different recensions, and all of the surviving texts should be seen as equally worthy of the title '*PRG*'.[21]

Though philologically unorthodox, this policy achieved a basic goal: it communicated all of the texts relevant to Andrieu's hypothesis with a minimum of editorial intervention. Thus in the *PRG* edition each of the 258 chapters is accompanied by its own list of sources and, in places where these sources differ substantially, competing readings are simply lined up in parallel columns; or, if necessary, they are quietly transferred into appendices. As might befit a tradition with no known primary source, the readings of the main text are not designed to be prejudiced towards a single witness, but are decided by the majority opinion of the sources with occasional interventions where grammar or sense require. Textual variants are easily accessible, and the wider context of each manuscript can be inferred from a concordance table which outlines the relative contents and shape of each manuscript source.[22] All

---

[18]   For details of the precise number of manuscripts used in the edition, see below.

[19]   Ibid., 1:xi: 'nous avons préféré nous en tenir à la tradition manuscrite effectivement conservée'. For a basic introduction to traditional text-critical methods see Paul Maas, *Textual Criticism*, trans. Barbara Flower (Oxford: Clarendon Press, 1958). On Karl Lachmann, the father-figure of these approaches, see Sebastiano Timpanaro, *The Genesis of Lachmann's Method*, trans. Glenn W. Most (Chicago: University of Chicago Press, 2005).

[20]   For the original claim that Group I is anterior see *OR*, 1:526–45. Group II's precedence was argued in respect of Coronation ritual in Percy Ernst Schramm, 'Die Krönung in Deutschland bis zu Beginn des Salischen Hauses (1028)', *Zeitschrift der Savigny-Stiftung für Rechtsgeschichte: kanonistische Abteilung* 24 (1935): 184–332, at 223–24 (where Group II equates to the so-called 'kürzere Fassung' of the *Mainzer Ordo*); and in Carl Erdmann, *Forschungen zur politischen Ideenwelt des Frühmittelalters*, ed. Friedrich Baethgen (Berlin: Akademie Verlag, 1951), 54–55 (where Group II equates to 'Fassung R').

[21]   *PRG*, 1:xv.

[22]   Found in ibid., vol. 1, after p. xxxi; beware several misprints in these tables.

of these decisions seem eminently reasonable. But there is a catch. Just as an edition of a single manuscript is relatively limited in what it can say, the trade-off for the *PRG*'s generously inclusive policy was that it represented no one historical reality. Without a privileged *Leithandschrift* (or 'best text') to lead the way, the editors had created something which technically never existed.[23] This was a critical weakness in their project, and later I shall consider the dire consequences it had for narratives of tenth- and eleventh-century liturgical history.

The editorial task might have been far less problematic, however, had the editors not sought to synthesize such a heterogeneous set of sources. While this may now provide the reader with a useful comparative tool, for the editors it meant forcing together conflicting texts, with the result that the edition is fundamentally predisposed to overstate the level of agreement among its sources. This is a serious issue if one considers that two of the most important texts, *PRG* chapters 63 (Episcopal Ordination) and 72 (Coronation), exist in quite different textual states in Group I and Group II manuscripts, a significant historical divergence which the printed edition actively subdues.[24] Similarly troubling is the fact that *PRG* chapters 190, 210–11 and 232 (Blessings) and 247 and 252 (Ordeals) comprise recensions which are dubiously related and have been stitched together editorially; and chapters 63 (Episcopal Ordination) and 214A/B (Blessing of Water for Crops) have each been subdivided for want of a legitimate connection between the different versions.[25]

No less problematic is the fact that, by means of the edition's inclusive policy, peripheral texts are valorized out of all proportion. Extraordinary as this may seem, those texts which are found in two sources or fewer far outnumber those which are common to all nine (Tables 4.1 and 4.2).[26] Thus is obscured one of the most troubling characteristics of the *PRG* edition: that only 16 of the 258 edited chapters (6 per cent) are common to all nine primary sources, of which only ten chapters (closer to 4 per cent) are reasonably free from significant variance from source to source. It is true that these 16 common chapters

---

[23] The 'best text' approach has the additional advantage of facilitating proofreading, as pointed out in D.L. d'Avray, *Medieval Marriage Sermons: Mass Communication in a Culture without Print* (Oxford: Oxford University Press, 2001), 40–41. The *PRG* edition is indeed littered with errata, some of which were belatedly listed in the third *PRG* volume of 1972.

[24] On these different textual states see Erdmann, *Forschungen*, 54–70; see also note 20, above.

[25] The printed text of *PRG* 190 completely mispresents what is in Source T; *PRG* 232 is only partially connected to Source T; and *PRG* 63 has an Appendix which treats Source A separately. In 'Précisions', at 161, Vogel sought to play down this aspect, stressing that 'Il ne faut pas au surplus s'éxagérer les différences ... elles sont minimes'.

[26] Vogel and Elze outwardly claimed to have used eleven sources, a confusion which is clarified below.

represent a core of texts which are among the most substantial (chapter 99 comprises approximately one quarter of the edition) and the most central to the fulfilment of episcopal office (the rituals of Ordination, Dedication and Coronation); and it is also true that by restricting ourselves to the manuscripts of Groups I and II, thereby removing statistical outliers from Groups III and IV, the total concordance is increased to 58 of the 258 edited chapters (22 per cent).[27] But having to fiddle the sources in this way makes that result no more satisfactory, and it does not detract from the underlying problem. The edition of Vogel and Elze presents a modern collection of texts which, though published under a single heading and regularly described as 'the *PRG*', simply never existed in that form. This point cannot be overstated.

Table 4.1   Texts of the *PRG* edition common to all nine primary sources[28]

PRG chapter	Description	Sources with significant variance
14	Explanation of clerical grades*	V
15	Ordination to minor orders	
16	Ordination to major orders	A
26	Ordination of abbot	A, C, D, T, V
40	Dedication of church	
50	Reconciliation of violated church	
51	Blessing of church bell	
63	Ordination of bishop	All, especially A
68	Mass for a bishop on the anniversary of his ordination	
75	Coronation of emperor (OR 45)	
78	Blessing of queen	
79	Holding a general synod	
80	Holding a provincial synod	
97	Explanation of mass (OR 7, nn. 6–26)	A
98	Explanation of episcopal mass (OR 10)	
99	Guide to church year (OR 50)	All

*This text was edited from eight sources, but is also present in Source V in an interpolated form.

---

27   On the arrangement of manuscript groups see note 12, above.
28   See note 1 for a key to manuscript sigla.

Table 4.2   Texts of the *PRG* edition found in two primary sources or fewer

PRG chapter	Description	Sources
64	Papal prayers at giving of *pallium*	C, D
101–02	A corrupt combination of *OR* 22 and *OR* 3	C, D
137	Mass after confession	V
138	Mass for the sick	C, V
181–82, 195, 212	Blessings and prayers	T
184, 186–93, 205–06, 215–24, 226–31, 233–40, 242, 245	Blessings and prayers	B, G
246	Ordeal of iron	B, G
248	Ordeal of water	B
249	Blessing of bread and cheese for ordeal	B, G
250–51	Ordeal of bread and cheese	T
253–58	Various texts on marriage, birth	B, G

A Reconstructed Archetype in All but Name

Strangely, although the editors were quick to deny that they had established an authoritative tenth-century archetype, they were also keen to play down the artificiality of their creation. That is, they saw the accumulation of different manuscript texts in the *PRG* edition as something of genuine historical import. According to the commentary, the edition was designed quite specifically 'to establish the content of the Mainz compilation between the years of 950 and 1000'.[29] This Vogel and Elze did by structuring the text according to the 'earliest' shape of the *PRG* tradition, which they located principally in Sources C and D (Group I), but which they also detected in Sources B and G (Group II).[30] When one bears in mind that not one of these manuscripts dates from the fifty years under consideration, all having been made in the eleventh century, such language bespeaks a fairly obvious attempt to recover some kind of legitimate 'original' document, even if not 'the original' which Andrieu had originally proposed.[31]

---

[29]   Vogel and Elze, *PRG*, 1:xii: 'établir la teneur de la compilation mayençaise entre les années 950 et 1000 environ'.

[30]   Vogel, 'Le PRG: éléments constitutifs', 114: 'la forme première du Romano-Germanique'. All of these foundations had been laid by Andrieu. For manuscript sigla see note 1.

[31]   These problems were afforded their most careful consideration by Vogel in a paper given in 1962, published as 'Contenu et ordonnance', 257–65. Rather less careful is the

Despite their protestations, evidence of the editors' underlying intentions can be seen in earlier boasts of 'restoring' the text as it was between 950 and 961/63.[32] It can be seen also in a later stemma of contributing manuscripts, first published in 1965 and then reprinted in the supplementary *PRG* volume of 1972, at the head of which is a single, imaginary source marked 'archétype commun'.[33]

What one finds in the *PRG* edition, therefore, is more than just an assembly of all the surviving texts. It is a hypothetical corpus of tenth-century material formed by surgically combining representatives of Andrieu's two principal manuscript groups. Chapters 1–170 follow the course of Source C, the eleventh-century Beneventan source from Group I which Andrieu had first proposed as the closest surviving representative of the Mainz archetype; and chapters 171–258 take their lead from Source B, the eleventh-century Bavarian manuscript from Group II whose blessings, prayers and ordeals were supposedly 'accidentally' omitted from the main branch of transmission.[34] It is important to recognize that this structure still accords with the edition's outwardly manuscript-neutral policy, since it incorporates unique readings from all of the other primary sources. Even so, with clear preference afforded to Source C, the spectre of an archetype looms large.

One further manuscript with unwarranted influence over the edition is Source T. This eleventh-century witness was sorted by Andrieu into Group IV, the group for miscellaneous remnants ('autres pontificaux'),[35] and perhaps deservedly so, because its collection of blessings, prayers and ordeals displays a marked reluctance to concord with other sources in the edition (see, in particular, *PRG* chapters 190, 210–11, 214, 232, 247 and 252). The editors might have been expected to remove these texts from contention, as they did with other parts of this manuscript, on the basis that they were copied in a codicologically separable section at the end.[36] The fact that Vogel and Elze decided against doing so, opting instead to reconcile the texts laboriously with the other contributing sources, probably relates to the manuscript's unique historical status. Source T is the only source of the *PRG* tradition known to have been copied at St Alban's, Mainz (supposedly the original wellspring); it was connected by Andrieu

---

earlier claim in Vogel, 'Le PRG: éléments constitutifs', 118, that 'nos 11 manuscrits suffisent pour restituer avec une fidélité presque absolue l'oeuvre hétéroclite du moine rhénan'.

[32]   Vogel, 'Précisions', 162.

[33]   Vogel, 'Contenu et ordonnance', 254; *PRG*, 3:56. Andrieu included a very similar diagram in *OR*, 5: 43.

[34]   This policy was first explained in Vogel, 'Le PRG: éléments constitutifs', 119–20; see also 'Précisions', 161–62. *PRG*, 1:xvi: 'les autres [*Benedictiones*] auront accidentellement disparu'.

[35]   *OR*, 1:542.

[36]   Henry Parkes, 'Liturgy and Music in Ottonian Mainz 950–1025', unpub. PhD dissertation (University of Cambridge, 2012), 240–42.

to archetypal Source C (Group I); and it was also considered to support the testimony of Source B (Group II).[37] By forcibly squeezing Source T into the wider *PRG* transmission, Vogel and Elze could lend their support to the very hypothesis underlying their editorial enterprise, that is, the putative existence of a Mainz archetype as the source behind Groups I and II. Had they admitted defeat at the hands of that same manuscript, they would have risked undermining the entire project. The credibility of the *PRG* edition was thus bolstered by this gentle manipulation of the evidence.

This is not the only instance of such behaviour. When Andrieu edited *Ordo Romanus* 50, the PRG's famous tract on the liturgical year, he did so from a generous twenty-one out of the forty or so known manuscripts.[38] By contrast, for their *PRG* edition Vogel and Elze initially settled on just eleven from that same corpus, a substantial reduction in scope.[39] In explaining this choice, Vogel pointed out that these were 'the best' examples from a cross-section of Andrieu's four manuscript groups.[40] Commendable as that decision may initially seem, there was more to this than merely representing a wide range of sources. As Vogel admitted elsewhere, the manuscripts were chosen principally 'because of their proximity to the archetype';[41] and in a further article he confessed to having eliminated some of the more troublesome witnesses from contention.[42] In other words, historical considerations had been fully subordinated to the task of establishing a single text. Given the magnitude of the task Andrieu had bequeathed, and with the benefit of hindsight, we might forgive the editors some of their actions. But, needless to say, had they opted to include any of the early or unstable witnesses which currently cower in historiographical limbo, the result would have been quite different.[43] Though significantly harder to establish and probably less loyal to Andrieu, such a creation would doubtless have been more honest to the true breadth of surviving '*PRG*' sources.

---

[37]   *OR*, 1:542–43; Vogel, 'Le PRG: éléments constitutifs', 120.

[38]   *OR*, 5:3–4.

[39]   That number was later reduced to the nine listed in note 1, above; on this confusion see below.

[40]   Vogel, 'Le PRG: éléments constitutifs', 114: '11 manuscrits ... qui sont les meilleurs parmi la quarantaine de témoins'.

[41]   Ibid., 118: 'surtout en raison de leur proximité avec l'archétype'. See also *PRG*, 1:xiii.

[42]   Vogel, 'Contenu et ordonnance', 255.

[43]   Among various manuscripts which need integrating into this narrative are: Munich, Bayerische Staatsbibliothek, Clm 6425 and Clm 21587; Milan, Biblioteca Ambrosiana, Ms. Z 52 sup.; Troyes, Bibliothèque Municipale, Ms. 2262; Schaffhausen, Ministerialbibliothek, Min. 94; Bamberg, Staatsbibliothek, Ms. Lit. 50 and Ms. Lit. 54. For an attempt to do so in relation to the rituals of excommunication see Sarah Hamilton's chapter 'Excommunication Rites in Eleventh-Century Pontificals' in this volume.

Editions Within Editions

Although outwardly Vogel and Elze chose eleven sources for their edition, that figure is itself somewhat misleading. This is partly due to the uneven transmission of texts, whereby no one source contains all 258 chapters and only sixteen chapters are common to all. But it also relates to the editors' occasional habit of moving the editorial goalposts from chapter to chapter according to the availability of relevant primary sources. In reality, Vogel and Elze based the *PRG* edition on just nine complete sources, which they then supplemented with other material where necessary or possible (see Table 4.3). They did not have full sight of Source J, presumably because Andrieu had only achieved a partial collation,[44] while Source P was effectively excluded from the final edition because of its near-identical relationship to Source V.[45] Another manuscript, the twelfth-century Source R, was called upon only to strengthen the testimony of certain coronation texts, an inconsistency which may have related to Reinhard Elze's particular expertise in that field. The editors also made selective use of Melchior Hittorp's sixteenth-century *De Divinis Catholicae Ecclesiae Officiis* – itself a selection of '*PRG*' texts from an unknown source or sources – as if it were a manuscript source in its own right.[46] Thus with an uneven mixture of contributing texts, the *PRG* edition was never technically a single entity. It was the sum total of several hundred self-contained editions.

But that is only part of the story. A sizeable proportion of the published *PRG* edition was not derived from primary sources at all. As Table 4.4 shows, this material was drawn from existing editions. The editors had been faced with a difficult problem. Andrieu had already edited a significant number of their texts in his series of *Ordines Romani* but from a different array of sources. Either they could edit the texts afresh from their limited corpus of nine *PRG* manuscripts (thereby retracing Andrieu's steps but with less information), or they could leave out those particular sections and defer to the existing editions (thereby impoverishing their own project).[47] In the end, they decided on a half-way solution: to reprint a skeleton text from Andrieu, allowing the casual reader to peruse, while directing the seasoned scholar to the relevant pages in the *Ordines Romani*.[48] Although the

---

[44]   See *OR*, 1:144–45. Andrieu's collation tables formed the basis of Vogel and Elze's edition.

[45]   On this relationship see Vogel and Elze, *PRG*, 1:xxxi; see also Pierre de Puniet, 'Formulaire grec de l'Epiphanie dans une traduction latine ancienne', *Revue bénédictine* 29 (1912): 26–46. It is curious that Source P was excluded but Source D (probable copy of Source C) and Source K (probable copy of Source L) were not.

[46]   Melchior Hittorp, *De Divinis Catholicae Ecclesiae Officiis et Mysteriis Varii Vetustorum Aliquot Ecclesiae Patrum ac Scriptorum Ecclesiasticorum Libri* (Cologne, 1568).

[47]   Vogel and Elze, *PRG*, 1:xxi–xxii.

[48]   Ibid., 1:xxi–xxii.

Table 4.3   Texts in the *PRG* edition which deviate from the nine primary sources

PRG chapter	Description	Source
56–63, 65–66	Episcopal ordination	Primary sources + J
72	Coronation ritual	Primary sources + R, with variants from Hittorp, *De Divinis Catholicae Ecclesiae Officiis*
73–74, 78	Coronation masses, Blessing of queen	Primary sources + R
93–96	Mass expositions	Primary sources + J
99	Guide to church year (*OR* 50)	Sources C and K only, with variants from Hittorp, *De Divinis Catholicae Ecclesiae Officiis*

editors spun this decision positively, repeatedly boasting of the 'benefit for the reader', this situation brings with it a host of editorial problems.[49] Chief among these is the fact that, because Andrieu's texts were established from different sources according to different editorial criteria, they are not strictly comparable to those of the *PRG* edition proper. The reader would not necessarily know that, though, because the *Ordines* were reprinted in the *PRG* edition without their editorial apparatus, and in specific textual recensions which were chosen silently at the discretion of the editors.[50] And while Vogel and Elze might have hoped that their readers simply called up Andrieu's original publications, parallel consultation is all but prohibited by the *PRG* edition's adoption of completely different manuscript sigla. Thus a considerable amount of information is obscured.

If that seems an unsatisfactory state of affairs, the treatment of *PRG* chapter 99 (*OR* 50) is no more encouraging. This substantial text, which amounts to around a quarter of the overall *PRG* edition, was edited separately by Andrieu before his death. At the stage that Vogel and Elze were working, however, the typescript was still with the printers, leaving the editors little choice but to establish a version themselves.[51] This they did with the help of just two manuscripts, Source C (representing Group I) and Source K (representing Group II), as well as Hittorp's edition for reference, a solution which

---

[49]   Ibid., 1:8–9 and passim: 'ad commodum lectoris'.

[50]   Each *Ordo Romanus* provided in the *PRG* edition is, as they put it, 'évidemment la recension donnée par les exemplaires du Romano-germanique qui a été retenu (et qui ne correspond donc pas nécessairement au texte établi par Mgr M. Andrieu)'. Ibid, 1:xxii.

[51]   Ibid. 1:xxii. The volume was ultimately published in 1961, some five years after Andrieu's death.

Table 4.4	Texts of the *PRG* edition drawn from existing editions

PRG chapter	Description	Source
7	Guide to Ember days (*OR* 37B)	*OR*, 4:249–54 (extract)
8	Guide to Ember days (*OR* 38)	Ibid., 4:267–69
63 Apx.	Ordination of a bishop (*OR* 35B)	Ibid., 4:99–110 (the second half is abbreviated, with *PRG* concordances indicated)
71	Ordination of pope (*OR* 40B)	Ibid., 4:307–8
72 Apx. 1	Coronation ritual (*Frühdeutscher Ordo*)	Erdmann, *Forschungen*, 83–87 (abbreviated, with *PRG* concordances indicated)
72 Apx. 2	Coronation ritual (*Ordo der Sieben Formeln*)	Ibid., 87–89 (abbreviated, with *PRG* concordances indicated)
75	Coronation of emperor (*OR* 45)	*OR*, 4:459–62
76	Coronation of emperor (*OR* 47)	Ibid., 4:503–5
77	Mass for emperor (*OR* 48)	Ibid., 4:517–19
92	Explanation of mass (*OR* 5)	Ibid., 2:209–27
97	Explanation of mass (*OR* 7, nn. 6–26)	Ibid., 2:295–305 (extract, with lines renumbered)
98	Explanation of episcopal mass (*OR* 10)	Ibid., 2:351–62
101	Guide to Lent (*OR* 22, nn. 1–15; fragmentary)	Ibid., 3:259–62 (given in full, but annotated to show where *PRG* sources cease)
102	Supplement to *OR* 1 (*OR* 3, nn. 4–6; fragmentary)	Ibid., 2:131–33 (given in full, but annotated to show where *PRG* sources cease)
103	Guide to office chants (*OR* 12)	Ibid., 2:459–66
104	Guide to clerical grades (*OR* 36)	Ibid., 4:195–205

reviewer Bernard Botte justly described as 'flawed'.[52] When one remembers that Andrieu had used 21 divergent manuscripts to establish the same text, the dangers of this economy become clear. The text of *OR* 50 in the *PRG* edition is not only unrepresentative of the wider manuscript situation, but also disconcertingly free of editorial paraphernalia, giving a wholly deceptive impression of harmony. This is of crucial importance when one considers that the original claim that the *PRG* was assembled by monks of St Alban's, Mainz – that rock of historical certainty upon which so many scholars have been

---

[52]	Bernard Botte's review of *PRG* Volumes 1 and 2 in *Revue d'histoire ecclésiastique* 59 (1964): 902–4, at 902: 'la solution est un peu boiteuse'.

content to lean – was largely premised upon a repertory of musical chants for Rogation only found in *PRG* Sources C, D and T.[53] Because *PRG* chapter 99 was established only from Sources C and K, the consequence is that Andrieu's favoured Group I and Group II recensions now appear unduly normative; and in the many places where Source K is silent – as happens with the crucial testimony of the 'Mainz' chants – the theory of a Mainz archetype appears all but incontrovertible.

A Modern Abstraction

By virtue of its reconstructive premise, the *PRG* edition is necessarily abstracted to some degree from its sources, and must be taken with a liberal pinch of salt accordingly. For example, one instinctively suspends disbelief when informed that Source C, from late eleventh-century Montecassino, most closely represents a principally German manuscript tradition from almost a thousand miles away and over a hundred years in the past.[54] And one can make the same adjustment whenever that same manuscript is held up as the 'first' witness to a particular text, when it is almost certainly not, or indeed whenever the wide chronologies and geographies of manuscript sources are collapsed to serve linear philological arguments. But there is another crucial kind of abstraction which remains largely concealed from view: the relationship between the manuscript and the printed page.

The issue here is that while the basic textual information is documented assiduously in the *PRG* edition, extending even to the recording of marginal additions and corrections, other potentially interesting details of transmission are not. The reader is in no position to know, for example, that in Vienna 701 the substantial *PRG* chapters 113, 111 and 112 number among a host of miscellaneous additions at the end of the manuscript, and were added by a later scribe. Nor is the reader equipped to find out that in Bamberg Ms. Lit. 53 the text is divided into four main codicological sections, shared unequally among two main scribes.[55] Such details are extremely difficult to record in a modern edition, without doubt, but they are also critical to the interpretation of the texts. Their absence, conversely, serves to strengthen the idea that 'the *PRG*' was a meaningfully singular creation.

---

[53] The most important of these chants is the *versus* 'Humili prece'. For the original claim of Mainz provenance see *OR*, 1:500–6; for the unpicking of that argument see Parkes, 'Liturgy and Music', ch. 2, esp. 113–16.

[54] According to the most recent assessment, this manuscript was produced in the years of Abbot Desiderius (1058–87). See Francis Newton, *The Scriptorium and Library at Monte Cassino, 1058–1105* (Cambridge: Cambridge University Press, 1999), 86.

[55] See Hamilton, 'Excommunication Rites in Eleventh-Century Pontificals', in this volume, 135.

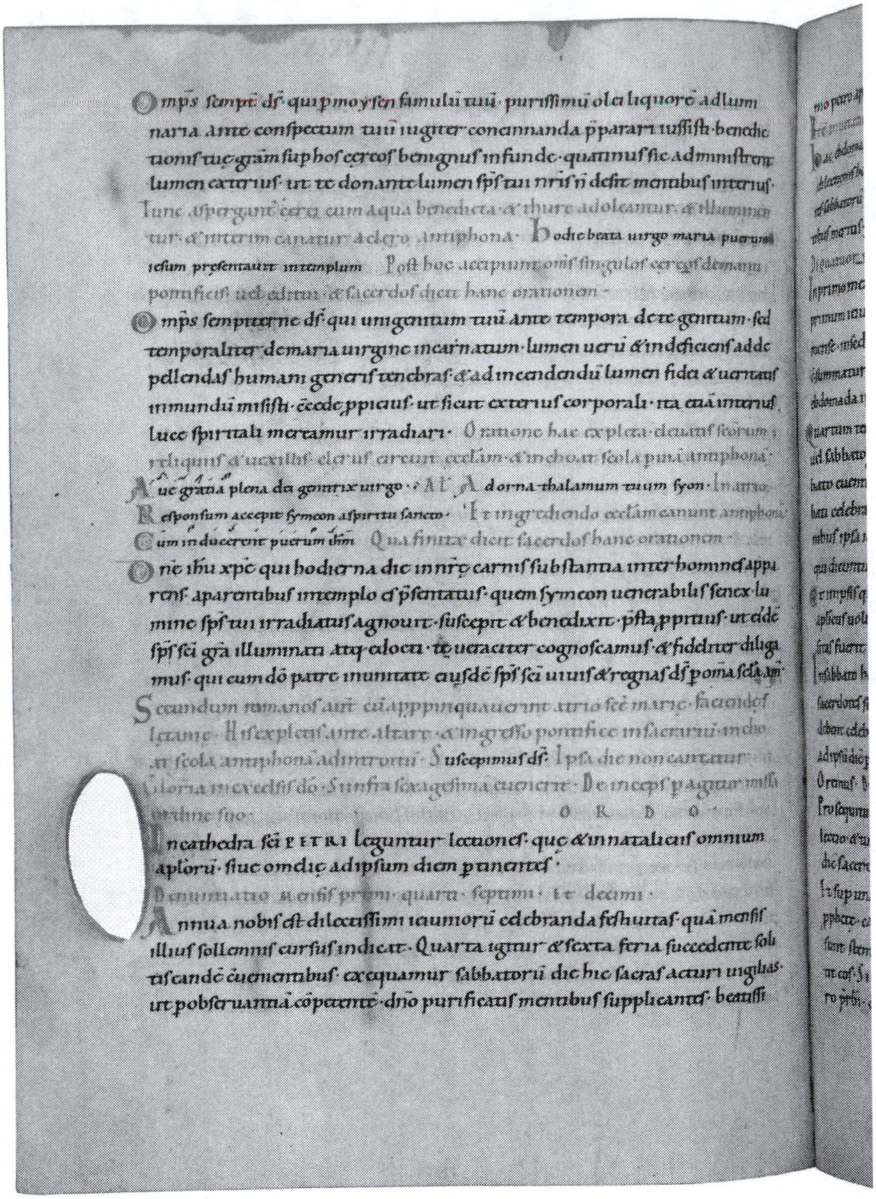

Omnipotens sempiterne deus qui per moysen famulum tuum purissimum olei liquorem ad luminaria ante conspectum tuum iugiter concinnanda preparari iussisti benedictionis tue gratiam super hos cereos benignus infunde quatinus sic administrent lumen exterius ut te donante lumen spiritus nostri non desit mentibus interius.

Tunc aspergantur cera cum aqua benedicta et thure adoleantur et illuminantur et interim canatur a clero antiphona. Hodie beata uirgo maria puerum iesum presentauit in templum. Post hec accipiunt omnes singulos cereos de manu pontificis uel editui et sacerdos dicat hanc orationem.

Omnipotens sempiterne deus qui unigenitum tuum ante tempora de te genitum sed temporaliter de maria uirgine incarnatum lumen uerum et indeficiens ad depellendas humani generis tenebras et ad incendendum lumen fide et ueritatis in mundum misisti cede propicius ut sicut exterius corporali ita etiam interius luce spirituali mereamur irradiari. Oratione hac expleta deinceps seorsum reliquis euntibus cleris areum ecclesiam et inchoat scola primam antiphonam.

Aue gratia plena dei genitrix uirgo. Al. Adorna thalamum tuum syon. In alio Responsum accepit symeon a spiritu sancto. Et ingrediendo ecclesiam canunt antiphona Cum inducerent puerum ihesum. Qua finita dicit sacerdos hanc orationem.

Domine ihesu christe qui hodierna die in nostre carnis substantia inter homines apparens a parentibus in templo es presentatus quem symeon uenerabilis senex lumine spiritus tui irradiatus agnouit suscepit et benedixit prestat propicius ut eiusdem spiritus sancti gratia illuminati atque docti te ueraciter cognoscamus et fideliter diligamus qui cum deo patre in unitate eiusdem spiritus sancti uiuis et regnas deus per omnia secula.

Secundum romanos aut cum appinquauerint atrio sancte marie sacerdos letanie. His expletis ante altare et ingresso pontifice in sacrarium inchoat scola antiphona. Ad introitum. Suscepimus deus. Ipsa die non cantatur Gloria in excelsis deo. Si infra sexagesima euenerit. Deinceps agitur missa ordine suo.   ORDO

In cathedra sancti petri leguntur lectiones que in natali eius omnium apostolorum siue omeliae ad ipsum diem pertinentes.

Denunciatio mensis primi quarta septima et decimi.

Annua nobis est dilectissimi ieiuniorum celebranda festiuitas qua mensis illius sollemnis cursus indicat. Quarta igitur et sexta feria succedente solutis candem euenientibus exequamur sabbatorum die hic sacras acturi uigilias. ut pro obseruantia competente dominio purificatis mentibus supplicantes beatissi

Figure 4.1   Hierarchy of scripts in Bamberg, Staatsbibliothek, Ms. Lit. 53, fol. 91v (photo: Gerald Raab), by kind permission of the Staatsbibliothek Bamberg

Omnipotens sempiterne Deus, qui per Moysen famulum tuum purissimum olei liquorem ad luminaria ante conspectum tuum iugiter concinnanda praeparari iussisti, benedictionis tuae gratiam super hos cereos benignus infunde, quatinus sic administrent lumen exterius, ut, te donante, lumen spiritus tui nostris non desit mentibus interius. Per.

Tunc aspergantur cerei cum aqua benedicta et thure adoleantur et illuminentur et interim canatur a clero antiphona: *Hodie beata virgo Maria puerum Iesum praesentavit in templum.* Post hoc accipiunt omnes singulos cereos de manu pontificis vel editui, et sacerdos dicit hanc orationem:

Omnipotens, sempiterne Deus, qui unigenitum tuum ante tempora de te genitum sed temporaliter de Maria virgine incarnatum, lumen verum et indeficiens, ad depellendas humani generis tenebras et ad incendendum lumen fidei et veritatis in mundum misisti, concede propitius, ut sicut exterius corporali, ita etiam interius luce spiritali mereamur irradiari. Per eundem.

Oratione hac expleta, elevatis sanctorum reliquiis et vexillis, clerus circuit aecclesiam et inchoat scola per viam primam antihonam: *Ave, gratia plena Dei genitrix virgo.* Alia: *Adorna thalamum tuum Syon.* In atrio: *Responsum accepit Symeon a spiritu sancto.* Et ingrediendo ecclesiam canunt antiphonam: *Cum inducerent puerum Iesum.* Qua finita, dicit sacerdos hanc orationem:

Domine Iesu Christe, qui hodierna die in nostrae carnis substantia inter homines apparens a parentibus in templo es presentatus quem Symeon venerabilis senex lumine spiritus tui irradiatus agnovit, suscepit et benedixit, praesta propitius, ut eiusdem spiritus sancti gratia illuminati atque edocti, te veraciter cognoscamus et fideliter diligamus. Qui cum Deo patre in unitate eiusdem spiritus sancti vivis et regnas deus per omnia secula. Amen.

Secundum Romanos autem, cum appropinquaverint atrio sanctae Mariae, faciendae sunt letaniae. His expletis ante altare, et ingresso pontifice in sacrarium, inchoat scola antiphonam ad introitum: *Suscepimus, Deus.* Ipsa die non cantatur *Gloria in excelsis Deo*, si infra sexagesimam evenerit. Deinceps peragitur missa ordine suo.

Ordo in cathedra sancti Petri. Leguntur lectiones quae et in nataliciis omnium apostolorum, sive omeliae ad ipsum diem pertinentes.

Denuntiatio mensis primi, quarti, septimi et decimi. *Annua nobis est, dilectissimi, ieiuniorum celebranda festivitas quam mensis illius sollempnis cursus indicat. Quarta igitur et sexta feria succedente, solitis eandem convenientibus exequamur, sabbatorum die hic sacras acturi vigilias, ut per observantiam competentem domino purificatis mentibus supplicantes, beatissi-*

Figure 4.2   The texts of Figure 4.1 typeset according to the house style of
Le pontifical romano-germanique, ed. Vogel and Elze, 2:8–10

A further dimension which is flattened in the edition is the manner in which each scribe interpreted the wide variety of textual types typically found in '*PRG*' sources. In certain key passages, such as in *Ordo Romanus* 50, the complex semantic hierarchy – of titles, subtitles, descriptive texts, instructional texts, explicatory texts, spoken texts and sung texts – attracts an equally complex visual hierarchy of scripts. Predictably, there is no standard arrangement. Rather, each scribe seems to have established a system according to his or her needs, with the different levels differentiated (or left undifferentiated) by a combination of ink colour, script size, script type, notation, line breaks and initial capitals (see Figure 4.1). In this context, the limits of our modern taxonomy (in other words, 'rubric') become painfully clear, as does the sheer variety of intellectual contexts in which a single text could potentially reside (for example, performance script, aide-mémoire, reference volume). The difficulty for the *PRG* edition is that while some scribes assiduously demarcated different levels of text, others made only basic concessions, presenting their materials almost as if continuous prose. Policies seem to have varied from section to section, too. The editors opted quietly to regularize these details, which certainly made their edition cleaner and more manageable. But to do so was also arguably to disavow a defining aspect of transmission and reception, and to impose upon the material an arbitrary and largely artificial visual hierarchy.[56] For a sense of this disjuncture compare Figure 4.1 with Figure 4.2.

This imposition of order represents another side to the abstraction problem. One surprisingly thorny aspect of the *PRG* edition is the parcelling up of its contents into 258 sections. Just as the book you are reading is divided into a number of complementary sections and chapters, instinct dictates that the same logic should apply to the subdivisions of the *PRG*. In fact, these are exceptionally uneven, both in size and content. While many *PRG* chapters transmit texts for 'complete' rituals, such as *PRG* 22 (Ordination of an Abbess) or *PRG* 40 (Dedication of a Church), others consist merely of subsections or related texts, such as *PRG* 62 (part of the Ordination of a Bishop), *PRG* 67 (mass prayers for the same), or *PRG* 60 (a single canon on Episcopal Ordination).[57] And while *PRG* 99 is a vast composite of ritual documents for the course of the church year, and was published by Andrieu in a volume of its own, *PRG* 222 is a one-line blessing for the fruit of a new tree. The editors could perhaps have organized their 'chapters' more efficiently, but it is by no means certain that these medieval scribes had any

---

[56] This family of problems is considered most carefully in Bernard Cerquiglini, *In Praise of the Variant: A Critical History of Philology*, trans. Betsy Wing (Baltimore, MD: Johns Hopkins University Press, 1999), 21–32. It is not clear that a workable solution for liturgical texts has yet been found.

[57] For a greater sense of this variety see the contributions to the present volume by S. Hamilton (*PRG* 85, 88, 90, 91), Chave-Mahir (*PRG* 114, 123), L. Hamilton and Birkedal Bruun (*PRG* 33, 40).

better sense of what defined a discrete unit of ritual text.[58] Vogel and Elze spoke of their collection as made up of separate *titres*, but these are inconsistent among the manuscript sources. Sometimes titles are afforded no special place within the visual hierarchy, perhaps for the reasons of scribal independence detailed above; sometimes they are absent altogether; and sometimes they do not correspond fully to the contents (applying only to the first section of many, for example), or exist in a variable form across all sources (as in the Excommunication rituals considered by Sarah Hamilton in Chapter 6). This state of uncertainty is put into relief in manuscripts where the scribes have attempted to use numbering systems, tables of contents or running titles to distinguish between different sections or rituals (see, for example, Wolfenbüttel, Herzog August Bibliothek, Cod. Guelf. 15 Weiss. (cat. no. 4099); Munich, Bayerische Staatsbibliothek, Clm. 6425; and Lucca, Biblioteca Capitolare Feliniana, Cod. 607). In such examples the dividing up of texts is inconsistent both within and across sources. Thus the very premise by which we assess variance and transmission within the *PRG* tradition – the 'chapter' – emerges as a problematic mode of enquiry, and it casts doubt on our most basic assumptions about the identity of a ritual text.

The Solidification of Hypothesis

Of all the shortcomings of the *PRG* edition, however, perhaps the greatest was the failure of the editors to acknowledge the true extent of these very shortcomings. Vogel and Elze may be absolved to the extent that they prefaced their edition with homage to Andrieu and with professions of inadequacy, and to the extent that a printed edition always tends to reinforce its object with artificial certainty and obstinacy. They might also be forgiven on the basis that the *PRG* tradition verges on being uneditable: Andrieu never got round to his edition, of course, and Bishop once referred to it presciently as 'that pitfall for the unwary'.[59] But at the same time there is much to suggest that the editors not only failed to emphasize sufficiently the edition's weaknesses, but also actively sought to strengthen its identity in spite of these problems. Narrowing the field

---

[58] This problem actually gave rise to a heated disagreement between Andrieu and Dom Pierre de Puniet on the identity of *Ordo Romanus Antiquus* (later published as *OR* 50), because in Hittorp's *De Divinis Catholicae Ecclesiae Officiis* it is not clear to which liturgical texts that title applies. See Andrieu, 'Melchior Hittorp et l'"Ordo Romanus Antiquus"', *Ephemerides liturgicae* 46 (1932): 3–21, at 9–12. What neither saw fit to concede is that Hittorp's publication may have preserved a long-standing medieval ambiguity.

[59] Edmund Bishop, *Liturgica Historica: Papers on the Liturgy and Religious Life of the Western Church* (Oxford: Clarendon Press, 1918), 112, referring to the text as found in Hittorp's edition.

of enquiry when it might have been broadened, they proclaimed an inconclusive theory as *fait accompli*.

Although they may not have intended it this way, much of the *PRG* edition's authority derives from the simple confidence of its presentation on the page. Redolent of the great liturgical monuments of the past, the edition bears on its first page the title 'Pontificale romano-germanicum saeculi decimi', a posturing faux-medievalism which is surrounded, somewhat sheepishly, by square brackets.[60] In a similar way, each chapter is furnished with a Latin title, even where that means inventing one (*PRG* 39, 63, 253), borrowing it from elsewhere (*PRG* 99, for which they used Hittorp's title *Ordo Romanus Antiquus*), or artificially separating one part of a ritual from another (see above). The edition even has Latinized editorial introductions to each *Ordo Romanus*, placed confusingly between the title and the text, and in a similar typeface, thereby blurring the distinction between text and commentary. Spurious authority is imparted, meanwhile, to the two fragmentary *Ordines Romani* (*PRG* 101, 102; found only in Sources C and D) which are mysteriously presented in the edition as if whole, and to the Coronation section, which includes in its appendices two rituals *not* found in any *PRG* source (*PRG* 72). Finally, in a highly suspicious anomaly of typesetting, several of the musical chants for Rogation – not least 'Humili prece', whose textual recension was critical to Andrieu's theory about the *PRG*'s origins in Mainz – are accorded special prominence, with ample spacing and distinct type.[61] No example is particularly significant on its own, but collectively such features endow the edition with certainty and immutability, qualities not wholly commensurate with the original anxieties of its assembly.

As I have already described, the *PRG* edition was further strengthened through the subtle amelioration of the very theory on which it rested, by which means the whole enterprise essentially became a self-fulfilling prophecy. The critical decision made by Vogel and Elze was to treat all surviving sources as 'originals', hence as equally valid witnesses to the liturgical activity at St Alban's, Mainz between 950 and 1000. Andrieu had argued nothing of the sort, visualizing the transmission of the *PRG* tradition instead as a gradual ripple effect outwards from Mainz, where the agency of each subsequent scribe in each subsequent institution was the key to its evolving identity.[62] Vogel did not seem to dissent from this view in his 1958 article, and so the airing of a new manuscript-neutral interpretation in 1960 strongly suggests that the intractable problems of source hierarchy – in particular, the claim that

---

[60]   *PRG*, 1:3.

[61]   Compare *PRG* 99.423 with 99.424. On 'Humili prece' see *OR*, 1:500–5. See also note 53, above.

[62]   Ibid., 1:505–9, 526.

the Group II versions of Coronation and Episcopal Ordination were actually earlier than those in Group I – had forced a change of tack.[63] If all manuscripts were to be presumed equal, of course, this greatly simplified the task of editing. But the historical implications are equally significant. According to this new view, no longer was the *PRG* merely a utilitarian textual collection whose historical success could be measured by the frequency of its copying, and by the changing complexion of its reception. If every source could trace its own distinct lineage back to Mainz, and to a diverse repertory of liturgical texts which (by Schramm's reckoning) was composed there over the course of many decades, then the *PRG* tradition was much more closely associated with that city than had previously been thought.[64] From this originated the idea that Mainz scribes had a kind of monopoly on *PRG* production, extending over the course of half a century or more.

Now firmly in the realm of fantasy, it was but a small step from here to suppose that this was not the work of a lone 'rédacteur' (Andrieu, 1931), but the achievement of a 'Werkstatt' (Schramm, 1935) or 'atelier' (Vogel, 1960) of copyists.[65] And while Andrieu had mooted the possibility of Archbishop William of Mainz's 'endorsement', for Schramm it was quite imaginable that William was the *PRG*'s 'protector' if not 'instigator'.[66] By 1960, doubt had dissolved altogether: 'it was *undoubtedly* by [William's] initiative and with his backing', wrote Vogel, 'that the Mainz scriptorium began work on the [*Pontifical*] *Romano-Germanique*'.[67] From a collection whose success derived purportedly from its general utility (Andrieu) came a collection proffered by the bishops to a German emperor 'preoccupied' with reform (Vogel).[68] And from something which the papacy might have wished to adopt (Andrieu) came something which Otto I brought to Rome principally 'to remedy a scandalous

---

[63]   Vogel, 'Le PRG: éléments constitutifs', esp. 117: 'Tous les manuscrits de ce deuxième groupe nous présentent une forme un peu plus récente du Romano-germanique que le groupe précédent'; Vogel, 'Précisions', 158. On the primacy of the Group II Coronation rite see note 20, above.

[64]   In 'Die Krönung', 223–24, 231, Schramm dates the Group II version of the Coronation rite, the 'kürzere Fassung', to some time before 961, and the Group I version, the 'längere', to the years around 980. Both versions are assumed to have been composed in Mainz, according to the (over-)literal interpretation of Coronation *ordines* as texts cultivated solely by their practitioners, that is, the Archbishops of Mainz.

[65]   *OR*, 1:526; Schramm, 'Die Krönung', 222; Vogel, 'Précisions', 148.

[66]   *OR*, 1:508: 'approbation'; Schramm, 'Die Krönung', 218: 'Man möchte sich den Erzbischof selbst als Protektor der Arbeit, vielleicht sogar als ihren Anreger vorstellen'.

[67]   Vogel, 'Précisions', 157: 'c'est *sans doute* sur son initiative et avec son appui que l'atelier mayençais mit en chantier le Romano-germanique' [my emphasis].

[68]   *OR*, 1:508; Vogel, 'Précisions', 151.

decadence' (Vogel),[69] this despite the fact that both authors saw the 'early' *PRG* as an imperfect and impractical invention.[70] Vogel was successful in embroidering Andrieu's narrative not because he had a greater insight into the sources, but because this entire *PRG* 'history' was pure, unadulterated fiction.

Lest there be any doubt, these claims must now be considered untenable. As far back as 1933, Gerald Ellard expressed robust doubts about Andrieu's hypotheses from the perspective of anointing rituals, questioning 'whether or not that ordinal [*Ordo Romanus Antiquus*, later edited as *Ordo Romanus* 50 and *PRG* 99] was known in Mayence itself, or elsewhere in Germany of which we have evidence, until at the earliest circa 1000'.[71] Roger Reynolds was later to reinforce that point when he showed that the *PRG* ordination rituals had no firm claim to tenth-century Italy, revising the arguably over-optimistic dating of Source L and extricating its ordination texts from their previous association with tenth-century popes Leo VIII and John XIII.[72] Since then, Sarah Hamilton has shown that *PRG* penance texts had limited geographical reach beyond Germany and no real monopoly on tenth- and eleventh-century liturgical practice.[73] And it is now by no means certain that Mainz's institutions or archbishops were involved in collection at all, at least in the tenth century. The pivotal 'Mainz' recension of 'Humili prece' can no longer be relied upon in questions of provenance, having entered a small branch of transmission at a demonstrably later stage; the capacity of Mainz's religious institutions to produce such a collection around 950 is gravely in doubt; and documented liturgical and musical traditions of tenth-century Mainz bear little or no relation to those found in the earliest surviving '*PRG*' sources.[74]

---

[69]   *OR*, 1:514; Vogel, 'Le PRG: nature, date et importance', 44: 'La principale raison de l'implantation à Rome du livre rhénan demeure cependant la volonté d'Otton de remédier à une décadance scandaleuse'. Vogel later sought to modify his view, dismissing the idea of the *PRG*'s 'brutal replacement' of Roman ritual practices, a confusing contradiction of his earlier speculation: ibid., 47.

[70]   Ibid., p. 42, note 68; *OR*, 1:526; also *OR*, 5:75–76.

[71]   Gerald Ellard, *Ordination Anointings in the Western Church before 1000 A.D.* (Cambridge, MA: Medieval Academy of America, 1933), 89. Ellard's argument, though, is compromised by questionable datings and manuscript locations, combined with a narrow range of source material, but it is possible that he knew more than he let on.

[72]   Roger E. Reynolds, 'Image and Text: The Liturgy of Clerical Ordination in Early Medieval Art', *Gesta* 22 (1983): 27–38, at 37–38; these ideas were fleshed out in Reynolds, 'The Ritual of Clerical Ordination of the Sacramentarium Gelasianum saec. VIII: Early Evidence from Southern Italy', in *Rituels: mélanges offerts à Pierre-Marie Gy*, ed. Paul de Clerck and Eric Palazzo (Paris: Editions de Cerf, 1990), 437–45, at 438–39.

[73]   Hamilton, *Practice of Penance*, esp. 219.

[74]   Parkes, 'Liturgy and Music', esp. chs. 2 and 4.

Of all the consequences of this speculative history, however, perhaps the most damaging has been the reification of 'the *PRG*' as a single, bounded object. While Andrieu's theory was at least relatively amenable to variance and scribal independence, Vogel's reinterpretation contended that the different sources were more or less equal visions of the same thing, a quality embodied in the printed edition. This latter version of events – pared down, self-justifying, and readily available in published form – has proved itself most seductive in subsequent scholarship, to the point that the edition is often misconstrued as a historical object. Palazzo's guide to the liturgy, for example, makes the elementary mistake of assuming that the *PRG* tradition 'comprises 258 sections' and is a 'carefully planned and organized compilation' – comments which are wholly antithetical to the state of manuscript survival.[75] Equally unhelpful has been the claim that 'the *PRG*' represented a turning point in liturgical history, when the wider evidence suggests nothing of the sort.[76] In conjunction with a widespread recognition that these are indeed historically interesting texts, the tangible singularity of Vogel and Elze's edition has distracted us from at least two potential misconceptions of the *PRG* phenomenon. First, it is dangerous to assume that a textual tradition characterized by its miscellaneous assembly, shifting identity and often archaic character necessarily had a single origin or single ontological existence. Second, it is by no means certain that the survival of a reasonably concordant family of liturgical texts, though noteworthy in its own right, necessarily reveals anything about wider changes in religious ritual practices in tenth- and eleventh-century Europe.

Future Directions

The shortcomings of Vogel and Elze's edition ultimately stem from the entanglement of two basic issues: the medieval phenomenon and its modern edition. While instinct dictates that these should be quite separable concerns, this chapter has shown how the reality is often more complicated. In this case, it was only through Andrieu's laborious collation of sources that a hierarchy of transmission could be constructed; and it was only through the construction of this hierarchy that historical information could be squeezed out of its otherwise elusive texts. Philology provided the window through which a lost tradition could be glimpsed. In fact, the relationship was probably even more involved

---

[75]   Palazzo, *Le moyen âge*, 210: 'Il se compose 258 sections'; 213: 'cette compilation réfléchie et organisée'; translation from Palazzo, *History*, 203 and 204.

[76]   In Vogel, 'Contenu et ordonnance', 243 (one of many examples), the *PRG* is hailed as 'le point de départ des pontificaux ultérieurs'. See also the flow diagram which first appeared in Vogel, 'Le PRG: date, nature et importance', and which was later reprinted in Vogel, *Introduction aux sources*, 235.

than that, since some of the philologically inferred history – above all the perceived importance of Mainz and Mainz sources – was fed back directly into the philology, making the entire creation circular and self-serving. The principal challenge for renewed engagement with these texts, therefore, is to bridge the chronological gap anew, re-examining our historical conception of these '*PRG*' manuscripts and establishing a suitable means of representing their testimony in edited form.

To that end, among the most pressing tasks is to topple the existing edition's artificial and outdated hierarchy of manuscript sources, by which the history and philology were inextricably intertwined. Andrieu clung resolutely to the idea that Group I manuscripts represented an antique form of the tradition – partly because he believed the sources to be earlier than they are, and partly because he had preconceptions about how the textual tradition had evolved – and Vogel and Elze did not demur, despite a strong challenge from the generally earlier-looking Group II.[77] That view must surely now be reconsidered. A simple reversal of Groups I and II might give the tradition a fresh new complexion, but the issue goes deeper than that. The real problem is in assigning heterogeneous manuscripts into two or more discrete groups when there is no clear division perceptible among surviving sources, and, more to the point, when many of the semblances of textual grouping tend to go firmly against the grain of manuscript chronology and context. Given that Vogel and Elze themselves believed in liturgical books as cultural objects, inseparable from the places in which they were copied, it is ironic that they could cling to two late eleventh-century Beneventan books (Group I) as valid representatives of tenth-century Mainz liturgy. What is required, therefore, is a historically sensitive reappraisal of the earliest sources, as far as that is possible without recourse to philology. Textual criticism clearly has a role to play, but it needs innovative treatment if we are retain the testimony of those problematic witnesses which Vogel and Elze sought to exclude, and it needs careful historical support such that sources from outside the central chronology and geography (such as those of late eleventh-century Montecassino) can be appreciated without prejudice to the other corners of the tradition.[78]

Another aspect of *PRG* orthodoxy that demands reconsideration is the assumption that these sources, as liturgical books, were necessarily active witnesses to local ritual practice and to local episcopal needs. Although modern liturgists might be inclined to endorse that statement, many of these sources exist in various and often ambiguous textual states, to the point of problematizing our very

---

[77] For information about the arrangement of groups see note 12, above.

[78] Such innovations might well be digital, as I consider further below; other approaches to editing liturgy are presently being explored within the *Ars Edendi* project, based in Stockholm: see n15.

vocabulary: *pontifical* and *liturgical book* are but two terms which merit significantly more scrutiny as a result.[79] Accordingly, the contents of these manuscripts regularly fail to accord with ritual traditions in the places they were copied, they often appear in non-episcopal contexts, and, as I have already described, they were often copied by scribes who display surprising levels of indifference towards the texts, employing a dense and continuous manner of inscription which is most uncharacteristic of liturgical sources more widely.[80] Whatever these books were, they do not fit comfortably into existing codicological categories, nor do they seem susceptible to any one satisfactory definition.

But the tradition's strange identity is not the only major issue at stake. Just as with collections of canon law from this period, the would-be editor must also contend with the fact that each scribe was at liberty to present and order his or her materials differently. Even if every collection had a more or less common basis, each was still a unique creation. This goes some way towards validating the basic editorial conception of Vogel and Elze, for all its faults, whereby the 258 individually edited chapters negotiate the precarious balance between *contenu* (the individual texts) and *ordonnance* (their arrangement as a whole).[81] It also suggests a good starting point for a modest future edition, where a basic section-by-section approach, arbitrarily ordered, might be complemented by rigorous appendices and comparative tables. But there quickly comes a point where this synthetic intent loses its meaning. If, as Tables 4.1 and 4.2 suggest, the *PRG* edition has already overstated the level of concordance among its sources, and has been rigged to favour only those witnesses which contribute to that impression, then a synoptic approach is fundamentally unsound. The various sources may present a recognizable core of texts based around *OR* 50 but, because that core was never transmitted without a substantial and highly variable body of ancillary texts, it means little to edit it alone. In fact, one source has since come to light which suggests that even *OR* 50 could be omitted: the mid-eleventh-century manuscript Schaffhausen, Ministerialbibliothek, Min. 94 displays a strong affinity to Bamberg Ms. Lit. 53, and is to all intents and purposes '*PRG*' in identity, but appears to have been copied without that

---

[79]   By Vogel's rather narrow reckoning, liturgical books must function directly in the service of worship, a definition which cannot fully account for '*PRG*' sources. See Vogel, 'Le PRG: nature, date et importance', 28–29. Andrieu memorably blamed the significant gulf between the *PRG* and other kinds of 'pontifical' on an inexperienced *PRG* scribe, an explanation which is patently untenable: 'Visiblement, le rédacteur primitif n'avait pas une claire notion de ce que devait être un pontifical'. See *OR*, 1:526. Both terms, it should be stressed, are anachronistic.

[80]   For some examples see Parkes, 'Liturgy and Music', 274–75.

[81]   See especially Vogel, 'Contenu et ordonnance'.

all-important section.[82] To the extent that the texts of the *Pontifical romano-germanique* can be understood as a tradition at all, therefore, they must surely be conceived of in terms of a nebulous scribal phenomenon without clearly defined boundaries. One might say that the sources exemplify a trend, but that trend does not necessarily explain the sources. Or to put it differently: to ask the question 'What was the *PRG*?' may be to seek a level of order in a tradition where none previously existed.

For this reason above all, the sanitized synthesis of the *PRG* edition needs to yield ground to the messy historical artefact, in line with the materialist principles of the so-called 'New' Philology.[83] Impractical as this may sound, this is an increasingly realistic proposition for the *PRG* tradition with the advent of digital facsimiles, and with the benefit of online indexing and analytical tools.[84] Such an approach is made all the more possible by Vogel and Elze's 1963 edition, which remains a substantial and invaluable source of reference provided it is used in a responsible way. Accordingly, references to the edition should take account of the sources and their dates, and they should always acknowledge the limited and biased sample of evidence. Andrieu's original *Ordines Romani* should always be consulted ahead of their compromised equivalents in the *PRG* edition, but with a similar degree of caution. And in view of the monolithic character of each collection one should always be mindful of the relationship of an individual 'chapter' to its neighbours, and to the overall scribal and intellectual context of the source. Finally, it must be re-emphasized that stories about Mainz, the monastery of St Alban, the period 950–63, archiepiscopal support, and imperial and papal reform are speculations bound up in a now discredited philological hypothesis.

What cannot be doubted is that a very significant textual tradition rose to prominence in late tenth- or early eleventh-century Germany, that its eclectic contents were broadly liturgical in scope, and that it metamorphosed wildly in its remarkable transmission across Europe in a manner which is not yet understood. There are far too many witnesses to claim that the *PRG* was a purely editorial fabrication. But this tradition is also far too interesting to be explained

---

[82]   Rudolf Gamper et al., *Katalog der mittelalterlichen Handschriften der Ministerialbibliothek Schaffhausen* (Dietikon: Graf, 1994), 209–14.

[83]   For an introduction to this movement and its principles see the special edition of *Speculum* 65 (1990). See also Cerquiglini, *In Praise of the Variant*, originally published as *Eloge de la variante: Histoire critique de la philologie* (Paris: Seuil, 1989).

[84]   One such tool is Henry Parkes, *PRG Database: A Tool for Navigating* Le Pontifical Romano-Germanique, ed. Cyrille Vogel and Reinhard Elze, currently available at http://database.prg.mus.cam.ac.uk. At the time of writing Bamberg, Ms. Lit. 53 is the only Vogel and Elze *PRG* source available; see online at http://bsbsbb.bsb.lrz-muenchen.de/~db/0000/sbb00000131/images/. From the wider corpus of '*PRG*' sources many manuscripts have been digitized, and an updated list may be found at http://database.prg.mus.cam.ac.uk.

away by a one-sentence summary, to be given a single title, or to be trapped in a 'definitive' edition. That is not to denigrate the achievements of Vogel and Elze, whose expeditious completion of Andrieu's skeleton edition was justly hailed as 'one of the most monumental works of liturgical history'.[85] Rather, it is to draw attention to the inherent problems and limitations of philology in dealing with complex liturgical material. While some text critical approaches are more helpful than others, none can fully account for the extraordinary scribal, ritual, intellectual and institutional divergence which we encounter in the different sources of the *PRG* tradition. The sense of authority and immutability in Vogel and Elze's edition is, therefore, in part a lesson in the importance of editorial disclosure and propriety. But it is also a lesson for the reader. If an all-encompassing and easily digestible theory about medieval ritual practices seems too good to be true, it probably is.

---

[85]   Botte's review of *PRG* volumes 1 and 2', 903: 'une des œuvres les plus monumentales de l'histoire liturgique'.

Chapter 5

Rethinking the Uses of Sarum and York: A Historiographical Essay

Matthew Cheung Salisbury

And whereas heretofore there hath been great diversity in saying and singing in Churches within this Realm; some following Salisbury Use, some Hereford Use, and some the Use of Bangor, some of York, some of Lincoln; now from henceforth all the whole Realm shall have but one Use.[1]

The Preface to the first Book of Common Prayer of 1549 points out the 'great diversity' in the liturgical practices which it replaced. This served to emphasize that the Prayer Book was the very first uniform liturgical text to be used in the English Church. Traditionally this statement has been understood as identifying all the medieval liturgical Uses (the patterns of text, movement, music and ceremonial associated with a particular venue or region). This is, however, a misinterpretation. Rhetorically speaking, the point seems to be to draw attention to the 'great diversity' in the liturgical practices that were being superseded rather than to identify the specific Uses the book was replacing. All five Uses undoubtedly existed – in some sense of that word – but so did the Use of the church of All Saints, Shorthampton. I mention this rural Oxfordshire church as an example because every church, cathedral, monastery and other venue for worship had its own distinct and authentic pattern of liturgical practice, but few of these were transmitted more widely, and so came to be labelled as the Use of that place. The key point is simply that there was a great deal more variety in liturgical practice than has sometimes been thought and this is masked by the often-used labels 'Use of Sarum' and 'Use of York'.

Whilst it is clear that the Uses of Sarum and York came to dominate the southern and northern ecclesiastical provinces of late medieval England respectively it is much less easy than might be expected to determine precisely what was meant by those terms. Both were widely used and were promulgated both in statutes of individual institutions and in episcopal and provincial orders. However, when one looks closely at a liturgical book said to be 'secundum usum Sarum' it becomes clear this does not guarantee that its contents are the same as those of another book with the same ascription, nor would both

---

[1] 'Concerning the Service of the Church', preface to *The Book of Common Prayer* (London: Edward Whitchurch, 1549 and succeeding editions).

books necessarily have contents which could be used together. The medieval identification of a liturgical book with a Use, often with an explicit ascription such as 'according to the use of Sarum' (*secundum usum Sarum*) sometimes seems to be more a label of accuracy and correctness than an association with the liturgy of Salisbury cathedral.[2]

The extent of the variation present in the manuscripts and early printed books associated with the major British uses is not widely appreciated. This is partly because books that have been labelled (either in the medieval or modern period) as being according to a particular Use are often not studied in detail, with individual copies assumed to possess the same characteristics as some already-surveyed exemplar. The second problem is that the available editions are misleading and often not representative of the surviving evidence; the modern edition of the Sarum Breviary, for instance, reprints a minority textual tradition. In the late nineteenth and early twentieth centuries a profusion of editions of medieval English liturgies, including ones associated with Sarum and York, emerged. The dominant methodology used by the editors of these books was the establishment of a fixed, authoritative text. In this analysis, I aim to show why so many editions were published at that time and why the prevailing editorial methodology must be resisted. This must be emphasized if scholars of the present and future wish to be liberated from inherited narratives and, instead, become sensitive to the nature, strengths and weaknesses of published editions of the liturgy in order to be able to use them carefully.

It will be shown that most of the early editions which have attained canonical status were produced in a time when scholars were particularly preoccupied with the re-discovery of ancient texts in their most genuine and incorrupt form (a tendency occasionally still seen), whereas the increasingly professionalized and 'scientific' disciplines of history, philology, musicology, and indeed 'medieval studies', have more recently insisted on an approach that is more faithful to the evidence. This must not, however, discredit the old editions entirely, but rather encourage us to take care to consider them for what they are: primarily transcriptions of single manuscripts or printed books, or in a few cases attempts at editorial judgement based on a few witnesses. Nor should their editors be faulted for their method, since their belief (in many cases) that their work was sufficient and representative was governed by the principle that medieval liturgical books themselves had texts and music which were the same in all cases, a principle which has only begun to be questioned in later years. It is not the intention of this study to suggest that liturgical scholars of the present should not make use of the substantial published legacy of their antecedents. Rather, it seeks to frame those publications within a historiographical context, so that

---

    [2]   This proposal is outlined in chapter 4 of my *The Secular Liturgical Office in Late Medieval England* (Turnhout: Brepols, 2015).

those wishing to make use of what is available are apprised of the implications. In order to do this it is important to identify the intellectual underpinnings of this preoccupation with definitive editions, and to illustrate some of the personal convictions of the scholars in various disciplines who worked on liturgy.

We also need to understand that the concept of the liturgical Use contributes to the notion that liturgies possessed any kind of practical uniformity. While all service books associated with a Use share a common set of properties, rather than concentrating attention on the production or identification of an authoritative version, it is more helpful to consider all such witnesses within a wider context which can illustrate local and regional tendencies and preferences. It is with a brief summary of this matter that this analysis will start, in order to lay out a case for challenging the concept of the definitive edition of a liturgical text.

'Great Diversity in Saying and Singing'

Although studies of liturgical texts and practices have always fallen within the conventional remit of philologists, local historians and theologians, many people engaged in liturgical research have been self-selecting on the basis of some personal attachment to the topic. Among the ranks of antiquarians interested in the topic there was a substantial clerical contingent: according to Nigel Yates, in the nineteenth century those in holy orders accounted for some twenty per cent of antiquarian researchers in general. This figure represents for Yates part of a search, from the 1820s onward, for the illumination and renewal of the 'Christian Society' of the Middle Ages, a time when, in contrast with nineteenth-century British exigencies, religion and politics were not at odds.[3] This had a significant impact on the way the subject of the liturgy was approached.

One of the most influential early discussions of the medieval liturgical situation in England was written by the antiquarian Richard Gough (1735–1809). The second volume of his *British Topography* (new edn., 1780) includes a substantial account, within the section on Wiltshire, of the service books and liturgical practices of the cathedral church of Salisbury.[4] Gough reports the institution of the Use by 'bishop Osmund [in] 1077', an attribution now

---

[3]   Nigel Yates, *Anglican Ritualism in Victorian Britain, 1830–1910* (Oxford: Clarendon Press, 1999), 43–44.

[4]   His descriptions of the various services and the books which contained them are well-intended but not always accurate, at one point stating 'The Breviary ... became a more compendious missal, containing the whole office of the mass ...'. Quoted from Richard Gough, *British Topography*, new edn. (London, 1780), 2:321. These were 'egregious blunders', according to William Maskell, in *A Dissertation upon the Ancient Service Books of the Church of England* (Oxford: Clarendon Press, 1882), x.

known to be false.[5] He also describes the spread of the pattern of Salisbury Cathedral 'almost all over England, Wales, and Ireland ...'. However, he also notes that 'the cathedrals of York, Lincoln, Hereford, Bangor, and Aberdeen, had their respective Uses', and mentions on the subject of Sarum's spread that 'the monks of Royston petitioned [Richard] Fitz-James, bishop of London, in the beginning of the 16th century, for leave to change that of Bangor for that of Sarum in their offices ...'.[6] Gough insightfully points out that the situation was rather different on the Continent, where a considerably greater number of local Uses enjoyed an unfettered existence,[7] but writes that he will 'leave it to the connoisseurs in music to determine whether the Sarum *chant* differed from that of York, Bangor or Hereford', distinctions supposedly discernible among the repertories of the Continental Uses.[8]

Here Gough shows a reliance on the passage from the preface, 'Concerning the Service of the Church' found in the Book of Common Prayer of the Church of England, which is presented as the epigraph to this chapter. Gough was not the only historian to become persuaded that the Prayer Book's assessment of liturgical variation in late medieval England (which, as suggested above, does not, in fact, presuppose that there existed *only* the five Uses stated, merely 'great diversity') was an accurate reflection of practice. The implication following from the Prayer Book's preface is that these Uses were a relatively fixed and identifiable set of liturgical texts, a belief which justifies the production of modern editions from one or a few allegedly homogeneous manuscript or printed sources.

The history outlined by Gough has been widely influential. It is certainly true that Sarum and York were important transregional patterns that enjoyed some substantial recognition, and indeed persistence, to the end of the Pre-Reformation English Church, and that Hereford Use, however restricted in remit, probably managed to survive in some form until the Prayer Book. However, to suggest as Gough did that churches adopted wholesale and unmodified one of the transregional Uses is to overlook the facts that each worshipping community had its own particular liturgical practices, codified or less codified, complex or less complex, and that these 'Uses', too, were understood as perfectly correct and normative when observed in their own constituencies. I have explained

---

5   The claim is disputed in Diana Greenway's 'The False *Institutio* of St Osmund', in *Tradition and Change: Essays in Honour of Marjorie Chibnall*, ed. Diana Greenway, Christopher Holdsworth and Jane Sayers (Cambridge: Cambridge University Press, 1970), 77–101.

6   '... alledging that the latter was imperfect in itself, and still more so in the performance from their torn and worn out books, which they were unwilling to change except for a better form'. Gough, *British Topography*, 2:319.

7   Gough, *British Topography*, 2:320.

8   Gough, *British Topography*, 2:323. Emphasis original.

elsewhere at length the justification for such a statement, both on the grounds of textual variation and on the principle that liturgical practice on more than a basic level must have varied from venue to venue even if practitioners were using exactly the same texts.[9]

The Exportation and Diversification of 'Sarum'

The Use of Salisbury Cathedral (commonly abbreviated to 'Sarum', often to distinguish the pattern which spread more widely from that of the cathedral) began as no more or less important, complex or codified than any other local practice. It is, however, easily accepted that 'Sarum' Use, at least in name, spread widely across the medieval South of England, a fact corroborated by the survival of liturgical books, by documents and foundation charters, and by contemporary historical accounts, but it has never been clear what the adoption of 'Sarum' might mean for a church or cathedral as regards particular changes in practice. Did 'adoption' mean the adoption of the Sarum liturgical kalendar, the list of feasts to be observed month by month? And from which exemplar would this kalendar have been drawn? Or did it mean the particular choice and order of proper texts used at Salisbury (and elsewhere) for the observance of feastdays? Or did it involve the appropriation of some practices from, for instance, the Sarum Ordinal and Customary, or the provision of new Sarum liturgical books? On the basis of the surviving evidence, the only answer must be that it varied according to circumstances, and therefore, for example, that any five worshipping communities who apparently observed the liturgical practices of 'Sarum' would have realized the particulars of services, readings, kalendars and other aspects in five very different ways. Moreover, unless the adoption of Sarum had taken place at the same time everywhere with an absolutely invariable set of texts, the exemplar followed by each of the five venues must have been different, considering that the Salisbury liturgy underwent several stages of development over several hundred years from its application at the new Cathedral of 1220 until its final suppression in the sixteenth century.[10] It is therefore fallacious to suggest that the *precise* liturgical pattern of Salisbury Cathedral was in any way adopted elsewhere, and dangerous to make the generalization that some text 'secundum usum Sarum', whether manuscript or printed book, whether contemporary or more ancient, accurately represents either the practice of

---

[9] Indeed the same variation may have existed within the many books belonging to a cathedral foundation of moderate size, because each, unless copied exactly from the same exemplar, would have been different from every other in a wide range of details which may or may not have affected the actual performance of the liturgy. See my *Secular Liturgical Office*.

[10] Salisbury, *Secular Liturgical Office*.

Salisbury or (more controversially) any venue in which 'Sarum' liturgy was said to have been used.

The assertion that there was never a fixed Use of Sarum or York in the Middle Ages can be supported by the recent work of Richard Pfaff (who draws together new research to show that an invariable Sarum Use is fallacious),[11] and Sherry Reames, in several important studies of the Breviary texts.[12] My own study of the kalendars and texts of 132 Sarum, York and English Benedictine manuscripts, proposes a heterogeneous promulgation of the Sarum liturgy which produced tensions between the dissemination of the Salisbury Cathedral rite, as it stood, to a wider constituency, and the creation of a more generic 'Sarum' liturgy modified for use in a wide range of venues.[13] Evidently, then, the provision of a critical edition or an edition otherwise purportedly authoritative for any more than a closely related family of witnesses is problematic at best.

'Essentially a Philological Enterprise': Editions, Evidence, Motives

The diversity evident in the surviving books and manuscripts is not, however, well represented in the editions of Sarum and York texts that were made in the nineteenth and early twentieth century. Instead, editors were interested in establishing good fixed forms of liturgical books. This was an outgrowth of a more general preoccupation with the establishment of texts. The prevailing climate was no doubt inspired by the Classical education of the practitioners and researchers of the nineteenth-century liturgical establishment.

That the purpose and function of Classical education (and scholarly enterprise) has always been the production of authoritative and faithful editions of primary texts must have made the perceived need for exemplary texts of the medieval English liturgy very strong indeed. This is one of the contexts in which the majority of modern editions were produced with great energy in the late nineteenth century. Witnesses of the Sarum Missal were published by F.H. Dickinson in 1861 and later by John Wickham Legg (1916), with the Sarum Breviary by Francis Procter and Christopher Wordsworth (1879–86), and the Ordinal and Customary edited and printed by Walter

---

[11]　Richard W. Pfaff, *The Liturgy in Medieval England: A History* (Cambridge: Cambridge University Press, 2009), ch. 13.

[12]　Most recently, Sherry L. Reames, 'Unexpected Texts for Saints in some Sarum Breviary Manuscripts', in *The Study of Medieval Manuscripts of England: Festschrift in Honor of Richard W. Pfaff*, ed. George Hardin Brown and Linda Ehrsam Voigts (Tempe: Arizona Center for Medieval and Renaissance Studies, 2010), 163–84.

[13]　*Secular Liturgical Office*, ch. 4.

Howard Frere somewhat later (1898–1901).[14] The York Missal was edited by W.G. Henderson (1872–74) and the Breviary by Stephen Lawley (1879–82).[15] The Hereford Breviary was edited by Frere and L.E.G. Brown in three volumes for the Henry Bradshaw Society between 1904 and 1915.[16] Other notable publications include facsimile editions of the Sarum Antiphonal and Gradual by Frere under the auspices of the Plainsong and Medieval Music Society.[17] Many of these projects were supported, if not published, by learned bodies such as the Henry Bradshaw Society, founded in 1890 'for the editing of rare liturgical texts', which were modelled on the antiquarian and regional historical societies that had been founded in great numbers in the early nineteenth century. It is worth pointing out that Procter and Wordsworth, at least, believed that a critical approach more rigorous than a mere transcription from a single printed edition was both possible and desirable, but realized that such a transcription was 'more manageable'.[18]

This study does not seek to question the groundwork laid by these editions, refute their contents, or indeed to suggest that they are unhelpful. But with Giuseppe Mazzotta, we now begin to question the ultimate satisfactoriness of their aim, that is, 'to reflect on the tendentious manipulations and ideological biases of those nineteenth-century masters, who were intent on concocting and peddling specific paradigms of textual origins for the vindication of one sort or another of political primacy'.[19] Whilst the canonical editions of liturgical observances may help to give an accurate picture for a few sources, representative

---

[14] *Missale ad usum insignis et praeclarae ecclesiae Sarum*, ed. F.H. Dickinson (Burntisland: Pitsligo, 1861–63); *The Sarum Missal: Edited from Three Early Manuscripts*, ed. John Wickham Legg (Oxford: Oxford University Press, 1916); *Breviarium ad usum insignis ecclesiae Sarum*, ed. Francis Procter and Christopher Wordsworth, 3 vols. (Cambridge: Cambridge University Press, 1879–86); *The Use of Sarum: The Original Texts Edited from the Mss*, ed. W.H. Frere, 2 vols. (Cambridge: Cambridge University Press, 1898–1901).

[15] *Missale ad usum ecclesiae Eboracensis*, ed. W.G. Henderson, Surtees Society 59, 60 (Durham: Surtees Society 1872–74); *Breviarium ad usum insignis ecclesiae Eboracensis*, ed. Stephen Lawley, Surtees Society 71, 75 (Durham: Surtees Society, 1879–82).

[16] *The Hereford Breviary*, ed. W.H. Frere and L.E.G. Brown, HBS 26, 40, 46 (London: HBS, 1904–15).

[17] *Antiphonale Sarisburiense: A Reproduction in Facsimile of a manuscript of the thirteenth century*, ed. W.H. Frere (London: Plainsong and Medieval Music Society, 1901–24; repr. Farnborough: Gregg Press, 1966); and *Graduale Sarisburiense: A Reproduction in Facsimile of a Manuscript of the Thirteenth Century* (London: Quaritch, 1894, repr. Farnborough: Gregg Press, 1966).

[18] *Breviarium … Sarum*, ed. Procter and Wordsworth, 2:vii. The unrepresentativeness of this edition was pointed out in the late nineteenth century but seems rarely to be remembered: see *Use of Sarum*, ed. Frere, 1:xli.

[19] Giuseppe Mazzotta, 'The Poet and the Critics', in *Dante Now: Current Trends in Dante Studies* (Notre Dame: University of Notre Dame Press, 1995), 63–79, at 67.

or otherwise, they must be considered as *witnesses* only, not as textual archetypes, and certainly not as transregionally valid without substantiation. In order to understand how these editions can usefully be used today it is necessary to understand more about the motivations and operating principles of some of the key players involved.

The origins of quantitative, evidence-based philological work for medieval texts had long been laid: Stuart Piggott writes that the necessary conditions for the scholarly study of antiquities had been produced by the seventeenth century, as a result of the 'nascent scientific disciplines'.[20] More importantly, Piggott points to the rise in interest in the Anglo-Saxon period during the later sixteenth century, for the purposes of national unity and identity, as part of an attempt to underpin 'the new fabric of government and society'.[21] The central motivation behind the multifarious efforts toward the reconstruction of the texts, music, architectural and material trappings of the medieval Church in Britain, was in many cases the same: namely, to show that the English Church was able to date its distinctive and self-sufficient identity from a much earlier time than the English Reformation. This search for the origins of pre-Reformation English Christianity followed the Catholic Relief Act of 1829 which was the final repeal of all anti-Catholic legislation in Britain. It was a striving for a past time when religion was not controversial or divisive, an important task for the Victorian scholar-priest. In practice antiquarians were also seeking evidence to support modifications, and augmentations of the Prayer Book liturgy. Justification for these changes could be found, according to the ritualists, in the so-called 'Ornaments Rubric' promulgated in the 1559 Elizabethan recension of the Prayer Book:

> the chauncels shall remain, as they have done in tymes past. And here is to be noted, that the Minister at the time of the communion, and at all other tymes in hys ministracion, shall use suche ornamentes in the church, as wer in use by aucthoritie of parliament in the second yere of the reygne of king Edward the VI.[22]

The 'catholic' nature of the Elizabethan prayer book has also been linked to its words of administration at Holy Communion.[23] It seems to reintroduce an understanding of the sacraments that was suppressed in the first and second Prayer Books of Edward VI which had a more ardently Protestant character. It is easy to see why the so-called 'Ritualists' would have seen the Ornaments Rubric

---

20   Stuart Piggott, *Ruins in a Landscape: Essays in Antiquarianism* (Edinburgh: Edinburgh University Press, 1976), 20.

21   Piggott, *Ruins in a Landscape*, 59, 64.

22   From the order for Morning Prayer, in the Book of Common Prayer, 1559.

23   Eamon Duffy, *The Stripping of the Altars: Traditional Religion in England c.1400–c.1580* (New Haven: Yale University Press, 1992), 567.

as an authoritative justification for the reintroduction of pre-Reformation decoration, vestments, architecture and liturgy. Proof of the catholicity of the Church itself could be found in the uncovering of a rite with apparently ancient origins, based on evidence from several surviving examples of the earliest known English liturgy. The natural approach to this issue would be an editorial project of the sort that has been described, with its objective being the synthesis of the earliest, most authoritative texts, and with the act of its creation taking precedence over the collation of several different versions and attention to their diversity. With a view to apostolicity, an ancient and preferably Roman origin for the English liturgy was highly desirable.

Among the various Anglo-Catholic camps, Ritualists were for the elaboration of ritual similar to that of the Roman Catholic Church, although the particular expression of this desire fell into two camps. Some were in favour of adopting *contemporary* Roman Catholic aesthetics and practice. Others, like the Reverend Percy Dearmer (1867–1936), vicar of St Mary's Primrose Hill and author of the *Parson's Handbook*, propounded a distinctively English realization of the liturgy and arts of the pre-Reformation Church.[24] This was the context in which the Alcuin Club was established in 1897: 'to encourage and assist in the practical study of ceremonial, and the arrangement of churches, their furniture and ornaments in accordance with the rubrics of the Book of Common Prayer'.[25] Not all of those involved in liturgical research were Ritualists, or Ritualists alone. High-Churchmen had a particular concern for the apostolic succession and authority of bishops and priests, and for the grace conveyed by the sacraments, which were celebrated in the context of formal worship. Tractarians, by definition, were those who were in particular sympathy with the membership and output of the Oxford Movement and its *Tracts for the Times*. The conditions were set for very considerable scholarly attention directed to and, in fact, no small reliance on, the establishment of the particular characteristics of pre-Reformation worship in England. All of these parties looked, with their own particular motivations, to the establishment of continuity of the Church of England from the medieval Church.

No matter the title ascribed to them, these efforts to reconstruct the trappings of the medieval English Church were not solely an aesthetic adjunct to a wider theological programme. In fact, they were seen as vital, since their historical exemplar had engaged the unlettered, uncultured, medieval layman with ceremonial, music and art writ large in its liturgies, buildings and other

---

[24] *The Parson's Handbook: Containing Practical Directions both for Parsons and Others as to the Management of the Parish Church and Its Services according to the Anglican Use, as Set Forth in the Book of Common Prayer*, ed. Percy Dearmer, 12th edn. (London: Humphrey Milford, 1932).

[25] Quoted in Yates, *Anglican Ritualism*, 336.

trappings of worship. This stance was embraced in particular by the Cambridge Camden Society, later the Ecclesiological Society.[26] Aside from the widely held aspiration for the medieval, and therefore compelling, trappings of church, the Camden Society held the belief that a Church which claimed a long and unbroken history stretching back to the Middle Ages should have appropriate church buildings and fixtures. Founding members John Mason Neale (1818–66) (better known for his contributions to hymnody) and Benjamin Webb (1819–85), despite their relative youth, were (to Stuart Piggott) 'vehement, tactless, and arrogant ... [with a] hideous consciousness of their own liturgical superiority'.[27] The Ecclesiologists employed quantitative, positivist methods to derive their desired model: 'The only safe way to arrive at any general principles', they wrote, 'is to observe and describe the details ... and from a large collection of such observations, if carefully recorded, much advantage may accrue to the science.'[28] The enormous interest in Sarum Use may be attributed, at least in part, to the assertion that it was an identifiable and historically viable, as well as irrefutably English, dialect of the liturgy of the medieval Church, and a vital part of the heritage of the (catholic) Church of England. A rediscovery of plainchant as an essential component of normative medieval worship was also considered important. Chant was to be a tangible expression of theological emphases; it was, '... to some extent, the aesthetic realization of high churchmanship ...'.[29] The revival in the Anglican church was also concomitant with the re-establishment of plainchant in Roman Catholic churches in Britain after the gradual repeal over the eighteenth century of the penal codes that made the trappings of worship impossible to enact.[30] In some respects the Church was also re-establishing the practice of Archbishop Cranmer, who had ordered 'the ancient Plain-Song' to be added to the First Prayer Book of Edward VI (1549).[31] Not all were in sympathy with this restoration, however. Of one parochial visit, the High-Churchman and future archbishop Edward White Benson (1829–96) wrote, 'All the music was Gregorian, gloomy'.[32] This stance, underlining an assessment of plainsong as otherworldly and hence abstruse, through the dissimilarity of plainsong to contemporary forms of sacred and secular music, was completely contradicted

---

[26]   There is a substantial account of the Society and its activities in James F. White, *The Cambridge Movement: The Ecclesiologists and the Gothic Revival* (Cambridge: Cambridge University Press, 1962).

[27]   Piggott, *Ruins in a Landscape*, 178.

[28]   White, *Cambridge Movement*, 50.

[29]   Bennett Zon, *The English Plainchant Revival* (Oxford: Oxford University Press, 1999), 251.

[30]   Zon, *English Plainchant Revival*, 7.

[31]   Thomas Helmore, *Plain-Song* (London: Novello & Co., 1877), 53.

[32]   Yates, *Anglican Ritualism*, 179.

by opinions such as those of the Catholic convert (and Oxford contemporary of John Henry Newman) the Reverend Henry Formby, who in 1848 suggested that it was this very character that made chant suitable to its purpose – namely, as an exposition of the mystery of faith.[33]

The Plainsong and Medieval Music Society played a substantial role in the revival of interest in medieval liturgical music. A tremendous amount of time and money was devoted to the production of Walter Howard Frere's *Antiphonale Sarisburiense* and the corresponding *Graduale*, both of which were issued in fascicles for a substantial period, under the direction of the 'small but learned group of "Sarum" scholars who formed [the] inner council',[34] a state which meant the Society by 1926 was 'little more than a propaganda group for adopting the Sarum chant (and no other) for English words'.[35] (Dom Anselm Hughes, a long-term member of the Society's Council, does point out that enthusiasm was dampened somewhat by the discovery that the liturgy of Salisbury Cathedral appeared to be very much Norman in origin.[36]) Similar sentiments are found in the words of Thomas Helmore, leading light in the Gregorian Association and Master of the Children of the Chapel Royal, who argued in the 1870s that 'the people's chant ... [should be] the same kind vocally now as in any century before us'.[37] He argued that the 'usages and traditions handed down from age to age' should not have been avoided simply because of the English Reformation.[38] 'In our opinion', confirmed the *Ecclesiologist*, vehicle of the Ecclesiological Society, 'the Plain Song of the Church is not only the most right, and the most beautiful method, of praising God, but also practically the most easy ...'.[39]

The search for historically inspired forms of worship was not, of course, restricted to those members of the Church of England who were particularly concerned with establishing the unbroken descent of the Anglican church from the Church universal. Some of the objectives of that particular liturgical revival were the same as those of the wider Liturgical Movement. This was a

---

[33] Zon, *English Plainchant Revival*, 235. One advertisement for recordings of chant read: '[Gramophone records] will be the allies of choirmasters, teaching choirs to interpret with exactitude the melodies which the *Motu Proprio* prescribes. By the aid of science, the literal voice of the Church may be heard in the land.' Printed in Katherine Bergeron, *Decadent Enchantments: The Revival of Gregorian Chant at Solesmes* (Berkeley: University of California Press, 1988), 134 illus.

[34] Anselm Hughes, *Septuagesima: Reminiscences of the Plainsong and Mediaeval Music Society, and of Other Things Personal and Musical* (London: Plainsong and Mediaeval Music Society, 1959), 21.

[35] Hughes, *Septuagesima*, 34.

[36] Hughes, *Septuagesima*, 33.

[37] Helmore, *Plain-Song*, 152.

[38] Helmore, *Plain-Song*, 48.

[39] Cited in White, *Cambridge Movement*, 216.

contemporary development which strove to re-assert the central role of public worship in Christian life. In part it was a reaction to what was considered an over-prioritization of the worldly implications of Christian living and in opposition to the tendency, at least among Roman Catholics, to practise various forms of private devotion in lieu of public worship in the form of the Eucharist. One of the most celebrated outgrowths of both the Liturgical Movement and the Romantic search for ancient origins was the Abbaye-de-Saint-Pierre at Solesmes (near Sablé in France), re-founded in 1837 on the site of an ancient priory by former parish priest Prosper Guéranger.[40] Katherine Bergeron, who has studied the foundation of the community in detail, compares the establishment of Solesmes to other post-Revolutionary efforts in France which tried to reconstruct through arts and spirituality a society which was thought to have lost both.[41] Guéranger and his followers believed that the most useful and authentic realization of the desired flavour of Benedictine spirituality could be achieved through accurate reconstruction not only of the buildings and administrative structure of the community, but also of its worship and music. To this end a growing number of scholar-monks were commissioned to probe the earliest medieval sources.[42] In any case the overall methodology had been anticipated by the community's first abbot: 'On possède la phrase gregorienne dans sa pureté', Dom Guéranger had written, '[si] les exemplaires de plusieurs églises éloignées s'accordent ....'[43] The establishment of authoritative forms of service in the style of performing editions was a necessary condition for the success of the enterprise. 'Solesmes guards an unchangeable idea', claimed Dom Gregorio Suñol, 'and in order to apprehend it rightly we must free ourselves from the tyranny of fashion, acquire the Gregorian temperament and recapture the antique soul.'[44]

In response to a growing desire for direction in light of the mixed messages on the subject issued by his predecessor Pope Leo XIII (r. 1878–1903), and under pressure from his musical adviser Angelo di Santi, who sympathized with the monks of Solesmes,[45] Pius X (r. 1903–14) decisively responded

---

[40]   For further observations on the re-foundation of Solesmes and its contributions to the chant revival, see Pierre Combe, *The Restoration of Gregorian Chant: Solesmes and the Vatican Edition*, trans. Theodore N. Marier and William Skinner (Washington, DC: Catholic University of America Press, 2003); and Katharine Ellis, *The Politics of Plainchant in Fin-de-Siècle France* (Farnham: Ashgate, 2013).

[41]   Bergeron, *Decadent Enchantments*, 4.

[42]   Bergeron, *Decadent Enchantments*, 93.

[43]   Prosper Guéranger, *Institutions liturgiques*, 3 vols. (Le Mans: Fleuriot, 1840–51), i, 306.

[44]   Gregorio Suñol, *Text Book of Gregorian Chant According to the Solesmes Method*, trans. G.M. Durnford (Tournai: Desclee and Society of St John the Evangelist, 1930), vii.

[45]   Bergeron, *Decadent Enchantments*, 130.

to the plainchant revival with the *motu proprio* 'Tra le sollecitudini' of 22 November 1903. He criticized the poor quality of contemporary sacred music as 'one of the [most common problems] ... even when everything else ... deserves the highest praise'.[46] The use of chant was a solution to the musical problem; indeed, the best qualities of sacred music, namely the 'holiness ... beauty [and] universality' which were to be elements of all liturgy were '... found most perfectly in Gregorian chant, which is therefore the proper chant of the Roman Church, [handed down from the Fathers], which has been so happily restored to its original perfection and purity by recent study'.[47] A sounder affirmation of the value of the work at Solesmes and elsewhere could not be desired. The document also gives some indication of the Pope's own preferences; it is interesting to note that under the heading 'Various Kinds of Sacred Music', he states that 'the more a musical composition for use in church is like plainchant ... so much the more is it right and liturgical'.[48]

The sometimes emotional or spiritual connexion between subject and researcher is sometimes as present for modern scholars as for the monks of Solesmes; Katherine Bergeron, for example, talks about having a particular affinity for her topic: 'I felt I was ... rediscovering my own [tradition]'.[49] In effect, whilst liturgical texts might be very fitting and conventional subjects for philological study, the driving force for many who have carried out the work has often been related to a doctrinal or aesthetic objective. For some the establishment of a fixed and identifiable text of the liturgy of medieval England was an indicator of continuity with the rest of the Church catholic (and, in the case of some in the Church of England, the identification of Sarum Use as a particularly insular form of the Roman rite); for others the musical and architectural supports to worship were meant to inspire an almost medieval fervency of devotion. These motivations were joined by a pan-Western Romantic rediscovery of ancient, long-lost origins and mythologies. All of these influences produced a scholarly milieu in which the establishment of authoritative editions was paramount. Even if their discoveries were not helping to shape a renewal of liturgical forms in practice, the editions themselves stood as a tangible record of medieval activity, which could be mobilized in order to support a variety of political or doctrinal stances.

---

[46]   Pius X, *Tra le sollecitudini*, quoted in Suñol, *Text Book*, 165.

[47]   Suñol, *Text Book*, 167.

[48]   Suñol, *Text Book*, 167.

[49]   Bergeron writes (*Decadent Enchantments*, xi): 'It was a tradition that had slipped by a whole generation of Catholics who, like me, had come of age after the Second Vatican Council, a generation raised on the flat vernacular of the suburban Church, with its plain-clothed celebrants and folksy guitar masses. For us, knowledge of the Latin liturgy had become esoteric, relegated to university curricula.'

Different Cloth: Edmund Bishop and William Maskell

If it appears that liturgical work was all carried out by researchers cut from the same cloth, two notable exceptions should be mentioned. The Reverend William Maskell, unlike many of his contemporaries, was not interested in the restoration of the liturgy in practice, and Edmund Bishop's investigations, which utilized an unusual degree of complexity in his information gathering, anticipate attitudes to the transmission of liturgical Uses which modern scholars are only now beginning to be able to substantiate. Maskell (1814–90), parish priest in the diocese of Salisbury and eventual Roman Catholic convert, was a theologian and also an accomplished bibliophile, who assembled collections of books and sold them to libraries:[50] many notable items from his liturgical collection are now in the British Library. Maskell's research, at least at an early stage, was by his own admission 'the illustration of our Common Prayer Book from ancient documents, and its original sources'.[51] In 1850, the year of his conversion to the Catholic Church, he wrote, 'I have never been drawn to, never been inclined to adopt, what people call (and rightly call) Roman practices, and books, and forms.'[52] Maskell in fact seems to have thought very poorly of Ritualists, particularly after his conversion, and if his objective had been to illustrate the history of the Prayer Book, this changed, to reject entirely the work of its compilers. In his pamphlet *Protestant Ritualists* (1872), he describes the order for Holy Communion as

> a pure jumble, unlike any ancient liturgy which was ever used in the Christian church. The compilers appear to have cut the Sarum ordinary and canon of the mass into pieces, and mixed the fragments with bits taken out of the Middleburg and other forms compiled by protestants abroad, and then taken them, as it were hap-hazard, out of a bag and stitched them together.[53]

Maskell's own involvement (as bishop's chaplain) in a particularly public and contentious case regarding baptismal theology[54] certainly coloured his opinions of the theology of the Ritualists, who in his mind

---

[50] Seymour de Ricci, *English Collectors of Books and Manuscripts (1530–1930) and Their Marks of Ownership*, Sandars Lectures 1929–30 (Cambridge: Cambridge University Press, 1930), 143.

[51] From the Dedication to vol. 3 of his *Monumenta Ritualia Ecclesiae Anglicanae*, 3 vols. (London: W. Pickering, 1846–47), unpaginated.

[52] William Maskell, *A Second Letter on the Present Position of the High Church Party in the Church of England*, subtitled *The Want of Dogmatic Teaching in the Reformed English Church* (London: W. Pickering, 1850), 11.

[53] William Maskell, *Protestant Ritualists*, 2nd edn. (London: J. Toovey, 1872), 30.

[54] The Gorham controversy, surrounding the presentation of the eponymous priest to a living, which diminished Maskell's faith in the Church of England; for which see *Gorham*

... are content to be suffered to hold their particular opinions ... to claim no higher authority than that which sends their next door neighbour into his pulpit to contradict them in every possible way ... to be allowed to put on copes and chasubles and make 'high celebrations' upon the strength of an old rubric which refers to the second year of Edward VI, although they well know that the vast majority of English ministers are no less borne out when they wear unseemly surplices and say the office of communion with every mark of carelessness ....[55]

A Ritualist, for Maskell, 'admits the lowest evangelical to his communion table because he has no authority to rest upon or to appeal to beyond his own private judgment',[56] a stance which echoes his own involvement with Gorham. Clearly Maskell's criticisms did not only lie with doctrine, for the matter of order and doctrine was laced together with remarks on the Ritualist attitude to liturgical reconstruction. The Ritualists were no more 'within the one true fold than their more protestant brethren, because they endeavour to base their ritual and liturgical restorations on Roman principles ....'[57] If his intentions had been at one time to illustrate 'the ancient liturgies of the Church of England', the second edition of his *Monumenta Ritualia* (issued in 1882) was far more kind to the Roman church than the first, published in 1846–47. Maskell was hardly a dispassionate, uninvolved researcher, but his tracts and other works demonstrate some views in direct contradiction to those of the Ritualists.

Maskell's contemporary Edmund Bishop (1846–1917) was a comparatively rare lay contributor to liturgiology, and just as opinionated about the necessity of Roman Catholic attention to the project of liturgical research. Bishop was a largely self-educated civil servant whose position allowed him a good deal of flexibility and free time with which to carry out his investigations. Like Maskell, he was a book-collector, and his substantial collection is now at Downside Abbey, where he spent a great deal of time living alongside the Benedictine community. As a layman, unaffiliated scholar and a Catholic, he was perhaps thwarted by Church of England '"clerical" monopolies'[58] on the subject, and sometimes exercised strong opinions about those persons whose work did not meet with his

---

v. the bishop of Exeter, a report of the arguments of counsel, before the judicial committee of the Privy council. To which is added, the judgment (London, 1850).

[55] Maskell, *Protestant Ritualists*, 13. John Henry Newman had already remarked on the apparent hypocrisy of Anglo-Catholics in his 1848 novel *Loss and Gain*: '"You forget," said Bateman to White, "you have, or might have, all this [the trappings of Catholic worship] in your church, without the Romish corruptions." *Loss and Gain*, new edn. (Oxford: Oxford University Press, 1986), 34.

[56] Maskell, *Protestant Ritualists*, 30.

[57] Maskell, *Protestant Ritualists*, 8.

[58] Nigel Abercrombie, *The Life and Work of Edmund Bishop* (London: Longmans, 1959).

requirements. Of the 1879 edition by F.E. Warren (of St John's College, Oxford) of the Irish Missal of Corpus Christi, Cambridge, Bishop wrote:

> Although the volume does not bear evidence of any very advanced stage of liturgical research within the University of Oxford, it is at least a welcome sign of the increasing activity in that department which the Editor assures us is manifesting itself in that ancient home of learning ... It is to be hoped that Catholics, to whom this branch of learning is, or should be, a natural inheritance, may not, through their own supineness and neglect, find it occupied by strangers.[59]

Bishop's hostility toward academe may be explained by his being 'one of the last great English autodidacts', in the words of David Knowles.[60] Though his work on regional cults of saints (to be discussed below) contributed to Roman Catholic liturgical renewal in England and Wales, Bishop seems to have been disdainful of some of the quasi-Ritualist activities of certain Catholic parties: he did not seem to approve of some of the 'modernizations' of Downside, commenting on 'some embellishments [in the liturgy] copied from or modelled on ... proprieties of Anglican "cathedral" "celebrations"'.[61] Of the renewal of monastic life at Solesmes, Bishop believed Dom Guéranger, first abbot of the community, to be

> a mere rechauffé of ideas which later research and method have superseded, whilst for the later period he is so passionate a partizan, and his work partakes, in spite of its size, so much of the character of a party pamphlet to serve a practical end, that he is to be used only with an amount of caution and discrimination that implies almost as much knowledge of the subject as that possessed by the author himself.[62]

He did subscribe to the nascent Henry Bradshaw Society at the request of John Wickham Legg, despite an undoubtedly unfriendly reaction to the attempt by the Protestants on the committee to serve as the sole office-holders.[63]

Bishop's hostility towards the gentleman-scholar's methodology which had dominated liturgical research for some time was supplemented by rigorous and methodical methods of his own devising, almost unprecedented at the time. Despite this energetic labour very little of his work was published within his lifetime: the few publications which came to light were relegated mainly to small-circulation Catholic periodicals and the *Downside Review*. His *Liturgica Historica* (Oxford: Clarendon Press, 1918), published posthumously, remains

---

59 Quoted in Abercrombie, *Bishop*, 100.

60 Knowles, in the preface to Abercrombie, *Bishop*, xi.

61 Quoted in Abercrombie, *Bishop*, 120.

62 Quoted in Abercrombie, *Bishop*, 273.

63 Abercrombie, *Bishop*, 162.

a useful body of essays on diverse topics of liturgical or antiquarian interest. But it is seemly here to illustrate an even more useful contribution of Bishop's, for which he has had little credit. He devoted substantial time to the study of liturgical kalendars and martyrologies as his contribution to a new English Catholic *Menology* (1887);[64] this had been commissioned by the bishops' conference, which had resolved to ask Rome for an augmentation in liturgical terms for the observance of the feastdays of local English saints. The principal research by Bishop for this new publication was to provide both names and hagiographies for a very substantial range of saints, many of whom had never before received official sanction. Bishop's painstaking transcriptions from a vast number of manuscript kalendars, in much greater detail than is represented in the final *Menology*, are now in the British Library in a series of notebooks which the editor, Father Richard Stanton, hoped 'may become generally available, as their publication would furnish an invaluable help to students of English Hagiology in all its branches'.[65]

Bishop's notebooks (now London, British Library, Additional Mss 36598–36602 and 39212) consist of lists and transcriptions organized synthetically and then by series of transcriptions of kalendars from Harley, Cotton and Royal manuscripts in the British Museum, expanding to include manuscripts from the Cotton, Arundel, Burney, Lansdowne, Sloane and King's collections. Fascinating to any liturgical scholar, they contain autograph sketches of some of the more ambiguous abbreviations and names, his notes on unusual lives of saints, and transcriptions of rare proper materials, including a rhymed office for St Neot, and a small amount of square notation. They betray some considerable concern for how his research would inform the modern practice of liturgy: in a section labelled 'jottings re. Martyrol.' he talks about 'the necessity for drawing the distinction between practical and devotional calendars' (a distinction which still concerns all who work on compiling such evidence of devotion); and how to deal with the convergence of the 'true' date of a feast in medieval kalendars with the date in the nineteenth-century Roman martyrology.[66] Another particular concern, entirely familiar to any researcher interested in regional considerations, was whether (and how) to use the current or medieval boundaries of dioceses and counties.[67] Most importantly, the transcriptions served as reference material for 'Skeleton Calendars' in each volume, which seem to have been the basis upon which that in the *Menology* was devised.

---

[64]   A more inclusive synonym for 'martyrology'.

[65]   *A menology of England and Wales or, Brief Memorials of their ancient British and English saints*, ed. Richard Stanton (London: Burns and Oates, 1887), ix.

[66]   Bishop notebook 1, British Library, Additional Ms. 36598, fol. 2.

[67]   Bishop notebook 1, British Library, Additional Ms. 36598, fol. 7.

The notebooks also illustrate Bishop's response to the Anglican appropriation of 'Sarum' as a distinctive and important medieval English liturgical forebear. In a section entitled 'Memoranda preparatory for a conversation with Revd Fr Stanton of the Oratory', Bishop wrote, 'The supposition cherished by *Anglicanism* in regard to "Sarum", who would raise it to a sort of national rite might well induce Catholics to investigate the origin, follow the extension & fix the best limits of the rite'.[68] Of the substantial spread of the cathedral liturgy of Salisbury, a subject of great interest, Bishop speculates:

> Its prevalence in England depended on 2 main causes: 1. the existence here of monastic cathedrals, whereby in many dioceses the Cathedral by the very nature of the case, could not serve as the liturgical model. 2. (the cause of less importance, but still a cause) the great size of the diocese of Lincoln and the situation of its Cathedral at the far end of it, whereby its influence, though it was held by secular canons, was necessarily weakened; moreover the invasion of Sarum in the Lincoln borders was facilitated by the fact that the diocese straggled down thro' dioceses with monastic cathedrals (Ely, Norwich, Coventry) the clergy of which had been reduced to seek for some rite not that of the cathedral.[69]

Inspired and informed by his investigation into the liturgical observance of saints, and his mastery of much of the extant material, Bishop was even able to comment substantively on the genericization of the Salisbury liturgy, its adoption within the widest range of local circumstances, and the increasing lack of fixity between manuscript evidence and apparent practice of the cathedral church and the 'Use of Sarum' adopted elsewhere. He realized that medieval churches that adopted Sarum would nonetheless have retained aspects of their pre-existent liturgy.[70]

Edmund Bishop's liturgical research did not bear fruit in the usual profusion of editions; rather, great quantities of his work, based on experience with a great many manuscripts, remains to be re-discovered within his notebooks. The

---

68   Bishop notebook 5, British Library, Additional Ms. 36602, fol. 223v.

69   Ibid.

70   'This gradual extension of the Sarum rite is contemporaneous with/marked by a gradual building up of the Sarum Kalendar until is obtained the form presented by the late prints. These printed books have made us overlook the earlier & simpler forms. I take it there was a practical barter: you take our books in your Church: we will take your Sts into our Kalendar. But is it ? question of all the feasts in the later Sarum Bks were observed in all places which these books were in use [sic]? *Progress towards Nationalization.* During the 15th Century there was a certain progress in the way of the Nationalization of Sarum, which on its side, so far as the Calendar goes, becomes gradually *un-diocesanized*.' Bishop notebook 5, British Library, Additional Ms. 36602, fol. 224v.

profundity of his knowledge touched upon issues which are still before scholars, namely the growth and development of the English Uses.

Conclusions

This analysis has sought to undermine the conventional understanding of the English liturgical Uses, held by medieval clerics and modern scholars, namely that there was such a thing as (for instance) inflexible 'Sarum' liturgy. In fact there was a degree of commonality in the choice and order of liturgical texts and chants associated with Salisbury Cathedral, but there was also much more divergence than previous generations have assumed, mainly because a textual pattern, even if copied wholesale from book to book, designed for one venue, could not possibly have been practised in the same way across wide swathes of medieval England. The ceremonial of a large cathedral could not possibly translate wholly into a small parish church with different furniture and clerical levels of professionalism. The same may be said for 'York Use' following the practices of the metropolitical church of York. Hereford, Lincoln and Bangor Uses (as mentioned in the Prayer Book's Preface) also existed, but these were the distinct patterns of liturgical text and ceremony practised at their respective cathedrals, wholly distinct from the practice of any other church, just as were Sarum and York.

The practice of liturgical research has shifted over the course of the twentieth century from a focus on the 'oldest' to a preoccupation with the 'most', and from the production of 'editions' to the production of 'lists'. There are, of course, implications for reading and analysis, because for the first time dissenting or discordant voices are permitted within a heterogeneous textual world, something so illegal to one scholar that he devised a method of eliminating infrequent variants from his quest for the earliest version.[71] Intertextual readings are made possible, and the liturgical 'act', conceived of as all iterations, written and otherwise, of an observance, including the way it was performed, begins to cohere as a concept never perfectly preserved in written prescriptions.[72]

The editions of the medieval English liturgy produced in the late nineteenth and early twentieth centuries have, since their publication, been presented to the modern researcher as the unassailable voice of authority, without qualification, and the researcher may be tempted to accept them, in the absence of any more

---

[71] See the sixth volume of *Corpus antiphonalium officii*, ed. René-Jean Hesbert, 6 vols., RED series maior, fontes 7–12 (Rome: Herder, 1963–79).

[72] See my 'Establishing a Liturgical "Text": Text for Performance, Performance as Text', in *The Experience of Late Medieval Worship*, ed. Paul Barnwell, Sally Harper and Magnus Williamson (forthcoming).

recent scholarship, as such. But future historical, literary and musicological investigations of topics where the liturgy is of interest must be aware of the mutability of the liturgical act. This raises questions about how much of the rite could have been based on, or adherent to, written prescriptions. Further questions are raised as to the purpose and function of liturgical books as one type of aide-mémoire within a complex network of aural/oral transmission, memory and precedent which must put paid to the notion of modest parish churches carrying out the exact liturgical practices of a cathedral.[73]

Attention to the variation in liturgical books can provide observations about the medieval Church and its liturgy at least as useful as those observations made possible by identifying what material is common among witnesses of the several Uses. Comparisons of liturgical kalendars, responsory series, post-Pentecost Alleluias, and of the contents of the Sanctorale, as well as more conventional textual analysis, will offer a more nuanced picture of the character of a liturgical book and how it may fit within its wider context. The modern researcher may have much to learn from M.R. James, who wrote of his own contribution to manuscript studies: 'If I have had a part to play, it has been that of making known, with what fullness of description I could, the existence of a mass of material, and assigning dates and provenances which in the main are, I hope, correct'.[74] It is with this optimistic statement that the reader is encouraged not to consign the idea of the medieval liturgy to the Procrustean bed of reductive and unrepresentative editions, but, rather, to respect variants as part of the signature, or unique character, of each manuscript or print, in future investigations. Such future work needs to be informed by the principle that every written witness to a liturgical observance, whether manuscript or print, is necessarily the result of interpretation on the part of its creators, scribes, redactors and users.

---

[73] Further attention to these topics is paid by Carol Symes, chapter 10 of this book.

[74] Richard Pfaff, *Montague Rhodes James* (London: Scolar Press, 1980), 330.

PART III
Diversity

Chapter 6

Interpreting Diversity: Excommunication Rites in the Tenth and Eleventh Centuries

Sarah Hamilton

Students of medieval rites are familiar with encountering variations in the surviving records.[1] It is common to find differences in a particular rite as it is recorded in various manuscripts, whether in the text of individual elements, the inclusion or omission of prayers, the order of service, or in terms of the level of detail specified in rubrics.[2] Overtly liturgical collections, such as pontificals, manuals or sacramentaries, often combine different rites, or record them in a different order from other manuscripts of the same type.[3] And rites are often recorded in diverse contexts, being sometimes copied alongside other ones in liturgical codices, and sometimes in more miscellaneous collections with paraliturgical, that is quasi-exegetical, and legal texts.[4] The disparate nature of the liturgical record is a particular feature of the manuscripts known to modern scholars as pontificals.[5] Here rites that can be performed only by a bishop are collected together in a single codex; the earliest examples to survive are from the ninth century but the genre seems to have developed more fully over the course of the late ninth and tenth centuries.[6] Although their contents vary greatly, they commonly include

---

[1]   As is made clear by other chapters in this volume, especially those by Helen Gittos and Matthew Salisbury. I should like to thank Helen Gittos and Henry Parkes and the anonymous reviewer for their helpful comments and suggestions on an earlier draft, although any errors that remain are, of course, my responsibility.

[2]   For example, see the differences in the *ordo* for confession recorded in two manuscripts made at, and for use by, the community at Fulda some fifty years apart: Sarah Hamilton, *The Practice of Penance, 900–1050* (Woodbridge: Boydell Press, 2001), 144–46.

[3]   See, for example, Henry Parkes' discussion of the Romano-German Pontifical manuscripts in Chapter 4.

[4]   Christopher A. Jones, 'Wulfstan's Liturgical Interests', in *Wulfstan, Archbishop of York: The Proceedings of the Second Alcuin Conference*, ed. Matthew Townend, Studies in the Early Middle Ages, 10 (Turnhout: Brepols, 2004), 325–52; Jones, 'The Book of the Liturgy in Anglo-Saxon England', *Speculum* 73 (1998): 659–702.

[5]   The term is early modern: Charles du Fresne, Seigneur du Cange, rev. D.P. Carpenterius and others, ed., *Glossarium mediae et infimae Latinitatis*, 10 vols. (Niort: L. Favre, 1886), 6:408.

[6]   For example, *Il Cosiddetto Pontificale di Poitiers: Paris, Bibliothèque de l'Arsenal, cod. 227*, ed. Aldo Martini (Rome: Herder, 1979); *Das Kollektar-Pontifikale des Bischofs Baturich von Regensburg 817–84: Cod. Vindob. Ser. N. 2762*, ed. Franz Unterkircher, SF 8 (Freiburg:

ordines for clerical ordination, the dedication of churches, the blessing of chrism, the administration of penance, holding synods, rites for public penance, and sometimes those for excommunication and confirmation. Alongside these rites which could only be administered by a bishop are often found others such as those for confession, baptism, administering to the dying, as well as other liturgical texts, including those for masses and benedictions, and also tracts of liturgical exegesis and commentary, legal and historical writings.[7]

These variations in what constituted the contents of pontificals raise particular problems for scholars seeking to explain the origins and purpose of these new collections. Two main explanations for the emergence of the pontifical as a distinct codex in the late ninth and tenth centuries have been proposed. Some researchers regard them as essentially didactic products of the growth of episcopal self-consciousness and increasing emphasis upon episcopal authority found in west Frankia in the second half of the ninth century, England during the tenth-century reforms, and mid-tenth-century Germany.[8] Such an approach tends to emphasize

---

Universitätsverlag, 1962). For analysis of the early pontificals see Niels Krogh Rasmussen with Marcel Haverals, *Les pontificaux du haut moyen âge: Genése du livre de l'évêque*, Spicilegium Sacrum Lovaniense: Etudes et Documents 49 (Leuven: Spicilegium Sacrum Lovaniense, 1998); for a summary of Rasmussen's work see Palazzo, *History*, 195–99. See also the manuscripts listed in Vogel, *Medieval Liturgy*, 226–30.

7   The collections known to modern scholars as pontificals went by a variety of different names in the Middle Ages, pointing to a certain ambiguity, perhaps, in both use and understanding arising from the heterogeneity of their contents; in Old English they were variously described as *halgungboc* (consecration book) and *bletsungboc* (blessing book; that is, benedictional which were often found together with collections of episcopal rites): see Helmut Gneuss, 'Liturgical Books in Anglo-Saxon England and their Old English Terminology', in *Learning and Literature in Anglo-Saxon England: Studies Presented to Peter Clemoes on the Occasion of His Sixty-Fifth Birthday*, ed. Michael Lapidge and Helmut Gneuss (Cambridge: Cambridge University Press, 1985), 91–141, at 131–33. I am not aware of any study of the medieval Latin terminology for these books although Henry Parkes is currently working on this topic. One eleventh-century churchman clearly envisaged them as bishop's books: Archbishop Lanfranc of Canterbury (1070–89) referred to an *ordo* 'in our codices of episcopal ordines' (in nostris episcopalis ordinis codicibus) in a letter dated 1070–77: see *The Letters of Lanfranc Archbishop of Canterbury*, ed. and trans. Helen Clover and Margaret Gibson (Oxford: Oxford Univeristy Press, 1979), Letter 14, p. 86; I owe this reference to Henry Parkes.

8   Eric Palazzo, 'La Liturgie de l'occident médiéval autour de l'an mil: Etat de la question', *Cahiers de civilisation médiévale* 43 (2000): 371–94; also Palazzo, *L'Evêque et son image: L'illustration du pontifical au moyen âge* (Turnhout: Brepols, 1999), 35–46; and Palazzo, *History*, 195–212; David N. Dumville, *Liturgy and the Ecclesiastical History of Late Anglo-Saxon England: Four Studies* (Woodbridge: Boydell, 1992), 91–95; Cyrille Vogel, 'Le pontifical romano-germanique du Xe siècle: nature, date et importance du document', *Cahiers de civilisation médiévale* 6 (1963): 27–48; Vogel, *Medieval Liturgy*, 235–36.

the importance of top-down reforming impulses and interpret pontificals as part of attempts to promote a unified episcopal liturgy. Henry Parkes has highlighted the problems with this approach to the German evidence in Chapter 4. Others, recognizing the lack of uniformity in the early pontificals, and the importance of local features, have instead argued that they were compiled for pragmatic reasons for use by bishops when touring their dioceses. They view pontificals as a consequence of the ninth-century pastoral reforms which promoted regular diocesan visitations, rather than as a vehicle for reform. For example, Niels Krogh Rasmussen argued in his study of the earliest pontificals that they were practical collections. He thought that the earliest pontificals were compilations of *ordines* recorded in separate *libelli* which had been brought together in a single codex for ease of use.[9] But as Richard Pfaff has pointed out, the lack of a contents list taken together with the variation in content between different codices would have made it difficult for those unfamiliar with a particular manuscript to find their way around it.[10] As Rasmussen himself acknowledged, many second-generation pontificals of the late tenth and eleventh centuries were larger and much more encyclopaedic in their coverage than the earliest ones.[11] He suggested that they may have been intended to serve as library copies; that is, authoritative records of liturgical rites which would then be copied into now-lost *libelli* for actual use. They might also serve as books for teaching and reflection, as is suggested by the inclusion of liturgical tracts in some of the manuscripts attributed to the Romano-German family. He therefore left open the question as to whether all pontificals were pragmatic texts to support the administration of rites or whether they were not sometimes intended to instruct bishops and their officers in how to administer rites, offering an aspirational view of how the rite should be conducted rather than a strict guide to use. Others have suggested that some collections point to a more academic interest in liturgy.[12]

---

[9] Rasmussen, *Les pontificaux du haut moyen âge*; see also Rasmussen, 'Célébration épiscopale et célébration presbyteriale: une essai de typologie', in *Segni e riti nella chiesa altomedievale occidentale: 11–17 aprile 1985*, Settimane di Studio del Centro italiano di studi sull'alto medioevo 33 (Spoleto: Centro italiano di studi sull'alto medioevo, 1987), 581–603; and 'Unité et diversité des pontificaux latins aux VIIIe, IXe, et Xe siècles', in *Liturgie de l'église particulière et liturgie de l'église universelle*, Bibliotheca Ephemerides liturgicae subsidia 7 (Rome: Edizioni Liturgiche, 1976), 393–410. On their relationship to practice see also Hamilton, *Practice of Penance*, esp. 104–72.

[10] Richard Pfaff, 'The Anglo-Saxon Bishop and His Book', *Bulletin of the John Rylands University Library of Manchester* 81 (1999): 3–24, esp. 7–12.

[11] Rasmussen, 'Unité et diversité', 404–7; *Les Pontificaux du haut moyen âge*, 479–83.

[12] Jones, 'Wulfstan's Liturgical Interests' and 'Book of the Liturgy'; Henry Parkes, 'Liturgy and Music in Ottonian Mainz 950–1025' (PhD diss., University of Cambridge, 2012), 231–78, and in particular his observation about Vienna, Österreichische Nationalbibliothek, Cod. 701: 'Vienna 701 was therefore far less a book of liturgy than a book for the liturgy, a monumental

This debate about why pontificals were created and how they were used is far from being resolved, in part because of the difficulties of finding investigative methods that can deal with the extent of variation in the evidence of the rites themselves. As Christopher A. Jones has suggested, it is necessary not only to work on books as a whole but also to proceed 'ritual by ritual'.[13] That is, in order to begin to think about why churchmen compiled a pontifical, it is important to think about the reasons why its individual elements were recorded. Investigating where churchmen chose to document a particular rite – that is, in what sorts of book, and at what stage in the book's compilation, and at the differences in how they recorded the rite – allows us to consider why churchmen sought to record this particular rite, and by extension how they thought about, and understood, the records of medieval rites more generally. Asking why a particular rite was written down in that particular book offers the possibility of insight into the wider problem of what early pontificals were for.

Some rites entered the liturgical record much earlier than others. For example, the practices of both baptism and excommunication are recorded in the New Testament, and the writings of early churchmen are peppered with references to each of them.[14] Such attention to the rites, whereby on the one hand Christians entered the community, and on the other were expelled for contravening its rules, is not surprising. What is odd is that whilst rites for baptism are recorded amongst the earliest liturgical books to survive, the earliest excommunication rites do not appear until much later, from c. 900 CE and first appear in collections of canon law; excommunication is not recorded in liturgical books until the early eleventh

---

library of knowledge and experience', 254. Ramussen was also aware of this dimension to pontifical manuscripts: Rasmussen, 'Unité et diversité', esp. 403–4.

[13] 'A fast rule in the study of liturgical manuscripts generally, and of pontificals especially, is that relations between books as wholes cannot be argued merely on the evidence of this or that single component. And yet the working out of such larger relationships has few options but to proceed ritual by ritual': Chrisopher A. Jones, 'The Chrism Mass in Later Anglo-Saxon England', in *The Liturgy of the Late Anglo-Saxon Church*, ed. Helen Gittos and M. Bradford Bedingfield, HBS Subsidia 5 (London: HBS, 2005), 105–42, at 128.

[14] Jesus Christ commands his disciples to baptize: Matt. 28:19; He commands them to excommunicate the obdurate after three warnings, first in private, then before witnesses, and finally before the church: Matt. 18:15–17. For the history of baptism see Bryan D. Spinks, *Early and Medieval Rituals and Theologies of Baptism: From the New Testament to the Council of Trent* (Aldershot: Ashgate, 2006), also J.D.C. Fisher, *Christian Initiation: Baptism in the Medieval West: A Study in the Distintegration of the Primitive Rite of Initiation*, Alcuin Club Collections 47 (London: SPCK, 1965); on that of excommunication see Paul Hinschius, *Das Kirchenrecht der Katholiken und Protestanten in Deutschland*, 6 vols. (Berlin: Guttentag, 1869–97; repr. Graz: Akademische Druck- und Verlagsanstalt, 1959), 4:691–864, 5:1–492; K. Hein, *Eucharist and Excommunication: A Study of Early Christian Doctrine and Discipline* (Frankfurt am Main: Herbert Lang, 1973); Elisabeth Vodola, *Excommunication in the Middle Ages* (Berkeley: University of California Press, 1986).

century. Thus there are detailed accounts of baptismal rites in Western Europe from the early sixth century and a complete *ordo* is preserved in the mid-seventh-century Old Gelasian Sacramentary.[15] By contrast, the earliest record of a service for the imposition of excommunication dates to c. 900 and evidence for concern about the regulation of this procedure only goes back some fifty years before that.[16] For, as Florence Chave-Mahir, Louis Hamilton and Mette Brunn also demonstrate in their chapters, the evidence of liturgical books is only ever part of the story for a particular rite. Letters, tracts, laws and sermons all suggest that both baptism and excommunication were administered long before rites for them were first set down. The relatively late arrival of a service for excommunication in the historic record allows us to think about why churchmen chose to document it. Baptismal *ordines* might be copied unthinkingly from earlier models; the decision to record an excommunication rite is likely to have been a much more conscious one for the churchmen of the tenth and eleventh centuries. Excommunication therefore offers a useful way into exploring the larger question about why pontificals were created and how they were used.

Between Law and Liturgy: The Early History of the Rite

As mentioned above, the earliest dateable text for the imposition of excommunication is in a tenth-century Rheims manuscript. Here, alongside a collection of canon law, is a record of the sentence imposed by the bishops of the province of Rheims (north-eastern France) upon the murderers of Archbishop Fulk, which is very precisely dated to 6 July 900 CE.[17] It sets out the particular formula used on that occasion in terms which are very similar to one found in the collection of church law compiled by the Lotharingian abbot Regino of Prüm a few years later.[18] Writing sometime between 906 and 913 for the archbishops

---

[15] *Liber Sacramentorum Romanae aeclesiae ordinis anni circuli (Cod. Vat. Reg. lat. 316/ Paris Bibl. Nat. 7193, 41/56): Sacramentarium Gelasianum*, ed. Leo C. Mohlberg, RED series maior, fontes 4 (Rome: Herder, 2nd edn. 1968), 32–33, 36, 39, 42–53, 67–68, 72–74; Spinks, *Early and Medieval Rituals*, 109–15. On the Old Gelasian, which now survives in a mid-eighth-century manuscript, see Vogel, *Medieval Liturgy*, 64–70.

[16] Berlin, Staatsbibliothek, Ms. Phillips 1765, fols. 95r–v; Isolde Schröder, *Die westfränkischen Synoden von 888 bis 987 und ihre Überlieferung*, MGH Hilfsmittel 3 (Munich: MGH, 1980), 153–57. On the ninth-century background see Wilfried Hartmann, *Kirche und Kirchenrecht um 900. Die Bedeutung der spätkarolingischen Zeit für Tradition und Innovation im kirchlichen Recht*, MGH, Schriften 38 (Hannover: Hahnsche Buchhandlung, 2008), 276–86.

[17] See n. 16 above.

[18] Regino of Prüm, *Libri duo de synodalibus causis et disciplinis ecclesiasticis*, II.416, ed. F.W.H. Wasserschleben, rev. Wilfried Hartmann (Darmstadt: Wissenschaftliche

of Trier and Mainz (Germany), Regino set out how a bishop should investigate the behaviour of both priests and laity within each local church, and provided a portable guide to canon law to support a bishop in his visitation. This includes an account of the process for the excommunication of contumacious sinners and the reconciliation of penitent excommunicants.[19] By following this rite the bishop proclaimed the separation of offenders from the community of the living and the services of the Church in this life, and the probability of their exclusion from the community of the saved in the afterlife. At the same time Regino made provision for the restoration of the truly penitent. Its very severity meant that the rite could only be performed by a bishop.

Regino's account of the rite for the imposition of excommunication has a number of features which are worth noting because he set out a structure which proved extremely popular:

- The rite takes place within the mass, after the reading of the Gospel, and before the consecration of the bread and wine.
- It begins with a formal address by the bishop to the clergy and people in which he names the person to be excommunicated, and outlines the nature of his offence.[20] The bishop explains that due legal process has been followed and the offender has already been warned three times by letter and priest, but has chosen to ignore these calls to 'emendation, satisfaction and penance'.[21] Citing precedents from the New Testament the bishop announces that he therefore cuts the offender off from the body of the Church with the sword of excommunication.
- The bishop then recites a formula to impose the excommunication sentence. Invoking the judgement of God, St Peter and the Petrine authority granted him to bind and to loose in heaven and on earth he

---

Buchgesellschaft, 2004), 444. On the similarities see Genevieve Steele Edwards, 'Ritual Excommunication in Medieval France and England, 900–1200' (PhD diss., Stanford University, 1997), 23–50.

19   Regino, *Libri duo*, II.412–18, 438–46. Hartmann's edition is slightly abridged and omits the second address and one of the alternative formulae, canons II.414–15; these are available in Wasserschleben's original 1840 edition or in the more problematic, but easily available edition in *PL* 132:361–62 where they are numbered cc. 411–12.

20   '**Allocutio.** Noverit caritas vestra, fratres mei, quod quidam vir nomine N. ... (**Address.** Let your affection know, my brothers, that a certain man named so-and-so ...)', Regino, *Libri duo*, II. 412, 438. *Note:* For reasons of brevity, the forms 'he', 'him', etc., are used throughout, although the same actions would apply to women offenders.

21   '... misimus ad eum presbyterum nostrum et literas commonitorias semel et iterum atque tertio, invitantes eum canonice ad emendationem et satisfactionem et poenitentiam, corripientes eum paterno affectu', Regino, *Libri duo*, II.412, 438.

excludes the offender 'from the boundaries of mother church in heaven and on earth'.[22]

- All those present should respond three times: 'Amen', or 'Fiat', or 'Let him be anathema'.[23]

- At the conclusion of the sentence twelve priests standing around the bishop with burning lights in their hands throw them to the ground and trample them out with their feet.

- Using the vernacular, the bishop explains the sentence to the people so that they understand that the excommunicant is damned and that anyone who communicates with him in any way will be similarly excommunicated.[24]

- Letters announcing the sentence should be sent to the priests of all the parishes in the diocese to be read out after the Gospel to ensure everyone avoids contact with the excommunicant.

- All the bishops of the province should be notified of the sentence, as should the archbishop.

Regino also includes various alternative texts: one for the bishop's initial address and three other versions of an actual excommunication formula.[25] These variants appear intended to allow the bishop to tailor his service to a particular situation. The first address is for someone who has attacked either church property or churchmen, devastating and plundering the Church, violently overwhelming and killing the poor of Christ and seizing their goods. The second version, however, is for a person who has 'withdrawn through apostasy from observance of the whole Christian religion' and is more appropriate for someone who has ignored the Church's injunctions, such as those on incest in marriage, for example.[26] The formulae similarly allow the minister to adjust the service to the nature of the offence and, perhaps, to the time available; they include one headed 'Another more terrible excommunication' and another 'A brief excommunication'.[27]

---

[22] '... et a liminibus sanctae matris ecclesiae in coelo et in terra excludimus', Regino, *Libri duo*, II.413, 442.

[23] 'Et respondeant omnes tertio: *Amen*, aut: *Fiat*, aut: *Anathema sit*', Regino, *Libri duo*, II.413, 442.

[24] 'Post haec episcopus plebi ipsam excommunicationem communibus verbis debet explanare, ut omnes intelligant, quam terribiliter damnatus sit', Regino, *Libri duo*, II.413, 442.

[25] Regino, *Libri duo*, II.414–17, 444; *PL* 138:361–62.

[26] 'Audistis, dilectissimi, quanta et quam horrenda pravitatis ac iniquitatis opera Ill. a diabolo instigatus perpetrare non timuerit et quomodo per apostasiam a totius christianae religionis cultu profana mente recesserit', Regino, *Libri duo*, II. 414.

[27] Regino, *Libri duo*, II.416–17, 444.

Regino envisaged the rite as being successful and leading, in time, to the submission of the sinner to the bishop's authority, because a description of how to conduct a service for the reconciliation of an excommunicant follows immediately.[28] Its main features again proved influential:

- The bishop, surrounded by twelve priests, meets the penitent in front of the doors of the church.
- He establishes whether the offender has already done penance, and if he has not, his willingness to do so.
- The bishop then takes the penitent by the hand and leads him into the church, restoring him to Christian communion and society.
- The bishop enjoins a formal penance on him.
- The bishop notifies the clergy in and outside the diocese of the penitent's reception back into Christian society.

Crucially, however, Regino made no mention of the prayers to be said on this occasion, confining himself to instructions as to how the service should be conducted.

Unlike his usual practice elsewhere in the collection, Regino failed to attribute any of his canons on excommunication to an earlier authority. It seems probable, however, that he drew on contemporary customs in Trier for his account.[29] But it is unlikely that he recorded a purely local custom, for his prescription for the rite fits with what is known of practice elsewhere within the ninth-century Frankish Church from surviving snippets. For example, the place of the service within the mass fits with another account written in the neighbouring province of Rheims a quarter of a century or so earlier: Archbishop Hincmar of Rheims (d. 882) instructed his diocesan clergy that although it was the usual practice to read excommunication sentences after the Gospel, they could, if they chose, read them before as some offenders had taken to leaving church before the Gospel in order to avoid public censure.[30] Further confirmation that Regino recorded current practice rather than proscribing a novel one comes from parallels in the

---

[28]   Regino, *Libri duo*, II.418, 446. On this particular rite see Sarah Hamilton, '*Absoluimus uos uice beati petri apostolorum principis*: Episcopal Authority and the Reconciliation of Excommunicants in England and Francia, c. 900–c. 1150', in *Frankland. The Franks and the World of the Early Middle Ages: Essays in Honour of Dame Jinty Nelson*, ed. Paul Fouracre and David Ganz (Manchester: Manchester University Press, 2008), 209–41.

[29]   As suggested by comparisons with other evidence undertaken by both Paul Fournier, 'L'oeuvre canonique de Réginon de Prüm', *Bibliothèque de l'Ecole des Chartes* 81 (1920): 5–44, at 11–12; and Wilfried Hartmann, 'Die *Capita incerta* im Sendhandbuch Reginos von Prüm', in *Scientia veritatis. Festschrift für Hubert Mordek zum 65. Geburtstag*, ed. Oliver Münsch and Thomas Zotz (Ostfildern: Thorbecke, 2004), 207–26.

[30]   Ep. 17: *PL* 126:101–4.

phrases and structure between the first formula in his collection and the slightly earlier formula for the murderers of Archbishop Fulk.[31] Combined together, the evidence from the provinces of Rheims and Trier suggests that the broad outline of the excommunication liturgy was already well established by the time it was first recorded at the beginning of the tenth century.

The two scholars who have studied the excommunication liturgy most recently, Roger Reynolds and Genevieve Steele Edwards, both concluded that the formal liturgy set out by Regino underwent relatively little change between the tenth and fifteenth centuries.[32] It quickly entered both the canon law and liturgical traditions. Regino's outline was thus copied by later legal compilers; Burchard of Worms (d. 1025) made a few alterations in his popular canon law collection, the *Decretum*, which served in turn as the source for the selections in Ivo of Chartres (d. 1116) and Gratian (c. 1140).[33] At the same time excommunication entered the liturgical tradition; five out of the ten eleventh-century manuscripts used by Cyrille Vogel and Reinhard Elze in their edition of the Romano-German Pontifical incorporated a service seemingly based on Regino's texts.[34] The rite seem to have been much less widely copied in twelfth-century liturgical collections.[35] In the late thirteenth century, however, when

---

[31]   See n. 17 above.

[32]   Roger E. Reynolds, 'Rites of Separation and Reconciliation in the Early Middle Ages', *Segni e riti nella chiesa altomedievale occidentale: 11–17 aprile 1985*, Settimane di Studio del Centro italiano di studi sull'alto medioevo 33 (Spoleto: Centro italiano di studi sull'alto medioevo, 1987), 405–33; Steele Edwards, 'Ritual Excommunication', 51–76. Christian Jaser reaches very similar conclusions in his recent study: *Ecclesia maledicens. Rituelle und zeremonielle Exkommunikationsformen im Mittelalter* (Tübingen: Mohr Siebeck, 2013).

[33]   Burchard, *Decretum*, XI.2–8, *PL* 140:856–61; Ivo of Chartres, *Decretum*, pars XIV, cc. 75–79, *PL* 161:844–48, and now the provisional edition by Martin Brett and Bruce Brasington at http://project.knowledgeforge.net/ivo/decretum.html (last accessed 25 June 2013) (Burchard XI.2–6 i.e. omits rubrics and reconciliation rite); Gratian, *Decretum*, C XI.q.3, cc. 106–8 (Burchard XI.3 (part), XI.7, XI.8 i.e. includes part of rubric for XI.3 and reconciliation rite): Gratian, *Decretum magistri Gratiani*, ed. E. Friedberg, Corpus iuris canonici 1 (Leipzig, 1879), digitized and available at Münchener DigitalisierungZentrum Digitiale Bibliothek http://geschichte.digitale-sammlungen.de/decretum-gratiani/online/angebot) (last accessed 25 June 2013).

[34]   Montecassino, Archivio della Badia, Ms. 451 (c. 1050), Rome, Biblioteca Vallicelliana, Cod. D. 5 (s. xi²), Eichstätt, Diözesanarchiv, Cod. B. 4 (1071–73), Vendôme, Bibliothèque municipale, Ms. 14 (s. xi¹); Henry Parkes, *PRG Database: A Tool for Navigating Le Pontifical Romano-Germanique, ed. Cyrille Vogel and Reinhard Elze* at http://database. prg.mus.cam.ac.uk/index.php (last accessed 25 June 2013). The excommunication rites in Bamberg, Staatsbibliothek, Ms. Lit. 53 will be considered below as they depart more substantially from those recorded in Regino and Burchard.

[35]   *Le pontifical romain au moyen âge*, ed. M. Andrieu, Studi e Testi 86–88, 99, 4 vols. (Vatican City: Biblioteca Apostolica Vaticana, 1938–41), 1:9–10, 93. This may be because

William Durandus wished to compose a comprehensive pontifical, he returned to Regino's texts to create his rite for excommunication.[36] Durandus' text was influential, circulating in the fourteenth and fifteenth centuries, before being printed as the *Pontificale Romanum* in 1485.[37] Consequently Durandus' rite remained current until the liturgical reforms of the Second Vatican Council. Scholars have, however, drawn attention to the varied formulae seemingly composed ad hoc in response to specific situations, such as that for the murderers of Archbishop Fulk, and which are recorded in medieval manuscripts from the tenth century onwards.[38] This chapter seeks to revise the prevailing view that the formal liturgy was essentially rather static.

What follows is a case study of the rites for excommunication recorded in four pontificals copied in one political region, the German Reich in the eleventh century. They represent some of the earliest examples of the rite to survive in liturgical collections. The myth of the Romano-German Pontifical, exposed by Henry Parkes in Chapter 4, means that the German Church in this period has often been viewed as having a relatively homogeneous pontifical tradition.[39] Investigating four examples of rites classified as belonging, in some way, to the group of Romano-German pontificals, allows us to explore the tensions between top-down reforming and bottom-up localizing factors in their production, and also those between law and liturgy, within a rite traditionally viewed as static and unchanging. These four examples have been chosen first for their chronological range; they cover the whole century. Secondly, they each include rites for both the imposition and reconciliation of excommunication, which allows us to compare like with like. Thirdly, a digitized version of each manuscript is freely available so readers are able to consult the manuscript evidence for themselves. The evidence of each manuscript will be reviewed in turn in chronological order.

The Bamberg Pontifical: Bamberg, Staatsbibliothek, Ms. Lit. 53

This pontifical was compiled at the instigation of King Henry II (1002–24) for the see of Bamberg (Franconia, Germany) which he founded in 1007.[40] It

---

free-form formulae were more widely used and copied at this time: see Steele Edwards, 'Ritual Excommunication', 58n30, 77–110.

36   *Le pontifical romain*, ed. Andrieu, 3:609–15.

37   *Le pontifical romain*, ed. Andrieu, 3:xv, 17–22.

38   Reynolds, 'Rites of Separation and Reconciliation'; Steele Edwards, 'Ritual Excommunication'.

39   See also the critique of this picture for penitential rites in Hamilton, *Practice of Penance*, 104–72.

40   H. Hoffmann, *Buchkunst und Königtum im ottonisch und frühsalischen Reich*, 2 vols., MGH Schriften 30 (Stuttgart: Hiersemann, 1986), 1:406–7; and his *Bamberger*

is a large and comprehensive collection of rites in 192 folios, measuring some 27.3 × 19.6 cm. Cyrille Vogel and Reinhard Elze used it as one of their base texts for the Romano-German Pontifical (*PRG*).[41] The excommunication rites in Bamberg Ms. Lit. 53 amply demonstrate Henry Parkes' interpretation of the *PRG* as a modern editorial construct; numbered 85 to 91 out of the 258 separate rites in the printed edition, here they constitute the final element in a varied and comprehensive collection, running from half way down fol. 191r (l.15) to half way down fol. 192v (l.18); the remainder of this folio is blank.[42] Hartmut Hoffmann suggested that this manuscript is the work of two scribes, near contemporaries of each other; the excommunication rites were copied by hand B who essentially supplemented the work of the main scribe, hand A.[43] Both their place in the manuscript, and the evidence of palaeography, suggest these rites were added as something of an afterthought to the main text.

The first text, rubricated 'the Excommunication of Pope Leo', takes the form of a letter from 'Pope Leo' to the 'archbishops and their suffragans and abbots and congregations of monks living in Francia'.[44] Masquerading as a papal letter, it is in fact a liturgical formula for the excommunication of those who take church property, following the structure for all such formulae in first identifying the offenders and their offences (invading the possessions of St Peter), then invoking God's curses on them, before making provision for him to lift the sentence if the reprobates repent, and concluding with the proclamation of anathema and excommunication.[45] It is distinguished from all of Regino's formulae by its harshness, as is clear from the text of the last of the eleven maledictions, that is, curses:

> And just as the Lord gave to Blessed Peter the Apostle and his successors, whose succession we hold, however unworthy, the power that whatever they bind on earth shall be bound on earth and in heaven, and whatever they loose on earth shall be loosed on earth and in heaven, thus to those [people], if they do not

---

Handschriften des 10. und 11. Jahrhunderts, MGH Schriften 39 (Hannover: Hahn, 1995), 145. For a full description of its contents see *OR*, 1: 41–63. A digitized copy is available at the Staatsbibliothek Bamberg Kaiser-Heinrich-Bibliothek, http://bsbsbb.bsb.lrz-muenchen. de/~db/0000/sbb00000131/images/index.html (last accessed 25 June 2013).

[41] *PRG*, 1:xiii, 3, 8.

[42] *PRG*, 1:308–21.

[43] Hoffmann, *Buchkunst*, 1:406–7.

[44] 'Leo episcopus seruus seruorum Dei, dilectissimis, fratribus et filiis archiepiscopis atque suffrageneis eorum, abbatibus et monachorum congregationibus in Francia commanentibus salutem perpetuam', Bamberg, Staatsbibliothek, Ms. Lit. 53, fol. 191r.

[45] Bamberg cathedral is dedicated to St Peter. It is difficult to know whether this is coincidence or reflects the fact that the rite has been tailored for the locality; some versions of the letter mention the attack on the possessions of St Peter, others on the lands of St Martin; see n. 48 below.

wish to be corrected, we close heaven and we deny the earth for burial and may they be plunged into the lower fire, and may they be consumed for what they did without end.[46]

This threat to bar the gates of heaven is a novel one, and justified by the author's supposed papal authority. The rite itself follows that outlined by Regino; those present should respond to each malediction with 'Amen'; the clergy should stamp out their lights at its conclusion. But this text is especially graphic; it ends: 'as this light is extinguished may their souls be extinguished in the stink of hell'.[47] The vividness of this allusion to the sulphurous smells of the inferno reminds us how rites relied on more than mere words to convey their message.

The Pope Leo formula in Bamberg, Ms. Lit. 53 is the earliest surviving manuscript copy of a text which seemingly circulated more widely across the former Carolingian Empire over the course of the later tenth and eleventh centuries. Its modern editor, Harold Zimmermann, argues it was a forgery originally written for the Abbey of St Martin's in Trier sometime before 947. It is now to be found in some fifteen pontifical collections from the eleventh and early twelfth centuries and four early modern copies of tenth-century monastic charters from Trier (Germany), Fleury (France) and Ripoll (Spain).[48] It is striking that whilst the Pope Leo formula is found in manuscripts and records produced in the Reich, west Frankia, Italy and even Catalonia, it is not recorded in any of the great canon law collections. Although probably composed too late for inclusion by Regino, it was not taken up by either Burchard of Worms or Ivo of Chartres. Instead its insertion into Bamberg, Ms. Lit. 53 testifies to how liturgical records could and did reflect wider contemporary interests, drawing on materials from a variety of sources. At the same time, the recording of a text which seems to have circulated in the context of both other rites and charters, but not canon law, undermines any attempt to postulate a simple shift from canon law to liturgy in the excommunication record.[49] The Bamberg codex

---

[46] 'Et sicut dominus beato petro apostolo eiusque successoribus cuius uicem tenemus quamuis indigni potestatem dedit ut quodcumque ligarent super terram ligarent esset et incaelis et quodcumque soluerent super terram solutum esset et incaelis ita illis si emendare noluerint caelum claudimus et terram ad sepeliendum negamus et dimergantur in inferno inferiori soluantque quod gesserunt sine fine. Amen.', Bamberg, Staatsbibliothek, Ms Lit. 53, fol. 191v.

[47] 'Et sicut lucerna ista extinguitur sic extinguantur animae eorum infetore inferni. Amen.', Bamberg, Staatsbibliothek, Ms Lit. 53, fol. 191v.

[48] Harold Zimmermann, ed., *Papsturkunden 896–1046*, 3 vols. (Vienna: Verlag der Österreichischen Akademie der Wissenschaften, 1984–89), 1:154–62.

[49] On the problematic nature of trying to categorize materials as one or the other, see Janet L. Nelson, 'Liturgy or Law: Misconceived Alternatives?', in *Early Medieval Studies in Memory of Patrick Wormald*, ed. Stephen Baxter et al. (Farnham: Ashgate, 2009), 433–47;

is also unusual in containing only the Pope Leo formula; other pontificals included it alongside other formulae, mostly drawn from Regino's collection. Understanding the wider context in which the Pope Leo formula was recorded is helpful, but it does not, of course, explain why those who requested scribe B add an excommunication rite to Bamberg, Ms. Lit. 53 chose to include this particular text and no others.

One possible explanation for the inclusion of this formula may lie in the insecurity generated by the fact that Bamberg had only been founded recently; its new bishop, Eberhard (1007–40) may have chosen to invoke papal as well as apostolic authority in order to boost his own claims to authority within the newly created and endowed diocese.[50] Another might be to look to the influence of specifically monastic traditions on the compiler, given the text's seeming origins in monastic charter material; the Bamberg pontifical was written by scribes from the monastery of Seeon in southern Bavaria.[51] But perhaps more convincing is the possibility of a direct link between the formula recorded here and the presentation of a royal privilege in favour of Bamberg; there are some very tempting parallels with Bishop Thietmar of Merseburg's description of events at Magdeburg in 979. Writing in the second decade of the eleventh century, Thietmar records how the Emperor Otto II issued a diploma granting the clergy of Magdeburg the privilege of electing their archbishop, and presented them with a book with splendid portraits in gold of himself and his wife, Theophanu; after the Gospel at mass (and thus at the very point where the excommunication sentence was usually proclaimed), the archbishop read the imperial diploma aloud in front of the emperor, and delivered a sermon. He then 'threatened anyone who might dare to infringe this privilege with a terrible excommunication and confirmed this as everyone shouted "Amen, so be it, so be it!"'.[52] The Bamberg excommunication formula is recorded in a similarly

---

also Adriaan Gaastra, 'Between Liturgy and Canon Law: A Study of Books of Confession and Penance in Eleventh- and Twelfth-Century Italy' (PhD diss, University of Utrecht, 2007).

[50]   On the early history of Bamberg, and in particular the need to placate the bishop of Würzburg in whose diocese and on whose lands it was established, see Bernd Schneidmüller, 'Die einzigartig geliebte Stadt – Heinrich II. und Bamberg', in *Kaiser Heinrich II. 1002–1024*, eds., Josef Kirmeier, Bernd Schneidmüller, Stefan Weinfurter and Evamaria Brockhoff (Stuttgart: Theiss, 2002), 30–51.

[51]   Hoffmann, *Bamberger Handschriften*, 145.

[52]   'Quod gratia cesaris et in presentia eius archiepiscopus, preparatus ad missam, cum perlecto euuangelio more solito optime predicasset, recitato coram precepto inperali, quo eleccio continebatur ostendit eundemque quicumque temerarius hoc umquam auderet infringere, terribili excommunicatione damnavit, cunctis prosequentibus 'Amen! Fiat! Fiat!' consolidavit': Thietmar, *Chronicon*, ed. R. Holtzmann, MGH SS rer ger n.s. 9 (Berlin: Weidmannsche Verlagsbuchhandlung, 1955), III.1, 96–98; English translation: *Ottonian*

splendid manuscript to that described by Thietmar, and includes a royal portrait, that of the founder of the see, Henry II, at the front.[53] There are further parallels: the bishoprics of both Magdeburg and Bamberg were recent royal-sponsored foundations; the archbishopric of Magdeburg was established by Otto I in 968, the bishopric of Bamberg by Henry II in 1007. It is therefore feasible that the Pope Leo formula might have been recorded for use on a similar occasion in which the presentation of the pontifical to the see in the presence of the ruler was accompanied by the recitation of a suitably grand excommunication formula against all those who threatened the possessions of the new see.

The text for absolution of excommunicants follows on immediately from the Pope Leo formula under the simple rubric 'Absolutio communicatorum (sic)'. The level of detail it includes offers some clues as to why this rite, and therefore perhaps also the Leonine formula, were recorded. In terms almost identical to those found in other manuscripts associated with the Romano-German group:

- The bishop begins by reciting Psalms 37, 50, 53 and 102, followed by the *Our Father* and ten versicles and responses, ending with Psalm 123.[54] These are set out continuously on the page.
- Six different alternative prayers follow, each written for a single penitent, each petitioning the Lord to show mercy and absolve the repentant sinner.[55]

Germany: The Chronicon of Thietmar of Merserburg, trans. David A. Warner (Manchester: Manchester University Press, 2001), 127. Geoffrey Koziol has highlighted how privileges in tenth-century west Frankia can also be interpreted as 'performative acts': *The Politics of Memory and Identity in Carolingian Royal Diplomas: The West Frankish Kingdom (840–987)* (Turnhout: Brepols, 2012), 17–62.

[53] Bamberg, Staatsbibliothek, Ms. Lit. 53, fol. 2v. Only one of Henry II's diplomata in favour of Bamberg includes a detailed anathema sanction clause: *Heinrici II et Arduini Diplomata*, ed H. Bresslau, H. Bloch, M. Meyer and R. Holtzman, MGH Diplomatum regum et imperatorum germaniae 3 (Berlin: Weidmannsche Verlagsbuchhandlung, 1957), 502, ll. 7–12 (no. 390). This is a grant to the monastery of Michaelsberg, Bamberg; it is a late eleventh-century forgery, but probably based on an original grant made at Aachen in May 1018. Furthermore other, genuine grants made by Henry II also include anathema sanction clauses so there is nothing inherently unlikely in this aspect being genuine as well; ibid., no. 111 (Magdeburg), pp. 136–37, no. 265 (Paderborn), pp. 314–16, no. 193 (Tegernsee), pp. 227–28, no. 343 (Paderborn), pp. 437–38.

[54] 'Primitus dicat episcopus psalmos ...', Bamberg, Staatsbibliothek, Ms. Lit. 53, fol. 192r; compare the edited version in *PRG*, 91.6, vol. 1:318.

[55] Bamberg, Staatsbibliothek, Ms. Lit. 53, fols. 192r–192v; compare those edited in *PRG*, 91.9, 10, 12, 13, 14, vol. 1: 319–20.

This rite is much shorter than others in the Romano-German group; it omits the prescriptive rubric drawn from Regino usually found at the beginning and end of the rite, which includes the scene-setting rubric at the beginning in which the bishop is instructed to check the offender is contrite, and that at the conclusion in which the bishop notifies the wider community of the lifting of the offender's sentence. The prayer for the absolution of several penitents and the text of the concluding blessings and sprinkling with holy water and incense found in some other manuscripts attributed to the Romano-German group are also left out.[56] The rite has been reduced to the psalm *incipits*, the versicles and responses, and prayer texts.

This manuscript thus contains the texts the officiant required to administer these two related rites, but lacks detailed instructions as to how they should be conducted. The minister would require further guidance, whether transmitted through oral traditions or by consulting other works, in order to conduct the rite successfully. The Leonine excommunication formula hints at a world concerned with the authority awarded the bishop in the text rather than the details of the service itself. Much more unusually, the evidence of Thietmar's account, when combined with that for the early history of the Bamberg bishopric, points to a possible context for its addition, namely the ceremonies which accompanied a royal visit rather than the actual imposition of a sentence of excommunication. The greater specificity of the absolution service could have served either as a practical aide-mémoire or as the basis for further reflection by someone interested in assembling materials for an excommunication liturgy. Read on their own, therefore, these rites can thus be variously interpreted as representing a general academic interest in the excommunication liturgy, the preservation of texts that were important to the cathedral's history, or as a guide to ministry for someone already familiar with these rituals.

The Freising Pontifical: Munich, Bayerische Staatsbibliothek, Clm 21587

The Freising Pontifical is also considered a member of the Romano-German group. It contains a more detailed and more legalistic account of excommunication than that provided in the Bamberg codex.[57] Written in the Bavarian diocese of Freising for its bishop sometime in the first half of the eleventh century, the

---

56   *PRG*, 19.16–18, vol. 1:321.

57   *OR*, 1:241–54; Vogel and Elze did not use this manuscript to compile their edition of the Romano-German Pontifical. A digital copy is accessible at Münchener DigitalisierungsZentrum Digitale Bibliothek, http://daten.digitale-sammlungen. de/~db/0006/bsb00060092/images/, fols. 152r–159v (accessed 25 June 2013). On this manuscript see now E. Klemm, *Die ottonischen und frühromanischen Handschriften der*

excommunication rites are copied in the hand of the main scribe.[58] Their inclusion in the codex was planned from the start; whereas they were added as a second thought at the end of the Bamberg Pontifical, in Munich, Clm 21587 they are found sandwiched between the *ordo* for holding a synod (fols. 146v-152r) and those for the administration of the ordeal and the exorcism of demons (fols. 159v–168v). Those for excommunication are thus copied alongside two other rites which also entered the liturgical repertoire late: ordeal and exorcism also seem to have been more peripheral to the content of pontificals in this period. Whereas exorcism left little trace at all, some elements of the rites for ordeal, like those for excommunication, were recorded in both pontificals and compilations of legal material from the ninth century onwards.[59] That the Freising rite for excommunication follows on from that for holding a synod may suggest an association of ideas on the part of the compiler, for excommunications were often imposed in the context of a provincial synod, as at Rheims in 900 CE.[60]

The rite itself is highly dependent on the one first described by Regino, and subsequently copied by Burchard, but it also has some differences which point perhaps to a different source, and possibly also to a degree of reflection on the part of the scribe. Andrieu argued that the compiler made use of Burchard of Worms' *Decretum* throughout the codex.[61] But, at least in the excommunication rites, the compiler included some telling differences which make it unlikely that Burchard

---

Bayerischen Staatsbibliothek, 2 vols. (Wiesbaden: Reichert, 2004), 1:96–97 (no. 71), 2:148 (pls 147–48).

[58]   *OR*, 1:241–43.

[59]   On exorcism see F. Chave-Mahir, Chapter 7 in this book. On the pontifical record of rites for ordeal, see especially S. Larratt Keefer, 'Ðonne se cirlisca man ordales weddigeð: The Anglo-Saxon Lay Ordeal', in *Early Medieval Studies in Memory of Patrick Wormald*, ed. S. Baxter et al. (Farnham: Ashgate, 2009), 353–67; also in the same volume, J.D. Niles, 'Trial by Ordeal in Anglo-Saxon England: What's the Problem with Barley?', 369–82; and on clerical ordeal see S. Larratt Keefer, '*Ut in omnibus honorificetur Deus*: The corsnæd Ordeal in Anglo-Saxon England', in *The Community, the Family and the Saint: Patterns of Power in Early Medieval Europe*, ed. J. Hill and M. Swan (Turnhout: Brepols, 1998), 237–64. In general see Robert Bartlett, *Trial by Fire and Water: The Medieval Judicial Ordeal* (Oxford: Clarendon Press, 1986), 2–33.

[60]   See n.16 above. Other examples of excommunication being promulgated at a synod include: Council of Trier (948), described in Flodoard, *Annales*, a. 948, in *Les Annales de Flodoard*, ed. Philippe Lauer (Paris: Alphonse Picard et Fils, 1905), and Richer's *Histories*, II. 82, ed. Hartmut Hoffmann, *Richeri Historiarum Libri IIII*, MGH SS 38 (Hannover: Hahnsche Buchhandlung, 2000); the Council of St Basle (991), the Council of Pavia (998), Council of Rome (998/99), c. 1, *Die Konzilien Deutchlands und Reichsitaliens 916–1001: Teil 2: 962–1001*, ed. Ernst-Dieter Hehl with Carlo Servatius, MGH Concilia 6.2 (Hannover: Hahnsche Buchhandlung, 2007), 439, 565–67, 574; Fulbert of Chartres, *The Letters and Poems of Fulbert of Chartres*, ed. F. Behrends (Oxford: Oxford University Press, 1976), Ep. 79, 138–40.

[61]   *OR*, 1:245n1.

was his immediate source. For example, he gave the rite for the imposition of excommunication a novel title; following Regino and Burchard, it is usually described as the excommunication of the unfaithful (*infideles*); the Freising pontifical introduces it as the *ordo* for excommunicating the *incorrigibiles*, the uncorrectable or incurable. This switch reflects local traditions; a similar title is also used in the roughly contemporary later recension of the Freising canon law collection – the *Collectio duodecim partium* – known as '1 CDP'.[62] The initial rubric in the Freising Pontifical goes into more detail than either Regino or Burchard about at what point in the mass the rite should be conducted, who should be present, and how the rite should be choreographed.[63] The phrases in italics signify the added details:

- When he is going to excommunicate anyone for certain and manifest crimes the bishop should do so in a *public* mass with the clergy and all the people, *entering in full procession from the sanctuary*, and sing the mass in the usual way up until after the Gospel.
- He should deliver the sentence *standing on the top step of the lectern*, surrounded by priests holding burning lights which they ought to throw down and trample with their feet at the conclusion of the anathema. *Then he should summon the rebel three times that he should return to the bosom of Holy Mother Church.*
- If the offender does not truly wish to change, the bishop should address the congregation. The text here is identical to that found in Regino and Burchard.
- An excommunication formula follows; the text is identical to that which is subsequent to this particular address in both Regino and Burchard's prescriptions for the service.[64] Three alternative formulae follow, as in Regino and Burchard.[65]

---

[62] Personal communication from Henry Parkes. On *Collectio duodecim partium* see Jörg Müller, *Untersuchungen zur Collectio Duodecim Partium* (Ebelsbach: Gremer, 1989) who identified 2CDP as the earlier recension of the text, and 1CDP as the later recension, finished around 1039; for a useful summary see Linda Fowler-Magerl, *Clavis Canonum. Selected Canon Law Collections Before 1140. Access with Data Processing*, MGH Hilfsmittel 21 (Hannover: Hahnsche Buchhandlung, 2005), 91–93; and on the relationship with Burchard's *Decretum* see now Greta Austin, 'Freising and Worms in the Early Eleventh Century: Revisiting the Relationship between the *Collectio duodecim partium* and Burchard's *Decretum*', *Zeitschrift der Savigny-Stiftung für Rechtsgeschichte: kanonistische Abteilung* 124 (2007): 45–108.

[63] Fols. 152r–v.

[64] Regino, *Libri duo*, II.412–13, pp. 438–42; Burchard, *Decretum*, XI.2–3, *PL* 140: 856–58; *PRG*, 85.2–3, vol. 1:308–10.

[65] He uses the same rubrics as Burchard (which are different from those in Regino) for the formulae: 'Prima excommunicatio', fol. 154r = Burchard, XI.3; 'Excommunicatio

- The service concludes with the bishop explaining the meaning and consequence of the sentence to the people in the vernacular; letters should be sent to all the priests of the diocese notifying them of the sentence and requesting that it is read out at Sunday mass. The sentence should also be notified to the bishops and metropolitan.[66]

The address in the Freising pontifical differs from that found in Regino and Burchard's legal collections in only one other substantial way: it makes provision for the minister to refer to multiple excommunicants by including a plural reading above the line; the compiler was anxious to ensure that the minister used the correct words for the situation. When this aspect is combined with the Freising rite's most novel feature, the duplication in both the rubric and the episcopal address of the reference to warning the excommunicant *three times* before imposing the sentence, it suggests a compiler interested in ensuring the rite was administered correctly and in conformance with church law. The Freising rite is thus encyclopaedic in its scope. Like those outlined in both Regino and Burchard, it provides the minister with the text of an alternative episcopal address to the congregation followed by three further excommunication formulae. Overall the language and order suggest that the compiler of this rite was building on a different redaction of the text from that in the law collections by Regino and Burchard which owes rather more to Freising local traditions.

The rite for the reconciliation of excommunication is similarly suggestive of a local tradition which shares many features with that recorded in both the 'Romano-German' tradition and Burchard's redaction of Regino. Thus the rubric is found elsewhere within the Romano-German group, but the prescription to recite the seven penitential psalms and the versicles and responses comes from Burchard. Two of the three prayers are those used by Burchard, although the compiler may have drawn them either from Burchard or an earlier Freising tradition.[67] Regino's instructions are again split, so that the initial rubric

---

secunda', fol. 156r = Burchard XI.5; 'Excommunicatio tertia', fol. 156v = Burchard XI.6; and 'Excommunicatio quarta', fol. 157r = Burchard XI.7.

[66]   Fols. 157v–158r; the rubric, although identical with that in Regino and Burchard, comes here at the end of the service rather than as in Regino and Burchard where it follows on from the text of the first excommunication formula: Regino, *Libri duo*, II.413, 442–44; Burchard, *Decretum*, XI.3, *PL* 140:858.

[67]   Fols. 158r–159v. Prayers: *Deus misericors* (Burchard XI.8), *Famulum tuum* (source unknown), *Maiestatem quaesumus* (Buchard XI.8). Unlike other manuscripts in the Romano-German group which incorporated prayers from both the Gregorian and Gelasian traditions, those in the rite in Burchard's *Decretum* have a solid Gelasian pedigree: Hamilton, '*Absoluimus*', 217, 236–41. The extent and nature of the relationship between Burchard's *Decretum* and Freising's *Collectio duodecim partium* is still debated; Müller, *Untersuchungen*; Hartmut Hoffmann and Rudolf Pokorny, *Das Dekret Burchard von Worms. Textstufen-Frühe*

instructs the bishop to receive the penitent, and introduce him to the church, where prayers of absolution are said, whilst the final rubric instructs the bishop to notify his fellow bishops that the sentence has been lifted.

It is clear that the compiler of the Freising rite drew up the rites for both excommunication and reconciliation with an eye to ensuring they were delivered in accordance with church law, but also gave thought to their structure in order to signal their message more clearly. It is the product of reflection on both the law and purpose of these rites, and it is significant that local canon law collections testify to a very similar practice. At the same time, the formal nature of the script, the hierarchy of scripts used to signify titles and rubrics, and the general *mise-en-page* of the rite in the manuscript itself, all point to considerable investment in a large and legible text which would have been easy for a minister to consult. The versicles and responses are set out in two parallel columns, for example, rather than running into each other.[68] Taken together, the content and physical features of the Freising Pontifical's excommunication rite suggest it was recorded by someone interested in promoting the effective delivery of the rite. At the same time it is evidence for the powerful influence of local tradition on a liturgy which did not yet have a long pedigree in liturgical books.

The Cambrai Pontifical: Cologne, Diözesan-und-Dombibliothek, Cod. 141

This pontifical was copied in the mid-eleventh century for the bishop of Cambrai at the monastery of Saint Vaast in Arras, northern France.[69] The excommunication rites come towards the end of the collection, copied between the *ordo* for the blessing of a pilgrim (fols. 177r–179r) and two blessings for meat on Easter Sunday, followed by one for fruits (fols. 183r–184r). This rite was a planned element in the whole corpus; the title, *ordo excommunicationis*, in uncial, is in blue; the rubrics are written in alternate red and blue lines; there are elaborate foliate initials for some of the major texts, coloured in gold, green, blue and red. This decoration accords with that used elsewhere in the book and testifies to the fact that this is a very high status and expensive manuscript.

Whilst similar to that found in other, earlier manuscripts associated with the Romano-German Pontifical group, the rite for the imposition of excommunication is by no means identical to them or to their precedents in

---

Verbreitung-Vorlagen, MGH Hilfsmittel 12 (Munich: MGH, 1991), 87–107. The evidence of the Freising pontifical needs to be placed against these wider debates about the extent and nature of the exchange between Worms and Freising in the second quarter of the eleventh century.

[68]   Munich, Bayerische Staatsbibliothek, Clm 21587, fol. 158v.

[69]   *OR*, 1:108–14. A digitized version is available at Codices Electronici Ecclesiae Coloniensis, http://www.ceec.uni-koeln.de/ (accessed 25 June 2013).

tenth-century law; the differences in the rubric, in particular, suggest that it has not been blindly copied. The *ordo* starts, as specified in Regino, with the bishop delivering the address 'Noverit caritas vestra, fratres' (Let your affection know, brothers) after the Gospel. But it includes the instructions that the bishop should 'climb the pulpit so that he can address the clergy and people'.[70] Note the similarity to the injunction in the Freising pontifical to deliver the sentence from the top step of the lectern. The address which follows is a significantly abbreviated version of that first recorded in Regino, and copied with only minor adjustments into both Burchard and various of the liturgical manuscripts in the Romano-German group. As Table 6.1 indicates, the text in the Cambrai pontifical is more straightforward, and therefore the message is much clearer.

In the Cambrai Pontifical, the bishop informs his brothers that N. has, disregarding his baptismal promise to renounce Satan, attacked the Church, overpowering and killing the poor of Christ, and seizing their goods. The bishop has therefore sent a legate to the offender with warning letters inviting him, according to the canon, to correction and satisfaction and penance. Because he has ignored these warnings he should now be condemned. It concludes: 'we commit him to the judgement of God with all his accomplices and fellow participants and supporters and we excommunicate him'. The Cambrai rite omits the lengthy references to the bishop's authority, to the ways in which the excommunicant has reneged on his baptismal promises, and the citation of different apostolic justifications for excommunication. Whilst many versions refer to the fact that the excommunicant has been warned three times, as set out in canon law, the Cambrai rite carefully does not specify a number. The address is followed by a rubric specifying that the priests should stand around the bishop with lighted candles which they should throw on the ground at the conclusion of the excommunication sentence.[71] In other texts the number of priests is specified as twelve; here the exact number is not prescribed. The result is a more straightforward text, which is more concerned to communicate its message clearly, less legalistic in tone, and more practical to use.

The formula for the imposition of excommunication then follows. Beginning 'Ex auctoritate dei', its text is not to be found in earlier legal collections or in other manuscripts associated with the Romano-German Pontifical group.[72] Such 'Ex auctoritate dei' formula are usually recorded ad hoc rather than as part of an *ordo*; whilst made up of existing phrases, they

---

[70] '... ascendat super pulpitum et sic alloquatur et clerum et populum', fol. 179r; compare rubric in Regino, *Libri duo*, II. 412, p. 438; Burchard, *Decretum*, XI.2, col. 856; *PRG*, 85.1, vol. 1:308.

[71] Fol. 180r.

[72] Fols. 180r–181r.

vary substantially from each other.[73] Through the authority conferred by God on the minister he separates those named from society and from Holy Mother Church both on earth and in heaven and petitions that they be condemned to perpetual fire along with Dathan and Abiron, Judas and Pilate, Nero and Simon Magus. This formula includes several responses in which those listening affirm and take part in the excommunication. They are asked, 'Do you excommunicate?' and reply, 'We excommunicate.' 'Do you damn? We damn. Do you anathematize? We anathematize.'[74] It provides, in other words, for an occasion in which all those clergy taking part participate in the rite itself. Whilst rites from Regino onwards had allowed some element of response, crying 'Amen' after the maledictions and 'So be it, so be it' (Fiat, fiat), at the conclusion of the sentence, this text is unusual in encouraging those assembled to join in the imposition of the sentence. It is not, however, unique: similar choruses are prescribed in a rite added to an existing manuscript at Worcester around c. 1100.[75] The Cambrai rite ends with instructions, found in other, seemingly earlier texts, in which the bishop explains the consequences of excommunication to the congregation in the vernacular (*communibus uerbis*) so that they all understand how terrible it is to be damned and so that they do not have any contact with the excommunicant.[76] The Cambrai pontifical therefore followed the structure and rubrics of other rites but inserted a different address and a different formula for imposition into the rite itself.

The next rubric reads 'Sequitur absolutio' (Absolution follows).[77] This presumably refers to absolution as accompanying the earlier rite rather than to a one-stop service! The reconciliation rite belongs to the Regino family. Unlike its precedents which were composed for a singular penitent excommunicant, the rite in the Cambrai pontifical is written for several penitents. Again, it also omits any reference to twelve priests, instead referring to the bishop being supported by his clergy. Instead of describing in detail how the bishop should introduce the

---

[73] Reynolds, 'Rites of Separation and Reconciliation', 416–17; Steele Edwards, 'Ritual Excommunication', 77–110. I intend to consider these ad hoc formulae in much greater detail in a forthcoming article; the variations in their texts suggest engagement with a lively tradition of excommunication in many sees, whilst the fact that such formulae were often added as one-offs to existing liturgical collections also has more to tell us about how liturgical rites were regarded and recorded than it is possible to consider here.

[74] 'Excommunicatis et vos. R. Excommunicamus. Dampnatis et vos. R. Dampnamus. Anathematizatis et vos. R. Anathematizamus', fol. 181r.

[75] Cambridge, Corpus Christi College, Ms. 146, p. 330; for digital images of this manuscript see Parker Library on the Web, at http://parkerweb.stanford.edu/ (last accessed 5 July 2013)

[76] Regino, *Libri duo*, II.413, 442–44; Burchard XI.3, *PL* 140:858. See also that edited in *PRG* 85.6, vol. 1:311.

[77] Fol. 181r.

Table 6.1 Comparison between the rite for the imposition of excommunication recorded in the Romano-German Pontifical tradition and that in the Cambrai Pontifical

PRG 85.2 (based very much on Regino, *Libri duo*, II.412)	Cambrai Pontifical Cologne, Cod. 141, fols. 179r–180r
Noverit caritas vestra fratres mei quod quidam vir nomine N. diabolo suadente postponens Christianam promissionem quam in baptismo professus est per apostasiam conversus post satanam cui abrenunciavit et omnibus operibus eius vineam Christi id est ecclesiam eius devastare et depraedare non pertimescit pauperes Christi quos pretioso sanguine suo redemit violenter opprimens et interficiens et bona eorum diripiens. Unde quia filius huius nostrae ecclesiae <u>cui Deo auctore praesidemus</u> debuerat esse <u>quia in ea per aquam et spiritum sanctum renatus est inter adoptivos filios Dei adnumeratus quamvis modo filius diaboli sit imitando diabolum</u> solliciti ne per negligentiam pastoralem <u>aliqua de ovibus nobis creditis</u> deperiret <u>pro qua in tremendo iudicio ante principem pastorum Dominum nostrum Iesum Christum rationem reddere compellemur iuxta quod ipse</u> terribiliter nobis comminatur dicens: *Si non adnunciaveris iniquo iniquitatem suam sanguinem eius de manu tua requiram* (Ezech. 3:18) misimus ad eum <u>presbyterum nostrum</u> et litteras commonitorias <u>semel et iterum atque tertio</u> invitantes <u>eum</u> canonice ad emendationem et satisfactionem et poenitentiam <u>corripientes eum paterno affectu</u>.	Noverit caritas vestra fratres mei quod quidam vir nomine N. diabolo suadente postponens Christianam pro- (fol. 179v) missionem quam in baptismo professus est per apostasiam conversus post satanam cui abrenunciavit et omnibus operibus eius vineam Christi id est ecclesiam eius devastare et depraedare non pertimescit pauperes Christi quos pretioso sanguine suo redemit violenter opprimens et interficiens et bona eorum diripiens. Unde quia filius nostrae ecclesiae debuerat solliciti ne per negligentiam pastoralem deperiret **unde dominus** terribiliter nobis comminatur dicens: *Si non adnunciaveris iniquo iniquitatem suam sanguinem eius de manu tua requiram* (Ezech. 3:18) misimus ad eum **legatum** nostram et litteras commonitorias invitantes canonice ad emendationem et satisfactionem et poenitentiam.

PRG 85.2 (based very much on Regino, *Libri duo*, II.412)	Cambrai Pontifical Cologne, Cod. 141, fols. 179r–180r
May your charity know, my brothers, that a certain man named N., having been persuaded by the devil, neglecting the Christian promise which he professed at baptism, turned back through apostasy to Satan, whom he had renounced with all his works, has not been afraid to devastate and pillage the vineyard of Christ, that is his Church, violently overwhelming and killing the poor of Christ whom he redeemed through his precious blood, and plundering their goods.	May your charity know, my brothers, that a certain man named N., having been persuaded by the devil, neglecting the Christian promise which he professed at baptism, turned back through apostasy to Satan, whom he had renounced with all his works, has not been afraid to devastate and pillage the vineyard of Christ, that is his Church, violently overwhelming and killing the poor of Christ whom he redeemed through his precious blood, and plundering their goods.
Whence, because he ought to be the son of this our Church <u>which we preside over by the authority of God because he was reborn in it through water and holy spirit and numbered amongst the adopted sons of God although like a son of the devil he imitates the devil</u>, careful lest through pastoral negligence any of the sheep entrusted to us be lost, for whom in the last judgement before the first prince of shepherds our Lord Jesus Christ we will be compelled to give account, just as he himself threatened us most terribly, saying 'If you will not make known his sin to the sinner, I will require his blood from your hand' (Ezech. 3:18); we sent to him <u>our priest</u> and warning letters <u>once and again and a third time</u>, inviting him according to the canon to emendation, and satisfaction and penance, <u>rebuking him with paternal affection</u>.	Whence, because he ought to be the son of this our Church, careful lest through pastoral negligence, **just as the Lord** threatened us most terribly saying 'If you will not make known his sin to the sinner, I will require his blood from your hand' (Ezech. 3:18), we sent to him our **legate** and warning letters inviting him according to the canon to emendation, and satisfaction and penance.

Sed ipse proh dolor diabolo cor eius indurante monita salutaria sprevit et incoepata malitia perseverans ecclesiae Dei quam laesit superbiae spiritu inflatus satisfacere dedignatur. De talibus itaque transgressoribus et sanctae religionis pacisque quam Christus suis discipulis dedit atque reliquit, violatoribus praecepta dominica et apostolica habemus quibus informamur quid de huiuscemodi praevaricatoribus agere non oporteat. Ait enim Dominus in evangelio *Si peccaverit in te frater tuus corripe eum* (Matt. 18:15). Fratres in unoquoque nostrum peccat quia in sanctam ecclesiam peccat. Si enim sancta ecclesia unum corpus est cuius corporis caput Christus est, singuli autem sumus alter alterius membra et cum patitur unum membrum compatiuntur omnia membra procul dubio in non peccat qui membra nostra laedit. Iubet ergo Dominus ut frater id est Christianus in nos peccans primo secrete corripiatur deinde cum testibus redarguatur novissime in conventu ecclesiae publice conveniatur. Quod si has tres admonitiones et pias correptiones contemnit et satisfacere despicit post haec *sit tibi,* inquit, *sicut ethnicus* (Matt. 18:17), id est gentilis atque paganus ut non iam pro Christiano sed pro pagano habeatur; et in alio loco membrum quod a sua compage resolvitur et a iunctura caritatis dissociatur et omne corpus scandalizat, Dominus abscindi et proici iubet, dicens Si oculus vel manus vel pes tuus

Sed pro dolor sprevit aecc-(fol. 180r)lesiae Dei satisfacere dedignatur.

Nunc autem quia has commonitiones et crebras uocationes contempnit. *Sit nobis sicut dominus praecepit sicut ethnicus et puplicanus* (Matt. 18:17). Hinc ergo eum cum universis complicibus et communicatoribus fautoribusque suis iudicio dei comittemus et eum excommunicamus.

But he, oh sorrow, <u>his heart hardened by the devil</u>, scorned <u>salutary admonishments and persevering in the evil begun against</u> the church of God, <u>whom he had injured, inflated with the spirit of pride</u>, refused to make satisfaction.

<u>We have the precepts of the Lord and the apostles about such great transgressors of holy religion and peace which Christ gave or left to his disciples about violators, which inform us what it is proper for us to do about these kinds of transgressor. For as the Lord said in the gospel: 'If your brother sins against you, rebuke him' (Matt. 18:15) That brother sins against everyone of us because he sins against holy Church. For if the holy Church is one body, the head of which is Christ, and we are each members of that body, one of another, and what is suffered by one member (of the body) is suffered by all members, it is beyond doubt that he who sins against wounds (all) our members. (Christ) orders therefore that he is secretly reproved, then refuted before witnesses, and lastly brought publicly into the assembly of the Church. But if he disregards these three warnings and pious reproofs and despises to make satisfaction, after this 'let him be to you as a heathen', that is as a gentile or pagan, so that he is not held to be a Christian but a pagan. And in another place the Lord orders the member which has been separated from its joint and become disassociated from the structure of charity and scandalises the</u>

But, oh sorrow, he scorned the church of God and refused to make satisfaction.

For now because he has shown contempt for these warnings and repeated callings, 'Let him be to us', as the Lord instructs, 'as a heathen and a publican' (Matt. 18:17). Hence therefore we commit him with all his accomplices and fellow participants and protectors to the judgement of God and we excommunicate him.

scandalizat te erue eum et proice abs te
(Matt. 8–9). Et apostolus: Auferte, inquit,
malum ex vobis (1. Cor. 5:13). Et item:
Infidelis si discedit, discedat (1. Cor. 7:15).
Et in alio loco rapaces a regno Dei excludit,
dicens; Neque rapaces regnum Dei
possidebunt (1. Cor. 6:10). Et alibi: Si quis
frater nominatur et est fornicator aut adulter
aut homicida aut rapax cum huiusmodi nec
cibum sumere licet (1. Cor. 5:11). Et
Iohannes dilectus prae ceteris Christi
discipulus talem nefarium hominem salutare
prohibebat dicens: Nec ei ave dixeris neque
eum in domum receperis. Qui enim ei ave
dicit communicat operibus eius malignis (2.
Ioh. 10–11). Dominica itaque atque
apostolica praecepta adimplementes
membrum putridum et insanabile quod
medicinam non recipit ferro
excommunicationis a corpore ecclesiae
abscidamus ne tam pestifero morbo reliqua
membra corporis veluti veneno inficiantur.

Key: bold represents text new to the Cologne manuscript not found in the *PRG* edition or earlier versions of this text. <u>Underline</u> indicates text omitted from that in the *PRG* edition in the Cologne manuscript. *Italics* indicate biblical quotes.

whole body to be cut off and thrust out saying 'If your eye, hand or foot scandalises you, cut it off and thrust it from you' (Matt. 18:8–9). And the Apostle said: 'Put away the evil person from among yourselves' (1 Cor. 5: 13). And also: 'If the unbeliever departs, let him depart' (1 Cor. 7:15). And in another place he excludes the grasping from the kingdom of God saying 'Nor will the rapacious possess the kingdom of God' (1 Cor. 6:10). And elsewhere: 'If any man that is called a brother is a fornicator or adulterer or murderer or thief, let no one eat dinner with such a person' (1 Cor. 5:11). And John the disciple beloved by Christ before others forbade greeting such an evil man saying: 'Neither say Ave nor receive him in the home. For whoever says Ave to him shares his evil works' (2 John 10–11). And so fulfilling the precepts of the Lord and the apostles we cut off with the sword of excommunication from the body of the Church this putrid and unhealthy member which will not receive medicine lest by such a destructive illness the remaining members of the body will be infected as if by poison.

penitent into the church and thus return him to Christian society, the bishop is instructed 'he should absolve them in this way'.[78] After an antiphon and the seven penitential psalms, various *preces*, that is versicles and responses, follow in a sequence which is almost identical (apart from one of the *preces*) to that used in the Metz pontifical. Three prayers petitioning the Lord to absolve the penitent follow, all of which are found in other manuscripts in the Romano-German tradition.[79] A simple prayer rubricated 'Absolutio' then follows: 'May the almighty and merciful Lord grant forgiveness and absolution and remission of all your sins and a period of penance and correction of your life'.[80]

The rite ends with a rubric instructing the bishop to introduce the penitents into the church and return them to communion and Christian society, and to enjoin penance on them. This particular text is found in earlier descriptions of the rite, where it is placed before the prayers of absolution; here it signifies the end of the rite; its placing is both practical and logical. Unlike the descriptions given in other accounts there is no mention of the need to publicize the reconciliation to other dioceses.

What are we to make of this seemingly more streamlined version of the rite? One possibility is that the compiler edited a rite similar to that cited in Regino, removing the references to legal niceties and the need for an elaborately manned ritual in order to produce a clearer one. The tenor is certainly very different from the legal concerns of that in the Freising Pontifical. But the evidence of canon law, for example, suggests that it was much more usual for compilers to expand upon existing texts, bringing in extra material, rather than excising extraneous material.[81] It is therefore more likely that the rite recorded in the Cambrai Pontifical reflects a local tradition related to, but independent of, that in Regino, and that both the Cambrai rite and Regino's texts have their roots in earlier ninth-century practice. Other rites within this pontifical can also be linked to localized, regional traditions which reinforce the likelihood of this possibility.[82]

---

[78]   'Absoluat eos hoc modo'. Compare the rubric on fol. 181r with that in Regino, *Libri duo*, II.418, 446; Burchard XI.8, *PL* 140:860–61, and *PRG* 91.1 and 91.3, vol. 1:317–18.

[79]   *PRG* 91.10, 9, 8, vol. 1:319–20.

[80]   'Veniam et absolutionem et remissionem omnium peccatorum vestrorum et spatium penitentiae et emendationem vitae tribuat vobis omnipotens et misericors domnus', fol. 183r.

[81]   See for example the examples considered by A.H. Gaastra, 'Penance and the Law: The Penitential Canons of the Collection in Nine Books', *Early Medieval Europe* 14 (2006): 85–102.

[82]   Rites for penance: Hamilton, *Practice of Penance*, 154–55, 160–61, and Appendix 2, Table 4. Coronation rite: *Ordines Coronationis Franciae: Texts and Ordines for the Coronation of Frankish and French Kings and Queens in the Middle Ages*, ed. Richard A. Jackson, 2 vols (Philadelphia: University of Pennsylvania Press, 1995–2000), 1:201–16.

The visual splendour of this manuscript testifies to the importance awarded to both the pontifical liturgy itself, and local liturgical traditions, in mid-eleventh-century Cambrai; the codex is a physical manifestation of the claims of Cambrai's bishop to authority. The contemporary *Deeds of the Bishops of Cambrai* testifies to how vulnerable this was at times.[83] The inclusion of an excommunication rite within such a statement is not surprising, for the rite itself articulated the bishop's claims to spiritual oversight and authority over his flock; he alone could exclude people from Christian society and the prospect of salvation in the afterlife. Its presence here tells us as much about episcopal ambitions as about the practice of excommunication within Cambrai.[84]

The Metz Pontifical: Paris, BN, Ms. latin 13313

Our final example is from late eleventh-century Metz (France).[85] This pontifical was probably originally written for Metz in the first quarter of the eleventh century and a supplement was added there in the second half of the eleventh century; various further texts were then added in Lotharingian hands in the later eleventh and twelfth centuries. The texts of an excommunication formula, together with penitential psalms and *preces* followed by four prayers for the reconciliation of excommunicants are amongst these late eleventh/twelfth-century additions. They were written in two different hands on the blank folios at the end of a quire in the middle of the manuscript as follows:

---

[83] *Gesta episcoporum Cameracensium*, ed. L.C. Bethmann, MGH SS 7 (Hannover: Hahn, 1846), 393–504. The pontifical could have been made for Bishop Gerard I of Cambrai-Arras (1012–51) or his nephew and successor Bishop Lietbert (1051–76). Both have been the subject of a great deal of scholarly attention; see especially most recently Laurent Jégou, 'L'évêque entre authorité sacrée et exercice du pouvoir. L'exemple de Gérard de Cambrai (1012–1051)', *Cahiers de civilisation médiévale* 47 (2004): 37–55; Theo M. Riches, 'Bishop Gerard I of Cambrai-Arras, the Three Orders and the Problem of Human Weakness', in *The Bishop Reformed: Studies of Episcopal Power and Culture in the Central Middle Ages*, ed. John S. Ott and Anna Trumbore Jones (Aldershot: Ashgate, 2007), 122–36; John S. Ott, '"Both Mary and Martha": Bishop Lietbert of Cambrai and the Construction of Episcopal Sanctity in a Border Diocese around 1100', in *The Bishop Reformed*, 137–60.

[84] It is perhaps worth noting here that Riches, in 'Bishop Gerard I of Cambrai', highlights the interest in excommunication within Gerard's circle.

[85] A digitized version is available at 'Pontifical de Trèves', Gallica, Bibliothèque nationale de France, http://gallica.bnf.fr/ark:/12148/btv1b90669992.r=lat+13313.langEN (last accessed 25 June 2013). The pontifical has an early modern Metz provenance and it seems likely that it was used there throughout the Middle Ages: Hoffmann, *Buchkunst*, 1:254–55. For a detailed description of its contents see Leroquais, *Pontificaux* 2:175–79.

- Excommunication formula (hand 1): fols. 102v, l. 6 to 103r, l. 13
- Antiphon, Psalms, 6, 31, 37, 101, 129, 142, *Our Father*, versicles and responses and three reconciliation prayers (hand 1): fols. 103r, l. 15 to 104r, l. 5
- Reconciliation prayer added in second hand (hand 2): fols. 104r, l. 6 to 104v, l. 14.

There is no mention in either the original collection, or the later supplement, of rites for excommunication; the readers of this codex only later felt the need to add the texts for them to this diverse collection of rites pertaining to the bishop.

There is no title for either the excommunication formula or the reconciliation prayers in the manuscript. The scribe left sufficient space for rubrication, but this was never completed; there are thus three blank lines between the end of the previous text and the start of the excommunication formula on fol. 102v; similarly there is a single blank line between the end of the formula for the imposition of excommunication and the start of the psalms and *preces* sequence which precedes the reconciliation of excommunication on fol. 103r at l. 14. As there is no list of contents either, it is clear that only someone very familiar with both this codex and the liturgy for excommunication would be able to identify these as the texts they needed to perform these rites; clearly experience or instruction would be needed in order to administer this rite using this book, as well as, perhaps, the consultation of other manuscripts.[86]

The text for the imposition of excommunication is identical to one of the formulae recorded in Regino of Prüm's *Libri duo* over a century and a half earlier; it is also to be found in Burchard of Worms' *Decretum*, and in various eleventh-century manuscripts classified by Andrieu as belonging to the Romano-German Pontifical group.[87] Regino classified it as 'Another, more terrible excommunication'.[88] However, the final sentence in the Metz version reads rather oddly: 'And just as these lights from our hands are extinguished today, so may the light of them be extinguished in eternity'.[89]

Other versions included the word *proiectae*, thrown down, after 'from our hands'; although by no means essential to the understanding of this sentence, the word acts as an important instruction to the clergy in the performance of the text. The failure to correct its omission here suggests either that this particular rite was not much read, or that those following it already knew what to do. The rite for the reconciliation of excommunicants similarly omits any rubrics

---

[86]   Indeed, its most recent cataloguer misidentified the initial absolution prayers as those for the reconciliation of penitents: Leroquais, *Pontificaux*, 2:176.

[87]   *PRG* 88, vol. 1:313–14; Burchard, *Decretum*, XI.6, *PL* 140:859–60.

[88]   Regino, *Libri duo*, II.416, 444.

[89]   'Et sicut hae lucernae de manibus nostris hodie extinguuntur, sic eorum lucerna in aeternum extinguatur', fol. 103r.

(and no room was left for them to be added later); it sets out the prayers and antiphons required for a service almost identical to that prescribed in Burchard's *Decretum*, XI.8. The order of service is thus:

- Antiphon: *Create a clean heart in me O God* (Psalm 50:12)
- Seven Penitential Psalms (6, 31, 37, 50, 101, 129, 142)
- *Pater noster*, and various versicles and responses, which are identical to those given in Burchard XI.8
- Prayers petitioning the Lord to absolve the sinner. The first three can be found in Burchard's early eleventh-century version of the rite.[90] A fourth was added in a second later hand: *Deus inmensae clementiae et inaestimabilis indulgentiae qui humane fragilitatis lapsum*. This prayer is not found in Burchard but was recorded in several manuscripts of the Romano-German Pontifical group.[91] The orator begs the God of immeasurable mercy and invaluable leniency to forgive the sinner and through the cure of His grace, restore him corrected and absolved to health.

The rite, in other words, seems designed to be used by someone who only requires the texts of the prayers; they can go elsewhere for instructions on how to conduct the service. It may perhaps have been intended to serve as an aide-mémoire to what was a well-known service or at least one for which guidance on how it should be delivered could be sought elsewhere, perhaps even in Burchard's *Decretum*. It is, however, also possible that these jottings reflect a more academic interest of someone seeking to complete the lacunae in the current collection.

Conclusions

This case study is limited to only four different excommunication rites recorded in pontificals from only one kingdom in one century, that is the eleventh-century German *Reich*; and yet it shows there are considerable differences. Although the sample is small, it suggests a pattern which is worth investigating further. In two instances, the early eleventh-century Bamberg and late eleventh-century Metz pontifical, these rites have been added to the manuscript at a later stage; in both these cases the rites consist of just the texts the bishop needs to conduct the rite without any instructions as to how to do so, or, in the case of Metz, even any titles to identify their purpose. Where rites

---

[90]   XI.8, *PL* 140:861; on its Gelasian origins, see Hamilton, '*Absoluimus*', 217, 237–38.

[91]   *PRG* 91, vol. 1:319. For example, the Bamberg Pontifical; Monte Cassino, Archivio della Badia, Ms. 451; Rome, Biblioteca Vallicelliana, Cod. D. 5; Eichstätt, Diözesanarchiv, Cod. B.4.

were included as a planned element of the whole codex, as in the Freising and Cambrai pontificals, they included a detailed rubric on how they should be conducted. This link between prestigious cathedral copies and more detailed prescriptive texts must be viewed in the light of Carol Symes' arguments for modern scholars taking the proscriptive nature of liturgical texts more seriously: such texts represent clear attempts to regulate rather than describe practice.[92] But attempting to impose a simple dichotomy on the manuscript evidence of didactic texts on the one hand, and pragmatic texts which support ministers who know what they are doing on the other, is more problematic.

While the shared features in the liturgies of the sample of manuscripts studied here hint at a common origin in the ninth-century Frankish practice which predated the earliest surviving account of it by Regino in the early tenth century, whether there was ever a single *Urtext* is much more doubtful. This microstudy demonstrates the varying levels of diversity which characterize the records of liturgical rites more generally, and at the same time highlights some challenges that the study of such texts poses for scholars. For historians interested in excommunication, it is clear that the simple narrative of a broadly static excommunication liturgy postulated by an earlier generation of scholars cannot be sustained. This case study also points to problems with the recent, revisionist accounts postulated by scholars for the pontifical's emergence as a genre. It is difficult to view such texts as the simple product of either reformist or pragmatic tendencies; both played a role, but so did local traditions and what is best described as a more academic interest in recording rites.

These manuscripts show that liturgists played with these rites, editing texts and composing them anew. They thought about both the words and the enactment of the rite. The variations outlined above therefore suggest a lively and ongoing interest in the practice of excommunication. Explaining the reasons for such variations is much less straightforward; each manuscript provides clues as to why that particular rite was copied but taken as a whole the evidence points in five different directions. First, the inclusion of rites without instructional rubrics, such as those for excommunication in the Metz and Bamberg pontificals, might reflect a simple, pragmatic addition for use in a particular service. But not all unrubricated texts fit easily into this category. The inclusion of a number of alternative prayers in the reconciliation service in these two manuscripts points to a second possible reason for their being set down: academic interest. These particular examples might represent the scholarly focus of an individual cleric, a completist anxious to ensure that his church had access to the full episcopal liturgy in one codex. Other examples suggest a

---

[92]　Carol Symes, 'Liturgical Texts and Performance Practices', Ch. 10 below; also her 'The Medieval Archive and the History of Theatre: Assessing the Written and Unwritten Evidence for Premodern Performance', *Theatre Survey* 52.1 (2011): 29–58.

third category: careful reading of individual excommunication rites alongside consideration of their place within the codex indicates a concern with bolstering and articulating episcopal authority, as in the Cambrai and perhaps also the Bamberg Pontificals. The Freising example, however, suggests a fourth reason, a reformist concern with ensuring due legal process. Differences between rites also points to the importance of local traditions, as at Cambrai. Comparison with records in canon law can help to explain how particular variations are indebted to the influence of local, diocesan traditions, as is particularly evident at Freising.

As the Freising Pontifical makes clear, looking beyond liturgical books for evidence can also help us to interpret the more overtly liturgical records that survive. Investigating where and how the rite of excommunication was recorded has revealed that excommunication was caught somewhere between canon law and liturgy. Although prescriptions as to how it should be conducted are first recorded in legal or quasi-legal collections from the early tenth century, it only begins to be written down in liturgical books from the early eleventh century onwards. This pattern is not dissimilar to that for penance, for example, where *ordines* for hearing confession were first attached to penitentials in the ninth century, before migrating into liturgical collections in the tenth and eleventh centuries.[93] But the pattern for penance is confused by the fact that some formulae for the older Late Antique rite of public penance, rather than confession, do appear in the earliest liturgical collections from the eighth century.[94] The chronology for excommunication is much clearer: the earliest surviving evidence for a formal rite is almost coterminous with the earliest pontifical collections. But unlike other episcopal rites, such as those for the dedication of churches and the ordination of clergy, excommunication did not get recorded in the early pontificals. And even after it did so, it seems not to have been a standard component of pontifical collections from the central middle ages; many from the eleventh and twelfth century do not include any excommunication rites.[95] It seems instead to belong with the more marginal rites such as those for ordeal or exorcism. And yet, it is clear from the way in which some east Frankish compilers incorporated the rite for excommunication into their liturgical collections over the course of the eleventh century that it was something which they often felt needed to be there, adding it later where necessary, as at Bamberg and Metz. Recording the rite tended to be the result of active choice; it had not become an 'expected' part of the pontifical repertoire, but was peripheral, entered as a response to particular situations or interests. Pontificals in this period were not, as Henry Parkes has demonstrated in Chapter 4, the static or rigid compilations

---

[93] Hamilton, *Practice of Penance.*

[94] *Sacramentarium Gelasianum*, ed. Mohlberg, 17–18, 56–58.

[95] Further research is required to establish how far excommunication became a more common feature of later medieval pontificals.

suggested by modern editions. And it is clear that by 1100 excommunication was not yet part of the liturgical canon.

It is perhaps easier to ask the question why excommunication was considered peripheral than to answer it. Does this mean that for some compilers it really belonged in the courtroom, and thus inside legal books? Franz Kerff has somewhat controversially argued on the basis of similar legal evidence that penance was a judicial rather than pastoral rite, suited to the episcopal court rather than the priest's ministry; might this be the case with excommunication?[96] But just as Kerff's arguments have been overturned both on the basis of the pastoral content of the texts of the penitential *ordines*, and because of their presence in priests' books, so the fact that eleventh-century compilers usually added excommunication rites to liturgical rather than other sorts of books suggests that at least some people regarded it as a liturgical rite.[97] The compilers of these books thought that it best belonged with other rites in a liturgical collection to which the cantor could make reference as necessary when preparing the bishop to conduct what, after all, must have been a formidable and frightening service for those who witnessed it.[98] Identifying patterns like this suggests that churchmen had very clear ideas about the purpose and scope of pontificals; more work on their contents, both those regarded as core as well those viewed as more marginal, will help to reveal more exactly what these were. It is, however, already clear that any attempt to come up with a single explanatory model for the emergence of pontificals is doomed to failure. As the rites for excommunication studied here testify, they were recorded for various ends, and this diversity in intention should be incorporated into future research on pontificals.

---

[96]   F. Kerff, '*Libri paenitentiales* und kirchliche Strafgerichtsbarkeit bis zum Decretum Gratiani: ein Diskussionsverschlag', *Zeitschrift der Savigny-Stiftung für Rechtsgeschichte: kanonistische Abteilung* 75 (1989): 23–57.

[97]   On Kerff see Raymund Kottje, 'Busspraxis und Bussritus', in *Segni e riti nella chiesa altomedievale occidentale, 11–17 aprile 1985*, Settimane di Studio del Centro italiano di studi sull'alto medioevo 33 (Spoleto: Centro italiano di studi sull'alto medioevo, 1987), 369–65; Rob Meens, 'The Frequency and Nature of Early Medieval Penance', in *Handling Sin: Confession in the Middle Ages*, ed. Peter Biller and A.J. Minnis (Woodbridge: York Medieval Press, 1998), 35–62. My research into ad hoc excommunication formulae suggests that these were more usually added to liturgical collections in this period; see n. 73 above.

[98]   On the cantor's role more generally see Margot Fassler, 'The Liturgical Framework of Time and the Representation of History', in *Representing History, 900–1300: Art, Music, History*, ed. R.A. Maxwell (University Park, PA: Pennsylvania State University Press, 2010), 149–71.

Chapter 7

Medieval Exorcism: Liturgical and Hagiographical Sources

Florence Chave-Mahir

The saints occupied an important place in medieval liturgy.[1] Their names were spoken many times in both prayers and litanies and they served as models for edification. This relationship is reflected back in saints' lives where they were sometimes depicted as clerics who were masters of liturgical rites. Saints were presented as examples of perfection to inspire the clergy, no more so than in the way that through their lives they continued Christ's own fight against the forces of evil. *Vitae* also presented exemplary models for how rituals could or should be performed. Hagiographic sources may therefore help to illuminate our understanding of liturgical practices, especially less well-documented ones, such as exorcism.[2]

Exorcism is not very visible in liturgical sources from the central Middle Ages. The ritual of exorcism was, however, practised much earlier than that. The minor orders of the Latin Church included the role of exorcist; the exorcist's role was to perform rites considered to be effective in rescuing a possessed person from evil spirits. The person could be either a man or a woman, young or old; they were considered as being possessed by a demon if they displayed forms of unusual behaviour, which are usually described in saints' lives as consisting of fits, shouting incomprehensible words in an unknown language, or committing acts of extreme violence. Liturgical sources which mention exorcisms of the possessed are quite rare before the later Middle Ages; the earliest book dedicated solely to the ritual of exorcism dates to the fifteenth century.[3] In this chapter I will consider what evidence there is for how exorcisms were conducted in the

---

[1]   I want to thank Alwyn Harrison for his translation of my text and Helen Gittos and Sarah Hamilton for their help and advice with writing it.

[2]   On the use of the liturgy by historians, see: Pierre-Marie Gy, *La liturgie dans l'histoire* (Paris: Cerf, 1990); Eric Palazzo, *Les sacramentaires de Fulda: Etude sur l'iconographie et la liturgie à l'époque ottonienne,* Liturgiewissenschaftliche Quellen und Forschungen 77 (Münster: Aschendorff, 1994) and *L'Evêque et son image: L'illustration du pontifical au moyen âge* (Turnhout: Brepols, 1999).

[3]   Munich, Bayerische Staatsbibliothek, Clm 10085; I am preparing an edition of this manuscript with Julien Véronèse: *Rituel d'exorcisme ou manuel de magie? Le manuscrit Clm 10085 de la Bayerische Staatsbibliothek de Munich* (Florence: Edizioni del Galluzzo, forthcoming).

Middle Ages, whether there were standard ways of conducting them, and, if so, whether they were actually followed in practice.

The practice of exorcism was clearly known in the early Middle Ages. Long reserved for the preparation of candidates for baptism, rites for exorcisms in baptismal contexts are first recorded in the Carolingian sacramentaries of the eighth century. All those who were to be baptised needed to be exorcised as they were thought to have been seized by the devil. In some tenth- and eleventh-century pontificals, the purification of catechumens by exorcism was separated from the baptismal liturgy.[4] However, there are few such liturgical sources concerning the treatment of the possessed and those that do survive are little concerned with describing the way in which the ritual should be conducted. What evidence does survive in liturgical books tends to consist of exorcism formulae rather than full *ordines* explaining how the clergy should lead the fight against the devil in this regard.

There are, though, several saints' lives from the central Middle Ages that record in some detail the staging of the conflicts against the devil present in the bodies of the possessed. Some of these texts emphasize accounts of the healing of the possessed and make such events into a significant moment of religious edification; these exorcisms become the grand finale of the story of the saint's life. This particular feature is intellectually and textually indebted to influential *vitae* from the early medieval period.[5] One such saint is St Norbert of Xanten (fl. 1080–1134), the influential clerical reformer and founder of the Premonstratensian order of regular canons, for whom two twelfth-century accounts of his life survive, the earlier *Vita A*, and the slightly later and much longer *Vita B*.[6] The earlier life focuses on its subject's virtues, whilst the later

---

[4]   See Bryan D. Spinks, *Early and Medieval Rituals and Theologies of Baptism: From the New Testament to the Council of Trent* (Aldershot: Ashgate, 2006); Peter Cramer, *Baptism and Change in the Early Middle Ages, c. 200–c. 1150* (Cambridge: Cambridge University Press, 1993).

[5]   The initial studies on exorcism using the hagiographic sources were undertaken by Peter Brown in his *The Cult of the Saints: Its Rise and Function in Latin Christianity* (Chicago: University of Chicago Press, 1981). See also: Dominique Barthélemy, 'La guérison des possédés dans les miracles de saint Benoît', in *Abbon, un abbé de l'an mil*, ed. Annie Dufour and Gillette Labory (Turnhout: Brepols, 2008), 343–67; and 'Devils in the Sanctuary: Violence in the Miracles of Saint Benedict', in *Feud, Violence and Practice: Essays in Medieval Studies in Honor of Stephen D. White*, ed. Belle S. Tuten and Tracey L. Billado (London: Ashgate, 2010), 71–94. I discuss the shortcomings of the liturgical sources compared with the riches of certain hagiographical texts in Florence Chave-Mahir, *L'exorcisme des possédés dans l'église d'occident (Xe–XIVe siècle)*, Bibliothéque d'histoire culturelle du moyen âge 10 (Turnhout: Brepols, 2011), 134–62.

[6]   See pp. 162–63 below for detailed consideration of the authorship and date of the lives and their relationship to one another.

life seeks to situate Norbert's life within the history of the order; both describe his involvement in healing several cases of possession in some detail. In this chapter I shall use the lives of Norbert as a case study, exploring how exorcisms are portrayed in these texts, and compare these descriptions with the scarce liturgical evidence from the same period. The accounts of exorcisms in the lives of Norbert are very detailed and full of references to liturgical texts. Given how little evidence actually survives in liturgical books of the period, it is especially worth investigating whether these hagiographical accounts can tell us anything about how exorcisms were performed in the central Middle Ages. There are two main questions to be considered. To what extent are these hagiographical tales mere echoes of the miracles performed by Christ and thus of *topoi* that had circulated in such writings from Late Antiquity onwards? Or do they provide evidence for how exorcisms were actually conducted in the twelfth century?[7]

The Sources

Liturgical Sources

In terms of the liturgical sources from Western Europe, examples of exorcistic formulae survive in various Carolingian manuscripts; these are derived, as I have mentioned above, from the rites for catechumens. These formulae were then incorporated into the Romano-German Pontifical (henceforth *PRG*) tradition.[8] Manuscripts in the *PRG* tradition, in turn, influenced liturgical sources produced in the same region of Germany, and around the same time, as the lives of Norbert.

---

[7]   The complementarity of liturgy and hagiography is found in other studies. See, for example: Patrick Henriet, *La parole et la prière au moyen âge* (Brussels: De Boeck Université, 2000); Louis I. Hamilton, 'Les dangers du rituel dans l'Italie du XIe siècle entre textes liturgiques et témoignages historiques', in *Mises en scène et mémoires de la consécration de l'Eglise dans l'Occident médiéval*, ed. Didier Méhu (Turnhout: Brepols, 2007), 159–88; and his contribution to the present volume, 'Rites for Dedicating Churches', Chapter 8. See also the recent studies on norms in the hagiographic sources, and in particular the colloquium M.-C. Isaïa and T. Granier, ed. *Normes et hagiographie dans l'occident latin (Ve–XVIe siècles), Lyon 4–6 octobre 2010* (Turnhout: Brepols, 2014), and the account given by Marie-Céline Isaïa in M.-C. Isaïa and T. Granier, ed. *Bulletin du centre d'études médiévales d'Auxerre* 15 (2011): 229–36.

[8]   On this subject, see: Henry Parkes, 'Questioning the Authority of Vogel and Elze's Pontifical Romano-Germanique', Chapter 4 of this book; and Sarah Hamilton's analysis of the study of excommunication in Chapter 6.

Three twelfth-century liturgical manuscripts containing material pertaining to exorcism survive from Germany.[9] The first is a twelfth-century ritual and penitential produced in the Rhine Valley for Cologne Cathedral (now Paris, Bibliothèque Nationale de France, Ms. latin 14833). It consists of a penitential, followed by a ritual – a priest's book – which includes ten or so folios of exorcism formulae.[10] This collection is quantitatively important and it contains many exorcism prayers which are also found in earlier manuscripts associated with the *PRG* tradition. A twelfth-century ritual from Prüm (now Munich, Bayerische Staatsbibliothek, Clm 100) includes a section of six folios dedicated to the exorcism of the possessed.[11] Finally, there is also a manuscript best described as a twelfth-century penitential-ritual (now Munich, Bayerische Staatsbibliothek, Clm 3909). The exorcism formulae for the possessed appear at the very end of this codex, and seem to have been copied from Carolingian sacramentaries via manuscripts in the *PRG* tradition.[12] These manuscripts contain only texts for use in exorcism rituals, not full *ordines* detailing how they were to be conducted.

For evidence as to how these formulae might have been used, we will now turn to the cases of possession described in the life of St Norbert of Xanten, in order to consider how far St Norbert (or rather his biographers) drew directly upon contemporary liturgical tradition in portraying his performance of exorcism. Can such narratives help provide evidence for how exorcism rituals were conducted at that time?

The Tales of Exorcisms in the Vitae *of St Norbert of Xanten: Presentation and Context*

As mentioned above, two different accounts now survive of the *vita* of St Norbert of Xanten, who died in 1134. Both were written soon after his death. The earliest, known as *Vita A*, was written at Magdeburg in Saxony (Germany) by a certain Evermode between 1145 and 1164; the second, called *Vita B*, was produced at Prémontré in Picardy (France) by Hugh de Fosses sometime

---

[9]   As noted by Sarah Hamilton (Chapter 6), the liturgy of excommunication is similar to that of exorcism in the sense that both appear to be 'peripheral' preoccupations in the pontificals of the eleventh and twelfth centuries; indeed exorcism interested the writers of liturgical books even less.

[10]   See Leroquais, *Pontificaux*, 441–42; Chave-Mahir, *L'exorcisme*, 127–28 for the description and 364–76 for the transcription.

[11]   See Adolf Franz, *Die Kirchlichen Benediktionen im Mittelalter* (Freiburg: Herder, 1909), 362; Gy, *La liturgie dans l'histoire*, 110; Chave-Mahir, *L'exorcisme*, 129 for the description and 376–80 for the transcription.

[12]   Chave-Mahir, *L'exorcisme*, 130 for the description and 380–84 for the transcription.

before 1163.[13] Both texts are closely related to each other and follow a similar structure. Although the exact relationship between the two accounts is not yet fully understood, B is twice as long and survives in many more copies. Both lives display a special interest in exorcism and there are several minor variations between them. The lives include six detailed accounts of exorcism and these are associated with decisive moments in the saint's life and the construction of his order.

Four of the examples occur in chapter 4 of both *vitae* A and B. The first of these is said to have happened in 1121 and depicts the spectacular healing of a young girl at Nivelles (France) at precisely the moment that the authority of St Norbert was challenged by certain people close to him.[14] The author of *Vita A* reports how this was a difficult time for Norbert; some people from the town had come to him in order to enter the religious life, but had left, unable to bear the austerity of his way of life and rule, and when he visited Nivelles they tried to turn the townspeople against him. Norbert set out a very high ideal of perfection for his brothers. As regular canons they combined a strict religious life with a commitment to pastoral preaching according to ideals directly influenced by the Gregorian reforms. Norbert adopted the Rule of Augustine, or rather the *ordo monasterii*, which predates that rule. It was in a climate of dispute with his followers over adherence to the life of rigorous discipline that a possessed young girl was presented to him.[15]

In the second example in the *vitae*, the object of Norbert's exorcism is the son of a lay brother at his foundation at Prémontré who had become possessed by the devil. Lay brothers, *fratres laici*, were men who joined Norbert's communities without taking holy orders; they often took care of physical tasks in order to lighten the burden of the monks, or administrative tasks if they were educated men. They sometimes included adult men who had already started a family, as in this case where the devil is described as taking one of the lay brother's sons.[16] At

---

[13] *Vita A*, in *Vita Norberti Archiepiscopi Magdeburgensis*, ed. R. Wilmans, MGH SS 12 (Hanover: Hahn, 1856), 670–706 [BHL 6248]; *Vita B, PL* 170:1253–1344 [BHL 6249]. See also Kasper Elm, ed., *Norbert von Xanten. Adliger, Ordensstifter, Kirchenfürst* (Cologne: Wienand, 1985); Wilfred Marcel Grauwen, *Norbert, Erzbischof von Magdeburg (1126–1134)* (Duisbourg: Prämonstratenser-Abtei S. Johann, 1986). For a translation, see *Norbert and Early Norbertine Spirituality*, ed. and trans. Theodore J. Antry and C. Neel (New York: Paulist Press, 2007).

[14] On the exorcism of Nivelles, see Wilfred Marcel Grauwen, 'De terugkeer van Hugo en de Duiveluitdrijving door Norbert te Nijvel, 1121', *Analecta praemonstratensia* 67, no. 3–4 (1991): 187–97.

[15] *Vita A Norberti*, c. 10, p. 650. On the early period of the order of Prémontré, see Bernard Ardura, *Prémontrés, histoire et spiritualité* (Saint-Etienne: Publications de l'Université de Saint-Etienne, 1995).

[16] *Vita A Norberti*, c. 14, p. 686.

the abbey of Saint-Martin de Laon, for example, there were 450 lay brothers and fifty canons. The lay brothers attended matins, the morning mass and compline, but devoted themselves to manual work or agriculture the rest of the time. The numerical imbalance between lay brothers and monks occasionally caused tensions within the community.[17] The portrayal of a demon attacking the son of one of the lay brothers shows how vulnerable such men were considered to be. As is clear from other sources, lay brothers were sometimes the object of criticism in the twelfth century. It is noteworthy that although the devil was a threat to someone within Norbert's monastery he did not seek to test the community as a whole, though he is depicted as being capable of approaching and attacking brothers close to the Premonstratensians, as the brothers of Prémontré are known. Satan was thus portrayed as a real threat to the order of St Norbert and from one exorcism to the next, he is reported as never forgetting the successive healing rites to which he had been subjected.[18]

In the next case, the devil attacked the porter of the monastery: this time he did not actually take possession, but rather just threatened the man.[19] The porter, as *Vita A* points out, is the brother charged with giving alms to the poor and with receiving guests. His main duty was to watch the entrance of the monastery and one night when he slept he found himself confronted with a terrifying image of Satan. After three successive nocturnal apparitions, the brother denounced the demon in order to make him leave. This example is not a matter of a possession but rather of a diabolic apparition which led the porter to utter a violent reprimand which is textually formally very similar to an exorcism.

In the final episode in this chapter, the devil attacked the steward of a lord of Maastricht.[20] The demon, probably still the same one as appeared to the porter and lay brother's son, is described as flying there. The steward, in charge of the property of his lord, may have committed some sort of crime for which he was punished with this crisis of possession, though the story does not say so specifically. In order to show that the demon attacks members from every group of society, *Vita A* reports that the next victim was a peasant from Vivières.[21] *Vita B* describes how the peasant became possessed whilst drawing water at a fountain. Carried to the local church of Vivières, he was cared for there by Norbert himself.[22] The final episode in *Vita A* recounts the diabolic possession of one of the soldiers of the Emperor Lothar II in Rome. Norbert is reported

---

[17]   See Ardura, *Prémontrés*, 45.

[18]   When Norbert asks the demon who he is, he answers that he is the one who was in the girl from Nivelles: 'Ei miser, quid agam? Ego sum, inquit, qui fui in puella Nivigellae coram Norberto magistro tuo, albo cane' (*Vita A Norberti*, c. 14, p. 686).

[19]   *Vita A Norberti*, c. 14, p. 687.

[20]   *Vita A Norberti*, c. 14, pp. 687–88.

[21]   *Vita A Norberti*, c. 15, p. 690.

[22]   *Vita B Norberti*, p. 843.

as healing him only because the pope had refused to do so.[23] As *Vita A* makes clear, Norbert had accompanied Lothar II to Rome in 1133, in order to show his support for Pope Innocent II whose authority had been challenged by the Antipope Anacletus II.

As this summary makes clear, the majority of the accounts of exorcism or diabolic episodes which pepper the story of Norbert's life serve to underline key moments in both his life and in the establishment of his order. They thus serve to validate the saint's authority during his life, and thus the development of his cult.

An Exorcism as Part of the Mass

Exorcism rituals were closely associated with the mass. Bernard of Clairvaux (d. 1153), for example, advocated performing exorcism at the moment of communion within the mass itself.[24] Norbert was not depicted in the *vitae* as actually carrying out his exorcisms whilst celebrating mass; nevertheless, the mass provides an important framework for exorcism in both the accounts in Norbert's *vitae*, and in the evidence of contemporary liturgical texts. As I will go on to discuss, in some of the more detailed stories in the lives, exorcism was associated with the gathering of the community brought about by the mass. The link between exorcism and the mass is also present in some of the twelfth-century liturgical manuscripts; the ritual and penitential of Cologne, for example, includes a 'missa pro demoniaco' at the end of the rite relating to exorcism of the possessed.[25]

One of the striking features of the exorcisms in the life of Norbert is that they are often connected with the mass. In the story of the liberation of the steward of Maastricht from the demon, the author of *Vita A* specifies that the possessed man was brought to St Norbert just after the celebration of the annual parish feast day. Norbert is described as still wearing his holy vestments, the alb and the stole, when the possessed man was brought before him; these vestments were considered to be highly effective against the demon, as the story emphasizes at several points.[26] The first exorcism in *Vita A*, the healing of the young girl

---

[23]   *Vita A Norberti*, c. 20, p. 702.

[24]   See Florence Chave-Mahir, 'Trois exorcismes eucharistiques de saint Bernard de Clairvaux', in *Pratiques de l'eucharistie dans les églises d'orient et d'occident*, ed. Nicole Bériou, Béatrice Caseau and Dominique Rigaux (Paris: Institut d'études augustiniennes, 2009), 987–1000.

[25]   See Paris, Bibliothèque Nationale de France, Ms. latin 14833, fol. 42v (Chave-Mahir, *L'exorcisme*, 376) and the 'Missa super demoniacum' (*PRG* 121, vol. II: 221–22).

[26]   'Cum sacris adhuc amictus vestibus immo sancti Spiritus virtute accinctus ad debellandum hostem importunissimum accederet, fratres quidam rogabant eum, ut imbecillitati suae parceret, quia iam vespera erat' (*Vita A Norberti*, c. 14, p. 687).

of Nivelles, does not specify when the encounter between the saint and the possessed took place. However, Norbert is described as still wearing his alb and stole, which suggests that he had very recently celebrated mass; then, faced with the demon's resistance, he went to rest and told the sick girl and those present to attend mass the next day.[27] In this case, the ritual is shown to be more effective when associated with the mass. This fits with the evidence in other sources that in the twelfth century at least some people thought that it was most appropriate to perform exorcisms during mass.

The stories in the *vitae* suggest certain other conditions were also considered propitious for conducting the rite. The search for the right time was accompanied by a search for the correct location; that is, the place which would be most effective against the devil. The possessed are usually reported as having been taken to sanctuaries and holy places, that is to churches. *Vita A* even describes how the possessed must be brought to the altar inside the church, which is also of course the spot where the mass was celebrated.[28] This confirms the *potentia* of place, to use Peter Brown's favoured term.[29] To the need for an appropriate context in which to carry out the exorcism Norbert adds the need for the minister himself to be on good form to fight the devil. To achieve this, Norbert advocates a strict regime of physical asceticism. Just as he imposed an austere rule on his order so he also imposed such conditions upon himself, including fasting. For example, during the exorcism carried out on the young girl of Nivelles, when he entered his lodgings, Norbert reportedly said he did not wish to eat until the possessed girl was healed.[30] Fasting is mentioned several times in relation to exorcism. It is a collective act in the case of the lay brother's son: the brothers of the house are all asked to submit themselves humbly to discipline, fasting and prayer.[31] Faced with the case of the steward of Maastricht, the saint himself fasted once again. Fasting was a useful means of penitential purification for the struggle against the devil. Several other twelfth-century works mention the state of ritual purity

---

[27] 'Iam vespertina hora erat, et videns pater Norbertus non exisse demonem, aliquantulum contristatus, iussit eam reddi patri et in crastinum ad missam perduci' (*Vita A Norberti*, c. 10, p. 681).

[28] 'Mandavit autem Norbertus duobus fratribus, ut tenerent puellam haut procul ab altari' (*Vita A Norberti*, c. 10, p. 681). The steward of Maastricht is also brought to the altar during the mass: 'Haec dixit et statuto demoniaco ante altare exorcismum aggressus est, demonem compellens ut exiret' (*Vita A Norberti*, c. 14, p. 687).

[29] See Brown, *Cult of the Saints*.

[30] 'Pater vero Norbertus ad hospicium se conferens, confirmavit in animo suo non gustare cibum donec puella sanaretur, et ita transegit diem et noctem illam sien cibo' (*Vita A Norberti*, c. 10, p. 681).

[31] 'Ad haec verba prior fratres convocat, qui cum humilitate corporalem disciplinam suscipiunt, ieiuniis et orationibus instituit. Dehinc cum aqua benedicta ad demonem accedunt' (*Vita A Norberti*, c. 10, p. 681).

necessary for one who engages the demon in combat. Peter Lombard, in his *Sentences*, explicitly refers to the necessity for the doctor to take care of himself just as the exorcist must purify himself from the evil that is in him.[32] It seems that a fast inspired by those practised by monks routinely in their communities was believed to be effective against such manifestations of the devil.

The stories of exorcisms in the *vitae* of Norbert, their length and their failures suggest it was sometimes difficult for medieval clerics to succeed in treating such cases of possession. They might have to go through the process several times in order to overcome an extremely resistant demon. As we have mentioned already, the lives twice refer to the alb (a white tunic worn by a priest when celebrating the eucharist) and the stole (worn as a scarf around the neck), the common insignia of a priest, as being effective instruments against the devil. St Norbert's first act when dealing with such a case was to put on these garments.[33] These two sacerdotal vestments here take on the sense of serving as armour in the fight against the devil. According to the *vitae*, Norbert used the stole several times and the devil even tried to strangle him with it.[34] When the devil realized that the saint was taking off his priestly vestments, he mocked him and suggested that he was abandoning the fight.[35] The *vitae* of Norbert of Xanten confirm a practice present in other hagiographic traditions such as that of Hildegard of Bingen (d. 1179), who recommends that priests administer the exorcism *ordo* she wrote using the stole.[36] Whilst contemporary liturgical books mention neither the alb nor the stole as being used in exorcisms, their use becomes progressively more evident during the later Middle Ages. Some liturgical manuscripts from the fifteenth century even refer to them as necessary items for exorcisms.[37] It may be that the hagiographical texts preserve evidence for a practice that was not recorded until much later in the liturgical sources. Alternatively, it may be that

---

[32] Peter Lombard (d. 1160) writes in the *Book of Sentences*: 'Debet autem spiritum mundum habere qui spiritibus imperat immundis, et malignum expellere de corde suo, quem expellit de corpore alieno, ne medicina quam alii facit sibi non prosit, et dicatur ei: Medice, cura te ipsum'. Peter Lombard, *Sententiae in IV libris distinctae*, Spicilegium Bonaventurianum 4–5, 2 vols. (Grottaferrata: Editiones Collegii S. Bonaventurae, 1971–1981), 2: 398.

[33] 'Cuius dolori et compatiens servus Dei, albis et stola vestitus super puellam iam duodennem exorcismum legit' (*Vita A Norberti*, c. 10, p. 680).

[34] 'Tunc puella manum iniecit ad stolam eius, ut collum ipsius astringeret' (*Vita A Norberti*, c. 10, p. 680).

[35] 'Ipase vero coepit se expoliare alba et aliis missae vestimentis. Quod videns demon insultando clamabat: "Ha, ha, he! Modo bene facis et nondum fecisti michi opus a Deo beneplacitum"' (*Vita A Norberti*, c. 10, p. 680).

[36] *Vita Sanctae Hildegardis*, ed. M. Klaes, CCCM 126 (Turnhout: Brepols, 1993), 3:21, 61; Chave-Mahir, *L'exorcisme*, 155–59, 197.

[37] For example, Munich, Bayerische Staatsbibliothek, Clm 10085, fol. 3v; also see n. 3 above.

hagiographical tales, such as those for Norbert, influenced the development of the recorded liturgy.

Returning to the first story in the life, that of the possessed girl from Nivelles, Norbert's initial efforts to exorcise her proved a failure. After a rest accompanied by fasting and prayer, Norbert is described as having been ready to attack the demon again. One of the more detailed stories tells how the little girl from Nivelles was finally delivered from the devil during the mass itself:

> The next day came and the priest of God prepared himself to celebrate the mysteries of the mass. The young girl was brought to him then in the presence of many people there to witness the outcome of the event. Norbert asked two brothers to hold the girl near the altar. Thus, when the mass had started and he came to read the Bible over the girl's head, the demon said mockingly that he had often heard nonsense of that kind. Afterwards, when the priest raised the host, the demon cried, 'Look! Look! He is holding his little god in his hands.' For demons confess that which the heretics deny. The priest of God shuddered at this and, having invoked the spirit of truth in prayer with great fervour, he began to act against the demon. The latter cried, 'I am burning, I am burning, I am dying! I want to go, I want to go! Let me go!' And as the brothers held the little girl, the unclean spirit fled: marking his foul passage with really vile urine, he abandoned the vessel he had possessed.[38]

The little girl was brought to the altar which is thus portrayed as simultaneously being the place of celebration for the eucharist and that of completion for the exorcism. The rite occurred at the point in the mass when there was the gospel reading. Many other saints' *vitae* also emphasize that a gospel reading was often required during exorcism.[39] There is also some evidence for this in liturgical sources. The exorcism formularies recorded in the *PRG* manuscripts

---

[38] 'Iam crastina dies advenerat et Dei sacerdos parat se ad celebranda missae mysteria, itemque puella adducitur, et fit multiplex populi concursus, finem rei praestolantis. Mandavit autem Norbertus duobus fratribus, ut tenerent puellam haut procul ab altari. Inchoata itaque missa ventum est ad evangelium, quod cum super caput eius legeretur, demon item irridendo respondit, se huiusmodi liras frequenter audisse. Postmodum sacerdote infra actionem levante hostiam, demon exclamavit: "Videte, videte, ecce iste deiculum suum manibus suis tenet". Fatentur enim demones, quod haereticis negant. Tunc vero sacerdos Dei inhorruit, et concepto spiritu veritatis in ipsa oratione sua instantius coepit agere contra demonem. At ille coactus clamabat: "En ardeo, en ardeo, en morior!" itemque: "Volo exire, volo exire, dimitte me!" Fratribus autem puellam fortiter tenentibus, spiritus immundus foetentissimee urinae foeda relinquens vestigia aufugit, vasque possessum reliquit' (*Vita A Norberti*, c. 10, p. 681).

[39] See Chave-Mahir, *L'exorcisme*, 150.

mention the possibility of such a reading[40] and the twelfth-century liturgical manuscripts actually recommend it.[41] In the fourteenth and fifteenth centuries this recommendation became more common in liturgical sources.[42] Norbert's *vita* specifies that the gospel book should be held upon the head of the possessed person as if it were itself considered effective and powerful in its own right against the devil.[43]

It is also worth noting one other feature in the story about the girl from Nivelles. In the account of the Nivelles exorcism it was at the actual moment of the raising of the host that the devil spoke to acknowledge the presence of Christ. The *Vita A* text also stresses that the demon recognized the quality of the Eucharist, but glosses the demon's speech with 'Demons confess what heretics deny'.[44] This aspect of the story can be linked to contemporary debates over the Eucharist. This controversy surfaces elsewhere in Norbert's life in the description of the heresy preached by Tanchelm in Antwerp. Norbert mobilized all his energy to go there to preach orthodoxy in 1124, as *Vita A* stresses; that is, three years after the exorcism of the little girl.[45] From the beginning of the 1110s Tanchelm was denounced for challenging the Church, the authority of the pope and the clerics, and the real presence of Christ in the host. This story in Norbert's *vita* therefore uses exorcism to affirm the truth of the real presence in the host, with the flight of the devil at the moment of the host's elevation just after the revelation of its authenticity by the devil himself.

---

[40]   The gospels are cited indirectly in the text found in at least seven manuscripts of the Romano-German Pontifical: 'Nam legimus in evangelio tuo quod cum imperio suo dominus Iesus filius tuus spiritus inmundos eiciebat et passiones ab ipsis illatas potenter curavit' (*PRG* 115, vol. II: 203).

[41]   'Tunc legantur super caput eius ista evangelia' – then Luke's gospel is read (9:1) and Luke 10:19 and 24–27 (Ritual of Prüm, Munich, Bayerische Staatsbibliothek, Clm 100, fol. 115v. See Chave-Mahir, *L'exorcisme*, 379–80). See also the manuscript at Munich Bayerische Staatsbibliothek Clm 3909, fol. 252v in Chave-Mahir, *L'exorcisme*, 383.

[42]   Chave-Mahir, *L'exorcisme*, 319.

[43]   On the question of the Bible as a book for carrying out exorcisms, see Chave-Mahir, *L'exorcisme*, 318ff.

[44]   'Fatentur enim demones quod haeretici negant', *Vita A Sancti Norberti*, c. 10, p. 681.

[45]   'Eo tempore apud Andverpiam, qui locus erat amplissimus et populosus, perniciosa haeresis oborta est. Haereticus enim quidam mirae subtilitatis et versutiae seductor, Tanchelm nomine, ad locum illum veniens suae seductionis ibidem oportunitatem invenit. Erat quidem idem ille sceleratissimus et christianae fidei et totius religionis inimicus in tantum ut obsequium episcoporum et sacerdotum nihil esse diceret, et sacrosancti corporis et sanguinis Domini nostri Iesu Christi perceptionem ad salutem perpetuam prodesse denegaret' (*Vita A Norberti*, c. 16, p. 691). On Tanchelm, see Uwe Brunn, *Des contestataires aux 'cathares'. Discours de réforme et propagande antihérétique dans les pays du Rhin et de la Meuse avant l'Inquisition* (Paris: Institut d'Etudes Augustiniennes, 2006), 61ff.

The most propitious circumstances for conducting an exorcism were seemingly to be found within the mass. The mass seems to have been favoured because it constituted a time when the faithful met, gathered around the saintly figure of Norbert. But the point of communion acquired particular importance at the time of Tanchelm's critique of the orthodox Church. In the *vitae*, the exorcism ritual gave the demon a chance to speak and, recognizing both the divinity of the host and Norbert's own powers, indirectly to denounce Tanchelm's heresy. Norbert's own fight again the devil through exorcism can thus be compared to the battle of the Church against heresy. Exorcism is also presented as being a liturgical practice which was not fixed, but could be adapted in response to different circumstances.

The Formulae of Exorcism Borrowed from Liturgical Books

The stories relating to exorcism in the Life of Norbert include many formulae – the words said by the saint during the rituals. *Vita A* in particular contains a good number of them. How far are these like or comparable with the texts found in contemporary liturgical books?

When the unnamed prior of the monastery of Prémontré (near Laon, France) tries to heal the son of a lay brother, he pronounces the formula:

> Adjuro te, per Iesum Christum filium Dei, qui tuas in cruce vicit insidias et potestatem, quam iniuste et fraudulenter rapueras super hominem, iuste et potenter recepit, ut quis sis celare non praesumas.

> I command you by Jesus Christ, Son of God, who triumphed over your tricks and your power upon the cross, who in all justice has taken back the power which you fraudulently usurped over man that you might not presume to hide it.[46]

In its construction this formula is completely faithful to the liturgical tradition. The operative *adjuro te* formula features many times in the formal liturgical record. This formulation seems to have been favoured for use against a demon who possesses an individual. (The words *exorcizo te* are more often used in rites for the exorcism of things, which are actually blessings for those objects, such as for the components of holy water.[47]) The initial words of Norbert's formula can be found many times in the various texts cited in the *PRG* tradition, such as in the phrase 'Adiuro te per Deum vivum et per Deum omnipotentem ...' (I

---

46   *Vita A Norberti*, c. 14, p. 686.

47   See J. Magne, 'Exploration généalogique dans les textes d'exorcisme', *Mélanges d'archéologie et d'histoire* 73 (1961): 323–64; Chave-Mahir, *L'exorcisme*, 97–99.

command you by the living God and by Almighty God ...).[48] One also finds some exorcism formulae which begin *adjuro te* in the German manuscripts of the twelfth century in versions which are longer than the 'model' in the *PRG* group.[49] Whilst this particular formula in *Vita A* is not identical to any I know of in the liturgical manuscripts, it is faithful to them in both its *incipit* and its invocation of Christ, which condemns the devil's usurpation of power. It also follows the same pattern as they do of referring to the story of the life of Christ and the battle in which He engaged with the forces of evil.

In the same account, the porter of Prémontré is reported as pronouncing an adjuration against the diabolical apparition that appeared to him. The demon is then cursed:

> Wretched creature, you were Lucifer, the star of the dawn; you were among the delights of paradise but that was not enough for you. You said, 'I shall sit upon the mountain of the gods, I shall be like the Most High.' So you have lost your former greatness, you have preferred the shadows to the light, wretchedness to beatitude, the filth of pigs to paradise. What a handsome exchange! What a splendid advantage for you! This is not where you belong – go wallow with the pigs in the filth and there in those stinking places await the moment of your judgement.[50]

---

48   *PRG*, 118.2, vol. II: 211 (from five manuscripts) and Paris, BNF, Ms. lat. 14833, fol. 40v; Chave-Mahir, *L'exorcisme*, 374. See also: 'Adiuro te, per Deum altissimum, maledicte Satanas, ne famulum suum artibus tuis temptare nitaris, neque eum violentium teneas ...' (*PRG* 115. 42 vol. II: 204–5 and Paris, BNF, Ms. lat. 14833, fol. 37; Chave-Mahir, *L'exorcisme*, 370).

49   'Adiuro ergo te serpens antique, per iudicem vivorum et mortuorum, factorem mundi, per creatorem omnium rerum, per patrem eternum et per unigenitum Ihesum Christum Filium eius Dominum nostrum ante secula genitum et in seculo ex matre [ex matre] virgine verum hominem temporaliter natum et per Spiritum sanctum ex Patre et Filio procedentem, coeternum et consubstantialem patri et filio qui trinus et unus vivens per immortalia secula et regnans sine fine, qui habet potestatem occidere et vivificare, perdere et salvare et mittere in gehennam, per eum te adiuro ut ab hoc famulo Dei cum omni malitia tua et cum omni militia exercitus tui festinus sine mora discedas. Adiuro te, non ex mea infirmitate eternum eiusdem patris et Filii et Spiritus sancti, ut exeas et recedas ab isto plasmate Dei quem ipse ad imaginem suam fecit'. This long formula is found in two manuscripts of Munich, Bayerische Staatsbibliothek, Clm 100, fol. 112ff (Chave-Mahir, *L'exorcisme*, 378). See also Munich, Bayerische Staatsbibliothek, Clm 3909, fol. 251 (Chave-Mahir, *L'exorcisme*, 382).

50   'Miser et misserrime tu quondam Lucifer, qui mane oriebaris, in deliciis paradysi fuisti, sed cum tibi non sufficerent haec et diceres: 'Ponam sedem meam ad aquilonem, ero similis Altissimo', idem quod eras amisisti, pro luce tenebras, pro beatitudine miseriam, pro loco deliciarum foetorem, cum porcis eligens commutasti. En dignum concambium, idonea commutatio. Eia non hic tibi locus est, sed in foetore cloacarum te volutans porcis assimilare et in locis putentibus districti tempus examinis praestolare' (*Vita A Norberti*, c. 14, p. 687).

This adjuration mentions both the devil's desire to get closer to paradise and his swift fall. This is very similar to adjurations in liturgical texts which also frequently recall Lucifer's primordial treason, citing, as did the porter, Isaiah 14:14 which attributes to the demon the desire to rule in paradise and be like God.[51] But the porter continues with a diatribe against the demon, likening him to the world of animals, and more specifically to the rank world of pigs. This particular comparison of the devil to a pig and to latrines does not feature in the liturgy of the *PRG* manuscripts although there are clear resonances with the Gospels.[52]

Finally, *Vita A*'s account of Norbert's life includes the words with which each exorcism should finish:

> Inde sacrae mos inolevit ecclesiae, ut omnium exorcizmorum conclusio in fine sic sonet: 'Exorcizo te per eum qui venturus et iudicare vivos et mortuos et saeculum per ignem'.

> Thenceforward arose the sacred Church's custom of ending every exorcism with the words 'I exorcise you through him who will come to judge the living and the dead and the age through the fire'.[53]

One of the exorcisms in the *PRG* tradition, called 'The exorcism of St Ambrose' in Vogel and Elze's edition, ends with almost exactly the same formula:

> Qui vivit et regnat cum spiritu sancto in gloria patris, quique venturus est iudicare vivos et mortuos et saeculum per ignem.

> He who lives and rules with the Holy Spirit in the glory of the Father and who will come to judge the living and the dead and the age by the fire.[54]

The phrase in the *vita* seems to come straight from a liturgical book.

The majority of the exorcism formulae presented in the *vitae* of Norbert of Xanten were clearly inspired by the rites recorded in the formal liturgy. The writers of these lives were sufficiently knowledgeable about the liturgy of

---

51 'Tu ab origine superbus et invidiosas artes machinans, Deo te esse similem voluisti dicens: 'Ascendam in nubem et ero similis altissimo [Isa. 14:14]'. Tibi enim parum visa fuit angelica dignitas, forma qua prius utebaris' (*PRG*, 118.3, vol. II: 213) ; this particular text appears in three manuscripts according to Vogel and Elze's edition.

52 See in particular the figure of the possessed man of Gerasa: Christ exorcises him and sends the demons that possessed him into some pigs which fall from a cliff (Luke 8:26–39; Mark 5:1–20; Matt. 8:28–34).

53 *Vita A Norberti*, c. 14, p. 687.

54 *PRG*, 118.2, vol. II: 212.

exorcism that they were able to find and use the right words against the demon.[55] *Vita A* of Norbert is certainly a text written with an eye for detail, but it is also the work of a cleric who was able to draw on the formal liturgy to write it. Because of its fidelity to the liturgical sources, this *vita* of Norbert is a very important document for students of the history of exorcism. But certain of the choices made in order to carry out the exorcisms in the narrative lead one to wonder if the writers did not sometimes take liberties with existing liturgical tradition.

A Free Liturgical Action?

In the manner of Christ, who knew how to improvise and find the appropriate actions and prayers for every situation, Norbert is shown as able to free himself from the constraints of the formal liturgy in his fight against Satan. Thus at certain moments in the story the saint seems to invent actions and techniques in his confrontation with the powers of evil.

The most surprising improvisations in the life are found in the extraordinary tale of the exorcism of the young girl of Nivelles. Having received the possessed girl and her father, Norbert, dressed in his alb and stole, began to read exorcisms over her. But his recitation was constantly interrupted by the demon's shows of bravado: the demon began by describing the words of the exorcism as 'nonsense' (*liras*); it then asked Norbert to renounce his faith by the blood of the martyrs and provided a distraction by reciting the entire *Song of Songs* in both French and German, declaring that it wished to possess one of the monks present and then make the church's vaults fall down on those in attendance. Although, when the possessed girl tried to strangle Norbert with his stole, the demon immediately lost its power. All these incidents led Norbert to take radical action, shaving the young girl's hair and plunging her in exorcised water.[56] The haircut of the young girl from Nivelles has no equivalent in the liturgy. It seems more closely related to the tonsure that medieval medical doctors gave to the insane in the hope of giving their head some fresh air. Otherwise, faced with continued symptoms, doctors might make recourse to trepanning. Was Norbert thought to have been inspired by

---

[55]   One example of a hagiographer who was also a liturgist seems to have been Goscelin of Saint-Bertin, working at St Augustine's, Canterbury (among other places) in the late eleventh century. See Richard Sharpe, 'Goscelin's St Augustine and St Mildreth: Hagiography and Liturgy in Context', *Journal of Theological Studies*, n.s. 41, no. 2 (1990): 502–16. I thank Helen Gittos for this reference.

[56]   'Iam itaque plurima parte diei cosumpta, pater Norbertus consilium habuit, ut in aqua exorzizata puella poneretur. Et ita factum est. Et quia flavis erat venusta capillis, sacerdos verens ne occasione crinium dyabolum in ea potestatem haberet, eam tonderi iussit' (*Vita A Norberti*, c. 10, p. 680).

this medical practice or did he simply decide, as the text says, to cut the girl's hair because it was reputed to attract the demon and to be the seat of vice?[57]

The lay brother's son is similarly plunged into exorcised water.[58] This surprising innovation, which has no equivalent in other hagiographic stories from the same period, has several possible explanations with regard to contemporary liturgical practice. Indeed, some liturgical books recommend changing the clothes of the possessed and sprinkling them with blessed water.[59] Another text, entitled 'On the fast required for the possessed', which is edited in the *PRG*, recommends 'washing the hands, face, feet and all other parts of the body with nothing but consecrated water for six weeks'.[60] This purification with blessed water is clearly analagous to the baptismal purification which also required exorcism; it is thus not surprising to see Norbert choose this kind of purification. Was this also intended to send a sign to the followers of Tanchelm who were said to have challenged all the sacraments of the Church by carrying out this kind of baptism by immersion?

The administration of exorcised water to the possessed was often accompanied by that of blessed salt. The steward of Maastricht gets salt in his mouth[61] and the peasant of Vivières has his gums rubbed with blessed salt:

> In response to the many people who requested it, father Norbert approached the possessed man and sprinkled him with blessed water. Then, rubbing his gums with blessed salt and washing him with blessed water, he commanded him to eat nothing during the following nine days that had not been seasoned with blessed salt and consecrated water. This done, the man returned home healed.[62]

---

[57] On the medical approaches to possession and the tonsure, see Chave-Mahir, *L'exorcisme*, 45.

[58] 'Cui cum praeceptum datum fuisset et alii discessissent, ille solus tenuit et ad aspectum vultus sui trementem eum ad aquam benedictam adduxit. Ponitur in aqua exorzizata, leguntur exorcismi et euangelia, orant et plorant fratres in disciplinis corporalibus, veniis et variis afflictionibus, tandem post nimias miserrimi corporis vexationes demon super linguam hominis residens in modum grani nigerrimae lenticulae' (*Vita A Norberti*, c. 14, p. 687).

[59] 'Tunc induat vestimentis novis, aspersis cum aqua benedicta, et tunc vadat ante altare ...': Vienna, Österreichische Nationalbibliothek, Ms. lat. 1888, fol. 81v–82 in Franz, *Die Kirchlichen Benediktionen*, 562.

[60] 'Manus autem neque faciem neque pedes neque ullum corporis membrum in illis sex ebdomadis lavet, nisi cum aqua benedicta' (*PRG*, 120, vol. II: 220). See the manuscript of the Library of Bamberg, Ms. Lit. 53, fol. 161v–162r; the Pontifical of Gundekar, Eichstätt, Diözesanarchiv, Cod. B4, fol. 163v; Vienna, Österreichische Nationalbibliothek, Ms. 701, fol. 111v–112r, and Vendôme, Bibliothèque Municipale, Ms. 14, fol. 124v.

[61] 'Haec dixit et statuto demoniaco ante altare exorcismum aggressus est, demonem compellens ut exiret. Et cum salem exorzizatum ori eius immisisset, ille magno impetu in faciem et in oculos sacerdotis exspuit': *Vita A Norberti*, c. 14, p. 687.

[62] 'Pater Norbertus multis postulantibus ad hominem obsessum accessit, eumque aqua benedicta aspersit. Dehinc gingivas eius sale benedicto fricans et aqua benedicta lavans,

This 'exorcistic regime', which is surprising at first sight, should also be linked to the common recommendations in liturgical rites of the period. In fact, the text referred to above entitled 'On the fast required for the possessed' demands that nothing be eaten apart from certain foods, preferably light, and dressed with blessed salt and water.[63] Abstaining from food is also recommended to the emperor's soldier.[64] This act indicates once again that the writers of Norbert's *vitae* were perfectly aware of contemporary liturgical practices.

It thus appears that through these immersions, the contact with blessed water and salt and even the haircut, the possessed underwent a process of renewal. This exorcism, which sometimes also had a penitential dimension, thus took the form of a new baptism with the use of water and salt.

Conclusions

Norbert is depicted in the life as a cleric who has mastered the liturgy of exorcism. The actions that the saint undertakes over the possessed are steeped in the rites for exorcism: the words and some of the actions even appear in the pontificals of the period. But the ritual is rendered as being far more dynamic than the liturgical sources suggest; the narrative in the life stages, relates and develops all the twists and turns of the combat. Whereas the liturgical formulae speak of the battle against the demon, the narrative tells of the difficulties of the struggle in which all exorcists are engaged from the moment they undertake to drive the demon from a possessed body. The fight is not a trivial encounter, it continues the ongoing combat against the devil led by Christ and continued by the saints throughout their *vitae*. The saint, like the cleric, must have his own arms, such as his stole. The liturgy and the lives of the saints are thus closely linked and these links allow us to better understand a religious practice that has left little trace in liturgical sources before the fifteenth century. Comparing the liturgical and hagiographical sources, as in this example, allows us to understand more about exorcism rituals in this period, even if we do not know whether they were actually often used against the possessed.

---

praecepit ei, ut per novem continuos sequentes dies nullis uteretur cibis, nisi sale benedicto et aqua benedicta conditis. Hoc facto sanatus homo in propiam domum rediit': *Vita A Norberti*, c. 15, p. 690.

[63] Chave-Mahir, *L'exorcisme*, 113–19.

[64] 'Vir autem Dei ad confesionem eum hortatus est, et tam pro praeteritorum peccatorum remissione quam pro gratiarum actione per dies aliquot a lautioribus cibis abstinere praecepit, in veritate denuncians, si constitutam praevaricaretur abstinentiae regulam, eandem quam evaserat poenam sibi affuturam': *Vita A Norberti*, c. 21, p. 702.

Chapter 8
Rites for Dedicating Churches

Mette Birkedal Bruun and Louis I. Hamilton[1]

Although the precise origins of Christian rites for dedication are murky and
the origin of Christian sacred space is itself debated, even the earliest Christians
shared with Judaism a sense of *terra sancta*.[2] In turn, the notion of Jerusalem as
the holy land *par excellence* became canonical through the orthodox acceptance
of the Book of Revelation as authentic. John's vision of the end of time
culminates (in Revelation 21:12) in the re-establishment of Jerusalem: 'the holy
city of Jerusalem coming down out of heaven from God'.[3] After the conversion of
Constantine, pilgrimage to Jerusalem rapidly became popular among Christians.[4]
It is also clear, that at least as early as Constantine, some churches were initiated
by a distinct form of dedication rite.[5] That is, almost as soon as Christianity was
licit and took on a public role in Roman society, we have evidence both for some
churches being dedicated in a distinct manner and for Jerusalem as a pilgrimage
site. Dedication sermons, and with them much stronger evidence for the rite,
soon followed.[6] The notion that the space was distinct within the community
and related to the Heavenly Jerusalem was commented on directly by Eusebius

---

[1]   Louis I. Hamilton wrote the introduction and the section on liturgical rites; Mette
Birkedal Brunn that on sermons; the final reflections were jointly authored.

[2]   For a survey of the earliest evidence, see Francis E. Peters, *Jerusalem: The Holy City
in the Eyes of Chroniclers, Visitors, Pilgrims, and Prophets from the Days of Abraham to the
Beginnings of Modern Times* (Princeton: Princeton University Press, 1985).

[3]   See the brief overview of the development of the allegorical reading of scripture
in early Christianity as it refers to the Temple in Ann R. Meyer, *Medieval Allegory and the
Building of the New Jerusalem* (Cambridge: D.S. Brewer, 2003), 1–23.

[4]   E.D. Hunt, *Holy Land Pilgrimage in the Later Roman Empire* (Oxford: Oxford
University Press, 1982).

[5]   Thaddeus S. Ziolkowski, *The Consecration and Blessing of Churches: A Historical
Synopsis and Commentary* (Washington, DC: Catholic University of America Press, 1943).

[6]   For fifth-century Gaul, for example, Ian Wood has found ample evidence, 'The
Audience of Architecture in Post-Roman Gaul', in *The Anglo-Saxon Church: Papers on
History, Architecture and Archaeology in Honour of Dr H.M. Taylor*, ed. L.A.S. Butler and
R.K. Morris (London: Council for British Archaeology, 1986), 74–79.

of Caesarea (260–341 CE).[7] The rapid emergence of practices of dedication may reflect an adaptation of preceding non-Christian practices and/or the existence of a Christian precedent lost to us.[8]

In the earliest centuries, an inaugural mass appears to have most commonly marked the dedication of the church.[9] The deposition of relics into a new altar became normative from at least 787, when it was prescribed at the second Council of Nicaea.[10] A rite for the deposition of relics in a new church appears in Roman *ordines* from about this time.[11] There was never one rite for the dedication of churches in the Middle Ages, nor was the rite uniformly practised or enforced. Tracing changes in how it was practised (as opposed to how it was presented in liturgical texts or commentaries) is exceedingly difficult and much work remains to be done.[12] The rite was unclear enough even to contemporaries that as late as the fifteenth century, a cleric complained that, 'Concerning the dedication or consecration of churches there is so much variety and various [customs] that, not only do they not agree in many points, but they often

---

[7]   Eusebius, *Historia ecclesiastica*, ed. Gustave Bardy, Sources chrétiennes, 31, 41, 55 and 73 (Paris: Cerf, 1952–60), Book X, cc. III–IV.

[8]   Louis I. Hamilton, *A Sacred City: Consecrating Churches and Reforming Society in Eleventh-Century Italy* (Manchester: Manchester University Press, 2010), 14. For an effort to further trace the origins of the rite, see Brian V. Repsher, 'The Abecedarium: Catechetical Symbolism in the Rite of Church Dedication', *Mediaevalia* 24 (2003): 1–18. See also Louis I. Hamilton, 'Les dangers du rituel dans l'Italie du XIe siècle: entre textes liturgiques et témoignages historiques', in *Mises en scène et mémoires de la consécration d'église dans l'occident médiéval*, ed. Didier Méhu (Turnhout: Brepols, 2008), 159–88.

[9]   Ziolkowski, *Consecration and Blessing of Churches*, 14–15.

[10]   Ziolkowski, *Consecration and Blessing of Churches*, 14–15.

[11]   *OR*, vol. 4, 336.

[12]   See Hamilton, *Sacred City*, 14. Physical evidence will prove essential in any effort to capture the earliest Christian notions of space. See, for example, the recent discoveries at Megiddo, described by Yotam Tepper and Leah Di Segni, *A Christian Prayer Hall of the Third Century CE at Kefar 'Othnay (Legio): Excavations at the Megiddo Prison 2005* (Jerusalem: Israel Antiquities Authority, 2006). The floor mosaics discovered certainly suggest a space set apart and marked for worship. Dominique Iogna-Prat and Collins both emphasize Paul's notion of the individual Christian as the temple: Dominique Iogna-Prat, *La maison dieu: une histoire monumentale de l'église au moyen âge (v. 800–v. 1200)* (Paris: Editions du Seuil, 2006), 30–33; Patrick Collins, *The Carolingian Debate over Sacred Space* (New York: Palgrave Macmillan, 2012), 7–8. Collins notes the wide range of views on sacred space in the first centuries of Christianity. It should be noted that Paul and the earliest Christians continued to worship at the Temple in Jerusalem, as at Acts 2:46 and 21:26. I am not convinced that Paul's notion of the body as Temple was intended as an assault on sacred space per se, or that early Christians understood it as such. See also Jennifer Harris, 'The Body as Temple in the High Middle Ages', in *Sacrifice in Religious Experience*, ed. Albert I. Baumgarten (Leiden: Brill, 2002), 233–56.

contradict themselves.'[13] It is clear, however, that during the Carolingian period in the ninth century and the so-called Gregorian reforms in the eleventh and early twelfth centuries there was intense clerical interest in the ritual in relation to larger debates about ecclesiology and sacrality.[14] The purpose of this chapter is to consider the problems and possibilities of a variety of sources associated with church dedications and the methods that will help reveal the multiple possible meanings of these rites. We wish to emphasize that each dedication event would have had its own range of possible significances.[15] For this reason we have divided the chapter into an initial section on the variety of the rites, and a second section on the interpretation of the rite through sermons. In discussing the rites we will use the term 'practised' in preference to the term 'performance', as the latter carries with it certain anthropological implications that emphasize rituals as being stable and reinforcing social stability.[16] Ritual had the capacity to generate power, rather than simply reflect power within a community; therefore, this instability ought to be expected and needs to be examined. The rite – as practised in that particular moment – would have contributed to those significances. The particular practice depended not only on the rite available, but the church itself, and the topography of its setting. From the fifth century, sermons would have attempted to direct the meaning of the event for participants, although we cannot assume that was the significance a participant perceived. The participants themselves, in addition, would have consciously or unconsciously shaped the event. This is most clearly revealed in the historical record when participants oppose the dedication through violence,

---

[13] The Pontifical of Charles de Neufchatel as transcribed in Leroquais, *Pontificaux*, 1: 77. Cited by Thomas Davies Kozacheck, 'The Repertory of Chant for Dedicating Churches in the Middle Ages: Music, Liturgy and Ritual', DPhil diss., Harvard University, 1995, 1. See also p. 16 above.

[14] For the Carolingian period, see Iogna-Prat, *La maison dieu*; Collins, *Carolingian Debate*; and D. Polanichka, 'Transforming Space, (Per)forming Community: Church Consecration in Carolingian Europe', *Viator* 43 (2012): 79–98 (emphasizing the uniting force of the ritual); on the Gregorian reformers' efforts to shape the meaning of the rite, see Hamilton, *Sacred City*.

[15] Hamilton intends a distinction between 'meaning' (that which may have been alluded to in rite, space or sermons) and 'significance' (that for which we have evidence as being perceived meaning by a participant). See Hamilton, 'Desecration and Consecration in Norman Capua, 1062–1122: Contesting Sacred Space during the Gregorian Reforms', *Haskins Society Journal* 14 (2003): 137–50.

[16] As rightly observed in the introduction to *The Appearances of Medieval Rituals*, ed. Nils Holger Petersen et al. (Turnhout: Brepols, 2003). Throughout this article Hamilton is emphasizing ritual instability in the dedication and the manner in which rites attracted opposition, noting that sermons asserted a meaning often in line with the notion of social stability in performance theory.

but their active support gave important force to the rite and made it important for the clergy to try to direct its meaning through sermons.

Liturgical Rites

Numerous studies concerning the dedication of churches have appeared in the last decade.[17] As a rule, these analyses of the liturgy and its significance have been indebted to the so-called *Ordo* 40 found in the edition of the *Pontifical romano-germanique* as edited by Cyrille Vogel and Reinhard Elze.[18] As Table 4.1 of Henry Parkes' article in this volume makes clear, *Ordo* 40 of the Vogel and Elze edition is a reconstruction based upon all nine of the manuscripts they consulted. It is contained in a tenth-century manuscript but is believed to be based on an earlier precedent.[19] The *Ordo* prescribes a rite of approximately thirty-one steps.[20]

1. Vesting of the clergy.
2. Vigil with the relics, outside of the church and inside a tent with the sung litany.
3. Procession from the tent to the church with the relics.
4. Triple circuit around the church. The bishop sprinkles the walls with holy water and knocks on the main doors at each circuit, reciting the antiphon, *Tollite portas*.
5. The church doors are opened from the interior and the bishop enters with a few clergy.
6. Litany and prostration.
7. Inscription of Greek and Latin alphabets in ash on the floor of the church in a cruciform pattern (the abecedarium).
8. Preparation of the 'Gregorian Water'.

---

[17]   To name some of the more prominent recent studies contributing to the study of the significance of the dedication rite: Thomas Kozachek, 'Repertory'; Brian V. Repsher, *The Rite of Church Dedication in the Early Medieval Era* (Lewiston, NY: Edwin Mellen Press, 1998); Eric Palazzo, *L'évêque et son image: l'illustration du pontifical au moyen âge* (Turnhout: Brepols, 1999); Didier Méhu, *Paix et communautés autour de l'abbaye de Cluny Xe–XVe siècle* (Lyon: Presses universitaires de Lyon, 2001); Iogna-Prat, *La maison dieu*; Méhu, ed., *Mises en scène et mémoires de la consécration de l'église dans l'occident médiéval* (Turnhout: Brepols, 2007); Hamilton, *Sacred City*; Polanichka, 'Transforming Space'; Helen Gittos, *Liturgy, Architecture, and Sacred Places in Anglo-Saxon England* (Oxford: Oxford University Press, 2013), ch. 6.

[18]   *PRG*.

[19]   See Polanichka, 'Transforming Space', 85.

[20]   For a more complete description, see Hamilton, *Sacred City*, 13–50.

9. Consecration of altar.
10. Aspersion of altar (seven times).
11. Aspersion of interior of church (three circuits).
12. Aspersion of length and width of interior.
13. Prayer of consecration.
14. Proceed to altar.
15. Preparation of mortar.
16. Incensing and anointing of altar with oil and chrism.
17. Anointing of interior walls with chrism.
18. Return to altar.
19. Incensing altar.
20. Prayer of consecration.
21. Blessing of linens, ornaments, vestments, etc.
22. Exit church to tent; change of vestments.
23. Prayers outside of doors; blessing of doors.
24. Process around exterior of church with laity.
25. Address to people, lord and constructor of church.
26. Entrance with relics.
27. Installation of relics into altar.
28. Anointing of altar with chrism.
29. Vesting of altar.
30. Illumination of church.
31. Mass.

The elaborateness of this rite as described in *Ordo* 40 clearly marks the space as distinct from others within the community. Scholars have expanded on this in multiple ways. Didier Méhu has observed that, in the dramatic example of Cluny, as dedicated by Urban II in 1095, the dedication rite, with its encircling of the church building, mirrored Cluny's own territorial circle of privilege, itself marked by a series of churches.[21] In this case, the liturgy reflected and reinforced Cluny's position within the landscape. Dominique Iogna-Prat has argued that the dedication at Cluny, coinciding as it did with Urban's call for Crusade, and when placed in the larger context of a debate over the sacrality of place, also marked a particular ordering of society that was increasingly intolerant of religious difference.[22] Moreover, this notion of sacred space as it developed primarily in the Carolingian era, but which came to the fore in the eleventh century, marked a rupture with early Christian notions of space, that Iogna-

---

[21] Méhu, *Paix et communautés*, 152–65.

[22] Iogna-Prat, *Order and Exclusion: Cluny and Christendom Face Heresy, Judaism, and Islam (1000–1150)* (Ithaca, NY: Cornell University Press, 2002), 168–79.

Prat describes as in opposition to pagan notions of the sacred.[23] Scholarship on the dedication, therefore, has emphasized how the rite marked communities of power, but it has paid less attention to the variety of ritual practice and, therefore, of meaning.

There was, however, a great variety in dedication rites and rarely can we be certain what rite was used where. For example, in southern Italy in the eleventh century, at least five different versions of the rite were available.[24] A still greater number of forms of the rite can be found on the Italian peninsula in the eleventh century. If we consider, for example, the rite as found in the central Italian manuscript Biblioteca Apostolica Vaticana Latina 4770, from the late tenth or early eleventh century, it contains fewer than half of the steps named above.[25] Its approximately fourteen steps share aspects of *Ordo* 40 but are in a different order: 6, 3, 5, 15, 10, 3, 26, 27, 28, 29, 11, 30, 31 of those listed above. Absent from Vat. Lat. 4770 are the triple circuits of the exterior of the church (step 4), the anointing of the interior walls (step 17) and the tracing of the alphabets on the floor (step 7) among other steps found in *Ordo* 40. Their absence or inclusion surely altered the significance of the rite for the participants. These last two aspects of the rite were to be conducted by the bishop and his clergy while alone inside the church and so their absence or presence would have changed the significance of the rite for them. The triple circumambulation, however, and with it the aspersions of the exterior walls, engaged the entire community visually. Moreover, Vat. Lat. 4770 also lacks the second exterior procession around the church that we see in *Ordo* 40 (step 24 above). That procession was intended to include the entire congregation. Also absent from Vat. Lat. 4770 is the instruction for the bishop directly to address the 'lay lord and constructor' of the church. The absence of these steps would have dramatically diminished the participation of the laity. Without the triple exterior circuits and the aspersion of the exterior walls, the most visible signs of the dedication as a kind of baptism of the church were removed.[26]

---

[23]   The full argument is presented in his *La Maison Dieu*, but see also Iogna-Prat, 'Churches in the Landscape', in *Early Medieval Christianities*, ed. Thomas F.X. Noble and Julia M.H. Smith (Cambridge: Cambridge University Press, 2008), 363–79.

[24]   For comparative tables see Roger E. Reynolds, 'Les cérémonies liturgiques de la cathédrale de Bénévent', in *La cathédrale de Bénévent*, ed. Thomas Forrest Kelly (Ghent: Ludion, 1999), 167–205; and Hamilton, *Sacred City*, Tables 1–3, pp. 27–50.

[25]   See the description in Reynolds, 'Les cérémonies liturgiques', 167–205; John Boe and Alejandro Planchart, eds., *Beneventanum Troporum Corpus 2: Ordinary Chants and Tropes for the Mass from Southern Italy, A.D. 1000–1250. Part 1 Kyrie Eleison*, 2 vols. (Madison, WI: A-R Editions, 1989), 1:2.

[26]   Repsher, studying the commentary known as the *Quid significent duodecim candelae*, argues that it is an interpretation of *Ordo* 40 as a baptism. Others have argued from the form of the rite and from sermons that the rite was understood as a baptism of the church: Iogna-

It should be remembered that liturgical texts are prescriptive, not descriptive sources. The rite may never have been practised as the pontifical said it must. Topography can provide important evidence in this regard. To give one example, churches built into mountainsides or existing infrastructure could not be readily circumambulated, if at all. Thus, in 1092, when Urban II dedicated Santissima Trinità at Cava, whose northern wall is partially built against the mountainside, it is difficult to imagine how a circumambulation could have been accomplished.[27] A monastic complex provides other problems as well, with multiple structures (cloister, dormitories, etc.) physically attached to the church. Therefore it is hard to imagine the circumambulation of Montecassino by Alexander II in 1071, even though the pontifical copied out under Desiderius, abbot of Montecassino (c. 1026–87), required an exterior circuit with the populus singing the *kyrie*.[28] The tenth-century manuscript produced at Montecassino or one of its dependencies, Montecassino, Biblioteca dell'Abbazia 451, contains *Ordines* 40 and 33, both of which call for exterior circumambulation.[29] It is possible, if *Ordo* 33 were used, that clerics (not Alexander) separately accomplished the one required exterior circuit, aspersing the church by means of a complicated route that would have taken them around the entire monastic complex and perilously close to the edge of the mountain itself.[30] Perhaps three dangerous and complicated circuits around the monastic complex were made. Topography reminds us, then, that these are prescriptive sources and that ritual analysis, while desirable, must be done with caution when based on texts.[31] In the broadest sense, the rite displayed the authority of the bishop and it clearly attempted to mark the church as set apart from the community as a whole. At a time when bishops were attempting to establish the 'Peace of God' (condemning violence against noncombatants and in sacred spaces) or their own position, the rite could have reinforced those themes. At the same time, a church's topographical location may indicate that it had a military or defensive purpose and was, despite the Peace, built in anticipation of its having a military role.[32]

Prat, *La maison dieu*; Lee Bowen, 'Tropology of Mediaeval Dedication Rites', *Speculum* 16 (1941): 469–79.

[27]   For the relationship of the church to the mountain, see Simeone Leone, 'La chiesa di S. Alferio fondatore della badia di Cava', *Benedictina* 27 (1980): 393–416.

[28]   Rome, Biblioteca Apostolica Vaticana, Ms. Barberini latinus 631.

[29]   See Hamilton, *Sacred City*, 110.

[30]   Herbert Bloch, *Monte Cassino in the Middle Ages*, 3 vols. (Cambridge: Cambridge University Press, 1986), 1072, fig. 54.

[31]   See Hamilton, 'Les dangers du rituel', 159–61, 173.

[32]   Hamilton, 'Memory, Symbol, and Arson: Was Rome Sacked in 1084?', *Speculum* 78 (2003): 378–99.

Without significant groups of people observing the rite, it must be noted, the rite would have been an impotent means to assert the bishop's authority or social norms, such as the Peace. We do have substantial evidence that rites did sometimes involve large numbers of clerics and laity from across the social spectrum.[33] Suger, abbot of Saint-Denis (France, 1122–51) reported that the crowds at the dedication of Saint-Denis were so great that during the rite of aspersing the exterior of the church the king and his soldiers beat back the crowd with branches and sticks in order to protect the doors; elsewhere Suger describes the crowd as forming a more joyful, more decorous procession: both may be true.[34] Bruno of Asti, bishop of Segni, cardinal legate, and abbot of Montecassino (d. 1123), observed in passing that it was fitting that 'large throngs of people gathered at the dedication of churches'.[35]

Clerics associated with these churches would tend to record the pious enthusiasm of the crowds who assembled at the dedication of a church and so their accounts should be treated with caution especially when lacking in detail. However, there is also evidence for resistance to both the building and the consecration of churches that may be considered more reliable. For example, in Italy, in a twenty-year period in the eleventh century, four different papal dedications were marked by some form of violence or threat of violence, in Bari (1092), Parma (1104), Modena (1106) and Capua (1108). The situations varied. In Bari in 1087, a group who stole the relics of St Nicholas (a group that included clergy, children of clergy, nobles, *boni homines* – civic notables of legal standing, merchants and sailors) fought a skirmish with, and defeated, the bishop's armed men in order to retain control over the relics and the right to build their own church for them. This group had already formed an alliance with a local abbot, Elias, who would later be consecrated bishop by Urban II, who also dedicated the church of San Nicola.[36] Thus, there were no clear divisions in Bari along civic or religious lines. In Modena, a group of eighteen armed

---

[33]   The evidence for eleventh-century Italy is discussed in detail in ch. 2 of Hamilton, *Sacred City*.

[34]   It is not entirely clear if the king and his retinue only were impeded by the crowd, or if the crowd was also impeding the rite although that seems most probable. Suger, *De consecratione*, in *Abt Suger von Saint-Denis ausgewählte schriften: Ordinatio, De consecratione, De administratione*, ed. Andreas Speer and Günther Binding. (Darmstadt: Wissenschaftliche Buchgesellschaft, 2000), 242; Suger, *De administratione*, in *Abt Suger*, 322. See also *Suger, Oeuvres 1*, ed. and trans. Françoise Gasparri (Paris: Les Belles Lettres, 1996), 44–47, 114–15; Günther Binding and Andreas Speer, *Abt Suger von Saint-Denis, De consecratione; kommentierte Studienausgabe* (Cologne: Abt. Architekturgeschichte, 1995); and *Abbot Suger: On the Abbey Church of St-Denis and Its Art Treasures*, ed. and trans. Erwin Panofsky (Princeton: Princeton University Press, 1946).

[35]   Bruno of Segni, *Libri sententiarum, PL* 165: 879c.

[36]   This is discussed in detail in Hamilton, *Sacred City*, 135–42.

knights and citizens, apparently mistrusting Matilda, countess of Tuscany, were permitted to be present at the deposition of the relics of St Geminiano into the altar of the basilica during the consecration. The rite was led by Pope Paschal II and among those present were Matilda, the new bishop, Dodo, and the architect Lanfranc along with the armed knights and citizens. It should be recalled that the deposition of the relics, according to every dedication rite from the period that I have studied, was supposed to take place only in the presence of the bishop and his clergy and certainly not an armed group of the laity. Thus, the explicit threat of violence was accommodated in the practice of the rite at Modena.[37]

In two other cases, Parma and Capua, a recently consecrated space elicited violence and destruction. In Parma in 1104, people destroyed a chapel Matilda built within the recently rebuilt cathedral, in opposition to an anti-imperial and reformist sermon preached by the papal legate. It was clear that the chapel represented Matilda's local authority, and a strong military response from her was required to exact payment for the damage and restore her authority.[38] In Capua, a chapel dedicated by Bruno of Segni in 1106 at Sant'Angelo in Formis (a few miles outside the city) was destroyed by soldiers of Sennes, archbishop of Capua. Sennes probably considered the dedication of a church closely linked to Montecassino by Bruno, then bishop of Segni and abbot of Montecassino, as a threat to his regional episcopal authority.

This example from Capua introduces another aspect of the rite's possible meanings, that given to it through its architecture and art.[39] In the case of Sant'Angelo, the very large image in the church's apse fresco of its builder, Abbot Desiderius (later Victor III, 1086–87), emphasized the authority and presence of the abbey of Montecassino in and around Capua. Interestingly, not

---

[37]   Hamilton, *Sacred City*, 187–95.

[38]   Hamilton, *Sacred City*, 196.

[39]   Examples of studies of art and architecture of particular interest to dedication rites include: Lucy E.G. Donkin, '*Usque ad ultimum terrae*: Mapping the Ends of the Earth in Two Medieval Floor Mosaics', in *Cartography in Antiquity and the Middle Ages: Fresh Perspectives, New Methods*, ed. Richard J.A. Talbert and Richard Watson Unger (Leiden: Brill, 2008), 189–218; Cécile Treffort, 'Une consécration "à la lettre". Place, rôle et autorité des textes incrits dans la sacralisation de l'église', *Mises en scène*, ed. Méhu, 219–52; Yann Codou, 'La consésecration du lieu de culte et ses traductions graphiques: inscriptions et marques lapidaires dans la Provence des XIe–XIIe siècles', in *Mises en scène*, ed. Méhu, 253–84; Donkin, 'Mosaici pavimentali medievali nell'Italia settentrionale e i loro rapporti con la liturgia', *Atti del X Convegno dell'Associazione Italiane per lo Studio e la Conservazione del Mosaico* (Tivoli: Edizioni Scripta Manent, 2005), 503–14; Elizabeth C. Parker, 'Architecture as Liturgical Setting', in *The Liturgy of the Medieval Church*, ed. Thomas J. Heffernan and E. Ann Matter (Kalamazoo: Western Michigan University, 2001), 273–326; Nancy Spatz, 'Church Porches and the Liturgy in Twelfth-Century Rome', in *Liturgy of the Medieval Church*, 327–67.

only did Paschal II censure Sennes, but he also joined Bruno in dedicating the church of San Benedetto in Capua in 1108. In this manner, Bruno and Paschal clearly employed the rite of consecration to reassert Bruno's authority.[40] These examples of participation in the rite expressed through violent opposition reveal the significance such rites could have and the diversity of interpretations of them and reactions to them. They also demonstrate the variety of views that could be held about these ceremonies in which monks and laity were pitted against bishops, the laity were confronting the reforming popes, and popes were confronting bishops. Clearly power was at stake in the consecration, but this was not a fixed performance with a fixed conclusion; it had no single 'function'.

If, as suggested, there is no single meaning for the rite and it was not uniformly practised, then clerical efforts to direct it or guide interpretation of it must be understood as precisely that, the efforts by a specific cleric to create significance for the rite for a specific audience. That a sermon or commentary attempted to shape the meaning of a rite reveals that it was clearly perceived as significant and worth shaping. Moreover, the emphasis placed on the rite in sermons and in liturgical sources during the Carolingian and Gregorian periods reflects an effort to assert meaning through ritual practice and interpretation, an effort whose success depended on the many factors discussed above that were largely beyond the control of papal or imperial authorities. Even though it can be difficult to connect a specific sermon to a specific rite, sermons, however, remain a central piece of evidence in the effort to shape the meaning of a particular church and it is to those that we now turn.[41]

Sermons

What did church dedication rites signify to medieval people? Which texts are we to turn to if we want to find out? The *ordines* spring to mind. They define the course of the rite and hint at symbolic connotations through biblical motifs evoked in readings and chants. But, as sources for significance, they pose two problems. How the rite ought to be performed is not the same as how it was actually practised,[42] and even if it was carried out by the book, the liturgy

---

[40] See Hamilton, 'Desecration and Consecration in Norman Capua', 143–50; and Hamilton, *Sacred City*, 200–1.

[41] A good example of the possibilities and limits of such an effort can be seen in Ugo Facchini, 'I sermoni *In cena Domini* ed *In dedicatione ecclesiae* di san Pier Damiani. Esame della ritualità', *Benedictina* 54 (2008): 212–32.

[42] On this general scholarly challenge, see, for example, Paul F. Bradshaw, *The Search for the Origins of Christian Worship: Sources and Methods for the Study of Early Liturgy*, 2nd ed. (Oxford: Oxford University Press, 2002), 1–20. Concerning dedication, see Hamilton, *Sacred City* and 'Les dangers du rituel', 159–88.

prescribed in the *ordines* is not the liturgy experienced by the participants. One part of the dedication was an inclusive and elaborate eight-day celebration with public processions and masses.[43] But much of the central activity, the anointings, the writing of the alphabet on the floor and so on, took place behind closed doors, involving only the bishop and his officiants.[44]

Other types of sources give a better sense of how the dedication was perceived, for example charters, chronicles and *vitae*.[45] This chapter focuses on the expositions in commentaries and sermons. First I examine a set of key motifs transmitted in early and high medieval texts, showing the meaning generally ascribed to the dedication. Secondly, I present three sermons that show the variation prompted by individual contexts and concerns.

Rite and Interpretation

Scholars of church dedication rituals stress the connection between contemporaneous liturgical rites, sermons and commentaries.[46] But sermons and commentaries are also connected to a prolific tradition of liturgical interpretations that serve not only to explain the liturgy, but also to mould Christian belief. They establish connections that reach backwards towards biblical origins and forwards towards eschatological fulfilment.

Early Christian and medieval liturgical interpretations hinged on allegorization. The platonically based pursuit of allegorical meaning occurs in the New Testament, but as a Christian interpretative strategy it was developed by Origen above all.[47] Origen's exegesis interpreted Old Testament books in

---

[43]   See Hamilton, 'To Consecrate the Church: Ecclesiastical Reform and the Dedication of Churches', in *Reforming the Church before Modernity: Patterns, Problems, and Approaches*, ed. C. Bellitto and L. Hamilton (Aldershot: Ashgate, 2005), 105–37, at 106–7 (early Middle Ages); Ruth Horie, *Perceptions of Ecclesia: Church and Soul in Medieval Dedication Sermons* (Turnhout: Brepols, 2006), 10–12 (historically unspecific).

[44]   Emphasized in Margrete Syrstad Andås, 'Art and Ritual in the Liminal Zone', in *The Medieval Cathedral of Trondheim: Architectural and Ritual Constructions in their European Context*, ed. Margrete Syrstad Andås et al., Ritus et artes: Traditions and Transformations 3 (Turnhout: Brepols, 2007), 47–126, at 59–60.

[45]   For example, Michel Lauwers, 'Consécration d'églises, réforme et ecclésiologie monastique', in *Mises en scène*, ed. Méhu, 93–142, see also Méhu, '*Historiae* et *imagines*', in ibid., 15–48, at 40–44; Hamilton, *Sacred City* and 'Les dangers du rituel'.

[46]   For example Méhu, '*Historiae* et *imagines*', 32.

[47]   Especially Galatians 4: 21–26 on Hagar and Sarah as allegories of the two covenants. The classic work is Henri de Lubac, *Medieval Exegesis: The Four Senses of Scripture* (Grand Rapids: W.B. Eerdmans, 1998; first publ. in French 1959); more accessible are Beryl Smalley, *The Study of the Bible in the Middle Ages* (Oxford: Blackwell, 1952 and later), 1–26; Daniel Boyarin, 'Origen as Theorist of Allegory: Alexandrian Contexts', in *The Cambridge Companion to Allegory*, ed. R. Copeland and P.T. Struck (Cambridge: Cambridge University

the light of the New Testament and argued that these texts are imbued with spiritual meanings beyond the straightforward literal or historical ones. Thereby texts remote in time and tenor became potentially relevant for all ages. The spiritual meanings came to be structured in three categories: the allegorical meaning speaks of Christ and the Church, the tropological or moral meaning offers guidelines for the Christian's conduct and the anagogical meaning deals with the afterlife. Read in this light, next to their literal meaning, biblical texts contain messages for each believer concerning belief, behaviour and beatitude. The four-fold approach is related to typology: the idea that the Old Testament prefigures the New while the New Testament fulfils the promise of the Old.[48] Owing to Fathers such as Ambrose, Augustine and Gregory the Great the typological-allegorical understanding came to permeate the religious mindset up to and including Dante.

General Motifs

Commentaries and sermons are important vehicles of liturgical interpretation. Those concerned with the dedication tend to focus on the constituents of the Church, and from the Carolingian age such interpretations became crucial frameworks for ecclesiological reflection.[49] Many commentaries and sermons on the dedication therefore come across as doctrinal compendia.

Scholars tend usually to read such commentaries and sermons as on a par. This chapter suggests that, while thematically related and both concerned with the spiritual and moral ramifications of the rite, commentaries and sermons abide by very different generic conventions.[50] The liturgical commentary is a strictly literary genre.[51] Some commentaries on church dedication rites, such as the Carolingian *Quid significent duodecim candelae*, stay close to the liturgy.[52] Others, such as Honorius of Autun's (d. 1154) *Gemma Animae*, with its nuptial

---

Press, 2010), 39–54; and Denys Turner, 'Allegory in Christian Late Antiquity', in ibid., 71–82.

[48]   Such as the crossing of the Red Sea as a type of Christ's Passion and the purging of sin in each individual baptism; Augustine, *De catechizandis rudibus*, 20.34: *Œvres de Saint Augustin 11/1: La première catéchèse, de catechizandis rudibus*, trans. Goulven Madec (Paris: Etudes augustiniennes, 1991), 166–68.

[49]   Méhu, '*Historiae* et *imagines*', 28.

[50]   Exemplified in Eric J. del Giacco, 'A Comparison of Bede's Commentary and Homilies on Luke', *Medieval Sermon Studies* 50 (2006): 9–29.

[51]   Treatises such as Ambrose's *De sacramentis*, Isidore of Seville's *De ecclesiasticis officiis* and Amalarius of Metz's commentaries, such as *Expositio Missae* and *Liber officialis*; for more examples see Méhu, '*Historiae* et *imagines*', 28–32; Iogna-Prat, *La maison dieu*, 285.

[52]   Published as *Tractatus de dedicatione ecclesiae* by Remigius of Auxerre in *PL* 131:845–66; an English translation appears in Repsher, *Rite of Church Dedication*.

vocabulary, are more independent.[53] By contrast, the sermon grows out of an oral situation.[54] Homiletic treatment of the dedication appears in sermons written for the annual feast of the dedication of the Jewish Temple, for the dedication of a church proper[55] and for the annual eight-day commemoration of the dedication instituted by Felix IV (526–30).[56]

It is true, however, that commentaries and sermons on the dedication share motifs. Both genres take their thematic cue from the dedication liturgy and, via four-fold interpretations, develop an array of themes whose spiritual connotations add further dimensions to the here and now of the rite.[57] The interpretations focus on fundamental doctrinal themes that are not particular to this rite. In the context of the dedication they are generally couched in a metaphorical vocabulary that favours architectural and spatial images as well as biblical references to building and building materials. A summary overview of key categories, motifs and biblical references will suffice:

Typology This category inscribes each community in salvation history. The church is associated with Solomon's Temple (1 Kings 7–8),[58] occasionally with a reference to the Temple as an inferior antecedent of the Church.[59] Sometimes an added typological dimension is offered through references to Moses' Tabernacle or to the description of the feast of the dedication of the Temple (John 10).[60] The typological tenor is augmented through allusions to Jacob's dream and its

---

[53]   *Gemma Animae* 1.150; *PL* 172:590. The allusion to the wedding between Christ and the Church is based on Eph. 5: 21–27; Lauwers, 'Consécration d'églises', 114.

[54]   See Beverly M. Kienzle, 'Medieval Sermons and Their Performance: Theory and Record', in *Preacher, Sermon and Audience in the Middle Ages*, ed. C. Muessig (Leiden: Brill, 2002), 89–124.

[55]   *OR* 40 prescribes a sermon after the triple procession with the relics.

[56]   Felix IV, *Epistula* 2, *PL* 65:16–21, including a full quotation of 1 Kings 8 on the Temple; see also Iogna-Prat, *La maison dieu*, 292; Repsher, *Rite of Church Dedication*, 20–21.

[57]   Finbarr C. Clancy, 'Augustine's Sermons for the Dedication of a Church', in *Papers Presented at the Thirteenth International Conference on Patristic Studies*, ed. M.F. Wiles and E.J. Yarnold, Studia Patristica 38 (2001): 48–55, at 48–50.

[58]   Augustine, *De civitate Dei*, 18.48; or to the synagogue as inferior to the church, *Quid significent duodecim candelae*, 5. These are but representative texts; for additional examples, see, for the early Middle Ages, Hamilton, *Sacred City*; Repsher, *Rite of Church Dedication*; for the late Middle Ages, see Horie, *Perceptions of Ecclesia*.

[59]   Hilary of Poitiers, *De dedicatione ecclesiae*, *PL* 10:881–83; Bede, *Homilia* 21, *PL* 94:247–8; *Homilia* 45, *PL* 94:434; Peter Damian, *Sermo* 72.9, *PL* 144:910.

[60]   For the Tabernacle, see Bede, *Homilia* 45, *PL* 94:434; Hrabanus Maurus, *De institutione clericorum*, 2.45, *PL* 107:358–9; *Homilia* 39, *PL* 110:73–4. The reference to John appears in Isidore of Seville, *De origine officiorum* 36.1, *PL* 83:771, reiterated in Hrabanus Maurus, *De institutione clericorum* 2.45, *PL* 107:358. See also Bede, *Homilia* 21, *PL* 94:243–49; Ivo of Chartres, *Decretum* 3.24, *PL* 161:204. The twelve-year-old Jesus in the

epiphany, grasped in the statement 'This place is terrifying' (*locus iste terribilis est*, Gen. 28:17), cued by readings in the rite.

Christology (The 'Allegorical' Meaning)   Allusions to the Christological implications of the dedication are complex and varied. They range from deliberations on Christ's passion and resurrection[61] to architectural images such as Christ as foundation (1 Cor. 3:11) and cornerstone (Ps. 117:22; Eph. 2:20–22).[62]

Ecclesiology (The 'Allegorical' Meaning)   The fundamental association between church (building) and Church (community) is present already in Eusebius's (d. c. 340) presentation of the Constantinian surge of dedications.[63] This association is reinforced with references to 1 Peter 2:4–5 (the Christians as living stones) or to Matthew 16:18 (Peter as the rock on which Christ built his Church) and elaborated with masonic metaphors.[64] Ecclesiological motifs create relations between communities across time and space, including Jews and pagans.[65] Both the Christological and the ecclesiological motifs are often developed in association with allegorical interpretations of parts of the church building or other architectural allegories.[66]

The Christian (The 'Moral' Meaning)   References to individual believers appear in the earliest expositions of the consecration.[67] The church is described

---

Temple (John 10: 24) is exploited allegorically in Bede, *Homilia* 21, *PL* 94:244; Hrabanus Maurus, *Homilia* 40, *PL* 110:74–75.

   61   Augustine, *Sermo* 163.3, *PL* 38:890; *Sermo* 336.3–5, *PL* 38:1473–75; Bede, *Homilia* 21, *PL* 94:244–45.

   62   Eusebius, *Historia ecclesiastica* 10.4; Bede, *Homilia* 45, *PL* 94:436; Haymo of Halberstadt, *Homilia* 141, *PL* 118:746 (defined by Henri Barré as Haymo of Auxerre in *Les homéliaires carolingiens de l'école d'Auxerre* (Vatican City: Biblioteca Apostolica Vaticana, 1962), 61.

   63   Eusebius, *Historia ecclesiastica* 10.3. See also Hilary of Poitiers, *De dedicatione ecclesiae*, *PL* 10:881; Bede, *Homilia* 21, *PL* 94:248; *Homilia* 45, *PL* 94:434.

   64   Méhu, '*Historiae* et *imagines*', 37.

   65   Augustine, *De civitate Dei* 18.48; Bede, *Homilia* 45, *PL* 94:434; Hrabanus Maurus, *De universo* 14.23, *PL* 111:401; Bruno of Segni, *Expositio in Exodum* 26, *PL* 164:318; Hugh of Saint-Victor, *De sacramentis* II.5.1, *PL* 176:439. Another form of historization appears in claims that the command to build churches was Christ's requirement to his disciples; Lauwers, 'Consécration d'églises', 117–21.

   66   Commentaries on Ezechiel, including his vision of the Temple; Bede's *De templo* and *De tabernaculo*; Hrabanus Maurus, *De universo* 14; G. Turville-Petre, 'The Old Norse Homily on the Dedication', *Medieval Studies* 11 (1949):206–18, at 207.

   67   Repsher, *Rite of Church Dedication*, 25 with reference to Ambrose's *Exhortatio ad virgines*, *PL* 16:380.

as being baptized into the universal Church in parallel with the baptism of the individual into the community.[68] Tropological or moral interpretations create links between the dedication and the Christian as God's temple (1 Cor. 3:16–17 and 6:19; 2 Cor. 6:16)[69] and latch on to associations between the Lord's temple and Christ's body (John 2:21).[70] This theme is developed ecclesiologically in the idea that the Church consists of the community of individual temples of the Lord.[71]

Eschatology (The 'Anagogical' Meaning)   The anagogical reading of the dedication turns towards beatitude. Authors emphasize the provisional character of the church building: what has been begun on earth will be completed in heaven.[72] The expositions stress the superiority of beatific immortality over earthly transience (1 Cor. 15:55–57) in representations of the heavenly abode which surpasses any earthly construction.[73]

The four-fold interpretation becomes a catalyst for expositions that position each church, community and believer within the Church and its comprehensive system of belief and which manifest the church building as the physical structure within which all of this is contained.

Three Sermons

These motifs are orchestrated in a variety of keys and degrees of sophistication. They are coloured by the theological mindset of individual authors, by the audience, as well as by institutional, social and textual conditions. The anti-arian Hilary of Poitiers (c. 300–c. 368) employs his dedication sermon to talk about the Trinity, while Augustine (354–430) uses one of his to propagate

---

68   Ivo of Chartres, *Sermo* 4; Repsher, *Rite of Church Dedication*, 17.

69   Eusebius, *Historia ecclesiastica* 10.4; Augustine, *Sermo* 163.1, *PL* 38:889; Bede, *Homilia* 21, *PL* 94:244; Hrabanus Maurus, *Homilia* 40, *PL* 110:75; Peter Damian, *Sermo* 72.11, *PL* 144:910. For associations of body and temple, see Harris, 'Body as Temple'.

70   Eric Palazzo, *Liturgies et société au moyen âge* (Paris: Aubier, 2000), 72.

71   Repsher, *Rite of Church Dedication*, 29–30.

72   Augustine, *Sermo* 336.1, *PL* 38:1473; *Sermo* 337, *PL* 38:1475–78, both arguing that believers, as houses of God, are built in this life and dedicated in the next; Hilary of Poitiers, *De dedicatione ecclesiae*, *PL* 10:884; Bede, *Homilia* 21, *PL* 94:245–46 and 248; *Homilia* 45, *PL* 94:434; Hrabanus Maurus, *Homilia* 40, *PL* 110:75–76.

73   Augustine, *Sermo* 163.7–12, *PL* 38:892–95; Bernard of Clairvaux, *In dedicatione ecclesiae, sermo* 4.4–6: *Bernhard von Clairvaux: Sämtliche Werke*, ed. Gerhard Winkler et al., 10 vols. (Innsbruck: Tyrolia Verlag, 1997), 8:840–46; *Sancti Bernardi opera*, ed. Jean Leclerq, Henri Rochais and Charles Talbot, 8 vols. (Rome: Editiones Cistercienses, 1957–77), 5: 385–88.

his anti-pelagian programme.[74] The interpretations hover in a tension between their shared adherence to an interpretative tradition and their individual historical context.

The meaning of the dedication is taught in both commentaries and sermons. But sermons are driven by a more acute communicative compulsion.[75] Méhu distinguishes between sermons inserted in historical narratives and the polished works by named authors, but even the latter, I argue, maintain a connection with the preaching situation, however stylized.[76] In its written form the sermon is defined by literary conventions and even allusions to oral practice may belong to a carefully crafted literary strategy.[77] At the same time sermons address, at the very least, an implied audience and by turning to sermons we approach the interpretative community for whom each of these texts made particular sense. This is an approach which is interested in the reader-response anticipated or prompted in a text and the questions in the audience which the author sought to answer.[78] If we examine three sermons, one for the dedication proper, two for its annual commemoration, we shall see that while all are permeated by the four-fold interpretation, their juxtaposition illustrates how understandings of the dedication vary from one text to another.

The Stave Church Sermon

We begin with the latest sermon of the three. The so-called 'Stave church sermon', an Old Norse homily for the dedication, is transmitted in Old Norse and Icelandic manuscripts from around 1200 to 1220, but the material is probably older.[79] Possibly a model sermon whose architectural description is

---

74   Gert Partoens, 'Prédication, orthodoxie et liturgie', in *Prédication et liturgie au moyen âge*, ed. N. Bériou and F. Morenzoni (Turnhout: Brepols, 2008), 23–51, at 50.

75   On medieval sermons, see B.M. Kienzle, ed., *The Sermon*, Typologie des sources du moyen âges occidental 81–83 (Turnhout: Brepols, 2000); and, briefer, Ann T. Thayer, 'The Medieval Sermon', in *Understanding Medieval Primary Sources: Using Historical Sources to Discover Medieval Europe*, ed. J.T. Rosenthal (London: Routledge, 2012), 43–58.

76   Méhu, '*Historiae et imagines*', 37.

77   See, for example, Bernard McGinn, 'Introduction', in *Isaac of Stella: Sermons on the Christian Year*, trans. H. McCaffery (Kalamazoo, MI: Cistercian Publications, 1979), xvii; *Bernard of Clairvaux: Sermons for the Summer Season*, trans. B.M. Kienzle (Kalamazoo, MI: Cistercian Publications, 1991), 4–6.

78   Related to the idea of the *Erwartungshorisont* addressed in a text, see Hans Robert Jauss, 'Literaturgeschichte als Provokation der Literaturwissenschaft', in *Literaturgeschichte als Provokation* (Frankfurt am Main: Suhrkamp, 1974), 144–207, esp. 183–89.

79   I am grateful to Nils Holger Petersen for his reference to this sermon. In its complete form it has been transmitted in two Icelandic and one Old Norse manuscripts; Hans Bekker-Nielsen, 'The Old Norse Dedication Liturgy', in *Festschrift für Konstantin Reichardt*, ed. C.

sufficiently vague to apply generally,[80] this homily does not speak of the rite, but offers an allegorical interpretation of the church building.[81] As a catalogue of commonplaces it makes a useful point of departure.

The sermon begins with Solomon's Temple in a paraphrase of 1 Kings 8–9 and then turns to the present community: 'From these origins, churches and all the celebration of dedication days began. And since, dear brethren, we are holding the feast of dedication today, it is of first importance that we realize how great is the grace we receive in the church.'[82] The author stresses how the church building and the grace bestowed inside it frame the life of a human being: baptism, the Eucharist, human beings' reconciliation with God, prayers and, when sin is so grave that God's friendship is lost, confession, as well as, finally, the funeral.[83] The meaning is expounded in pedagogic vein, associating the Christian community with the hall of God (1 Cor. 6:19). First, the parts of the building are interpreted as an image of the different peoples who share the Christian faith; the Christians who are already with God (signified by the choir) and those still on earth (the nave). The altar is Christ, and the entry to the church is the right faith that leads believers into the Christian community. The floorboards are the humble: the more they are trodden on, the more they

---

Gellinek with H. Zauchenberger (Bern: Francke Verlag, 1969), 127–34, at 127–28. An edition of the Old Norse text has been published as *Gamal Norsk Homiliebok*, ed. Gustav Indrebø (Oslo: Oslo Universitetsforlaget, 1966; first publ. 1931). Turville-Petre's English translation is published in 'The Old Norse Homily', 206–18, at 215–18. The homily was previously dated to the early twelfth century, but recent research associates it with the beginning of the thirteenth century when preaching to lay people became a consolidated practice; Arnved Nedkvitne, *Lay Belief in Norse Society 1000–1350* (Copenhagen: Museum Tusculanum Press, 2009), 52–53. However, the earlier dating is maintained in Kirsten M. Berg, 'On the Use of Mnemonic Schemes in Sermon Composition: The *Old Norwegian Homily Book*', in *Constructing the Medieval Sermon*, ed. Roger Andersson (Turnhout: Brepols, 2007), 221–36, at 232. On the commemoration of the dedication according to the Nidaros ordinal, see Andås, 'Art and Ritual', 60; on dedication in the Old Norse context see Andås, 'Imagery and Ritual', 85–91 and 119–22.

[80]   Although Turville-Petre sees the absence of the commonplace reference to living stones as a pointer to the wooden construction typical of stave churches; 'Old Norse Homily', 209.

[81]   Bekker-Nielsen, 'Old Norse Dedication Liturgy', 130. Influences can be traced from, among others, Richard of Saint-Victor's homilies on the dedication, Honorius of Autun's *Gemma Animae* and Hrabanus Maurus's *De universo*; *Gammelnorsk Homiliebok*, ed. Erik Gunnes, trans. Astrid Salvesen (Oslo: Universitetsforlaget, 1971), 176; Turville-Petre, 'Old Norse Homily', 207–11.

[82]   'Old Norse Homily', 215; this part is influenced by Origen's *De tabernaculo*, in part transmitted via Bede's *De templo*; *Gammelnorsk Homiliebok*, 176.

[83]   It is worth bearing in mind that also secular reconciliations could take place in the church; Nedkvitne, *Lay Belief*, 92; Andås, 'Imagery and Ritual', 151–55.

bear the weight of the Christians. The long walls are the pagans and the Jews, the cross wall at the West is Christ who unites them and the rood-screen the Holy Spirit by way of which one passes into heaven. The corner posts are the gospels and the roof an image of the believer who looks towards heaven.[84]

Midway through the sermon, the author shifts focus from Christianity at large to the individual Christian 'who verily makes himself the temple of the Holy Spirit by his good works. For every man shall fashion a spiritual church within himself, not with timbers or stones, but rather with good works.'[85] In *this* church the choir is prayer and psalms and the altar love, the cross walls are the love of neighbour (the outer wall) and of God (the inner). The entry into *this* church signifies control of the tongue. The corner posts are the key virtues: wisdom, justice, strength and temperance; the floorboards are humility and the roof is hope. The crucifixes are the burdens laid on our bodies in fasts and vigils. The sermon ends on an anagogical note: 'it is for this reason that we celebrate the feast of dedication annually on earth, that we may celebrate an eternal day of dedication, which is true rejoicing of all the saints in heaven.'[86] The road to this eternity goes by way partly of charity towards the neighbour: bemoan and punish them for their sins, help them in their needs; partly of tending to the souls of the dead with prayers.[87]

With a focus on the building the preacher has a material point of reference at hand: a physical anchoring of his instruction that aids memorization.[88] The architecture provides a spatial structure which sustains messages both about relations (Christ mediating between Jews and pagans as a cross wall between two long walls) and about movement (the entry into the church, that is, via faith into the community, or the progression from nave to choir, that is, from life to death) and which allows for a coherent doctrinal structure which embraces widely different components: communal and individual, historical and contemporary, material and spiritual.

---

[84] 'Old Norse Homily', 216.

[85] 'Old Norse Homily', 216.

[86] 'Old Norse Homily', 217.

[87] 'Old Norse Homily', 218. In his three dedication homilies Richard of Saint-Victor presents an interpretation which resembles the 'Stave church sermon's' but has more theological finesse, including both the *imago Dei* and the five senses of the soul; *PL* 177:901–07; Hideki Nakamura, '*Talem vitam agamus, ut Dei lapides esse possimus*: Kirchweihpredigten Richards von Sankt Viktor', in '*Das Haus Gottes, das seid ihr selbst*': *Mittelalterliches und barockes Kirchenverständnis im Spiegel der Kirchweihe*, ed. R.M.W. Stammberger and C. Sticher (Berlin: Akademie Verlag, 2006), 293–327.

[88] Berg, 'On the Use of Mnemonic Schemes'. The homily comes across as an accessible counterpart to Hugh of Saint-Victor's ark of Noah; see Mary Carruthers, *The Book of Memory: A Study of Memory in Medieval Culture* (Cambridge: Cambridge University Press, 2008; first publ. 1990), 53–55.

The sermon rehearses standard motifs. It goes through allegorical, tropological and, albeit less elaborately, anagogical explications of the church. When searching for the specificities of this model sermon, we may notice, parenthetically, the striking difference between the preacher's anticipation of the community's intent focus on the architecture and the sagas' descriptions of the general coming and going during mass.[89] Putting aside whether it was listened to or not, the sermon stresses the role of the church in human life as the locus of baptism, confession and burial, and gives clear-cut directions concerning charity for the needy and prayers for the dead. The church is positioned at the centre of the community's life, embracing generations and social segments. The dedication ceremony is present only tacitly as the initiation of the relation between God and the congregation which is manifested in the church and which has a bearing on individual and familial life cycles as well as the daily conduct for which the listeners would expect guidelines.

Ivo of Chartres: Sermo 4, De sacramentis dedicationis

Ivo of Chartres (c. 1040–1115) was prior of the Abbey of Saint-Quentin (France) from 1069 to 1090 when he became bishop of Chartres. He was an influential author of texts on canon law, working under the auspices of Gregorian reform.[90] Ivo's *Sermo 4, De sacramentis dedicationis*, is written for a dedication proper.[91] This is not yet a familiar space, but the preacher invests it with a meaning that relates it to the believers, employing baptism as the central point of identification. The sermon is closely connected to the sacramental ponderings in the bishop's remaining oeuvre and to his reform agenda; as Louis Hamilton has demonstrated, the dedication feast is well suited to this end.[92] It is indicative of the sermon's doctrinal character that several of Ivo's points were taken over in Hugh of Saint-Victor's *De sacramentis*, including the dedication as the sacramental framework for all other sacraments.[93] This raises, again,

---

[89] Nedkvitne, *Lay Belief*, 94–95.

[90] For Ivo's biography, see Christof Rolker, *Canon Law and the Letters of Ivo of Chartres* (Cambridge: Cambridge University Press, 2010), 1–49; Margot E. Fassler, *The Virgin of Chartres: Making History through Liturgy and the Arts* (New Haven: Yale University Press, 2010), 133–36; Bruce C. Brasington, 'Lessons of Love: Bishop Ivo of Chartres as Teacher', in *Teaching and Learning in Northern Europe, 1000–1200*, ed. S.N. Vaughan and J. Rubenstein (Brepols: Turnhout, 2006), 129–47.

[91] *PL* 162:527–35.

[92] See above and Hamilton, *Sacred City*; Fassler, *Virgin of Chartres*, 136–40.

[93] *De sacramentis* II.5.1, *PL* 176:439; Margot E. Fassler, *Gothic Song: Victorine Sequences and Augustinian Reform in Twelfth-Century Paris* (Cambridge: Cambridge University Press, 1993), 333–34; Hanns P. Neuheuser, 'Ritus und Theologie der Kirchweihe bei Hugo von St. Viktor', in *'Das Haus Gottes'*, 251–92, esp. 273–76.

the question of genre. Méhu argues that the most theoretical sermons on the dedication do not differ substantially from treatises.[94] But even with the flux in generic definitions in mind, an identification as *sermo* and its particular connotations are not to be lightly dismissed – no matter how theoretical the text. Ivo's sermon feeds rhetorically on the implied presence of an audience: a community who shares the view of the bishop knocking on the church door and partakes in the festivities. The sermon has a speech-act character that unites the community, the feast and the Scripture differently from a treatise.

Ivo addresses his audience directly: 'Since you have come devoutly to the dedication of this basilica today, it is necessary that you understand that what you see done to this saintly man-made [edifice] has all been fulfilled in you.'[95] His ample introduction reminds them that through baptism they have been made temples of the Lord, athletes of Christ, dedicated to a life-long combat against the devil. This sacramental association flavours the entire sermon which revolves around two powerful images. The first is the dedication as a mimesis of baptism: 'We circulate and asperse the church with water on the outside because when there cannot be a triple immersion [of the church] in the same way as of those baptized, it is necessary that there is a triple aspersion so that we can make it resemble the sacrament.'[96] The second is the entry of the bishop which is presented as a critical exorcistic moment. Bearing in mind Ivo's inclination for reform, it is unsurprising that he lingers over episcopal power: the bishop's admission into the church is described as a veritable conquest. Ivo ponders the 'Quis est iste rex gloriae?' (Who is this king of Glory?) of Psalm 24 which sounds from within the church when the bishop knocks after each circulation. The voice of the Psalm – and of the deacon from inside the church – is ascribed to the church itself. Before the bishop enters, the church is a type, Ivo states, of an ignorant people immersed in the darkness of faithlessness; they do not recognize the Petrine power bestowed by the Lord. But the bishop commands the demons and vices to open their doors. He enters the church and, prostrate on the floor, calls to God to sanctify the place. Associations between liturgy and dramaturgy are controversial, but it does seem that Ivo exploits the dramatic potential of the entry to the full.

Each ritual element is commented on and put in perspective by biblical references, some of which recur in readings and chants during the rite. After having zoomed in, as it were, on the church, Ivo employs the elements of the

---

94   Méhu, '*Historiae* et *imagines*', 37.

95   'Quoniam ad dedicationem praesentis basilicae hodie devote convenistis, oportet ut quod in his sanctis manufactis fieri videtis, totum impletum esse in vobis cognoscatis.' *Sermo* 4, *PL* 162:527.

96   'Ista aqua ad quamdam baptismi imaginem gyrando ecclesiam tunc exterius aspergimus, quia ubi more baptizatorum non potest fieri trina mersio, necesse est ut qua possumus sacramenti similitudine trina fiat aspersio.' *Sermo* 4, *PL* 162:529.

dedication ceremony to open the view towards a wider doctrinal horizon. The symbolism is dense and knotted. The diagonal writing of the alphabets is associated with the first rudimentary version of sacred doctrine which reaches Jews and Gentiles. The episcopal staff used for writing signifies the salvation reaching to the ends of the world through the sacerdotal office.[97] The association of the alphabet with Jews and Gentiles is in tune with other interpretations, but it is in contrast to the 'Stave church sermon's' association of the people with the church walls.[98] This reminds us that while motifs are relatively stable, their interpretations are not schematic. Doctrinal motifs are accumulated in Ivo's homiletic compendium: salt and ashes are mixed just as divine insight must merge with faith in the Passion; water mixed with wine signifies Christ's double nature, and the aspersion of the inner walls shows that exterior appearances must be complemented by interior saintliness. The seven-fold aspersion of the altar is done with water and hyssop. Hyssop is a humble, purging herb; it signifies Christ's humility which cured human pride when he aspersed it with his blood. The bishop wipes the altar with linen; linen comes from the earth and is bleached with much labour: this is Christ's flesh emerging from earth, signifying the Virgin, and he who reached resurrection through suffering.[99]

After a rich and dense explanation the bishop reaches his anagogical conclusion with Psalm 29:12: 'You have turned for me my mourning into joy'. This makes for a dialectical juxtaposition of the mournful present life and the vision of peace. Lamentation, Ivo states, will be turned to joy when we are brought through to the fatherland from which we are now exiled. The feast establishes a link to this eternal joy: it is the delightful and festive dedication of God's man-made temple in its wedding clothes, and he will preserve this temple until the eternal dedication.[100]

Ivo of Chartres exploits the stock repertory of dedication themes: the community as living stones, the universal Church and each baptized member of it, the completion of the dedication in beatitude. But their exact form and organization are shaped by his preoccupation with episcopal power and his intent to make the audience see the dedication of this new church in relation to their baptism. This intent he shares, to some extent, with the Stave church preacher, but whereas the Old Norse text centres on life cycles and guidelines for behaviour, Ivo's focus rests on the divine purging imparted in the sacrament and mediated by the bishop; he addresses the sacramental and salvational coherence

---

[97] *Sermo* 4, *PL* 162:530–31.

[98] Whose interpretation in turn equals Hugh of Saint-Victor's *De sacramentis* II.5.1, *PL* 176:439.

[99] *Sermo* 4, *PL* 162:534.

[100] *Sermo* 4, *PL* 162:535.

between the Bible, the building and the doctrine, between the baptized and their church. We can only begin to surmise that these may have been issues that the audience was querying too.

Bernard of Clairvaux: In dedicatione ecclesiae, sermo 1

The Cistercian Bernard of Clairvaux (1090–1153) was a crusade preacher, church politician and prolific author. In his six sermons *In dedicatione ecclesiae*, completed after 1150, he writes, above all, as abbot. The commemoration of the dedication is one of the feasts for which the Cistercian manual *Ecclesiastica officia* prescribes that a sermon be delivered in the chapter, preferably by the abbot.[101] The audience was the Cistercian community at its most comprehensive, including lay brothers, guests and *familiares*.[102] Kienzle suggests that this retinue may have entailed straightforward, vernacular preaching.[103] But in the written version Bernard's dedication sermons are literary compositions which presumably circulated among audiences beyond Clairvaux.[104] Meyer considers the sermons to be a liturgical commentary on the rite.[105] But again it seems well-advised to maintain a distinction between sermon and commentary. The texts retain an association with the idea of the abbot preaching to a monastic community; for instance, Bernard appears to survey his audience, observing 'so many youngsters, so many adolescents, so many noblemen';[106] elsewhere he speaks of the mood in which the audience will leave having heard the sermon.[107] At the same time Bernard's dedication sermons form a coherent literary unit

---

[101] *Ecclesiastica officia* 67.5, *Les 'Ecclesiastica officia' cisterciens du XIIème siècle*, ed. D. Choisselet and P. Vernet (Reiningue: Abbaye d'Oelenberg, 1989), 190; Chrysogonus Waddell, 'The Liturgical Dimension of Twelfth-Century Cistercian Preaching', in *Medieval Monastic Preaching*, ed. C. Muessig (Leiden: Brill, 1998), 335–49, at 336–39.

[102] Chrysogonus Waddell, 'The Early Cistercian Experience of Liturgy', in *Rule and Life: An Interdisciplinary Symposium*, edited by M.B. Pennington (Spencer, MA: Cistercian Publications, 1971), 77–116 at 112nn107–8; *Cistercian Lay Brothers: Twelfth-Century Usages with Related Texts* ed. Chrysogonus Waddell (Cîteaux: Commentarii Cistercienses, 2000), 184, nn 2–4.

[103] B.M. Kienzle, 'The Twelfth-Century Monastic Sermon', in *The Sermon*, ed. Kienzle, 271–323, at 279n41; M.B. Bruun, 'Mapping the Monastery: Hélinand of Froidmont's Second Sermon for Palm Sunday', in *Prédication et liturgie au moyen âge*, ed. Bériou and Morenzoni, 183–99, at 187–90.

[104] Méhu, *'Historiae* et *imagines'*, 35.

[105] Meyer, *Medieval Allegory*, 91.

[106] '... tot iuvenes, tot adolescents, tot nobiles ...', *In ded., sermo* 1.2, *Bernhard*, ed. Winkler, 8: 812; *Sancti Bernardi opera*, ed. Leclercq, 5: 371.

[107] *In ded., sermo* 5.2: *Bernhard*, ed. Winkler, 8: 848; *Sancti Bernardi opera*, ed. Leclerq, 5: 389.

with conscious development of motifs and escalating density.[108] They are permeated by the allegorical dynamic and carefully crafted rhetoric typical of the abbot and thereby linked to the remainder of Bernard's work as much as to other dedication texts.[109]

Like Ivo of Chartres and the Stave church preacher Bernard begins by approaching his audience, but the abbot addresses a 'we' that is considered as a group apart from the Church at large: 'Today's feast, brothers, must for us be so much more worthy of devotion, as it is more related to us. For we have the other saints' feast in common with the other churches, but this one is our own since it is celebrated by no one but us.'[110] Then the abbot introduces one of his main themes: the relation between the building, each monk's body, and the soul which God beatifies on earth and sanctifies in heaven.[111] Bernard rehearses the motif of the individual believer as the Lord's temple, but he dwells upon the corporeal aspect, speaking about the wonder which takes place when men decide to estrange themselves from gluttony, drunkenness and lasciviousness for the rest of their lives. He speaks in the language of Exodus about their individual paths: each knows the wonder that brought him to leave Egypt and traverse the desert of renunciation. The perspective is exclusively monastic.

The monks' conversion stories prove that the Holy Spirit inhabits their bodies. They have been dedicated to the Lord; not only those who were present at the consecration, but 'anybody who does service for God in this place to the end of time'.[112] With this prelude the abbot reaches his Christological peak:

---

[108] On the relation between oral markers and literary style see the positions of Jean Leclercq, 'Les sermons sur les cantiques ont-ils été prononcés?', in *Recueil d'études sur S. Bernard et ses écrits*, 3 vols. (Rome: Storia et Letteratura, 1962), 2: 193–212, esp. 199–200, summarized in his introduction to *Bernard of Clairvaux: Sermons on the Song of Songs II*, trans. K. Walsh (Kalamazoo, MI: Cistercian Publications, 1983), vii–xxx; Christopher Holdsworth, 'Were the Sermons of Bernard on the Song of Songs ever Preached?', in *Medieval Monastic Preaching*, ed. Meussig, 295–318, esp. 308–11; and Wim Verbaal, 'Réalités quotidiennes et fiction littéraire dans les *Sermons sur le Cantique* de Bernard de Clairvaux', *Cîteaux* 51 (2000): 201–18.

[109] This is against Horie's view that Bernard 'allows his thoughts to flow freely'; Horie, *Perceptions of Ecclesia*, 31.

[110] 'Festivitas hodierna, fratres, tanto nobis debet esse devotior, quanto familiarior est. Nam ceteras quidem Sanctorum sollemnitates cum ecclesiis aliis habemus communes; haec vero sic nobis est propria, ut necesse sit, vel a nobis eam, vel a nemine celebrari. Nostra est, quia de ecclesia nostra, magis autem nostra est, quia de nobis ipsis.' *In ded., sermo* 1.1: *Bernhard*, ed. Winkler, 8:811 (*Sancti Bernardi opera*, ed. Leclerq, 5:370).

[111] *In ded., sermo* 1.1: *Bernhard*, ed. Winkler, 8:810 (*Sancti Bernardi opera*, ed. Leclerq, 5:369); see also Harris, 'Body as Temple', 248–49.

[112] '... quicumque usque in finem saeculi Domino sunt in hoc loco militaturi.' *In ded., sermo* 1.3: *Bernhard*, ed. Winkler, 8:814 (*Sancti Bernardi opera*, ed. Leclerq, 5:372). The second Clairvaux was built in 1135 and some members of the audience may have

'Thus in us must be carried out spiritually what earlier happened visibly on the walls. And that, if you want to know, is aspersion, inscription, unction, illumination and benediction. This have the bishops carried out visibly in this house; this Christ [...] carries out invisibly in us each day.'[113] We recognize the association of the ritual action and the interior work of grace from Ivo's sermon, but instead of speaking of the work of grace in association with baptism, the abbot describes it as an ongoing process. Bernard elaborates each element: the purging is brought about by the hyssop of humility, the aspersion by the tears of confession and the water from Christ's side wound, the source of love. For both Ivo and Bernard hyssop signifies humility. But while Ivo associated the herb with Christ, Bernard links it to the humility demanded of monks. Bernard's notion of humility is related to Christ's example but has its particular place in the monastic mindset, revolving around the Rule of Benedict's twelve steps of humility. The diagonal alphabets signify the law written not in stone, but in hearts, with God's exorcizing finger. Once again we see that motifs resonate, but in other tonalities.

Across the next five sermons Bernard traces a grand loop, intertwining the threads of the three spiritual modes of interpretation. He moves via the soul as God's lodging, a soldier's tent (*sermo* 2) and a walled camp attacked by enemies (*sermo* 3), to the ascent to the peace of beatitude (*sermo* 4) and the recognition of the darkness of sin and the light of hope (*sermo* 5) before he brings his elaboration to a safe landing in the present:

> For us this dedication of our house is a family celebration, even more familial, however, is the dedication of ourselves. Ours was that aspersion, ours that benediction and ours that consecration, which was carried out by the holy hands of the bishop, and which, with the anniversary recurring today, is called to memory through solemn praises.[114]

---

remembered its dedication; Thomas Coomans, 'Cistercian Architecture or Architecture of the Cistercians?', in *The Cambridge Companion to the Cistercian Order*, ed. Mette Birkedal Bruun (Cambridge: Cambridge University Press, 2012), 151–69, at 157.

[113] 'In nobis proinde spiritualiter impleri necesse est, quae in parietibus visibiliter praecesserunt. Et si vultis scire, haec utique sunt: aspersio, inscriptio, inunctio, illuminatio, benedictio. Haec quidem in hac visibili domo fecere pontifices; haec Christus [...] invisibiliter quotidie operatur in nobis.' *In ded., sermo* 1.4: *Bernhard*, ed. Winkler, 8:814 (*Sancti Bernardi opera*, ed. Leclerq, 5:372).

[114] 'Domestica nobis celebritas dedicatio domus nostrae, magis autem domestica nostra ipsorum dedicatio est. Nostra siquidem illa aspersio, nostra illa benedictio, nostra consecratio fuit, quae per manus sanctorum celebrata Pontificum, etiam hodie anniversario reditu votivis laudibus ad memoriam revocatur.' *In ded., sermo* 6.1: *Bernhard*, ed. Winkler, 8:862 (*Sancti Bernardi opera*, ed. Leclerq, 5:396).

Bernard takes his point of departure from the material world. References to the building recur throughout, but he also lingers over each monk's individual combat with vice. His is a metaphorical construction: what the bishop does in the dedication resembles Christ's actions in the soul. In order for the metaphor to function, one part must make immediate sense; the dedication must connote an event at which things are done to the building.[115] The association between the building and the soul is not unique to Bernard.[116] However, in his portrayal of the things done to the building and to the soul Bernard evokes his basic interpretative principle: the development from an understanding *in carne* (according to the flesh) to an understanding *in spiritu* (according to the spirit).[117] Envisioning the dedication will help his audience understand the ineffable workings of Christ in their own souls. From this basis the abbot proceeds into a dense elaboration of typically Bernardine themes. The dedication is the point of departure, but it seems that, for author and audience, the real interest rests less with the interpretation of the dedication than with the dedication as a cognitive tool for the understanding of how Christ works in each monk as he proceeds towards beatitude. We recognize key dedication motifs, but the tone is distinctly Bernardine.

Conclusions

What did the dedication signify to medieval people? Which texts are we to turn to if we want to find out? A reading across commentaries and sermons shows dominant motifs. But if we want to gain the slightest idea – and slight it is – of the audience's understanding, one way is to turn to specific texts and the queries they address. In this respect, sermons are arguably more suggestive than commentaries, owing to their communicative obligation to a specific audience. No matter how literary or how theoretical, sermons speak to a particular

---

[115] Hamilton suggests a similar interpretation for Bruno of Segni's comparison of the crowds gathering for dedication to the crowds in Noah's ark: the comparison only works if crowds did in fact gather; *Sacred City*, 61.

[116] It echoes Augustine's 'Quod hic factum corporaliter videmus in parietibus, spiritualiter fiat in mentibus', *Sermo* 336, *PL* 38:1475, and reappears in Hugh of Saint-Victor's *De sacramentis* II.5.1, *PL* 176:439.

[117] For example *Super cantica canticorum, sermo* 6.3: *Bernhard*, ed. Winkler, 5:102 (*Sancti Bernardi opera*, ed. Leclerq, 1:27); *In Adventu, sermo* 1.10: *Bernhard*, ed. Winkler, 7:72–73 (*Sancti Bernardi opera*, ed. Leclerq, 4:168–69); Denis Farkasfalvy, 'Use and Interpretation of St John's Prologue in the Writings of Saint Bernard', *Analecta cisterciensia* 35 (1979): 205–66; M.B. Pranger, *Bernard of Clairvaux and the Shape of Monastic Thought: Broken Dreams* (Leiden: Brill, 1994); M.B. Bruun, *Parables: Bernard of Clairvaux's Mapping of Spiritual Topography* (Leiden: Brill, 2007), 37–39 and 283–85.

interpretative community. The contours of such communities, however vague, begin to appear when we examine the ways in which particular authors shaped stock motifs and made them relevant in a given context – even when this was not done as explicitly as in Bernard of Clairvaux's 'Ours was that aspersion, ours that benediction, ours that consecration ...'.

The dedication consecrates the church as a place that is holy and in which one encounters the holy. Interpretations of the rite reflect on the life and faith framed by the building. These interpretations are often rooted in the four-fold method of interpreting scripture. They tend to be all-inclusive, comprehending, albeit rudimentarily, ecclesiology, Christology and eschatology as well as the belief and conduct of the community and its individual members. Interpretations tend to reproduce an overarching set of motifs, even as diversity abounds. Genre is key. Therefore dedication commentaries and sermons must be considered not only within the semantic universe established by the rite, but also within their individual conceptual worlds, emerging against the backdrop of generic conventions, communities of interpretation and authorial perspectives.

Reflections

If ritual matters to history, then differences and nuances in ritual also matter. The more generic our understanding of the ritual is, the more generic our conclusions about its import will be: in the example of the dedication rite, that it marked communal identity and power and conveyed particular typological structures. The more precise our understanding of the ritual employed, the more subtle our analysis of its significance can become. If we can analyse precise rituals and how they were practised and perceived, then we can, in turn, discern the interpretive communities that they address and the subcommunities of antipathy and amity that they establish. Ideally, we can see how ritual generates, not simply reflects, power. It is no surprise that bishops wished to mark themselves and their actions as politically and soteriologically powerful. What is more interesting, and more difficult, is to understand how these efforts were received as that tells us about both the resistance to, and the generation of, power.

New methods are needed to coordinate the multiple sources and varieties of evidence that enable multivocal readings of a liturgy and to trace the changing significances of a space and a practice over time. One promising area of development is the growing interest in the possibilities of geographic information systems (GIS) as a tool for historical analysis. GIS enables us to locate multiple forms of evidence (visual and textual) at a precise latitude and longitude. That permits the analysis of the historical evidence in its geographic context on a map. With such tools one can analyse how the larger built environment, either within a church, city or landscape, and the multiple levels of meaning it signified to contemporaries, helped shape the local significances of specific liturgical events. While modern historians have begun to exploit these tools, medievalists have yet to fully embrace them.[118] The closest efforts so far by medievalists that we know of, is the work being done on medieval Chester.[119]

This method is particularly helpful to capture the allegorical approach to space as it enables the coordinated analysis of texts and objects within a landscape, what Mette Bruun has called, 'the textual representation of topography'.[120] Sermons for the dedication and its annual commemoration create a form of palimpsest. They map a spiritual topography onto the physical topography of the church and its surroundings, elaborating on the topographical allusions of the rite. This spiritual topography encompasses Old Testament locales such as Solomon's Temple and the *terribilis locus* where Jacob encountered God as well as the eternal heavenly homeland. We cannot know how this palimpsestic speech-act was conceived by the participants. The medieval allegorical climate was such that the association between a particular church and its specific political context and location on the one hand and the celestial beatitude on the other would not seem foreign. But individual perceptions must be surmised from reactions: be they the violent resistance

---

[118] See Louis I. Hamilton, 'The Rituals of Renaissance: Liturgy and Mythic History in *The Marvels of Rome*', in *Rome Re-Imagined: Twelfth-Century Jews, Christians, and Muslims Encounter the Eternal City*, ed. Louis I. Hamilton and Stefano Riccioni (Leiden: Brill, 2012), 417–38; Hamilton, 'Virtual Cities: GIS as a Tool for the Analysis of Dante's *Commedia*', *Pedagogy: Critical Approaches to Teaching Literature, Language, Composition, and Culture* 13, no. 1 (2013): 115–24. While archaeologists have been earlier adaptors of GIS, the application of this tool to the analysis of texts and images by medievalists has been slow. See the proposed application of digital technologies to liturgical sources, including a mention of GIS possibilities, in James Cummings, 'Liturgy, Drama, and the Archive: Three Conversions from Legacy Formats to TEI XML', *Digital Medievalist* 1 (2006), at http://www.digitalmedievalist.org/journal/2.1/cummings/ at §41 (accessed 1 March 2013). Textual representation of topography proposed is much broader than the digital study of medieval maps, per se; on the latter see the important work of Martin K. Foys and Shannon Bradshaw, 'Developing Digital Mappaemundi: An Agile Mode for Annotating Medieval Maps', *Digital Medievalist* 7 (2011), at www.digitalmedievalist.org/journal/7/foys/ (accessed 1 March 2013). On the field of historical GIS and its possibilities as explored by modern historians, see Jordi Martí-Henneberg, 'Geographical Information Systems and the Study of History', *Journal of Interdisciplinary History* 42 (2011): 1–13; David Cooper and Ian N. Gregory, 'Mapping the English Lake District: A Literary GIS', *Transactions of the Institute of British Geographers* 36 (2011): 89–108; Donald A. DeBats and Ian N. Gregory, 'Introduction to Historical GIS and the Study of Urban History', *Social Science History* 35 (2011): 455–63.

[119] Catherine Clarke et al., 'Mapping Medieval Chester', at http://www.medievalchester.ac.uk/about/mappings.html (accessed 1 March 2013).

[120] See Bruun, *Parables*, 19–24.

against episcopal authority or the more peaceful responses anticipated or evoked by sermons.

The consecration of a church drew its possible meanings from a broad range of local and pan-European sources. When we work with the dedication rite, we must make an effort to coordinate those sources – and to do so with an acute consciousness of the range of information which may be gathered from each particular source. Only thus can we counter the risk of confusing one asserted meaning for the totality of its significances, or the significance imparted to any given viewer.

PART IV
Texts and Performances

Chapter 9

Architecture as Evidence for Liturgical Performance

Carolyn Marino Malone

Customaries and ordinals can be used as evidence for clarifying the function of medieval churches, but architecture, in turn, can augment our understanding of the liturgy outlined in these laconic texts and, in conjunction with them, can provide evidence for liturgical performance. On the basis of the routes of processions indicated in these texts, this chapter attempts in two case studies to visualize particular liturgical moments by identifying the architectural sites for singing specific chants. The first case study analyses the processions for the feasts of the Purification of the Virgin and Palm Sunday in the eleventh-century abbey of Saint-Bénigne in Dijon, France. The second concentrates on the Palm Sunday procession in front of the thirteenth-century façade of the church of secular canons of St Andrew in Wells, England.[1]

Saint-Bénigne in Dijon

Saint-Bénigne's basilica and its eastern rotunda were begun in 1001; the basilica was consecrated to St Bénigne in 1016, and its attached three-storeyed rotunda was dedicated to the Virgin and All the Martyrs in 1018.[2] Although only the crypt of Saint-Bénigne's chevet and rotunda survive, the unusual design of the rotunda is known from plans and drawings, made between 1719 and 1722 by Dom Urbain Plancher; the reliability of this visual record of the early eleventh-century arrangement is supported by a detailed description of the building in the chronicle of Saint-Bénigne, written between 1058 and 1065 (Figures 9.1,

---

[1]   I dedicate this chapter to my son, Jesse David Kramer, for his 29th birthday, and I thank Helen Gittos for her helpful comments on it. I have written monographs on both of these buildings: see Carolyn Marino Malone, *Façade as Spectacle: Ritual and Ideology at Wells Cathedral* (Leiden: Brill, 2004); Malone, *Saint-Bénigne et sa rotonde. Archéologie d'une église bourguignonne de l'an mil* (Dijon: Editions universitaires de Dijon, 2008); Malone, *Saint-Bénigne de Dijon en l'an mil, totius Galliae basilicis mirabilior: Interprétation politique, liturgique et théologique*, Disciplina monastica 5 (Turnhout: Brepols, 2009). Additional photographs of Saint-Bénigne can be found at the following website: Saint-Bénigne et sa rotonde, http://rcf.usc.edu/~cmalone.

[2]   Malone, *Saint-Bénigne de Dijon*, 32–34; Malone, *Saint-Bénigne et sa rotonde*, 11–12.

9.2, 9.3).[3] Reconstruction of the basilica is based on the chronicle's description and excavations conducted between 1976 and 1978 and in 2003 (Figure 9.4).[4]

Saint-Bénigne's Customaries

Saint-Bénigne was an independent Benedictine monastery, but its abbot, William, had been trained in the monastery of Cluny by Abbot Mayeul, who sent him to reform the Dijon abbey in 989. Abbot William's interest in liturgical chant is well documented,[5] and he must have thought about how the new church would be used liturgically when it was designed in 1001.[6] Saint-Bénigne's three successive customaries provide evidence about the liturgy practised in this church which survived with only a few modifications until the end of the thirteenth century. The first customary was written at the beginning of the eleventh century, the second towards the end of that century, and the third at the end of the twelfth or the beginning of the thirteenth century.[7] Although all three customaries are based on Cluniac practice, they each include modifications specific to Saint-Bénigne. Nonetheless, the degree to which they describe the liturgy of Saint-Bénigne, as practised in the early

---

3   Dom Urbain Plancher, *Histoire générale et particulière de la Bourgogne*, 3 vols. (Dijon: De Fay, 1739–48, repr. Farnborough: Gregg International, 1968), 1:489–99. The eleventh-century basilica was replaced by the existing Gothic church in 1271, but St Bénigne's tomb, the hemicycle of the basilica and the rotunda with its axial chapel were preserved to the east of this later church until 1792. Between 1843 and 1900 St Bénigne's tomb and the crypt of the rotunda with its axial chapel were excavated and reconstructed

4   Andrew Martindale, 'The Romanesque Church of S. Bénigne at Dijon and Ms. 591 in the Bibliothèque Municipale', *Journal of the British Archaeological Association* 25 (1962): 21–54, at 47, edited the chronicle's description of the church and the rotunda. For the Latin text and a French translation of this edition by Jacques Ménard, see Malone, *Saint-Bénigne de Dijon*, 287–93. For the excavation of the basilica and St Bénigne's tomb, see Carolyn Marino Malone, 'Les fouilles de Saint-Bénigne de Dijon (1976–1978) et le problème de l'église de l'an mil', *Bulletin monumental* 138 (1980): 253–84; Malone, *Saint-Bénigne et sa rotonde*, 13, 44–69, 121–28, 156–60. For an archaeological study of the lower storey of the axial chapel of the rotunda and also St Bénigne's tomb see Christian Sapin and Carolyn Marino Malone, 'Oratoire Est', in *Rapport préliminaire sur les recherches archéologiques conduites dans la crypte de Saint-Bénigne de Dijon en août 2003*, ed. Christian Sapin, submitted 2005 to the Service Archéologique de Dijon, 49–58.

5   Rodulfus Glaber, *Vita Domni Willelmi Abbatis*, ed. Neithard Bulst and John France, trans. John France and Paul Reynolds (Oxford: Clarendon Press, 1989), 81–82, 166–67, 288; Ruth Steiner, 'Marian Antiphons at Cluny and Lewes', in *Music in the Medieval English Liturgy*, ed. Susan Rankin and David Hiley (Oxford: Oxford University Press, 1999), 175–204, at 183, 198–202.

6   Malone, *Saint-Bénigne de Dijon*, 80; Glaber, *Vita*, 266–68.

7   Malone, *Saint-Bénigne de Dijon*, 171–77.

eleventh-century church, must be addressed before using them as evidence to identify specific architectural sites and chants sung during processions.

Saint-Bénigne's first customary (Paris, BnF, Ms. latin 4339 (fols. 77v–88r), which Kassius Hallinger called B², probably dates from the early eleventh century.[8] It is part of the earliest group of manuscripts describing Cluniac liturgy, the *Consuetudines antiquiores*. Yet none of the monasteries owning these texts, written in the late tenth or early eleventh century, were controlled by Cluny.[9] Kassius Hallinger believed that the *Consuetudines antiquiores* were produced by Cluny for Cluny, a view that prevailed until Isabelle Cochelin pointed out that Cluniac sources never mention their existence; she considers them to be inspirational texts made for powerful non-Cluniac houses wishing to 'measure themselves against Cluny'.[10] Still, she concludes that the first customary of Saint-Bénigne was much 'reworked to fit Saint-Bénigne's reality' and played an integral role in the life of its monastery because it records modifications intended for Dijon, such as those for the Palm Sunday procession to be discussed later.[11] According to Jeremiah Brady, this customary, which he edited a few years before Hallinger, differs from others in the group not only in

> addition, omission, and contradiction, but even in the use of a flowery and idiomatic Latin in contrast to the terse and paratactic style characteristic of the part that is common to all three versions ... The Dijon version emerged not so much as blood-brother or even a first cousin to the others, with only the minor differences and accommodations to be expected in the transmission of a text of this sort, but rather as an individual work drawn to some extent from common material.[12]

---

[8]   *Consuetudinum saeculi X/XI/XII monumenta. Introductiones*, ed. Kassius Hallinger, CCM 7.1 (Siegburg: Franz Schmitt, 1984), 101–4; Jeremiah D. Brady, 'Review of *Untersuchungen zu den Klosterreformen Wilhelms von Dijon (962–1031)* by Neithard Bulst', *Speculum* 52 (1977): 355–59, at 352. Brady dated this customary during the lifetime of Abbot William because of its similarities to William's foundation charter for Fruttuaria.

[9]   *Consuetudinum saeculi*, 119–26.

[10]   Isabelle Cochelin, 'Customaries as Inspirational Sources', in *Constitutiones et regulae: Sources for Monastic Life in the Middle Ages and Early Modern Period*, ed. Carolyn Marino Malone and Clark Maines, Disciplina monastica 10 (Turnhout: Brepols, 2014), 27–55.

[11]   Ibid., 51.

[12]   Jeremiah D. Brady, 'Critical Edition of the Earliest Monastic Customary of Saint-Bénigne of Dijon (Paris, Bibliothèque Nationale, Ms. lat. 4339)', PhD diss., Harvard University, 1972, 66–68. He compared it to related texts (as edited by Bruno Albers) B and C of Saint-André de Villeneuve-lès-Avignon (Rome: Biblioteca Apostolica Vaticana, Ms. Barberini latinus 477, fols. 110v–123v, 130r–147v) and B¹ from Nonantola (Rome: Biblioteca Casanatense, Ms. 54, fols. 14r–21v).

Moreover, the Dijon customary includes a reference to Saint-Bénigne's abbot and the unusual command for Holy Saturday that 'on the order of Abbot William, they should not eat eggs'.[13] This interdiction is related to Cluniac restrictions on fast days but is not found elsewhere in the *Consuetudines antiquiores*. The redactor thus emphasized the rigour with which William observed restrictions on Holy Saturday.

Hallinger and the editors of the *Consuetudines antiquiores* considered that Abbot William himself transformed this Cluniac text for Saint-Bénigne.[14] Cochelin considers this to be possible because the text no doubt dates from before Abbot William's death in 1031, but she disagrees with the related hypothesis that William brought a text with him from Cluny and instead proposes an oral transmission of the customs.[15] Still, she questions whether it can be considered a normative customary because she doubts that the monks considered it as a list of required regulations. Given that it is included in a manuscript containing the Rule of St Benedict and the necrology of the abbey, it had been suggested that it was used as a *texte de référence* for the resolution of conflicts – to be kept in the chapter house where the affairs of the community were discussed daily.[16] Although numerous spaces were left blank, probably with the intention to fill them in later with local customs alongside those from Cluny,[17] Cochelin finds that, if the manuscript had been used frequently as a normative text by the senior monks, it is strange that the spaces were not filled in to give the text greater authority. Moreover, because the hand that started the customary added elementary glosses to the Rule of St Benedict in the manuscript, such as synonyms for words and etymological explanations of simple concepts such as *monachus* and *abbas*, she suggests that the customary was created to help adult converts, which she believes was the purpose for the late eleventh-century

---

[13]   *Consuetudines Cluniacensium antiquiores cum redactionibus derivatis*, ed. Kassius Hallinger, Maria Wegener and Candida Elvert, CCM 7.2 (Siegburg: Franz Schmitt, 1983), 92 line 26: Secundum iussionem abbatis VV<illihalmi>nec oues comedant; Malone, *Saint-Bénigne de Dijon*, 212–13. This is the only reference to William in Saint-Bénigne's first or later customaries.

[14]   *Consuetudines Cluniacensium antiquiores*, ed. Hallinger et al., 198 line 26.

[15]   Cochelin, 'Customaries', 52n121.

[16]   Ibid., 52. Jean-Loup Lemaître, "*Liber capituli*." Le livre du chapitre, des origines au XVIe siècle, l'exemple français', in *Memoria. Der geschichtliche Zeugniswert des liturgischen Gedenkens im Mittelalter*, ed. Karl Schmid and Joachim Wollasch (Munich: Wilhelm Fink Verlag, 1984), 625–48, at 626–27.

[17]   Cochelin, 'Customaries', 51; see, for instance, *Consuetudines Cluniacensium antiquiores*, ed. Hallinger et al., 129 lines 17–19 for the feast of the Exaltation of the Cross B²; the first customary leaves blank the hymn, verse and antiphon (indicated by stars) whereas B¹ from Nonantola (Rome, Biblioteca Casanatense, Ms. 54, fols. 14r–21v) cites *Vexilla regis, Salua nos Christe*, and *Super Omnia*.

Cluniac customary of Bernard of Cluny.[18] Under the abbacy of William, Saint-Bénigne had an influx of adult converts speaking various mother tongues, and Cochelin reasons that this text could have served as a common Latin reference for explaining otherwise oral customs.[19]

For these reasons, the first customary is likely to indicate the liturgy that was performed at Saint-Bénigne. In fact, its writer acknowledges practising these customs when, on a few folios, he uses the first person plural, 'we do this' and 'we do not do that', a feature that is absent from the other versions of the *Consuetudines antiquiores*.[20] Sometimes he supplies information not found in the other texts; for example, he alone gives the following information for the Christmas Vigil: 'When light appears, the guardian sounds the bell, and we go to sing Prime. Then we say *Miserere mei deus* for the dead ...'.[21] This habitual monastic practice of bell ringing at daybreak was probably implicit for the other monasteries owning texts of the *Consuetudines antiquiores*, but its inclusion shows that the writer of the Saint-Bénigne text was recording what he knew about his monastery's customs. As will be pointed out later, sometimes additions, such as the chant *Venit lumen*, which is not found elsewhere in the *Consuetudines antiquiores* or in any other Cluniac text for the feast of the Presentation in the Temple, seem to have been unique to Saint-Bénigne at the beginning of the eleventh century.

Saint-Bénigne's second customary, probably written between 1086 and 1092, was also used in the early eleventh-century church because it is anterior to the fire of 1137 and the subsequent addition of a new west portal. Unfortunately, it has not survived, except for extracts made during the seventeenth century by Hugues Lanthenas and Edmond Martène. Lanthenas copied several chapters from the original manuscript then in Saint-Bénigne's library in preparation for the *Acta sanctorum ordinis Sancti Benedicti*, edited by Jean Luc d'Achery and Jean Mabillon.[22] Unfortunately Lanthenas often copied only the beginning and end of a chapter. More numerous extracts were made by Dom Edmond Martène

---

[18] Cochelin, 'Customaries', 52.

[19] Ibid., 52n125; Glaber, *Vita*, 280–81.

[20] Cochelin, 'Customaries', 50n116.

[21] *Consuetudines Cluniacensium antiquiores*, ed. Hallinger et al., 26: 'Cum autem apparuerit lux, sonet custus signum et ambulamus Primam cantare. Post haec dicimus Miserere mei deus pro defunctis ...'.

[22] For Lanthenas' copies see Paris, Bibliothèque Nationale de France, Collection de Bourgogne, t. 11, fols. 83r–100r, 128r–138v and 171r–172v; some of these were published and translated by Carol Heitz, 'Lumières anciennes et nouvelles sur Saint-Bénigne de Dijon', in *Du VIIIe au XIe siècles: Edifices monastiques et culte en Lorraine et en Bourgogne*, ed. Carol Heitz and François Héber-Suffrin, Université de Paris-Nanterre, Centre de recherches sur l'antiquité tardive et le haut moyen âge, Cahier 2 (Nanterre: Imprimerie de l'Université de Paris X, 1977), 63–106. Lanthenas' list of the second customary's seventy-three chapters

and are dispersed, according to feast day, throughout his collection of monastic customs.[23] This second customary was probably commissioned by Abbot Jarenton (1077–1113), who undertook a new reform of Saint-Bénigne in 1077 when he brought to Dijon eight monks from Cluny, one of whom, probably named Jobert, became prior.[24] This customary and innovations in the customs have been attributed to Laurent de Liège, one of the monks from Saint-Vanne de Verdun who took refuge at Saint-Bénigne in 1085 and then served as claustral prior for seven years.[25]

Hallinger mentioned Saint-Bénigne's second customary as a probable copy, somewhat modified for its site, of the no-longer-extant first version of Bernard of Cluny's customary, which predated that available in Herrgott's eighteenth-century edition.[26] Cochelin strengthened this identification by comparing the order and content of the chapter titles of Saint-Bénigne's second customary to a similar copy of Bernard's customs.[27] As with the first customary of Saint-

was published by Louis Chomton, *Histoire de l'église de S. Bénigne de Dijon* (Dijon: Jobard, 1900), 346–47.

[23]   Edmond Martène, ed., *De antiquis ecclesiae ritibus*, 2nd edn., 4 vols. (Antwerp: Johannis Baptistae de la Bry, 1736–38; repr. Hildesheim: Georg Olms, 1969). This edition as well as the first, dating from 1690, can be found on Google Books. For a discussion of the *Divionenses S. Benigni consuetudines* used by Martène see Aimé-Georges Martimort, *La documentation liturgique de Dom Edmond Martène: Etude codicologique*, Studi e Testi 279 (Vatican City: Biblioteca Apostolica Vaticana, 1978), 102–3.

[24]   *Chartes et documents de Saint-Bénigne de Dijon, prieurés et dépendances des origines à 1300*, ed. Georges Chevrier and Maurice Chaume, Analecta Burgundica, 2 vols. (Dijon: Bernigaud and Privat, 1943), 2:253.

[25]   Ibid., 2:254. Chevrier and Chaume cite Laurentius of Leodio, *Gesta Virdunensium Episcoporum* in *PL* 204:919A–970D, at 967A: 'he removed or modified many of the superfluous traditions that he found there and added others more worthy' ('multa superfluae traditionis ibi inventa delevit vel mutavit, aliaque superinseruit honestiora'); H.R. Philippeau, 'Pour l'histoire de la coutume de Cluny', *Revue Mabillon* 44 (1954): 141–52.

[26]   Kassius Hallinger, 'Klunys Bräuche zur Zeit Hugos des Grossen (1049–1109). Prolegomena zur Neuherausgabe des Bernhard und Udalrich von Kluny', *Zeitschrift der Savigny-Stiftung für Rechtsgeschichte: kanonistische Abteilung* 45 (1959): 99–140, at 103; Bernard of Cluny, 'Ordo cluniacensis', in *Vetus disciplina monastica*, ed. Marquard Herrgott (Paris: Osmont, 1726), reproduced by Pius Engelbert (Siegburg: Franz Schmitt, 1999), 134–364.

[27]   Cochelin, 'Customaries', 41n72; Cochelin, 'Appendix: The Relation between the Last Cluniac Customaries, *Udal* and *Bern*', in *Constitutiones et Regulae: Monastic and Regular Life in the Middle Ages and the Early Modern Period*, ed. Carolyn Marino Malone and Clark Maines, Disciplina monastica 10 (Turnhout: Brepols, 2014), 56, 70–72. The similar manuscript is from Monreale: Palermo, Biblioteca central FM 7. She dates the first redaction of Bernard of Cluny's customs to around 1080 and believes that they were probably written at Cluny for Cluny. See also Cochelin, 'Evolution des coutumiers monastiques dessinée à

Bénigne, adjustments were made to Cluniac practices in the second. Because the infirmary chapel in Dijon was consecrated to Benedict instead of to Mary as at Cluny, 'ecclesiam Sancti Benedicti' was substituted for 'ecclesia Sanctae Mariae', as in the case of the death of a monk.[28] In the event of an urgent necessity, the relics were to be carried to the limits of the cemetery and not to the walls of the monastery, as at Cluny.[29] The veneration of the tomb of St Bénigne is added to the Sunday procession.[30] But most importantly, only the second customary contains a list locating the altars of Saint-Bénigne which is also found in the chronicle of Saint-Bénigne written about thirty years earlier.[31]

Although more detailed, Saint-Bénigne's third customary closely resembles the abbey's earlier customaries. It was probably written between 1170 and 1215, thus, after the addition of the west portal but before the destruction of the eleventh-century basilica in 1287.[32] Just as Saint-Bénigne's second customary was an adaptation of the first version of Bernard of Cluny's customary, so Saint-Bénigne's third customary was an adaptation of his second version, published by Herrgott. One of many examples that distinguish it from Bernard's second customary is the veneration of the tomb of St Bénigne during the Sunday procession; this is also found in Saint-Bénigne's second customary, but the third adds further information about when the tomb was not to be visited, as on Palm Sunday.[33] By comparing the second and third customaries, Guy de Valous concluded that Saint-Bénigne conserved its customs practically without interruption or great change during the Middle Ages.[34]

---

partir de l'étude de Bernard', in *From Dead of Night to End of Day: The Medieval Customs of Cluny*, ed. Susan Boynton and Isabelle Cochelin, Disciplina monastica 3 (Turnhout: Brepols, 2005), 29–66, at 54.

[28]   Malone, *Saint-Bénigne de Dijon*, 40, 294 line 37; Martène, *De antiquis*, vol. 4, book 5, col. 734–40; *Liber tramitis aevi Odilonis abbatis*, CCM 10, ed. Petrus Dinter (Siegburg: Franz Schmitt, 1980), 10: 205; Bernard of Cluny, 'Ordo', 262.

[29]   Malone, *Saint-Bénigne de Dijon*, 25; Bernard of Cluny, 'Ordo', 251.

[30]   Malone, *Saint-Bénigne de Dijon*, 206, 215; Martène, *De antiquis*, vol. 4, book 2, col. 140.

[31]   Malone, *Saint-Bénigne de Dijon*, 294–95, for Jacques Ménard's French translation of the second customary which is based on the transcription of the Latin made by Heitz, 'Lumières', 77.

[32]   Chomton, *Histoire*, 338–41, edited and published its recension in a fifteenth- or sixteenth-century manuscript (Dijon, Archives de la Côte d'Or, 1H72). According to Brady, 'Critical Edition', 91n3, an older copy is conserved in Montpellier, Bibliothèque de la Faculté de Médecine H. 449. The customary is dated before 1215, because it includes the elevation of the host after consecration.

[33]   Malone, *Saint-Bénigne de Dijon*, 206, 215; Chomton, *Histoire*, 100–1, 363–64 and 403. See also details about churches visited in Dijon below n. 59.

[34]   Guy de Valous, 'L'*ordo monasterii sancti Benigni*. Fragments d'un coutumier clunisien du XIe siècle', in *A Cluny, congrès scientifique, fêtes et cérémonies liturgiques en l'honneur des*

Cochelin believes that all of Saint-Bénigne's customaries were intended to be used more actively than just for inspiration, not as regulations to be followed to the letter but as referential tools allowing for flexibility and acclimatization between the ideal distant community of Cluny and local practices. She concludes that Saint-Bénigne's ownership of three versions of Cluniac customaries indicates a wilful adoption of Cluniac customs.[35] More importantly, the continuity of Saint-Bénigne's customaries reinforces a conclusion that they describe practices observed at Saint-Bénigne. Their similar descriptions of liturgical procedures make it possible occasionally to use all three for identifying specific sites in the early eleventh-century church. Because the third gives far more detail, it can sometimes be used to supplement information in the first. Because Saint-Bénigne's customs, for the most part, are those of Cluny with site-specific modifications, it is also possible in some cases to use information described in greater detail in other Cluniac-based texts to amplify our understanding of early practices at Saint-Bénigne. For example, although there are significant differences among the texts of the *Consuetudines antiquiores*, as pointed out above, the liturgy described is usually the same. Nonetheless, even when the practice described is identical to the other texts of the group, the participants' experience of the liturgy in Dijon would have been different because of an extremely different architectural setting. For example, because the altar of the Virgin was located at Saint-Bénigne in the axial chapel of the second level of the rotunda instead of to the east of the chapter house, as at Cluny, the path of processions to it from the choir and, hence, the monks' visual experience of the liturgy differed significantly.

The Rotunda of Saint-Bénigne

The three-storeyed eastern rotunda attached to the chevet of the basilica of Saint-Bénigne played an important part in the liturgy. The entire rotunda was dedicated to 'Mary, ever Virgin and all the martyrs,'[36] and its second level was

---

saints Abbés Odon et Odilon, 9–11 juillet 1949 (Dijon: Société des Amis de Cluny, 1950), 233–43, at 236, 239–42. For evidence that the musical tradition of Saint-Bénigne had the same continuity, see Michel Huglo, 'Le tonaire de Saint-Bénigne de Dijon (Montpellier H. 159)', *Annales musicologique, moyen-âge et renaissance* 4 (1956): 7–18; Martimort, *La documentation liturgique*, 99–102, discusses other liturgical sources for Saint-Bénigne known to have been in its library during the seventeenth century, as were the second and third customaries; some are still extant, as, for example, a twelfth-century lectionary, martyrology and necrology, and extracts of relics from a breviary.

[35] Cochelin, 'Customaries', 53.

[36] Malone, *Saint-Bénigne de Dijon*, 33n23, 66n223, 71; Chomton, *Histoire*, 123, cites *Martyrologium Sancti Benigni Divionnensis* (Dijon, Bibliothèque Municipale, Ms. 379, fol. 25): 'in honore semper virginis Mariae et omnium martyrum dedicavit'.

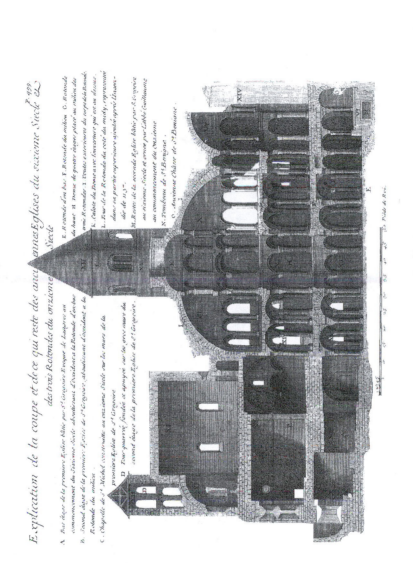

Figure 9.1 Saint-Bénigne, rotunda, longitudinal section, from Dom Urbain Plancher, *Histoire générale et particulière de la Bourgogne*, 3 vols. (Dijon: De Fay, 1739–48, repr. Farnborough: Gregg International, 1968), 1:499 (photo: C. Malone)

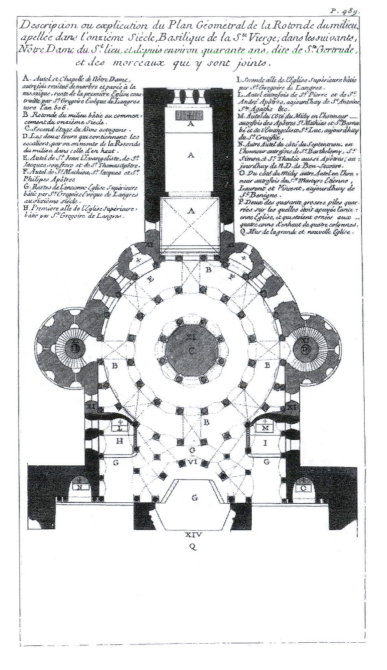

Figure 9.2   Saint-Bénigne, rotunda, plan of the second level, from Plancher, *Histoire*, 1: 489 (photo: C. Malone)

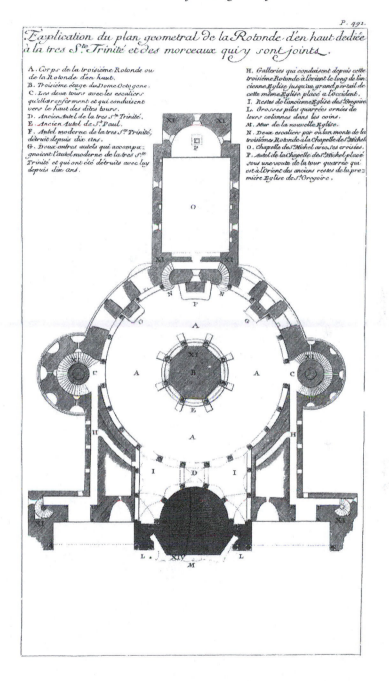

Figure 9.3   Saint-Bénigne, rotunda, plan of the third level, from
Plancher, *Histoire*, 1:491 (photo: C. Malone)

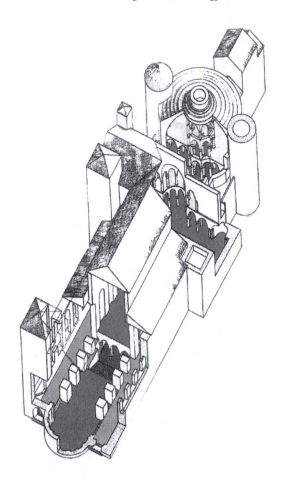

Figure 9.4   Saint-Bénigne, reconstruction, C. Malone, drawn by G. Monthel

known as the 'church of St Mary' with the altar in its axial chapter dedicated to her.[37] The second level was on the same level as the choir of the basilica, and the altar of the Virgin in its axial chapel was aligned with the main altar dedicated to St Bénigne, located in the basilica's hemicycle, directly above his tomb in the

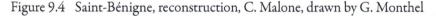

[37]   Malone, *Saint-Bénigne de Dijon*, 294 line 1: the second customary refers to the second level as 'the church of St Mary' and states that its altar was dedicated 'to the Mother of our Lord and saviour Jesus Christ' (ecclesia Sanctae Maria ... in honorem eiusdem Dei et Domini nostri Jesu Christi, Genitricis suntque); ibid., 71, 290 line 69: the chronicle of Saint-Bénigne confirms not only that its second storey was the 'church of St Mary, mother of God' but also that the altar in its axial chapel was dedicated to 'Mary ever virgin' (basilicam sanctae Dei genitricis Mariae ... perpetuae virginis).

crypt below (Figures 9.1, 9.2, 9.4).[38] The altar of the Virgin was frequently the destination of monastic processions from the choir, and her altar could only be reached by going through the rotunda. Because of the open arcades of the hemicycle and the rotunda's central light-well, her altar was visible from the choir, and red and green columns supporting the arcading visually linked it with the main altar by creating a west–east axis across the rotunda (Figure 9.2).[39]

The third level of the rotunda was dedicated to the Trinity. The chronicle describes it as 'constructed in the form of a crown, supported by thirty-six columns; the light shines with an exceptional brightness from the windows on all sides and from the open sky above.'[40] The 'open sky' refers to the central *oculus* depicted in Plancher's eighteenth-century drawing and plan (Figures 9.1, 9.3). The chronicle adds that 'the altar of the Trinity is so placed that for those entering and standing anywhere in the church it may easily be seen.'[41] This was possible because the altar was located in the middle of the hemicycle's gallery in alignment with the altar of Saint-Bénigne in the hemicyle below.[42] Thus, for the monks in the choir, light descending from the rotunda's *oculus* through the arcaded gallery of the hemicycle would have united visually the Trinity altar with the main altar of Saint-Bénigne.[43] This simultaneous illumination of altars was probably also visible to the laity in the nave which was located at a lower level than the choir to the west of the crypt (Figures 9.1, 9.4).[44]

The Feast of the Purification of the Virgin at Saint-Bénigne

Analysis of the procession for the feast of the Purification of the Virgin allows us to see how its three successive customaries, and related Cluniac customaries, can

---

[38] The monks' choir included the transept of the church. The main altar was in the hemicycle of the monks' choir. The term 'hemicycle' refers to the semicircular termination of the choir when it is surrounded by columns instead of an apse wall. A hemicycle is often surrounded by an ambulatory and in conjunction with a crown of chapels constitutes the chevet of a basilica.

[39] Malone, *Saint-Bénigne et sa rotonde*, 134, 153n124.

[40] Ibid., 290 line 77: 'Haec in modum coronae constructa. triginta quoque et sex innixa columnis. fenestris undique ac desuper patulo caelo lumen infundentibus micat eximia claritate'.

[41] Ibid., 290 line 80: 'Altare sanctae trinitatis ita est positum. ut undecumque ingredientibus ac ubicumque per aecclesiam consistentibus sit perspicuum'.

[42] Ibid., 161n99, 246. In the fifteenth century the Trinity altar was moved from the west to the east of the *oculus*, as shown in Plancher's plan (Figure 9.3).

[43] Because the openings of the gallery of the hemicyle directed light from all sides of the *oculus* onto the main altar below, any light, no matter what its intensity or angle of its projection, would have descended onto the altar.

[44] Malone, *Saint-Bénigne de Dijon*, 158.

be used to locate the architectural site where specific chants were intended to be sung. This procession on 2 February celebrated Christ's arrival as the new light during a re-enactment of his presentation in the Temple following the office of terce around 9:00 in the morning.[45] After the blessing of the candles at the Marian altar on that day, the monks made a procession towards the choir for mass. The only route between this altar and the choir at Saint-Bénigne was across the rotunda; hence, it is possible to visualize how the light from the rotunda's *oculus*, descending through the arcading of the rotunda's central light-well, would have resonated with the words of the chants specified for this procession and with the candles carried by the monks, symbolizing Christ as the new light.

Saint-Bénigne's first customary says that there should be a procession after terce 'to the place where the candles are blessed'.[46] This place can be identified as the altar of the Virgin on the basis of information in the contemporaneous Cluniac-inspired customary from Nonantola which specifies, as do two others in the *Consuetudines antiquiores*, that the procession was to go 'to the oratory of St Mary'.[47] Additionally, Saint-Bénigne's second and third customary refer to 'the oratory of St Mary' as the site for the blessing of the candles.[48] The altar of the Virgin in 'the oratory of St Mary' was located on the second level of the eastern chapel of the rotunda (Figures 9.1, 9.2). Then, the first customary states: 'the [candles] having been given to all the brothers; when they will have begun to light them, the singer begins the antiphon *Venit lumen*. The same with *Lumen ad revelationem* ... They sing Mass'.[49] Thus, on their way from the altar of the Virgin towards the choir for mass the monks would have crossed the rotunda

---

[45]   Terce corresponds to the third hour of a day in which sext and none correspond to the sixth and ninth hours and thus follow the zero hour of lauds that begins at approximately 6:00 am. Depending on the weather, the intensity of the light would have varied within the rotunda, but even on a cloudy day some light would have descended from the *oculus*.

[46]   *Consuetudines Cluniacensium antiquiores*, ed. Hallinger et al., 39 lines 25–7 (B²): 'ubi benedicendi sunt cerei, faciant orationem'.

[47]   Ibid., 39 line 20 (B¹): 'ad oratorium sanctae Mariae'.

[48]   Martène, *De antiquis*, vol. 4, book 3, col. 300: 'oratorio B. Mariae'; Chomton, *Histoire*, 401.

[49]   *Consuetudines Cluniacensium antiquiores*, ed. Hallinger et al., 40 lines 6–11 and line 29: B² (donare [cereos] ad omnes fratres. Cumque caeperint accendi incipiat cantor antiphonam Venit lumen. Item Lumen ad revelationem ... Cantent missam). Candles *[cereos]* are specified in the similar text of B¹. See also Malone, *Saint-Bénigne de Dijon*, 181–84. *Liber tramitis*, ed. Dinter, 42, adds that 'before the mass began the monks offered the candles that they carried to the priest'. See *Corpus antiphonalium officii*, ed. René-Jean Hesbert, RED series maior, fontes 7–12, 6 vols. (Rome: Herder, 1963–79), 4: Responsoria, Versus, Hymni et Varia (1970), for *Venit lumen*, as an antiphon (no. 5344) and as a response (no. 7833) as well as *Lumen ad revelationem* as an antiphon (no. 3645) and later as a response (no 601338). An antiphon is a verse or a series of verses sung as a prelude or conclusion to some part of the service. A response responds to a psalm or other part of a religious service.

with the words of *Venit lumen*, 'Thou light comes oh Jerusalem, and the glory of God rises above you; the people walk in your light', resonating with the beam of light from the oculus which illuminated their path.[50] This dramatic visual effect, along with the sound of the chant, the smell of the incense and the tactile warmth of the candles would have created a synergy of sensations enhancing their spiritual experience of Christ as the new and eternal light. This chant, which is documented as part of Abbot William's musical tradition, is included neither in Cluniac customaries nor in Saint-Bénigne's third customary for the feast of the Purification.[51] Perhaps Abbot William added *Venit lumen* to the Cluniac celebration of this feast with the *oculus* and procession in mind or even designed the *oculus* in relation to this and other processions that he envisioned between the altar of the Virgin and the choir.[52]

According to the first customary, following *Venit lumen* but before mass in the choir, the monks sang the more usual chant of *Lumen ad revelationem*, 'A light to illuminate the nations', which is based on the primary text for this feast,

---

[50]   *Venit lumen tuum, Jerusalem, et gloria Domini super te orta est; et ambulabunt gentes in lumine tuo, alleluia. Venit Lumen* is based on Isaiah 60:1–7: 'Arise be enlightened, O Jerusalem; for thy light is come, and the glory of the Lord is risen upon thee. For behold darkness shall cover the earth, and a mist the people: but the Lord shall arise upon thee, and his glory shall be seen upon thee. And the Gentiles shall walk in thy light, and kings in the brightness of thy rising. Lift up thine eyes round about, and see ...'. (These and other Bible translations are from the Latin Vulgate Bible, Douay-Rheims Version, http://www.latinvulgate.com/).

[51]   For a more complete explanation of *Venit lumen*, including its earlier use, see Malone, *Saint-Bénigne de Dijon*, 183. According to Raymond Le Roux, *Venit lumen* was part of William's musical tradition, appearing in twelfth-century breviaries from Norman abbeys that he reformed as well as in the fourteenth-century Breviary of Saint-Bénigne but not in Cluniac customaries. See R. Le Roux, 'Guillaume de Volpiano, son cursus liturgique au Mont Saint-Michel et dans les abbayes normandes', in *Millénaire monastique du Mont Saint-Michel, vol. 1: Histoire et vie monastiques*, ed. Jean Laporte (Paris: P. Lethielleux, 1966), 417–72, at 443, 445–46, 468–72.

[52]   The use of *Venit lumen* for the Feast of the Purification is unusual. It is usually used as a response for Epiphany. *Venit lumen* was, however, also sung as an antiphon for the feast of the Purification in the *Consuetudines Fructuarienses* II of Fruttuaria, an abbey founded by William on his family estate in northern Italy. In Saint-Bénigne's first customary, *Venit lumen* is cited additionally as a response at vespers for the Vigil of Epiphany (*Corpus antiphonalium offici*, ed. Hesbert, 7:2, 36) and in its third customary as a response for the octave of Epiphany (Chomton, *Histoire*, 400). Likewise, *Venit lumen* is indicated as a response for Epiphany in the *Redactio Galeatensis* de San Ilaro di Galeata, a customary based on the first customary of Saint-Bénigne (Poppi, Bibliotheca Communale, Ms. 63, fols. 2r–22v). The *Cantus* data base, http://publish.uwo.ca/~cantus, includes *Venit lumen* only as an antiphon or as a response for Epiphany, not for the Purification of the Virgin.

Luke 2.[53] According to the second customary, relics and 'an image of the Christ Child depicted on a gilded tablet' were carried at the head of this procession.[54] The monks carried candles to imitate Mary carrying Christ, as the new light, into the world in anticipation of their future entrance into the Heavenly Jerusalem.[55] Around the year 1000, Ælfric of Eynsham (c. 955–1010) concluded his sermon for this day with the words, 'Though some men cannot sing, they can, nevertheless, bear the light in their hands; for on this day was Christ, the true Light, borne to the temple, who redeemed us from darkness and bringeth us to the Eternal Light ...'.[56] Accordingly, during the feast of the Purification which celebrated the Incarnation, the architectural frame afforded a ritual experience of God's descent to mankind from the invisible to the visible as light.

Palm Sunday in Dijon

Further comparison of Saint-Bénigne's three successive customaries reveals a change in the site for singing the *Gloria laus* hymn during the procession on Palm Sunday between the eleventh and late twelfth century. The change can be interpreted as enhancing the performance and meaning of this major feature of the procession that took place after terce and re-enacted Christ's triumphal entry into the city of Jerusalem as an anticipation of mankind's future entrance into the Heavenly Jerusalem. According to the first customary, the children sang the *Gloria laus* at the gate of the fortress (*portam castellum*) in Dijon.[57] If they sang

---

53   According to the Gospel of Luke 2:30–32, Simeon, a priest in the Temple recognized Christ as the Messiah and exclaimed, 'Because my eyes have seen thy salvation, which thou hast prepared before the face of all peoples: A light to the revelation of the Gentiles and the glory of thy people Israel.'

54   Malone, *Saint-Bénigne de Dijon*, 180n40; Heitz, 'Lumieres', 94: 'pueri Jesu (imago) quae depicta est in tabula aurata'. It was also carried during the processions of Christmas and the Assumption of the Virgin.

55   Malone, *Saint-Bénigne de Dijon*, 183–84; Margot Fassler, 'Liturgy and Sacred History in the Twelfth-Century Tympana at Chartres', *Art Bulletin* 57 (1993): 499–520, at 513. Early prayers and sermons allude to the similarity of those in this lighted procession with those who wait with lighted lamps for the bridegroom's return at the end of time; Thomas Dale, 'The Nude at Moissac; Vision, Phantasia and the Experience of Romanesque Sculpture', in *Current Directions in Eleventh- and Twelfth-Century Sculpture Studies*, ed. Robert Maxwell and Kirk Ambrose, Studies in the Visual Cultures of the Middle Ages 5 (Turnhout: Brepols, 2011), 74. The words accompanying the antiphons for the feast of the Presentation in a twelfth-century processional from Moissac (Paris, BN, Ms. latin 2819) cast this celebration of the Child's reception in the Temple as the participants' entry into heaven.

56   Aelfric, *Homilies of Aelfric: The Homilies of the Anglo-Saxon Church*, ed. and trans. Benjamin Thorpe (London: Taylor for Aelfric Society, 1844), 1:151.

57   Malone, *Saint-Bénigne de Dijon*, 206–11; *Consuetudines Cluniacensium antiquiores*, ed. Hallinger et al., 65. Saint-Bénigne's first customary (B²) differs from the contemporaneous

it from above the gate, the singers would have corresponded to the 'company of angels ... praising thee on high', invoked in the *Gloria laus* hymn.[58] Yet, by the time of the third customary the *Gloria laus* is to be sung as the procession entered the church. The new location is similar to Cluniac custom, but the third customary is clearly describing the practice at Saint-Bénigne because it names other churches in Dijon to be visited earlier during the procession.[59]

According to the third customary, the singers are in the nave, and 'while the procession is entering the church, these singers intoned the *Gloria laus* ... When finished ... the procession mounted to the choir.'[60] At the entrance to the church the procession would have passed beneath a tympanum depicting the *Maiestas domini* flanked by angels, which was added in the mid-twelfth century. This carved image is a promise of the face-to-face encounter with God that will be realized at the end of time and can now only be seen by angels

---

texts of the *Consuetudines antiquiores* in which the *Gloria laus* is sung before the procession enters the door of the church (*portam aecclesiae*); Jean Richard, 'Histoire topographique de Dijon', *Mémoires de la Commission des antiquités du département de la Côte-D'Or* 22 (1951): 316–50, at 317. This gate (*portam castellum*) in Dijon seems to correspond to the later gate of the Bourg on the west of the fortress which can be seen in plans of Dijon in 1574 but is no longer present in 1595.

[58] David Chadd, 'The Ritual of Palm Sunday: Reading Nidaros', in *The Medieval Cathedral of Trondheim: Architectural and Ritual Constructions in Their European Context*, ed. Margrete Syrstad Andås et al., Ritus et artes: Traditions and Transformations 3 (Turnhout: Brepols, 2007), 253–78, at 268. This location was repeated at Fécamp, also reformed by Abbot William. City gates and the entrance of the church were the most popular locations for this Palm Sunday station. See also Susan Boynton, 'The Liturgical Role of Children in Monastic Customaries', *Studia liturgica* 28 (1998): 194–209, at 208.

[59] Chomton, *Histoire*, 404: the procession proceeds to the nearby churches of Saint-Jean and Saint-Philibert before returning to Saint-Bénigne for the *Gloria laus*. Likewise, the procedure to be taken for this procession during an interdict species that the monks pass through the chapter house in order to get to the infirmary chapel dedicated to St Benedict, a dedication and route specific to Saint-Bénigne.

[60] Ibid., 403–4: 'Et dum processio in ecclesiam venerit, illi cantores simul incipiunt Gloria laus, quem versum simul conventus reincipit et finit sedentibus cunctis ... Quo finit, simul incipiunt resp. *Ingrediente Domino*, tunc ascendit processio in chorum.' This part of the second customary was not copied by Lanthenas or Martène; however, Martène, *De antiquis*, vol. 4, book. 3, col. 345, states that it was identical to the customs of Udalrich: 'Returning to the vestibule of the church with these verses: *Gloria Laus*' ('Redeundo vestibulo ecclesiae cum his versibus: Gloria laus'); this is similar to Bernard of Cluny, 'Ordo', 307: 'let them receive the procession in the vestibule [narthex] of the church with such verses as these, *Gloria laus*; and when these verses are finished, the responsory *Ingrediente* is sung at the entrance to the church' ('Processionem in vestibulo ecclesiae cum huiusmodi versibus, & cum eisdem cappis regant chorum ad Missam, Gloria, laus; quibus finitis, ad introitum ecclesiae cantatur Resp. *Ingrediente*').

of the highest order.[61] As the procession passed beneath this visual reference to heaven and entered the church, the earthly equivalent of the Heavenly Jerusalem, the congregation heard the angels' song of praise, the *Gloria laus*, 'All glory, laud, and honour to thee, Redeemer, King'.[62] Moreover, once inside the nave, they would have seen on axis with this tympanum the altar of the Trinity in the gallery of the hemicycle which, according to the chronicle, 'is so placed that for those entering ... the church it may easily be seen'.[63] As the monks ascended to the choir to celebrate mass the light from the oculus would have united the Trinity altar with the Host on the altar of Saint-Bénigne below, perhaps evoking for them the union of his spiritual and corporal natures.

Saint-Bénigne: Conclusions

Thus, the sequence of Saint-Bénigne's three customaries, considered in conjunction with its architecture, permits one to observe continuity and change in ritual performance. The first customary provides information about the liturgy that William, its abbot-builder, seems to have intended, such as the chanting of *Venit lumen* in the rotunda during the procession for the feast of the Purification of the Virgin and the singing of the *Gloria laus* at the gate of the fortress on Palm Sunday.[64] In the later customaries these

---

61   The *Maiestas domini* is based on Revelation 4 and Revelation 1:8, 'I am Alpha and Omega, the beginning and the end, saith the Lord God, who is, and who was, and who is to come, the Almighty.'

62   Although no texts from Saint-Bénigne or Cluny refer to laity in reference to any specific procession, it is likely that the laity, as well as the monks, were present during this procession that went outside the church. The mid-eleventh century customary from Farfa, which describes the customs of Cluny, refers to the laity in a general way during processions in front of the door to the church. See *Liber tramitis*, ed. Dinter, 204: 'two towers are placed in front of this galilee [narthex]. Underneath is an atrium where the laity stands so as not to impede the processions' ('duae turrae sunt ipsius galileae in fronte constitute et subter ipsas atrium est ubi laici stant, ut non impediant processionem').

63   See above note 41.

64   *Consuetudines Cluniacensium antiquiores*, ed. Hallinger et al., 62. Abbot William's involvement in the liturgy may also be apparent in an additional practice on Palm Sunday described in the first customary, which is found neither in the later customaries nor any Cluniac text: after Matins an *osanna* was taken to an unspecified 'meeting place', perhaps another church outside the monastery, where it was met by the procession coming from the blessing of the palms en route to sing the *Gloria laus*. Chadd, 'Ritual of Palm Sunday', 263–69, believes that the term *osanna* may indicate relics, if not the host. A similar reference to *osanna* in the customary of Fruttuaria, an Italian abbey reformed by William, seems, according to Chadd, to refer to relics. On the other hand, Elizabeth Lipsmeyer, 'Devotion and Decorum: Intention and Quality in Medieval German Sculpture', *Gesta* 34 (1995): 20–27, at 21, 26, understands the *osanna* in the Fruttuaria text, which is carried to another

two liturgical moments are more similar to Cluniac practice. Moreover, the relocation of the place where the *Gloria laus* was sung on Palm Sunday had visual consequences for the participants in Dijon because it created a greater correspondence between what the participants heard (the angels' chant from 'on high') and what they saw at the entrance to the church (the heavenly imagery in the tympanum). Visual emphasis on the words of the chant, however, seems to have been a recurring aspect of liturgical performance. This emphasis occurred early in the eleventh century when both *Venit lumen* and *Lumen ad revelationem* would have resonated with the light descending from the *oculus* in the rotunda. Although *Venit lumen* later disappears from Saint-Bénigne's customaries, a similar experience was still possible because *Lumen ad revelationem* continued to be sung according to the third customary. These attempts to localize the architectural sites where textually documented chants were sung at Saint-Bénigne not only add to our understanding of liturgical processions but also make it possible to visualize the ways in which the church building was able to enhance the performance of the liturgy.

St Andrew at Wells

During the thirteenth century, simulation of a heavenly setting for the performance of the choristers singing the *Gloria laus* hymn on Palm Sunday was to be developed even further at St Andrew in Wells where the façade depicted the Heavenly Jerusalem and was constructed with a hidden passage for singers behind a row of carved angels once present in the lower row of quatrefoils above the central door (Figures 9.5, 9.6).[65] The facade was built around 1220 by Bishop Jocelin (1206–42),[66] but the earliest account of liturgical processions for Wells is an ordinal, forming the second and third sections of a fourteenth-century consuetudinary which was probably based on a lost ordinal written in

---

church, to have been most likely an image on a panel, as may have been the *osanna* referred to in Saint-Bénigne's first customary, given that its second customary mentions a gilded tablet with an image of the Christ Child which was carried during processions at Christmas, the Purification and the Assumption.

[65] Malone, *Façade*, 43–83, for the sculptural programme which depicts the descent of the Heavenly Jerusalem described in Revelation 21:2: 'And I, John, saw the holy city, new Jerusalem, coming down out of heaven from God, prepared as a bride adorned for her husband'. The image of the Coronation of the Virgin above the centre portal refers to the Church Triumphant, crowned in the image of Mary and reigning with Christ as His Bride in the palace of heaven.

[66] Malone, *Façade*, 20–26, for the dating of the facade.

Figure 9.5   St Andrew, Wells, façade (photo: C. Malone)

1298.[67] Scholars concur that this ordinal was adapted from the Sarum Use.[68]

[67]   Herbert Edward Reynolds, ed., *Wells Cathedral, Its Foundation, Constitutional History, and Statutes* (Leeds: M'Corquodale, 1880); Aelred Watkin, ed., *Dean Cosyn and Wells Cathedral Miscellanea*, Somerset Record Society 56 (Frome: Somerset Record Society, 1941), xxviii, 27–52, 111–34, translated the text and concluded that 'in its present form [it] is identical with that introduced from Salisbury c. 1270 and is not a later redaction of it'. In 1241, during the episcopate of Jocelin, the chapter at Wells had ordered the correction of the existing ordinal, and in 1273 the order was repeated. Finally, in 1298 a statute referred to the ordinal with satisfaction. Arnold Klukas, 'The *Liber Ruber* and the Rebuilding of the East End of Wells', in *Medieval Art and Architecture at Wells and Glastonbury*, British Archaeological Association Conference Transactions for the Year 1978 (London: British Archaeological Association, 1981), 30–36, at 31, dates the text (found in the *Liber Ruber* which is written in a late fourteenth- or early fifteenth-century hand) to after 1318 but states that 'the major portion of the text is certainly that of the ordinal required by statute in 1298'. See also Terence Bailey, *The Processions of Sarum and the Western Church*, Studies and Texts 21 (Toronto: Pontifical Institute of Medieval Studies, 1971), 62; Pfaff, *Liturgy*, 505–7, concludes that 'Salisbury seems to be the model [for Wells] as early as, and to the extent that, we can derive any concrete information about its liturgy' (quote on 505).

[68]   *The Use of Sarum: The Original Texts edited from the Mss*, ed. Walter Howard Frere, vol. 1: *The Sarum Customs* (Cambridge: Cambridge University Press, 1898), xix, and vol. 2: *The Ordinal and Tonal* (Cambridge: Cambridge University Press, 1901), xxix. Frere fixed the date of the *Sarum Use* to around 1210, certainly between 1173 and 1220 because it mentions the

Figure 9.6　St Andrew, Wells, quatrefoils above the portal
(photo: C. Malone)

Because Wells relied on Salisbury's customs at the beginning of the thirteenth century and because the processions described in the later Wells ordinal are similar to the Sarum Use, it is possible to reconstruct the Palm Sunday procession for Wells at the time of the facade's design around 1220. The order of stations in this ordinal indicates that the second station took place in front of the west front and that during this station the *Gloria laus* was sung; the rubrics of the later Sarum Missal add that this hymn was performed by 'boys

---

martyrdom but not the translation of St Thomas at Canterbury, hence, to the time of Richard Poore (dean of Salisbury in 1197 and bishop in 1217), who was a close associate of Bishop Jocelin. Reynolds, *Wells Cathedral*, cxxxvii, supported Frere's assessment that Wells had been dependent on Sarum customs since the twelfth or early thirteenth century by pointing out that the Dean and Canons at Wells in 1213 were to consult the Sarum chapter concerning the customs in case the Deanery was vacant. Matthew Salisbury, Chapter 5 in this book, notes the usefulness of Frere's editions. Pfaff, *Liturgy*, 364, 505–6, believes that Sarum usages would have certainly been present at Wells by time of Reginald fitz Jocelin (1174–91), if not earlier under Robert of Lewes (1136–66), and that the Sarum ordinal could predate Richard Poore and could date from the reign of Jocelin de Bohun, bishop of Sarum (1142–84).

singing in an elevated place'.[69] The passage constructed in the lower zone of the facade accommodates well these rubrics as an ideal location for singers of the *Gloria laus*. No other account of processions specifies singers in an elevated position, as does that of Palm Sunday, although stations were made in front of the facade, according to the Wells ordinal, on Ascension Day and Pentecost.[70]

Whilst at York a temporary platform appears to have been erected in front of the facade of the cathedral for choristers to sing from an 'elevated place' during the Palm Sunday procession,[71] at Wells a permanent, hidden passage was constructed in the thickness of the west wall of the facade. Because it does not open into the nave, it was clearly intended to communicate only with the area in front of the facade through splayed *oculi* that were once concealed behind busts of angels in the lower band of quatrefoils on each side of the central portal (Figure 9.6).[72] These openings are splayed outward, like a reversed megaphone, and are located at two levels in the west wall of the passage: the upper openings are five and a half feet (1.67 metres) above the floor of the passage while the lower are four feet (1.23 metres) above the floor, indicating choristers of two heights.[73]

A similar system of passages and *oculi* once existed in the later facade of Salisbury Cathedral where eight small quatrefoils formerly opened onto the exterior but are now concealed by nineteenth-century statues.[74] Here, however,

---

[69]   *The Sarum Missal: Edited from Three Early Manuscripts*, ed. John Wickham Legg (Oxford: Oxford University Press, 1916), v–ix, 96: 'pueri in eminenciori loco canentes'. The chants used during the Wells processions are preserved in the *Sarum Missal* (c. 1264), certainly dated between 1150 and 1319.

[70]   Malone, *Façade*, 140.

[71]   For a reference to the York Use and Missal see Daniel Rock, *The Church of Our Fathers, as Seen in St. Osmund's Rite for the Cathedral of Salisbury*, 4 vols. (London: John Hodges, 1904), vol. 4, pt. 2, 269–70n62; Mark Spurrell, 'The Procession of Palms and West-Front Galleries', *The Downside Review* 415 (2001): 125–44, at 131–32.

[72]   The passage for the choristers is the lower of two superposed passages constructed within the west wall of the facade. The upper passage at triforium level opens onto the nave and is fully visible within the church. The lower passage is invisible from within the church because it is closed to the nave with solid masonry. Several steps leading down from the triforium give access to this lower passage; the low height of its entrance makes it suitable for choristers but unlikely for maintenance. In this lower passage twelve *oculi*, arranged in triangular groups of three, within the outer west wall, are now visible within the four lower quatrefoils adjacent to the Coronation of the Virgin, located above the central portal, because the angel busts here have been destroyed. The higher *oculi* are behind the top lobe of each quatrefoil, while the lower pairs are behind the side lobes.

[73]   In a text message to the author on 15 March 2012 Susan Boynton stated 'that the different heights of the openings could be related to younger boys of different heights'.

[74]   Jerry Sampson, *Wells Cathedral West Front* (Stroud: Sutton Publishing, 1998), 172; Spurrell, 'Procession', 124–35. Similar openings to the west, as at Wells, occur later in the thirteenth century at Kilkenny, Ireland, which is built of Somerset limestone and had

this passage with quatrefoils is open to the nave through an arcaded gallery. H. Shortt first pointed out that the choristers probably sang the *Gloria laus* from this passage behind the quatrefoil openings above the entrance at Salisbury and noted the similar arrangement at Wells; his observations were developed by Pamela Blum and Jerry Sampson.[75] Sarum scholars, however, have not accepted this location for the second station at Salisbury, and some have also questioned the use of the openings at Wells for singers of the *Gloria laus* during the second station. Putting aside discussion of the route of the procession at Salisbury, consideration of its route at Wells might be helpful.

Let us first take a look at the route for the Palm Sunday procession as described in the Wells ordinal:

> First it goes through the north door of the choir, goes round the choir and cloister, out into the big graveyard [the lay cemetery to the west of the facade] through the choristers' house [on the west side of the cloister] and round the graveyard up to the place of the first station ... The procession then moves off to the second station, the precentor intoning the anthem. The second station is made before the door where the boys sing the *Gloria laus*. The station ended, the procession goes to the place of the third station, which is usually made before another door of the Church on the same side where three priests in the doorway sing the verses facing the people without changing their choir-dress. This done, the procession goes to the west door and then enters, passing under the box of relics which is lifted up across the doorway. Finally a station is made before the rood ... all enter the choir ....[76]

---

adopted the Sarum Use in 1172, and at Lichfield, which did not follow the Sarum Use. J. Philip McAleer, 'Particularly English? Screen Facades of the Type of Salisbury and Wells Cathedrals', *Journal of the British Archaeological Association* 141 (1988): 124–58, at 148–50, believed, without textual evidence, that twelfth-century passages in the thickness of the facade wall behind arcading at Lindisfarne, Rochester, St Botolph's, Colchester, and perhaps Croyland and Malmesbury could have had a similar liturgical use.

[75] Hugh de Sausmarez Shortt, *Salisbury Cathedral and Indications of the Sarum Use* (Salisbury: Friends of Salisbury Cathedral, 1970), 4; Pamela Blum, 'Liturgical Influences on the Design of the West Front of Wells and Salisbury', *Gesta* 25, no. 1 (1986): 145–50; Sampson, *Wells*, 169.

[76] Watkin, *Dean Cosyn*, 116; Reynolds, *Wells Cathedral*, 29: 'In primis eant per ostiu boriali chori circuens choru et claustru et exeant in cimiterio magno per domu Choristaru circuens cimiterium usq ad locum prime stationis ... Deinde eat processio ad locum secunde stationis Precentore incipiente Antiphona fit autem secunda statio ante ostiu ubi pueri cantant Gloria laus peracta autem statione eat processio ad locu tertie stationis que fieri solet ante aliud ostium ipsius ecclesie, ex eodem latere ubi tres sacerdotes in ipso ostio habitu non mutato conversi ad populu dicant versu: his peractis eat processio ad ostiu occidentale et ibi intret sub capsula reliquiaru ex transverso ostii elevate, et fiat statio ante crucem ... intrent choru ...'.

Mark Spurrell believes that the processional route at Wells should have been similar to that in the Sarum Use, although he admitted that the Wells ordinal changed the route between the choir and the first station by having it go into the cemetery of the laity to the west of the facade.[77] Although this first station in the cemetery, in turn, oriented the procession towards the facade for the second station, he suggested that the second station was in front of the north porch at Wells. Nonetheless, he placed the third station in front of the north door of the facade although, according to the ordinal, it is 'on the same side' of the church as the second. At Wells the north door of the facade would not have been conceived as being on the same side of the church as the north porch because it is separated clearly from the north side by the massive projecting north facade tower. Spurrell also objected to the use of the openings at Wells for singing the *Gloria laus* because they were hidden and felt that, if they had served this use, the procession 'seems to dither under the west front'.[78] He concluded, however, 'It is probably impossible to be certain of the route of the Palm Procession at Wells.'[79]

Spurrell did not take into account adequately the relocation of the first station to the west of the facade and the consequent orientation of the procession towards the *oculi* and the fact that their elevated position on the facade corresponds to the rubrics in the Sarum Missal for the singing of the *Gloria laus* during the second station. Furthermore, he seems not to have understood the dramatic reasons for hiding singers behind carved angels for the performance of this hymn of angelic praise and for having the procession linger before a facade that depicts the Heavenly Jerusalem, the ultimate goal of the procession. On the other hand, although William Mahrt, a specialist in Sarum liturgy, does not believe that the second station took place in front of Salisbury's west facade,[80] he understands that the relocation of the first station of the Sarum procession to the new cemetery facing the facade at Wells coincided with a logical and meaningful relocation of the second station, stating that 'the ceremonial books prescribe this hymn exactly at the proper point to be sung from the singers' holes in the Palm Sunday procession'.[81]

---

[77]   Spurrell, 'Procession', 136–37.

[78]   Ibid., 134.

[79]   Ibid., 139.

[80]   William Peter Mahrt, 'The Role of Old Sarum in the Processions of Salisbury Cathedral', in *The Study of Medieval Manuscripts of England: Festschrift in Honor of Richard W. Pfaff*, ed. George Hardin Brons and Linda Ehrsam Voigts (Turnhout: Brepols, 2010), 129–41; he does not mention Wells.

[81]   William Peter Mahrt, 'Review of *Façade as Spectacle: Ritual and Ideology at Wells Cathedral*. Leiden and Boston: Brill, 2004, by Carolyn Marino Malone', *The Medieval Review*, at tmr-l@wmich.edu, 17 March 2005. Mahrt also believes that 'Wells is the place

Although Christopher Hohler in a letter written around 1990 considered it 'manifest and incontestable' that the openings at both Salisbury and Wells were for singers responding to other singers outside the west door, he questioned whether they were specifically intended for the *Gloria laus* and denied 'that it was ever Salisbury use (as opposed to York use) for the *Gloria laus* to be sung over the west door, though [he added] I should not contemplate trying to maintain that it was never in practice occasionally sung there at Salisbury or at Wells'.[82] He believed that if the openings were devised for the Palm Sunday procession, which took place only once each year, they would

> ... seem a disproportionate expenditure of money and effort ... It looks to me like an architect's brainstorm, sold to a couple of patrons as calculated to add grace and solemnity to every sort of ceremonial entry into the church, which proved a complete failure ... and I expect ... that the effect is better if the singers are in the open air.[83]

Certainly, the passage and openings could have been used on other occasions, such as for the reception of distinguished visitors, although there is no evidence for this in the textual sources.[84] Moreover, actual experiments were tried at Wells of having the choir sing from the passage, demonstrating that voices were clearly audible across the Cathedral Green (the previous lay cemetery) and that the passage functioned as a resonating chamber.[85] Instead of having the sound scatter in the open air, the back wall of the passage acted as a sounding-board from which the sound was reflected and collected within the splay of the holes and released loudly.[86]

All scholars concur that Wells is the first example of a passage with *oculi* hidden behind carved angels in a facade wall.[87] This staging device for singing

---

where their purpose is most clearly demonstrable. Malone correctly describes the adaptation of the Sarum rite to the topography of Wells.'

[82] Christopher Hohler, 'The Palm Sunday Procession and the West Front of Salisbury Cathedral', in *Medieval Cathedral of Trondheim*, 285–90, at 285.

[83] Ibid., 289–90.

[84] Watkin, *Dean Cosyn*, 116, 121; Reynolds, *Wells Cathedral*, 34. During the procession for the reception of distinguished guests, a station was made before the choir screen and verses were sung by three of the choir from the screen facing the people. The procession then went out through the west door to the appointed place to receive the king, archbishop, bishop or papal legate who was then led back through the portals of both the facade and choir screen to the high altar.

[85] Sampson, *Wells*, 17.

[86] L.S. Colchester, *Wells Cathedral*, New Bell's Cathedral Guide (London: HarperCollins, 1987), 38.

[87] Spurrell, 'Procession', 137; McAleer, 'Particularly English?', 9.

may have been conceived at Wells, in part, because the lower zone of the facade was based on the design of choir screens. The exceptionally small doors of the facade are about the height of doors in choir screens, which were sometimes decorated with bands of quatrefoils or angels.[88] A facade screens the nave as the choir screen does the choir, and singers often stood on top of choir screens.[89] The tradition of processions stopping for a station first in front of the facade and then before the choir screen, in fact, might have stimulated the idea for the facade's choir screen design. Within this context, the hymn of the *Gloria laus*, itself, which was often sung at the entrance to churches, could have suggested designing the passage at Wells, given that the *Gloria laus* implicitly identifies the boy singers as angels 'praising thee on high'. Hence, it was a logical step to locate the singers in an elevated passage concealed behind carved angels in a facade programme depicting the Heavenly Jerusalem.[90] Later, William Durandus (1230–96) developed this idea implicit in the *Gloria laus* hymn when he stated that 'the boys, who by their purity signify the angels, offer the hymn of praise with a joyful noise, with their faces turned as if they were meeting the Lord as he comes to open heaven ...'.[91]

Having identified the passage above the central portal at Wells as the site for the boys singing the *Gloria laus*, let us integrate the rubrics and chant in the Sarum Missal with the processional stations described in the Wells ordinal in order to understand better the participants' experience. Following the blessing and the distribution of the palms in the choir, the shrine with relics was carried around the cloister on the south of the church, then around the lay cemetery to the west of the facade, up to the place of the first station where the deacon read the Gospel of Christ's entry (Matthew 21:1–9). Then three clerics facing the people sang the anthem and verse:

Behold, thy king cometh unto thee ...

---

[88]   Malone, *Façade*, 119–27, 162–63, for additional similarities; Sampson, *Wells*, 179. The heights of the side doors are eight feet (2.4 metres), the centre doors twenty feet (6 metres).

[89]   E.K. Doberer, 'Die deutschen Lettner bis 1300' (PhD diss., University of Vienna, 1946), 117; Watkin, *Dean Cosyn*, 116. On the feast of the Purification of the Virgin in the Wells ordinal, there is a station before the rood in which verses are sung 'in the choir screen facing the people' ('in pulpito conversi ad populum').

[90]   Chadd, 'Ritual of Palm Sunday', 268, documents a long tradition for this station at the west door.

[91]   William Durandus, *Guilelmi Durandi rationale divinorum officiorum*, ed. A. Davril and T.M. Thibodeau, CCCM 140 (Turnhout: Brepols, 1998), 323, lines 74–76: 'Significat id quod cantus et occursus illorum puerorum significabat; prefigurabat enim concursum et letitiam angelorum recipientium Christum in celum post resurrectionem ...'.

Hail, light of the world, king of kings, glory of heaven ...[92]

The procession then moved off to the second station which was made before the door where 'boy choristers in an elevated place sang the *Gloria laus*':

> All glory, laud, and honour
> To thee, Redeemer, King,
> To whom the lips of children
> Made sweet Hosannas ring. [93]

Then, the choir below in response repeated the *Gloria laus* after each of the following stanzas sung by the boys:

> Thou art the King of Israel,
> Thou David's royal Son,
> Who in the Lord's name comest,
> The King and blessed One.

> The company of angels
> Are praising thee on high ...
> Our praise and prayer and anthems
> Before thee we present

> The people of the Hebrews
> With palms before thee went;
> Our praise and prayer and anthems
> Before thee we present.[94]

After a third station at another door on the same side of the church,[95] the procession went to the west door (presumably the central portal) where the shrine was lifted up so that the procession could pass beneath it singing the response:

---

[92] *Sarum Missal*, ed. Legg, 95; *The Sarum Missal in English*, trans. Frederick E. Warren, 2 vols. (London: A. Moring, 1911), pt. 1, 222.

[93] *Sarum Missal*, ed. Legg, 96; Reynolds, *Wells Cathedral*, 29: 'secunda statio ante ostiu ubi pueri cantant Gloria laus ...'; *Sarum Missal*, trans. Warren, pt. 1, 224, translates the *Gloria laus* hymn.

[94] *Sarum Missal*, ed. Legg, 96. Following the stanza of the *Gloria laus*, the text states 'let the chorus repeat the same after each verse' ('chorus idem repetat post unumquem uersum'); *Sarum Missal*, trans. Warren, pt.1, 224–25, translates the following three stanzas.

[95] See n. 76 above.

> As the Lord was entering into the holy city the children of the Hebrews proclaimed the resurrection of life, and with branches of palms, cried out: Hosanna in the Highest.[96]

The procession then entered into the church, where in front of the choir screen the fourth station was made and the following anthem was intoned:

> Hail, our King ... Hosanna to the Son of David. Blessed is he that cometh in the name of the Lord. Hosanna in the highest.

Finally, all genuflected, entered the choir, and mass began.[97]

The fact that the rubrics of the Sarum Missal state that the *Gloria laus* was sung from an elevated position indicates that a heavenly source was always intended, but at Wells having carved angels in clouds appear to sing this hymn just overhead more dramatically signalled heaven and thus would have heightened the emotional response of those in the procession below. The chorus acknowledged the heavenly source of the music when they sang, 'All glory, laud, and honour to thee, Redeemer, King', in response to the boys' verse, 'the company of angels are praising thee on high', and this reciprocal dialogue united heaven and mankind in a shared joyful exchange. In addition, an angel carved in a quatrefoil on a buttress to the south of the portal once held a palm, as those in the Palm Sunday procession would have done, reinforcing the rapport between the earthly participants and the singing angels.[98] Above the busts of the angels, the statues of the blessed, enshrined in heavenly mansions, beneath a frieze depicting their resurrection, and Christ at the apex of the central gable created an elaborate *scaenae frons* that further confirmed heaven as the setting for the performance of the *Gloria laus* during the second station.[99]

Beneath Christ, the gable is pierced with eight *oculi*, which are accessed from a walkway on top of the facade wall at the level of the top of the nave vault hidden beneath the roof. The height of the *oculi* above the walkway is similar

---

[96] *Sarum Missal*, trans. Warren, pt. 1, 225–26, translated the following two stanzas.

[97] *Sarum Missal*, ed. Legg, 96–97; Watkin, *Dean Cosyn*, 116; Reynolds, *Wells Cathedral*, 29.

[98] Sampson, *Wells*, 257, states that the dexter hand of this angel holds a broken staff or martyr's palm, the top of which is lost. W.H. St John Hope and W.R. Lethaby, 'The Imagery and Sculptures on the West Front of Wells Cathedral', *Archaeologia* 59 (1904): 143–206, at 187, however, could still see that it was a palm.

[99] Malone, *Façade*, 50; Sampson, *Wells*, 183. The figure of Christ, now in the museum at Wells, is a later replacement made when the towers were added in the late fourteenth and early fifteenth century, but the presence of the thirteenth-century mandorla indicates that such a figure existed earlier.

to the height of the upper *oculi* in the lower passage behind the quatrefoils.[100] Yet, because these openings are located 75 feet (23 metres) above the ground, the passage probably was not intended for singers: these splayed openings are 4 feet 2 inches (1.27 metres) deep, nearly twice the depth of the *oculi* for singers, and capable of accommodating a thirteenth-century trumpet with its bell hidden from the ground.[101] Although trumpets are not mentioned in any textual source, these *oculi* suggest that hidden trumpeters might well have announced the triumphant moment when the Palm Sunday procession, and perhaps other processions, entered the church. Because the *oculi* are located at the level of trumpeting angels carved at the top of the buttresses, the angels would have appeared to sound the descent of the Heavenly Jerusalem described in Revelation 21:2, the sculptural theme of the facade.[102] This fanfare may have stimulated the participants in the procession to anticipate, as part of the ritual experience on Palm Sunday, their final joyful entry into the Heavenly Jerusalem as they passed into the church, its earthly representation. A Palm Sunday sermon written around 1200 in a West-Saxon dialect, when describing this procession re-enacting Christ's triumphal entry into the city of Jerusalem, admonishes the participants 'to follow his holy earthly procession, that we may be in the holy procession which he will make with his chosen on Doomsday from judgement into heaven'.[103] En route to the culmination of the Palm Sunday ritual, eucharistic union with Christ and the eternal Church during the mass, the procession passed beneath relics and through the central portal. Above this portal the sculptural image of the Coronation of the Virgin visually presented the concept of the union of the faithful with Christ as the Church Triumphant; that is, the Heavenly Jerusalem descending as described in Revelation 21:2, a concept made

---

[100] Sampson, *Wells*, 175–76, 283n269. The outside diameter of the *oculi* is 10 inches (25 cm), but they splay inwards to around 28 inches (70 cm). The walkway, which is on the top of the facade wall, is about five and a half feet (1.67 metres) below the centre of the *oculi*. Neither structural nor functional reasons warrant their presence, not even for ventilation. Shaped stone plugs survive on the walkway showing that the *oculi* were sometimes blocked. Sampson points out that the stairs in the towers remain very wide up to this level, perhaps for this liturgical purpose.

[101] Ibid.

[102] Malone, *Façade*, 51; Hope and Lethaby, 'Imagery and Sculptures', 163; Sampson, *Wells*, 187–88. The eight *oculi* are located between statues of the nine orders of angels, which are now fifteenth-century; however, it is likely that during the thirteenth century similar statues filled the niches.

[103] Malone, *Façade*, 138; *Old English Homilies of the Twelfth Century*, ed. Richard Morris, Early English Text Society, original series 53 (London: Early English Text Society 1873), 92.

familiar in the hymn, *Urbs beata Ierusalem*, which was sung, according to the Sarum Missal, during the annual rededication of the church (Figure 9.6).[104]

The design of the façade and its sculpture thus provide evidence that cannot be learned from textual descriptions about the performance of the Palm Sunday procession. Although the sculptural programme, as a representation of the blessed in the Heavenly Jerusalem, provided an appropriate backdrop for other processions and for burials in the cemetery of the laity, it would have created a sensational stage-set on Palm Sunday with angels in clouds singing the *Gloria laus* and angels on top of the buttresses trumpeting the descent of the Heavenly Jerusalem at the end of time.[105]

Conclusion

Although it is impossible to know the reality of what actually happened during any one procession, the textual sources for liturgical processions at Saint-Bénigne and at Wells, in conjunction with the architectural design of these churches, makes it possible to visualize what probably was intended and did occur. Specific sites for the performance of certain chants can be inferred from the routes that processions would have taken between altars or stations described in the texts. This attempt to locate processions and chants in relation to their architectural frame allows one to envision not only the setting of a performance but also to a certain extent what the participants experienced. At Saint-Bénigne the presence of the rotunda's *oculus* indicates that a beam of light could have illuminated monastic processions, such as the re-enactment of Christ's presentation in the Temple, when the descending light would have dramatized his birth as the new light. At Wells the material evidence of a passage and stone megaphones helps to identify the location for singing the *Gloria laus* hymn and reveals how hidden musical accompaniment may have encouraged an emotional reaction that helped the participants anticipate their final joyful entrance into the Heavenly Jerusalem. Music is essential to the sacred experience of the liturgy and material light as a manifestation of divine light was fundamental to medieval church

---

[104] Malone, *Façade*, 46; *Sarum Missal*, trans. Warren, pt. 1, 414–21; *Sarum Missal*, ed. Legg, 202–4. In the Sarum Missal the Epistle for the feast of the Dedication cites Revelation 21:2: the 'new Jerusalem, coming down out of heaven from God, prepared as a bride adorned for her husband,' and the Sequences that follow discuss as a symbol for the triumph of the Church the marriage of Christ and the Virgin, His Bride; that is, the congregation of the faithful. The blessed city, Jerusalem, is built in the sky from living rocks and crowned by the angels as one promised in marriage for her husband; the New City descends from heaven prepared for her nuptials as a bride to join with God.

[105] For funerals see Malone, *Façade*, 141–43; Watkin, *Dean Cosyn*, 128–30; Reynolds, *Wells Cathedral*, 47–48.

design.[106] Both were always intended to engender a spiritual response, but, because of the unusual design of the rotunda at Saint-Bénigne, the resonance of light and chant created an exceptional setting for conveying the significance of the liturgy, as did the innovation of passages for hidden singers and trumpeters behind carved angels at Wells.

Our understanding of the ideal liturgy as presented in texts can thus be enhanced by visualizing its performance within the specific architectural context for which it was intended. When liturgical documentation can be paired with architectural and sculptural evidence, it is possible to suggest how the liturgy interacted with its material frame to engage the participants. Architecture and its sculpture were an integral part of the liturgical performance during the Middle Ages and can serve as evidence for past ritual in ways that texts cannot.

[106] Malone, *Saint-Bénigne de Dijon*, 150–262, 271–73.

Chapter 10
Liturgical Texts and Performance Practices

Carol Symes

The study of medieval liturgy is largely dependent on surviving manuscript sources, but the nature of those sources and their bearing on the most fundamental aspect of liturgy – its enactment – is very difficult to reconstruct. We cannot assume that any written rite captures or prompts performance in a straightforward manner. The reasons for this include the low survival rate of the texts most often and most directly implemented in the course of worship, the dearth of explicit evidence for the ways such texts were used, the longevity of oral methods for transmitting information about performance, significant local and regional differences in the scripting of ritual activity, and changes in recording practices over time. Above all, our understanding of medieval liturgy is fundamentally fettered by the modern academic and confessional agendas that have manipulated and framed its study, beginning with the competing ideologies that shaped the concept of 'liturgy' during and after the Reformation, and continuing up to the present day in the retroactive designation of certain medieval texts as 'liturgical', 'paraliturgical' or 'non-liturgical'.[1] The very word 'liturgy' (in English and other European languages) came into use only in the mid-sixteenth century, at precisely the time when the parameters and meanings of religious ceremonial were at the heart of confessional controversies.[2]

Although the medieval vocabulary used to describe the wide parameters of religious worship was large and rich, it did not – at least in the Latin West – include the word 'liturgy'. The classical Greek λειτουργία meant, originally, the performance of any kind of public service or duty (religious, civic, military); it

---

[1] The degree to which post-medieval editorial choices and scholarly chauvinism have shaped the study of medieval texts – while generating the modern genres and typologies to which these texts are assigned – has been the subject of intense critique by scholars in many disciplines for several decades. Yet this sort of scrutiny is only just beginning to inform the way we conceptualize and study such phenomena as medieval worship, preaching and dramatic performance. I address these issues in 'The Appearance of Early Vernacular Plays: Forms, Functions, and the Future of Medieval Theater', *Speculum* 77.3 (2002): 778–831 and 'A Few Odd Visits: Unusual Settings of the *Visitatio sepulchri*', in *Music and Medieval Manuscripts: Paleography and Performance: Essays Dedicated to Andrew Hughes*, ed. John Haines and Randall Rosenfeld (Aldershot: Ashgate, 2004), 300–22.

[2] Lesley Brown, ed. *The New Shorter Oxford English Dictionary on Historical Principles*, 2 vols. (Oxford: Clarendon Press, 1993), 1:1608.

was later pressed into use by the translators of the Septuagint and the writers of the Greek New Testament, where it was associated with worship in the Temple.[3] But its Latin cognate, *liturgia*, appears nowhere in the Latin Vulgate Bible, the most important source of ritual language in Western Christendom. And there are only seven separate instances of its use in the corpus of Christian writings assembled in the *Patrologia Latina*, all of which signal its association with exotic, foreign rites.[4] 'Liturgy' is thus an anachronistic and rather unhelpful term that masks a wide spectrum of worshipful activities practised during the Middle Ages.[5] The difficulty of understanding the medieval sources that we

---

[3]   Thomas J. Heffernan and E. Ann Matter, 'Introduction to the Liturgy of the Medieval Church', in *The Liturgy of the Medieval Church*, ed. Thomas J. Heffernan and E. Ann Matter (Kalamazoo: Western Michigan University, 2001), 1–10, at 1.

[4]   This was determined through a search for *liturgia* and its variants in the Patrologia Latina Database, which initially yields seventy-three mentions (in thirty-six entries), of which the majority occur in modern commentaries. (The less anachronistic word *ordo* and its variants, by contrast, yields some 18,614 mentions in 2,555 separate entries.) The seven authentic medieval references to 'liturgy' in this sample occur as follows: 1. in a Latin translation of a Greek letter sent by Pope Julius I (r. 337–52) to the followers of the schismatic bishop Eusebius of Emesa at Antioch (*PL* 8:896a); 2. in St Augustine's sermon on Psalm 135, referencing the Greek word for worship (*PL* 37:1757); 3. in a letter by Pope Leo I (r. 440–61) to Turribius, bishop of Asturia, condemning the heresies of the Priscillianists (*PL* 55:1041d); 4. in the laws of the Emperor Justinian relating to bishops and clerics in Constantinople (*PL* 72:1054c); 5. in the *Canons* of Ælfric of Eynsham (c. 955–c. 1010), where the term refers explicitly to debates at the Council of Nicea (*PL* 139:1471b); 6. in the *Opusculum* XII of Odorannus of Sens (c. 985– c. 1045), which is an important early source for the description of the Cluniac 'liturgical day' of constant prayer (*PL* 142:826a); 7, in Peter Lombard's commentary on the Corinthians I, where he is referencing Augustine (above) in the context of a discussion of idolatry (*PL* 191:1604c). To summarize: during the first thousand years of Christianity in the Latin West, the word 'liturgy' was sparingly used to refer to outlandish (Greek, heretical or pagan) practices of worship or – at Cluniac monasteries – as a consciously chosen marker of their own special commitment to the *opus Dei*. On the Cluniac liturgy, see Susan Boynton and Isabelle Cochelin, eds., *From Dead of Night to End of Day: The Medieval Customs of Cluny*, Disciplina monastica 3 (Turnhout: Brepols, 2005) and Chapters 9 in this book.

[5]   It is important to note that many modern translators of medieval sources insert the word 'liturgy' or its variants into texts that use a different (larger and more specific) vocabulary. For example, Cyril Vogel uses the term five times in his translation of a short text (the preface to a famous sacramentary) which contains no such word: *Introduction aux sources de l'histoire du culte chrétien au moyen âge* (Spoleto: Centro italiano di studi sull'alto medioeva, 1966); trans. Vogel, *Medieval Liturgy*, 87. The text in question, known by its *incipit* as the *Hucusque*, is appended to the Hadrianum in various ninth-century manuscripts; it has been edited in *The Gregorian Sacramentary under Charles the Great*, ed. Henry Austin Wilson, HBS 49 (London: HBS, 1915), 145–46; and *Le sacramentaire grégorien: Ses principales formes d'après les plus anciens manuscrits*, edited by Jean Deshusses, 3 vols., SF 16, 24, 28 (Fribourg: Editions

call 'liturgical' is further compounded by the ways that they have been selected, packaged and interpreted for hundreds of years. So while we may continue to use the word 'liturgy' and its variants, we must remain aware of their limitations and connotations.

These issues have already been underscored by the preceding contributions to this volume, which have also introduced the problematic connection between texts and performance.[6] The contributions in Part I deal with the challenges of interpreting primary materials and the necessity of placing these sources within a broader historical framework, raising many questions about how they would have been realized in performance. Those in Part II have critiqued the received understanding of prescriptive Uses and other compilations that were intended to dictate the parameters of performance. And those in Part III have investigated ritual performances that were clearly important and yet were not (for various reasons) fully documented.

This chapter places the nature of liturgical texts and their relationship to performance at the centre of inquiry. It argues that such texts often resulted from attempts to capture or control performance, by recording local practices in order to guard against faulty memories and to ensure future transmission, or by censoring innovations that were deemed unorthodox by replacing them with approved practices, or by eliding the differences among local variations in an effort to create a generic style of worship. The written records resulting from these efforts *might* have been carefully replicated in ritualized performances; but they might also have been resisted or altered. They must accordingly be analysed differently from modern liturgical books, dramatic scripts or musical scores. Such modern texts are usually the *points of origin* for performance and are furthermore accepted as establishing rules which are more or less binding on performers. By contrast, medieval liturgies often came into being as part of a compositional, performative and social *process*. This means that we must work both backward and forward from the moment of inscription in order to glimpse the activities that a particular text was designed to bolster, supplant or curtail. And we must bear in mind that these texts were often created at the behest of certain powerful people with specific agendas – and yet they were not always implemented in ways that conformed to those agendas. Furthermore, we must be on the lookout for sources and actors that have been dismissed or overlooked, but which deserve to be studied as liturgical. As research in performance theory and cultural anthropology suggests, we can make a useful distinction between

universitaires, 1971–82), 1:351–53. This 'supplement' used to be attributed to Alcuin, but Deshusses ascribes it to Benedict of Aniane.

[6]   See also the comments of Richard W. Pfaff, 'Liturgical Books', in *The Cambridge History of the Book in Britain, vol. 1: c. 400–1100*, ed. Richard Gameson (Cambridge: Cambridge University Press, 2011), 449–59.

the performance archive – a canon made up of carefully selected templates or recorded examples – and the living repertoire of performative possibilities: 'what people do in the activity of their doing it'.[7] This is why it is important to know as much as possible about the specific conditions in which a given source was generated, used and passed down to posterity.

In many cases, the very precision of a text describing liturgical performance practices should make us sceptical about what occurred in performance. For example, the famous *Quem quaeritis?* trope for Easter Matins was long regarded as the earliest instance of liturgical drama – a genre which allegedly came into being only in the late tenth century, when scripts like this begin to appear, scripts that insist on the decorous and uniform presentation of ceremonial performances. On the contrary, I have argued that this type of text reflects an effort to regulate an *existing* performance tradition which may have been more colourful and varied.[8] The trope's most famous exemplar actually proclaims this: the so-called *Regularis concordia* ('concordance of rules') was promulgated by Bishop Æthelwold of Winchester (r. 963–84) as part of an attempt to reform monastic worship in the realm of the Anglo-Saxon king, Edgar.[9] In addition to thinking about its relationship to performance, then,

---

[7]   Richard Schechner, *Performance Theory*, 2nd rev. edn. (London: Routledge, 2003), 1 and Schechner, 'Drama, Script, Theater, and Performance', in the same book, 66–111, at 68. See also Diana Taylor, *The Archive and the Repertoire: Performing Cultural Memory in the Americas* (Durham, NC: Duke University Press, 2003); Dennis Tedlock, *The Spoken Word and the Work of Interpretation* (Philadelphia: University of Pennsylvania Press, 1983); and Max Harris, *Carnival and Other Christian Festivals: Folk Theology and Folk Performance* (Austin: University of Texas Press, 2003).

[8]   Carol Symes, 'The Medieval Archive and the History of Theatre: Assessing the Written and Unwritten Evidence for Premodern Performance', *Theatre Survey* 52.1 (2011): 29–58. The germ of this argument can be found in O.B. Hardison, *Christian Rite and Christian Drama in the Middle Ages* (Baltimore: Johns Hopkins University Press, 1965).

[9]   See the edition by Lucia Kornexl of *Die* Regularis Concordia *und ihre altenglische Interlinearversion* (Munich: Wilhelm Fink, 1993), § 51. Susan Rankin's facsimile edition of a later version of this trope allows one to examine it within a manuscript that reflects the influence of the *Regularis concordia*: see *The Winchester Troper*, Early English Church Music 50 (London: Published for the British Academy by Stainer and Bell, 2007), fol. 26v. On the musical and codicological contexts of this trope, see Michel Huglo, 'Remarks on the Alleluia and Responsory Series in the Winchester Troper', and Susan Rankin, 'Winchester Polyphony: The Early Theory and Practice of Organum', in *Music in the Medieval English Liturgy: Plainsong and Medieval Music Centennial Essays*, ed. Susan Rankin and David Hiley (Oxford: Clarendon Press, 1993), 47–58 and 59–99 respectively. On the possible sources and patterns of transmission affecting its inscription, see David A. Bjork, 'On the Dissemination of *Quem quaeritis* and the *Visitatio sepulchri* and the Chronology of Their Early Sources', *Comparative Drama* 14 (1980): 46–69; and Susan Rankin, 'Musical and Ritual Aspects of *Quem queritis*', in *Liturgische Tropen: Referate zweier Colloquien des Corpus*

we need to think about its 'performativity': the functions it would have performed for those who made it, copied it and used it. We also need to think seriously about what role(s) it performed for those who later extracted it from the historical record and held it up for scrutiny as a liturgical prototype.[10] What this particular text of the *Quem quaeritis?* performs, most obviously, is Æthelwold's authority to impose this model.[11] The extent to which it was subsequently adopted, with or without amendment, is unclear; although the evidence of later manuscript witnesses suggests that it was implemented and modified in different ways according to different needs.[12] We also do not really know what practices it was intended to replace, although the fact that it insists on a quiet, measured, melodious ceremony may indicate that it was a reaction against unscripted, even boisterous, enactments; and that these (now lost) were what Æthelwold successfully suppressed. We might also conclude that this text's popularity among scholars stems from the way that it confirms modern expectations of what medieval liturgy should be: staid, formalized, boring.

As this brief case study demonstrates, we need to pose some essential questions as we seek to understand how any liturgical text may have been realized in performance by any given community on any given occasion.

- How did it become a text in the first place?
- Does the text predate a performance tradition, or does it respond to existing practices?
- Were performers likely to have followed it closely?
- If they did not, why was it made and kept?
- If they did, how did they make use of it?
- When did this text come to be designated as 'liturgical'? How have the interventions of later scholars reshaped its meanings?

Troporum in München (1983) und Canterbury (1984), ed. Gabriel Silagi (Munich: Arbeo-Gesellschaft, 1985), 181–89. Anselme Davril has argued that the first scripted version of this liturgy may ultimately derive from Saint-Benoît-sur-Loire (Fleury): 'L'origine du *Quem quæritis*', in *Requirentes modos musicos: Mélanges offerts à Dom Jean Claire*, ed. Daniel Saulnier (Solesmes: Abbaye Saint-Pierre, 1995), 119–34.

[10] For a definition of 'performativity', see Andrew Parker and Eve Kosofsky Sedgwick, eds., 'Introduction' to *Performativity and Performance* (New York: Routledge, 1995), 1–18, at 2.

[11] On reading for agency and performance in medieval texts, see Jody Enders, *Murder by Accident: Medieval Theater, Modern Media, and Critical Intentions* (Chicago: University of Chicago Press, 2009), 3, 12, 113–14.

[12] For discussion of the subsequent use of the *Regularis concordia*, see Pfaff, *Liturgy*, 85–87; Helen Gittos, *Liturgy, Architecture, and Sacred Places in Anglo-Saxon England* (Oxford: Oxford University Press, 2013), 120–28.

- Are there other – seemingly 'non-liturgical' – texts that are also relevant to the study of liturgy in the same place and time?

In general, as I will demonstrate below, the evidence suggests that medieval liturgical texts are apt to function as *prescriptive* templates for what should occur in performance (but might not), or as *proscriptive* documents dictating what should not occur (hinting at resistance and the existence of alternative variations). They are highly unlikely to be *transcriptions* of events.[13] That is, such texts tend to function as recipes do: those who need them may adhere to them, but renegades and experts will adapt, annotate or abandon them at will. How can we tell? In many cases, we cannot. Ingredients added to an established recipe may be left out by a later practitioner without any indication of this; or a practitioner may subtract or substitute ingredients without changing the written record to reflect that. Meanwhile, a collector of recipes may organize them in novel, idiosyncratic ways which may or may not correspond to the feasts for which they were intended. The key thing is to remain aware of the possibilities. In the following pages, we will take up the questions outlined above and explore their wider implications.

On the Erratic Survival of Liturgical Texts

Around the year 1119, an ambitious Norman cleric called Geoffrey de Gorron left his home diocese of Rouen to become a schoolmaster at the abbey of St Albans. Because his arrival in England was delayed, the post he had been promised was given to someone else. So Geoffrey opened a school in the nearby village of Dunstable and, perhaps in an effort to impress his erstwhile employers, taught his students to perform a play about St Catherine of Alexandria. It was the kind of play 'which we commonly call "miracles"', and the abbey loaned Geoffrey a number of ceremonial vestments in order to enhance the show.[14] Was this, then, a liturgical drama? Was there a script? The chronicler does not say. All we are told is that the borrowed vestments accidentally burned the night after the performance, and that the hapless Geoffrey pledged himself as a 'burnt offering' (*holocaustum*) to make amends for their loss. That is, he became a monk of St Albans. We only know about the incident because he eventually became abbot, so this sketch of his picaresque youth was included in the abbey's history.

---

[13] I adapt this terminology from the work of Gregory Nagy, *Poetry as Performance: Homer and Beyond* (Cambridge: Cambridge University Press, 1996), 110–12. See also Symes, 'Appearance of Early Vernacular Plays', and 'Medieval Archive'.

[14] *Gesta abbatum monasterii Sancti Albani*, ed. Henry Thomas Riley, 3 vols. (London: Rolls Series, 1897), 1:72–73: 'quemdam ludum de Sancta Katerina – quem miracula vulgariter appellamus'.

This story illustrates two common fates that could befall the records of medieval performance, as well as raising other issues to which I will return. Scripts could easily be damaged or destroyed, but they might not be made at all; they might not even surface as anecdotes. The extant collections of medieval liturgical texts bear witness to this in various ways. Some are collections of *libelli* assembled and annotated by successive generations of users, thereby testifying to living traditions of performance in the communities that made these books.[15] But compositions that did not find their way into *libelli*, and those *libelli* not enclosed between covers, are likely to have perished.[16] This cannot be stressed too heavily, because it means that some of the most prevalent varieties of local liturgical practice may have disappeared from view; and by the same logic, those that we have now could have been those that were highly experimental, very occasional, or (literally) shelved as useless curiosities.

Testifying to the contemporary forces that have preserved only *some* texts for posterity is a memorandum written by Burchard of Michaelsberg (Bamberg, Germany) in the first half of the twelfth century. In it, Burchard announces that he has finally 'sorted through' the library's *diversis libellis* 'with a great deal of effort', because 'the slimness of the books made them seem less apt to be noticed, and because any small thing can so easily vanish by stealth or theft'. He then had all of these little booklets enclosed into 'four huge volumes'.[17] Burchard is talking mostly about individual saints' lives, *historiæ* and *passiones*, that were read on feast days and around which liturgies were created; we know that many of the texts supporting such liturgies were transcribed and kept in similar booklets. These sorts of liturgical manuscripts were often stored in the sacristy or cantor's room.[18] This means that (1) they were seldom included in a library catalogue

---

[15] An excellent example is the so-called Durham Collectar: see Karen Louise Jolly, 'Dismembering and Reconstructing Ms. Durham, Cathedral Library, A.IV.19', in *Scraped, Stroked, and Bound: Materially Engaged Readings of Medieval Manuscripts*, ed. Jonathan Wilcox (Turnhout: Brepols, 2013), 177–200.

[16] Pierre-Marie Gy, 'The Different Forms of Liturgical "Libelli"', in *Fountain of Life*, ed. Gerard Austin (Washington, DC: Pastoral Press, 1991), 24–34, at 26–27. See also Eric Palazzo, 'Le rôle des *libelli* dans la pratique liturgique du haut moyen âge: histoire et typologie', *Revue Mabillon* n.s. 62 (1990): 9–36; and Nils Krogh Rasmussen, with Marcel Haverals, *Les pontificaux du haut moyen âge: Genèse du livre de l'évêque*, Spicilegium Sacrum Lovaniense: Etudes et Documents 49 (Leuven: Spicilegium Sacrum Lovaniense, 1998).

[17] Karin Dengler-Schreiber, *Scriptorium und Bibliothek des Klosters Michelsberg in Bamberg* (Graz: Akademische Druck- und Verlagsanstalt 1979), 184: 'congessit ... magno labore ... in quatuor magna volumina ... quia parvitas librorum videbatur minus apta cernentibus, et facile porterat furto vel qualibet surrepcione perire res modica'. This example is also cited (but differently interpreted) by Palazzo, 'Le rôle des *libelli*', 10.

[18] The library catalogue of the abbey of Schaffhausen (made between c. 1083 and 1096) notes that there are *alii libelli, quae* [*sic*] *in choro habentur*, and so these are not listed in the

like Burchard's and (2) never acquired the protective armour of a binding. It also means (3) that they were in constant use and (4) employed in the instruction of schoolboys or novices, further lessening their chances of survival.[19] It is telling that the librarians at Muri Abbey (Switzerland), writing in the twelfth century, lamented the loss of *libelli* 'which ought to be saved and better cared for and not destroyed'. Many were in such poor condition that they could not be deciphered and transcribed, to the detriment of the whole community.[20] These stray references remind us of the fragmentary nature of the surviving sources and allow us to glimpse some of the strategies that preserved certain kinds of texts – but not others.

The Discordance between the Codification of Liturgical Texts and Living Performance Practices

The earliest extant text in the Castilian vernacular is a sung processional for the feast of the Epiphany; it is now known as the *Auto de los reyes magos* (The Play of the Magi Kings). By dramatizing the heathen kings' journey towards enlightenment, it also advanced the aims of the 'Reconquista': a political, military and cultural campaign to 'reconquer' the lands of Christian Spain. Largely launched from Castile, the Reconquista eventually elevated the regional vernacular featured in the *Auto* to a position of prominence – while eradicating the Muslim kingdoms of medieval al-Andalus. This particular liturgical text was probably transcribed around 1200 at the behest of Archbishop Rodrigo Jiménez de Rada of Toledo (c. 1170–1247), a powerful proponent of the crusade against Muslims. Yet the text alone betrays nothing of its performative or political context. It preserves only enough information to serve as an aide-mémoire for experienced enactors: the words of the (sung) dialogue, but with no accompanying musical notation,

---

inventory. See Gustave Becker, *Catalogi bibliothecarum antiqui* (Bonn: M. Cohen et filium, 1885), 157 (no. 69).

[19] For example, three tattered *libelli* of the twelfth-century Latin comedy *Babio* (which would have been used to teach Latin verse and Roman mythology) were evidently used in the school of Lincoln Cathedral and were only saved from imminent destruction by being bound together: Lincoln, Cathedral Chapter Library, Ms. 105. For a liturgical *libellus* that was rudely dismembered and barely survived, see André Wilmart, 'Un livret bénédictin composé à Gellone au commencement du IXe siècle', *Revue Mabillon* 12 (1922): 119–33.

[20] Becker, *Catalogi*, 252 (no. 122): 'que oportet servare et meliorare et non destruere ... quia nos non potuimus ea hic sigillatim describere. Libros autem oportet semper describere et augere et meliorare et ornare et annotare cum istis, quia vita omnium spiritalium hominum sine libris nichil est'.

rubrics or performance instructions of any kind.[21] Moreover, it is inexpertly copied onto the flyleaves of a 'non-liturgical' miscellany.

This text illustrates some of the motives that could undergird the collection of certain liturgical materials, as well as the frustrating (to us) partiality and often baffling locations of those materials. Although a great deal of effort has been expended on drawing up definitive taxonomies of medieval liturgical sources, these compendia do not help us to understand how such sources came into existence, and whether or not they reflect contemporary performance practices. Eric Palazzo has noted the need to pay 'special attention to the process that formed each of the liturgical books' that have come down to us, while carefully tracing 'the crucial passage from oral practice to the written document'.[22] Yet this passage was not teleological, as Palazzo suggests, and it was never complete. From the beginning, the notation that came to be called 'Gregorian' chant was designed to transmit aspects of a liturgical language – a grammar of worship – from which performers could select and combine elements. As Andrew Hughes has put it, '[w]hen the performance practice was written down, the fluid tradition had to be frozen into a fixed form'. But the singers who used these texts knew that the form was *not* fixed, and prided themselves on reviving and varying it.[23]

Although Carolingian initiatives aimed at codifying liturgical practices may have resulted in the eradication of many largely unscripted performance practices, this initiative was unevenly carried out and constantly productive of intriguing hybrids. It was not, as some have argued, a single-minded attempt at standardization.[24] The most prominent intellectual at Charlemagne's

---

[21]   The manuscript is now Madrid, Biblioteca Nacional de España, Vitr. 5–9, fols. 67v–68r; it was originally Toledo, Biblioteca del Cabildo, Cax-6, 8. For an edition and English translation, see Charles E. Stebbins, 'The "Auto de los reyes magos": An Old Spanish Mystery Play of the Twelfth Century', *Allegorica* 2 (1977): 118–43. I discuss this example in 'Medieval Archive'. See also Lucy Pick, *Conflict and Coexistence: Archbishop Rodrigo and the Muslims and Jews of Medieval Spain* (Ann Arbor: University of Michigan Press, 2004), 185–201.

[22]   Palazzo, *History*, xxx.

[23]   Andrew Hughes, *Medieval Music: The Sixth Liberal Art*, rev. edn. (Toronto: University of Toronto Press, 1980), 453–54, 460. See also Leo Treitler, 'Oral, Written, and Literate Process in the Transmission of Medieval Music', *Speculum* 56 (1981): 471–91; and Treitler, 'Reading and Singing: On the Genesis of Occidental Music-Writing', *Early Music History* 4 (1984): 135–208. This 'new historical view of chant transmission' has been evaluated and tested by Peter Jeffrey with reference to the methods of ethnomusicology: *Re-Envisioning Past Musical Cultures: Ethnomusicology in the Study of Gregorian Chant* (Chicago: University of Chicago Press, 1992). See also Christopher Page, *The Christian West and Its Singers: The First Thousand Years* (New Haven: Yale University Press, 2010), 360–78.

[24]   See Richard E. Sullivan, 'The Carolingian Age: Reflections on Its Place in the History of the Middle Ages', *Speculum* 64, no. 2 (1989): 267–306; Yitzhak Hen, *The Royal Patronage*

court, Alcuin of York (c. 740–804), says as much in an oft-cited (and often misinterpreted) letter to Archbishop Eanbald of York. In it, Alcuin gently chides his former schoolmate for worrying about the format and organization of *libelli* used in the performance of the mass: 'Can it be possible that you don't already have a very large number of ritual booklets arranged according to Roman custom? You certainly have more than enough of the older type in those big sacramentaries'. The task at hand, Alcuin said, was not to replace venerable traditions with new ones, wholesale, but to use all available resources to enhance the worship of God in the best possible way. At the same time, he recognized that few practitioners would want to do that sort of work themselves; hence the need for those willing to cull and combine available sources.[25]

Despite these initiatives, or in defiance of them, the making of books did not replace oral methods of creating, learning and circulating liturgical practices – especially in those liturgical powerhouses, monasteries.[26] It is significant that we owe our knowledge of liturgical education at Cluny in the eleventh century to the customary made by one of the few monks who had not been a child oblate there: because Ulrich of Zell had entered monastic life as a teenager, he envied his contemporaries' status as embodied repositories of liturgical knowledge gained through oral instruction and memorization over many years. He even couched his *ordo* in the form of a dialogue, since that was how liturgical knowledge was usually transmitted.[27] All of the systems of musical notation and textual transcription being developed at this time would have required personalized instruction to render them intelligible; they were not transparent. Experienced singers would also need to learn how to locate and 'combine the

---

of Liturgy in Frankish Gaul to the Death of Charles the Bald (877) (Woodbridge: Boydell and Brewer, 2001); Susan A. Keefe, *Water and the Word: Baptism and the Education of the Clergy in the Carolingian Empire*, 2 vols. (Notre Dame, IN: University of Notre Dame Press, 2002) and Chapter 1 in this book.

[25]   Alcuin, *Epistolae*, ed. E. Dümmler, *MGH Epistolae*, vol. 4 (Berlin: Weidmann, 1895), 370 (no. 226). 'De ordinatione et dispositione missalis libelli nescio cur demandasti. Numquid non habes Romano more ordinatos libellos sacratorios abundanter? Habes quoque et veteris consuetudinis sufficienter sacramentaria maiora. Quid opus est nova condere, dum vetera sufficiunt? Aliquid voluissem tuam incepisse auctoritatem Romani ordinis in clero tuo; ut exempla a te sumantur, et ecclesiastica officia venerabiliter et laudabiliter vobiscum agantur. Sed "Rari sunt adiutores" forte dicis'. On the rich resources of the library at York in this era, see Mary Garrison, 'The Library of Alcuin's York', in *Cambridge History of the Book*, 1: 633–64.

[26]   See the excellent collection of essays in Steven Vanderputten, ed., *Understanding Monastic Practices of Oral Communication (Western Europe, Tenth–Thirteenth Centuries)* Utrecht Studies in Medieval Literacy 21 (Turnhout: Brepols, 2011).

[27]   Susan Boynton, 'Oral Transmission of Liturgical Practice in the Eleventh-Century Customaries of Cluny', in *Understanding Monastic Practices*, 67–83, at 71.

various elements of the office in the order of their performance', using multiple kinds of books.[28] In Ulrich's time, as Susan Boynton observes, 'the increasing dependence upon written materials in monastic liturgical and musical practice' meant that the office of the cantor and that of the *armarius* (librarian-archivist) became fused.[29] At the same time, in the words of David Hughes, the use of notation to record a community's traditions became 'a kind of defensive weapon by means of which a cantor could say, "Our way is the right way, *and we have this notated gradual to prove it*".[30]

Again, we note the absence of any one-way movement from text to performance, or replacement of performance by text. Continuing alongside efforts to preserve the liturgy in textual form was a strong tradition of creativity and improvisation in performance.[31] Tellingly, the classic example for the use of a liturgical *libellus* is a story about how St Sidonius Apollinarus, bishop of Auvergne (d. 489), easily performed a service without it, because the book was stolen.[32] He had probably compiled the text himself, as a mnemonic aid, and was more than familiar with its contents anyway.[33] Indeed, the ad hoc assembly of personalized liturgical materials was another practice that would continue alongside attempts to produce authoritative codifications. In

[28]   Boynton, 'Oral Transmission', 81, 71. On text-based education, see Diane J. Reilly, 'Education, Liturgy and Practice in Early Cîteaux', in *Understanding Monastic Practices*, 85–114, at 99–107.

[29]   Margot E. Fassler, 'The Office of the Cantor in Early Western Monastic Rules and Customaries: A Preliminary Investigation', *Early Music History* 5 (1985): 29–51, at 46. See also Monika Otter, 'Entrances and Exits: Performing the Psalms in Goscelin's *Liber confortatorius*', *Speculum* 83, no. 2 (2008): 283–302.

[30]   David Hughes, 'From the Advent Project to the Late Middle Ages: Some Issues of Transmission', in *Western Plainchant in the First Millennium: Studies in the Medieval Liturgy and Its Music*, ed. Sean Gallagher et al. (Aldershot: Ashgate, 2003), 181–98, at 184.

[31]   Hughes, 'From the Advent Project', 184. See also László Dobszay, 'Concerning a Chronology for Chant', in *Western Plainchant*, 217–29. On the persistence and control of improvisation, see Allan Bouley, *From Freedom to Formula: The Evolution of the Eucharistic Prayer from Oral Improvisation to Written Texts* (Washington, DC: Catholic University of America Press, 1981); and Thomas William Elich, 'Le context oral de la liturgie médiévale et le rôle du texte écrit', 3 vols. (Paris: unpub. PhD diss., Paris IV-Sorbonne, 1988). Paul de Clerck provides an overview that stretches from the second century to Vatican II: 'Improvisation et livres liturgiques: leçons d'une histoire', *Communauté et liturgie* 50 (1978): 109–26.

[32]   Gregory of Tours, *Historiarum libri X*, ed. Bruno Krusch and Wilhelm Levison, MGH SS rerum Merovingicarum 1.1 (Hannover: Hansche Buchhandlung, 1951), 67 (II.22). See Gy, 'Different Forms', 27–28. Compare Palazzo, 'Le rôle des *libelli*', 13.

[33]   Gennadius of Marseille (d. c. 496) mentions similar 'little books' (*libellum ... parvum/ parvum volumen*) made by individuals for their own use: *Liber de scriptoribus ecclesiasticis* in *PL* 58:1103a (c. 76) and 1104a (c. 79).

the eleventh century, the library of the abbey at Gorze (near Metz, modern France) included an anonymous meditation 'on how a priest should prepare himself beforehand to celebrate mass, written in a tiny little booklet'.[34] In the twelfth century, old-fashioned *libelli* were still being used to disseminate new services in honour of the Blessed Virgin and, in the thirteenth century, to popularize the feast of Corpus Christi or the *ordines* composed by Thomas Aquinas.[35] The liturgy was always a work in progress and no single set of practices or texts determined it.[36]

Despite such evidence, many scholars have wanted to see the ultimate triumph of a 'definitive form' of liturgical book, which would make earlier, 'embryonic forms' obsolete.[37] And while it is true that efforts to standardize the liturgy (and to enforce these standards) were more strenuous after the Fourth Lateran Council of 1215, the subsequent manuscript tradition continues to register variations and adaptations.[38] Evidence of parallel, popular forms of liturgy shows little concern for conformity to 'official' templates, and Vogel himself was at pains to stress the variety of medieval liturgical practice – all the while working to create an elaborate textual fiction of uniformity.[39] In this, he shared the philological and editorial goals of his predecessors and contemporaries, who were heavily influenced by a Darwinian method of extraction and interpretation that was having an equally deleterious effect on the study of other medieval cultural artefacts.[40] The assumption that the liturgy develops through an 'evolutionary

---

[34]   A. Wagner, 'Les manuscrits de la Bibliothèque de Gorze. Remarques à propos du catalogue', in *Religion et culture autour de l'an mil: Royaume capétien et Lotharingie*, ed. Dominique Iogna-Prat and Jean-Charles Picard (Paris: Picard, 1990), 111–17, at 114: 'Qualiter vel presbyter se preparet ad missa celebranda in quaterniunculis scriptum'.

[35]   Palazzo, 'Le rôle des *libelli*', 23–24; Gy, 'Different Forms', 27–28.

[36]   This is underscored by the essays in John Haines, ed., *The Calligraphy of Medieval Music* (Turnhout: Brepols, 2011).

[37]   Palazzo, 'Le rôle des *libelli*', 25; Palazzo, *History*, 188.

[38]   Mary C. Mansfield, *The Humiliation of Sinners: Public Penance in Thirteenth-Century France* (Ithaca, NY: Cornell University Press, 1995). See also Chapter 7 in this book.

[39]   He notes that 'liturgical uniformity was unknown in the Middle Ages' and that 'celebrants could pick and choose among the various options' of which they were aware: Vogel, *Introduction aux sources*, 4–5; cf. Eng. trans. *Medieval Liturgy*, 62, 135. Vogel's acknowledgment of the slippage between extant texts and actual performance is especially evident in his analysis (*Medieval Liturgy*, 87) of the so-called *Hucusque*, which describes liturgical practice in Rome (see note 5, above). This awareness also undergirds Vogel's discussion of 'Non-Roman Western Rites' that have been 'lost': *Medieval Liturgy*, Appendix II, 273. On Vogel's editorial practices see Chapter 4 in this book.

[40]   Symes, 'Appearance', and 'Manuscript Matrix, Modern Canon', in *Oxford Twenty-First Century Approaches to Literature: Middle English*, ed. Paul Strohm (Oxford: Oxford University Press, 2007), 7–22.

process' is still common.[41] So is the notion that medieval liturgical performance is 'well documented' and relatively transparent.[42] As Richard Crocker has argued, these convictions are (in part) a legacy of the influential Solesmes movement of the late nineteenth century, which adapted one type of medieval chant notation and held it up as the norm, making it hard to recognize 'signs of nuance' in liturgical manuscripts that do not adhere to this post-medieval standard.[43] It is therefore crucially important to re-assess what has been frequently misconstrued as a closed and closely regulated system. The making of liturgical texts occurred in the context of living liturgical practices that were neither fully reflected in texts nor confined to them.

On the Varied Reasons for the Textual Preservation of New or Unique Performance Traditions

The chancy survival of liturgical texts has already been stressed: we have noted how accident and negligence (on the one hand) or reliance on oral tradition and improvisation (on the other) can affect the frequency with which certain practices are preserved and the formats in which they are preserved. We have also observed that some kinds of liturgical texts, like the tropers of the tenth century, are not witnesses to the genesis of a practice so much as they are attempts to harness it. When trying to interpret any source it is therefore essential to ask *why it was created at all*, because the many different possible answers to that question will have a direct bearing on how a given text may (or may not) relate to performance. In this section, we will consider some of the motivations for inscribing liturgical practices.

Beginning in the eighth century, the invention and/or dissemination of more precise recording technologies enabled the preservation of older liturgical repertoires. These technologies, the precursors of musical notation, included new methods of *mise-en-page*, varieties of punctuation and rubrication and the creative use of neumes. On the one hand, their deployment could lead to the fossilization of a particular style or local use; on the other, they facilitated the transmission of novel compositions and could inspire experimentation.

---

[41] For example, Joanne Pierce, 'The Evolution of the *ordo missae* in the Early Middle Ages', in *Medieval Liturgy: A Book of Essays*, ed. Lizette Larson-Miller (New York: Garland, 1997), 3–24.

[42] For example, Jeanne E. Krochalis and E. Ann Matter, 'Manuscripts of the Liturgy', in *Liturgy of the Medieval Church*, 433–72, at 434.

[43] Richard Crocker, 'Singing the *Nuance* in Communion Antiphons', in *Western Plainchant in the First Millennium*, 453–60, and accompanying CD. This valuable account by a scholar-performer explains the process of interpreting and reproducing the sounds notated in a particular chant manuscript.

The multiple dimensions of this process make the difference between newer and older practices difficult to discern on the page; this is yet another reason to distrust evolutionary models of liturgical development, which frequently hinge on the creative redating of manuscript sources according to the prejudices of individual researchers.[44] 'Simple' rites are not necessarily earlier rites, and many of those that *seem* simple can mask hidden complexities. For instance, musicologists have observed that the performance of polyphony in some locales actually predates the thirteenth-century development of mensural notation (delineating rhythmic values) by at least two hundred years; these earlier methods for expressing polyphony in writing were 'hidden' and therefore unrecognizable to modern scholars until they were decoded in the 1960s.[45] Any type of notation has severe limitations, and medieval scribes often struggled to capture complex traditions or individual feats of virtuosic performance that were 'still well known but in danger of spiralling out of control', in the words of David Hiley.[46] (Anyone who has ever tried to transcribe or re-enact a jazz solo from a musical score will have experienced similar frustrations.) There was, in other words, no universal trend and no simple chronology of progress. While some monastic communities appear to have been resistant to novelty, clinging to older (unscripted) repertoires and ways of learning them, others were capable of generating and/or recording an extraordinary amount of material within a relatively short period of time.[47]

For many communities, liturgical innovation was a medium for confronting and processing internal and external changes. Liturgical texts therefore tend to appear and proliferate at times of crisis, either to create or to dramatize customs, identity, and claims to property. Susan Boynton and Margot Fassler have independently shown that the composition of liturgical texts was a way of making and writing history.[48] Nor was this strategy confined to powerful

---

[44]   Symes, 'Appearance', and 'Manuscript Matrix'.

[45]   Symes, 'Appearance', 792–93. Pioneering studies include Judith Marshall, 'Hidden Polyphony in a Manuscript from Saint Martial de Limoges', *Journal of the American Musicological Society* 15 (1962): 131–44; and Sarah Fuller, 'Hidden Polyphony: A Reappraisal', *Journal of the American Musicological Society* 24 (1971): 169–92. See also Hendrick van der Werf, *Oldest Extant Part Music and the Origin of Western Polyphony*, 2 vols. (Rochester, NY: H. van der Werf, 1993), 1:155.

[46]   David Hiley, *Western Plainchant: A Handbook* (Oxford: Clarendon Press, 1993), 518.

[47]   Such as the abbey of Saint-Martial at Limoges: see Michel Huglo, *Les livres de chant liturgique*, Typologie de sources du moyen âge occidental 52 (Turnhout: Brepols, 1988), 29.

[48]   Susan Boynton, *Shaping a Monastic Identity: Liturgy and History at the Imperial Abbey of Farfa, 1000–1125* (Ithaca, NY: Cornell University Press, 2006); Margot E. Fassler, *The Virgin of Chartres: Making History through Liturgy and the Arts* (New Haven: Yale University Press, 2010).

episcopal and monastic communities like Cluny, Chartres, Metz or Farfa; documentation was frequently generated by real or perceived threats to the survival of unique local practices in much smaller places. A case in point is the extraordinarily precise effort to safeguard the impressive and eclectic oeuvre of Hildegard of Bingen, an effort which can be tied to her nuns' resistance of censorship by local authorities, as well as to their awareness of her advanced age and the fear that her artistic legacy might die with her. As a result, the liturgical compendium known as the Riesencodex was probably copied under Hildegard's direct supervision in the years immediately before her death in 1179, at the age of 81. It was undertaken in the context of an ominous quarrel with the bishop of Mainz, who had placed the convent under interdict. Since Hildegard had probably devised liturgical ceremonies and music orally, the very novelty and flexibility of her compositions were inimical to their survival; if she and her nuns were going to outwit the male prelates, they had to beat them at their own game.[49] The resulting manuscript would have ensured that future performances of her works were based on an authorized text, and it may also have been intended as a posthumous source for the canonization dossier submitted to (and twice rejected by) the papal curia.[50]

This was not the only time that the imminent death of an inspired performer was the catalyst for record-making campaigns. In the 1160s, the monks of Durham Priory vied with one another to record the mystical vernacular songs spontaneously composed by the hermit Godric of Finchale (d. 1170), a former merchant-adventurer who claimed to have been taught to sing by the Virgin herself.[51] The resulting texts constitute the oldest extant notated songs in the English vernacular, inscribed at a time 'when very little musical notation is found outside the context of liturgical books' and when the status of 'English' itself was being renegotiated after the Norman Conquest. Helen Deeming has demonstrated that the manuscripts conveying these songs betray the difficulties of inscribing them – and of ensuring that they would remain firmly attached to

---

[49]   The codex is now Wiesbaden, Hessische Landesbibliothek Clm 2. See Albert Derolez, 'The Manuscript Transmission of Hildegard of Bingen's Writings: The State of the Problem', in *Hildegard of Bingen: The Context of Her Thought and Art*, ed. Charles Burnett and Peter Dronke (London: Warburg Institute, 1998), 17–28; and Margot Fassler, 'Composer and Dramatist: "Melodious Singing and the Freshness of Remorse"', in *Voice of the Living Light: Hildegard of Bingen and Her World*, ed. Barbara Newman (Berkeley: University of California Press, 1998), 145–79. Some of the materials in this codex were recycled by Hildegard in the final segment of her *Liber Scivias* (III.13), in which her divine revelations are accompanied by antiphons, responsory, prosæ and the *Ordo Virtutum*.

[50]   Hildegard did not achieve canonization until 2012.

[51]   Reginald of Durham, *Libellus de vita et miraculis S. Godrici, heremitae de Finchale*, Surtees Society 20 (London: J.B. Nichols and Son [1847]), 117–20 (c. 50).

the saint's cult, and in the priory's control.[52] At least one of the saint's inspired performances was so intricate that it could not be replicated. As Reginald of Durham tells us, Godric once burst out in a joyful, nearly wordless melody that gradually resolved into the repetition of the phrase *Welcume, Simund* ('Welcome, Simon'), on which the aged singer improvised for a very long time. Reginald could only listen in wonder. Later, though, he could at least ensure that his *vita* of the saint took the form of a liturgical *libellus* suitable for performance.[53] The other contemporary manuscripts of Godric's songs also circulated as portable (but frail) booklets, and display marked evidence of annotation and use.[54] Some were probably lost or destroyed.

These examples show that we are often indebted to specific initiatives for preserving a precarious, locally prized liturgical corpus. And fundamentally, the very great difficulty of capturing liturgical – especially musical – performance in writing is a constant vein of anxiety running through our sources.[55] It even surfaces as a leitmotif in the various origin myths that purport to explain the dissemination of Roman chant in the eighth century. As Notker of Saint-Gall (d. c. 912) narrates the story, Charlemagne had requested that a dozen singers be dispatched from the papal choir to his court at Aachen, to teach their Frankish counterparts. But because the Roman emissaries were jealous guardians of their own traditions, they each taught the Franks a different, erroneous way of singing. When this subterfuge was discovered, the enterprising Franks went to Rome in disguise, where they listened carefully to the services in the papal basilica, memorized what they heard, and later wrote the chants down.[56] The young Mozart's legendary 'theft' of Gregorio Allegri's *Miserere* – on the basis of two hearings in the Sistine Chapel – falls neatly into this medieval tradition of liturgical *ars memoriæ* buttressed by the creation of texts.[57]

---

[52]   Helen Deeming, 'The Songs of St Godric: A Neglected Context', *Music and Letters* 86 (2005): 169–85, at 169. On the persistence of post-Conquest English vernacular writing, see Elaine Treharne, *Living through Conquest: The Politics of Early English, 1020–1220* (Oxford: Oxford University Press, 2012); and Elaine Treharne and Mary Swan, eds., *Rewriting Old English in the Twelfth Century* (Cambridge: Cambridge University Press, 2000).

[53]   Reginald of Durham, *Libellus*, 306–9 (c. 161).

[54]   Julius Zupitza, 'Cantus beati Godrici', *Englische Studien* 11 (1888): 401–32.

[55]   On the situation in Anglo-Saxon England, see Susan Rankin, 'Music Books', in *Cambridge History of the Book*, 1, ed. Gameson, 482–506.

[56]   Notker Balbulus, *Gesta Karoli Magni Imperatoris*, ed. Hans F. Haefele, MGH SS rer ger n. s. 12 (Berlin: Weidmann, 1959), 12–15. This episode is discussed by Page, *Christian West*, 290 (among others). On the politics of chant dissemination see also Hiley, *Western Plainchant*, 514–18; and Andrew Hughes, 'Charlemagne's Chant or the Great Vocal Shift', *Speculum* 77 (2002): 1069–1106.

[57]   This famously mystical setting of Psalm 51(50), composed in the 1630s, was supposed to be performed exclusively in the papal chapel at the service of Tenebrae (at the beginning

The historian Orderic Vitalis (d. c. 1142) opens a particularly vivid window onto the organic and haphazard ways that a community's liturgical repertoire could develop and the role that writing played in the process. He mentions that the liturgical office (*historia*) for his own abbey's patron, Saint Evroul, was first developed at the behest of Abbot Robert (r. 1040–61), who had refounded the monastery and accordingly needed to start a ceremonial tradition from scratch. So Robert asked Arnulf, a famous cantor of Chartres Cathedral, to create something for the saint's feast. Arnulf accordingly 'composed' an office: here, Orderic uses the verb *ediderat*, 'he pronounced' or even 'he brought forth'. This act of composition involved no writing, and it was transmitted from Chartres to Saint-Evroul by two young monks who had been sent to record Arnulf's singing of it, by hearing it sung and learning it by ear. These human recorders (chosen, as Orderic hints, because of their youth and faculties of retention) then conveyed the office orally to their brethren at Saint-Evroul, who must have continued to sing and transmit it from memory for at least a decade thereafter. We can infer this because Orderic says that it was not 'completed' (*perfecit*) until a new monk with formal scholastic training came to Saint-Evroul and 'set it down' (*condiderat*) along with other antiphons and responsories of his own. And yet this learned monk must also have been skilled at oral composition, too, because he simultaneously 'brought forth' (*edidit*) many lovely chants which were later preserved in the abbey's troper and antiphonary, presumably by someone else.

Orderic's use of different verbs invites us to distinguish among various modes of liturgical invention. In this same passage, he says that a novel responsory 'was sung by' a certain Reginald, implying that he was the instrument for its creation, and that this Reginald had also 'brought forth' (*ediderat*) some antiphons. Still other monks 'dictated' (*dictaverunt*) hymns that were eventually preserved in the library of Saint-Evroul, implying some sort of collaboration between gifted musicians and the scribes who made *libelli*.[58] Orderic's pride in his abbey's liturgical repertoire is therefore compounded by his pride in the technical skills that preserved it. His own *historia* is, in essence, a gigantic extension of the liturgical office (*historia*) that had crystallized around the monastery's patron

---

of the Holy Week Triduum) and again on Good Friday. Mozart's feat was to transcribe it from memory on the basis of a single hearing, with a return visit to check the accuracy of his text. See Ilias Chrissochoidis, 'London Mozartiana: Wolfgang's Disputed Age and Early Performances of Allegri's *Miserere*', *The Musical Times* 151, no. 1911 (2010): 83–89.

58   Orderic Vitalis, *The Ecclesiastical History of Orderic Vitalis*, ed. and trans. Marjorie Chibnall, 6 vols. (Oxford: Clarendon Press, 1969–80), III.3 (vol. 3, 108), my translation. Chibnall notes that there is a twelfth-century neumed troper from Saint-Evroul in the Bibliothèque nationale, Ms. latin 10508.

saint.[59] (As noted above, the work of the cantor and that of the historian were often undertaken by the same person.[60]) Orderic's massive *Ecclesiastical History*, accordingly, may have begun as a modest *libellus* before it metastasized into our best source for the events of its author's lifetime – a source which incidentally illuminates some of the reasons for the written preservation of liturgical performance practices.

The Use of Liturgical Texts in Performance

It might seem to go without saying that texts were used in the course of liturgical performances. But *how* were they used? Was any given text *required* for the successful enactment of the ritual, either as a script or as a memory aid? Or was it merely *incidental*, a kind of stage property? Exploring the answers to such questions can be revealing. In many cases, surviving liturgical manuscripts offer visual clues designed for performers, suggesting that such instructions were necessary: eye-catching rubrics describing gestures and bodily postures, careful formatting, clear notation, meticulous correction of musical or textual errors. Sometimes the very size of manuscript books indicates how they were used. For example, the large-format volumes that came into use in the later Middle Ages were meant to serve a new class of professional: non-monastic singers who were not trained to perform from memory – who had to 'sing unto the Lord a new song' they had only just learned.[61] But at other times, texts were used in performance even if they were not necessary. A seasoned celebrant of the mass, especially one with the prodigious memory of a medieval religious, would hardly have needed a script to prompt his daily observances. And yet books containing the mass were ubiquitous because they helped to validate the rite's sanctity, whether these were large and gorgeously bejewelled sacramentaries or humble missals. For similar reasons, the text of the *Exultet* sung at the Great Vigil of Easter retained (at least in some regions) the ancient

[59] Fassler, 'Office of the Cantor'. See also her essay, 'The Liturgical Framework of Time and the Representation of History', in *Representing History, 900–1300: Art, Music, History*, ed. Robert A. Maxwell (University Park, PA: Pennsylvania State University Press, 2010), 149–71. On the close connection between institutional memory, history, and the liturgy more generally, see her *Virgin of Chartres*.

[60] Michel Huglo, 'Codicologie et musicologie', in *Miscellanea codicologica F. Masai: dicata MCMLXXIX*, ed. Pierre Cockshaw et al., 2 vols. (Ghent: E. Story-Scientia, 1979), 1: 71–82; Fassler, 'Office of the Cantor'.

[61] Hiley, *Western Plainchant*, 392 and 418–21 (plates); Katherine Zieman, *Singing the New Song: Literacy and Liturgy in Late Medieval England* (Philadelphia: University of Pennsylvania Press, 2008). The illuminated miniature accompanying Psalm 96 in such manuscripts is often a *mise-en-abîme* of this scene.

form of the scroll, often elaborately illuminated.[62] This had everything to do with its visual impact in performance and almost nothing to do with the deacon's own needs, since the words and melody of that chant would have been familiar to any cantor from childhood.

By contrast, the ivory covers of a *libellus* belonging to the Swiss abbey of Pfävers (made c. 1030, but otherwise unidentified) remind us that some very specialized rites would definitely require a script that could also be a pleasing theatrical object.[63] The elaborate service for the dedication of a church, to take an obvious example, would have been one that relatively few bishops would have performed routinely over the course of their pontificates.[64] Most would need a text. Accordingly, some prelates may have preferred a book whose slim size would make it easily portable during a long and intricate performance: a book like the ivory-covered *libellus* of Pfävers. Moreover, because a new church might be far away from the bishop's city, a pocket-sized *libellus* would leave more room in overstuffed saddlebags for vestments, mitre, crozier, relics and other accoutrements.[65] The so-called Pontifical of Lanalet (probably made for the abbey of St Germans in Cornwall, in the early eleventh century) allows us to glimpse such a *libellus* in action. It features a full-page image of a moment from the consecration ceremony – the bishop at the door of the church, backed by clergy and surrounded by a crowd of parishioners – as well as an image of a praying bishop reading from a *libellus* held open by an acolyte (see cover image).[66] *Dedicatio* manuscripts also exhibit design elements that would have guided overworked prelates in the successful execution of this long and demanding ritual. A twelfth-century pontifical from Ely (England)

---

[62]   On the decoration of these *rotulae*, see Palazzo, *History*, 78–79.

[63]   Bernhard Bischoff, *Mittelalterliche Schatzverzeichnisse* (Munich: Prestel-Verlag, 1967), 1:75 (no. 68). Palazzo expresses surprise that a 'humble *libellus*' would be bound in ivory: 'Le rôle des *libelli*', 17.

[64]   On the mechanics and performance of this rite, see the essays edited by Didier Méhu, *Mises en scène et mémoires de la consécration de l'église dans l'occident médiéval* (Turnhout: Brepols, 2007) and Chapter 8 in this book.

[65]   An example of such a book is London, British Library, Additional Ms. 82956: this is an early eleventh-century sacramentary from Noyons with various additions (including an excommunication formula) made by or for a bishop, which has been identified as a 'saddle book' based on its dimensions (long and thin) and size (portable). I am grateful to Sarah Hamilton for bringing this codex to my attention. On the practical usage of pontificals, see Richard Pfaff, 'The Anglo-Saxon Bishop and His Book', *Bulletin of the John Rylands University Library of Manchester* 81 (1999): 3–24.

[66]   Rouen, Bibliothèque municipale, Ms. 368, fols. 2v and 1v, respectively. See Eric Palazzo, *L'évêque et son image: L'illustration du pontifical au moyen âge* (Turnout: Brepols, 1999), 318–20 and fig.14; and Palazzo, 'L'illustration des livres liturgiques autour de l'an mil', in *L'Europe de l'an mil*, ed. Pierre Riché (Saint-Léger-Vauban: Zodiaque, 2001), 291–307.

includes very explicit instructions for performing a key aspect of the rite: the act of intoning the letters of the Greek alphabet while tracing them in sand sprinkled on the floor of the church. The book carefully notes that the bishop should begin at the eastern (left) corner and work toward the western (right) corner. A later hand, anxious lest this not be entirely clear, has noted in the margin that the eastern corner is also the 'NORTH CORNER'. Helpfully, too, the rubrics not only supply the letters of the Greek alphabet but also provide a key to their pronunciation.[67] Yet no such aid is needed for the Latin alphabet, to be intoned and inscribed from the opposite corners, and which every bishop had internalized: hence even the most complete liturgical books may leave out information that was commonly known.

Alongside all of the other performative dimensions outlined in this chapter, these examples indicate that examination of the actual manuscript of a medieval liturgical text should be a key component of any investigation, as should informed speculation as to its possible uses in the context of performance. If large and heavy, a liturgical book would need to rest on a lectern. If no lectern was available, it would need to be hefted by a sturdy deacon, which means that we can infer the need for other liturgical actors from the size of the book alone. In the ninth through twelfth centuries, the possession of a large Bible would be symbolic of a community's commitment to liturgical reform: not only were these books costly, their purpose was to ensure that no scriptural readings were omitted, especially from the Night Office. The larger size of their script also made readings and chanting by candlelight easier, while their distinctive illuminations would have assisted readers in remembering individual readings and could even have been glimpsed by listeners while open on the lectern.[68] By contrast, a small Bible or missal conveyed different messages. Fitting into a pocket or a palm, it might never be opened in the course of the service; the writing would be too small to read anyway, in a dim church. The mere presence of the book was important.[69] This can often be confirmed by a worn binding coupled with a pristine interior. Indeed, assumptions about the influence of some liturgical texts may need to be subjected to fresh scrutiny when these manuscripts show no signs of use. If the St Albans Psalter was made for the anchoress Christina of Markyate (c. 1096–c. 1156), any argument for its influence on her spiritual

---

[67]   Cambridge University Library Ll. 2.10, fol. 19r: 'ANGULO AQUILO'. A plate is reproduced in Hiley, *Western Plainchant*, 424–25.

[68]   Diane J. Reilly, 'Lectern Bibles and Liturgical Reform in the Central Middle Ages', in *The Practice of the Bible in the Middle Ages: Production, Reception, and Performance in Western Christianity*, ed. Susan Boynton and Diane J. Reilly (New York: Columbia University Press, 2011), 105–25.

[69]   See Huglo, *Les livres*, 75 and 124–25.

practices is complicated by the fact that she does not seem to have looked at it very carefully, if at all.[70]

In addition to scrutinizing individual liturgical texts for information about their use in performance, it is also worth considering the liturgical roles played by other texts that frequently functioned as liturgical objects or ritual scripts. Chief among these are charters and other legal instruments, which were frequently negotiated, sealed, read aloud, and displayed in churches, on altars, and carried in processions.[71] Monastic cartularies and chronicles (like Orderic's *historia*) were also exhibited and read in the course of liturgical ceremonies on certain occasions. Like the services in which they featured, they represented the patrimony of a religious house. Domesday Book, that vast repository of data assembled at the behest of William the Conqueror in 1086, was another text displayed and treated in this manner. For whatever the original purposes underlying its making, its two volumes functioned as impressive ceremonial artefacts, more so than as legal or administrative documents.[72] The important role of ritual in most medieval claims to property or rights, and in the settlement of disputes, means that liturgy would often help to frame such transactions, especially those involving an oath.[73]

As important as liturgical texts undoubtedly were, then, the evidence we have gathered so far shows that their role(s) in performance would be conditioned by many factors. Some books and *libelli* may never have appeared in a church; they were instructional or memorial aids. Others would have been carried into church, but never opened. Still others might have been needed to prompt certain

---

[70] It is now Hildesheim, Dombibliothek Ms St. Godehard 1. This argument is put forward most forcefully by Jane Geddes, *The St. Albans Psalter: A Book for Christina of Markyate* (London: British Library, 2005).

[71] See the articles in Marco Mostert and P.S. Barnwell, eds., *Medieval Legal Process: Physical, Spoken, and Written Performance in the Middle Ages* (Turnhout: Brepols, 2011), esp. Bernhard Zeller's 'Writing Charters as a Public Activity: The Example of the Carolingian Charters of St Gall' (27–37), Charles Insley's 'Rhetoric and Ritual in Late Anglo-Saxon Charters' (109–21), and Michael H. Gelting's 'Circumstantial Evidence: Danish Charters of the Thirteenth Century' (157–95). A particularly evocative description of a charter's ceremonial making and meaning is Geoffrey Koziol's 'A Father, His Son, Memory, and Hope: A Joint Diploma of Lothar and Louis V (Pentecost Monday, 979) and the Limits of Performativity', in *Geschichtswissenschaft und 'Performative Turn': Ritual, Inszenierung und Performanz vom Mittelalter bis zur Neuzeit*, ed. Jürgen Martschukat and Steffen Patzold (Cologne: Böhlau Verlag, 2003), 83–103.

[72] Michael T. Clanchy, *From Memory to Written Record: England 1066–1307*, 3rd edn. (Oxford: Wiley-Blackwell, 2013), 156, 164–65.

[73] See, for example, Geoffrey Koziol, *Begging, Pardon and Favor: Ritual and Political Order in Early Medieval France* (Ithaca, NY: Cornell University Press, 1992); Warren Brown 'Charters as Weapons. On the Role Played by Early Medieval Dispute Records in the Disputes They Record', *Journal of Medieval History* 28 (2002): 227–48.

performers at certain times, and afterward laid aside. Within each book, text, rubrics, notation, illuminations and other features may have been absolutely essential to the performance of a rite – or merely incidental, decorative. Every text was designed for a particular context, user or audience. Every text therefore includes and omits certain kinds of information. Moreover, liturgical texts are not the only sources of information for the ways liturgies were conducted, nor were they the only texts featured in religious rituals. We might even begin to wonder whether we can always tell which texts are liturgical ones.[74]

On the Difficulty of Determining What Is and Is Not a 'Liturgical Text', and the Possible Benefits to be Gained from Expanding Our Definition

As I noted at the outset, we have inherited an anachronistic and narrow idea of what 'liturgy' is. 'The liturgy' is usually conceptualized as a set of fixed, 'top-down' directives issued by a monolithic authority. There are many compelling reasons to challenge and expand that conventional understanding. We can go back to the Greek verb λειτουργέω, 'to perform public service', or the basic elements of the noun λειτουργία: 'people' (λεώς) and 'work' (ἔργον).[75] Liturgy is the public work of a particular group of people, the shared performances that comes to define that group. By this definition, not every kind of liturgy propagated by clerical authorities was relevant to every community, or adopted by every community in a uniform manner. At the same time, every community had its own liturgical formulae – some scripted, some not. In the course of the eleventh century, for example, many of the miracles recorded at the shrine of Sainte-Foy at Conques witness successful resistance to the 'reforming' efforts of foreigners from Cluny or Rome, on the part of laypeople and the shrine's monastic custodians. They also show 'how many ritual activities [were] performed by non-specialists' and 'how unmarked the boundary [was] between "official" liturgical practice and what might be considered paraliturgical or even non-liturgical activities'.[76] Now, clearly, this is a special case: the monks and people of Conques were in an unusually strong position to assert and protect their own community's traditions, given the extraordinary powers accorded to their saint. They were also equipped to ensure that their efforts to safeguard her cult were recorded for posterity in writing. But these caveats merely underscore the fact that less

---

[74]   See Chapter 6 in this book.

[75]   C. Clifford Flanigan, Kathleen Ashley and Pamela Sheingorn, 'Liturgy as Social Performance: Expanding the Definitions', in *Liturgy of the Medieval Church*, 695–714, at 698. See the definition of 'liturgy' in F.L. Cross and E.A. Livingstone, eds., *The Oxford Dictionary of the Christian Church*, 3rd rev. edn (Oxford: Oxford University Press, 2005), 356.

[76]   Flanigan et al., 'Liturgy as Social Performance', 699.

powerful communities might have had no less valued traditions, even if they are now obscured from view.[77] How might we go about recovering them?

We might begin by looking for alternative sources of information, in sources both familiar and strange.[78] Bede's *Ecclesiastical History*, for instance, seems to serve no obvious liturgical function; but it does include many narratives of miracles and conversions that could derive from older homilies, *historiæ* or liturgical *lectiones* prepared by his predecessors. Moreover, his famous story of Cædmon's hymn is a story about how vernacular song was 'converted' to Christianity in England, along with its inhabitants. As Bruce Holsinger has shown, the song was formally constructed and received by contemporaries as a hymn. A later Anglo-Saxon translation of Bede's entire history even seems to have been used as a liturgical book.[79]

We might also ask 'What constitutes a liturgical text?' That is, we can become better sensitized to recognizing *as* liturgical an array of texts that have been misidentified or passed over due to the assumptions of modern scholarship.[80] The correspondence of the philosopher and teacher Peter Abelard (c. 1079–1142) and his former pupil and wife, Heloise (d. 1164) is a striking example. These letters have inspired prurient fascination since the end of the thirteenth century, when they were construed by later readers as private admissions of hypocrisy, arrogance and frustrated passion. (Even arguments alleging the letters' inauthenticity rest on this key assumption.[81]) But as Morgan Powell has argued, the correspondence was probably crafted or revised for contemplative, structured reading at the convent the couple jointly founded, and at its half-dozen daughter houses. So, far from being an exposé of illicit love, these letters

---

[77] For an example, see Pamela Sheingorn and Kathleen Ashley, '*Discordia et lis*: Negotiating Power, Property, and Performance in Medieval Sélestat', *Journal of Medieval and Early Modern Studies* 26 (1996): 419–46.

[78] Perhaps the best study of the way that liturgical performance pervaded and shaped a single urban locale in its totality is Susannah Crowder's 'Performance Culture in Medieval Metz, c. 200–1200', unpub. PhD diss., (City University of New York, 2008).

[79] *Bede's Ecclesiastical History of the English People*, ed. and trans. Bertram Colgrave and R.A.B. Mynors (Oxford: Clarendon Press, 1969), 4.24 (pp. 414–17). See Bruce Holsinger, 'The Parable of Caedmon's *Hymn*: Liturgical Invention and Literary Tradition', *Journal of English and Germanic Philology* 106 (2007): 149–75. On the liturgical uses of other Old English works, see Holsinger, 'Liturgy', in *Oxford Twenty-First Century Approaches*, ed. Strohm, 295–314, at 301. See also Christopher A. Jones, 'The Book of the Liturgy in Anglo-Saxon England', *Speculum* 73 (1998): 659–702; and also his 'Performing Christianity: Liturgical and Devotional Writing', in *The Cambridge History of Early Medieval English Literature*, ed. Clare A. Lees (Cambridge: Cambridge University Press, 2013), 427–50.

[80] This point is also stressed by Helen Gittos: see Chapter 1 in this book.

[81] For a brief summary of the letters' historical reception and interpretation, see M.T. Clanchy, 'The Letters of Abelard and Heloise in Today's Scholarship', in *The Letters of Abelard and Heloise*, trans. Betty Radice, rev. edn. (London: Penguin, 2003), lviii–lxxxiv.

were supposed to be didactic, inspirational and liturgical.[82] They narrate how a new monastic rule for women was devised by the founders of the Paraclete, and they dramatize the often painful process of worldly renunciation that any female postulant would need to undergo. Couched in an epistolary and dialogic format, featuring passages of brilliant lyricism, they draw upon well-known Biblical and patristic genres that had already been thoroughly integrated into the liturgy: the Psalms, the Song of Songs, the letters of St Paul and St Jerome, the *Confessions* of St Augustine.[83] Like the body of hymns and songs jointly composed by Heloise and Abelard, they would have formed the basis of ritual life within a new religious order.[84] We can appreciate their significance only if we expand our understanding of medieval liturgy.

That understanding could further profit from embracing the vastly important activity of preaching, which took place in every conceivable venue, reached every stratum of society, and generated a relatively large amount of documentation. Even more vitally, it should take account of the liturgy's 'formal, authorial and economic impact' on all vernacular literature, much of which could be considered relevant to the history of liturgy's reception and practice.[85] How might the study of the liturgy be transformed if we consider the enormous archive of writings that would have supported family prayers, private devotions and daily worship in household chapels? Devotional texts in the vernacular, as well as Latin prayerbooks, proliferate from the thirteenth century onward and continued to do so after the advent of print. Indeed, rather than standardizing the liturgy, the late medieval printing press created a still larger array of genres and opened up new markets for them. As Holsinger notes, there are more liturgical texts (in English and in Latin) among the surviving incunabula from the British Isles

---

[82]   Morgan Powell, 'Listening to Heloise at the Paraclete: Of Scholarly Diversion and a Woman's Conversion', in *Listening to Heloise: The Voice of a Twelfth-Century Woman*, ed. Bonnie Wheeler (New York: St. Martin's Press, 2000), 255–86.

[83]   A recent translation of the letters renders the meter and rhythm of Heloise's literary *cursus*, thereby helping to make their performative character more apparent: *Abelard and Heloise: The Letters and Other Writings*, trans. William Levitan (Indianapolis: Hackett, 2007).

[84]   Susan Boynton, 'Religious Soundscapes: Liturgy and Music', in *The Cambridge History of Christianity, vol. 4: Christianity in Western Europe, c.1100–c.1500*, ed. Miri Rubin and Walter Simons (Cambridge: Cambridge University Press, 2009), 238–53, at 240–43; David Wulstan, '*Novi modulaminis melos*: The Music of Heloise and Abelard', in *Plainsong and Medieval Music* 11 (2002): 1–23; Constant Mews, 'Heloise and Liturgical Experience at the Paraclete', *Plainsong and Medieval Music* 11 (2002): 25–35; Marc Stewart and David Wulstan, *The Poetic and Musical Legacy of Heloise and Abelard: An Anthology of Essays by Various Authors* (Ottawa: Institute of Medieval Music, 2003).

[85]   Holsinger, 'Liturgy', 296.

than there are works by classical, medieval or early modern authors *combined*.[86] Deepening and extending our research on medieval liturgy entails reconsidering *what liturgy was* and where the sources for it might be found.

Concerning the Evidence for Lay Liturgical Performance

Reckoning with the usually unscripted role performed by the laity at different times and in all regions of Christendom is yet another important task for future scholars of the medieval liturgy. Nor is this a task limited to the study of the later Middle Ages. Rosamund McKitterick reminds us that the liturgy of the Carolingian Reform was above all a mode of instruction, aimed at the conversion of pagan tribes subjugated by Charlemagne, but also at the consolidation of a wider community. The presence, engagement and responses of the laity were crucial to this endeavour and to the formation of Western Christendom.[87] If this is not explicit in surviving texts, it is because the makers of those texts were trying to promote the interests and authority of a small class of professionalized clergy.

Occasionally, though, early sources do allow us to glimpse some of the forms that lay participation could take. Although the use of the vernacular is not necessarily a marker of lay practice or outreach, it is instructive that the earliest surviving liturgical dramas with vernacular elements witness efforts to formalize the liturgical role of local dialects which may have featured in worship services for a long time, and to reframe certain Biblical stories or characters in immediate, effective ways.[88] It is also significant that the earliest vernacular songs tend to be preserved in liturgical manuscripts.[89] This may be related to the ways that popular performance traditions crystallized, very early on, into some of the most canonical of liturgical texts. Edward Foley has noted that ancient dialogic responses were included in the Ordinary of the Mass due to congregational demand, and that many processional chants in Latin have absorbed 'popular

---

[86]   Holsinger, 'Liturgy', 300.

[87]   Rosamond McKitterick, *The Frankish Church and the Carolingian Reforms, 789–895* (London: Royal Historical Society, 1977), 115–54.

[88]   The *Ludus de Passione* (Passion Play) of Benediktbeuern (c. 1250) is a particularly good example. See Peter Loewen, 'The Conversion of Mary Magdalene and the Musical Legacy of Franciscan Piety in the Early German Passion Plays', in *Speculum sermonis: Interdisciplinary Reflections on the Medieval Sermon*, ed. Georgiana Donivan et al. (Turnhout: Brepols, 2004), 235–58.

[89]   For example, the earliest Occitan songs are preserved in a liturgical manuscript from the abbey of Saint-Martial at Limoges (Paris, Bibliothèque nationale de France Ms. latin 1139) and the oldest extant Anglo-Norman text, the *Chanson de saint Alexis*, survives in the Saint Albans Psalter. See Symes, 'Appearance'.

religious songs' and carols.[90] John Haines has argued that vernacular song, often unwritten, was a vital part of devotional music-making throughout the premodern period.[91] Els Rose has shown that the early Latin of the mass was *not* an elevated, 'hieratic' language designed to remove the sacred liturgy beyond the realm of everyday speech; on the contrary, early regional missals show that vocabulary and syntax reflect common speech.[92] Although many diocesan and provincial synods would try to suppress vernacular elements in the liturgy from time to time – just as they tried to maintain clear distinctions between clerics and laymen – these efforts were often fruitless.[93] We have already noted Godric of Finchale's celebrity status among the monks of Durham Priory.

In fact, most laypeople would have been liturgical practitioners at one time or another in their lives. Although some couples would have entered into informal partnerships that were recognized as legal marriages without the public exchange of vows, many communities and nearly all propertied families would have insisted on a solemn church ceremony. In any case, marriages vows (even clandestine ones) constituted a sacramental rite that was canonically valid regardless of clerical involvement.[94] The baptism of infants was another sacrament that could be performed by laypeople because of its crucial importance for the salvation of the newborn soul; and it was usually done by women, especially midwives. In at least some regions, by around 1200, parents of both sexes were being instructed in the wording of the rite, using either the Latin words (*ego baptizo te in nomine patris et filii et spiritus sancti*) or their vernacular equivalent.[95]

---

[90] Edward Foley, 'The Song of the Assembly in Medieval Eucharist', in *Medieval Liturgy*, ed. Larson-Miller, 203–34.

[91] John Haines, *Medieval Song in Romance Languages* (Cambridge: Cambridge University Press, 2010), 116–43. He also calls for a new history of music (and the liturgy) that eschews the 'great man' grand narratives still prevalent.

[92] Rose thus argues against the influential work of Christine Mohrmann; for example, *Liturgical Latin, Its Origins and Character; Three Lectures* (Washington, DC: Catholic University of America Press, 1957). For a summary of her findings, see Els Rose, 'Liturgical Latin in Early Medieval Gaul', in *Spoken and Written Language: Relations between Latin and the Vernacular Languages in the Earlier Middles Ages*, ed. Mary Garrison, A.P. Orbán and Marco Mostert (Turnhout: Brepols, 2013), 303–13.

[93] Foley, 'Song of the Assembly'.

[94] John K. Leonard, 'Rites of Marriage in the Western Middle Ages', in *Medieval Liturgy*, ed. Larson-Miller, 165–202; Carol Symes, *A Common Stage: Theater and Public Life in Medieval Arras* (Ithaca, NY: Cornell University Press, 2007), 173–74. On the formal and informal modes of marriage formation – and the complications that often arose from the practical application of canon law – see Charles Donahue, Jr., *Law, Marriage, and Society in the Later Middle Ages: Arguments about Marriage in Five Courts* (Cambridge: Cambridge University Press, 2007).

[95] Kathryn Taglia, 'Delivering a Christian Identity: Midwives in Northern French Synodal Legislation, c. 1200–1550', in *Religion and Medicine in the Middle Ages*, ed. Peter

Funeral services were also overwhelmingly organized by laypeople and, from at least the twelfth century onward, the formulation and enactment of elaborate commemorative liturgies was central to the mission of urban confraternities.[96] In the wealthy Franco-Flemish city of Arras, the oldest of such confraternities provides a particularly striking example of laity-driven liturgy. This charitable fellowship was formed by an alliance of jongleurs (professional entertainers) and townspeople, and it became one of the most powerful religious and social institutions in the region. The confraternity's spiritual authority derived from its possession of the Sainte Chandelle, a candle legendarily bestowed on its founders by the Blessed Virgin; its wax, when mixed with water, was believed to heal the terrible burning sensations caused by the convulsive and gangrenous disease of ergotism (also known as Saint Anthony's Fire). This cult, fostered by the Carité de Nostre Dame des Ardents ('the Confraternity of Our Lady of the Burning Ones'), was officially sponsored by the bishop of Arras and, by the middle of the thirteenth century, received papal approval. Until the time of the French Revolution, it was at the centre of an annual cycle of urban celebrations supported by diocesan clergy and also by their local rivals, the monks of the abbey of Saint-Vaast. These rites attracted pilgrims from all over Europe, and secondary relics of the holy candle were used to found chapels throughout Flanders, Brabant and Wallonia. A few of the texts drawn up by the confraternity survive and can be used to reconstruct its liturgy: they include Latin and vernacular versions of the foundation legend and subsequent Marian *miracula*, a set of protocols for the conduct of funerals, a memorial register of the dead (maintained over a period of 167 years and listing the names of over 10,500 individuals), and an *ordo* partially describing the preparations for a major annual feast. It is largely thanks to the precocious vernacular literacy of Arras that we know something about how these liturgical activities became central to the spiritual and civic lives of many thousands of laypeople over a period of at least five hundred years. Yet explicit evidence for them is hard to find in the conventional liturgical sources generated by the abbey or cathedral; we need to look in other places. When we do, we begin to discern – with a sense of irony – that the jongleurs' methods were being copied by the most mainline establishments in Arras. In 1308, the monks of Saint-Vaast even translated portions of their venerable liturgical ordinal into the local Picard vernacular, as part of a larger project that encompassed popular preaching. Their obvious goal was to compete with

---

Biller and Joseph Ziegler (York: York Medieval Press, 2001), 77–90; Symes, *Common Stage*, 173.

[96]   Lester K. Little, *Liberty, Charity, Fraternity: Lay Religious Confraternities in Bergamo in the Age of the Commune* (Bergamo: P. Lubrina, 1988), 57–81. For a general overview, see Catherine Vincent, *Les confréries médiévales dans le royaume de France, XIIIe–XVe siècle* (Paris: A. Michel, 1994).

the populist approaches of the mendicant orders, using the techniques of popular entertainers.[97]

The widely held notion that laypeople were excluded from meaningful participation in religious rites derives in part from the successful propaganda of some medieval authorities, but it has been even more effectively propagated since the middle of the sixteenth century. Once again, it is to the modern era that we owe the myths that there was no communal singing in churches before the Protestant Reformation, or that the vernacular did not come into liturgical use within the Catholic Church until after the Second Vatican Council (1962–65).[98] Recent scholarship strongly demonstrates that the liturgical roles of the medieval laity require significant re-assessment. While we will never be able to overcome the gap between the mostly canonical texts we have and the wider world of liturgical practice, a more holistic and critical engagement with the evidence is in order, and could yield a good deal of fresh evidence.

In Conclusion

This chapter has focused on the problematic relationship between medieval texts and contemporary performance practices in the many contexts that could be considered 'liturgical'. It has insisted that the recognition of this relationship *as* problematic is a very fruitful place to begin any inquiry. It calls for a fresh evaluation of extant sources and an expansion of efforts to find new ones. It urges researchers to pay special attention to the possible performance dynamics of particular communities at particular times, to investigate the extent to which local authorities sought to influence or control these dynamics, and to question whether those participating in the liturgy relied on literate forms of communication at all, or to what extent. It insists on asking what kinds of information liturgical manuscripts were intended to convey, and how enactors would have used that information. It maintains that such questions will empower us to learn more about even well-known sources, including those that have long been regarded as canonical and which seem impervious to new interpretations. Moreover, and perhaps more importantly, it holds out hope that this approach will help us to locate texts that have been ignored or overlooked, while allowing us to access extra-textual or contextual evidence that can further assist in apprehending what occurred in performance. We need to know this, because we

---

[97] Arras, Bibliothèque municipale 230. It has been edited by Louis Brou as *The Monastic Ordinale of St.-Vedast's Abbey, Arras*, 2 vols, HBS, 86–87 (London: HBS, 1957). See Symes, *Common Stage*, 68–126 and 171–72.

[98] Foley, 'Song of the Assembly'; Flanigan et al., 'Liturgy as Social Performance', 709. See also Symes, *Common Stage*, 159–74, and Gittos in Chapter 1 of this book.

need to know how the liturgy *worked*: how it intersected with spiritual, political, economic, social and cultural exchanges – and helped to enact them. If we do not understand medieval liturgy, it is hard to imagine how we can understand any aspect of the Middle Ages.

Bibliography

Primary sources

Abbot Suger: On the Abbey Church of St-Denis and Its Art Treasures, edited and translated by Erwin Panofsky. Princeton: Princeton University Press, 1946.

Abt Suger von Saint-Denis ausgewählte schriften: Ordinatio, De consecratione, De administratione, edited by Andreas Speer and Günther Binding. Darmstadt: Wissenschaftliche Buchgesellschaft, 2000.

Abelard and Heloise: The Letters and Other Writings. Translated by William Levitan. Indianapolis: Hackett Publishing, 2007.

Adémar de Chabannes. *Opera liturgica et poetica: Musica cum textibus*, edited by James Grier. Ademari Cabannensis, Opera Omnia Pars II, CCCM 245, 245a. Turnhout: Brepols, 2012.

Aelfric, *Homilies of Aelfric: The Homilies of the Anglo-Saxon Church*, vol. 1, edited and translated by Benjamin Thorpe. London: Taylor for Aelfric Society, 1844.

Alcuin, *Epistolae*, edited by E. Dümmler. *MGH Epistolae*, vol. 4. Berlin: Weidmann, 1895.

Antiphonale missarum sextuplex, edited by René-Jean Hesbert. Brussels: Vromont, 1935; reprinted Rome: Herder, 1967.

Antiphonale Sarisburiense: A Reproduction in Facsimile of a Manuscript of the Thirteenth Century, edited by W.H. Frere. London, Plainsong and Medieval Music Society, 1901–24; repr. Farnborough: Gregg Press, 1966.

Bede's Ecclesiastical History of the English People, edited and translated by Bertram Colgrave and R.A.B. Mynors. Oxford: Clarendon Press, 1969.

Bernard of Clairvaux. *Sancti Bernardi opera*, edited by Jean Leclercq, Henri Rochais and Charles Talbot. 8 vols. Rome: Editiones Cistercienses, 1957–77.

Bernard of Clairvaux: Sermons for the Summer Season. Translated by B.M. Kienzle. Kalamazoo, MI: Cistercian Publications, 1991.

Bernard of Clairvaux: Sermons on the Song of Songs II. Translated by K. Walsh. Kalamazoo, MI: Cistercian Publications, 1983.

Bernard of Cluny. 'Ordo cluniacensis'. In *Vetus disciplina monastica*, edited by Marquard Herrgott. Paris: Osmont, 1726; reproduced by Pius Engelbert, 134–364. Siegburg: Franz Schmitt, 1999.

Bernhard von Clairvaux: Sämtliche Werke, edited by G. Winkler, Alberich Altermatt, Denis Farkasfalvy and Polykarp Zakar. 10 vols. Innsbruck: Tyrolia Verlag, 1997.

Biblia sacra iuxta vulgatam versionem, edited by B. Fischer et al. Stuttgart: Deutsche Bibelgesellschaft, 1994.

Bibliotheca hagiographica latina antiquae et media aetatis, edited by Socii Bollandiani. Brussels: Société des Bollandistes 1898–.

The Bobbio Missal: A Gallican Mass-Book, edited by E.A. Lowe and J. Wickham Legg. HBS 53, 58, 61. London: HBS, 1917, 1920, 1924.

The Book of Common Prayer. London: Edward Whitchurch, 1549.

Breviarium ad usum insignis ecclesiae Eboracensis, edited by Stephen Lawley. Surtees Society 71, 75. Durham: Surtees Society, 1879–82.

Breviarium ad usum insignis ecclesiae Sarum, edited by Francis Procter and Christopher Wordsworth. 3 vols. Cambridge: Cambridge University Press, 1879–86.

The Canterbury Benedictional (British Museum, Harl. Ms 2892), edited by R.M. Woolley. HBS 51. London: HBS, 1917.

Chartes et documents de Saint-Bénigne de Dijon, prieurés et dépendances des origines à 1300, edited by Georges Chevrier and Maurice Chaume. Analecta Burgundica. 2 vols. Dijon: Bernigaud and Privat, 1943.

Consuetudines Benedictinae variae. Saec XI–Saec XIV, edited by Giles Constable. CCM 6. Siegburg: Franz Schmitt, 1975.

Consuetudines Cluniacensium antiquiores cum redactionibus derivatis, edited by Kassius Hallinger, Maria Wegener and Candida Elvert. CCM 7.2. Siegburg: Franz Schmitt, 1983.

Consuetudinum saeculi X/XI/XII monumenta. Introductiones, edited by Kassius Hallinger. CCM 7.1. Siegburg: Franz Schmitt, 1984.

Corpus antiphonalium officii, edited by René-Jean Hesbert. 6 vols. RED series maior, fontes 7–12. Rome: Herder, 1963–79.

Corpus consuetudinum monasticarum, edited by Kassius Hallinger et al., vols. 1–9. Siegburg: Franz Schmitt, 1963–76.

Corpus orationum, edited by Eugene Moeller and Jean-Marie Clément, completed by Bertrand Coppieters 't Wallant. 13 vols. CCSL 160. Turnhout: Brepols, 1993–2003.

Il Cosiddetto Pontificale di Poitiers: Paris, Bibliothèque de l'Arsenal, cod 227, edited by Aldo Martini. Rome: Herder, 1979.

The Customary of the Benedictine Abbey of Eynsham in Oxfordshire, edited by Antonia Gransden. CCM 2. Siegburg: Franz Schmitt, 1963.

d'Achery, Luc. *Spicilegium sive Collectio veterum aliquot scriptorum qui in Galliae bibliothecis maxime Benedictinorum delituerant*. 3 vols. Paris: Montalant, 1723.

Les 'Ecclesiastica officia' cisterciens du XIIème siècle, edited by D. Choisselet and P. Vernet. Reiningue: Abbaye d'Oelenberg, 1989.

English Monastic Litanies of the Saints after 1100, edited by Nigel J. Morgan. 2 vols. HBS 119–20. London: HBS, 2012–13.

Eusebius of Caesarea. *Historia ecclesiastica*, edited by Gustave Bardy. Sources chrétiennes 31, 41, 55 and 73. Paris: Cerf, 1952–60.

Flodoard. *Les annales de Flodoard*, edited by Philippe Lauer. Paris: Alphonse Picard et Fils, 1905.

Fulbert of Chartres. *The Letters and Poems of Fulbert of Chartres*, edited by F. Behrends. Oxford: Oxford University Press, 1976.

Gamal Norsk Homiliebok, edited by Gustav Indrebø. Oslo: Oslo Universitetsforlaget, 1966; first published 1931.

Gammelnorsk Homiliebok, edited by Erik Gunnes, translated by Astrid Salvesen. Oslo: Universitetsforlaget, 1971.

Gennadius of Marseille. *Liber de scriptoribus ecclesiasticis*. *PL* 58.

Gesta abbatum monasterii Sancti Albani, edited by Henry Thomas Riley. 3 vols. London: Rolls Series, 1897.

Gesta episcoporum Cameracensium, edited by L.C. Bethmann, MGH SS 7. Hannover: Hahn, 1846.

Gorham v. the bishop of Exeter, a report of the arguments of counsel, before the judicial committee of the Privy council. To which is added, the judgment. London, 1850.

Graduale Sarisburiense: A Reproduction in Facsimile of a Manuscript of the Thirteenth Century, edited by W.H. Frere. London: Quaritch, 1894, repr. Farnborough: Gregg Press, 1966.

Gratian. 1.I, *Decretum magistri Gratiani*, edited by Emil Friedberg. *Corpus iuris canonici*, Leipzig, 1879.

The Gregorian Sacramentary under Charles the Great, edited by Henry Austin Wilson. HBS 49. London: HBS, 1915.

Gregory of Tours. *Historiarum libri X*, edited by Bruno Krusch and Wilhelm Levison. MGH SS rerum Merovingicarum 1.1. Hannover: Hansche Buchhandlung, 1951.

Harting-Corrêa, Alice L. *Walahfrid Strabo's* Libellus de exordiis et incrementis quarundam in observationibus ecclesiasticis rerum: *A Translation and Liturgical Commentary*. Mittellateinische Studien und Texte 19. Leiden: E.J. Brill, 1996.

Heinrici II et Arduini Diplomata, edited by H. Bresslau, H. Bloch, M. Meyer and R. Holtzman. MGH Diplomatum regum et imperatorum germaniae III Berlin: Weidmannsche Verlagsbuchhandlung, 1957.

The Hereford Breviary, edited by W.H. Frere and L.E.G. Brown. HBS 26, 40, 46. London: HBS, 1904–15.

Herrgott, Marquard, *Vetus Disciplina Monastica*. Paris: Osmont, 1726; reprinted Siegburg: Schmitt, 1999.

Hittorp, Melchior, *De Divinis Catholicae Ecclesiae Officiis et Mysteriis Varii Vetustorum Aliquot Ecclesiae Patrum ac Scriptorum Ecclesiasticorum Libri*. Cologne, 1568.

Holy Bible, Douay-Rheims version. Baltimore: John Murphy Company, 1899.

Hymn Collections from the Paraclete, edited by C. Waddell. 2 vols. CLS 8–9.

Jones, Christopher A. *Ælfric's Letter to the Monks of Eynsham*. Cambridge: Cambridge University Press, 1998.

Das Kollektar-Pontifikale des Bischofs Baturich von Regensburg 817-84: Cod. Vindob. Ser. N. 2762, edited by Franz Unterkircher. SF 8. Freiburg: Universitäts Verlag, 1962.

Die Konzilien Deutchlands und Reichsitaliens 916–1001: Teil 2: 962–1001, edited by Ernst-Dieter Hehl with Carlo Servatius. MGH Concilia 6.2. Hannover: Hahnsche Buchhandlung, 2007.

Lanfranc, *The Monastic Constitutions of Lanfranc*, edited and translated by Dom David Knowles. London: Thomas Nelson and Sons, 1951; rev. edn. by Christopher Brooke, 2002; 1951 edition reprinted with minor corrections and a slightly revised introduction as *Decreta Lanfranci monachis Cantuariensibus transmissa*, CCM 3, Siegburg: Franz Schmitt, 1967.

The Letters of Lanfranc Archbishop of Canterbury, edited and translated by Helen Clover and Margaret Gibson. Oxford: Oxford University Press, 1979.

The Leofric Missal, edited by Nicholas Orchard. 2 vols. HBS 113–14. London: HBS, 2002.

Le liber ordinum en usage dans l'église wisigothique et mozarabe d'Espagne du cinquième au onzième siècle, edited by Marius Férotin. Monumenta Ecclesiae Liturgica 5. Paris: Firmin-Didot, 1904; repr. with bibliographical supplement on the Spanish liturgy, Rome: Edizioni Liturgiche, 1996.

Liber ordinum sacerdotal, edited by José Janini. Studia Silensia. Silos: Abadia de Silos, 1981.

Liber sacramentorum Augustudonensis, edited by Odilo Heiming. CCSL 159B. Turnhout: Brepols, 1984.

Liber sacramentorum Gellonensis, edited by Antoine Dumas. CCSL 159A. Turnhout: Brepols, 1981.

Liber sacramentorum Romanae aeclesiae ordinis anni circuli (Cod. Vat. Reg. lat. 316/Paris Bibl. Nat. 7193, 41/56): Sacramentarium Gelasianum, edited by Leo C. Mohlberg. RED series maior, fontes 4. Rome: Herder, 1960, 2nd edn. 1968, 3rd edn. 1981.

Liber tramitis aevi Odilonis abbatis, edited by Peter Dinter. CCM 10. Siegburg: Franz Schmitt, 1980.

Marbach, Karl, *Carmina scripturarum, scilicet Antiphonas et Responsoria ex sacra scripturae fonte in libros liturgicos*. Strasbourg: F.-X. Le Roux, 1907; repr. Hildesheim: Georg Olms, 1963.

Martène, Edmond, ed. *De antiquis ecclesiae ritibus*. 2nd edn., 4 vols. Antwerp: Joannis Baptistae de la Bry, 1736–38; repr. Hildesheim: Georg Olms, 1969.

Maskell, William *Monumenta Ritualia Ecclesiae Anglicanae*. 3 vols. London: W. Pickering, 1846–47.

A Menology of England and Wales or, Brief Memorials of their Ancient British and English Saints, edited by Richard Stanton. London: Burns and Oates, 1887.

Missale ad usum ecclesiae Eboracensis, edited by W.G. Henderson. Surtees Society 59, 60. Durham: Surtees Society, 1872–74.

Missale ad usum ecclesie Westmonasteriensis, edited by John Wickham Legg. 3 vols. HBS 1, 5, 12. London: HBS, 1891, 1893, 1897.

Missale ad usum insignis et praeclarae ecclesiae Sarum, edited by F.H. Dickinson. Burntisland: Pitsligo, 1861–63.

Missale Francorum, edited by L.C. Mohlberg. RED series maior, fontes 2. Rome: Herder, 1957.

Missale Gallicanum vetus, edited by L.C. Mohlberg. RED series maior, fontes 3. Rome: Herder, 1958.

Missale Gothicum, edited by L.C. Mohlberg. RED series maior, fontes 5. Rome: Herder, 1961.

The Monastic Ordinale of St-Vedast's Abbey, Arras, edited by L. Brou. 2 vols. London: HBS, 1957.

Newman, John Henry. *Loss and Gain*, new edn. Oxford: Oxford University Press, 1986.

Norbert and Early Norbertine Spirituality, edited and translated by Theodore J. Antry and C. Neel. New York: Paulist Press, 2007.

Notker Balbulus, *Gesta Karoli Magni Imperatoris*, edited by Hans F. Haefele. MGH SS rer ger n.s. 12. Berlin: Weidmann, 1959.

Œvres de Saint Augustin 11/1: La première catéchèse, De catechizandis rudibis, trans. Goulven Madec. Paris: Etudes augustiniennes, 1991.

Old English Homilies of the Twelfth Century, edited by Richard Morris. Early English Text Society, original series 53. London: Early English Text Society, 1873.

The Old French Paraclete Ordinary: Edition, edited by C. Waddell. CLS 4. Trappist, KY: Gethsemani Abbey, 1983.

The Old French Paraclete Ordinary: Paris Bibliothèque Nationale Ms français 14410 and the Paraclete Breviary: Chaumont, Bibliothèque Municipale Ms 31: Introduction and Commentary, edited by C. Waddell. CLS 3. Trappist, KY: Gethsemani Abbey, 1985.

Orderic Vitalis, *The Ecclesiastical History of Orderic Vitalis*, edited and translated by Marjorie Chibnall. 6 vols. Oxford: Clarendon Press, 1969–80.

Ordines Coronationis Franciae: Texts and Ordines for the Coronation of Frankish and French Kings and Queens in the Middle Ages, edited by Richard A. Jackson, 2vols. Philadelphia: University of Pennsylvania Press, 1995–2000.

Les ordines romani du haut moyen âge, edited by Michel Andrieu. 5 vols. Spicilegium Sacrum Lovaniense, Etudes et Documents, 11, 23, 24, 28 and 29. Louvain: Université Catholique et Collèges Théologiques de Louvain, 1931–61.

The Paraclete Breviary: Edition, edited by C. Waddell. 3 vols. CLS 5–7. Trappist, KY: Gethsemani Abbey, 1983.

The Paraclete Statutes, Institutiones Nostrae: Introduction, Edition and Commentary, edited by C. Waddell. CLS 20. Trappist, KY: Gethsemani Abbey, 1987.

The Parson's Handbook: Containing Practical Directions Both for Parsons and Others as to the Management of the Parish Church and Its Services According to the Anglican Use, as Set Forth in the Book of Common Prayer, edited by Percy Dearmer, 12th edn. London: Humphrey Milford, 1932.

Patrologia cursus completus, series latina, edited by J.-P. Migne. Paris: Garnier, 1844–64. Cited in notes as *PL*.

Peter Lombard, *Sententiae in IV libris distinctae*. Spicilegium Bonaventurum 4–5, 2 vols. Grottaferrata: Editiones Collegii S. Bonaventurae, 1971–1981.

Pontificale ecclesiæ S. Andreæ: The Pontifical Offices Used by David de Bernham, Bishop of S. Andrews, edited by C. Wordsworth. Edinburgh: Pitsligo Press, 1885.

Le pontifical romain au moyen âge, edited by Michel Andrieu. 4 vols. Studi e Testi 86–88, 99. Vatican City: Biblioteca Apostolica Vaticana, 1938–41.

Le pontifical romano-germanique du dixième siècle, edited by Cyrille Vogel and Reinhard Elze. Studi e Testi 226, 227, 269. 3 vols. Vatican City: Biblioteca Apostolica Vaticana, 1963–72.

Reginald of Durham, *Libellus de vita et miraculis S. Godrici, heremitae de Finchale*. Surtees Society 20. London: J.B. Nichols and Son [1847].

Regino of Prüm, *Libri duo de synodalibus causis et disciplinis ecclesiasticis*, edited by F.W.H. Wasserschleben, rev. Wilfried Hartmann. Darmstadt: Wissenschaftliche Buchgesellschaft, 2004.

Die Regularis Concordia *und ihre altenglische Interlinearversion*, edited with commentary by Lucia Kornexl. Munich: Wilhelm Fink, 1993.

Das Rheinauer Rituale (Zürich Rh 114, Anfang 12. Jh.), edited by Gebhard Hürlimann. SF 5. Freiburg: Universitätsverlag, 1959.

Richer of Reims, *Richeri Historiarum Libri IIII*, edited by Hartmut Hoffmann. MGH SS 38. Hanover: Hahnsche Buchhandlung, 2000.

Rodulfus Glaber. *Vita Domni Willelmi Abbatis*, edited by Neithard Bulst and John France. Translated by John France and Paul Reynolds. Oxford: Clarendon Press, 1989.

Le sacramentaire grégorien: Ses principales formes d'après les plus anciens manuscrits, edited by Jean Deshusses. 3 vols. SF 16, 24, 28. Fribourg: Editions Universitaire, 1971–1982; 2nd and 3rd revised and corrected edns 1988–92.

Sacramentarium Rhenaugiense, edited by Anton Hänggi and Alfons Schönherr. SF 15. Freiburg: Universitätsverlag, 1970.

Sacramentarium Veronense, edited by Leo Cunibert Mohlberg, Leo Eizenhöfer and Petrus Siffren. RED series maior, fontes 1. Rome: Herder, 1956; 2nd edn. 1966, 3rd edn. 1978.

The Sacramentary of Echternach. Paris, Bibliothèque Nationale, Ms lat. 9433, edited by Yitzhak Hen. HBS 110. London: HBS, 1997.

The Sacramentary of Ratoldus. Paris, Bibliothèque nationale de France, lat 12052, edited by Nicholas Orchard. HBS 116. London: HBS, 2005.

La sainte Bible, translated by Louis-Claude Fillion. Paris: Libraire Letouzey et Ané, 1889.

The Sarum Missal: Edited from Three Early Manuscripts, edited by John Wickham Legg. Oxford: Oxford University Press, 1916.

The Sarum Missal in English. Translated by Frederick E. Warren. 2 vols. London: A. Moring, 1911.

The Stowe Missal, edited by George F. Warner. HBS 32. London: HBS, 1915.

Suger. *Oeuvres 1*, edited and translated by Françoise Gasparri. Paris: Les Belles Lettres, 1996.

Thietmar of Merseburg. *Chronicon*, edited by R. Holtzmann. MGH SS rer ger n.s. 9. Berlin: Weidmannsche Verlagsbuchhandlung, 1955.

Thietmar of Merseburg. *Ottonian Germany: The Chronicon of Thietmar of Merseburg.* Translated by David A. Warner. Manchester: Manchester University Press, 2001.

Two Anglo-Saxon Pontificals (The Egbert and Sidney Sussex Pontificals), edited by H.M.J. Banting. HBS 104. London: HBS, 1989.

Ulrich of Cluny. *Antiquiores consuetudines cluniacensi monasterii*. PL 149:643–778.

The Use of Sarum: The Original Texts Edited from the Mss, edited by Walter Howard Frere. 2 vols. Cambridge: Cambridge University Press, 1898–1901.

Vita Norberti A, Vita Norberti Archiepiscopi Magdeburgensis, edited by R. Wilmans, 670–706. MGH SS 12. Hanover: Hahn, 1856.

Vita Sanctae Hildegardis, edited by M. Klaes. CCCM 126. Turnhout: Brepols, 1993.

Vita Norberti B, Vita S. Norberti Auctore Canonico Praemonstrantensi Coaevo. PL 170:1253–1344.

The Vulgate Bible. Dumbarton Oaks Medieval Library. Cambridge, MA: Harvard University Press, 2010, 170:1253–1344.

Watkin, Aelred, ed. *Dean Cosyn and Wells Cathedral Miscellanea*. Somerset Record Society 56. Frome: Somerset Record Society, 1941.

Whitaker, E.C., and Maxwell E. Johnson. *Documents of the Baptismal Liturgy*. 3rd edn. Alcuin Club Collections 79. London: SPCK, 2003.

William Durandus. *Guilelmi Durandi rationale divinorum officiorum*, edited by A. Davril and T.M. Thibodeau. CCCM 140. Turnhout: Brepols, 1998.

The Winchester Troper, edited by Susan Rankin. Early English Church Music 50. London: Published for the British Academy by Stainer and Bell, 2007.

Wormald, Francis, ed. *English Benedictine Kalendars before AD 1100*. HBS 72. London: HBS, 1934.

Zimmermann, Harold, ed. *Papsturkunden 896–1046*. 3 vols. Vienna: Verlag der Österreichischen Akademie der Wissenschaften, 1984–89.

Secondary sources

Abercrombie, Nigel. *The Life and Work of Edmund Bishop*. London: Longmans, 1959.

Andås, Margrete Syrstad. 'Art and Ritual in the Liminal Zone'. In *The Medieval Cathedral of Trondheim: Architectural and Ritual Constructions in their European Context*, edited by Margrete Syrstad Andås, Øystein Ekroll, Andreas Haug and Nils Holger Petersen. Ritus et artes: Traditions and Transformations 3, 47–126. Turnhout: Brepols, 2007.

Andrieu, Michel. *Immixtio et consecratio: La consécration par contact dans les documents liturgiques du moyen âge*. Paris: Picard, 1924.

_____. 'Melchior Hittorp et l'"Ordo Romanus Antiquus"'. *Ephemerides liturgicae* 46 (1932): 3–21.

Angenendt, Arnold. *Geschichte der Religiosität im Mittelalter*. Darmstadt: Wissenschaftliche Buchgesellschaft, 1997.

_____. *Liturgik und Historik Gab es eine organische Liturgie-Entwicklung?* Freiburg: Herder, 2001.

Apel, Willi. *Gregorian Chant*. Bloomington: Indiana University Press, 1958.

Ardura, Bernard. *Prémontrés, histoire et spiritualité*. Saint-Etienne: Publications de l'Université de Saint-Etienne, 1995.

Ariès, Philippe. *L'homme devant le mort*. Paris: Editions de Seuil, 1977. English translation by Helen Weaver as *The Hour of Our Death*. New York: Knopf, 1981.

_____. *Western Attitudes towards Death*. English translation by Patricia M. Ranum. Baltimore: Johns Hopkins University Press, 1974.

Austin, Greta. 'Freising and Worms in the Early Eleventh Century: Revisiting the Relationship between the *Collectio duodecim partium* and Burchard's *Decretum*'. *Zeitschrift der Savigny-Stiftung für Rechtsgeschichte: kanonistische Abteilung* 124 (2007): 45–108.

Backhouse, Janet, and Shelley Jones. 'D.H. Turner (1931–1985): A Portrait'. *British Library Journal* 13, no. 2 (1987): 111–17.

Bailey, Terence. *The Processions of Sarum and the Western Church*. Studies and Texts 21. Toronto: Pontifical Institute of Medieval Studies, 1971.

Barnwell, P.S. 'The Laity, the Clergy and the Divine Presence: The Use of Space in Smaller Churches of the Eleventh and Twelfth Centuries'. *Journal of the British Archaeological Association* 157 (2004): 41–60.

Barré, Henri. *Les homéliaires carolingiens de l'école d'Auxerre*. Vatican City: Biblioteca Apostolica Vaticana, 1962.

Barthélemy, Dominique. 'Devils in the Sanctuary: Violence in the Miracles of Saint Benedict'. In *Feud, Violence and Practice: Essays in Medieval Studies in Honor of Stephen D. White*, edited by Belle S. Tuten and Tracey L. Billado, 71–94. London: Ashgate, 2010.

———. 'La guérison des possédés dans les miracles de saint Benoît'. In *Abbon, un abbé de l'an mil*, edited by Annie Dufour and Gillette Labory, 343–67. Turnhout: Brepols, 2008.

Bartlett, Robert. *Trial by Fire and Water: The Medieval Judicial Ordeal*. Oxford: Clarendon Press, 1986.

Baud, Anne. *Cluny, un grand chantier médiéval au cœur de l'Europe*. Paris: Picard, 2003.

———. 'La place des morts dans l'abbaye de cluny, état de la question'. *Archéologie mediévale* 29 (2000): 99–114.

Baud, Anne, and Gilles Rollier. 'Liturgie et espace monastique à Cluny à la lecture du *Liber tramitis*, '*descriptione monasterii*' et données archéologiques'. In *Espace ecclesial et liturgie au moyen âge*, edited by Anne Baud, 27–42. Lyon: Maison de l'Orient et de la Méditerranée, 2010.

Becker, Gustave. *Catalogi bibliothecarum antiqui*. Bonn: M. Cohen et filium, 1885.

Bekker-Nielsen, Hans. 'The Old Norse Dedication Liturgy'. In *Festschrift für Konstantin Reichardt*, edited by C. Gellinek with H. Zauchenberger, 127–34. Bern: Francke Verlag, 1969.

Berg, Kirsten M. 'On the Use of Mnemonic Schemes in Sermon Composition: The *Old Norwegian Homily Book*'. In *Constructing the Medieval Sermon*, edited by Roger Andersson, 221–36. Turnhout: Brepols, 2007.

Bergeron, Katherine. *Decadent Enchantments: The Revival of Gregorian Chant at Solesmes*. Berkeley: University of California Press, 1998.

Billet, Jesse. 'The Liturgy of the "Roman" Office in England from the Conversion to the Conquest'. In *Rome Across Time and Space: Cultural Transmission and the Exchange of Ideas, c. 500–1400*, edited by Claudia Bolgia, Rosamond McKitterick and John Osborne, 84–110. Cambridge: Cambridge University Press, 2011.

Binding, Günther and Andreas Speer. *Abt Suger von Saint-Denis, De consecratione; kommentierte Studienausgabe*. Cologne: Abt. Architekturgeschichte, 1995.

Bischoff, Bernhard. *Mittelalterliche Schatzverzeichnisse*, vol. 1. Munich: Prestel-Verlag, 1967.

Bishop, Edmund. *Liturgica Historica: Papers on the Liturgy and Religious Life of the Western Church*. Oxford: Clarendon Press, 1918.

Bjork, David A. 'On the Dissemination of *Quem quaeritis* and the *Visitatio sepulchri* and the Chronology of Their Early Sources', *Comparative Drama* 14 (1980): 46–69.

Blair, John. *The Church in Anglo-Saxon Society*. Oxford: Oxford University Press, 2005.

———. 'The Prehistory of English Fonts'. In *Intersections: The Archaeology and History of Christianity in England, 400–1200: Papers in Honour of Martin Biddle and Birthe Kjølbye-Biddle*, edited by Martin Henig and Nigel Ramsay, 149–77. British Archaeological Reports, British Series 505. Oxford: Archaeopress, 2010.

Bloch, Herbert. *Monte Cassino in the Middle Ages*, 3 vols. Cambridge: Cambridge University Press, 1986.

Bloch, R. Howard. *God's Plagiarist: Being an Account of the Fabulous Industry and Irregular Commerce of the Abbé Migne*. Chicago: University of Chicago Press, 1994.

Blum, Pamela. 'Liturgical Influences on the Design of the West Front of Wells and Salisbury'. *Gesta* 25, no. 1 (1986): 145–50.

Bobrycki, Shane. 'The Royal Consecration *Ordines* of the Pontifical of Sens from a New Perspective'. *Bulletin du centre d'études médiévales d'Auxerre* 13 (2009): 131–142.

Boe, John, and Alejandro Planchart, eds. *Beneventanum Troporum Corpus 2: Ordinary Chants and Tropes for the Mass from Southern Italy A.D. 1000–1250. Part 1 Kyrie eleison*. 2 vols. Madison, WI: A-R Editions, 1989.

Borg, Alan, and Andrew Martindale, eds. *The Vanishing Past: Studies of Medieval Art, Liturgy and Metrology Presented to Christopher Hohler*. British Archaeological Reports, International Series 111, Oxford: British Archaeological Reports, 1981.

Botte, Bernard. ['Review of *PRG* volumes 1 and 2'.] *Revue d'histoire ecclésiastique*, 59 (1964): 902–04.

Bouley, Allan. *From Freedom to Formula: The Evolution of the Eucharistic Prayer from Oral Improvisation to Written Texts*. Washington, DC: Catholic University of America Press, 1981.

Bouman, Cornelius. *Sacring and Crowning: The Development of the Latin Ritual for the Anointing of Kings and the Coronation of an Emperor before the Eleventh Century*. Groningen: J.B. Wolters, 1957.

Bowen, Lee. 'Tropology of Mediaeval Dedication Rites'. *Speculum* 16 (1941): 469–79.

Boyarin, Daniel. 'Origen as Theorist of Allegory: Alexandrian Contexts'. In *The Cambridge Companion to Allegory*, edited by R. Copeland and P.T. Struck, 39–54. Cambridge: Cambridge University Press, 2010.

Boynton, Susan. 'The Liturgical Role of Children in Monastic Customaries' *Studia liturgica* 28 (1998): 194–209.

_____. 'Oral Transmission of Liturgical Practice in the Eleventh-Century Customaries of Cluny'. In *Understanding Monastic Practices of Oral Communication (Western Europe, Tenth–Thirteenth Centuries)*, edited by Steven Vanderputten, 67–83. Turnhout: Brepols, 2011.

_____. 'Religious Soundscapes: Liturgy and Music'. In *The Cambridge History of Christianity, vol. 4: Christianity in Western Europe, c.1100–c.1500*, edited by Miri Rubin and Walter Simons, 238–53. Cambridge: Cambridge University Press, 2009.

_____. *Shaping a Monastic Identity: Liturgy and History at the Imperial Abbey of Farfa, 1000–1125*. Ithaca, NY: Cornell University Press, 2006.

Boynton, Susan, and Isabelle Cochelin, eds., *From Dead of Night to End of Day: The Medieval Customs of Cluny*. Disciplina monastica 3. Turnhout: Brepols, 2005.

Bradshaw, Paul F. *Reconstructing Early Christian Worship*. London: SPCK, 2009.

_____. *The Search for the Origins of Christian Worship: Sources and Methods for the Study of Early Liturgy*, 2nd ed. Oxford: Oxford University Press, 2002.

Bradshaw, Paul F., ed., *The New SCM Dictionary of Liturgy and Worship*. London: SCM Press, 2002.

Brady, Jeremiah D. 'Review of *Untersuchungen zu den Klosterreformen Wilhelms von Dijon (962–1031)*, by Neithard Bulst'. *Speculum* 52 (1977): 355–59.

Brasington, Bruce C. 'Lessons of Love: Bishop Ivo of Chartres as Teacher'. In *Teaching and Learning in Northern Europe, 1000–1200*, edited by S.N. Vaughan and J. Rubenstein, 129–47. Brepols: Turnhout, 2006.

Brooks, Nicholas. *The Early History of the Church of Canterbury: Christ Church from 597 to 1066*. London: Leicester University Press, 1984.

Brown, Lesley, ed., *The New Shorter Oxford English Dictionary on Historical Principles*, 2 vols. Oxford: Clarendon Press, 1993.

Brown, Peter. *The Cult of the Saints: Its Rise and Function in Latin Christianity*. Chicago: University of Chicago Press, 1981.

Brown, Warren. 'Charters as Weapons. On the Role Played by Early Medieval Dispute Records in the Disputes They Record'. *Journal of Medieval History* 28 (2002): 227–48.

Brückmann, J. 'The Ordines of the Third Recension of the Medieval English Coronation Order'. In *Essays in Medieval History Presented to Bertie Wilkinson*, edited by T.A. Sandquist and M.R. Powicke, 99–115. Toronto: University of Toronto Press, 1969.

Bruun, M.B. 'Mapping the Monastery: Hélinand of Froidmont's Second Sermon for Palm Sunday'. In *Prédication et liturgie au moyen âge*, edited by N. Bériou and F. Morenzoni, 183–99. Turnhout: Brepols, 2008.

_____. *Parables: Bernard of Clairvaux's Mapping of Spiritual Topography.* Leiden: Brill, 2007.

Brunn, Uwe. *Des contestataires aux 'cathares'. Discours de réforme et propagande antihérétique dans les pays du Rhin et de la Meuse avant l'Inquisition.* Paris: Institut d'études Augustiniennes, 2006.

Buc, Philippe. *The Dangers of Ritual: Between Early Medieval Texts and Social Scientific Theory*, 164–202. Princeton, NJ: Princeton University Press, 2001.

Busse Berger, Anna Maria. *Medieval Music and the Art of Memory.* Berkeley: University of California Press, 2005.

Cardine, Eugène. *Gregorian Semiology*, translated by Robert M. Fowels. Sablé-sur-Sarthe, France: Solesmes, 1982.

Carruthers, Mary. *The Book of Memory: A Study of Memory in Medieval Culture.* Cambridge: Cambridge University Press, 2008, first publ. 1990.

Caspary, G.E. *Politics and Exegesis: Origen and the Two Swords.* Berkeley: University of California Press, 1979.

Cerquiglini, Bernard. *Eloge de la variante: Histoire critique de la philologie.* Paris: Seuil, 1989.

_____. *In Praise of the Variant: A Critical History of Philology*, translated by Betsy Wing. Baltimore, MD: Johns Hopkins University Press. 1999.

Chadd, David. 'The Ritual of Palm Sunday: Reading Nidaros'. In *The Medieval Cathedral of Trondheim: Architectural and Ritual Constructions in Their European Context*, edited by Margrete Syrstad Andås, Øystein Ekroll, Andreas Haug and Nils Holger Peterson. Ritus et artes: Traditions and Transformation 3, 253–78. Turnhout: Brepols, 2007.

Chave-Mahir, Florence. *L'exorcisme des possédés dans l'église d'occident (Xe–XIVe siècle).* Bibliothèque d'histoire culturelle du moyen âge 10. Turnhout: Brepols, 2011.

_____. 'Trois exorcismes eucharistiques de saint Bernard de Clairvaux'. In *Pratiques de l'eucharistie dans les églises d'orient et d'occident*, edited by Nicole Bériou, Béatrice Caseau, Dominique Rigaux, 987–1000. Paris: Institut d'études Augustiniennes, 2009.

Chave-Mahir, Florence, and Julien Véronèse. *Rituel d'exorcisme ou manuel de magie? Le manuscrit Clm 10085 de la Bayerische Staatsbibliothek de Munich.* Florence: Edizioni del Galluzzo, forthcoming.

Chomton, Louis. *Histoire de l'église de S. Bénigne de Dijon.* Dijon: Jobard, 1900.

Chrissochoidis, Ilias. 'London Mozartiana: Wolfgang's Disputed Age and Early Performances of Allegri's *Miserere*'. *The Musical Times* 151, no. 1911 (2010): 83–89.

Cistercian Lay Brothers: Twelfth-Century Usages with Related Texts, edited by Chrysogonus Waddell. Cîteaux: Commentarii Cistercienses, 2000.

Clanchy, Michael T. *From Memory to Written Record: England 1066–1307*, 3rd edn. Oxford: Wiley-Blackwell, 2013.

――――. 'The Letters of Abelard and Heloise in Today's Scholarship'. In *The Letters of Abelard and Heloise*, translated by Betty Radice, rev. edn. London: Penguin, 2003.

Clancy, Finbarr C. 'Augustine's Sermons for the Dedication of a Church'. In *Papers Presented at the Thirteenth International Conference on Patristic Studies*, edited by M.F. Wiles and E.J. Yarnold. Studia Patristica 38 (2001), 48–55.

Cochelin, Isabelle. 'Appendix: The Relation between the Last Cluniac Customaries, *Udal* and *Bern*'. In *Consuetudines et Regulae: Sources for Monastic Life in the Middle Ages and the Early Modern Period*, edited by Carolyn Marino Malone and Clark Maines, 56–72. Disciplina monastica 10. Turnhout: Brepols, 2014.

――――. 'Customaries as Inspirational Sources'. In *Consuetudines et Regulae: Sources for Monastic Life in the Middle Ages and the Early Modern Period*, edited by Carolyn Marino Malone and Clark Maines, 27–72. Disciplina monastica 10. Turnhout: Brepols, 2014.

――――. 'Evolution des coutumiers monastiques dessinée à partir de l'étude de Bernard'. In *From Dead of Night to End of Day: The Medieval Customs of Cluny*, edited by Susan Boynton and Isabelle Cochelin, 29–66. Disciplina monastica 3. Turnhout: Brepols, 2005.

――――. 'Peut-on parler de noviciat à Cluny pour les Xe–XIe siècles?' *Revue Mabillon*, n.s. 9, no. 70 (1998): 17–52.

――――. 'Le pour qui et le pourquoi (des manuscrits) des coutumiers clunisiens'. In *Ad libros! Mélanges d'études médiévales offerts à Denise Angers et Claude Poulin*, edited by J.-F. Cottier, Martin Gravel and Sébastien Rossignol, 121–38. Montreal: Presses de l'Université de Montréal, 2010.

Codou, Yann. 'La consésecration du lieu de culte et ses traductions graphiques: inscriptions et marques lapidaires dans la Provence des XIe–XIIe siècles'. In *Mises en scène et mémoires de la consécration de l'église dans l'occident médiéval*, edited by Didier Méhu, 253–84. Turnhout: Brepols, 2007.

Colchester, L.S. *Wells Cathedral*. New Bell's Cathedral Guide. London: HarperCollins, 1987.

Collins, Patrick. *The Carolingian Debate over Sacred Space*. New York: Palgrave Macmillan, 2012.

Combe, Pierre. *The Restoration of Gregorian Chant: Solesmes and the Vatican Edition*, translated by Theodore N. Marier and William Skinner. Washington, DC: Catholic University of America Press, 2003.

Coomans, Thomas. 'Cistercian Architecture or Architecture of the Cistercians?'. In *The Cambridge Companion to the Cistercian Order*, edited by Mette Birkedal Bruun, 151–69. Cambridge: Cambridge University Press, 2012.

Coon, Lynda L. *Dark Ages Bodies: Gender and Monastic Practice in the Early Medieval West*. Philadelphia: University of Pennsylvania Press, 2010.

Cooper, David, and Ian N. Gregory. 'Mapping the English Lake District: A Literary GIS'. *Transactions of the Institute of British Geographers* 36 (2011): 89–108.

Cooper, Tracey-Anne. 'Episcopal Power and Performance: The Fugitive-Thief Rite in Textus Roffensis (Also Known as the Cattle-Theft Charm). In *Textus Roffensis: Law, Language and Libraries in Early Medieval England*, edited by Bruce O'Brien and Barbara Bombi. Turnhout: Brepols, forthcoming.

Cramer, Peter. *Baptism and Change in the Early Middle Ages, c. 200–c. 1150*. Cambridge: Cambridge University Press, 1993.

Crocker, Richard. 'Singing the *Nuance* in Communion Antiphons'. In *Western Plainchant in the First Millennium: Studies in the Medieval Liturgy and Its Music*, edited by Sean Gallagher et al., 453–60. Aldershot: Ashgate, 2003.

Cross, F.L. and Livingstone, E.A., eds. *The Oxford Dictionary of the Christian Church*. 3rd rev. edn. Oxford: Oxford University Press, 2005.

Crossley, Paul. '*Ductus* and *Memoria*: Chartres Cathedral and the Workings of Rhetoric'. In *Rhetoric Beyond Words: Delight and Persuasion in the Arts of the Middle Ages*, edited by Mary Carruthers, 214–49. Cambridge: Cambridge University Press, 2010.

Cummings, James. 'Liturgy, Drama, and the Archive: Three Conversions from Legacy Formats to TEI XML'. *Digital Medievalist* 1 (2006), available at http://www.digitalmedievalist.org/journal/2.1/cummings/.

Dale, Thomas. 'The Nude at Moissac: Vision, Phantasia and the Experience of Romanesque Sculpture'. In *Current Directions in Eleventh- and Twelfth-Century Sculpture Studies*, edited by Robert Maxwell and Kirk Ambrose. Studies in the Visual Cultures of the Middle Ages 5. Turnhout: Brepols, 2011.

d'Avray, D.L. *Medieval Marriage Sermons: Mass Communication in a Culture without Print*. Oxford: Oxford University Press, 2001.

Davril, Anselme. 'L'origine du *Quem quæritis*'. In *Requirentes modos musicos: Mélanges offerts à Dom Jean Claire*, edited by Daniel Saulnier, 119–34. Solesmes: Abbaye Saint-Pierre, 1995.

DeBats, Donald A., and Ian N. Gregory. 'Introduction to Historical GIS and the Study of Urban History'. *Social Science History* 35 (2011): 455–63.

de Blaauw, Sible. 'Architecture and Liturgy in Late Antiquity and the Middle Ages: Traditions and Trends in Modern Scholarship', *Archiv für Liturgiewissenschaft* 33 (1991): 1–34.

de Clerck, Paul. 'Improvisation et livres liturgiques: leçons d'une histoire'. *Communauté et liturgie* 50 (1978): 109–26.

Deeming, Helen. 'The Songs of St Godric: A Neglected Context'. *Music and Letters* 86 (2005): 169–85.

del Giacco, Eric J. 'A Comparison of Bede's Commentary and Homilies on Luke'. *Medieval Sermon Studies* 50 (2006): 9–29.

de Lubac, Henri. *Medieval Exegesis: The Four Senses of Scripture*. Grand Rapids: W.B. Eerdmans, 1998 [first publ. in French, 1959].

Dengler-Schreiber, Karin. *Scriptorium und Bibliothek des Klosters Michelsberg in Bamberg*. Graz: Akademische Druck- und Verlagsanstalt, 1979.

de Puniet, Pierre. 'Formulaire grec de l'Epiphanie dans une traduction latine ancienne', *Revue bénédictine* 29 (1912): 26–46.

de Ricci, Seymour. *English Collectors of Books and Manuscripts (1530–1930) and Their Marks of Ownership*. Sandars Lectures 1929–30. Cambridge: Cambridge University Press, 1930.

Derolez, Albert. 'The Manuscript Transmission of Hildegard of Bingen's Writings: The State of the Problem'. In *Hildegard of Bingen: The Context of Her Thought and Art*, edited by Charles Burnett and Peter Dronke, 17–28. London: Warburg Institute, 1998.

Deshusses, Jean. 'Chronologie des grands sacramentaires de Saint-Amand'. *Revue bénédictine* 87 (1977): 230–37.

———. 'Encore des sacramentaires de Saint-Amand', *Revue bénédictine* 89 (1979): 310–12.

———. 'Le "Supplément" au sacramentaire grégorien: Alcuin ou Benoît de Aniane?' *Archiv für Liturgiewissenschaft* 9 (1965): 48–71.

Deshusses, Jean, and Benoît Darragon. *Concordances et tableaux pour l'étude des grands sacramentaires*. SF subsidia, 9–14, 6 vols. Fribourg: Editions Universitaires, 1982–83.

de Valous, Guy. 'L'*ordo monasterii sancti Benigni*. Fragments d'un coutumier clunisien du XIe siècle'. In *A Cluny, congrès scientifique. Fêtes et cérémonies liturgiques en l'honneur des saints Abbés Odon et Odilon, 9–11 juillet 1949*, 233–43. Dijon: Société des Amis de Cluny, 1950.

Ditchfield, Simon. 'Giving Tridentine Worship Back Its History'. In *Continuity and Change in Christian Worship*, edited by R.N. Swanson, 199–226, Studies in Church History 35. Woodbridge: Boydell Press, 1999.

———. *Liturgy, Sanctity and History in Tridentine Italy: Pietro Maria Campi and the Preservation of the Particular*. Cambridge: Cambridge University Press, 1995.

Dix, Gregory. *The Shape of the Liturgy*, 2nd edn. London: A. and C. Black, 1945.

Dobszay, László. 'Concerning a Chronology for Chant'. In *Western Plainchant in the First Millennium: Studies in the Medieval Liturgy and Its Music*, edited by Sean Gallagher et al., 217–29. Aldershot: Ashgate, 2003.

Donahue, Jr, Charles. *Law, Marriage, and Society in the Later Middle Ages: Arguments about Marriage in Five Courts*. Cambridge: Cambridge University Press, 2007.

Donkin, Lucy E.G. 'Mosaici pavimentali medievali nell'Italia settentrionale e i loro rapporti con la liturgia'. *Atti del X Convegno dell'Associazione Italiane per lo Studio e la Conservazione del Mosaico*, 503–14. Tivoli: Edizioni Scripta Manent, 2005.

Donkin, Lucy E.G. '*Usque ad ultimum terrae*: Mapping the Ends of the Earth in Two Medieval Floor Mosaics'. In *Cartography in Antiquity and the Middle Ages: Fresh Perspectives, New Methods*, edited by Richard J.A. Talbert and Richard Watson Unger, 189–218. Leiden: Brill, 2008.

Duffy, Eamon. *The Stripping of the Altars: Traditional Religion in England c. 1400–c. 1580*. New Haven: Yale University Press, 1992.

Dumville, David N. *Liturgy and the Ecclesiastical History of Late Anglo-Saxon England: Four Studies*. Woodbridge: Boydell, 1992.

Ebner, Adalbert. *Quellen und Forschungen zur Geschichte und Kunstgeschichte des Missale Romanum im Mittelalter Iter italicum*. Freiburg: Herder, 1896.

Ellard, Gerald. *Ordination Anointings in the Western Church before 1000 AD*. Cambridge, MA: Medieval Academy of America, 1933.

Ellis, Katharine, *The Politics of Plainchant in Fin-de-Siècle France*. Farnham: Ashgate, 2013.

Elm, Kaspar, ed. *Norbert von Xanten. Adliger, Ordensstifter, Kirchenfürst*. Cologne: Wienand, 1985.

Enders, Jody. *Murder by Accident: Medieval Theater, Modern Media, and Critical Intentions*. Chicago: University of Chicago Press, 2009.

Erdmann, Carl. *Forschungen zur politischen Ideenwelt des Frühmittelalters*, edited by Friedrich Baethgen. Berlin: Akademie Verlag, 1951.

Everson, Paul, and David Stocker. 'The Common Steeple? Church, Liturgy, and Settlement in Early Medieval Lincolnshire'. In *Anglo-Norman Studies 28: Proceedings of the Battle Conference 2005*, edited by C.P. Lewis, 103–23. Woodbridge: Boydell Press, 2006.

Facchini, Ugo. 'I sermoni *In cena Domini* ed *In dedicatione ecclesiae* di san Pier Damiani. Esame della ritualità'. *Benedictina* 54 (2008): 212–32.

Farkasfalvy, Denis. 'Use and Interpretation of St John's Prologue in the Writings of Saint Bernard'. *Analecta cisterciensia* 35 (1979): 205–66.

Fassler, Margot. 'Composer and Dramatist: 'Melodious Singing and the Freshness of Remorse'. In *Voice of the Living Light: Hildegard of Bingen and Her World*, edited by Barbara Newman, 145–79. Berkeley: University of California Press, 1998.

———. *Gothic Song: Victorine Sequences and Augustinian Reform in Twelfth-Century Paris*. Cambridge: Cambridge University Press, 1993; 2nd rev. edn. Notre Dame, IN: Notre Dame Press, 2011.

———. 'The Liturgical Framework of Time and the Representation of History'. In *Representing History, 900–1300: Art, Music, History*, edited by Robert A. Maxwell, 149–71. University Park, PA: Pennsylvania State University Press, 2010.

_____. 'Liturgy and Sacred History in the Twelfth-Century Tympana at Chartres'. *Art Bulletin* 57 (1993): 499–520.

_____. 'The Office of the Cantor in Early Western Monastic Rules and Customaries: A Preliminary Investigation'. *Early Music History* 5 (1985): 29–51.

_____. *The Virgin of Chartres: Making History through Liturgy and the Arts*. New Haven: Yale University Press, 2010.

Fisher, J.D.C. *Christian Initiation: Baptism in the Medieval West: A Study in the Disintegration of the Primitive Rite of Initiation*. Alcuin Club Collections 47. London: SPCK, 1965.

Fisher, Rebecca M.C. 'The Anglo-Saxon Charms: Texts in Context'. In *Approaching Methodology*, edited by Frog and Pauliina Latvala with Helen F. Leslie, 221–47. Helsinki: Finnish Academy of Science and Letters, 2012.

_____. 'Genre, Prayers and the Anglo-Saxon Charms'. In *Genre, Text, Interpretation: Multidisciplinary Perspectives on Folklore and Beyond*, edited by Kaarina Koski. Helsinki: University of Helsinki, forthcoming.

Flanigan, C. Clifford, Kathleen Ashley and Pamela Sheingorn. 'Liturgy as Social Performance: Expanding the Definitions'. In *The Liturgy of the Medieval Church*, edited by Thomas J. Heffernan and E. Ann Matter, 695–714. Kalamazoo: Western Michigan University, 2001.

Flynn, William T. 'Abelard and Rhetoric: Widows and Virgins at the Paraclete'. In *Rethinking Abelard: A Collection of Critical Essays*, edited by Babette S. Heelemans, 155–86. Leiden: Brill, 2014.

_____. '*Ductus figuratis et subtilis*: Rhetorical Interventions for Women in Two Twelfth-Century Liturgies'. In *Rhetoric Beyond Words: Delight and Persuasion in the Arts of the Middle Ages*, edited by Mary Carruthers, 250–80. Cambridge: Cambridge University Press, 2010.

_____. 'Letters, Liturgy, and Identity: The Use of *Epithalamica* at the Paraclete'. In *Sapientia et Eloquentia: Meaning and Function in Liturgical Poetry, Music, Drama, and Biblical Commentary in the Middle Ages*, edited by Gunilla Iversen and Nicolas Bell, 301–48. Turnhout: Brepols, 2009.

_____. *Medieval Music as Medieval Exegesis*. Lanham, MD and London: Scarecrow Press, 1999.

_____. 'Reading Hildegard of Bingen's Antiphons for the 11,000 Virgin-Martyrs of Cologne: Rhetorical *Ductus* and Liturgical Rubrics'. *Nottingham Medieval Studies* 56 (2012): 171–89.

_____. 'Review of T.J.H. McCarthy, *Music, Scholasticism and Reform: Salian Germany, 1024–1125*'. *German History* 28 (2010): 572–73.

Flynn, William, and Jane Flynn, 'Review of Anna Maria Busse Berger, *Medieval Music and the Art of Memory*'. *Early Music History* 28 (2009): 249–62.

Foley, Edward. 'The Song of the Assembly in Medieval Eucharist'. In *Medieval Liturgy: A Book of Essays*, edited by Lizette Larson-Miller, 203–34. New York: Garland, 1997.

Fournier, Paul. 'L'oeuvre canonique de Réginon de Prüm'. *Bibliothèque de l'Ecole des Chartes* 81 (1920): 5–44.

Fowler-Magerl, Linda. *Clavis Canonum. Selected Canon Law Collections Before 1140 Access with Data Processing*, MGH Hilfsmittel 21. Hannover: Hahnsche Buchhandlung, 2005.

Foys, Martin K., and Shannon Bradshaw. 'Developing Digital Mappaemundi: An Agile Mode for Annotating Medieval Maps'. *Digital Medievalist* 7 (2011), available at www.digitalmedievalist.org/journal/7/foys/.

Franz, Adolf. *Die Kirchlichen Benediktionen im Mittelalter*. Freiburg: Herder, 1909.

Fresne, Charles du, Seigneur du Cange, revised by D.P. Carpenterius and others, *Glossarium mediae et infimae Latinitatis*, 10 vols. Niort: L. Favre, 1886.

Fuller, Sarah. 'Hidden Polyphony: A Reappraisal'. *Journal of the American Musicological Society* 24 (1971): 169–92.

Gaastra, A.H. 'Penance and the Law: The Penitential Canons of the Collection in Nine Books'. *Early Medieval Europe* 14 (2006): 85–102.

Gamber, Klaus. *Codices liturgici latini antiquiores*. SF subsidia 1, 2nd edn., Freiburg, Schweiz: Universitätsverlag, 1968.

Gamper, Rudolf, et al. *Katalog der mittelalterlichen Handschriften der Ministerialbibliothek Schaffhausen*. Dietikon: Graf, 1994.

Gaposchkin, M.C. 'Origins and Development of the Pilgrimage and Cross Blessings in the Roman Pontificals of the Twelfth and Thirteenth Centuries'. *Mediaeval Studies* 73 (2011): 261–86.

Garrison, Mary. 'The Library of Alcuin's York'. In *The Cambridge History of the Book in Britain, vol. 1: c. 400–1100*, edited by Richard Gameson, 633–64. Cambridge: Cambridge University Press, 2011.

Geddes, Jane. *The St Albans Psalter: A Book for Christina of Markyate*. London: British Library, 2005.

Gelting, Michael H. 'Circumstantial Evidence: Danish Charters of the Thirteenth Century'. In *Medieval Legal Process: Physical, Spoken, and Written Performance in the Middle Ages*, edited by Marco Mostert and P.S. Barnwell, 157–95. Turnhout: Brepols, 2011.

Gem, Richard. 'How Much Can Anglo-Saxon Buildings Tell Us About Liturgy?'. In *The Liturgy of the Late Anglo-Saxon Church*, edited by Helen Gittos and M. Bradford Bedingfield, 271–89. HBS Subsidia 5. London: HBS, 2005.

Gennep, Arnold van. *Rites of Passage*. Translated by Monika B. Vizedom and Gabrielle L. Caffee. Chicago: University of Chicago Press, 1960.

Gittos, Helen. 'Hallowing the Rood: Consecrating Crosses in Late Anglo-Saxon England'. In *Cross and Culture in Anglo-Saxon England: Studies in Honor of*

George Hardin Brown, edited by Karen Louise Jolly, Catherine E. Karkov and Sarah Larratt Keefer, 242–75. Morgantown: West Virginia University Press, 2008.

———. 'Introduction'. In *The Liturgy of the Late Anglo-Saxon Church*, edited by Helen Gittos and M Bradford Bedingfield, 1–11. HBS Subsidia 5. London: HBS, 2005.

———. 'Is There Any Evidence for the Liturgy of Parish Churches in Late Anglo-Saxon England? The Red Book of Darley and the Status of Old English'. In *Pastoral Care in Late Anglo-Saxon England*, edited by Francesca Tinti, 63–83. Anglo-Saxon Studies 6. Woodbridge: Boydell Press, 2005.

———. *Liturgy, Architecture, and Sacred Places in Anglo-Saxon England*. Oxford: Oxford University Press, 2013.

———. 'Sources for the Liturgy of Canterbury Cathedral in the Central Middle Ages'. In *Medieval Art, Architecture and Archaeology at Canterbury*, edited by Alixe Bovey, 41–58. Leeds: British Archaeological Association, 2013.

———. 'The Use of English in the Liturgy in the Middle Ages: A Case Study from York' (working title). Forthcoming.

Gittos, Helen, and M. Bradford Bedingfield, eds. *The Liturgy of the Late Anglo-Saxon Church*. HBS Subsidia 5. London: HBS, 2005.

Gneuss, Helmut. 'Liturgical Books in Anglo-Saxon England and Their Old English Terminology'. In *Learning and Literature in Anglo-Saxon England: Studies Presented to Peter Clemoes on the Occasion of his Sixty-Fifth Birthday*, edited by Michael Lapidge and Helmut Gneuss, 91–141. Cambridge: Cambridge University Press, 1985.

Gougaud, Louis. *Anciennes coutumes claustrales*. Ligugé: Abbaye Saint-Martin, 1930.

Gough, Richard. *British Topography*, new edn. London, 1780.

Grafton, Anthony. 'Church History in Early Modern Europe: Tradition and Innovation'. In *Sacred History: Uses of the Christian Past in the Renaissance World*, edited by Katherine Van Liere, Simon Ditchfield and Howard Louthan, 1–26. Oxford: Oxford University Press, 2012.

Grauwen, Wilfred Marcel. *Norbert, Erzbischof von Magdeburg (1126–1134)*. Duisbourg: Prämonstratenser-Abtei S. Johann, 1986.

———. 'De terugkeer van Hugo en de Duiveluitdrijving door Norbert te Nijvel, 1121'. *Analecta praemonstratensia* 67, no. 3–4 (1991): 187–97.

Greenway, Diana. 'The False *Institutio* of St Osmund'. In *Tradition and Change: Essays in Honour of Marjorie Chibnall*, edited by Diana Greenway, Christopher Holdsworth and Jane Sayers, 77–101. Cambridge: Cambridge University Press, 1970.

Grelot, Pierre, et al. 'Liturgie et vie spirituelle'. In *Dictionnaire de spiritualité ascétique et mystique, doctrine et histoire*, edited by Marcel Viller et al. 17 vols., vol. 9, cols. 873–939. Paris: Beauchesne, 1932–95. Reprinted as *Liturgie et vie spirituelle*. Paris: Beauchesne, 1977.

Grier, James. 'Adémar de Chabannes (989–1034) and Musical Literacy'. *Journal of the American Musicological Society* 66 (2013): 605–38.

———. 'The Musical Autographs of Adémar de Chabannes (989–1034)'. *Early Music History* 24 (2005): 125–68.

———. *The Musical World of a Medieval Monk: Adémar de Chabannes in Eleventh-Century Aquitaine*. Cambridge: Cambridge University Press, 2006.

Guéranger, Prosper. *Institutions liturgiques*. 3 vols. Le Mans: Fleuriot, 1840–51.

Gullick, Michael, and Susan Rankin, 'Review of K.D. Hartzell, *Catalogue*'. *Early Music History* 28 (2009): 262–85.

Gy, Pierre-Marie. 'The Different Forms of Liturgical "Libelli"'. In *Fountain of Life*, edited by Gerard Austin, 24–34. Washington, DC: Pastoral Press, 1991.

———. *La liturgie dans l'histoire*. Paris: Cerf, 1990.

Haggh, Barbara. 'Foundations or Institutions? On Bringing the Middle Ages into the History of Medieval Music'. *Acta Musicologica* 68 (1996): 87–128.

Haines, John., ed. *The Calligraphy of Medieval Music*. Turnhout: Brepols, 2011.

Haines, John. *Medieval Song in Romance Languages*. Cambridge: Cambridge University Press, 2010.

Hallinger, Kassius. 'Klunys Bräuche zur Zeit Hugos des Grossen (1049–1109). Prolegomena zur Neuherausgabe des Bernhard und Udalrich von Kluny'. *Zeitschrift der Savigny-Stiftung für Rechtsgeschichte: kanonistische Abteilung* 45 (1959): 99–140.

Hamilton, Louis I. 'Les dangers du rituel dans l'Italie du XIe siècle entre textes liturgiques et témoignages historiques'. In *Mises en scène et mémoires de la consécration de l'église dans l'occident médiéval*, edited by Didier Méhu, 159–88.Turnhout: Brepols, 2007.

———. 'Desecration and Consecration in Norman Capua, 1062–1122: Contesting Sacred Space during the Gregorian Reforms'. *Haskins Society Journal* 14 (2003): 137–50.

———. 'Memory, Symbol, and Arson: Was Rome Sacked in 1084?'. *Speculum* 78 (2003): 378–99.

———. 'The Rituals of Renaissance: Liturgy and Mythic History in *The Marvels of Rome*'. In *Rome Re-Imagined: Twelfth-Century Jews, Christians, and Muslims Encounter the Eternal City*, edited by Louis I. Hamilton and Stefano Riccioni, 417–38. Leiden: Brill, 2012.

———. *A Sacred City: Consecrating Churches and Reforming Society in Eleventh-Century Italy*. Manchester: Manchester University Press, 2010.

———. 'To Consecrate the Church: Ecclesiastical Reform and the Dedication of Churches'. In *Reforming the Church before Modernity: Patterns, Problems, and Approaches*, edited by C. Bellitto and L. Hamilton, 105–37. Aldershot: Ashgate, 2005.

————. 'Virtual Cities: GIS as a Tool for the Analysis of Dante's *Commedia*'. *Pedagogy: Critical Approaches to Teaching Literature, Language, Composition, and Culture* 13, no. 1 (2013): 115–24.

Hamilton, Sarah. '*Absoluimus uos uice beati petri apostolorum principis*: Episcopal Authority and the Reconciliation of Excommunicants in England and Francia, c. 900–c. 1150'. In *Frankland: The Franks and the World of the Early Middle Ages: Essays in Honour of Dame Jinty Nelson*, edited by Paul Fouracre and David Ganz, 209–41. Manchester: Manchester University Press, 2008.

————. *Church and People in the Medieval West, 900–1200*. Harlow: Pearson, 2013.

————. 'The Early Pontificals: The Anglo-Saxon Evidence Reconsidered from a Continental Perspective'. In *England and the Continent in the Tenth Century: Studies in Honour of Wilhelm Levison (1876–1947)*, edited by David Rollason, Conrad Leyser and Hannah Williams, 411–28. Studies in the Early Middle Ages 37. Turnhout: Brepols, 2010.

————. *The Practice of Penance, 900–1050*. Woodbridge: Boydell Press, 2001.

————. 'Rites for Public Penance in Late Anglo-Saxon England'. In *The Liturgy of the Late Anglo-Saxon Church*, edited by Helen Gittos and M. Bradford Bedingfield, 65–103. HBS Subsidia 5. London: HBS, 2005.

Hardison, O.B. *Christian Rite and Christian Drama in the Middle Ages*. Baltimore: Johns Hopkins University Press, 1965.

Harper, John. *The Forms and Orders of Western Liturgy from the Tenth to the Eighteenth Century: A Historical Introduction and Guide for Students and Musicians*. Oxford: Clarendon Press, 1991.

Harris, Jennifer. 'The Body as Temple in the High Middle Ages'. In *Sacrifice in Religious Experience*, edited by Albert I. Baumgarten, 233–56. Leiden: Brill, 2002.

Harris, Max. *Carnival and Other Christian Festivals: Folk Theology and Folk Performance*. Austin: University of Texas Press, 2003.

Hartmann, Wilfried. 'Die *Capita incerta* im Sendhandbuch Reginos von Prüm'. In *Scientia veritatis. Festschrift für Hubert Mordek zum 65. Geburtstag*, edited by Oliver Münsch and Thomas Zotz, 207–26. Ostfildern: Thorbecke, 2004.

————. *Kirche und Kirchenrecht um 900. Die Bedeutung der spätkarolingischen Zeit für Tradition und Innovation im kirchlichen Recht*. MGH Schriften 38. Hannover: Hahnsche Buchhandlung, 2008.

Hartzell, K.D. *Catalogue of Manuscripts Written or Owned in England up to 1200 containing Music*. Woodbridge: Boydell Press in association with the Plainsong and Medieval Music Society, 2006.

Häussling, Angelus A., Martin Klöckener and Burkhard Neunheuser. 'Der Gottesdienst der Kirche: Texte, Quellen, Studien'. *Archiv für Liturgiewissenschaft* 42 (2000): 106–202; 43/44 (2001–02): 97–221.

Heffernan, Thomas J., and E. Ann Matter. 'Introduction to the Liturgy of the Medieval Church'. In *The Liturgy of the Medieval Church*, edited by Thomas J. Heffernan and E. Ann Matter, 1–10. Kalamazoo: Western Michigan University, 2001.

Heffernan, Thomas J., and E. Ann Matter, eds. *The Liturgy of the Medieval Church*. Kalamazoo: Western Michigan University, 2001.

Hein, K. *Eucharist and Excommunication: A Study of Early Christian Doctrine and Discipline*. Frankfurt am Main: Herbert Lang, 1973.

Heitz, Carol. 'Lumières anciennes et nouvelles sur Saint-Bénigne de Dijon'. In *Du VIIe au XIe siècles: Edifices monastiques et culte en Lorraine et en Bourgogne*, edited by Carol Heitz and François Héber-Suffrin, 63–106. Université de Paris-Nanterre, Centre de recherches sur l'antiquité tardive et le haut moyen âge, Cahier 2. Nanterre: Imprimerie de l'Université de Paris X, 1977.

Helmore, Thomas. *Plain-Song*. London: Novello & Co., 1877.

Hen, Yitzhak. 'A Liturgical Handbook for the Use of a Rural Priest. Brussels, Br 10127–10144'. In *Organising the Written Word: Scripts, Manuscripts, and Texts*, edited by Marco Mostert. Turnhout: Brepols, forthcoming.

———. 'Knowledge of Canon Law among Rural Priests: The Evidence of Two Carolingian Manuscripts from around 800'. *Journal of Theological Studies* n.s. 50, no. 1 (1999): 117–34.

———. 'Priests and Books in the Merovingian Period'. In *Early Medieval Priests*, edited by Yitzhak Hen and Rob Meens. Hilversum: Verloren, forthcoming.

———. *The Royal Patronage of Liturgy in Frankish Gaul to the Death of Charles the Bald (877)*. Woodbridge: Boydell and Brewer, 2001.

Hen, Yitzak, and Rob Meens, eds. *The Bobbio Missal: Liturgy and Religious Culture in Merovingian Gaul*. Cambridge Studies in Palaeography and Codicology 11. Cambridge: Cambridge University Press, 2004.

Henriet, Patrick. *La parole et la prière au moyen âge*. Brussels: De Boeck Université, 2000.

Hiley, David. *Western Plainchant: A Handbook*. Oxford: Clarendon Press, 1993.

Hinschius, Paul. *Das Kirchenrecht der Katholiken und Protestanten in Deutschland*. 6 vols. Berlin: Guttentag, 1869–97; repr. Graz: Akademische Druck- und Verlagsanstalt, 1959.

Hoffmann, H. *Bamberger Handschriften des 10. und 11. Jahrhunderts*. MGH Schriften 39. Hannover: Hahn, 1995.

———. *Buchkunst und Königtum im ottonisch und frühsalischen Reich*. 2 vols. MGH Schriften 30. Stuttgart: Hiersemann, 1986.

Hoffmann, Hartmut, and Rudolf Pokorny. *Das Dekret Burchard von Worms. Textstufen-Frühe Verbreitung-Vorlagen*, MGH Hilfsmittel 12. Munich: MGH, 1991.

Hohler, Christopher. 'The Palm Sunday Procession and the West Front of Salisbury Cathedral'. In *The Medieval Cathedral of Trondheim: Architectural and Ritual Constructions in Their European Context*, edited by Margrete Syrstad Andås, Øystein Ekroll, Andreas Haug, and Nils Holger Petersen, 285–90. Ritus et Artes: Traditions and Transformation 3. Turnhout: Brepols, 2007.

———. 'The Red Book of Darley'. In *Nordiskt Kollokvium II: I Latinsk Liturgiforskning 12–13 Maj 1972, Hässelby Slott*, 39–47. Stockholm: Institutionen för Klassiska Språk vid Stockholms Universitet, [1972].

Holdsworth, Christopher. 'Were the Sermons of Bernard on the Song of Songs ever Preached?'. In *Medieval Monastic Preaching*, edited by C. Muessig, 295–318. Leiden: Brill, 1998.

Hollis, Stephanie. 'Scientific and Medical Writings'. In *A Companion to Anglo-Saxon Literature*, edited by Phillip Pulsiano and Elaine Treharne, 188–208. Oxford: Blackwell, 2001.

Holsinger, Bruce. 'Liturgy'. In *Oxford Twenty-First Century Approaches to Literature: Middle English*, edited by Paul Strohm, 295–314. Oxford: Oxford University Press, 2007.

———. 'The Parable of Caedmon's *Hymn*: Liturgical Invention and Literary Tradition'. *Journal of English and Germanic Philology* 106 (2007): 149–75.

———. *The Work of God: Liturgical Culture and Vernacular Writing in Britain, 550–1550*. Chicago: University of Chicago Press, forthcoming.

Horie, Ruth. *Perceptions of Ecclesia: Church and Soul in Medieval Dedication Sermons*. Turnhout: Brepols, 2006.

Hornby, Emma. *Gregorian and Old Roman Eighth Mode Tracts: A Case Study in the Transmission of Western Chant*. Aldershot: Ashgate, 2002.

———. *Medieval Liturgical Chant and Patristic Exegesis: Words and Music in the Second-Mode Tracts*. Woodbridge: Boydell and Brewer, 2009.

Hornby, Emma, and Rebecca Maloy. *Music and Meaning in Old Hispanic Lenten Chants: Psalmi, Threni and Easter Vigil Canticles*. Woodbridge: Boydell and Brewer, 2013.

Hughes, Andrew. 'Charlemagne's Chant or the Great Vocal Shift'. *Speculum* 77 (2002): 1069–1106.

———. *Medieval Manuscripts for Mass and Office: A Guide to Their Organization and Terminology*. Toronto: University of Toronto Press, 1982.

———. *Medieval Music: The Sixth Liberal Art*, rev. edn. Toronto: University of Toronto Press, 1980.

Hughes, Anselm. *Septuagesima: Reminiscences of the Plainsong and Mediaeval Music Society, and of Other Things Personal and Musical*. London: Plainsong and Mediaeval Music Society, 1959.

Hughes, David. 'From the Advent Project to the Late Middle Ages: Some Issues of Transmission'. In *Western Plainchant in the First Millennium: Studies in the Medieval Liturgy and Its Music*, edited by Sean Gallagher, James Haar, John Nádas and Timothy Striplin, 181–98. Aldershot: Ashgate, 2003.

Hughes, David G. 'The Implications of Variants for Chant Transmission'. In *De musica et cantu: Helmut Hucke zum 60. Geburtstag*, edited by Peter Cahn and Ann-Katrin Heimer, 65–73. Hildesheim: Olms, 1993.

Huglo, Michel. 'Codicologie et musicologie'. In *Miscellanea codicologica F. Masai: dicata MCMLXXIX*, edited by Pierre Cockshaw, Monique-Cécile Garland and Pierre Jodogne. 2 vols., 1: 71–82. Ghent: E. Story-Scientia, 1979.

———. *Les livres de chant liturgique*. Typologie de sources du moyen âge occidental 52. Turnhout: Brepols, 1988.

———. 'Remarks on the Alleluia and Responsory Series in the Winchester Troper'. In *Music in the Medieval English Liturgy: Plainsong and Medieval Music Centennial Essays*, edited by Susan Rankin and David Hiley, 47–58. Oxford: Clarendon Press, 1993.

———. 'Le tonaire de Saint-Bénigne de Dijon (Monpellier H. 159)'. *Annales musicologiques, moyen-âge et renaissance* 4 (1956): 7–18.

Huglo, Michel, Barbara Haggh and Leofranc Holford-Strevens. 'The Topography of Music Theory in Paris, 900–1450'. In *City, Chant, and the Topography of Early Music: In Honour of Thomas Forrest Kelly*, edited by Michael Scott Cuthbert, Sean Gallagher and Christoph Wolff, 275–334. Cambridge, MA: Harvard University Press, 2013.

Hunt, E.D. *Holy Land Pilgrimage in the Later Roman Empire*. Oxford: Oxford University Press, 1982.

Insley, Charles, 'Rhetoric and Ritual in Late Anglo-Saxon Charters'. In *Medieval Legal Process: Physical, Spoken, and Written Performance in the Middle Ages*, edited by Marco Mostert and P.S. Barnwell, 109–21. Turnhout: Brepols, 2011.

Iogna-Prat, Dominique. 'Churches in the Landscape'. In *Early Medieval Christianities*, edited by Thomas F.X. Noble and Julia M.H. Smith, 363–79. Cambridge: Cambridge University Press, 2008.

———. *La maison Dieu: une histoire monumentale de l'église au moyen âge (v 800–v 1200)*. Paris: Editions du Seuil, 2006.

———. 'Des morts très spéciaux aux morts ordinaires: le pastorale funéraire clunisienne (XIe–XIIe siècles)', *Médiévales* 31 (1996): 79–91.

———. 'Les morts dans la comptabilité céleste des Clunisiens de l'an mil'. In *Religion et culture autour de l'an mil: royaume capétien et Lotharingie. Actes du colloque international 'Hugues Capet 987–1987. La France de l'an mil', Auxerre, 26–27 juin, Metz, 11–12 septembre 1987*, edited by Dominique Iogna-Prat and Jean-Charles Picard. Paris: Picard, 1990, 55–69. English translation: 'The Dead in the Celestial Bookkeeping of the Cluniac Monks Around the Year 1000'. In *Debating the Middle Ages*, edited by Lester K. Little and Barbara H. Rosenwein. Malden, MA: Blackwell, 1998.

————. *Order and Exclusion: Cluny and Christendom Face Heresy, Judaism, and Islam (1000–1150)*. Ithaca, NY: Cornell University Press, 2002.

Isaïa, Marie-Céline. 'Normes et hagiographie dans l'occident latin (Ve–XVIe siècle)'. *Bulletin du centre d'études médiévales d'Auxerre* 15 (2011): 229–36.

Isäia M.C. and Granier, T., ed. *Normes et hagiographie dans l'occident latin (Ve–XVIe siècle), Lyon 4–6 octobre 2010*. Turnhout: Brepols, 2014.

Iversen, Gunilla. *Laus Angelica: Poetry in the Medieval Mass*, translated by W. Flynn, edited by J. Flynn. Turnhout: Brepols, 2010.

Jaser, Christian. *Ecclesia maledicens. Rituelle und zeremonielle Exkommunikationsformen im Mittelalter*. Tübingen: Mohr Siebeck, 2013.

Jauss, Hans Robert. 'Literaturgeschichte als Provokation der Literaturwissenschaft'. In *Literaturgeschichte als Provokation*, 144–207. Frankfurt am Main: Suhrkamp, 1974.

Jeffrey, Peter. *Re-Envisioning Past Musical Cultures: Ethnomusicology in the Study of Gregorian Chant*. Chicago: University of Chicago Press, 1992.

Jégou, Laurent. 'L'évêque entre authorité sacrée et exercice du pouvoir. L'exemple de Gérard de Cambrai (1012–1051)'. *Cahiers de civilisation médiévale* 47 (2004): 37–55.

Jolly, Karen Louise. 'Dismembering and Reconstructing Ms Durham, Cathedral Library, A.IV.19'. In *Scraped, Stroked, and Bound: Materially Engaged Readings of Medieval Manuscripts*, edited by Jonathan Wilcox, 177–200. Turnhout: Brepols, 2013.

————. *Popular Religion in Late Saxon England: Elf Charms in Context*. Chapel Hill: University of North Carolina Press, 1996.

Jones, Christopher A. 'The Book of the Liturgy in Anglo-Saxon England'. *Speculum* 73 (1998): 659–702.

————. 'The Chrism Mass in Later Anglo-Saxon England'. In *The Liturgy of the Late Anglo-Saxon Church*, edited by Helen Gittos and M. Bradford Bedingfield, 105–42. HBS Subsidia 5. London: HBS, 2005.

————. 'The Origins of the 'Sarum' Chrism Mass at Eleventh-Century Christ Church, Canterbury'. *Mediaeval Studies* 67 (2005): 219–315.

————. 'Performing Christianity: Liturgical and Devotional Writing'. In *The Cambridge History of Early Medieval English Literature*, edited by Clare A. Lees, 427–50. Cambridge: Cambridge University Press, 2013.

————. 'Wulfstan's Liturgical Interests'. In *Wulfstan, Archbishop of York: The Proceedings of the Second Alcuin Conference*, edited by Matthew Townend, 325–52. Studies in the Early Middle Ages 10. Turnhout: Brepols, 2004.

Jorden, Willibald. *Das cluniazensische Totengedächtniswesen vornehmlich unter den drei ersten Äbten Berno, Odo und Aymard (910–954), Zugleich ein Beitrag zu den cluniazensischen Traditionsurkunden*. Münsterische Beiträge zur Theologie 15. Münster: Aschendorff, 1930.

Jotischky, Andrew. 'Holy Fire and Holy Sepulchre: Ritual and Space in Jerusalem from the Ninth to the Fourteenth Centuries'. In *Ritual and Space in the Middle Ages: Proceedings of the 2009 Harlaxton Symposium*, edited by Frances Andrews, 44–60. Harlaxton Medieval Studies 21. Donington: Shaun Tyas, 2011.

Jungmann, Josef A. *Missarum sollemnia: eine genetische Erklärung der römischen Messe*. 2 vols. 2nd rev. edn., Vienna: Herder, 1949. Translated by Francis A. Brunner as *The Mass of the Roman Rite: Its Origins and Development*, 2 vols., New York: Benziger Brothers, 1951–55.

Kantorowicz, Ernst H. *Laudes regiae: A Study in Liturgical Acclamations and Mediaeval Ruler Worship*, University of California Publications in History 33. Berkeley: University of California Press, 1946).

Kay, Richard. *Pontificalia: A Repertory of Latin Manuscript Pontificals and Benedictionals*. Lawrence, KA: published online by Digital Publishing Services, University of Kansas Libraries, at http://hdlhandlenet/1808/4406, 2007.

Keefe, Susan A. *Water and the Word: Baptism and the Education of the Clergy in the Carolingian Empire*. 2 vols. Notre Dame, IN: University of Notre Dame Press, 2002.

Keefer, S. Larratt. 'Ðonne se cirlisca man ordales weddigeð: The Anglo-Saxon Lay Ordeal'. In *Early Medieval Studies in Memory of Patrick Wormald*, edited by S. Baxter, C. Karkov, J. L. Nelson and D. Pelteret, 353–67. Farnham: Ashgate, 2009.

———. '*Ut in omnibus honorificetur Deus*: The *corsnæd* Ordeal in Anglo-Saxon England'. In *The Community, the Family and the Saint: Patterns of Power in Early Medieval Europe*, edited by Joyce Hill and Mary Swan, 237–64. Turnhout: Brepols, 1998.

Kelly, Thomas Forrest, ed. *Chant and Its Origins*. Farnham: Ashgate, 2009.

———, ed. *Oral and Written Transmission in Chant*. Farnham: Ashgate, 2009.

Kerff, F. '*Libri paenitentiales* und kirchliche Strafgerichtsbarkeit bis zum Decretum Gratiani: ein Diskussionsverschlag'. *Zeitschrift der Savigny-Stiftung für Rechtsgeschichte: kanonistische Abteilung* 75 (1989): 23–57.

Kienzle, Beverly M. 'Medieval Sermons and Their Performance: Theory and Record'. In *Preacher, Sermon and Audience in the Middle Ages*, edited by C. Muessig, 89–124. Leiden: Brill, 2002.

———. 'The Twelfth-Century Monastic Sermon'. In *The Sermon*, edited by B.M. Kienzle, 271–323. Typologie des sources du moyen âges occidental 81–83. Turnhout: Brepols, 2000.

Kienzle, B.M., ed. *The Sermon*. Typologie des sources du moyen âges occidental 81–83. Turnhout: Brepols, 2000.

Klauser, Theodor. *A Short History of the Western Liturgy: An Account and Some Reflections*. 2nd edn. Oxford: Oxford University Press, 1979. [Originally published as *Kleine abenländische Liturgiegeschichte*, 5th edn. 1969, translated by John Halliburton.]

Klemm, E. *Die ottonischen und frühromanischen Handschriften der Bayerischen Staatsbibliothek.* 2 vols. Wiesbaden: Reichert, 2004.

Klukas, Arnold. 'The *Liber Ruber* and the Rebuilding of the East End of Wells'. In *Medieval Art and Architecture at Wells and Glastonbury*, 30–36. British Archaeological Association Conference Transactions for the Year 1978. London: British Archaeological Association, 1981.

Kottje, Raymund. 'Busspraxis und Bussritus'. In *Segni e riti nella chiesa altomedievale occidentale: 11–17 aprile 1985*, 369–65. Settimane di Studio del Centro italiano di studi sull'alto medioevo 33. Spoleto: Centro italiano di studi sull'alto medioevo, 1987.

Koziol, Geoffrey. *Begging, Pardon and Favor: Ritual and Political Order in Early Medieval France*. Ithaca, NY: Cornell University Press, 1992.

——. 'The Early History of Rites of Supplication'. In *Suppliques et requêtes: le gouvernement par la Grâce en Occident, XIIe–XVe siècle*, edited by Hélène Millet, 21–36. Rome: Ecole française de Rome, 2003.

——. 'A Father, His Son, Memory, and Hope: A Joint Diploma of Lothar and Louis V (Pentecost Monday, 979) and the Limits of Performativity'. In *Geschichtswissenschaft und 'Performative Turn': Ritual, Inszenierung und Performanz vom Mittelalter bis zur Neuzeit*, edited by Jürgen Martschukat and Steffen Patzold, 83–103. Cologne: Böhlau Verlag, 2003.

——. *The Politics of Memory and Identity in Carolingian Royal Diplomas: The West Frankish Kingdom (840–987)*. Turnhout: Brepols, 2012.

Krochalis, Jeanne E., and E. Ann Matter. 'Manuscripts of the Liturgy'. In *The Liturgy of the Medieval Church*, edited by Thomas J. Heffernan and E. Ann Matter, 433–72. Kalamazoo: Western Michigan University, 2001.

Krüger, Kristina. 'Architecture and Liturgical Practice: The Cluniac *galilaea*'. In *The White Mantle of Churches: Architecture, Liturgy, and Art around the Millennium*, edited by Nigel Hiscock, 138–59. International Medieval Research 10; Art History Subseries 2. Turnhout: Brepols, 2003.

——. 'Monastic Customs and Liturgy in the Light of the Architectural Evidence: A Case Study on Processions (Eleventh–Twelfth Centuries)'. In *From Dead of Night to End of Day: The Medieval Customs of Cluny*, edited by Susan Boynton and Isabelle Cochelin, 191–220. Disciplina monastica 3. Turnhout: Brepols, 2005.

Larson-Miller, Lizette, ed. *Medieval Liturgy: A Book of Essays*. New York: Garland, 1997.

Lauwers, Michel. 'Consécration d'églises, réforme et ecclésiologie monastique'. In *Mises en scène et mémoires de la consécration de l'église dans l'occident medieval*, edited by Didier Méhu, 93–142. Turnhout: Brepols, 2007.

Leclercq, Jean. 'Les sermons sur les cantiques ont-ils été prononcés?'. In *Recueil d'études sur S. Bernard et ses écrits*. 3 vols., vol. 2, 193–212. Rome: Storia et Letteratura, 1962.

Lemaître, Jean-Loup. '"*Liber capituli*". Le livre du chapitre, des origines au XVIe siècle, l'exemple français'. In *Memoria. Der geschichtliche Zeugnisswert des liturgischen Gedenkens im Mittelalter*, edited by Karl Schmid and Joachim Wollasch, 625–48. Munich: Wilhelm Fink Verlag, 1984.

Lenker, Ursula. 'The Rites and Ministries of the Canons: Liturgical Rubrics to Vernacular Gospels and Their Functions in a European Context'. In *The Liturgy of the Late Anglo-Saxon Church*, edited by Helen Gittos and M. Bradford Bedingfield, 185–212. HBS Subsidia 5. London: HBS, 2005.

Leonard, John K. 'Rites of Marriage in the Western Middle Ages'. In *Medieval Liturgy: A Book of Essays*, edited by Lizette Larson-Miller, 165–202. New York: Garland, 1997.

Leone, Simeone. 'La chiesa di S. Alferio fondatore della badia di Cava'. *Benedictina* 27 (1980): 393–416.

Leroquais, V. *Les pontificaux manuscrits des bibliothèques publiques de France*. 4 vols. Paris, 1937.

———. *Les sacramentaires et les missels manuscrits des bibliothèques publiques de France*. 4 vols. Paris: n.p., 1924.

Le Roux, Raymond. 'Guillaume de Volpiano, son cursus liturgique au Mont Saint-Michel et dans les abbayes normandes'. In *Millénaire monastique du Mont Saint-Michel, vol. 1: Historie et vie monastiques*, edited by Jean Laporte, 417–72. Paris: P. Lethielleux, 1966.

Lipsmeyer, Elizabeth. 'Devotion and Decorum: Intention and Quality in Medieval German Sculpture', *Gesta* 34 (1995): 20–27.

Little, Lester K. *Liberty, Charity, Fraternity: Lay Religious Confraternities in Bergamo in the Age of the Commune*. Bergamo: P. Lubrina, 1988.

Liuzza, R.M. 'Prayers and/or Charms to the Cross'. In *Cross and Culture in Anglo-Saxon England: Studies in Honor of George Hardin Brown*, edited by Karen Louise Jolly, Catherine E. Karkov and Sarah Larratt Keefer, 279–323. Morgantown: West Virginia University Press, 2007.

Loewen, Peter. 'The Conversion of Mary Magdalene and the Musical Legacy of Franciscan Piety in the Early German Passion Plays'. In *Speculum sermonis: Interdisciplinary Reflections on the Medieval Sermon*, edited by Georgiana Donivan et al., 235–58. Turnhout: Brepols, 2004.

Lutz, Angelika. 'The Study of the Anglo-Saxon Chronicle in the Seventeenth Century and the Establishment of Old English Studies in the Universities'. In *The Recovery of Old English: Anglo-Saxon Studies in the Sixteenth and Seventeenth Centuries*, edited by Timothy Graham, 1–82. Kalamazoo, MI: Medieval Institute Publications, Western Michigan University, 2000.

Lynch, Joseph H. *Christianizing Kinship: Ritual Sponsorship in Anglo-Saxon England*. Ithaca, NY: Cornell University Press, 1998.

Maas, Paul. *Textual Criticism*. Translated by Barbara Flower. Oxford: Clarendon Press, 1958.

Magne, J. 'Exploration généalogique dans les textes d'exorcisme'. *Mélanges d'archéologie et d'histoire* 73 (1961): 323–64.

Mahrt, William Peter. 'Review of *Façade as Spectacle: Ritual and Ideology at Wells Cathedral*, Leiden and Boston: Brill, 2004, by Carolyn Marino Malone'. *The Medieval Review*, available at tmr-l@wmich.edu, 17 March 2005.

———. 'The Role of Old Sarum in the Processions of Salisbury Cathedral'. In *The Study of Medieval Manuscripts of England: Festschrift in Honor of Richard W. Pfaff*, edited by George Hardin Brons and Linda Ehrsam Voigts, 129–41. Turnhout: Brepols, 2010.

Malone, Carolyn Marino. *Façade as Spectacle: Ritual and Ideology at Wells Cathedral*. Leiden: Brill, 2004.

———. 'Les fouilles de Saint-Bénigne de Dijon (1976–1978) et le problème de l'église de l'an mil'. *Bulletin monumental* 138 (1980): 253–84.

———. *Saint-Bénigne de Dijon en l'an mil, totius Galliae basilicis mirabilior: Interprétation politique, liturgique et théologique*. Disciplina monastica 5. Turnhout: Brepols, 2009.

———. *Saint-Bénigne et sa rotonde. Archéologie d'une église bourguignonne de l'an mil*. Dijon: Editions universitaires de Dijon, 2008.

Maloy, Rebecca. *Inside the Offertory: Aspects of Chronology and Transmission*. New York: Oxford University Press, 2010.

Mansfield, Mary C. *The Humiliation of Sinners: Public Penance in Thirteenth-Century France*. Ithaca, NY: Cornell University Press, 1995.

Marshall, Judith. 'Hidden Polyphony in a Manuscript from Saint Martial de Limoges'. *Journal of the American Musicological Society* 15 (1962): 131–44.

Martí-Henneberg, Jordi. 'Geographical Information Systems and the Study of History'. *Journal of Interdisciplinary History* 42 (2011): 1–13.

Martimort, Aimé-Georges. *La documentation liturgique de Dom Edmond Martène: Etude codicologique*. Studi e Testi 279. Vatican City: Biblioteca Apostolica Vaticana, 1978.

Martindale, Andrew. 'The Romanesque Church of S. Bénigne at Dijon and Ms 591 in the Bibliothèque Municipale'. *Journal of the British Archaeological Association* 25 (1962): 21–54.

Maskell, William. *A Dissertation upon the Ancient Service Books of the Church of England*. Oxford: Clarendon Press, 1882.

———. *Protestant Ritualists*. 2nd edn. London: J. Toovey, 1872.

———, *A Second Letter on the Present Position of the High Church Party in the Church of England: The Want of Dogmatic Teaching in the Reformed English Church*. London: W. Pickering, 1850.

Mazzotta, Giuseppe. 'The Poet and the Critics'. In *Dante Now: Current Trends in Dante Studies*, 63–79. Notre Dame, IN: University of Notre Dame Press, 1995.

McAleer, J. Philip. 'Particularly English? Screen Facades of the Type of Salisbury and Wells Cathedrals'. *Journal of the British Archaeological Association* 141 (1988): 124–58.

McCarthy, T.J.H. *Music, Scholasticism and Reform: Salian Germany, 1024–1125*. Manchester: Manchester University Press, 2009.

McGinn, Bernard. 'Introduction'. In *Isaac of Stella: Sermons on the Christian Year*, translated by H. McCaffery. Kalamazoo, MI: Cistercian Publications, 1979.

McKitterick, Rosamond. *The Frankish Church and the Carolingian Reforms, 789–895*. London: Royal Historical Society, 1977.

McMillan, Sharon L. *Episcopal Ordination and Ecclesial Consensus*. Collegeville, MN: Liturgical Press, 2005.

Meeder, Sven. 'The Early Irish Stowe Missal's Destination and Function'. *Early Medieval Europe* 13 (2005): 179–94.

Meens, Rob. 'The Frequency and Nature of Early Medieval Penance'. In *Handling Sin: Confession in the Middle Ages*, edited by Peter Biller and A.J. Minnis, 35–62. Woodbridge: York Medieval Press, 1998.

Méhu, Didier. '*Historiae* et *imagines*'. In *Mises en scène et mémoires de la consécration de l'église dans l'occident médiéval*, edited by Didier Méhu, 15–48. Turnhout: Brepols, 2007.

———. *Paix et communautés autour de l'abbaye de Cluny Xe–XVe siècle*. Lyon: Presses universitaires de Lyon, 2001.

Méhu, Didier, ed. *Mises en scène et mémoires de la consécration de l'église dans l'occident médiéval*. Turnhout: Brepols, 2007.

Mélanges en l'honneur de Mgr Andrieu. Revue des Sciences Religieuses, Volume Hors Série. Strasbourg, 1956.

Mews, Constant. 'Heloise and Liturgical Experience at the Paraclete'. *Plainsong and Medieval Music* 11 (2002): 25–35.

Meyer, Ann R. *Medieval Allegory and the Building of the New Jerusalem*. Cambridge: D.S. Brewer, 2003.

Mohrmann, Christine. *Liturgical Latin, Its Origins and Character; Three Lectures*. Washington, DC: Catholic University of America Press, 1957.

Moreton, Bernard. *The Eighth-Century Gelasian Sacramentary: A Study in Tradition*. Oxford: Oxford University Press, 1975.

Mostert, Marco, and P.S. Barnwell, eds. *Medieval Legal Process: Physical, Spoken, and Written Performance in the Middle Ages*. Turnhout: Brepols, 2011.

Müller, Jörg. *Untersuchungen zur Collectio Duodecim Partium*. Ebelsbach: Gremer, 1989.

Nagy, Gregory. *Poetry as Performance: Homer and Beyond*. Cambridge: Cambridge University Press, 1996.

Nakamura, Hideki. '*Talem vitam agamus, ut Dei lapides esse possimus*: Kirchweihpredigten Richards von Sankt Viktor'. In '*Das Haus Gottes, das seid ihr selbst': Mittelalterliches und barockes Kirchenverständnis im Spiegel der Kirchweihe*, edited by R.M.W. Stammberger and C. Sticher, 293–327. Berlin: Akademie Verlag, 2006.

Nedkvitne, Arnved. *Lay Belief in Norse Society 1000–1350*. Copenhagen: Museum Tusculanum Press, 2009.

Nelson, Jinty. 'Coronation Rituals and Related Materials'. In *Understanding Medieval Primary Sources: Using Historical Sources to Discover Medieval Europe*, edited by Joel T. Rosenthal, 114–30. London: Routledge, 2012.

———. 'Liturgy or Law: Misconceived Alternatives?'. In *Early Medieval Studies in Memory of Patrick Wormald*, edited by Stephen Baxter et al., 433–47. Farnham: Ashgate, 2009.

Neuheuser, Hanns P. 'Ritus und Theologie der Kirchweihe bei Hugo von St Viktor'. In '*Das Haus Gottes, das seid ihr selbst': Mittelalterliches und barockes Kirchenverständnis im Spiegel der Kirchweihe*, edited by R.M.W. Stammberger and C. Sticher, 251–92. Berlin: Akademie Verlag, 2006.

Newton, Francis. *The Scriptorium and Library at Monte Cassino, 1058–1105*. Cambridge: Cambridge University Press, 1999.

Niles, John D. 'The Æcerbot Ritual in Context'. In *Old English Literature in Context: Ten Essays*, edited by John D. Niles, 44–56, 163–64. Cambridge: D.S. Brewer, 1980.

———. 'Trial by Ordeal in Anglo-Saxon England: What's the Problem with Barley?'. In *Early Medieval Studies in Memory of Patrick Wormald*, edited by S. Baxter, C. Karkov, J.L. Nelson and D. Pelteret, 369–82. Farnham: Ashgate, 2009.

Noble, Thomas F.X., and Smith, Julia M.H. eds.,*The Cambridge History of Christianity, vol. 3: Early Medieval Christianities, c. 600–c. 1100*. Cambridge: Cambridge University Press, 2008.

Nowakowska, Natalia. 'From Strassburg to Trent: Bishops, Printing and Liturgical Reform in the Fifteenth Century'. *Past and Present* 213 (2011): 3–39.

Ó Carragáin, Tomás. 'Archaeology of Early Medieval Baptism at St Mullin's, Co Carlow'. *Peritia: Journal of the Medieval Academy of Ireland* 21 (2010): 285–302.

Ott, John S. '"Both Mary and Martha": Bishop Lietbert of Cambrai and the Construction of Episcopal Sanctity in a Border Diocese around 1100'. In *The Bishop Reformed: Studies of Episcopal Power and Culture in the Central Middle Ages*, edited by John S. Ott and Anna Trumbore Jones, 137–60. Aldershot: Ashgate, 2007.

Otter, Monika. 'Entrances and Exits: Performing the Psalms in Goscelin's *Liber confortatorius*'. *Speculum* 83, no. 2 (2008): 283–302.

Page, Christopher. *The Christian West and Its Singers: The First Thousand Years*. New Haven: Yale University Press, 2010.

Palazzo, Eric. 'Art and Liturgy in the Middle Ages: Survey of Research (1980–2003) and Some Reflections on Method'. *Journal of English and Germanic Philology* 105, no. 1 (2006): 170–84.

———. *A History of Liturgical Books from the Beginning to the Thirteenth Century*, translation by Madeleine Beaumont of *Le moyen âge* (q.v.). Collegeville, MN: Liturgical Press, 1998.

———. 'L'illustration des livres liturgiques autour de l'an mil'. In *L'Europe de l'an mil*, edited by Pierre Riché, 291–307. Saint-Léger-Vauban: Zodiaque, 2001.

———. 'La liturgie de l'occident médiéval autour de l'an mil: Etat de la question'. *Cahiers de civilisation médiévale* 43 (2000): 371–94.

———. *L'évêque et son image: L'illustration du pontifical au moyen âge*. Turnhout: Brepols, 1999.

———. *Le moyen âge: des origines au XIIIème siècle*. Paris: Beauchesne, 1993.

———. 'Le rôle des *libelli* dans la pratique liturgique du haut moyen âge: histoire et typologie', *Revue Mabillon* n.s. 62 (1990): 9–36.

———. *Les sacramentaires de Fulda: Etude sur l'iconographie et la liturgie à l'époque ottonienne*. Liturgiewissenschaftliche Quellen und Forschungen 77. Münster: Aschendorff, 1994.

———. *Liturgie et société au moyen âge*. Paris: Aubier, 2000.

Parker, Andrew, and Eve Kosofsky Sedgwick, eds. 'Introduction'. In *Performativity and Performance*, 1–18. New York: Routledge, 1995.

Parker, Elizabeth C. 'Architecture as Liturgical Setting'. In *The Liturgy of the Medieval Church*, edited by Thomas J. Heffernan and E. Ann Matter, 273–326. Kalamazoo: Western Michigan University, 2001.

Parkes, Henry. *The Making of Liturgy in the Ottonian Church: Books, Music and Ritual in Mainz 950–1050*. Cambridge: Cambridge University Press, 2015.

Partoens, Gert. 'Prédication, orthodoxie et liturgie'. In *Prédication et liturgie au moyen âge*, edited by N. Bériou and F. Morenzoni, 23–51. Turnhout: Brepols, 2008.

Paxton, Frederick S. *Anchoress and Abbess in Ninth-Century Saxony: The Lives of Liutbirga of Wendhausen and Hathumoda of Gandersheim*. Washington, DC: Catholic University of America Press, 2009.

———. 'Birth and Death'. In *The Cambridge History of Christianity, vol. 3: Early Medieval Christianities, c. 600–c. 1100*, edited by Thomas F.X. Noble and Julia M.H. Smith, 381–98. Cambridge: Cambridge University Press, 2008.

———. '*Bonus Liber*: A Late Carolingian Clerical Manual from Lorsch (Bibliotheca Vaticana Ms Pal. lat. 485)'. In *The Two Laws: Studies in Medieval*

Legal History Dedicated to Stephan Kuttner, edited by Laurent Mayali and Stephanie A.J. Tibbetts, 1–30. Studies in Medieval and Early Modern Canon Law 1. Washington, DC: Catholic University of America Press, 1990.

———. *Christianizing Death: The Creation of a Ritual Process in Early Medieval Europe*. Ithaca, NY: Cornell University Press, 1990.

———. 'Death by Customary at Eleventh-Century Cluny'. In *From Dead of Night to End of Day: The Medieval Customs of Cluny*, edited by Susan Boynton and Isabelle Cochelin, 297–318. Disciplina monastica 3. Turnhout: Brepols, 2005.

———. *The Death Ritual at Cluny in the Central Middle Ages/Le rituel de la mort à Cluny au moyen âge central*. Disciplina monastica 9, fontes 2. Turnhout: Brepols, 2013.

———. 'The Early Growth of the Medieval Economy of Salvation in Latin Christianity'. In *Death in Jewish Life: Burial and Mourning Customs among the Jews of Europe and nearby Communities*, edited by Stefan Reif, Andreas Lenhardt and Avriel Bar-Levav, 17–41. Studia Judaica 78. Berlin: W. De Gruyter, 2014.

———. 'Gratian's Thirteenth Case and the Composition of the *Decretum*'. In *Proceedings of the Eleventh International Congress of Medieval Canon Law*, edited by Manlio Bellomo and Orazio Condorelli, 119–29. Monumenta Iuris Canonici Series C: Subsidia 12. Vatican City: Biblioteca Apostolica Vaticana, 2006.

———. 'Listening to the Monks of Cluny'. In *Why the Middle Ages Matter: Medieval Light on Modern Injustice*, edited by Celia Chazelle, Simon Doubleday, Felice Lifshitz and Amy G. Remensnyder, 41–53. London: Routledge, 2012.

———. 'Musical and Ritual Aspects of *Quem queritis*'. In *Liturgische Tropen: Referate zweier Colloquien des Corpus Troporum in München (1983) und Canterbury (1984)*, edited by Gabriel Silagi, 181–89. Munich: Arbeo-Gesellschaft, 1985.

———. *A Medieval Latin Death Ritual: The Monastic Customaries of Bernard and Ulrich of Cluny*. Studies in Music-Thanatology 1. Missoula, MT: St. Dunstan's Press, 1993.

———. 'Musical and Ritual Aspects of *Quem queritis*'. In *Liturgische Tropen: Referate zweier Colloquien des Corpus Troporum in München (1983) und Canterbury (1984)*, edited by Gabriel Silagi, 181–89. Munich: Arbeo-Gesellschaft, 1985.

———. 'Review of *The Bobbio Missal: Liturgy and Religious Culture in Merovingian Gaul*, edited by Yitzhak Hen and Rob Meens'. *Journal of English and Germanic Philology* 105 (2006): 345–47.

Peters, Francis E. *Jerusalem: The Holy City in the Eyes of Chroniclers, Visitors, Pilgrims, and Prophets from the Days of Abraham to the Beginnings of Modern Times*. Princeton: Princeton University Press, 1985.

Petersen, Nils Holger, Mette Birkedal Bruun, Jeremy Llewellyn and Eyolf Østrem, eds. *The Appearances of Medieval Rituals*. Turnhout: Brepols, 2003.

Pfaff, Richard. 'The Anglo-Saxon Bishop and His Book'. *Bulletin of the John Rylands University Library of Manchester* 81 (1999): 3–24.

Pfaff, Richard W. 'Liturgical Books'. In *The Cambridge History of the Book in Britain, vol. 1: c. 400–1100*, edited by Richard Gameson, 449–59. Cambridge: Cambridge University Press, 2011.

––––––. 'Musical and Ritual Aspects of *Quem queritis*'. In *Liturgische Tropen: Referate zweier Colloquien des Corpus Troporum in München (1983) und Canterbury (1984)*, edited by Gabriel Silagi, 181–89. Munich: Arbeo-Gesellschaft, 1985. *The Liturgy in Medieval England: A History*. Cambridge: Cambridge University Press, 2009.

––––––. 'Musical and Ritual Aspects of *Quem queritis*'. In *Liturgische Tropen: Referate zweier Colloquien des Corpus Troporum in München (1983) und Canterbury (1984)*, edited by Gabriel Silagi, 181–89. Munich: Arbeo-Gesellschaft, 1985. *Medieval Latin Liturgy: A Select Bibliography*. Toronto Medieval Bibliographies 9. Toronto: University of Toronto Press, 1982.

––––––. 'Musical and Ritual Aspects of *Quem queritis*'. In *Liturgische Tropen: Referate zweier Colloquien des Corpus Troporum in München (1983) und Canterbury (1984)*, edited by Gabriel Silagi, 181–89. Munich: Arbeo-Gesellschaft, 1985. *Montague Rhodes James*. London: Scolar Press, 1980.

Philippeau, H.R. 'Pour l'histoire de la coutume de Cluny'. *Revue Mabillon* 44 (1954): 141–51.

Pick, Lucy. *Conflict and Coexistence: Archbishop Rodrigo and the Muslims and Jews of Medieval Spain*. Ann Arbor: University of Michigan Press, 2004.

Pierce, Joanne. 'The Evolution of the *ordo missae* in the Early Middle Ages'. In *Medieval Liturgy: A Book of Essays*, edited by Lizette Larson-Miller, 3–24. New York: Garland, 1997.

Piggott, Stuart. *Ruins in a Landscape: Essays in Antiquarianism*. Edinburgh: Edinburgh University Press, 1976.

Plancher, Urbain. *Histoire générale et particulière de la Bourgogne*. 3 vols. Dijon: De Fay, 1739–48; reprinted Farnborough: Gregg International, 1968.

Polanichka, D. 'Transforming Space, (Per)forming Community: Church Consecration in Carolingian Europe'. *Viator* 43 (2012): 79–98.

Powell, Morgan. 'Listening to Heloise at the Paraclete: Of Scholarly Diversion and a Woman's Conversion'. In *Listening to Heloise: The Voice of a Twelfth-Century Woman*, edited by Bonnie Wheeler, 255–86. New York: St. Martin's Press, 2000.

Pranger, M.B. *Bernard of Clairvaux and the Shape of Monastic Thought: Broken Dreams*. Leiden: Brill, 1994.

Rankin, Susan. 'Beyond the Boundaries of Roman-Frankish Chant: Alcuin's *De laude Dei* and Other Early Medieval Sources of Office Chants'. In *City, Chant, and the Topography of Early Music: In Honour of Thomas Forrest Kelly*, edited by Michael Scott Cuthbert, Sean Gallagher and Christoph Wolff, 229–62. Cambridge, MA: Harvard University Press, 2013.

――――. 'From Memory to Record: Musical Notations in Manuscripts from Exeter'. *Anglo-Saxon England* 13 (1984): 97–112.

――――. 'The Making of Carolingian Mass Chant Books'. In *Quomodo cantabimus canticum: Studies in Honor of Edward H. Roesner*, edited by Rena Mueller and John Nadas, 37–63. American Institute of Musicology Miscellanea 7. Middleton, WI: A-R Editions, 2008.

――――. 'Musical and Ritual Aspects of *Quem queritis*'. In *Liturgische Tropen: Referate zweier Colloquien des Corpus Troporum in München (1983) und Canterbury (1984)*, edited by Gabriel Silagi, 181–89. Munich: Arbeo-Gesellschaft, 1985.

――――. 'Music Books'. In *The Cambridge History of the Book in Britain, vol. 1: c. 400–1100*, edited by Richard Gameson, 482–506. Cambridge: Cambridge University Press, 2011.

――――. *The Music of the Medieval Liturgical Drama in France and England*. 2 vols. New York: Garland, 1989.

――――. 'Winchester Polyphony: The Early Theory and Practice of Organum'. In *Music in the Medieval English Liturgy: Plainsong and Medieval Music Centennial Essays*, edited by Susan Rankin and David Hiley, 59–99. Oxford: Clarendon Press, 1993.

Rasmussen, Neils Krogh. 'Célébration épiscopale et célébration presbyteriale: une essai de typologie'. In *Segni e riti nella chiesa altomedievale occidentale: 11–17 aprile 1985*, 581–603. Settimane di Studio del Centro italiano di studi sull'alto medioevo 33. Spoleto: Centro italiano di studi sull'alto medioevo, 1987.

――――. 'Unité et diversité des pontificaux latins aux VIIIe, IXe, et Xe siècles'. In *Liturgie de l'église particulière et liturgie de l'église universelle*, 393–410. Bibliotheca Ephemerides liturgicae subsidia 7. Rome: Edizioni Liturgiche, 1976.

Rasmussen, Niels Krogh, with Marcel Haverals. *Les pontificaux du haut moyen âge: Genèse du livre de l'évêque*. Spicilegium Sacrum Lovaniense: Etudes et Documents 49. Leuven: Spicilegium Sacrum Lovaniense, 1998.

Reames, Sherry L. 'Unexpected Texts for Saints in some Sarum Breviary Manuscripts'. In *The Study of Medieval Manuscripts of England: Festschrift in Honor of Richard W. Pfaff*, edited by George Hardin Brown and Linda

Ehrsam Voigts, 163–84. Tempe: Arizona Center for Medieval and Renaissance Studies, 2010.

Reilly, Diane J. 'Education, Liturgy and Practice in Early Cîteaux'. In *Understanding Monastic Practices of Oral Communication (Western Europe, Tenth–Thirteenth Centuries)*, edited by Steven Vanderputten, 85–114. Utrecht Studies in Medieval Literacy. Turnhout: Brepols, 2011.

―――. 'Lectern Bibles and Liturgical Reform in the Central Middle Ages'. In *The Practice of the Bible in the Middle Ages: Production, Reception, and Performance in Western Christianity*, edited by Susan Boynton and Diane J. Reilly, 105–25. New York: Columbia University Press, 2011.

Reinburg, Virginia. 'Liturgy and the Laity in Late Medieval and Reformation France'. *The Sixteenth Century Journal* 233, no. 3 (1992): 526–47.

Repsher, Brian V. 'The Abecedarium: Catechetical Symbolism in the Rite of Church Dedication'. *Mediaevalia* 24 (2003): 1–18.

―――. *The Rite of Church Dedication in the Early Medieval Era*. Lewiston, NY: Edwin Mellen Press, 1998.

Reynolds, Herbert Edward. *Wells Cathedral, Its Foundation, Constitutional History, and Statutes*. Leeds: M'Corquodale, 1880.

Reynolds, Roger E. 'Les cérémonies liturgiques de la cathédrale de Bénévent'. In *La cathédrale de Bénévent*, edited by Thomas Forrest Kelly, 167–205. Ghent: Ludion, 1999.

―――. 'Image and Text: The Liturgy of Clerical Ordination in Early Medieval Art'. *Gesta* 22 (1983): 27–38.

―――. 'Rites of Separation and Reconciliation in the Early Middle Ages'. In *Segni e riti nella chiesa altomedievale occidentale: 11–17 aprile 1985*, 405–33. Settimane di Studio del Centro italiano di studi sull'alto medioevo 33. Spoleto: Centro italiano di studi sull'alto medioevo, 1987.

―――. 'The Ritual of Clerical Ordination of the Sacramentarium Gelasianum saec. VIII: Early Evidence from Southern Italy'. In *Rituels: mélanges offerts à Pierre-Marie Gy*, edited by Paul de Clerck and Eric Palazzo, 437–45. Paris: Editions de Cerf, 1990.

Rhijn, Carine van. 'The Local Church, Priests' Handbooks and Pastoral Care in the Carolingian Period'. *Chiese locali e chiese regionali nell'alto medioevo*. Settimane di studio del Centro italiano di studi sull'alto medioevo 61, 2 vols. 2: 689–710. Spoleto: Fondazione Centro Italiano di Studi Sull'alto Medioevo, 2014.

Richard, Jean. 'Histoire topographique de Dijon'. *Mémoires de la Commission des antiquités du département de la Côte-D'Or* 22 (1951): 316–50.

Richards, Jeffrey. *Consul of God: The Life and Times of Gregory the Great*. London: Routledge & Kegan Paul, 1980.

Riches, Theo M. 'Bishop Gerard I of Cambrai-Arras, the Three Orders and the Problem of Human Weakness'. In *The Bishop Reformed: Studies of Episcopal*

Power and Culture in the Central Middle Ages, edited by John S. Ott and Anna Trumbore Jones, 122–36. Aldershot: Ashgate, 2007.

Rock, Daniel. *The Church of Our Fathers, as Seen in St Osmund's Rite for the Cathedral of Salisbury*. 4 vols. London: John Hodges, 1904.

Rolker, Christof. *Canon Law and the Letters of Ivo of Chartres*. Cambridge: Cambridge University Press, 2010.

Romano, John F. 'Joy in Waiting?: The History of Gaudete Sunday'. *Mediaeval Studies* 72 (2010): 75–124.

Rose, Els. 'Liturgical Latin in Early Medieval Gaul'. In *Spoken and Written Language: Relations between Latin and the Vernacular Languages in the Earlier Middles Ages*, edited by Mary Garrison, A.P. Orbán and Marco Mostert, 303–13. Turnhout: Brepols, 2013.

St John Hope, W.H. and W.R. Lethaby. 'The Imagery and Sculptures on the West Front of Wells Cathedral'. *Archaeologia* 59 (1904): 143–206.

Salisbury, Matthew Cheung. 'Establishing a Liturgical "Text": Text for Performance, Performance as Text'. In *The Experience of Late Medieval Worship*, edited by Paul Barnwell, Sally Harper and Magnus Williamson. 2015.

_____. *Hear My Voice, O God: Functional Dimensions of Christian Worship*. Collegeville, MN: Liturgical Press, 2014.

_____. *The Secular Liturgical Office in Late Medieval England*. Turnhout: Brepols, 2015.

_____. *The Use of York: Characteristics of the Medieval Liturgical Office in York*, Borthwick Paper 113. York: Borthwick Institute, University of York, 2008.

Sampson, Jerry. *Wells Cathedral West Front*. Stroud: Sutton Publishing, 1998.

Sanders, Vivienne. 'The Household of Archbishop Parker and the Influencing of Public Opinion'. *Journal of Ecclesiastical History* 34, no. 4 (1983): 534–47.

Saurette, Marc. 'Excavating and Renovating Ancient Texts: Seventeenth- and Eighteenth-Century Editions of Bernard of Cluny's *Consuetudines* and Early Modern Monastic Scholarship'. *From Dead of Night to End of Day: The Medieval Customs of Cluny*, edited by Susan Boynton and Isabelle Cochelin, 85–107. Disciplina monastica 3. Turnhout: Brepols, 2005.

Schechner, Richard. *Performance Theory*. 2nd rev. edn. London: Routledge, 2003.

Schmid, Karl, and Joachim Wollasch. 'Die Gemeinschaft der Lebenden und Verstorbenen in Zeugnissen des Mittelalters'. *Frühmittelalterliche Studien* 1 (1967): 365–405.

Schneidmüller, Bernd. 'Die einzigartig geliebte Stadt – Heinrich II. und Bamberg'. In *Kaiser Heinrich II 1002–1024*, edited by Josef Kirmeier, Bernd Schneidmüller, Stefan Weinfurter and Evamaria Brockhoff, 30–51. Stuttgart: Theiss, 2002.

Schramm, Percy Ernst. 'Die Krönung in Deutschland bis zu Beginn des Salischen Hauses (1028)'. *Zeitschrift der Savigny-Stiftung für Rechtsgeschichte: kanonistische Abteilung* 24 (1935): 184–332.

Schröder, Isolde. *Die westfränkischen Synoden von 888 bis 987 und ihre Überlieferung.* MGH Hilfsmittel 3. Munich: MGH, 1980.

Schroeder Sheker, Therese. *Transitus: A Blessed Death in the Modern World.* Missoula, MT: St Dunstan's Press, 2001.

Sharpe, Richard. 'Goscelin's St Augustine and St Mildreth: Hagiography and Liturgy in Context'. *Journal of Theological Studies* n.s. 41, no. 2 (1990): 502–16.

Sheingorn, Pamela, and Kathleen Ashley. '*Discordia et lis:* Negotiating Power, Property, and Performance in Medieval Sélestat'. *Journal of Medieval and Early Modern Studies* 26 (1996): 419–46.

Shortt, Hugh de Sausmarez. *Salisbury Cathedral and Indications of the Sarum Use* (pamphlet). Salisbury: Friends of Salisbury Cathedral, 1970.

Sicard, Damien. *La liturgie de la mort dans l'église latine des origines à la réforme carolingienne.* Liturgiewissenschaftliche Quellen und Forschungen 63. Münster: Aschendorff, 1978.

Siffrin, Petrus. *Konkordanztabellen zu den römischen lateinischen Sakramentarien.* 3 vols. RED series minor 4–6. Rome: Herder, 1958–61.

Smalley, Beryl. *The Study of the Bible in the Middle Ages.* Oxford: Blackwell, 1952.

Smith, Julia M.H. 'The Problem of Female Sanctity in Carolingian Europe, c 780–920', *Past and Present* 146 (February 1995): 3–37.

Spatz, Nancy. 'Church Porches and the Liturgy in Twelfth-Century Rome'. In *The Liturgy of the Medieval Church*, edited by Thomas J. Heffernan and E. Ann Matter, 327–67. Kalamazoo: Western Michigan University, 2001.

Spinks, Bryan D. *Early and Medieval Rituals and Theologies of Baptism: From the New Testament to the Council of Trent.* Aldershot: Ashgate, 2006.

Spurrell, Mark. 'The Procession of Palms and West-Front Galleries'. *The Downside Review* 415 (2001): 125–44.

Stebbins, Charles E. 'The "Auto de los reyes magos": An Old Spanish Mystery Play of the Twelfth Century'. *Allegorica* 2 (1977): 118–43.

Steiner, Ruth. 'Marian Antiphons at Cluny and Lewes'. In *Music in the Medieval English Liturgy*, edited by Susan Rankin and David Hiley, 175–204. Oxford: Oxford University Press, 1999.

Stewart, Marc, and David Wulstan. *The Poetic and Musical Legacy of Heloise and Abelard: An Anthology of Essays by Various Authors.* Ottawa: Institute of Medieval Music, 2003.

Stratford, Neil. 'Les bâtiments de l'abbaye de Cluny à l'époque médiévale: Etat des questions'. *Bulletin monumental* 150 (1992): 383–411.

Sullivan, Richard E. 'The Carolingian Age: Reflections on Its Place in the History of the Middle Ages'. *Speculum* 64, no. 2 (1989): 267–306.

Suñol, Gregorio. *Text Book of Gregorian Chant According to the Solesmes Method*, translated by G.M. Durnford. Tournai: Desclee and Society of St John the Evangelist, 1930.

Swanson, R.N., ed. *Unity and Diversity in the Church: Papers Read at the 1994 Summer Meeting and the 1995 Winter Meeting of the Ecclesiastical History Society*. Studies in Church History 32. Oxford: Blackwell, 1996.

Symes, Carol. 'The Appearance of Early Vernacular Plays: Forms, Functions, and the Future of Medieval Theater'. *Speculum* 77, no. 3 (2002): 778–831.

———. *A Common Stage: Theater and Public Life in Medieval Arras*. Ithaca, NY: Cornell University Press, 2007.

———. 'A Few Odd Visits: Unusual Settings of the *Visitatio sepulchri*'. In *Music and Medieval Manuscripts: Paleography and Performance: Essays Dedicated to Andrew Hughes*, edited by John Haines and Randall Rosenfeld, 300–22. Aldershot and Brookfield, VT: Ashgate, 2004.

———. 'Manuscript Matrix, Modern Canon'. In *Oxford Twenty-First Century Approaches to Literature: Middle English*, edited by Paul Strohm, 7–22. Oxford: Oxford University Press, 2007.

———. 'The Medieval Archive and the History of Theater: Assessing the Written and Unwritten Evidence for Premodern Performance'. *Theatre Survey* 52, no. 1 (2011): 29–58.

Taft, Robert. 'The Structural Analysis of Liturgical Units: An Essay in Methodology'. *Worship* 52 (1978): 314–29.

Taglia, Kathryn. 'Delivering a Christian Identity: Midwives in Northern French Synodal Legislation, c. 1200–1550'. In *Religion and Medicine in the Middle Ages*, edited by Peter Biller and Joseph Ziegler, 77–90. York: York Medieval Press, 2001.

Taylor, Diana. *The Archive and the Repertoire: Performing Cultural Memory in the Americas*. Durham, NC: Duke University Press, 2003.

Tedlock, Dennis. *The Spoken Word and the Work of Interpretation*. Philadelphia: University of Pennsylvania Press, 1983.

Tepper, Yotam, and Leah Di Segni. *A Christian Prayer Hall of the Third Century CE at Kefar 'Othnay (Legio): Excavations at the Megiddo Prison 2005*. Jerusalem: Israel Antiquities Authority, 2006.

Thayer, Ann T. 'The Medieval Sermon'. In *Understanding Medieval Primary Sources: Using Historical Sources to Discover Medieval Europe*, edited by J.T. Rosenthal, 43–58. London: Routledge, 2012.

Thomas, Keith. *Religion and the Decline of Magic: Studies in Popular Beliefs in Sixteenth- and Seventeenth-Century England*. London: Weidenfeld and Nicolson, 1971.

Timpanaro, Sebastiano. *The Genesis of Lachmann's Method*. Translated by Glenn W. Most. Chicago: University of Chicago Press, 2005.

Treffort, Cécile. 'Une consécration "à la lettre". Place, rôle et autorité des textes incrits dans la sacralisation de l'église'. In *Mises en scène et mémoires de la consécration de l'église dans l'occident médiéval*, edited by Didier Méhu, 219–52. Turnhout: Brepols, 2007.

Treharne, Elaine. *Living through Conquest: The Politics of Early English, 1020–1220*. Oxford: Oxford University Press, 2012.

Treharne, Elaine, and Mary Swan, eds. *Rewriting Old English in the Twelfth Century*. Cambridge: Cambridge University Press, 2000.

Treitler, Leo. 'Oral, Written, and Literate Process in the Transmission of Medieval Music'. *Speculum* 56 (1981): 471–91.

———. 'Reading and Singing: On the Genesis of Occidental Music-Writing'. *Early Music History* 4 (1984): 135–208.

Turner, Denys. 'Allegory in Christian Late Antiquity'. In *The Cambridge Companion to Allegory*, edited by R. Copeland and P.T. Struck, 71–82. Cambridge: Cambridge University Press, 2010.

Turner, Victor. 'Betwixt and Between: The Liminal Period in Rites de Passage'. In idem, *The Forest of Symbols*. Ithaca, NY: Cornell University Press, 1967.

———. *Dramas, Fields, and Metaphors: Symbolic Action in Human Society*. Ithaca, NY: Cornell University Press, 1974.

Turner, Victor, with Edith Turner. *Image and Pilgrimage in Christian Culture: Anthropological Perspectives*. New York: Columbia University Press, 1978.

Turville-Petre, G. 'The Old Norse Homily on the Dedication'. *Medieval Studies* 11 (1949): 206–18.

Tutsch, Burkhardt. 'Die Consuetudines Bernhards und Ulrichs von Cluny im Spiegel ihrer handschriftlichen Überlieferung'. *Frühmittelalterliche Studien* 30 (1996): 248–93.

———. *Studien zur Rezeptionsgeschichte der Consuetudines Ulrichs von Cluny*. Vita Regularis 6. Münster: LIT, 1998.

Vanderputten, Steven, ed. *Understanding Monastic Practices of Oral Communication. (Western Europe, Tenth–Thirteenth Centuries)*. Utrecht Studies in Medieval Literacy 21. Turnhout: Brepols, 2011.

Verbaal, Wim. 'Réalités quotidiennes et fiction littéraire dans les *Sermons sur le Cantique* de Bernard de Clairvaux'. *Cîteaux* 51 (2000): 201–18.

Vincent, Catherine. *Les confréries médiévales dans le royaume de France, XIIIe–XVe siècle*. Paris: A. Michel, 1994.

Vodola, Elisabeth. *Excommunication in the Middle Ages*. Berkeley: University of California Press, 1986.

Vogel, Cyrille. 'Contenu et ordonnance du pontifical romano-germanique'. In *Atti del VI Congresso Internazionale di Archeologia Cristiana, Ravenna 23–*

30 Settembre 1962, 243–65. Vatican City: Pontifico Istituto di Archeologia Cristiana, 1965.

———. *Introduction aux sources de l'histoire du culte chrétien au moyen âge*. Spoleto: Centro italiano di studi sull'alto medioeva, 1966. Revised and translated by William G. Storey and Niels Krogh Rasmussen as *Medieval Liturgy: An Introduction to the Sources*. Washington, DC: Pastoral Press, 1986.

———. 'Mgr Michel Andrieu (1886–1956)'. *Ephemerides liturgicae* 71 (1957): 34–36.

———. 'Le pontifical romano-germanique du Xe siècle: éléments constitutifs avec indication des sections imprimées'. *Revue des sciences religieuses* 32 (1958): 113–67.

———. 'Le pontifical romano-germanique du Xe siècle: nature, date et importance du document'. *Cahiers de civilisation médiévale* 6 (1963): 27–48.

———. 'Précisions sur la date et l'ordonnance primitive du pontifical romano-germanique'. *Ephemerides liturgicae* 74 (1960): 145–62.

Waddell, Chrysogonus. 'The Early Cistercian Experience of Liturgy'. In *Rule and Life: An Interdisciplinary Symposium*, edited by M.B. Pennington, 77–116. Spencer, MA: Cistercian Publications, 1971.

———. 'The Liturgical Dimension of Twelfth-Century Cistercian Preaching'. In *Medieval Monastic Preaching*, edited by C. Muessig, 335–49. Leiden: Brill, 1998.

Wagner, A. 'Les manuscrits de la Bibliothèque de Gorze. Remarques à propos du catalogue'. In *Religion et culture autour de l'an mil: Royaume capétien et Lotharingie*, edited by Dominique Iona-Prat and Jean-Charles Picard, 111–17. Paris: Picard, 1990.

Werf, Hendrick van der. *Oldest Extant Part Music and the Origin of Western Polyphony*. 2 vols. Rochester, NY: H. van der Werf, 1993.

White, James F. *The Cambridge Movement: The Ecclesiologists and the Gothic Revival*. Cambridge: Cambridge University Press, 1962.

Wickham, Chris. 'Problems in Doing Comparative History'. In *Challenging the Boundaries of Medieval History: The Legacy of Timothy Reuter*, edited by Patricia Skinner, 5–28. Studies in the Early Middle Ages 22. Turnhout: Brepols, 2009.

Wilmart, André. 'Un livret bénédictin composé à Gellone au commencement du IXe siècle'. *Revue Mabillon* 12 (1922): 119–33.

Wollasch, Joachim. 'Ein cluniacensisches Totenbuch aus der Zeit Abt Hugos von Cluny'. *Frühmittelalterliche Studien* 1 (1967): 406–43.

Wollasch, Joachim. 'Zur Erforschung Clunys'. *Frühmittelalterliche Studien* 31 (1997): 32–45.

———. 'Zur Verschriftlichung der klösterlichen Lebensgewohnheiten unter Abt Hugo von Cluny'. *Frühmittelalterliche Studien* 27 (1993): 317–49.

Wood, Ian. 'The Audience of Architecture in Post-Roman Gaul'. In *The Anglo-Saxon Church: Papers on History, Architecture and Archaeology in Honour of Dr H.M. Taylor*, edited by L.A.S. Butler and R.K. Morris, 74–79. London: Council for British Archaeology, 1986.

Wranovix, Matthew. 'Ulrich Pfeffel's Library: Parish Priests, Preachers, and Books in the Fifteenth Century'. *Speculum* 87, no. 4 (2012): 1125–55.

Wright, Craig. 'Quantification in Medieval Paris and How it Changed Western Music'. In *City, Chant, and the Topography of Early Music: In Honour of Thomas Forrest Kelly*, edited by Michael Scott Cuthbert, Sean Gallagher and Christoph Wolff, 3–26. Cambridge, MA: Harvard University Press, 2013.

Wulstan, David. '*Novi modulaminis melos*: The Music of Heloise and Abelard'. *Plainsong and Medieval Music* 11 (2002): 1–23.

Yates, Nigel. *Anglican Ritualism in Victorian Britain, 1830–1910*. Oxford: Clarendon Press, 1999.

Zeller, Bernhard. 'Writing Charters as a Public Activity: The Example of the Carolingian Charters of St Gall'. In *Medieval Legal Process: Physical, Spoken, and Written Performance in the Middle Ages*, edited by Marco Mostert and P.S. Barnwell, 27–37. Turnhout: Brepols, 2011.

Zieman, Katherine. *Singing the New Song: Literacy and Liturgy in Late Medieval England*. Philadelphia: University of Pennsylvania Press, 2008.

Ziolkowski, Thaddeus S. *The Consecration and Blessing of Churches: A Historical Synopsis and Commentary*. Washington, DC: Catholic University of America Press, 1943.

Zon, Bennett. *The English Plainchant Revival*. Oxford: Oxford University Press, 1999.

Zupitza, Julius. 'Cantus beati Godrici', *Englische Studien* 11 (1888): 401–32.

Unpublished works

Andås, Margrete S. 'Imagery and Ritual in the Liminal Zone: A Study of Texts and Architectural Sculpture from the Nidaros Province c. 1100–1300'. PhD diss., University of Copenhagen, 2012.

Arthur, Ciaran, 'The Liturgy of Charms in Anglo-Saxon England' [working title]. PhD diss., University of Kent, in progress.

Aubert, Eduardo Henrik. 'Ecrire, chanter, agir: Les graduels et missels notés en notation aquitaine avant 1100'. PhD thesis, l'Ecole des Hautes Etudes en Sciences Sociales, Paris, 2011.

Brady, Jeremiah D, ed. 'Critical Edition of the Earliest Monastic Customary of Saint-Bénigne of Dijon (Paris, Bibliothèque Nationale, Ms lat. 4339)'. PhD diss., Harvard University, 1972.

Crowder, Susannah. 'Performance Culture in Medieval Metz, c. 200–1200'. PhD diss., City University of New York, 2008.

DiCenso, Daniel. 'Sacramentary-Antiphoners as Sources of Gregorian Chant in the Eighth and Ninth Centuries'. PhD thesis, University of Cambridge, 2012.

Doberer, E.K. 'Die deutschen Lettner bis 1300'. PhD diss., University of Vienna, 1946.

Edwards, Genevieve Steele. 'Ritual Excommunication in Medieval France and England, 900–1200'. PhD diss., Stanford University, 1997.

Elich, Thomas William. 'Le context oral de la liturgie médiévale et le rôle du texte écrit'. 3 vols. PhD dissertation, Paris IV-Sorbonne, 1988.

Gaastra, Adriaan. 'Between Liturgy and Canon Law: A Study of Books of Confession and Penance in Eleventh- and Twelfth-Century Italy'. PhD diss., University of Utrecht, 2007.

Helsen, Katherine Eve. 'The Great Responsories of the Divine Office: Aspects of Structure and Transmission'. PhD thesis, University of Regensberg, 2008.

Kozachek, Thomas Davies. 'The Repertory of Chant for Dedicating Churches in the Middle Ages: Music, Liturgy, and Ritual'. DPhil thesis, Harvard University, 1995.

Mascareñas Garza, Óscar Octavio. 'Exposing the *Play* in Gregorian Chant: The Manuscript as an *Opening* of *Re-Presentation*'. PhD thesis, University of Limerick, 2010.

Parkes, Henry. 'Liturgy and Music in Ottonian Mainz 950–1025'. PhD diss., University of Cambridge, 2012.

Sapin, Christian, and Carolyn Marino Malone. 'Oratoire est'. In *Rapport préliminaire sur les recherches archéologiques conduites dans la crypte de Saint-Bénigne de Dijon en août 2003*, edited by Christian Sapin, 49–58. Submitted 2005 to the Service Archéologique de Dijon.

Wackett, Jayne, 'The Litlyngton Missal: Its Patrons, Iconography and Messages'. PhD thesis, University of Kent, 2015.

Databases

Biblia sacra juxta vulgatam clementinam, editio electronica, Michael Tweedale. London, 2005, available at http://vulsearch.sourceforge.net/html/index.html

Cantus: A Database for Latin Ecclesiastical Chant, available at http://cantus.uwaterloo.ca

Parkes, Henry, *PRG Database: A Tool for Navigating* Le Pontifical Romano-Germanique, *ed. Cyrille Vogel and Reinhard Elze*, currently available at http://database.prg.mus.cam.ac.uk

Index